An A to Z of
BRITISH LIFE

ADRIAN ROOM

Oxford University Press
Walton Street, Oxford OX2 6DP

Oxford New York
Athens Auckland Bangkok Bombay
Calcutta Cape Town Dar es Salaam
Delhi Florence Hong Kong Istanbul
Karachi Kuala Lumpur Madras Madrid
Melbourne Mexico City Nairobi Paris
Singapore Taipei Tokyo Toronto

and associated companies in
Berlin Ibadan

OXFORD and OXFORD ENGLISH
are trade marks of Oxford
University Press

ISBN 0 19 431144 9

First published 1990
Fourth (updated and revised)
impression 1994

Previously published as
Dictionary of Britain 1986, 1987.

The *Dictionary of Britain* was
originally adapted from *Great
Britain*, written by Adrian Room
and a group of Soviet authors and
first published in the USSR by
Russkij Yazyk in 1978.

Filmset in Palatino by Interactive
Sciences, Gloucester.

Printed in Hong Kong

Contents

Introduction

An A to Z of British Life gives up-to-date information on all aspects of British life and institutions. It explains everything that other nationalities find interesting, amusing, puzzling or even frustrating about Britain and the British. Important public events, major government posts and well-known organizations of all kinds are described. Also included are events, institutions and people that show a typically British set of values or an important facet of British life. Entries on regional foods shed light on the culinary variety within Britain, while descriptions of sports, crafts and societies show what the British do in their spare time.

Extensive cross-references and a thematically arranged index make the dictionary easy to use. Finally, information that can most usefully be summarized in list or map form is included towards the back of the book and cross-referred to from the main text.

Adrian Room
Stamford, Lincolnshire

Key to phonetic symbols

Vowels and diphthongs

1	iː	*as in*	**see** /siː/		11	ɜː	*as in*	**fur** /fɜː(r)/
2	ɪ	*as in*	**sit** /sɪt/		12	ə	*as in*	**ago** /əˈɡəʊ/
3	e	*as in*	**ten** /ten/		13	eɪ	*as in*	**page** /peɪdʒ/
4	æ	*as in*	**hat** /hæt/		14	əʊ	*as in*	**home** /həʊm/
5	ɑː	*as in*	**arm** /ɑːm/		15	aɪ	*as in*	**five** /faɪv/
6	ɒ	*as in*	**got** /ɡɒt/		16	aʊ	*as in*	**now** /naʊ/
7	ɔː	*as in*	**saw** /sɔː/		17	ɔɪ	*as in*	**join** /dʒɔɪn/
8	ʊ	*as in*	**put** /pʊt/		18	ɪə	*as in*	**near** /nɪə(r)/
9	uː	*as in*	**too** /tuː/		19	eə	*as in*	**hair** /heə(r)/
10	ʌ	*as in*	**cup** /kʌp/		20	ʊə	*as in*	**pure** /pjʊə(r)/

Consonants

1	p	*as in*	**pen** /pen/		13	s	*as in*	**so** /səʊ/
2	b	*as in*	**bad** /bæd/		14	z	*as in*	**zoo** /zuː/
3	t	*as in*	**tea** /tiː/		15	ʃ	*as in*	**she** /ʃiː/
4	d	*as in*	**did** /dɪd/		16	ʒ	*as in*	**vision** /ˈvɪʒn/
5	k	*as in*	**cat** /kæt/		17	h	*as in*	**how** /haʊ/
6	ɡ	*as in*	**got** /ɡɒt/		18	m	*as in*	**man** /mæn/
7	tʃ	*as in*	**chin** /tʃɪn/		19	n	*as in*	**no** /nəʊ/
8	dʒ	*as in*	**June** /dʒuːn/		20	ŋ	*as in*	**sing** /sɪŋ/
9	f	*as in*	**fall** /fɔːl/		21	l	*as in*	**leg** /leɡ/
10	v	*as in*	**voice** /vɔɪs/		22	r	*as in*	**red** /red/
11	θ	*as in*	**thin** /θɪn/		23	j	*as in*	**yes** /jes/
12	ð	*as in*	**then** /ðen/		24	w	*as in*	**wet** /wet/

Pronunciation

For each entry a recommended pronunciation is given. The model followed is RP, a non-regional accent of British English. In this accent *r* is sounded only before vowels. Final *r* in the spelling is silent unless the word is followed by one beginning with a vowel. This 'linking r' is shown in brackets as in *welfare officer* /ɒfɪsə(r)/: the *r* is to be sounded only when the next word begins with a vowel. When a linking *r* is possible within a headphrase, it is shown as at the end of *welfare*. Thus /'welfeər ˌɒfɪsə(r)/. The high mark /'/ shows the main stress in the phrase, and the low mark /ˌ/ shows the secondary stress. Sometimes the stress changes when a word is added to a headphrase. In such cases the pronunciation for the expanded phrase is shown in full in brackets. For example, *trilby* (*hat*) /'trɪlbɪ (ˌtrɪlbɪ 'hæt)/. When the addition of a word does not affect the position of the main stress, the additional word alone is shown in brackets. For example, *bring-and-buy* (*sale*) /ˌbrɪŋ ən 'baɪ (seɪl)/. The style of pronunciation shown is a careful one. For instance, *first class* is given as /ˌfɜːst 'klɑːs/, although in fluent colloquial speech the /t/ is very likely to be omitted. A /t/ is also shown in *hot cross bun* where native speakers of English are likely to say /ˌhɒk krɒs 'bʌn/. Users of the dictionary who want systematic information on such features are referred to *An English Pronunciation Companion* by A C Gimson and S M Ramsaran (OUP 1982).

Susan Ramsaran
University College, London

The Lion and the Unicorn
were fighting for the Crown;
The Lion beat the Unicorn
all round about the town.

Some gave them white bread,
and some gave them brown;
Some gave them plum-cake,
and sent them out of town.

Traditional English nursery rhyme

A N Other /ˌeɪ ˌen ˈʌðə(r)/ (language) A way of giving the name of a member of a sports team when his or her name is not yet known or when the member has not yet been selected. It is also used as a specimen name in other circumstances, such as on a form, to show how it should be completed. [from 'another']

A to Z /ˌeɪ tə ˈzed/ (daily life) A book giving a detailed plan of *London* or some other town, with a list of all its streets. [from the alphabetical listing; name is properly that of the maps published by the A–Z Geographers' Map Co *Ltd*]

AA /ˌeɪ ˈeɪ/ see *Alcoholics Anonymous* (charities)

AA /ˌeɪ ˈeɪ/, **the (Automobile Association, the)** (transport) One of the two leading British *clubs* for motorists, which offers its members practical advice and assistance, legal aid and a range of specialized services. Compare *RAC*.

Abbeyfield home /ˈæbɪfiːld ˈhəʊm/ (charities) A home for an elderly person living on his or her own, run by the Abbeyfield Society, a charity founded in 1956. The person lives in a *bedsit(ter)* in a large house, often with a private bathroom, and is provided with two main meals a day, with overall charges deliberately kept low. [first house was in Abbeyfield Road, *London*]

Abdication /ˌæbdɪˈkeɪʃn/, **the** (history) The formal giving up of the throne in 1936 by King Edward VIII, so that he could marry an American divorcee, Mrs Wallis Simpson.

Aberdeen Angus /ˌæbədiːn ˈæŋɡəs/ (animal world) A breed of black, hornless, beef cattle, originally reared in the Scottish counties of Aberdeen and Angus.

Aberdonian /ˌæbəˈdəʊnɪən/ (geography) Someone born or living in Aberdeen or the former county of Aberdeenshire, *Scotland*.

academic year /ˌækədemɪk ˈjɪə(r)/ (education) The year beginning in October in universities and establishments of *further education* or *higher education*, and September in schools (see *school year*), and ending in late June or early July. The year, which is usually divided into three *terms[1]*, ends with important examinations, such as the *GCSE* and *A-level* in schools or a *first degree* in a university.

academy /əˈkædəmɪ/ (education) The name of certain schools and *colleges[3]*, in particular some *private secondary schools* and a number of *public schools[1]* in *Scotland* (eg, *Edinburgh Academy*).

Academy /əˈkædəmɪ/**, the** (arts) The short title of a famous *academy*, especially the *Royal Academy* (*of Arts*) or the *British Academy*.

Academy of St Martin-in-the-Fields /əˌkædəmɪ əv snt ˌmɑːtɪn ɪn ðə ˈfiːldz/**, the** (arts) A leading *London* chamber orchestra, whose first concerts in the 1960s were held in the *church* of St Martin-in-the-Fields.

ACAS /ˈeɪkæs/ **(Advisory, Conciliation and Arbitration Service, the)** (work) An organization set up by the government in 1975 to provide mediation and arbitration as a means of avoiding or ending strikes or other industrial disputes. The Service also advises on industrial relations and encourages *collective bargaining*.

accumulator /əˈkjuːmjʊleɪtə(r)/ (sport and leisure) A progressive bet in horse-racing, especially on four or more races, in which the bet and winnings on the first race are placed on the second, those of the second on the third, and so on, so that the *punter* finally either wins everything or loses everything. Compare *double[3]*.

Act (of Parliament) /ækt (əv ˈpɑːləmənt)/ (law) A law that has been passed by the *House of Commons* and *House of Lords* and given the *royal assent*.

act of God /ˌækt əv ˈgɒd/ (law) A legal term used for damage caused by a sudden natural force such as a flood, hail storm or landslide, and not by man.

Act of Supremacy /ˌækt əv suːˈpreməsɪ/**, the** (history) The *Act* of 1534 that declared the sovereign to be the secular head of the *Church of England*.

Act of Union /ˌækt əv ˈjuːnɪən/**, the** (history) The *Act* of 1707 that declared the union of *England* and *Wales* and *Scotland* as a single kingdom under the name of *Great Britain*.

Adam (style) /ˈædəm (ˌædəm ˈstaɪl)/ (style) An elegant, neo-classical style of architecture and furniture created by the two Scots brothers Robert and James Adam in the 18th century.

Adie, Kate /ˈeɪdɪ, keɪt/ (people) Kate Adie (born 1945) is one of the *BBC*'s best known foreign news reporters. She is noted for her calm but vivid reports from scenes of conflict and violence, such as the siege at the Iranian Embassy, *London* in 1980, the student uprising in Tiananmen Square, Beijing in 1989 (when a bullet hit her arm and killed a young man nearby) and the Gulf War in 1991. Kate Adie has been awarded the *OBE* for her courageous reporting.

Admiral's Cup /ˌædmərəlz ˈkʌp/, **the** (sport and leisure) The main prize for the biennial international yachting contest of four races (the *Fastnet*, the Britannia Cup and two others). It is presented by the admiral who is the head of the Royal Ocean Racing Club, which established the prize in 1957.

Admiralty /ˈædmərəltɪ/, **the** (1 defence 2 government) **1** The former name (to 1964) of the *Royal Navy department* of the Ministry of Defence. **2** The government building in *Whitehall*, *London*, where the Admiralty was and where now the headquarters of the *Civil Service* is.

Admiralty Arch /ˌædmərəltɪ ˈɑːtʃ/ (London) A triumphal arch at the east end of The Mall, *London*, built as a memorial to *Queen Victoria* and named after the *Admiralty²*, next to which it stands.

adult education /ˌædʌlt edʒʊˈkeɪʃn/ (education) Any education or educational course taken by someone who has left school, whether with the aim of gaining a basic academic qualification, such as a *GCSE* grade, or simply for personal satisfaction and pleasure. Adult educational courses, which are fee-paying, are usually held in a school building or *community centre* at a time when people are free to attend, such as in the evening or at a *weekend*. The courses themselves, which are normally weekly and start in the autumn, range from the purely academic, such as mathematics or foreign languages, to the recreational, such as 'keep fit', calligraphy and gardening. Some courses are specially designed for *OAP*s. In other instances, adults are allowed to join normal *sixth form* classes at a *secondary school*, especially if they are studying for an *A-level* examination.

Advent /ˈædvənt/ (religion) For Christians, the time of preparation for the celebration of Christ's birth at *Christmas*, lasting from the *Sunday* nearest 30 November (called Advent Sunday) to Christmas. [from the *advent* or coming of Christ]

Advertising Standards Authority /ˌædvətaızıŋ 'stændədz ɔːˌθɒrətı/, **the (ASA, the)** (daily life) The independent (non-governmental) body that monitors professional standards of advertising in the interests of the public and of industry, in particular by means of the British Code of Advertising Practice. This Code aims to ensure that all advertisements are truthful, within the law, and morally decent (their slogan is 'legal, decent, honest and truthful'). Members of the public have the right to complain to the ASA about any specific advertisement, and the Authority may subsequently ask for the offending advertisement to be reworded or withdrawn altogether.

AEEU /ˌeɪ iː iː 'juː/, **the (Amalgamated Engineering and Electrical Union, the)** (work) A large trade union of about 1 million engineering and electrical employees, formed in 1992 through the merger of two separate unions.

Age Concern /'eɪdʒ kənˌsɜːn/ (charities) A charity organization that cares for the elderly. It was founded in 1940, and has nearly 1,000 local groups round the country working with volunteers to provide a range of services. These include day centres, lunch *clubs*, visits to the elderly in their homes, etc. A separate Age Concern organization cares for the elderly in *London*.

age of consent /ˌeɪdʒ əv kən'sent/, **the** (law) The minimum age, at present 16, at which a young person may legally have sexual intercourse.

age of discretion /ˌeɪdʒ əv dɪ'skreʃn/, **the** (law) The minimum age, at present 14, at which a young person is judged legally competent to manage his or her own affairs.

agony aunt /'ægənɪ aːnt/ (media) A journalist (usually but not necessarily a woman) who has a regular column or page in a newspaper or magazine to give personal advice to readers who write in. Some agony aunts carry out the same task on *local radio* stations, answering listeners by telephone during a programme.

Aintree /'eɪntriː/ (sport and leisure) A horse-racing course near Liverpool, where the *Grand National* is run annually.

Air Miles /ˌeə 'maɪlz/ (transport) A promotional scheme operated by *British Airways,* whereby the purchase of goods or services from certain shops and companies gives the purchaser the right to travel free for a stated number of miles on a BA air route. For example, the purchase of a man's suit costing £100 or more from the chain store Debenhams gives

250 Air Miles, or over half the cost of the return flight from *London* to Paris (rated at 450 Air Miles). The Air Miles distance is an approximation (to a multiple of 50) of the true distance by air from London, so that a return flight to Rome counts as 1,800 Air Miles, to New York 6,800, and to Hong Kong 11,500.

Airedale (terrier) /ˈeədeɪl (ˌeədeɪl ˈterɪə(r))/ (animal world) A large, rough-haired, tan-coloured breed of dog with black back and sides. [originally bred in the valley of the river Aire, Yorkshire]

Albert Hall /ˌælbət ˈhɔːl/, **the** (London) A large hall in *London*, with seating for 8,000, where the annual *Promenade Concerts* are held, as well as a number of other concerts, parades, meetings and ceremonial and sporting events. [in full, the *Royal Albert Hall*, built in 1867–71 and named in honour of Prince Albert, the husband of *Queen Victoria*]

Albert Memorial /ˌælbət məˈmɔːrɪəl/, **the** (London) A large monument opposite the *Albert Hall, London*, and containing a seated bronze figure of Prince Albert, to whom it was built as a national memorial in 1863–76.

Alcoholics Anonymous /ˌælkəˌhɒlɪks əˈnɒnɪməs/ **(AA)** (charities) A voluntary organization founded in 1947 for people who need help in fighting alcoholism. It currently has over 35,000 members, and operates through more than 2,000 branches.

Alcohol Concern /ˌælkəhɒl kənˈsɜːn/ (charities) A national voluntary agency that aims to prevent the misuse of alcohol by training helpers and advisers at a local level. In 1990 it began a special campaign directed at factory and office workers. It is funded by the government.

Aldeburgh Festival /ˌɔːldbrə ˈfestəvl/, **the** (arts) An annual music festival at Aldeburgh, Suffolk, where it was started in 1948 by the composer Benjamin *Britten* (1913–76), who lived in Aldeburgh.

alderman /ˈɔːldəmən/ (government) The title of a senior governor of the *City (of London)* and, before 1974, that of a senior member of a local council, elected by other *councillors*. Aldermen were not members of the *Greater London* Council from the time of the 1977 elections, and they have not been members of London *borough*[2] councils since 1978.

Aldermaston /ˈɔːldəmɑːstən/ (defence) A village in Berkshire where the Atomic Weapons Research Establishment is, and one of the main places selected by *CND* for anti-nuclear demonstrations, especially the marches to and from *London* in 1958–63.

Alderney (cow) /'ɔ:ldənɪ (ˌɔ:ldənɪ 'kaʊ)/ (animal world) A breed of light brown dairy cow, originally from Alderney, *Channel Islands*.

A-level /'eɪ ˌlevl/ **(Advanced level)** (education) A higher-level examination, usually taken at the age of 17 or 18, two years after the *GCSE* examination. It is the standard for entrance to university and other *higher education*, and to many forms of professional training.

Alexandra Palace /ˌælɪgzɑːndrə 'pælɪs/ (London) A large building on a hill in north *London*, used mainly for conferences, exhibitions and concerts. It formerly housed the main television studios of the *BBC*. The Palace is in a park with a racecourse. [named for Princess Alexandra, wife of the future king Edward VII]

All England Club /ˌɔ:l 'ɪŋglənd klʌb/, **the** (sport and leisure) A tennis *club* in *Wimbledon, London*, on whose courts the annual open lawn tennis championships are held. [full title: All England Lawn Tennis and Croquet Club]

all-in wrestling /ˌɔ:l ɪn 'reslɪŋ/ (sport and leisure) Freestyle wrestling, with no restriction on the type of holds, and with no international agreement on the rules.

Alliance Party (of Northern Ireland) /ə'laɪəns ˌpɑ:tɪ (əˌlaɪəns ˌpɑ:tɪ əv ˌnɔ:ðən 'aɪələnd)/, **the** (politics) The Party was formed in 1970 as a reaction to the *Troubles*. It aims to break down divisions between Protestants and Catholics in *Northern Ireland* and to unite both sections of the community by working for moderate policies.

allotment /ə'lɒtmənt/ (daily life) A small piece of land, often on the outskirts of a town, that is rented by a private individual (often from a *local authority*) who grows vegetables there. Usually several allotments are grouped together. They were started during the First World War.

Ally Pally /ˌælɪ 'pælɪ/ (London) A nickname for *Alexandra Palace*.

almshouse /'ɑ:mzhaʊs/ (charities) A house provided by the *church* or a charitable organization for poor or elderly people. [from 'alms', donations made to the poor or elderly]

Alsatian /æl'seɪʃn/ (animal world) A large, wolf-like dog kept as a pet or for use as a guide dog or guard dog, or for police work. It is more correctly known as a German shepherd dog.

Alton Towers /ˌɔ:ltən 'taʊəz/ (sport and leisure) A popular

allotment

leisure park near Stoke-on-Trent, Staffordshire. It is one of the largest of its kind in *Britain*, with an average 2 million visitors annually.

Amateur Athletic Association /ˌæmətər æθˈletɪk əsəʊsɪˌeɪʃn/, **the (AAA, the/three As, the)** (sport and leisure) The national governing body of men's amateur athletics in *England*, founded in 1880. The corresponding organization for women is the Women's AAA, founded in 1922. ['amateur' as opposed to 'professional']

Amis, Kingsley /ˈeɪmɪs, ˈkɪŋzlɪ/ (people) Kingsley Amis (born 1922) is an established novelist who writes in an imaginative but original manner about the inner feelings and hidden worries of ordinary people. Some people compare him to Anthony *Burgess*, but his style is more straightforward, and his language generally easier to understand. His best-known novel is perhaps his first, 'Lucky Jim' (1954), whose hero, a *lower middle class* lecturer, was regarded as a typical anti-*Establishment* 'angry young man'. In 1986 Amis won the *Booker prize* with 'The Old Devils', a perceptive study of growing old, centring on a group of old friends in South *Wales*.

Amnesty International /ˌæmnəstɪ ɪntəˈnæʃnəl/ (charities) A human rights movement funded by members' fees and gifts of money. It was founded in *Britain* in 1961. It works to release people who have been imprisoned, in any country, for their beliefs, colour, language, ethnic origin or religion, provided that they have not used or advocated violence. Such prisoners are called 'prisoners of conscience'. The movement, which also campaigns against torture and *capital punishment*, has over 100,000 members today in more than 70 countries.

ancient monument /ˌeɪnʃənt ˈmɒnjʊmənt/ (history) A monument or other building officially listed as being of historic, architectural or archaeological interest and so protected by *Act (of Parliament)* from being damaged or destroyed.

Andy Capp /ˌændɪ ˈkæp/ (media) A character in a strip cartoon by the artist Reg Smythe in the *Daily Mirror*. He represents, in humorously exaggerated form, a typical *working class* man, and has what are supposed to be the two main characteristics of the working man, that is, idleness and flippancy. These are usually shown in his treatment of his wife, Florrie, and his reaction to daily life. [from a pun on 'handicap', and with a reference to the flat *cap*[1] which many working men wear, and which Andy Capp himself wears]

Anfield Road /ˌænfiːld ˈrəʊd/ (sport and leisure) The home *football* ground in Liverpool of *Liverpool Football Club*.

Anglesey /ˈæŋɡlsɪ/ (geography) A Welsh island in the Irish Sea, close to mainland *Britain* and joined to it by a rail bridge and a road bridge. It is a popular tourist centre and the town of Holyhead on Anglesey is one of the main departure points for sea crossings to *Ireland*.

Anglia TV /ˌæŋɡlɪə tiː ˈviː/ (media) One of the 15 regional television companies of the *ITC*, based in Norwich and broadcasting mainly to *East Anglia*.

Anglican /ˈæŋɡlɪkən/ (religion) A member of the *Church of England*.

Anglo-Catholic /ˌæŋɡləʊ ˈkæθəlɪk/ (religion) An *Anglican* who accepts much of the teaching of the *Roman Catholic Church*, without wishing to join it. He usually regards *church* ritual as important, and believes in the authority of the clergy. See *High Church*.

Anglo-Irish Agreement /ˌæŋɡləʊ ˌaɪərɪʃ əˈgriːmənt/, **the** (law) An agreement set up in 1985 between the British and Irish governments with the aim of promoting peace and stability in *Northern Ireland*, encouraging friendship and cooperation between the British and Irish peoples, and improving methods of fighting terrorism. Formal political talks between *Britain* and Ireland have been taking place since 1991.

Anglo-Saxon /ˌæŋgləʊ ˈsæksn/ (language) **1** The language of the Anglo-Saxons, the Germanic people who were dominant in *Britain* from the 5th century to the *Norman Conquest* in 1066. The language is also known as Old English. **2** Another term for 'plain' English, especially containing *four-letter words* and other normally taboo words and phrases.

Anne Hathaway's Cottage /ˌæn ˌhæθəweɪz ˈkɒtɪdʒ/ (history) The old house near *Stratford-(up)on-Avon* in which *Shakespeare*'s wife, Anne Hathaway (1557-1623), was born. Today the house is a museum and a popular tourist attraction.

Anne Hathaway's Cottage

Anne, Princess /ˈæn ˌprɪnses/ (royal family) See *Princess Royal*.

annual /ˈænjʊəl/ (media) A book or magazine published once a year, usually just before *Christmas* (for the following year). The term often applies to a children's book that has the title of a comic, for example 'The *Dandy* Annual 1992'. Such a book contains longer versions of many of the comic's regular features.

another place /əˌnʌðə ˈpleɪs/ (government) A parliamentary phrase used in the *House of Commons* to refer to the *House of Lords* and in the House of Lords to refer to the House of Commons. Compare *other place*.

Antonine Wall /ˌæntənaɪn ˈwɔːl/, **the** (history) A wall in southern *Scotland* running from the river *Forth* in the east to *Clyde* in the west. It was built in the reign of the Roman emperor Antoninus Pius (86-161 AD). Compare *Hadrian's Wall*.

Any Questions? /ˌenɪ ˈkwestʃənz/ (media) A popular radio programme broadcast weekly since 1948 in which questions of topical interest are put by members of an audience to members of a specially selected panel, who answer them spontaneously. The programme is made from a different location in *Britain* each week. The panel members usually include noted public figures such as *MP*s, writers and broadcasters.

A1 /ˌeɪ ˈwʌn/ (transport) **1** The classification of a ship in *Lloyd's Register* when it is in first class condition. **2** The *A-road* that runs from *London* to *Edinburgh*.

APEX/Apex /ˈeɪpeks/ (transport) A form of cheap travel ticket issued to people who book in advance. They are mostly used by holiday-makers travelling by air or by *BR* passengers planning a train journey. [abbreviation of 'advance purchase excursion']

Apprentice Boys' Parade /əˌprentɪs ˌbɔɪz pəˈreɪd/, **the** (tradition) An annual parade of *Orangemen* in Derry (Londonderry) and other towns in *Northern Ireland*, on 12 August. The parade marks the defeat of the Catholics by the Protestants in the siege of Derry in 1688, in which Protestant apprentice boys took part. In recent years the parade has led to scenes of violence between Catholics and Protestants in Northern Ireland.

APR /ˌeɪ pi: ˈɑː(r)/ (annual percentage rate) (finance) The gross annual interest rate, expressed as a percentage, charged by a financial company when lending money or when a person buys goods through a hire purchase scheme. The rate is usually quoted together with the monthly interest rate charged to holders of *credit cards*, for example 'monthly rate 2% (equivalent to an APR of 27.5%)'.

April Fools' Day /ˌeɪprəl ˈfuːlz deɪ/ (tradition) 1 April, when, traditionally, practical jokes are played. The day is also known as All Fools' Day.

Archbishop of Canterbury /ˌɑːtʃbɪʃəp əv ˈkæntəbrɪ/, **the** (religion) The title of the religious head of the *Church of England*, who is also bishop of *Canterbury*. His official title is *Primate of All England*. Compare *Archbishop of York*.

Archbishop of York /ˌɑːtʃbɪʃəp əv ˈjɔːk/, **the** (religion) The title of the deputy religious head of the *Church of England*, who is also bishop of York. His official title is *Primate of England*. Compare *Archbishop of Canterbury*.

Archers /ˈɑːtʃəz/, **the** (media) A popular daily radio programme on *Radio 4* telling of the day-to-day life of an imaginary farming family, which has been broadcast since 1950, thus being the longest-running radio serial. Each episode continues the story from the previous programme.

area of outstanding natural beauty (AONB) /ˌeərɪə əv aʊtˌstændɪŋ ˌnætʃrəl ˈbjuːtɪ/ (geography) An area of the countryside designated for conservation and public recreation by the *Countryside Commission* in *England* or the *Countryside Council for Wales* in *Wales*. An AONB has attractive scenery but lacks the wide stretches of open country that a *National Park* has. There are now 39 AONBs in England and Wales.

ARELS /ˈɑːrelz/ **(Association of Recognized English Language Schools, the)** (education) A professional body that promotes the teaching of English to foreign students visiting *Britain*, and that aims to ensure their proper welfare while they are in the country. It officially approves nearly 200 teaching establishments (language schools), and sets its own examinations at three levels (Preliminary, Higher and Diploma) in speaking and listening to English in a language laboratory.

Armada /ɑːˈmɑːdə/**, the** (history) The name of the Spanish fleet sent by Philip II, King of Spain, in 1588 against *England* but defeated by the English navy. [in full, 'Spanish Armada']

Armistice Day /ˈɑːmɪstɪs ˌdeɪ/ (history) 11 November 1918, the final day of the First World War. See also *Remembrance Sunday*.

Army /ˈɑːmɪ/**, the** (defence) The present British Army developed from the New Model Army of Oliver Cromwell in the 17th century, and has been under the control of *Parliament* since then. As a result of conscription, there were almost 4 million men and women in the Army in the First World War and nearly 3 million in the Second. Conscription in the form of *national service* ended in 1957, however. The strength of the Army is now down to 145,500, and will be reduced further as a result of defence cuts and regiment mergers.

A-road /ˈeɪ rəʊd/ (transport) The designation of a trunk road, usually running between major towns and *cities*. The best known are those that radiate clockwise from *London*: the A1 to *Edinburgh*, mainly following the route of the *Great North Road*, A2 to Dover, A3 to Portsmouth, A4 to Bristol, A5 to Holyhead, north *Wales*, and A6 to Carlisle, northeast *England*.

The A40 London to *Oxford*[1] and south Wales is also well known. *Motorways* have superseded some sections of A-roads, and have the same numbers. The M4, for example, runs more or less parallel to the A4. ['A' as first letter of alphabet, implying importance]

A-road

Arsenal /ˈɑːsənl/ (sport and leisure) A popular *football club* with a stadium at Highbury, north *London*, and nicknamed the Gunners. [formerly based near Woolwich Arsenal, south *London*, a government arsenal closed in 1966]

Arts Council (of Great Britain) /ˈɑːts ˌkaʊnsl (ˌɑːts ˌkaʊnsl əv ˌgreɪt ˈbrɪtn)/, **the** (media) A government organization established in 1946 to promote the arts generally in *Britain*, and in particular drama, music and the visual arts.

Ascension Day /əˈsenʃn deɪ/ (religion) A festival day for Christians, celebrating the ascension of Christ to heaven, and held on the 40th day after *Easter* (always a Thursday). Unlike other major *church* festivals, it is not a *bank holiday*.

Ascot /ˈæskət/ (sport and leisure) A racecourse near Windsor. Each year the *Royal Ascot* four-day meeting is held there. [named after village there]

ASH /æʃ/ **(Action on Smoking and Health)** (charities) A voluntary organization founded in 1971 to discourage smoking and to find ways for decreasing the damage done to health by smoking. The organization has 14 branches and about 1,400 members. [name partly chosen to indicate cigarette ash]

Ash Wednesday /æʃ ˈwenzdɪ/ (religion) The first day of *Lent* in the Christian *church*. [from the practice of sprinkling ashes on the heads of penitents]

Ashdown, Paddy /'æʃdaʊn, 'pædɪ/ (people) A former *Royal Marines* officer and *MP*, Paddy Ashdown (born 1941) was elected as the first leader of the new *SLD* in 1988. He continued as leader when that party became the *Liberal Democrats* in 1989. In recent years he has won increasing popularity and respect, and has done much to raise the status and influence of his party.

Ashmolean (Museum) /æʃ'məʊlɪən (æʃˌməʊlɪən mjuːˈzɪəm)/, **the** (arts) A museum and library of ancient history, fine arts and archaeology at *Oxford University*, founded in 1683 by Elias Ashmole (1617-92).

Aslef /'æzlef/ **(Associated Society of Locomotive Engineers and Firemen, the)** (work) An influential trade union for railway workers, traditionally regarded as left-wing. Its current membership is over 18,000. Compare *RMI*.

AS-level /eɪ 'es ˌlevl/ **(Advanced Supplementary level)** (education) An examination that is an alternative to *A-level* or additional to it. A combination of A-level and AS-level passes is usually required for *higher education*.

assisted area /əˌsɪstɪd 'eərɪə/ (work) A region of high unemployment where the government encourages industrial development by means of special grants and loans of money. There are two types of assisted area: *development areas* and *intermediate areas*.

association football /əˌsəʊsɪeɪʃn 'fʊtbɔːl/ (sport and leisure) The formal name of *football*, as distinct from *rugby football*. See the *FA* and the *Football League* and compare *rugby league* and *rugby union*. [from the FA, who established the rules of football, and whose title gave the term 'soccer' as a colloquial word for football]

Aston (University) /'æstən (ˌæstən juːnɪˈvɜːsətɪ)/ (education) A university in Birmingham, founded in 1966. [from the district of Birmingham where it is]

Aston Villa /ˌæstən 'vɪlə/ (sport and leisure) A popular Birmingham *football club*, with a stadium, Villa Park, in the district of Aston.

Astronomer Royal /əˌstrɒnəmə 'rɔɪəl/, **the** (science and technology) The title of the director of the *Royal Greenwich Observatory* to 1972, and since then an honorary title awarded to an outstanding astronomer.

ATL /ˌeɪ tiː 'el/, **the (Association of Teachers and Lecturers,**

the) (education) A union of teachers and lecturers, mainly in independent *secondary schools* and *colleges*[2] of *further education*. It was founded in 1978 (as the Assistant Masters and Mistresses Association), and adopted its present name in 1993. It has a current membership of about 145,000, but is not affiliated to the *TUC*.

Attenborough, David /ˈætnbrə, ˈdeɪvɪd/ (people) David Attenborough (born 1926) is well known for his popular but carefully presented television programmes on natural history, documented in a clear and precise style. He is a professional broadcaster, and was the first Controller of *BBC 2*, later becoming Director of Programmes. David Attenborough was knighted in 1985.

attendance centre /əˈtendəns ˌsentə(r)/ (law) A centre that a young offender (under 21) is ordered to attend for a stated number of hours, with a minimum of 12 hours and a maximum of 36 (24 hours for a person under 16). The longest period of attendance in any one day is three hours. Compare *community service, young offender institution*.

attorney /əˈtɜːnɪ/ (law) A person, especially a lawyer, appointed to act for someone in business or legal matters.

Attorney General /əˌtɜːnɪ ˈdʒenrəl/, **the** (law) In *England* and *Wales*, the senior law officer and chief legal counsel to the *Crown*[1].

August Bank Holiday /ˌɔːgəst bæŋk ˈhɒlədeɪ/, **the** (daily life) An alternative name for the *Summer Bank Holiday*.

Auld Lang Syne /ˌɔːld læŋ ˈsaɪn/ (tradition) A traditional song sung at the end of a gathering, to remember times past, especially as midnight strikes on *New Year's Eve*. Compare *Burns' Night*. [Scottish, literally 'good times long ago'. The words of the song are from a poem by Robert Burns (1759-96)]

Aunt Sally /ˌɑːnt ˈsælɪ/ (tradition) **1** A figure, usually of an old woman's head, that is set up at fairgrounds and *fêtes* as a target for balls or other objects. The aim is to knock off the head or to knock the figure down. **2** A person or thing that is a target for attack or criticism.

Auntie/Aunty /ˈɑːntɪ/ (media) An affectionate name for the *BBC*. [seen as a staid old aunt, or keeper of moral values]

Austen, Jane /ˈɒstɪn, dʒeɪn/ (people) The novels of Jane Austen (1775–1817) are remarkable for the skilful and sensitive way in which the day-to-day *upper class* lives of the characters are described, either in *country houses* or in the *city* of Bath which was then very fashionable and elegant. The society of such people, with all their loves and ambitions, was one that Jane Austen knew well, and her novels remain as realistic portraits of the period. The main novels are: 'Pride and Prejudice' (1813), 'Sense and Sensibility' (1811), 'Northanger Abbey' (a satire on the *Gothic novel*[1]) (1818), 'Mansfield Park' (1814), 'Emma' (1815) and 'Persuasion' (1818). Devotees of Jane Austen and her novels are still sometimes known as 'Janeites'.

Authorized Version /ˌɔːθəraɪzd ˈvɜːʃn/, **the (AV, the)** (religion) An English translation of the Bible made in 1611 and 'authorized' by King James I (James VI of Scotland), for which reason it is also known as the *King James Bible*. The Authorized Version is used in many *Anglican churches*, although some *churches* today favour the use of a more modern translation of the Bible.

Autocar & Motor /ˌɔːtəʊkaːr ən ˈməʊtə(r)/ (media) A weekly magazine for car owners and motoring enthusiasts. It was founded in 1988 on the merger of two separate magazines: 'Autocar', first published in 1895, and 'The Motor', founded in 1902. Its current circulation is about 96,500.

autumn double /ˌɔːtəm ˈdʌbl/, **the** (sport and leisure) A bet placed simultaneously on two horse races held in the autumn—the Cesarewitch and the Cambridgeshire.

Avebury /ˈeɪvbrɪ/ (tradition) A village in Wiltshire where one of the largest pre-Celtic temples in Europe is located. The site, which probably dates back to about 2000 BC, includes Silbury Hill, the largest ancient man-made mound in Europe. Despite several attempts to excavate it, the exact purpose of the hill remains uncertain. Over the centuries, many of the standing stones have either been destroyed or removed, and although some remain to form an impressive display, Avebury has never been as popular with tourists and visitors as *Stonehenge*.

avoirdupois /ˌævədəˈpɔɪz/ (daily life) A system of weights based on the pound divided into 16 ounces. [from Old French 'aver de peis', 'goods of weight']

Ayckbourn, Alan /ˈeɪkbɔːn, ˈælən/ (people) Alan Ayckbourn (born 1939) is a popular and prolific playwright, whose plays have been running almost continuously in *London* and New York since the 1960s. Although basically farces, his plays are in fact accurately observed studies of English *middle class* life and society, with its many domestic clashes and problems of personality. His plays are always carefully constructed, often with a simultaneous 'overlay' of time or place. For example, in one of his best works, 'Absurd Person Singular' (1973), three married couples are shown on three successive *Christmas Eves*, with the action set in the kitchen of each in turn.

Aylesbury (duck) /ˈeɪlzbrɪ (ˌeɪlzbrɪ ˈdʌk)/ (animal world) A breed of white domestic duck, regarded as of good quality for eating. [originating from Aylesbury, Buckinghamshire]

Ayrshire (cow) /ˈeəʃə(r) (ˌeəʃə ˈkaʊ)/ (animal world) A breed of brown and white dairy cow. [originally from Ayrshire, *Scotland*]

BA /ˌbiː ˈeɪ/ **(Bachelor of Arts)** (education) A degree obtained by the student at a university or *polytechnic* on successfully completing a course of studies, usually in a non-science subject. However, at *Oxford*[2] and *Cambridge*[2], as well as at some of the newer universities, the BA is a *first degree* in either non-science or science subjects.

BAA /ˌbiː eɪ ˈeɪ/ (transport) The private company that owns and operates seven major airports in *Britain*, including *Heathrow*, *Gatwick* and *Stansted*. Together, the seven handle three out of four air passengers in Britain. [abbreviation of British Airports Authority, the former name of the company when state-run]

Bach Choir /ˌbɑːk ˈkwaɪə(r)/, **the** (arts) A well-known *London choir* that performs not only the works of J S Bach but those of other important composers. Bach Choirs also exist in other towns and *cities*.

backbencher /ˌbæk ˈbentʃə(r)/ (government) An *MP* who does not hold any special office and who, therefore, in the *House of Commons* sits on the back benches (as distinct from the *front benches*, on which sit *ministers*[2] and members of the *Shadow Cabinet*).

Backs /bæks/, **the** (education) The attractive gardens and lawns in *Cambridge*[1], between several *colleges*[1] and the river Cam. Each garden belongs to a particular college, and is at the back of it.

bacon and eggs /ˌbeɪkən ən ˈegz/ (food and drink) A popular main dish of a traditional *English breakfast*: fried rashers (slices) of bacon and one or more fried eggs.

Bacon, Francis /ˈbeɪkən, ˈfrɑːnsɪs/ (people) The painter Francis Bacon (1909–92) was famous for the 'tortured' style of his pictures, many of which were portraits. Bacon deliberately distorted his human figures to express their conflicting emotions. His paintings of screaming popes, based on Velázquez's portrait of Innocent X, are particularly striking. Bacon destroyed much of his earlier work, but 'Three Studies for Figures at the base of a Crucifixion' (1944) is in the *Tate Gallery* as an early example of his mature style.

bacon sarnie /ˌbeɪkən 'sɑːnɪ/ (food and drink) A bacon sandwich, eaten as a popular snack or meal in the *North* of England. ['sarnie' is a northern colloquial abbreviation of 'sandwich']

BACS /bækz/ (finance) An automated payment system used by banks and *building societies* for *standing orders* and *direct debits*. [abbreviation of its original name, Bank Associated Clearing Services]

Badger /'bædzə(r)/ (sport and leisure) A boy or girl aged 6 to 10 who is a member of the junior branch of the *St John Ambulance (Brigade)*. Compare *Beaver*. [so named from their black and white uniform]

bagpipes /'bægpaɪps/ (arts) A wind instrument played by forcing air through reed pipes from a bag held under the player's arm. It is traditionally associated with Scottish *highlanders*[1,2], but is also played in other parts of the *British Isles*, such as northern *England* and *Ireland*.

Badminton (Horse Trials) /'bædmɪntən (ˌbædmɪntən 'hɔːs traɪəlz)/, **the** (sport and leisure) The most important *three-day event* in *Britain*, held annually in the grounds of Badminton House, Avon. The event is usually attended by members of the *royal family*.

bailiff /'beɪlɪf/ (law) An officer employed to serve *writ*s and *summons*es, make arrests, collect fines, and ensure that a *court*[3] sentence is carried out.

Baker Street /'beɪkə striːt/ (London) A central street in *London*. It was at number 221B Baker Street that the famous fictional detective Sherlock *Holmes* lived.

Bakewell tart /ˌbeɪkwel 'tɑːt/ (food and drink) An open tart made of pastry lined with a layer of jam and filled with almond-flavoured sponge cake. [originally made in Bakewell, Derbyshire]

ballboy/ballgirl /'bɔːlbɔɪ/'bɔːlgɜːl/ (sport and leisure) A boy or girl who retrieves the balls on tennis courts, especially at *Wimbledon* and other important tennis matches.

ballot paper /'bælət ˌpeɪpə(r)/ (government) The special slip of paper on which an elector records his vote in a political election such as a *by-election* or a *general election*. It has the names of the candidates and their parties printed on it, and the voter makes his choice by marking a letter 'X' against the name of the candidate he supports. He does this in a *polling booth* where no-one else can see which candidate he has voted for.

Balmoral (Castle) /bæl'mɒrəl (bæl'mɒrəl 'kɑːsl)/ (royal family) A castle in northeast *Scotland* that has been a private home of the *royal family* since 1852, when it was bought by the *Prince Consort*.

Baltic (Exchange) /'bɔːltɪk (ˌbɔːltɪk ɪks'tʃeɪndʒ)/, **the** (finance) An important market in *London* for the chartering of cargo vessels of all nationalities. It also deals with marine insurance. [in full, the Baltic Mercantile and Shipping Exchange, named after the coffee-house where merchants involved in the Baltic trade met in the 18th century]

Bampton fair /ˌbæmptən 'feə(r)/ (tradition) An annual fair at Bampton, Devon, famous for its sale of *Exmoor ponies*.

Banbury cake /'bænbrɪ keɪk/ (food and drink) A cake containing currants, raisins, candied peel and sugar, and with a criss-cross pattern on top. [originally made at Banbury, Oxfordshire]

bangers and mash /ˌbæŋəz ən 'mæʃ/ (food and drink) A colloquial term for sausages and mashed potatoes.

bank holiday /ˌbæŋk 'hɒlədeɪ/ (daily life) An official holiday (on a day other than Saturday or *Sunday*) when banks, post offices and factories are closed as well as many shops. At present the bank holidays in *England* and *Wales* are: *New Year's Day* (or the first working day after it), *Good Friday*, *Easter Monday*, the first Monday in May (*May Day* bank holiday), the last Monday in May (*Spring Bank Holiday*), the last Monday in August (*Summer Bank Holiday*), *Christmas Day* (or the Monday following, if it falls on a Saturday or Sunday) and *Boxing Day* (or the next working day after Christmas Day). In 1995 the May Day Bank Holiday will be on 8th May, the 50th anniversary of VE day which marked the end of the war in Europe. *Scotland* and *Northern Ireland* have some extra bank holidays.

Bank Holiday Monday /ˌbæŋk 'hɒlədeɪ ˌmʌndɪ/ (daily life) A name for any *bank holiday* that always falls on a Monday, as many do.

Bank of England /ˌbæŋk əv 'ɪŋglənd/, **the** (finance) The central bank of *England* and *Wales*, in *London*, founded in 1694 and nationalized in 1946. It issues bank notes and advises the government on financial matters.

Bank of Scotland /ˌbæŋk əv ˈskɒtlənd/**, the** (finance) The second largest of the three main Scottish banks (after the *Royal Bank of Scotland* and before the *Clydesdale Bank*). It was founded in 1695. Like the other two Scottish banks (but unlike English banks, except for the *Bank of England*), it issues its own banknotes (for values from £5 to £100). These notes are not legal tender. However, in *Scotland* and almost always in *England* they are given the same status as notes issued by the Bank of England.

bannock /ˈbænək/ (food and drink) A round, flat cake, made from wheat or barley and sometimes filled with currants. It is specially popular in *Scotland* and the north of *England*.

Banqueting House /ˈbæŋkwɪtɪŋ haʊs/**, the** (London) One of the most famous buildings in *Whitehall[1]*, *London*, and the only surviving part (built 1622) of Whitehall Palace, which was mostly destroyed by fire in 1698. Today it is used for official receptions.

bap /bæp/ (food and drink) A kind of soft, round, flat bread roll.

Baptists /ˈbæptɪsts/ (religion) A large Protestant (but non-Anglican) *church* that has about 160,000 members and that is mainly organized in groups of churches. Most of these belong to the Baptist Union of Great Britain (formed in 1812). There is a traditionally strong Baptist following in *Wales*. Baptists reject infant baptism on the grounds that there is no evidence of it in the Bible. Only adults are therefore baptised. At the ceremony of baptism, the person being admitted to the church is completely immersed in water.

bar /bɑː(r)/ (**1** food and drink **2, 3** law) **1** A counter or room for the sale and consumption of alcoholic drinks (*public bar, saloon bar, lounge bar*) in a *pub*, or in general in a hotel, restaurant, or other public place such as a theatre or concert hall. **2** The area in a law *court[3]* separating the part reserved for the judge or *magistrate* and *QC* from the part reserved for junior *barristers, solicitors* and the general public. **3** The place in a law court where the accused person ('prisoner at the bar') stands during his or her trial.

bar billiards /bɑː ˈbɪliədz/ (sport and leisure) A version of billiards popular in *pubs*, in which the balls are hit into holes on the surface of the billiard table.

bar snacks /'bɑː snæks/ (food and drink) A light meal in one of the *bars[1]* of a *pub,* such as a *ploughman's lunch* or a snack of sandwiches or meat pies.

Barbarians /bɑːˈbeərɪənz/**, the** (sport and leisure) The name of the *rugby football club* whose members are the best players of *Britain,* France and the *Commonwealth[1].*

Barbican (Centre) /'bɑːbɪkən (ˌsentə(r))/**, the** (arts) A large cultural complex in the *City of London* opened in 1982. It contains the Barbican Theatre, as the *London* base of the *Royal Shakespeare Company,* a smaller theatre known as The Pit, and the Barbican Hall, as the home of the *London Symphony Orchestra.* It also houses three cinemas, an art gallery, a sculpture court, a large lending library, and facilities for exhibitions and conferences, as well as *bars* and restaurants.

Barbour jacket /'bɑːbə 'dzækɪt/ (clothing) A type of strong waterproof coat, usually green in colour and typically worn by *upper class* people in the country, together with *green wellies.* [properly a trade name; the coat was originally made by John Barbour in South Shields, northeast *England,* for sailors visiting this port]

Barchester Chronicles /ˌbɑːtʃɪstə 'krɒnɪklz/**, the** (arts) The collective title of six novels by Anthony Trollope (1815–92), set in the fictional *cathedral city* of Barchester (believed to be based on either Salisbury or Wells) and portraying the intrigues and struggle for power of the local *Anglican* clergy.

Barclays (Bank) /'bɑːklɪz (ˌbɑːklɪz 'bæŋk)/ (finance) The second largest British bank, founded in 1896 and with branches in most towns and *cities.*

bard /bɑːd/ (arts) The title of the poet who wins a competition at an *eisteddfod,* especially in *Wales.* (A bard was originally a wandering musician who sang about the deeds of his tribe.)

Bard of Avon /ˌbɑːd əv 'eɪvn/**, the** (arts) A nickname for William *Shakespeare* (1564–1616), the great poet (*bard*) and dramatist who was born, and is buried, at *Stratford-(up)on-Avon.*

bargain basement /'bɑːgɪn ˌbeɪsmənt/ (commerce) **1** In some large shops and stores, a basement (floor below street level) where goods are sold at reduced prices. **2** In some local papers, a section where second-hand goods for sale can be advertised at low rates, or even free of charge.

Barnardos /bəˈnɑːdəʊz/ (charities) A charity that runs homes, schools and other centres for orphans and deprived children, including those with physical or mental handicaps. [founded

'THE PARENTS WHO CAME BY CHARABANC'

Bateman Cartoon

by an Irish doctor, Thomas John Barnardo (1845–1905) in
1870, who worked among such children in *London*]

barrister /'bærɪstə(r)/ (law) In *England*, a lawyer who has been
'called to the bar' (see *bar*[2]), or admitted to the *Inns of Court*.
He can advise on legal problems submitted through a
solicitor, and present a case in the higher *courts*[3].

Bart's /bɑːts/ (medicine) A colloquial abbreviation for *St
Bartholomew's Hospital*.

base rate /'beɪs reɪt/ (finance) **1** The rate of interest at which
individual banks lend money. **2** The rate at which the *Bank of
England* lends money to the *discount houses*, thus effectively
controlling interest rates generally throughout the banking
system. In 1994 the base rate was $5\frac{1}{4}$%.

Basic English /ˌbeɪsɪk 'ɪŋglɪʃ/ (language) A simplified form of
English intended as an international language. It contains a
vocabulary of 850 basic words and was invented by I A
Richards (1893–1979). The psychologist Charles Ogden
(1889–1957) was also involved. [pun on 'basic' and initials of
'British American Scientific International Commercial']

Bateman cartoon /ˌbeɪtmən kɑː'tuːn/ (arts) A cartoon (comic
drawing) by H M Bateman (1887–1974), portraying a man in
an embarrassing situation, especially one who has
unknowingly broken some code of social conduct. The
cartoons usually have a caption beginning, 'The Man

Who. . . . . .', or something similar, for example, 'The Guest who Called "Pâté de Foie Gras" Potted Meat'.

Bath and West /ˌbɑːθ ən 'west/, **the** (tradition) The short name of the Royal Bath and West of England Show, an important agricultural show, originally held in Bath, Avon, but now held in a permanent ground at Shepton Mallet, Somerset, in the *West Country*.

Bath bun /ˌbɑːθ 'bʌn/ (food and drink) A type of sweet bun containing spices and dried fruit. [originally made in Bath, Avon]

Bath Festival /ˌbɑːθ 'festɪvl/, **the** (arts) An annual music festival held in Bath, Avon, and running at the same time as various theatre and ballet performances, exhibitions, lectures, etc.

Bath Oliver /ˌbɑːθ 'ɒlɪvə(r)/ (food and drink) A type of unsweetened dry biscuit, whose recipe was originally invented in the 17th century by William Oliver, a doctor, of Bath, Avon.

Battersea Dogs' Home /ˌbætəsɪ 'dɒgz həʊm/, **the** (animal world) A *London* centre for lost and unwanted dogs and cats, founded in 1860. [situated in Battersea]

Battle of Britain /ˌbætl əv 'brɪtn/, **the** (history) The battle between British and German aircraft over *London* and the south of *England* in the early years of the Second World War, in particular 1940. The Battle was to have been the start of the German invasion of *Britain*.

Battle of Britain Day /ˌbætl əv 'brɪtn deɪ/ (history) 15 September, when a fly-past of aircraft is held over *London* to mark the anniversary of the climax of the *Battle of Britain* in 1940. On the following *Sunday* a special commemorative service is held in *Westminster Abbey*.

BBC /ˌbiː biː 'siː/, **the (British Broadcasting Corporation, the)** (media) One of two major television and radio broadcasting bodies in *Britain*. Its board of 12 governors is appointed by the *Queen* on the advice of the government. Its two television networks are *BBC1* and *BBC2* and its five national radio stations are *Radio 1*, *Radio 2*, *Radio 3*, *Radio 4* and *Radio 5 Live*. Outside Britain, it broadcasts on the *BBC World Service*. See also *Broadcasting House, Bush House, BBC Television Centre*, and compare *ITC*.

BBC English /ˌbiː biː siː 'ɪŋglɪʃ/ (language) Traditionally correct English, especially as formerly spoken by *BBC* announcers and news readers.

BBC 1 /ˌbiː biː siː 'wʌn/ (media) The main television channel of the *BBC*, transmitting mostly programmes of general interest such as light entertainment, news, sport, current affairs and children's programmes.

BBC Television Centre /ˌbiː biː siː 'telɪvɪʒn ˌsentə(r)/, **the** (media) The main television studios of the *BBC* in west *London*.

BBC 2 /ˌbiː biː siː 'tuː/ (media) The second television channel of the *BBC*, transmitting mainly programmes that are more specialized than those of *BBC 1*, such as documentaries, travel programmes, serious plays, concert performances, programmes on leisure interests and international (foreign language) films.

BBC World Service /ˌbiː biː siː ˌwɜːld 'sɜːvɪs/, **the** (media) The service of the *BBC* that broadcasts to other countries of the world, in both English and foreign languages. There are radio broadcasts for 24 hours a day in English, and in 1991 a television service was added. See also *Bush House*.

beagle /'biːgl/ (animal world) A small breed of hound used for hunting hares, and with a short, smooth black and white or brown and white coat. Hunting hares with such hounds is known as 'beagling'.

Beano /'biːnəʊ/, **the** (media) A popular weekly comic for children, founded in 1938. ['beano', a colloquial term for 'good time', 'party']

bear /beə(r)/ (finance) On the *Stock Exchange*, a term for a speculator who sells his shares hoping that the price will fall and that he can then make a profit by buying them back. Compare *bull*. [probably from the proverb, 'sell the bear's skin before you have caught the bear']

beating the bounds /ˌbiːtɪŋ ðə 'baʊndz/ (tradition) An old custom, still kept in some parts of *Britain*, of marking the boundaries of a parish by marching round them and beating the ground, or certain boundary marks, with rods. The custom usually takes place annually on either *Ascension Day* or before *Easter*. In former times, small boys were beaten at boundary marks so that they would remember the boundaries of their parish.

Beatles /'biːtlz/, **the** (people) One of *Britain*'s most influential pop groups, first performing in 1959 in Liverpool. The group included Paul McCartney (born 1942), John Lennon (1940–80), George Harrison (born 1943) and Ringo Starr—real name Richard Starkey—(born 1940). At first, the group performed music that was influenced by American rock 'n' roll and rhythm-and-blues. Lennon and McCartney's songs, however, became increasingly sophisticated and experimental, and their imaginative lyrics and memorable melodies soon contributed to the distinctive *Mersey sound*. Their records were consistently top of the pop music charts in the mid-1960s, their first great success being 'Please Please Me' in 1962. They also made several successful films. In the late 1960s the group studied Indian mysticism and used hallucinatory drugs, and both activities influenced their music. The Beatles broke up in 1971. Paul McCartney then formed the successful group 'Wings' while John Lennon wrote and recorded music in America with his second wife Yoko Ono. Lennon was murdered in New York in 1980.

Beaujolais Nouveau /ˌbəʊʒəleɪ 'nuːvəʊ/ (food and drink) Standard Beaujolais wine imported newly-bottled to *Britain* from France every mid-November and sold by wine shops, *pubs* and restaurants as a commercial attraction. [French, 'new Beaujolais', the vintage of the current year]

Beaulieu /'bjuːlɪ/ (transport) A village near the sea in Hampshire noted for its yachting and famous for the Montagu Motor Museum, formerly known as the National Motor Museum.

Beaver (Scout) /'biːvə (skaʊt)/ (sport and leisure) A boy aged 6 to 8 who is a member of the youngest branch of the *Scout Association*. Compare *Badger*. [movement originated in Canada, where beaver is a familiar forest animal]

Becher's Brook /ˌbiːtʃəz 'brʊk/ (sport and leisure) A difficult jump in the course of the *Grand National*. [named after Captain Becher, who fell there with his horse in the first Grand National in 1839]

BEd /ˌbiːˈed/ **(Bachelor of Education)** (education) The degree awarded to a qualified teacher, either after a four-year course or, for a person already having some qualifications, after a two-year course. A *graduate* usually takes a one-year course leading to a *PGCE*.

bed and breakfast /ˌbed ən 'brekfəst/ (daily life) A bed for the night and breakfast the following morning in a hotel, boarding house or private house, charged to a guest as a single unit. The term is often used colloquially to refer to private houses which provide such a service.

bedsit(ter) /bed'sɪt(ə(r))/ (daily life) A combined sitting-room and bedroom, often with cooking and washing facilities, and usually rented out in a private house to a single tenant.

Beeb /biːb/**, the** (media) A familiar nickname for the *BBC*. [from the pronunciation of BBC]

Beefeater /'biːfiːtə(r)/ (tradition) The nickname of a *Yeoman Warder* at the *Tower of London*. [in the sense 'one who eats beef', 'one who is well fed']

beer garden /'bɪə gɑːdn/ (daily life) The garden of a *pub* in which customers can sit in fine weather to eat the food and drink bought inside the pub. Beer gardens are popular with families in the summer months since young children, who are not allowed inside a pub, can be with their parents.

beer tent /'bɪə tent/ (sport and leisure) A marquee or large tent in which drinks and refreshments are served at an outdoor sporting event or entertainment, such as the *Henley Regatta* or a *fête*. The beer tent is a popular place for people to go to when bad weather stops the sport, while some people prefer to spend most of their time there, regarding the tent as a kind of temporary *pub*.

Belfast /'belfɑːst/ (geography) The capital of *Northern Ireland*, and in normal times the *seat* of the government of Northern Ireland. The *city*, which has a population of almost 300,000, is an important industrial centre (in particular ship-building and the manufacture of aircraft), but at the same time has relatively high unemployment. Most of its buildings are comparatively modern. Since the 1960s it has been almost continuously one of the key points in the *Troubles*.

Belgravia /bel'greɪvɪə/ (London) A fashionable residential district of *London* centring on Belgrave Square, near *Hyde Park*.

Belisha beacon /bə'liːʃə 'biːkən/ (transport) A road sign in the form of a flashing light in an orange globe on a striped pole, marking a pedestrian crossing. See *zebra crossing* and *pelican crossing*. [named after Leslie Hore-Belisha, minister of transport in the 1930s, when such signs were introduced]

bell ringing /'bel rɪŋɪŋ/ see *change ringing* (tradition)

Bellamy, David /'beləmɪ, 'deɪvɪd/ (people) David Bellamy (born 1933) is a popular botanist who appears regularly on television to present programmes on the subject. He is particularly interested in the protection of the environment and in the preservation of wild life of all kinds. David Bellamy has an enthusiastic but 'rough' style of speech which not all viewers find attractive.

Belisha beacon

BEM /ˌbiː iː ˈem/, **the (British Empire Medal, the)** (life and society) A medal awarded to both military personnel and civilians 'for meritorious service'.

Ben Nevis /ˌben ˈnevɪs/ (geography) The highest mountain in *Britain*, in western *Scotland*. Its height is 1,343 metres.

benchmark /ˈbentʃmɑːk/ (geography) A mark in the form of a broad arrow below a horizontal line, engraved on a wall, pillar, etc to indicate a particular height above sea level at that point and so serve as a reference mark in surveying.

Benn, Tony /ˈben, ˈtəʊnɪ/ (people) Tony Benn (born 1925) became a Labour MP (see *Labour Party*) in 1950. However, he was the son of a viscount, and when his father died in 1960 he had to relinquish his *seat* in the *House of Commons* since he had legally inherited his father's title. He refused to accept it, and started a campaign to introduce a law that would enable those inheriting titles to disclaim them, if they wished. His campaign resulted in the passing of the Peerage Act of 1963, whereupon Tony Benn disclaimed his title (he would have been The *Right Honourable* Anthony Wedgwood Benn, 2nd Viscount Stansgate) and was re-elected as an *MP*. He had wished to become leader of the Labour Party.

Bennett, Alan /ˈbenɪt, ˈælən/ (people) Alan Bennett (born 1934) is an actor and writer who is renowned for his witty but perceptive and sensitive plays about ordinary people preoccupied with the details of everyday life. His characters are typically lonely middle-aged women who live in the *North* of England (where Bennett himself was born) and who are absorbed in their past lives and relationships while reflecting on the present and on what the future will hold. Alan Bennett has gained recent success with a series of monologues for television, 'Talking Heads' (1988), one of which he appears in himself.

Bentley /ˈbentlɪ/ (transport) A luxury car made by the *Rolls-Royce* Company.

best man /ˌbest ˈmæn/ (tradition) The chief attendant on the bridegroom at a wedding. Traditionally, he presents the ring at the moment when the bride is ready to put it on, and after the wedding makes the leading speech at the *wedding breakfast* or reception.

Betjeman, John /ˈbetʃəmən, dʒɒn/ (people) John Betjeman (1906–84) was one of the most popular English poets of the present century. His poems are both easy to read and evocative, and reflect his deep love of the traditional British way of life and of established customs and daily routines. Some of his poems are sombre and introspective, and are about the unspoken fear of death that everyone has, or the fact that the Christian religion is a matter of hope, rather than faith. Betjeman was particularly interested in old churches and *Victorian* architecture, and he also had a special affection for old railways and railway stations.

betting shop /ˈbetɪŋ ʃɒp/ (sport and leisure) The licensed premises of a *bookmaker* in a town. Such premises take nearly 90% of all money staked on horse and *greyhound racing*.

B'ham /ˈbɜːmɪŋəm/ (geography) A conventional abbreviation, for example on road signs and lanes, for Birmingham.

Big Ben /ˌbɪg ˈben/ (London) The clock in the clock tower of the *Houses of Parliament, London*, famous for its accurate time-keeping and for its use as a broadcast time signal by the *BBC*. The name properly refers to the bell of the clock, so nicknamed after Benjamin Hall, Chief Commissioner of Works when it was cast in 1856.

bill /bɪl/ (government) The term for the draft of an *Act of Parliament*, which when under discussion in the *Houses of Parliament* passes through five stages: *first reading, second reading*, committee stage, report stage and *third reading*.

Bill, The /ˈbɪl, ðə/ (media) A popular television series about

bingo

the day-to-day incidents at a London police station, involving the different police officers working there. The series began in 1984 and is screened by *ITV* in three weekly episodes. [from 'the Old Bill', a nickname for the police, itself perhaps from 'Old Bill', an old soldier who was a popular cartoon character in the First World War]

Billy Bunter /ˌbɪlɪ ˈbʌntə(r)/ (education) A famous fat and greedy boy in the stories about *Greyfriars*.

bingo /ˈbɪŋgəʊ/ (sport and leisure) A popular gambling game. It is normally played in halls and converted cinemas. Players buy cards printed with rows of numbers and cross off the numbers as they are called out at random. The winner is the first player to cross out all the numbers on his or her card. In recent years it has also been possible to play bingo by filling in similar cards published in *popular papers*. [said to represent a cry of joy on winning or achieving something]

Birkbeck (College) /ˈbɜːkbek (ˌbɜːkbek ˈkɒlɪdʒ)/ (education) A *college¹*, of *London University*, founded in 1823 by George Birkbeck as an institute of mechanics.

Birmingham Royal Ballet, the /ˌbɜːmɪŋəm ˌrɔɪə ˈbæleɪ/, **the** (arts) The name of the former Sadler's Wells Royal Ballet after it moved from *London* to Birmingham in 1990. See *Sadler's Wells (Theatre)*.

Birthday Honours /ˌbɜːθdeɪ ˈɒnəz/, **the** (life and society) The announcement of honorary titles, orders and medals awarded annually on the sovereign's *Official Birthday*. Compare *New Year Honours*.

Birtwistle, Harrison /ˈbɜːtwɪsl, ˈhærɪsn/ (people) Harrison Birtwistle (born 1934) is a musical composer whose works have gained increasing appreciation. Much of his music is avant-garde, although his opera 'The Mask of Orpheus' (1973–83) and some recent orchestral works have proved rather more accessible. Harrison Birtwistle was knighted in 1988.

Bisley /ˈbɪzlɪ/ (sport and leisure) A shooting range near Woking, Surrey, where international and other important shooting contests are held. [from the name of the village near to it]

bitter /ˈbɪtə(r)/ (food and drink) A type of draught beer with a high hop content and a rather bitter taste. Compare *light ale*.

Black, Cilla /ˈblæk, ˈsɪlə/ (people) Cilla Black (born Priscilla White in 1943) is a talented television presenter who originally gained fame as a pop singer in the 1960s. She then appeared in various forms of entertainment such as *pantomime* and the *Royal Variety Show*, before becoming the host of two very popular *ITV* shows, 'Surprise Surprise', first shown in 1984, in which long-lost friends and relatives are reunited, and 'Blind Date', first shown in 1985, in which young couples are introduced to each other in the hope that they will fall in love and marry. Cilla Black comes from Liverpool and her *Scouse*[2] accent makes both participants and viewers feel at home.

black /blæk/, **the** (finance) A colloquial term for a bank account in credit, said to be 'in the black'. [as opposed to a debit account 'in the *red*'. Credit entries were originally written in black ink and debit entries were written in red ink]

Black Country /ˈblæk ˌkʌntrɪ/, **the** (geography) The industrialized region of the West *Midlands*, where there are many collieries and steelworks. [from the black smoke and blackened buildings there]

Black Maria /ˌblæk məˈraɪə/ (law) A police van for taking prisoners to and from prison. [from the original colour of the vans: Black Maria was said to be the name of a strong black woman in Boston, USA, who helped the police in the handling of prisoners]

Black Prince /ˌblæk ˈprɪns/, **the** (history) The nickname of

Edward, *Prince of Wales* (1330–76), son of King Edward III. [either from the colour of his armour or for his cruelty]

black pudding /ˌblæk ˈpʊdɪŋ/ (food and drink) A kind of black sausage made mainly from minced pork fat and pig's blood.

Black Rod /ˌblæk ˈrɒd/ (government) In the *House of Lords*, an officer whose main duty is calling the members of the *House of Commons* to attend the annual *Speech from the Throne* at the opening of *Parliament*. [from the black rod topped by a gold *lion* that he carries during this ceremony]

black tie /ˌblæk ˈtaɪ/ (clothing) **1** A black bow tie worn with a *dinner jacket*. **2** A conventional indication on an official invitation that *evening dress* must be worn. Compare *white tie*.

Black Watch /ˌblæk ˈwɒtʃ/, **the** (defence) The nickname of the *Royal Highland Regiment* in the British *Army*. [from the dark colour of the *tartan* of the men's *kilts*]

blacking /ˈblækɪŋ/ (work) The boycott of specific goods, work, etc by a trade union in a firm where there are *blacklegs*.

blackleg /ˈblækleg/ (work) A strike-breaker or person who works in place of another striker when ordered not to by his trade union.

Blackpool /ˈblækpuːl/ (geography) *Britain*'s most popular seaside resort, in Lancashire, famous for its Tower (Blackpool Tower), its 'Pleasure Beach', its seafront, with its trams and decorative lighting ('illuminations'), and its *conference centre*.

Blackwell's /ˈblækwelz/ (commerce) A famous bookshop in *Oxford*. [founded by Benjamin Blackwell in 1846]

blazer /ˈbleɪzə(r)/ (clothing) A distinctive jacket, usually with a badge on the breast pocket, and often having gold or silver buttons, worn by a pupil as part of a school uniform, by a member of a sports team, or by a member, or former member, of an association or organization of some kind.

Blenheim /ˈblenɪm/ **(Battle of Blenheim, the)** (history) The battle of 1704 in which the Anglo-Austrian forces won a victory over the French and Bavarian troops in the War of the Spanish Succession. [from the name of the village, now Blindheim, West Germany, where it was fought]

Blenheim Orange /ˌblenɪm ˈɒrɪndʒ/ (food and drink) A type of winter eating apple, with large, round, golden fruit. [first grown in the gardens of *Blenheim Palace*]

Blenheim Palace /ˌblenɪm ˈpælɪs/ (history) A large country house and estate near *Oxford¹*, built for the Duke of Marlborough, leader of the English forces in the Battle of *Blenheim*, in memory of his victory in this battle.

blimp /blɪmp/ (life and society) A short name for someone like *Colonel Blimp*.

Blitz /blɪts/**, the** (history) The bombing of *Britain*, and especially *London*, by the German air force in the Second World War, in particular 1940–1. [from German 'Blitzkrieg', 'lightning war']

block release /ˌblɒk rɪ'liːs/ (work) The release of employees from their place of work for an extended period so that they can attend a *college²* of *further education* or *higher education* with the aim of obtaining a qualification related to their work. The release may even be for a whole *term¹*. Compare *day release*.

block vote /ˌblɒk 'vəʊt/ (work) A method of voting in which a single delegate's vote represents not one vote but the total number of votes cast by the section he represents. Such a method is commonly used by the *TUC*.

blood donor /'blʌd ˌdəʊnə(r)/ (medicine) A person who voluntarily gives blood for use in blood transfusions in hospitals. The collection of blood in this way is operated by the state-run Blood Transfusion Service, which set up regional transfusion centres and organize donor sessions in towns, villages, factories, offices and in the armed services. Blood donors must be in good health and between the ages of 18 and 60.

blood sports /'blʌd spɔːts/ (sport and leisure) The hunting of wild animals such as foxes, hares and otters with the aim of killing them. Such hunting has been increasingly opposed by supporters of the *League Against Cruel Sports* and similar bodies. ['blood' from the blood that is shed]

Bloody Mary /ˌblʌdɪ 'meərɪ/ (**1** history **2** food and drink) **1** A nickname of Queen Mary Tudor (1516–58), given her by the Protestants whom she persecuted cruelly. **2** A type of cocktail, made from vodka and tomato juice. [from its red colouring]

Bloody Tower /ˌblʌdɪ 'taʊə(r)/**, the** (history) A tower in the *Tower of London* built in the 14th century and supposedly where the *Princes in the Tower* were murdered.

Bloomsbury Group /'bluːmzbrɪ gruːp/**, the** (arts) A group of writers, artists and intellectuals living and working in the early 20th century in the *London* district of Bloomsbury, near the *British Museum*. Among them were the writers E M Forster (1879–1970), Virginia Woolf (1882–1941) and Lytton Strachey (1880–1932), the philosopher and mathematician

Bertrand Russell (1872–1970) and the economist John
Maynard Keynes (1883–1946). The Group were critical of
many aspects of contemporary society, notably morality,
religion and aesthetics.

blue /bluː/ (**1** politics **2**, **3** sport and leisure) **1** A member of
the *Conservative Party*, whose campaigning colour is blue. **2**
A member of a sports team playing for *Oxford University* (and
wearing dark blue) or *Cambridge University* (wearing light
blue). **3** An award at either Oxford University or Cambridge
University to such a member.

blue chip /ˌbluː ˈtʃɪp/ (finance) On the *Stock Exchange*, a share
regarded as reliable for providing a good *dividend* and for
retaining a high value. [from gambling jargon: in poker a
blue 'chip' (counter) has a high value]

Blue Ensign /ˌbluː ˈensən/ (defence) A flag flown by ships
chartered by the government (and formerly by ships under
the command of naval reserve officers). The flag is blue, with
a *Union Jack* in the upper left quarter.

Blue Peter /ˌbluː ˈpiːtə(r)/ (media) A twice-weekly informative
and entertaining television programme for children,
broadcast on *BBC 1* since 1958. [from the 'blue peter', a flag
hoisted by a ship about to leave port]

blue plaque /ˌbluː ˈplɑːk/ (London) A round blue-coloured
notice on the wall of a *London* house showing that a famous
person lived there. The plaques are placed by the local
borough council and give the person's name and occupation,
dates of birth and death, and the period during which they
lived in the house. The first plaque was placed in 1867 on the
house near *Oxford Street* where Byron was born in 1788. To
qualify for a plaque, the person must have been dead for at
least 20 years and have been born more than 100 years ago.
The City of *Westminster*[1] has its own special green plaques.

Bluebell Railway /ˌbluːbel ˈreɪlweɪ/, **the** (transport) A private
railway line in Sussex, operating with old-style steam
engines and coaches. The track runs for five miles from
Sheffield Park to Horsted Keynes, and follows a picturesque
route along a track bordered by bluebells in spring.

Bluebird /ˈbluːbɜːd/ (sport and leisure) The name of a series of
racing cars and speed boats in which the racing drivers
(father and son) Malcolm and Donald Campbell set several
world speed records over the period 1935–67.

blue-collar worker /bluː ˈkɒlə wɜːkə(r)/ (work) A nickname for an industrial worker, who often wears blue overalls. [as distinct from a *white-collar worker*]

Blues and Royals /ˌbluːz ən ˈrɔɪəlz/**, the** (defence) One of the two regiments of the *Household Cavalry*, formed in 1969 when the *Royal Horse Guards*, nicknamed 'The Blues' from the colour of their uniform, merged with the Royal Dragoons. Compare *Life Guards*.

bluestocking /ˈbluːstɒkɪŋ/ (life and society) A (usually disparaging) name for a scholarly woman. [from the blue stockings originally worn by male members of an 18th century literary society]

Blyton, Enid /ˈblaɪtn, ˈiːnɪd/ (people) Enid Blyton (1896–1968) was a highly popular writer of children's books, many featuring the same characters, such as Noddy and Big Ears, two puppet friends, and the Famous Five and Secret Seven, groups of child adventurers. Although her writing has been criticized by some adults as sexist and racist, the books themselves remain as popular as ever among her young readers.

BMA /ˌbiː em ˈeɪ/**, the (British Medical Association, the)** (medicine) The professional body that promotes medical and related sciences in *Britain* and that represents the interests of doctors and surgeons. It is thus effectively the trade union of all *GP*s. It was founded in 1852, and its early campaigning work resulted in the establishment of the *General Medical Council* in 1858.

Boat Race /ˈbəʊt reɪs/**, the** (sport and leisure) The traditional annual rowing race between teams (eight rowers and a cox) from *Oxford University* and *Cambridge University*, held on a section of the river Thames in *London* in March or April. The length of the course is 7.2 km. [in full, University Boat Race]

Boat Show /ˈbəʊt ʃəʊ/**, the** (sport and leisure) A short name for one of the two annual International Boat Shows, held respectively at *Earls Court, London* in January and in Southampton in September.

boater /ˈbəʊtə(r)/ (clothing) A stiff straw hat with a low, flat crown, straight brim, and broad ribbon round it, in fashion at cricket matches, boating parties and picnics in the 1920s. Today it still forms part of the uniform of some *public schools*[1] (notably *Harrow*) and *college*[1] sports *clubs*.

bob /bɒb/ (daily life) A nickname for a *shilling*, for some time also used for the 5 pence piece which superseded it in 1971,

bobby

and still sometimes heard in colloquial expressions such as 'a couple of bob', or 'a bob or two', meaning simply 'money'.

bobby /'bɒbɪ/ (law) A common nickname for a policeman, especially one regarded as friendly and helpful, for example when controlling traffic or giving directions to a passer-by. The word often occurs in such phrases as 'the British bobby' or 'the bobby on the beat' (one making a regular patrol of a district on foot or by bicycle). [from the name Bobby, a form of Robert, referring to Sir Robert Peel, the *Home Secretary* who founded the *Metropolitan Police* in 1828]

Bodleian (Library) /'bɒdlɪən (ˌbɒdlɪən 'laɪbrərɪ)/, **the** (arts) The main library of *Oxford University*, with about 5 million printed volumes and many thousands of manuscripts. It is a *copyright library*. [from Thomas Bodley, who refounded the old library with new furnishings and books in 1598]

Boer War /ˌbɔː 'wɔː(r)/, **the** (history) The Anglo-Boer War of 1899–1902, in which *Britain* fought against the South African Boer republics of Transvaal and Orange Free State and gained control of them.

boiler suit /'bɔːlə suːt/ (clothing) A type of garment in one piece worn for rough or dirty work, especially by older men. [formerly worn by men working on boilers]

Bond Street /'bɒnd striːt/ (London) One of the main shopping streets of *London*, famous for its fashion stores and in particular its jewellers' shops and private picture galleries. [named after Sir Thomas Bond, who built it in the 17th century]

Bonfire Night /'bɒnfaɪə naɪt/ (tradition) A popular name for *Guy Fawkes' Night*.

Bonnie Prince Charlie /ˌbɒnɪ prɪns 'tʃɑːlɪ/ (history) One of the nicknames of the Scottish prince Charles Edward Stuart (1720–88), the son of James Edward Stuart. See also *Young Pretender, Culloden*. [from Scottish 'bonnie' meaning 'handsome']

Book of Common Prayer /ˌbʊk əv ˌkɒmən 'preə(r)/, **the** (religion) The official prayer and service book of the *Church of England*, first published in 1549 and later in a new version in 1662. Many *churches* today use a modernized and simplified version of it, the Alternative Service Book.

book token /'bʊk ˌtəʊkən/ (commerce) A voucher, usually in the form of a greetings card, which can be exchanged at a bookshop for a book or books at the stated value of the card. Book tokens are frequently given as presents or prizes, especially when the giver wishes to leave the choice of gift or prize to the receiver. They were first introduced in the 1930s. Compare *gift token*.

Book Trust /'bʊk trʌst/ (life and society) A charitable trust founded in 1986 to encourage an interest in books and reading, especially among young people. It organizes the *Booker Prize* and is funded partly by the *Arts Council (of Great Britain)* and partly by booksellers and publishers.

Booker prize /ˌbʊkə 'praɪz/, **the** (arts) The leading British literary prize, sponsored by Booker *Plc* and awarded annually for the best novel written in English and published for the first time in *Britain* by a British publisher. The prize is administered by *Book Trust* and is worth £20,000.

bookie /'bʊkɪ/ (sport and leisure) A colloquial term for a *bookmaker*.

bookmaker /'bʊkmeɪkə(r)/ (sport and leisure) A man whose business is to accept bets, especially on horse and dog races, and to pay out the winnings. See *betting shop*. [literally, 'one who makes a betting book']

Border TV /'bɔːdə ti: ˌviː/ (media) One of the 15 regional television companies of the *ITC*, based in Carlisle and broadcasting to the *Borders* as well as to the *Isle of Man*.

Borders /'bɔːdəz/, **the** (geography) The district either side of the border between *England* and *Scotland*. Compare *Border TV*.

borough /'bʌrə/ (government) **1** A town that forms the *constituency* of an *MP* or that was granted the ceremonial title of 'borough' by royal authority. **2** One of the 32 ˙ administrative districts of *Greater London*. Compare *burgh*.

borough council /ˌbʌrə ˈkaʊnsl/ (government) A *local authority* within a *borough*. Like a *district council*, it deals mainly with local services, for example, environmental health, housing, decisions on *planning permission* and rubbish collection.

borstal /ˈbɔːstl/ (law) The former name of a *young offender institution*. [The first such institution opened in 1902 in Borstal, now a suburb of Rochester, Kent]

Boston Stump /ˌbɒstən ˈstʌmp/**, the** (geography) The colloquial name of the main *church* in Boston, Lincolnshire, whose tall tower serves as a landmark for ships.

bottle bank /ˈbɒtl bæŋk/ (daily life) A large, round iron container in which people can put empty bottles so that the glass can be used to make new bottles. The containers are placed by the *local authority* in a public place such as a car park and are usually in groups of three, coloured respectively white, green and brown for the different colours of the bottles. Bottle banks are not intended for milk bottles, as these are collected daily by the *milkman*.

bottle party /ˈbɒtl ˌpɑːtɪ/ (life and society) An evening party to which each guest brings a bottle of drink. See also *BYOB*.

bouncy castle /ˌbaʊnsɪ ˈkɑːsl/ (sport and leisure) A large toy castle made from rubber, plastic or other material that is inflated so that young children can jump about on it.

Boundary Commission /ˈbaʊndrɪ kəˌmɪʃn/ (government) One of the four government bodies (respectively for *England, Scotland, Wales* and *Northern Ireland*) that decide the boundaries of parliamentary *constituencies*. They carry out their surveys every 10 or 15 years and make recommendations in the light of shifts in population and alterations to *local government* boundaries. The overall number of constituencies in *Britain* is thus subject to change. When *Parliament* approved the Commissions' reports in 1983, for example, the number of constituencies rose from 635 to 650.

bound over /ˌbaʊnd ˈəʊvə/ (law) A legal term meaning that a person has been ordered by a court of law to behave in a proper manner, and especially to 'keep the peace'. A person who is bound over is thus in a sense 'on *probation*'.

Bournemouth /ˈbɔːnməθ/ (geography) A large and fashionable seaside town and resort in Dorset, well known also as a *conference centre*.

bowls

Bow Bells /ˌbəʊ ˈbelz/ (London) The bells of the *London* church *St Mary-le-Bow*. According to tradition, a true Londoner or *cockney²* is a person who was born within the sound of these bells.

Bow Group /ˈbəʊ gruːp/, **the** (politics) An influential society of younger members of the *Conservative Party*, whose first meeting in 1951 was held in the Bow and Bromley Club, southeast *London*.

Bow Street /ˈbəʊ striːt/ (law) The chief police criminal court in *London*, formerly in the street of this name, but now in new premises at *Charing Cross*.

Bowie, David /ˈbəʊɪ, ˈdeɪvɪd/ (people) David Bowie (born 1947), whose original name was David Jones, is generally regarded as one of the most original pop musicians after the *Beatles* and the *Rolling Stones*. He became a cult figure for his many surrealistic costumes and 'images'. More recently he has become an effective stage and film actor.

bowl /bəʊl/ (sport and leisure) A large, heavy, wooden ball used in the game of *bowls*, with flattened sides to make it run on a course.

bowler /ˈbəʊlə(r)/ (clothing) A type of man's hat, usually black, and rigid with a round crown, traditionally worn by businessmen in the *City (of London)*. [in full, 'bowler hat', named after John Bowler, a 19th-century *London* hatter]

bowling /ˈbəʊlɪŋ/ (sport and leisure) **1** An alternative name for *bowls*. **2** The sport of tenpin bowling.

box junction

bowls /bəʊlz/ (sport and leisure) A game in which a heavy wooden ball (*bowl*) is rolled over a smooth lawn (bowling green) in such a way that it stops as close as possible to a small white ball (jack). The game has from two to eight players, each bowling two or more bowls.

box junction /ˈbɒks dʒʌŋkʃn/ (transport) A special marking on the road at a crossroad or junction, consisting of a yellow square ('box') marked with criss-cross lines. In order to control traffic flow at the junction, no vehicle is supposed to drive onto the box unless its exit is clear.

Boxing Day /ˈbɒksɪŋ deɪ/ (tradition) The day (26 December) following *Christmas Day*, and celebrated as a *bank holiday*. It was formerly the custom to give 'Christmas boxes', or gifts of money, to servants and tradesmen on this day. Today many people still give an annual Christmas gift to regular callers such as dustmen and *paperboys/girls*.

boy scout /ˌbɔɪ ˈskaʊt/ (sport and leisure) A term still used for a *scout¹*.

Boyne /bɔɪn/, **the (Battle of the Boyne, the)** (history) A battle in 1690 on the river Boyne, *Ireland*. The Roman Catholics in Ireland rose in favour of the former King James II (reigned 1685–89), but their rebellion was crushed by his successor, the Protestant King William III (reigned 1689–1702). See also *Orangemen*.

BP /ˌbiː'piː/ **(British Petroleum)** (science and technology) One of the two leading oil companies in *Britain*. It was formerly state-run, but was privatized in 1987.

BR /ˌbiː'ɑː(r)/ **(British Rail)** (transport) The state company that controls the railways of *Britain*. It has five business sectors. *InterCity*, *Network SouthEast* and *Regional Railways* are responsible for the passenger services, while Railfreight Distribution and Trainload Freight are concerned with freight. There are plans to privatize parts of BR.

Braemar Gathering /ˌbreɪmɑː'gæðərɪŋ/**, the** (sport and leisure) The annual *Highland gathering* held at Braemar, *Scotland*, in September and traditionally attended by members of the *royal family*. The activities include *tossing the caber*, wrestling and Scottish country (ie, folk) dancing.

Bragg, Melvyn /'bræg, 'melvɪn/ (people) Melvyn Bragg (born 1939) is a novelist and television presenter (on the *South Bank Show*) who has done much to popularize 'serious' literature and the arts.

Brain of Britain /ˌbreɪn əv 'brɪtn/ (media) A regular general knowledge quiz programme on *Radio 4*, in which contestants answer questions in front of a studio audience. The winner at the end of the series is declared 'Brain of Britain' for that year.

Bramley's (Seedling) /'bræmlɪz (ˌbræmlɪz 'siːdlɪŋ)/ (food and drink) A type of winter cooking apple with large, juicy, greenish-yellow fruit. [said to have been first grown in the 19th century by Matthew Bramley, an English butcher]

Branagh, Kenneth /'brænə, 'kenɪθ/ (people) Kenneth Branagh (born 1960) is a film and stage actor and director who has gained praise for his imaginative productions and memorable acting. He is particularly known for his interpretation of *Shakespeare*'s plays, both in the theatre and in the cinema. In 1989 he married the actress Emma Thompson and the two often act together in his productions. In 1993, for example, they played the lovers Benedick and Beatrice in the film of Shakespeare's *Much Ado About Nothing*.

Brand's Hatch /ˌbrændz 'hætʃ/ (sport and leisure) The name of a motor racing track in Kent, near the village of that name. The *British Grand Prix[1]* is held there every second year.

Branson, Richard /'brænsn, 'rɪtʃəd/ (people) Richard Branson (born 1950) is a successful pop music promoter and record company director who has become a millionaire through his commercial expertise and enthusiasm. He set up his record company in 1970, and in 1984 launched his own transatlantic airline, both under the commercial name of Virgin. In 1985 he won the Business Enterprise Award. In 1986 he broke the transatlantic record for the fastest crossing by power boat. In 1987 he set up another record by being the first man to cross the Atlantic in a hot-air balloon. In 1992 he sold his music company to Thorn EMI.

brass band /ˌbrɑːs 'bænd/ (arts) A band or orchestra of players of brass musical instruments, often together with other wind instruments and almost always with drums. Brass bands are found throughout *Britain*, but are particularly popular in the north of *England*. Their players come from a wide range of commercial and voluntary organizations, although some of the best have players from factories (so called 'works bands'), coal mines and religious or charitable organizations such as the *Salvation Army*. There are also good bands with young players, especially in schools.

bread and butter pudding /ˌbred ən ˌbʌtə 'pʊdɪŋ/ (food and drink) A hot sweet dish consisting of slices of bread baked in egg *custard* with raisins and sugar.

breakfast TV /ˌbrekfəst tiː 'viː/ (media) A colloquial name for early morning television, watched by people as they are having breakfast. The main breakfast television programmes are 'BBC Breakfast News' on *BBC 1* and 'The Big Breakfast' on *Channel 4*, while a separate company, *GMTV*, broadcasts on *ITV*. The satellite channel MTV (see *BSkyB*) has 'Awake on the Wildside' at this time.

Brecon Beacons /ˌbrekən 'biːkənz/, **the** (geography) The name of two high hills in Powys (formerly in Breconshire), South *Wales*, on which signal fires were lit in medieval times. They are now part of a *national park*.

Brewer /'bruːə(r)/ (language) The short title of 'Brewer's Dictionary of Phrase and Fable', a reference book explaining the origins of words and phrases from mythology, history, religion, art and related themes, and originally compiled in 1870 by a clergyman, Ebenezer Brewer.

Bridge of Sighs /ˌbrɪdʒ əv 'saɪz/, **the** (style) A picturesque covered bridge over the river Cam at *Cambridge*[1] belonging to St John's *College*[1]. A bridge like this and with the same name links two of the buildings of Hertford *College*[1], Oxford. [from its appearance, similar to the Bridge of Sighs in Venice]

bridleway /'braɪdlweɪ/ (geography) A public track or path along which a horse may be ridden or led.

Brighton /'braɪtn/ (geography) A large seaside resort in East

Sussex, famous for its *Regency* architecture (especially the *Royal Pavilion*), its long, broad seafront, its nudist beach, its pier and its *conference centre*. The pier, officially the Palace Pier, is the most popular in *Britain*, with over 3 million visitors annually.

bring-and-buy (sale) /ˌbrɪŋ ən 'baɪ (seɪl)/ (daily life) A sale, in which people bring goods they wish to sell, and buy the goods brought by others. It is usually held to raise money for a charity.

Bristol Cream /ˌbrɪstl 'kri:m/ (food and drink) The brand name of a type of superior full-bodied, medium sweet sherry. [named in the 19th century by comparison with *Bristol Milk*]

Bristol Milk /ˌbrɪstl 'mɪlk/ (food and drink) The brand name of a type of superior fine, medium dry sherry. [originally a nickname for sherry, as this was imported to *England* from Spain via the port of Bristol]

Brit /brɪt/ (geography) A colloquial term, sometimes used critically, for a British person.

Britain /'brɪtn/ (geography) A frequently-used name for *Great Britain*. See also *United Kingdom* and *British Isles* and maps on p 466.

Britannia /brɪ'tænjə/ (1 history 2 tradition 3 royal family) 1 The Roman name for the southern part of *Great Britain*. 2 A personification of Great Britain on coins, etc in the form of a seated woman holding a trident in one hand and wearing a helmet. 3 The name of the *Royal Yacht*.

Britannia Royal Naval College /brɪˌtænjə ˌrɔɪəl 'neɪvl ˌkɒlɪdʒ/, **the** (education) A *college*[2] for officer cadets of the *Royal Navy*, at Dartmouth, Devon. [college originated on board *HMS* 'Britannia' in 1863]

British Academy /ˌbrɪtɪʃ ə'kædəmɪ/, **the** (arts) A learned society founded in 1901 for the purpose of promoting historical, philosophical and philological studies, and which fulfils almost the same role for the humanities as the *Royal Society* does for the natural sciences.

British Aerospace /ˌbrɪtɪʃ 'eərəʊspeɪs/ **(BAe)** (science and technology) The leading British aircraft company, manufacturing civil and military aircraft, satellites, space systems, and guided weapons. It was formed from various aircraft companies as a single nationalized company in 1977 but was privatized in 1981.

British Airways (Plc) /ˌbrɪtɪʃ 'eəweɪz (ˌpi: el 'si:)/ **(BA)** (transport) The largest airline in *Britain*, set up in 1974 as a state company formed from British European Airways (BEA) and the British Overseas Airways Corporation (BOAC). British Airways was privatized in 1987.

British Association /ˌbrɪtɪʃ əsəʊsɪˈeɪʃn/, **the** (science and technology) An organization founded in 1831 to promote general interest in science in all its branches by means of lectures, exhibitions and the publication of pamphlets. [full name: the British Association for the Advancement of Science]

British Board of Film Classification /ˌbrɪtɪʃ ˌbɔːd əv ˈfɪlm klæsɪfɪˌkeɪʃn/, **the** (arts) The body that decides the category in which a film must be placed for public showing. There are at present five categories: *U*, *PG*, *12*, *15* and *18*. The Board also classifies videos in similar categories.

British Broadcasting Corporation /ˌbrɪtɪʃ ˈbrɔːdkɑːstɪŋ kɔːpəˌreɪʃn/ see *BBC* (media)

British Coal /ˌbrɪtɪʃ ˈkəʊl/ (work) The state body that manages coal mines in *Britain*. In 1992 there were 50 British Coal collieries in Britain, with 44,000 miners, compared with 850 collieries and 695,000 miners in 1955. The closure of pits in the *Midlands*, northeast *England*, south *Wales* and central *Scotland* has contributed to high unemployment in these traditional mining regions. It is planned to privatize British Coal.

British Council /ˌbrɪtɪʃ ˈkaʊnsl/, **the** (education) A government organization founded in 1934 to promote a wider knowledge of *Britain* and the English language abroad and to develop closer cultural ties with other countries.

British Empire /ˌbrɪtɪʃ ˈempaɪə(r)/, **the** (history) A term formerly used for *Great Britain* and its overseas dominions and colonial possessions, today replaced by the *Commonwealth[1]*. The British Empire was at its greatest in about 1920, when it included approximately 25% of the world's population and more than a quarter of the world's land territory.

British Film Institute /ˌbrɪtɪʃ ˈfɪlm ˌɪnstɪtjuːt/, **the** (arts) An organization founded in 1933 to encourage film making. It administers the *National Film Theatre* and has a large library of scripts and books on film and television. It is financed mainly by the government.

British Gas /ˌbrɪtɪʃ ˈgæs / (science and technology) The company that supplies gas throughout *Britain*, operating in

12 administrative regions. British Gas was formerly state-owned but was privatized in 1986.

British Grand Prix /ˌbrɪtɪʃ ˌɡrɑːn ˈpriː/, **the** (sport and leisure) **1** An important motor racing championship held in alternate years at *Brands Hatch* and *Silverstone*. **2** An important motorcycle racing championship held annually at Silverstone.

British Isles /ˌbrɪtɪʃ ˈaɪlz/, **the** (geography) A frequently-used name for *England, Scotland, Wales* and the whole of *Ireland.* Compare *Great Britain* and the *United Kingdom.* See p 466.

British Legion /ˌbrɪtɪʃ ˈliːdʒən/ see *Royal British Legion* (charities)

British Leyland /ˌbrɪtɪʃ ˈleɪlənd/ see *Rover* (transport)

British Library /ˌbrɪtɪʃ ˈlaɪbrərɪ/, **the (BL, the)** (arts) The national library of *Britain*, with its headquarters in *London* and its interlibrary lending centre at Boston Spa, West Yorkshire. The main library opened in new and larger premises near *St Pancras* station in 1994.

British Lions /ˌbrɪtɪʃ ˈlaɪənz/, **the** (sport and leisure) A party of *rugby union football* players chosen from the best amateur players in the *United Kingdom.* They play as a team on tours overseas.

British Museum /ˌbrɪtɪʃ mjuːˈzɪəm/, **the (BM, the)** (arts) A museum in *London* noted for its collections of antiquities, coins and medals, prints and drawings. Until 1994 its famous circular reading room also housed the reference division of the *British Library.*

British National Party /ˌbrɪtɪʃ ˈnæʃnəl ˌpɑːtɪ/, **the (BNP, the)** (politics) A small political party of the extreme right wing, with neo-Nazi and racist views. It was founded in 1980 as a 'breakaway' party from the *National Front*, and adopted its present name in 1982. In 1993 its first *councillor* was elected in a *borough* in the *East End* of *London*, where a number of Asian people live.

British Nuclear Fuels /ˌbrɪtɪʃ ˌnjuːklɪə ˈfjuːəlz/ **(BNFL)** (science and technology) The state-owned company that manufactures nuclear fuel and reprocesses nuclear waste. Its reprocessing plant at *Sellafield* has gained adverse publicity because of its faulty operating procedures.

British Open (Championship) /ˌbrɪtɪʃ ˈəʊpən (ˌbrɪtɪʃ ˌəʊpən ˈtʃæmpɪənʃɪp)/, **the** (sport and leisure) The most important annual golf tournament in *Britain*, open to professional and amateur players, and held since 1860 at different courses in the *British Isles*.

British Philatelic Bureau /ˌbrɪtɪʃ fɪləˈtelɪk ˌbjʊərəʊ/, **the** (commerce) An organization set up by the *Post Office* in 1963 to provide stamp collectors with information about British stamps, and to sell new issues of stamps and other philatelic items by post from its headquarters in *Edinburgh*.

British Shipbuilders /ˌbrɪtɪʃ ˈʃɪpbɪldəz/ (transport) A state corporation established in 1977 to manage all publicly owned shipyards in *Britain*. The corporation was privatized in 1989.

British Steel /ˌbrɪtɪʃ ˈstiːl/ (science and technology) The former state company, privatized in 1988, that manufactures iron and steel at a number of plants in *Britain*.

British Technology Group /ˌbrɪtɪʃ tekˈnɒlədʒɪ gruːp/, **the (BTG, the)** (science and technology) An organization that promotes and finances the development of new technology into commercial products, whether in industry or at universities and state-run research centres.

British Telecom /ˌbrɪtɪʃ ˈtelɪkɒm/ (commerce) The former name (to 1991) of *BT*.

Briton /ˈbrɪtn/ (1 geography 2 history) 1 A native or inhabitant of *Britain*, or a citizen of the *United Kingdom*. 2 An early Celtic inhabitant of southern Britain before the 5th century, also sometimes called an Ancient Briton.

Britten, Benjamin /ˈbrɪtn, ˈbendʒəmɪn/ (people) Benjamin Britten (1913–76), a noted composer, pianist and conductor, wrote works that range widely from arrangements of simple folk songs for voice and piano to such large, dramatic executions as the children's opera 'Noyes Fludde' (1958) and the sombre, serious 'War Requiem' (1962). He was noted for his skill as an opera writer and for his use of children's voices in both religious and secular works. His output also extended to music for radio and films. Benjamin Britten was awarded the *Companion of Honour* in 1953, the *Order of Merit* in 1965, and was made a *life peer* in 1976. See also *Aldeburgh Festival*.

BRMB /biː ˈɑːr em ˌbiː/ (media) One of *Britain*'s oldest *ILR* stations, based in Birmingham and first broadcasting in 1974. The station is famous for the annual 'walkathon' (*sponsored walk*) that it has organized since 1983. [initials from full name of original company, *Bir*mingham *B*roadcasting *Ltd*. See also *Brum*.]

B-road

B-road /'bi: rəʊd/ (transport) A secondary or minor road (compare *A-road*), often running cross country to connect two A-roads.

Broadcasting House /ˌbrɔːdkɑːstɪŋ 'haʊs/ (media) The main building and central office of the *BBC* in *London*, where a number of radio and television studios are. Compare *Bush House*.

Broadmoor /'brɔːdmɔː(r)/ (law) An institution (officially Broadmoor Hospital) in Berkshire where patients suffering from mental illness are treated and, in particular, where there is a residential centre for people who have been convicted of a criminal offence but who cannot be sent to an ordinary prison as they are seriously mentally disturbed. [opened in 1873 as Broadmoor Asylum]

Broads /brɔːdz/**, the** (geography) A group of shallow navigable lakes, interconnected by rivers, in *East Anglia* (Norfolk and Suffolk). They are popular as a tourist centre and for their many bird sanctuaries. In 1988 the Broads were officially designated a *national park*.

brogues /brəʊgz/ (clothing) A type of stout walking shoe, often with ornamental decorations in the form of small holes. [The holes were originally punched through the leather to let water drain out when the wearer was walking over wet ground]

brogues

broker /'brəʊkə(r) (**1** commerce **2** finance) **1** An agent who buys or sells goods on someone's behalf in return for payment. **2** A short word for a *stockbroker*.

Brookside /'brʊksaɪd/ (media) A popular 'soap opera' (melodramatic series about the lives of a family or group of people) shown on *Channel 4* since 1982. It is broadcast three times weekly, and centres on the daily lives of various families and individuals living in a *close³* in Liverpool. It is generally regarded as one of the more 'intelligent' series of this type.

brother /'brʌðə(r)/ (life and society) A form of address in some religious organizations and in trade unions, used to show a friendly relationship between members of the group.

brown sign /ˌbraʊn 'saɪn/ (transport) A brown-coloured road sign, indicating a tourist attraction such as a *stately home*, a place for family outings and holidays such as a caravan site or picnic site, or an *ancient monument* under the care of *English Heritage*.

Brownie (Guide) /'braʊnɪ (ˌbraʊnɪ 'gaɪd)/ (sport and leisure) A girl aged 7 to 11 who is a member of the junior branch of the *Guides Association*. [originally named after the helpful children in the stories 'The Brownies and Other Tales' (1870) by Juliana Ewing, but later associated with the girls' brown uniform]

Brum /brʌm/ (geography) A colloquial nickname for Birmingham. Compare *Brummie*.

Brummie /'brʌmɪ/ (geography) A colloquial name for a native or inhabitant of Birmingham. Compare *Brum*.

BSc /ˌbiː es 'siː/ **(Bachelor of Science)** (education) A degree obtained by the student of a university or *polytechnic* on successfully completing a course of studies in one of the sciences.

BSI /ˌbiː es 'aɪ/, **the (British Standards Institution, the)** (science and technology) An association formed in 1901 to establish and maintain standards relating to the dimensions, performance and safety criteria, and testing methods, of a wide range of products and processes. See also *Kitemark*.

BSkyB /ˌbiː skaɪ 'biː/ **British Sky Broadcasting** (media) A satellite television service introduced in 1989 (as Sky Television). It is beamed to *Britain* from the Astra satellite and by 1994 was offering 18 channels: Sky One (entertainment), Sky News (news reports round the clock), Sky Sports (sports programmes), The Movie Channel (films), Sky Movies Plus (mainly recent films), Sky Movies Gold (film 'classics'), The Children's Channel (children's programmes), MTV (Music Television, pop programmes), UK Gold (past popular programmes from Thames Television [succeeded by *Carlton TV*] and the *BBC*), Nickelodeon (programmes for young children), Nick at Nite (complementing it), Bravo (a mix of programmes), Discovery (documentary programmes), CMTV (Country Music Television), The Family Channel (past popular programmes for 'clean' family viewing), UK Living (programmes for women), QVC (Quality, Value and Convenience, a home shopping channel) and VH1 (Video Hits 1). BSkyB actually owns only the first two of these. Viewers need a special dish aerial to receive the channels and pay an annual subscription for them.

BST /ˌbiː es 'tiː/ **(British Summer Time)** (daily life) A period in the summer, usually from March to October, when clocks are advanced one hour ahead of *GMT* in order to gain maximum use of daylight hours.

BT /ˌbiː 'tiː/ (commerce) The private company that is the largest operator of telephone networks in *Britain*, as well as a number of more specialized services such as *Prestel*. Compare *Mercury*. [the abbreviation of *British Telecom*, the company's former name, itself short for British Telecommunications]

BTA /ˌbiː tiː 'eɪ/, **the (British Tourist Authority, the)**

(commerce) The state industry established in 1969 for the promotion overseas of tourism in *Great Britain*. It co-operates with the three national tourist boards (English, Scottish and Wales).

bubble and squeak /ˌbʌbl ən ˈskwiːk/ (food and drink) A dish made from cold cabbage and potatoes left over after a meal. The cold, already cooked, ingredients are heated together and served. [so named for the sound made when being cooked]

Buck House /ˌbʌk ˈhaʊs/ (royal family) A colloquial name sometimes used for *Buckingham Palace*.

bucket shop /ˈbʌkɪt ʃɒp/ (transport) A shop or agency that sells airline tickets unofficially at reduced prices. [said to be from a shop that sold small quantities of liquor in buckets]

Buckingham Palace /ˌbʌkɪŋəm ˈpælɪs/ (royal family) The official *London* residence of the sovereign. The daily ceremony of the *Changing of the Guard* takes place in its courtyard. The palace was built in 1703 by the Duke of Buckingham.

buck's fizz /ˌbʌks ˈfɪz/ (food and drink) An alcoholic drink of champagne and orange juice. [from the slang words 'buck', meaning 'dandy', and 'fizz', meaning 'champagne']

budgerigar /ˈbʌdʒərɪɡaː(r)/ (animal world) A small Australian parrot popular in many homes as a cage bird. It can be trained to talk.

Budget /ˈbʌdʒɪt/, **the** (government) The annual proposals made by *Parliament* for taxation, government spending, and related financial matters. It is presented by the *Chancellor of the Exchequer* in the *House of Commons* in a special speech made in November (until 1993 it was in March).

budgie /ˈbʌdʒɪ/ (animal world) A colloquial term for a *budgerigar*.

building society /ˈbɪldɪŋ səˌsaɪətɪ/ (finance) A banking organization financed by deposits from members of the public on which interest is paid and from which loans called *mortgages* are made to people who wish to build or buy a house. In recent years building societies have been increasingly competing with banks to offer investors such facilities as cheque books, credit cards and *standing orders*.

built-up area /ˌbɪlt-ʌp ˈearɪə/ (geography) An area with many buildings, such as a town or the suburbs of a town, where traffic must observe a special *speed limit*.

bull /bʊl/ (finance) On the *Stock Exchange*, a term for a

speculator who buys shares hoping that their value will rise
so that he can make a profit when he sells them. [perhaps by
association with *bear*, the opposite term]

Bull Ring /'bʊl rɪŋ/**, the** (commerce) A large shopping centre
in Birmingham, built in the 1960s on the site of a covered
market where bulls were once sold.

bull terrier /ˌbʊl 'terɪə(r)/ (animal world) A stocky breed of
working dog that is a cross between a *bulldog* and a terrier. It
has a short smooth coat and is usually white in colour.

bulldog /'bʊldɒg/ (animal world) A sturdy breed of dog with
a broad head, the lower jaw projecting beyond the upper,
and a short, smooth coat on a muscular body. The aggressive
appearance of the dog and the association of its name with
that of *John Bull* have caused it to be used as a personification
of *Britain*, especially in a military context. [named from its
former use in the sport of bull-baiting—exciting bulls with dogs]

bullseye /'bʊlzaɪ/ (food and drink) A round, hard,
peppermint-flavoured boiled sweet, usually striped black
and white. [from its supposed likeness to a bull's eye]

Bunty /'bʌntɪ/ (media) A weekly comic for young girls,
founded in 1958. [girl's name]

BUPA /'buːpə/ (medicine) An insurance association
providing financial cover for private medical treatment for
regular subscribers. [in full, British United Provident
Association]

Burberry /'bɜːbərɪ/ (clothing) The trade name of a make of
light, good quality raincoat. [first made by Thomas Burberry
in 1856]

Burgess, Anthony /'bɜːdʒɪs, 'æntənɪ/ (people) Anthony
Burgess (1917–93) has become well known as a novelist and
literary critic, and has won a reputation as a writer in a
number of cultural fields, from language to music. His fiction
often has a 'visionary' quality, such as the acclaimed 'A
Clockwork Orange' (1962), later turned into a successful film,
and the ambitious 'Earthly Powers' (1980), in which real and
imaginary characters combine to give a sort of panoramic
view of the 20th century. Some of Burgess's writing is
difficult, since he invents words (from Greek and Latin roots)
when he feels the need.

burgh /'bʌrə/ (government) A Scottish town that has
approximately the same status as an English *borough*[1].

Burke('s Peerage) /bɜːk(s 'pɪərɪdʒ)/ (life and society) An
annual reference work that lists biographical details of

members of the *peerage* and other titled people. Compare *Debrett*. [from John Burke, who first published 'Burke's Peerage, Baronetage and Knightage' in 1826]

Burlington House /ˌbɜːlɪŋtən ˈhaʊs/ (London) A large building in *Piccadilly*, *London*, in which are the *Royal Academy* and other learned societies (including the *Royal Society* to 1967). In it is held the annual summer exhibition of contemporary works by the Royal Academy. [originally built for Richard Boyle, Earl of Burlington, in the 17th century]

Burns' Night /ˈbɜːnz naɪt/ (tradition) A celebration held every year on 25 January, the anniversary of the birth of Robert Burns (1759–96), *Scotland*'s great 'national' poet. The celebration usually takes the form of a supper at which traditional Scottish dishes are eaten (including *haggis* and mashed potatoes and turnips, known as 'bashed tatties and neeps') and during which a Scottish piper plays, wearing traditional Highland dress. Some of Burns' most popular poems are recited and there may be Scottish dancing after the meal is finished. Burns' Night celebrations are held not only in Scotland and in many places in *England*, but also amongst British people living in other countries, with several British embassies regarding Burns' Night as one of the social events of the year. See also *Auld Lang Syne*.

Burrell Collection /ˌbʌrəl kəˌlekʃn/, **the** (arts) An important collection of paintings, tapestries, porcelain, and bronzes given in 1944 to the city of *Glasgow* by Sir William Burrell (1861–1958). In 1983, the collection was put on show in a special gallery in Glasgow now called the Burrell Gallery.

bursar /ˈbɜːsə(r)/ (finance) An official in charge of the finances of a school, *college*[1,2] or other establishment.

bus pass /ˈbʌs pɑːs/ (transport) A special ticket entitling an *OAP* to travel free on a bus. The phrase is sometimes used humorously to denote a newly retired person, as in 'He's got his bus pass'.

busby /ˈbʌzbɪ/ (clothing) A special type of tall fur hat or helmet, with a bag hanging from the top to the right side, worn as part of their ceremonial uniform by certain regiments of the British *Army*.

Bush House /ˌbʊʃ ˈhaʊs/ (media) A large building in central *London* containing the headquarters and studios of the *BBC World Service*. [named after its designer in 1931, the American business executive Irving T. Bush]

busker

busker /ˈbʌskə(r)/ (tradition) A performer who makes money
by singing, playing, acting, etc in public places, for example,
in front of theatre queues or in *Underground* railway stations.
but and ben /ˌbʌt ən ˈben/ (style) In *Scotland*, a small cottage
with two rooms, 'but' being the outer room and 'ben' the
inner.
Butlin's /ˈbʌtlɪnz/ (sport and leisure) A name for self-
contained holiday centres, run by a company with the same
name. The centres are often by the sea and are designed so
that the holidaymaker has a wide range of amenities and
entertainments, and need not leave the centre. The first such
centre was opened at Skegness, Lincolnshire, in 1936 by Billy
Butlin (later Sir William Butlin) (1899–1980).
butterscotch /ˈbʌtəskɒtʃ/ (food and drink) A kind of hard,
brittle toffee made chiefly from butter and burnt sugar. [said
to have been originally made in *Scotland*]
butty /ˈbʊtɪ/ (food and drink) In the north of *England*, a
colloquial word for a sandwich, for example, a jam butty.
Compare *bacon sarnie*. [from 'buttered bread']
by-election /ˈbaɪɪlekʃn/ (politics) An election held in a single

constituency between one *general election* and the next. It may be held because an *MP* has retired or died, or because he has been transferred to the *House of Lords*.

by-law /'baɪlɔː/ (law) A law passed by a *local authority* such as a *town council*.

BYOB /ˌbiː waɪ əʊ 'biː/ **(bring your own bottle/booze/beer)** (life and society) An abbreviation used on an invitation to a party indicating that the person invited should bring a contribution of (usually alcoholic) drink with them. The party will often be a *bottle party*.

CAT'S EYES

CAA /ˌsiː eɪ ˈeɪ/, **the (Civil Aviation Authority, the)**
(transport) An independent organization that supervises the
operation of British airline companies and provides air
navigation facilities.

CAB /ˌsiː eɪ ˈbiː/, **the (Citizens Advice Bureau, the)** (daily
life) A voluntary organization found in over 1,300 centres in
most towns and cities. It gives advice to people who are
uncertain about their rights or who seek special state or
voluntary aid but do not know where to find it.

Cabinet /ˈkæbɪnɪt/, **the** (government) The executive group of
ministers[2,4], usually about 20 in number, who are chosen by
the *Prime Minister* to determine government policies. A
minister so selected is usually the head of a *department*, and
all *Secretaries of State* are traditionally members. The Cabinet
usually meets for a few hours once a week in private at *No 10,
Downing Street* while *Parliament* is sitting, and less often
when it is not.

Caernarfon /kəˈnɑːvn/ (geography) A town and tourist resort
in North *Wales*, famous for its 13th-century castle where the
ceremony of the investiture of the *Prince of Wales* is held.

Caerphilly /keəˈfɪlɪ/ (food and drink) A type of white, mild-
flavoured cheese originally made in Caerphilly, South *Wales*.

caff /kæf/ (daily life) A colloquial word for a snack bar,
especially a cheap one. [alteration of 'café']

cairn (terrier) /keən (ˈterɪə(r))/ (animal world) A small breed
of rough-haired terrier, once used for hunting foxes and other
animals in hilly country, and originating from *Scotland*,
where it worked among cairns, ie, mounds of stones built as
landmarks on mountain tracks.

Cairngorms /ˈkeəngɔːmz/, **the** (geography) A group of

mountains in north central *Scotland*, in the larger *Grampians*.
They have become popular in recent years as a winter sports
centre, with good facilities for skiing, and are a year-round
centre for climbing and walking.

Caledonia /ˌkælɪˈdəʊnɪə/ (geography) A poetic name for
Scotland, also found in adjective form (Caledonian) in the
name of commercial companies and other Scottish
organizations. See also *Caledonian Canal*. [originally the
Roman name for northern *Britain*]

Caledonian Canal /ˌkælɪdəʊnɪən kəˈnæl/, **the** (geography) A
canal in northern *Scotland*, running across the country
through a series of lochs (lakes) (including *Loch Ness*) from
the North Sea at its northeast end to the Atlantic at the
southwest end.

Caledonian Market /ˌkælɪdəʊnɪən ˈmɑːkɪt/, **the** (London) A
market held on Friday mornings by antique dealers in
Bermondsey Street, in the *East End* of *London*. [properly, the
New Caledonian Market, as it was originally on the
Caledonian Road in North London]

Cambria /ˈkæmbrɪə/ (geography) A poetic name for *Wales*,
found in adjective form (Cambrian) in the names of
commercial organizations and in some specialist uses.
[originally the medieval Latin name for Wales]

Cambridge /ˈkeɪmbrɪdʒ/ (**1** geography **2** education) **1** The
chief *city* and administrative centre of Cambridgeshire,
famous for its university, and a major tourist centre. **2** A
short name for *Cambridge University*. Compare *Oxford*[2].

Cambridge blue /ˌkeɪmbrɪdʒ ˈbluː/ (**1** daily life **2** sport and
leisure) **1** A light blue colour. Compare *Oxford blue*[1]. **2** A
blue[3] at *Cambridge University*.

Cambridge Certificate /ˌkeɪmbrɪdʒ səˈtɪfɪkət/, **the** (education)
The short name of one of two examinations in English as a
foreign language operated by an examinations board of
Cambridge University. The lower examination is officially
called the First Certificate in English, and the higher is
known as the Certificate of Proficiency in English. Both
examinations consist of five papers to test different aspects of
reading, writing, understanding and speaking English.

Cambridge University /ˌkeɪmbrɪdʒ juːnɪˈvɜːsɪtɪ/ (education)
One of the two oldest and most famous universities in
England, the other being *Oxford University*. It was founded in
the 13th century. There are at present 28 *colleges*[1], of which
two are for women only. The remaining 26 take both men

and women. Among the best known colleges are: King's College, founded in 1441, famed for its fine *chapel²* in the *Perpendicular* (*style*) and for the *choir* that sings there; Trinity College, founded in 1546, with its large *court²* and excellent library; Magdalene College, founded in 1542, with a famous library containing the original diaries of Samuel Pepys (1633–1703); and St John's College, founded in 1511, with its well-known *Bridge of Sighs*. There are at present about 6,000 male and 4,000 female students in residence. Cambridge University has made the city of *Cambridge¹* an internationally famous tourist centre. See also *Backs, Fitzwilliam Museum, Mays*.

CAMRA /'kæmrə/ **(Campaign for Real Ale, the)** (daily life) A voluntary organization (also a *limited company*) formed in 1971 with the aim of conserving and promoting the brewing and drinking of *real ale* (beer made without additives by small traditional brewers). The organization also promotes the traditional *pub* that sells such beer.

Canterbury /'kæntəbrɪ/ (geography) A historic walled city in Kent, famous for its cathedral, built in the 11th–15th centuries, which became a place of pilgrimage in medieval times after the murder of Thomas à Becket, *Archbishop of Canterbury*.

Canterbury bell /ˌkæntəbrɪ 'bel/ (tradition) A plant with blue, violet or white bell-shaped flowers, and said to be so named since the flowers look like (or, remind one of) the bells on the horses of pilgrims riding to *Canterbury*, or else the metal badges, called St Thomas's Bells, sold to these pilgrims.

cap /kæp/ (**1** clothing **2, 5** education **3, 4, 6, 7** sport and leisure) **1** The traditional headwear of the *working class* man, especially a flat cloth cap (see *Andy Capp*). **2** Part of the uniform of some boys' *public schools¹* and *preparatory schools*. **3** Part of the uniform of the member of a sports team, especially one representing his *county*, university, school, etc. **4** A player awarded a *cap³* as a team member. **5** A *mortarboard* worn with a gown by a university student or *graduate*, especially in the phrase 'cap and *gown¹*'. **6** A contribution of money to a *hunt* by a follower who is not a member of that hunt, to allow him or her to join in hunting for a day, and traditionally collected in a huntsman's cap before the start of the day's hunting. **7** A collection of money for charity taken by a hunt before the start of the day's hunting, traditionally made in a huntsman's cap.

capital gains tax /ˌkæpɪtl 'ɡeɪnz tæks/ (finance) A special tax charged at the appropriate rate of *income tax* (i.e. 25% or 40%) on profit of £5,800 or more made from the sale of goods, property or assets.

capital punishment /ˌkæpɪtl ˈpʌnɪʃmənt/ (law) The execution of a criminal by hanging. This was abolished in *Britain* in 1965, but can still, at least in theory, be the punishment awarded for treason. Capital punishment (also known as the 'death penalty') has been replaced by a life sentence, which usually means imprisonment for a minimum of 20 years.

Capital Radio /ˌkæpɪtl ˈreɪdɪəʊ/ (media) A leading *ILR* station in *London* operating under the *Radio Authority*. It opened in 1973 and broadcasts mainly popular music, entertainment programmes and news reports.

car boot sale /kɑː ˈbuːt seɪl/ (daily life) A sale held on an agreed site by car owners, who each pay a fee (usually about £5) in order to sell secondhand or homemade goods to the public from the boot of their car. Such sales are usually held at a *weekend*, or on a *bank holiday*. The fee paid often goes to a charity or other cause, much as in a *fête*.

cardboard city /ˌkɑːdbɔːd ˈsɪti/ (life and society) A nickname for an area where homeless people live and sleep out on the streets, often in large cardboard boxes. A well-known cardboard city is the one in *London* on the *South Bank* near the *Royal Festival Hall*.

Cardiff /ˈkɑːdɪf/ (geography) The capital city of *Wales*, in the southeast, and an important industrial centre and port.

cardphone /ˈkɑːdfəʊn/ (commerce) A public telephone from which calls are made by a *phonecard*, not using coins. Some cardphones will accept standard credit cards. See also *payphone*.

Carey, George /ˈkeəri, dʒɔːdʒ/ (people) George Carey (born 1935) was appointed *Archbishop of Canterbury* in 1991. He inclines to *Low Church* views.

Carlton House Terrace /ˌkɑːltən ˌhaʊs ˈterəs/ (London) A short but fashionable street in central *London* where the official residence of the *Foreign Secretary* is, and where famous British statesmen have lived in the past, among them Gladstone, Palmerston and Lord Curzon.

Carlton TV /ˌkɑːltən tiː ˈviː/ (media) One of the 15 regional television companies of the *ITC*, based in *London* but broadcasting only on weekdays. Its *weekend* equivalent is *LWT*.

Carnaby Street /ˈkɑːnəbi striːt/ (London) A small street in central *London* famous in the 1960s for its fashion shops.

carol service /ˈkærəl ˌsɜːvɪs/ (religion) A special religious
service held in the weeks before *Christmas* either in a *church*
or in a public place such as a town square, and consisting
chiefly of carols (Christmas hymns) and readings from the Bible.

Carroll, Lewis /ˈkærəl ˈluːɪs/ (people) Although by profession
a mathematician at *Oxford University*, Lewis Carroll (1832–98,
real name Charles Lutwidge Dodgson) is known
internationally as the author of 'Alice in Wonderland' (1865)
and 'Through the Looking-Glass' (1871). These two books are
very popular not only with children but with adults. Both
books tell stories of exciting and unusual adventures and
have humorous characters. In the original editions, the
imaginative illustrations by John Tenniel added to the
attractiveness of the text.

Cartland, Barbara /ˈkɑːtlənd, ˈbɑːbrə/ (people) Barbara
Cartland (born 1900) became widely known from the 1950s as
the author of a large number of romantic and historical
novels and biographies, and as an expert on fashion, health
and physical fitness. In some senses, she has become a sort of
'national granny', much as *Queen Elizabeth, the Queen Mother*
has, although Barbara Cartland's personality is much more
extrovert, and her colourful dresses (usually pink) are much
more extravagant.

cathedral city /kəˌθiːdrəl ˈsɪtɪ/ (geography) A term sometimes
used for an ancient *city* with a cathedral, especially one that is
popular with tourists. Examples of cathedral cities are Exeter,
Gloucester, Salisbury and Winchester.

cathedral school /kəˈθiːdrəl skuːl/ (education) A school in a
cathedral city, usually a *preparatory school* or, occasionally, a
public school[1], some of whose pupils sing in the cathedral
choir. Compare *choir school*.

Catholic Herald /ˌkæθlɪk ˈherəld/, **the** (media) A weekly
newspaper for Roman Catholics, with articles and features of
general interest as well as specifically on religious matters. It
has a current circulation of about 25,000.

Catholic Times /ˌkæθlɪk ˈtaɪmz/, **the** (media) A weekly
newspaper for Roman Catholics founded in 1993, partly to
cater for the growing number of Catholics in *Britain*.

cat's-eyes /ˈkæts aɪz/ (transport) Glass reflectors set into
rubber pads down the centre of a road to indicate traffic lanes
at night. [from their resemblance to the eyes of a cat, which
glow in the dark when facing a light]

caution /ˈkɔːʃn/ (law) An official warning given by a police officer to a person suspected or accused of an offence. The traditional words of the caution are: 'I must warn you that anything you say may be taken down and used in evidence' (formerly ending 'against you').

cavalry twill /ˌkævlrɪ 'twɪl/ (clothing) A strong wool fabric used for trousers and woven with a 'twill' or ribbed effect. [originally worn by soldiers on horseback]

CBI /ˌsi: bi: 'aɪ/, **the (Confederation of British Industry, the)** (work) An organization set up in 1965 to represent the employers of industrial companies (currently about 250,000) with the aim of ensuring that both the government and the public understand the needs and objectives of British business.

Ceefax /'si:fæks/ (media) A teletext service provided by the *BBC*. Compare *Teletext*. [a stylized spelling of 'see facts']

ceilidh /'keɪlɪ/ (tradition) In *Scotland* and *Ireland*, an informal gathering with folk music, singing, dancing and story telling. [*Gaelic* word, meaning 'visit']

Celtic /'seltɪk/ (sport and leisure) A popular Scottish *football club* with its stadium at Parkhead in *Glasgow*. It draws support especially from the local Roman Catholic community and its traditional rivals are *Rangers*.

Celtic fringe /ˌkeltɪk 'frɪndʒ/, **the** (geography) A name for those parts of the *United Kingdom* whose population is of Celtic origin—*Wales*, *Cornwall*, *Scotland* and *Northern Ireland*, such parts being on the 'fringe' or borders of *England*.

Cenotaph /'senətɑ:f/, **the** (London) A war memorial in *Whitehall*, *London*, built after the First World War in memory of the dead. On *Remembrance Sunday* every year there is a short memorial service there, with the laying of wreaths, to commemorate those who died in both world wars. The ceremony is attended by the sovereign, the *Prime Minister* and other leading figures of state. See also *two-minute silence*.

Central Criminal Court /ˌsentrəl 'krɪmɪnl kɔ:t/, **the** (law) The official name of the leading criminal court in *Britain*, at the *Old Bailey*, *London*.

Central TV /ˌsentrəl ti: 'vi:/ (media) One of the 15 regional television companies of the *ITC*, based in Birmingham and broadcasting to the *Midlands*.

Centre Point /ˌsentə 'pɔɪnt/ (London) A modern 33-storey office building in central *London*. It contains the offices of the *CBI* and part of it is used as a night shelter for young and homeless people.

Cerne Giant

Ceremony of the Keys /ˌserɪmənɪ əv ðə ˈkiːz/**, the** (tradition) A ceremony held every night at 10.00 at the *Tower of London*. The Chief Warder closes the gates and after exchanging passwords with a sentry hands him the keys of the Tower for safe-keeping with the Resident Governor.

Cerne Giant /ˌsɜːn ˈdʒaɪənt/**, the** (geography) A huge figure of a man holding a club, carved out of the chalk hillside near the village of Cerne Abbas, Dorset. The figure, 55 m in length, dates back to at least the 2nd century AD and may represent Hercules.

CFE /ˌsiː ef ˈiː/ **(college of further education)** (education) An educational establishment, other than a *polytechnic* or university, where students can go after they leave school for additional full-time or part-time education. See *further education* and compare *higher education*.

chamber of commerce /ˌtʃeɪmbər əv ˈkɒmɜːs/ (commerce) An association of local businessmen, shop owners and industrialists in a town, formed to promote, regulate and protect their interests.

Chamber of Horrors /ˌtʃeɪmbər əv ˈhɒrəz/**, the** (London) At *Madame Tussaud's* waxworks museum, *London*, a special exhibition room containing models of famous criminals, murder scenes, etc.

change ringing

chambers /'tʃeɪmbəz/ (law) **1** The room of a *barrister* where clients are interviewed. In *London*, such rooms are mostly in the *Inns of Court*. **2** A judge's room in which cases are heard 'in camera' and in which he also hears minor cases.

chancellor /'tʃɑ:nsələ(r)/ (education) The title of the nominal head of a university. He is appointed for life and attends the university only on formal occasions once or twice a year. Compare *vice-chancellor*.

Chancellor of the Duchy of Lancaster /ˌtʃɑːnsələr əv ðə ˌdʌtʃɪ əv ˈlæŋkəstə(r)/, **the** (government) The title of the *minister*[4] in the *Cabinet* who is responsible for royal estates in Lancashire (see *Privy Purse*). He has few or no departmental duties, so is free to carry out any special tasks that the *Prime Minister* may require.

Chancellor of the Exchequer /ˌtʃɑːnsələr əv ðɪ ɪksˈtʃekə(r)/, **the** (government) The title of the British finance minister. He is a member of the *Cabinet* and responsible for the annual *Budget*, which makes him one of the most important *ministers*[2] in the government.

Chancery /ˈtʃɑːnsərɪ/ (**1** law **2** government) **1** A division in the *High Court of Justice* that examines civilian cases (in full, Chancery Division). **2** A section in a British embassy or legation that deals with political matters, the head of such a section usually being called a counsellor.

change ringing /ˈtʃeɪndʒ ˌrɪŋɪŋ/ (tradition) The special method of ringing *church* bells in *England*, especially those of an *Anglican* church. Members of a team of ringers (usually six, but depending on the number of bells) stand some way below the bells and pull on the end of a long rope attached to the bells (one rope to each bell) so that the bell swings, causing the clapper inside the bell to strike the side of the bell. Each bell is rung according to a mathematical sequence, instead of being rung to give the notes of a melody.

Changing of the Guard /ˌtʃeɪndʒɪŋ əv ðə ˈɡɑːd/, **the** (London) The formal ceremony of changing the royal guard in *London*, held every morning in the forecourt of *Buckingham Palace* and also in front of the main building of the *Royal Horse Guards* in *Whitehall*[1]. The sight is a popular tourist attraction.

Channel 4 /ˌtʃænl ˈfɔː(r)/ (media) One of the two main television channels of the *ITC*, broadcasting to the whole of the *United Kingdom* except *Wales*, which has *S4C*. It complements *ITV* but its programmes are more innovative and it caters for tastes and interests that are not met by ITV. These include documentaries, 'permissive' plays, and detailed news reports. ['4' as the fourth channel to appear after *BBC 1*, *BBC 2* and *ITV*]

Channel Islands /ˈtʃænl ˌaɪləndz/, **the** (geography) A group of islands off the northwest coast of France that since the *Norman Conquest* have belonged to *Britain*. Like the *Isle of Man*, they are not officially part of the *United Kingdom* and are a self-governing crown dependency with their own parliaments (called the 'States' in the three main islands of Jersey, Guernsey and Alderney, and the 'Court of Chief Pleas' in the smaller island of Sark). They also have their own systems of local administration and their own courts. They are popular with British tourists, because of their mild, sunny climate and their favourable tax rates. The official languages of the islands are French and English, although English has virtually supplanted French. A local Norman-French dialect is still spoken, however, in some of the rural districts.

Channel Tunnel /ˌtʃænl ˈtʌnl/, **the** (transport) The railway tunnel under the English Channel that links *Britain* and France. It opened in 1994. A colloquial name for the Channel Tunnel is the *Chunnel*.

Channel TV /ˌtʃænl tiː ˈviː/ (media) One of the 15 regional television companies of the *ITC*, based in St Helier, Jersey, and broadcasting to the *Channel Islands*. [name puns on 'channel' in sense of 'television station']

chapel /ˈtʃæpl/ (**1, 2, 3, 4,** religion **5, 6** work) **1** A separate place of worship, with an altar, in a cathedral or *church*. **2** A private church or place of worship in a *college[1]*, school, hospital, military barracks, prison, etc. **3** A *Nonconformist* (non-*Anglican*) church or place of worship, sometimes used as a term of criticism by contrast with the *Church of England*. **4** A *chapel royal*. **5** A division of a trade union, usually in a newspaper press or a publishing house. **6** A meeting of the members of a chapel[5].

chapel of rest /ˌtʃæpl əv ˈrest/ (daily life) A euphemistic expression for an undertaker's mortuary. It usually does not have any specific Christian or even religious furnishings in the normal sense of 'chapel', except in the most general way.

chapel royal /ˌtʃæpl ˈrɔɪəl/ (religion) A *chapel[2]* or *church* belonging to a royal palace or residence, such as the one at *Windsor Castle*.

CHAPS /ˌtʃæpz/ (finance) An electronic system used by banks for making high payments the same day, [abbreviation of Clearing House Automated Payment System. See also *clearing bank*]

Charing Cross /ˌtʃærɪŋ ˈkrɒs/ (**1, 4** London **2, 3** transport) **1** A busy crossroads in *London* between *Trafalgar Square* and *Whitehall[1]*, regarded as the centre of London for purposes of measuring distances in miles from London. **2** A main line railway station and terminus there, from which trains leave for south and southeast *England*. **3** A station of the *Underground* nearby. **4** A superior hotel near the station, on the *Strand*. ['Charing' from an Old English word meaning 'bend', referring to an old road that altered course here; 'Cross' from the *Eleanor Cross* set up here]

Charing Cross Hospital /ˌtʃærɪŋ krɒs ˈhɒspɪtl/ (medicine) A large *London* hospital founded in 1818 near *Charing Cross*[1] but in 1971 transferred to the district of Fulham, west *London*.

Charity Commission /ˈtʃærətɪ kəˌmɪʃn/, **the** (charities) A government body that keeps a record of all charities and controls charitable trusts.

Charles, Prince /ˈtʃɑːlz, prɪns/ see *Prince of Wales* (royal family)

chartered accountant /ˌtʃɑːtəd əˈkaʊntənt/ (finance) An accountant who has passed the examinations of the Institute of Chartered Accountants and so is professionally qualified.

Charterhouse (School) /ˈtʃɑːtəhaʊs (ˌtʃɑːtəhaʊs ˈskuːl)/ (education) A leading *public school*[1] founded in 1611 on the site of a former 'charterhouse' (Carthusian monastery) in *London*, but in 1872 transferred to Surrey. It has about 700 students.

Chartwell /ˈtʃɑːtwel/ (history) A *country house* (in full Chartwell Manor) in Kent that for many years was the home of Winston *Churchill* (1874–1965) and which is now open to the public as a museum.

Chat /tʃæt/ (media) A popular weekly magazine for women, first published in 1985. It has a current circulation of about 515,000.

Cheddar (cheese) /ˈtʃedə(r) (ˌtʃedə ˈtʃiːz)/ (food and drink) One of several types of smooth, firm, yellow cheese, originally made in the village of Cheddar, Somerset.

Chelsea /ˈtʃelsɪ/ (**1** London **2** sport) **1** A fashionable district in west *London*, famous as an artists' quarter. **2** A London *football club* with a stadium in Fulham, west of Chelsea[1].

Chelsea bun /ˌtʃelsɪ ˈbʌn/ (food and drink) A type of rolled currant bun sprinkled with sugar. [originally made in *Chelsea*[1]]

Chelsea Flower Show /ˌtʃelsɪ ˈflaʊə ʃəʊ/, **the** (London) The most important flower show in *Britain*, held in May every year in the grounds of *Chelsea Hospital*.

Chelsea Hospital /ˌtʃelsɪ ˈhɒspɪtl/ (London) A home for about 450 old or invalid soldiers (*Chelsea Pensioners*) in *Chelsea*[1], founded in 1682. [full title, Chelsea Royal Hospital]

Chelsea Pensioners /ˌtʃelsɪ ˈpenʃənəz/ (tradition) Former

Chelsea Pensioners

soldiers who live in *Chelsea Hospital*, famous for their traditional, knee-length coats, scarlet in summer and navy blue in winter. On *Oak Apple Day* they wear a special three-cornered hat.

Cheltenham /'tʃeltnəm/ (geography) A fashionable town and former health resort in Gloucestershire, famous for its *public schools[1]*, mineral springs and race course. See *Cheltenham Gold Cup*.

Cheltenham Festival /ˌtʃeltnəm 'festɪvl/, **the** (arts) An annual music festival in *Cheltenham*, Gloucestershire, where mainly modern British music is performed.

Cheltenham Gold Cup /ˌtʃeltnəm gəʊld 'kʌp/, **the** (sport and leisure) An annual horse race at *Cheltenham*, for which the prize is a gold cup.

Chequers /'tʃekəz/ (government) The *country house* in Buckinghamshire that is the official country residence of the *Prime Minister*. Compare *Downing Street, No 10*. [full name Chequers Court]

Cheshire (cheese) /'tʃeʃə(r) (ˌtʃeʃə 'tʃiːz)/ (food and drink) One of several types of cheese, of various colours, flavours and textures, the most common being white, mild and crumbly, and originally produced in Cheshire.

Cheshire Homes /ˌtʃeʃə ˈhəʊmz/ (charities) Special homes for the permanently disabled and incurably sick, run by the Leonard Cheshire Foundation, a charity set up in 1948 by Leonard Cheshire (1917-92), a heroic *RAF* pilot who was awarded the *VC* in the Second World War.

Chessington Zoo /ˈtʃesɪŋtən ˈzuː/ (animal world) A popular zoo and leisure park near Kingston, southwest *London*. [officially the Chessington World of Adventure]

Cheviot (sheep) /ˈtʃevɪət (ˌtʃevɪət ˈʃiːp)/ (animal world) A breed of hill sheep famous for their wool, and reared in the south of *Scotland* and in the English county of Northumberland, through which run the Cheviot Hills.

Chichester Festival /ˌtʃɪtʃɪstə ˈfestəvl/, **the** (arts) An annual drama festival in the *cathedral city* of Chichester, West Sussex, held since 1962.

Chief Constable /ˌtʃiːf ˈkʌnstəbl/ (law) The rank of a senior police officer who is in command of an administrative area, usually corresponding to that of an English *county* or a Scottish region. He is responsible for the direction and control of the police forces in his area, and for the appointment, promotion and discipline of all police officers below assistant chief constable. He is also responsible for all *traffic wardens* in his area.

Chief Scout /ˌtʃiːf ˈskaʊt/, **the** (sport and leisure) The official title of the head of the *Scout Association*.

Chief Whip /ˌtʃiːf ˈwɪp/, **the** (politics) In the *House of Commons*, a leading member of a political party who is appointed to keep party discipline, encourage active support for the party and its policies, and make sure party members attend meetings and vote. See *whip[1]*, *three-line whip*.

chieftain /ˈtʃiːftən/ (life and society) In *Scotland*, the title of the leader or hereditary head of a *clan*.

child benefit /ˈtʃaɪld ˌbenɪfɪt/ (finance) A state payment made for all the children in a family. The current rate is £9.65 per week for the first or only child and £7.80 for each subsequent child.

ChildLine /ˈtʃaɪldlaɪn/ (charities) A charity set up in 1986, enabling children who are being physically or sexually abused to ring a special telephone number for confidential help and advice.

childminder /ˈtʃaɪldmaɪndə(r)/ (life and society) A woman employed to look after a family's young children when the parents are out at work. She often does this in her own home, where she looks after the children in the same way as their mother would, feeding them, playing with them, washing their clothes, taking them to a *playgroup*, etc. Many childminders are registered with the National Childminding Association, which currently has about 36,000 members. For her services, five days a week, a childminder will be paid about £60. Childminders were first employed during the Second World War, when many mothers were involved in war work (for example in factories), or were working as nurses or in the armed services. Compare *nanny*.

Chiltern Hundreds /ˌtʃɪltən 'hʌndrədz/, **the** (government) A historic administrative division (see *hundred*) of Buckinghamshire, used when an *MP* retires. He 'applies for the Chiltern Hundreds' and thus gives up his seat, since the (purely nominal) position of managing the Chiltern Hundreds is incompatible with his post as an MP in the *House of Commons*.

Chilterns /'tʃɪltənz/, **the** (geography) A range of chalk hills between *London* and *Oxford[1]*, famous for their beautiful scenery and old houses, including *Chequers*. The hills have been designated an *area of outstanding natural beauty*.

Chippendale /'tʃɪpəndeɪl/ (style) A style of 18th-century furniture characterized by flowing lines, carved work, and a combination of strength and elegance. Compare *Hepplewhite*, *Sheraton*. [from the cabinet-maker and furniture designer Thomas Chippendale (?1718–79)]

chippy /'tʃɪpɪ/ (**1** food and drink **2** work) **1** A colloquial name for a shop selling *fish and chips*. **2** A colloquial name for a carpenter.

choir /'kwaɪə(r)/ (arts) A group of singers formed to perform choral works, whether accompanied or unaccompanied. There is strong British tradition of choral singing, both by choirs in *churches* and by local 'choral societies'. Some choirs in cathedrals or *Oxford[2]* and *Cambridge[2] colleges[1]* are internationally famous. Choral singing is particularly associated with *Wales*, where *chapel[3]* and miners' choirs are well known for their enthusiastic and fine singing.

choir school /'kwaɪə skuːl/ (education) A *preparatory school* or *public school[1]* attached to a *church*, cathedral or *chapel[2]* (especially that of a *college[1]* at *Oxford University* or *Cambridge University*), in which certain pupils, apart from receiving a normal school education, are trained to sing in the choir of the church, cathedral or chapel. Compare *cathedral school*.

Christian Aid /ˌkrɪstʃən ˈeɪd/ (charities) A well-known charity organization raising funds for practical aid and relief operations in developing countries. It was founded in 1945.

Christie, Agatha /ˈkrɪstɪ, ˈæɡəθə/ (people) Agatha Christie (1890–1976) was one of *Britain's* most popular and successful writers of detective novels, many of them featuring an elderly spinster detective, Miss Marple. Agatha Christie's play 'The Mousetrap', also a detective drama, has been running continuously in *London* since 1952. Her fiction is noted for its ingenious plots, sustained suspense, and for its ever-present congenial humour.

Christie, Linford /ˈkrɪstɪ ˈlɪnfəd/ (people) Linford Christie (born 1960) is one of *Britain's* finest athletes. He is World, Olympic, Commonwealth and European champion in the 100-metre race, winning a gold medal in the 1992 Olympics and almost achieving a world record at the 1993 World Championships.

Christie's /ˈkrɪstɪz/ (commerce) A well-known firm of *London* auctioneers, famous for its fine art sale-room. Compare *Sotheby's*. [founded in 1766 by James Christie]

Christmas /ˈkrɪsməs/ (religion) The second greatest religious festival (after *Easter*) in the Christian year. It is the most popular family holiday season after the summer, and centres on *Christmas Day*. At this time presents and Christmas greetings cards are exchanged, a *Christmas tree* (traditionally a fir tree) is decorated, parties are held, and *pantomimes* and *carol services* take place. The Christmas season traditionally begins on *Christmas Eve* and continues until *Twelfth Night*. See also *Advent*, *Christmas dinner* and *Boxing Day*.

Christmas bonus /ˌkrɪsməs ˌbəʊnəs/ (finance) A state supplementary payment made once a year before *Christmas* to all *OAP*s. At present the Christmas bonus is £10.

Christmas Day /ˌkrɪsməs ˈdeɪ/ (tradition) 25 December, the central day of the *Christmas* season, and a traditional family reunion day. On this day, many people attend a *church* service, open their presents, eat a *Christmas dinner* and watch the sovereign's annual Christmas broadcast on television (or listen to it on the radio). The day is regarded as a special one for children, who receive much attention from their families and friends.

Christmas dinner /ˌkrɪsməs ˈdɪnə(r)/ (food and drink) A traditional midday meal eaten on *Christmas Day*, and usually including roast turkey and *Christmas pudding* with *mince pies*, and accompanied by wine. Often *crackers* are pulled and the paper hats they contain are worn throughout the meal.

Christmas Eve /ˌkrɪsməs ˈiːv/ (tradition) 24 December, the day before *Christmas Day*, when all preparations for *Christmas* are complete and when almost everyone starts a holiday of several days (in recent times, often until the next working day after *New Year's Day*). It is a traditional time for parties, especially the annual *office party*, and many work places, including shops and banks, close earlier than usual. In the late evening, many people go to a *church* service (in the *Church of England* and the *Roman Catholic Church* often called a 'midnight mass'), and children, on going to bed, traditionally hang up an old sock ('stocking') at the head of their bed for *Santa Claus* to fill with presents during the night. (This role is actually played by the child's parents.)

Christmas pudding /ˌkrɪsməs ˈpʊdɪŋ/ (food and drink) A rich steamed pudding containing dried fruit, spices and often brandy, served as part of a *Christmas dinner* and traditionally decorated with a small piece of *holly* 'planted' in the top. Compare *plum pudding*.

Christmas tree /ˈkrɪsməs triː/ (tradition) A fir tree that is decorated with small, brightly-coloured lights and small coloured glass ornaments. Decorating the tree is part of the *Christmas* festivities.

Christ's Hospital /ˌkraɪsts ˈhɒspɪtl/ (education) A *public school*[1] in Horsham, West Sussex, also known as the 'Bluecoat School' from the long blue coats that form part of its traditional uniform. It was founded in *London* in 1552 as a 'hospital' (religious home) to educate children of poor parents. The boys' section moved to Sussex in 1902, where it was joined in 1985 by the girls' section from Hertford. Unusually, its fees depend on the income of the parents, and are graded accordingly. It currently has about 800 students.

Chubb (lock) /ˈtʃʌb (lɒk)/ (daily life) The trade name of a type of patent lock that contains a special device to prevent it from being picked. [from the name of its inventor, Charles Chubb (1773–1845), a *London* locksmith]

Chunnel /ˈtʃʌnl/, **the** (transport) A colloquial name for the *Channel Tunnel*. [a blend of *Ch*annel and t*unnel*]

church /tʃɜːtʃ/ (religion) A term sometimes used to apply to the *Church of England*, or other established church, by contrast with *chapel*[3].

Church Army /ˌtʃɜːtʃ ˈɑːmɪ/, **the** (charities) An evangelistic organization within the *Church of England*, founded in 1882 with the aim of aiding all who are disadvantaged, such as the poor, the homeless and the elderly, by offering them homes, hostels and practical assistance on Christian lines.

Church Commissioners /ˌtʃɜːtʃ kəˈmɪʃənəz/, **the** (religion) An organization appointed by the government to manage the finances of the *Church of England*.

Church House /ˌtʃɜːtʃ ˈhaʊs/ (religion) The headquarters in *London* of the *General Synod* of the *Church of England*.

Church of England /ˌtʃɜːtʃ əv ˈɪŋɡlənd/, **the** (religion) The official (established) *church* of *England*, created in the 16th century as a protestant church by the *Act of Supremacy*. Its secular head is the sovereign, and its religious head, the *Archbishop of Canterbury*. Its senior clergy—archbishops, bishops and *deans*[3]—are appointed by the sovereign on the recommendation of the *Prime Minister*. It is one of the main forces of the *Establishment* in *Britain*. See also *High Church, Low Church, Anglo-Catholic, General Synod*.

Church of Scotland /ˌtʃɜːtʃ əv ˈskɒtlənd/, **the** (religion) The national Presbyterian church of *Scotland*, governed by local '*Kirk* Sessions' that consist of *ministers*[1] and elders (elected senior members). Both men and women may join the ministry, and all its members are ordained. The total adult membership of the Church of Scotland is currently about 790,000.

church school /ˈtʃɜːtʃ skuːl/ (education) A *state school* subsidized by the *Church of England* and under its authority. See *voluntary school*.

Church Times /ˌtʃɜːtʃ ˈtaɪmz/, **the** (media) A weekly newspaper for members of the *Church of England*, whether clergy or laity. It inclines to *High Church* views. It was first published in 1863 and has a current circulation of about 42,000.

Church Urban Fund /ˌtʃɜːtʃ ˈɜːbən fʌnd/, **the** (charity) A voluntary organization set up by the *Church of England* in 1988 to raise money for the Church's work in *inner cities* and other poor urban areas.

Churchill, Winston /ˈtʃɜːtʃɪl, ˈwɪnstən/ (people) Winston Churchill (1874–1965) became a major political figure during the Second World War. In 1940 he became both *Prime Minister* (of a *coalition* government) and Minister of Defence. He inspired the confidence of the British people in their struggle for victory and his radio speeches did much to boost the nation's morale at a time of crisis and deprivation. Churchill was a gifted orator and many of his speeches contained memorable phrases, for example, 'This was their finest hour', and, of fighter pilots in the *Battle of Britain*, 'Never in the field of human conflict was so much owed by so many to so few'.

churchwarden /ˌtʃɜːtʃˈwɔːdn/ (religion) An elected representative of a parish (not a priest) in the *Church of England*. He helps with the day-to-day running of a *church*, such as showing people to seats, taking the collection and managing church money and other business.

CID /ˌsiː aɪ ˈdiː/, **the (Criminal Investigation Department, the)** (law) A regional crime and detection department of the British police force, with the best known being that of the *Metropolitan Police* in *London*. This operates at *New Scotland Yard* and is divided into a number of branches, including the *Special Branch*, the Criminal Record Office and the *Flying Squad*.

Cinque Ports /ˈsɪŋk pɔːts/ (geography) The collective historic title of the five coastal towns (some now no longer on the coast) of Hastings, Dover, Sandwich, Romney and Hythe (and, later, Winchelsea and Rye), all in southeast *England* (Sussex and Kent), which formerly had special privileges as ports. [Old French, 'five ports']

citizen's arrest /ˌsɪtɪznz əˈrest/ (law) The right of a British citizen to arrest any person he suspects of committing an arrestable offence, or of having committed such an offence. An arrestable offence is one which has a fixed penalty by law (eg, a number of years' imprisonment), such as murder, theft, rape or unlawful wounding. Most arrests, however, are made by police officers.

Citizen's Charter /ˌsɪtɪznz ˈtʃɑːtə(r)/, **the** (government) A social programme introduced in 1991 by the *Prime Minister*, John *Major*, to improve the standard of service to the public. Its aims include: a reduction in the time people wait to enter hospital, the sending of school reports to parents, the publishing of exam results, better run *council estates*, better railways, a better postal service, more efficient *local authorities*, and the wearing of name badges by government employees who deal direct with the public.

city /ˈsɪtɪ/ (geography) The title of many large towns in *Britain*, traditionally ones with a cathedral, but also of a smaller town awarded the title as an honour.

City Action Team /ˌsɪtɪ ˈækʃn ˌtiːm/ (government) One of a number of local teams organized by the government to encourage cooperation between private and state enterprises in *inner cities* and to promote business projects there.

City (of London) /'sɪtɪ (ˌsɪtɪ əv 'lʌndən)/, **the** (London) A self-governing administrative region, with its own police force, in the east of *London*, and the historic centre of London as a whole. It is one of the chief financial and commercial centres of the western world, and its territory of just over one square mile contains several banks, including the *Bank of England*, the *Stock Exchange* and the offices of many financial companies.

city technology college /ˌsɪtɪ tek'nɒlədʒɪ kɒlɪdʒ/ **(CTC)** (education) A type of state college set up by the government in 1987 to provide young people with practical training and educational opportunities in selected urban areas where educational standards are below the average. There are currently 13 CTCs, five of them in *London*.

civic centre /ˌsɪvɪk 'sentə(r)/ (government) The public administrative buildings of a town, where the *town council* offices are, as well as other local government offices and, often, recreational facilities.

Civic Trust /ˌsɪvɪk 'trʌst/, **the** (charities) A non-government organization founded in 1957 to encourage the preservation and maintenance of *ancient monuments*, historic buildings and picturesque areas of the country, and to protect and improve the aesthetic environment.

Civil List /ˌsɪvl 'lɪst/, **the** (royal family) An annual payment made by *Parliament* to the *Queen* and members of the *royal family* to cover the cost of their public duties. The amount paid is the same every year for ten years (at present to 2000). No payment is made to the *Prince of Wales* as he derives his income from the *Duchy of Cornwall*. The Queen's private expenses as sovereign are paid by the *Privy Purse*.

civil servant /ˌsɪvl 'sɜːvənt/ (government) A person employed as a member of the *Civil Service*, that is, a civilian employed by the government. As such he has no right to be actively engaged in politics or to become an *MP*. His position is not affected by a change of government. ['civil' as not military, 'servant' as serving both the government and the public]

Civil Service /ˌsɪvl 'sɜːvɪs/, **the** (government) The state organization, composed of several *ministries* or *departments*, that is responsible for carrying out the work of the government at all levels. See also *civil servant*.

clan /klæn/ (life and society) In *Scotland* and (mainly historically) *Ireland*, the collective term for members of a family having a common ancestor and, usually, bearing the same surname and acknowledging the same leader. See *chieftain*.

Clansman /'klænzmən/, **the** (transport) The name of a daily express train that runs between *London* and Inverness, *Scotland*. [literally, 'member of a *clan*']

Clapham Junction /ˌklæpəm 'dʒʌŋkʃn/ (transport) A large and busy railway junction in south *London*. There have been serious railway accidents there in the past.

Clarence House /ˌklærəns 'haʊs/ (royal family) The house in *London* that is the residence of *Queen Elizabeth, the Queen Mother*, next to *St James's Palace*. The house has had royal associations since it was built in 1829 for William IV, then Duke of Clarence. *Queen Elizabeth* lived there before she came to the throne, and the *Princess Royal*, her only daughter, was born there.

Claridges /'klærɪdʒɪz/ (London) A fashionable hotel in the *West End* of *London*, where rich people and members of the aristocracy traditionally stay. [originally built as a small hotel by William Claridge, a butler in an aristocratic household in the mid-19th century]

Classic FM /'klæsɪk ef ˌem/ (media) The *INR* station that came into operation in 1992 as INR1. It broadcasts mainly classical music, together with news and information.

clearing bank /'klɪərɪŋ bæŋk/ (finance) A formal term for any of the major banks in *Britain* that transfers credits and cheques through one of the three payment systems: *BACS*, *CHAPS* or *Town Clearing*.

clearway /'klɪəweɪ/ (transport) A stretch of road that is of *A-road* status but is not a *motorway*, on which traffic may stop only in an emergency.

Cleese, John /'kliːz, dʒɒn/ (people) John Cleese (born 1939) is one of the most popular British comedy actors of modern times. He became particularly well known through his brilliant characterization of Basil Fawlty, the central figure in the television comedy series 'Fawlty Towers' (1975 and 1979), telling of the misunderstandings and mishaps that occur in a country hotel, where Basil Fawlty is the owner. Cleese closely identified with his role, which was that of a manic but typically 'English' *gentleman*[2], who openly expresses the many prejudices and attitudes that remain unexpressed by most people. Cleese has subsequently starred in several successful films, notably 'A Fish Called Wanda' (1988).

Cleopatra's Needle /ˌklɪəpætrəz 'niːdl/ (London) An obelisk of pink granite placed on the (*Thames*) *Embankment, London* in 1878. It is one of two such obelisks originally standing at Heliopolis, Egypt, in about 1500 BC. The other was placed in Central Park, New York, USA, in 1880.

clerihew /'klerɪhjuː/ (language) A humorous verse in four lines usually serving as a 'mini-biography' of some famous person, for example:

George the Third

Ought never to have occurred.

One can only wonder

At so grotesque a blunder.

[named after their inventor, Edmund Clerihew Bentley (1875–1956), whose first such verse appeared in 1905]

Clerk of the House (of Commons) /ˌklɑːk əv ðə 'haʊs (ˌklɑːk əv ðə ˌhaʊs əv 'kɒmənz)/**, the** (government) A senior official of the *House of Commons*. He is the principal adviser to the *Speaker* on matters of procedure and he attends all sittings of the *House*[1].

clerk of works /ˌklɑːk əv 'wɜːks/ (work) A person who supervises building work in progress or who is responsible for the maintenance of existing buildings.

Clifton (College) /'klɪftən (ˌklɪftən 'kɒlɪdʒ)/ (education) A leading *public school*[1] in Bristol, founded in 1862 and having 670 students. [named for its location on Clifton Down]

Clifton Suspension Bridge /ˌklɪftən sə'spenʃn brɪdʒ/**, the** (transport) A road and pedestrian bridge high over the river Avon in Bristol, Avon, and notorious for the suicides committed by people jumping from it.

clock golf /ˌklɒk 'ɡɒlf/ (sport and leisure) A type of *putting* played on a lawn on which a course is laid out in the form of a clock face, with 12 numbers. Players start at figure 1 and move round the clock face in turn, driving their ball into a hole at the centre of the 'clock'.

close /kləʊs/ (**1** style **2** religion) **1** A courtyard enclosed by buildings, or the entry to such a courtyard. **2** The land surrounding a cathedral, usually with houses facing inwards on roads that form the four sides of a square, with lawns extending between the roads and the cathedral. **3** A small, quiet, residential road, in a street name such as 'Park Close'.

closed shop /ˌkləʊzd 'ʃɒp/ (work) An arrangement whereby the whole of the work force of a factory or other establishment is obliged to join one of the trade unions recognized in that establishment. Compare *open shop*.

closing price /ˈkləʊzɪŋ praɪs/, **the** (finance) The price of stocks and shares recorded at the end of the working day at the *London Stock Exchange*.

cloth cap /ˌklɒθ ˈkæp/ (clothing) A flat *cap¹* made of cloth that has become the symbol of the *working-class* man. Compare *Andy Capp*.

clotted cream /ˌklɒtɪd ˈkriːm/ (food and drink) A thick, rich cream made with very hot milk, produced chiefly in Devon and *Cornwall*, and regarded as especially tasty. It is usually eaten with fruit, or added to jam on bread or in cakes. [so called as the cream is not liquid but has *clotted* or thickened to a soft but firm consistency]

club /klʌb/ (life and society) An association of people, linked by a common interest, such as sport, who have their own premises for meetings and relaxation. Many clubs have a restricted membership (some *London* clubs still do not admit women) and charge a high entrance fee and annual subscription.

Clubland /ˈklʌblænd/ (London) A nickname for the area of *London* near *St James's Park*, where there are many *clubs*.

Clyde /klaɪd/, **the** (geography) The most important river of southwest *Scotland*, long famous for the industries that have developed on its banks and at its estuary, especially where it flows through *Glasgow*. Its length is about 106 miles (170 km).

Clydesdale (horse) /ˈklaɪdzdeɪl (ˌklaɪdzdeɪl ˈhɔːs)/ (animal world) A heavy breed of powerful cart-horse, usually reddish-brown in colour. [originally from the valley of the river *Clyde, Scotland*]

Clydesdale Bank /ˌklaɪdzdeɪl ˈbæŋk/, **the** (finance) The third largest of the major Scottish banks (after the *Royal Bank of Scotland* and the *Bank of Scotland*). It was founded in 1838 and has its head office in *Glasgow*. Unlike English banks, but like the other two main Scottish banks, it issues its own banknotes (for values of £5 to £100). Such notes are not legal tender, but in *Scotland* have a status equal to a note issued by the *Bank of England*. [called this because Glasgow is in Clydesdale, a general name for the region that lies in the broad valley of the river Clyde]

coalition /ˌkəʊəˈlɪʃn/ (politics) A government formed from the alliance of normally opposed political parties, especially at a time of crisis, as during war. There have been coalition governments in *Britain* in the periods 1915–16, 1916–22, 1931–5 and 1940–5.

Coalport /'kəʊlpɔːt/ (style) A type of fine porcelain made at the potteries in the village of this name in Shropshire since the end of the 18th century.

cock-a-leekie /ˌkɒkə'liːkɪ/ (food and drink) A type of soup popular in *Scotland*, made from chicken boiled with leeks. [from *cock*, 'chicken', and *leek*]

cocker (spaniel) /'kɒkə(r) (ˌkɒkə 'spænjəl)/ (animal world) A breed of working spaniel with a short, silky, black, reddish or golden coloured coat and long ears. [from its use in hunting woodcock]

cockney /'kɒknɪ/ (London) **1** The standard *London* dialect, with characteristic pronunciation and the use of *rhyming slang*. **2** A native Londoner, who speaks such a dialect, traditionally a person born within hearing of *Bow Bells*.

cod war /ˌkɒd 'wɔː(r)/ (politics) A dispute between *Britain* and Iceland concerning Iceland's extension of her fishing limits and involving the deliberate collisions of British and Icelandic fishing boats at sea. Such disputes occurred in 1958, 1972–3 and 1975–6.

coffee-table book /'kɒfɪ ˌteɪbl bʊk/ (arts) A large, and usually expensive size illustrated book printed on good quality paper and designed to be glanced at rather than read. [from its display on a coffee-table — a low table on which coffee is served in a sitting-room]

COI /ˌsiː əʊ 'aɪ/, **the (Central Office of Information, the)** (government) A state organization responsible for the preparation and dissemination of government information, both at home and abroad. It publishes booklets and brochures, organizes exhibitions and film shows, and arranges the distribution of British publications, television films, etc overseas.

Coldstream Guards /ˌkəʊldstriːm 'gɑːdz/, **the** (defence) The second oldest regiment in the British *Army* (after the *Royal Scots*), raised in 1650 and forming part of the *Guards Division*. [originating in the village of Coldstream, *Scotland*]

Coliseum (Theatre) /ˌkɒlɪ'sɪəm (ˌkɒlɪsɪəm 'θɪətə(r))/, **the** (arts) A large *London* theatre, also known as the London Coliseum, that is the home of the *English National Opera*.

collective bargaining /kəˌlektɪv 'bɑːgɪnɪŋ/ (work) A term used for joint negotiation and discussion between employers and trade unions in order to agree wages and conditions of employment, especially when employers and employees are in dispute. When collective bargaining fails to resolve a dispute, matters are usually referred to *ACAS*.

college /'kɒlɪdʒ/ (education) **1** An independent institution of *higher education* within a university, typically one at *Oxford University* or *Cambridge University*. **2** A specialized professional institution of secondary or higher education, such as a college of music or a *college of education*. **3** The official title of certain *public schools[1]*, such as *Eton College*. **4** The building or buildings of any of these.

College of Arms /ˌkɒlɪdʒ əv 'ɑːmz/**, the** (life and society) An organization established in the 15th century that grants armorial bearings and is responsible for all matters relating to the coats of arms and pedigrees of English, Irish and Commonwealth[1] families. Its head is the *Earl Marshal*. It is also known as the College of Heralds.

college of education /ˌkɒlɪdʒ əv edʒʊ'keɪʃn/ (education) A *college[2]* where teachers are trained.

collie /'kɒlɪ/ (animal world) A breed of Scottish sheepdog with a long or short silky coat, usually reddish or black in colour and with a long narrow head. [said to be so called as its coat was as black as coal]

Collins, Phil /'kɒlɪnz, fɪl/ (people) Phil Collins (born 1951) became well known as a pop musician in the 1980s, when he began his solo career as a singer after performing as a drummer with the group 'Genesis'. His most popular songs include 'In the Air Tonight' and 'You Can't Hurry Love', while later albums such as 'No Jacket Required' and 'Face Value' became internationally famous. Although his appearance is not striking, his distinctive voice has won him public acclaim.

Colonel Blimp /ˌkɜːnl 'blɪmp/ (life and society) A character drawn by the cartoonist David Low in the 1930s, representing a plump and pompous elderly army officer with a keen dislike of anything new. The name, often shortened to the word 'blimp', and having a corresponding adjective 'blimpish', is used of anyone felt to be like this character. [character's name originated from 'blimp' as a word for an airship in the First World War]

colours /'kʌləz/ (sport and leisure) A distinguishing badge or item of clothing, such as a tie, awarded to a player who has become a member of a particular sports team, especially at a school or *college*[1]. Compare *blue*[2,3], *cap*[3,4].

coming of age /ˌkʌmɪŋ əv 'eɪdʒ/ (law) The 18th birthday of a young person, when he or she legally becomes an adult. At 18, a person gains several additional rights, including the ability to vote at a political election, to serve on a *jury* (if asked to), to see a film rated *'18'*, drink alcohol in a *pub* (or buy it from an *off-licence*) and marry without the consent of his or her parents (although in *Scotland* a person has always been able to, and can still, marry at 16 without such consent).

Commandos /kə'mɑːndəʊz/, **the** (defence) A branch of the *Royal Marines* specially trained to carry out landings on enemy coasts and to prepare the way for landings by sea, air or land forces. [originating as an Afrikaans word for troops used in the *Boer War*]

Commission for Racial Equality /kəˌmɪʃn fə ˌreɪʃl ɪ'kwɒlətɪ/, **the** **(CRE, the)** (life and society) An official body established by the Race Relations Act of 1976 in order to eliminate racial discrimination and to promote equality of opportunity and good relations between people of different racial groups.

Common Agricultural Policy /ˌkɒmən ægrɪ'kʌltʃərəl pɒləsɪ/, **the** **(CAP, the)** (government) The *EC* policy set up in order to increase agricultural production, provide a fair standard of living for farmers, and enable food to be bought at reasonable prices. However, the CAP caused overproduction, resulting in a surplus of food (popularly known by such terms as 'butter mountain' or 'wine lake'), so that various reforms were introduced in *Britain* and other countries from 1992. See *set-aside*.

Common Entrance /ˌkɒmən 'entrəns/ (education) In *preparatory schools*, a school-leaving examination taken to gain entrance to a *public school*[1] (usually by boys at age 13, girls at age 10). [from the examination being used by all schools in common to gain entrance]

common law /ˌkɒmən 'lɔː/ (law) The traditional unwritten law of *England*, based on judges' decisions and custom rather than on written laws passed by *Parliament*.

common law husband/wife /ˌkɒmən lɔː 'hʌzbənd/'waɪf/ (law) A husband or wife recognized by *common law* only—that is, one who is not married but who has lived for some time with his or her partner.

Common Market /ˌkɒmən 'mɑːkɪt/, **the** (government) A rather dated term for the *EC*.

commoner /ˈkɒmənə(r)/ (**1** education **2** life and society) **1** A student at a university, especially *Oxford²* or *Cambridge²*, who is not receiving a *scholarship*. **2** A person who is not a *peer*.

Commons /ˈkɒmənz/, **the** (government) A short name for the *House of Commons*.

Commonwealth /ˈkɒmənwelθ/, **the 1** The free association of (currently) 50 countries that were mostly at one time part of the *British Empire*. The *Queen* is the head of the Commonwealth, and is the actual head of state in some of the countries. See also *High Commissioner*. **2** The republic that existed in *England* from 1649 to 1660, and especially the five years from 1553 when Oliver Cromwell governed the country.

community centre /kəˈmjuːnɪtɪ ˌsentə(r)/ (daily life) A building used by members of a community, such as a town or village, for social gatherings, sports meetings, etc.

community council /kəˌmjuːnɪtɪ ˈkaʊnsl/ (government) A *local authority* in *Wales* that has replaced the former *parish council*, county borough council, *borough* council or urban district council. There are also community councils in *Scotland*, but these are merely local advisory bodies and do not have the status of a local authority.

Companion of Honour /kəmˌpænɪən əv ˈɒnə(r)/, **the (CH, the)** (life and society) An order instituted in 1917 as an award to someone who has performed a special service of national importance. It is similar to the *Order of Merit*.

Company /ˈkʌmpənɪ/ (media) A glossy monthly magazine for women, aimed at independent and intelligent young readers. Its current circulation is about 220,000.

comprehensive school /ˌkɒmprɪˈhensɪv skuːl/ (education) A large state *secondary school* for children of all abilities within a single district, offering a wide ('comprehensive') education. About 90% of all secondary school students attend a comprehensive school. Compare *grammar school²*, *secondary modern school, technical school*.

Concorde /ˈkɒŋkɔːd/ (transport) The name of the first commercial supersonic airliner, of joint British and French design and construction, first flown in 1969 and entering into passenger service in 1976.

conference centre /ˈkɒnfərəns ˌsentə(r)/ (**1** daily life **2** geography) **1** A large, usually modern building in a town or *city*, especially a seaside resort, that contains an auditorium where meetings or conferences can be held, and

conkers

which provides facilities for those attending. There are well-known conference centres in *Blackpool*, *Bournemouth*, *Brighton* and *Harrogate*, and the centres are mainly used by large organizations such as trade unions and political parties. **2** A town having such a centre.

Conference (pear) /'kɒnfərəns (ˌkɒfərəns 'peə(r))/ (food and drink) A popular type of autumn pear with a good flavour and a long, tapering, brownish-coloured fruit.

Congress House /ˌkɒŋgres 'haʊs/ (work) The headquarters of the *TUC*, in central *London*.

conkers /'kɒŋkəz/ (sport and leisure) A game popular among children in the autumn. One player threads a shelled horse chestnut ('conker') onto a string and with this strikes the conker of another player, with the aim of breaking it.

Conqueror /'kɒŋkərə(r)/, **the** (history) The nickname of King William I, Duke of Normandy (1028–87), who in 1066 led the Normans to victory in *Britain*. See *Norman Conquest*.

Conquest /'kɒŋkwest/, **the** (history) A short name for the *Norman Conquest*.

conservation area /kɒnsə'veɪʃn ˌeərɪə/ (geography) An area of particular architectural or historic interest, usually in a town or *city*, where building and development is carefully controlled by the *local authority*. There are about 6,000 conservation areas in *England* alone.

Conservative Party /kən'sɜːvətɪv ˌpɑːtɪ/, **the** (politics) One of the three main political parties in *Britain*, together with the *Labour Party* and the *Liberal Democrats*. It is the leading right-wing party, supporting free enterprise, private ownership, and social reform. Its supporters are mainly *middle class* or *upper class*, and are chiefly in the south of *England* or in rural areas. Although continuously in power since 1979, public support for the Party has declined in recent years and it has lost several *by-elections*. ['conservative' as it aims to conserve traditional values and practices]

constable /'kʌnstəbl/ (**1** law **2** life and society) **1** A police officer (in full, police constable (PC) or woman police constable (WPC)) of the lowest rank. See *Chief Constable*. **2** The title of the commandant or governor of a royal castle or fortress, such as the *Tower of London* or *Windsor Castle*. This title is always written with a capital C, ie, Constable.

Constable country /'kʌnstəbl ˌkʌntrɪ/ (geography) A tourist name for the picturesque rural districts of Suffolk and Essex, especially along the river Stour, where the landscape painter John Constable (1776–1837) lived and worked.

constituency /kən'stɪtjʊənsɪ/ (government) A political administrative district whose voters elect a single *MP* to represent them in the *House of Commons*.

constitutional monarchy /ˌkɒnstɪtjuːʃənl 'mɒnəkɪ/ (government) The official status in *Britain* of the monarchy, meaning that the power of the monarch is limited by the country's constitution. The legal authority (the passing of acts) is given to *Parliament*, and executive authority (the carrying out of laws) to the government.

Consumers Association /kən'sjuːməz əsəʊsɪˌeɪʃn/, **the (CA, the)** (commerce) A non-governmental organization that works to promote the interests of consumers and everyday shoppers by monitoring and testing the quality and cost of goods and services. It publishes its findings in the magazine *Which?* It was founded in 1956.

continental breakfast /ˌkɒntɪnentl 'brekfəst/ (food and drink) A light breakfast without a cooked dish, and usually consisting of fruit juice or cereal, rolls or *toast* and *marmalade* and coffee. Such a breakfast has become increasingly popular in *Britain* in recent years. Compare *English breakfast*.[regarded as typical of the 'continent' or mainland Europe]

convenience store /kən'viːnɪəns ˌstɔː(r)/ (commerce) A shop similar to a *corner shop*, but larger and more modern, which has the convenience of its customers in mind. It stays open longer than other shops, and stocks a wide range of household goods, including food and drink.

Cook Report /'kʊk rɪˌpɔːt/, **The** (media) A weekly television programme on *ITV* broadcast in several series since 1987. In the programme, the presenter, Roger Cook, investigates corrupt or illegal practices in different parts of the world, and is filmed confronting the organizer of the practice wherever possible.

Co-op /ˈkəʊ ɒp/ (commerce) A retail shop or store run by the *Co-operative Wholesale Society*. Most towns and cities have a Co-op. The majority are either department stores, selling food, furniture, electrical goods and household products on different floors, or convenience stores.

Co-operative Movement /kəʊˈɒpərətɪv ˌmuːvmənt/, **the** (commerce) The Co-operative Movement began in the 19th century to help poorly-paid factory workers in early industrialized *Britain*. Individual workers contributed small amounts of money so that, as a group, they could afford to produce and sell goods to earn more money than they would earn in factories. The groups also bought important items of food and household goods more cheaply than any one person could. This part of the movement's activities became the *Co-operative Wholesale Society*. The Co-operative Movement also worked to improve housing, education and employment conditions. Today, the Movement has about 9.5 million members in retail, wholesale and manufacturing sectors, and over 400,000 in the agricultural sector.

Co-operative Wholesale Society /kəʊˌɒpərətɪv ˈhəʊlseɪl səˌsaɪətɪ/, **the (CWS, the)** (commerce) The national trading and manufacturing organization of the *Co-operative Movement* in *England* and *Wales*, established in 1863, and producing mainly consumer goods. The Scottish Co-operative Wholesale Society (SCWS), set up in 1868, amalgamated with the CWS in 1973 to form a single co-operative wholesale and productive organization for the *United Kingdom*. Customers of the CWS are encouraged to become shareholders in the company and to attend local company policy meetings. The CWS also operates its own bank, the Co-operative Bank. See also *Co-op*.

copper /ˈkɒpə(r)/ (**1** daily life **2** law) **1** A low-value coin (1p, 2p) which is made of bronze, and is copper-coloured. **2** A colloquial term for a policeman. [from colloquial 'to cop', meaning 'to catch']

copyright library /ˈkɒpɪraɪt ˌlaɪbrərɪ/ (arts) One of six libraries in the *British Isles* entitled to receive a free copy of every book published in the *United Kingdom*. They are: the *British Library*,

Bodleian Library, University Library, *Cambridge²*, National Library of *Scotland*, *Edinburgh*, National Library of Wales, Aberystwyth and the library of Trinity College, Dublin.

corgi /ˈkɔːgɪ/ (animal world) A breed of small dog with a smooth coat and usually reddish-brown in colour. Corgis are popular with the *royal family*. [from Welsh meaning 'dwarf dog']

corn exchange /ˈkɔːn ɪksˌtʃeɪndʒ/ (tradition) A building where corn was, or still is, bought and sold. In many towns the corn exchange serves as a public hall for concerts, exhibitions, etc.

corner shop /ˈkɔːnə ʃɒp/ (commerce) A small, often privately owned, general shop frequently on or near a street corner in the residential district of a town or *city*. See also *Sunday*, and compare *convenience store*.

Cornish pasty /ˌkɔːnɪʃ ˈpæstɪ/ (food and drink) A pastry case filled with meat and vegetables and usually eaten hot. The pasty was a traditional product in *Cornwall*, where it often served as a complete midday meal for fishermen, miners, farmers and schoolchildren.

Cornish Riviera /ˌkɔːnɪʃ rɪˈvɪeərə/**, the** (transport) A daily express train running between *London* and Penzance, *Cornwall*. [from the Cornish Riviera, the southern coast of Cornwall with its many resorts]

Cornwall /ˈkɔːnwəl/ (geography) The county at the western end of the southwestern peninsula of *England*. It is an historically distinct part of *Britain*, with its own Celtic language (Cornish, once extinct, but now revived by experts). Cornwall is a popular tourist centre and has a picturesque indented coastline.

Coronation /ˌkɒrəˈneɪʃn/**, the** (history) The religious ceremony when a new *king* or *queen* is crowned in *Westminster Abbey*. The year when this takes place is regarded as a historic milestone. The present sovereign, *Queen Elizabeth*, had her Coronation in 1953.

Coronation Chair /ˌkɒrəneɪʃn ˈtʃeə(r)/**, the** (history) The special throne in *Westminster Abbey* on which the sovereign sits during the *Coronation* ceremony. In an open box under the seat of the throne is the *Stone of Scone*.

Coronation Street /kɒrəˈneɪʃn striːt/ (media) A popular television series on *ITV* about the everyday life of several families who live in the same street in a town in the *North* of *England*, with a *pub* at one end and a *corner shop* at the other. The programme is broadcast three times a week and has been

Coronation

running since 1960. It currently has about 15 million viewers. Compare *EastEnders*. [named after a typical residential street, itself built (or named) shortly after the *Coronation* of a British sovereign]

coroner /ˈkɒrənə(r)/ (law) A local government officer responsible for investigating sudden deaths, especially in suspicious circumstances. Compare *procurator fiscal*.

corporal punishment /ˌkɔːpərəl ˈpʌnɪʃmənt/ (life and society) The punishment of criminals or offending children by physically striking or beating them, either with the hand or with a cane or other object (such as a slipper or strap). Corporal punishment was abolished in all *state schools* in 1986.

corporation tax /ˌkɔːpəˈreɪʃn tæks/ (finance) A tax paid by a company on its profits. For large companies the current rate is 33%, and for small companies it is 25%. Compare *capital gains tax*.

correspondence college /ˌkɒrɪˈspɒndəns ˌkɒlɪdʒ/ (education) A *college*² that prepares students for examination by means of correspondence, the student working at home and sending his work to the college by post for assessment and return.

correspondence course /ˌkɒrɪˈspɒndəns kɔːs/ (education) An educational course, usually for an official examination, in which a student studies by means of correspondence (by post) with a particular tutor or lecturer, either at a standard educational establishment or at a special *correspondence college*. Especially well known are the correspondence courses run by *London University* and the *Open University*, with both leading to a *first degree*.

Cosmopolitan /ˌkɒzmə'pɒlɪtən/ (media) A glossy monthly magazine for young women, with emphasis on romantic relationships and careers. It was first published in 1972 and has a current circulation of about 441,000.

cottage /'kɒtɪdʒ/ (style) A small house, usually in the country and often old and picturesque, and having an attractive garden. Some people, especially those living in towns and *cities*, rent a cottage as a holiday home in the summer or to live in at *weekends*.

cottage hospital /ˌkɒtɪdʒ 'hɒspɪtl/ (medicine) A small hospital in a town or rural district, often laid out as several individual buildings resembling *cottages*.

cottage loaf /ˌkɒtɪdʒ 'ləʊf/ (food and drink) A type of loaf baked in the form of a round bread base with a smaller piece on top. [once traditionally made in *cottages*]

cottage pie /ˌkɒtɪdʒ 'paɪ/ (food and drink) Another name for *shepherd's pie*.

council estate /'kaʊnsl ɪˌsteɪt/ (daily life) A residential, usually modern, district of a town or *city* consisting of *council houses*.

council house /'kaʊnsl haʊs/ (1 daily life 2 government) 1 A house provided by a *local authority* at a low rent. Such houses are mainly occupied by *working class* people who cannot afford to buy or rent a house privately. Most council house tenants have the right to buy their house at a specially reduced rate. 2 In *Scotland*, and in some towns elsewhere in *Britain*, an alternative name for a *town hall*.

council tax /'kaʊnsl ˌtæks/ (finance) A tax charged to help pay for the spending of a *local authority* such as a *county council*, *district council* or *parish council*. It is based on the value of an individual dwelling, and is paid by the residents on the assumption that each household consists of at least two adults. (A 25% discount is given to people living alone.) The tax was introduced in 1993 and replaced earlier forms of local tax.

councillor /'kaʊnsələ(r)/ (government) A member elected to serve, without pay, under the chairman of a *local authority* council such as a *town council* or *county council*.

Countdown /'kaʊntdaʊn/ (media) A popular daily television programme on *Channel 4*, first broadcast in 1982. Contestants have to form a word from jumbled letters while a clock 'counts down' the seconds.

Country Code /ˌkʌntrɪ ˈkəʊd/**, the** (life and society) A code of conduct issued by the *Countryside Commission* for visitors to the countryside, recommending a considerate attitude to the property of country people such as farmers and respect for the natural environment, for example: Guard against risks of fire, Fasten all gates, Keep dogs under control, etc.

country house /ˌkʌntrɪ ˈhaʊs/ (style) A large, often historic and privately owned, house in the country. Some such houses, together with their estates or gardens, are open to the public for an admission fee. See also *stately home*.

Country Life /ˌkʌntrɪ ˈlaɪf/ (media) A quality illustrated weekly magazine with features on country life and living, including *field sports*, wildlife, rural events, social history, and all that interests *upper class* country dwellers. It was founded in 1897 and has a current circulation of about 46,000.

Countryside Commission /ˈkʌntrɪsaɪd kəˌmɪʃn/**, the** (government) The government organization responsible for conserving and improving the natural beauty and amenities of the countryside in *England*. One of its tasks is to encourage *local authorities* and others to provide facilities such as parks and picnic sites. The equivalent body in *Wales* is the *Countryside Council for Wales* and in *Scotland* it is *Scottish Natural Heritage*. Compare *English Nature*.

Countryside Council for Wales /ˈkʌntrɪsaɪd ˈkaʊnsl fə ˌweɪlz/**, the (CCW, the)** (government) The *government* body for *Wales* that corresponds to the *Countryside Commission* in *England*.

county /ˈkaʊntɪ/ (geography) **1** One of the 50 territorial divisions of *England* (12 of *Wales*, 37 of *Scotland*) that evolved in historic times and that served as administrative units before 1974 (1975 in Scotland). **2** One of the 47 territorial units into which, outside *Greater London*, England and Wales have been divided for purposes of local government since 1974. There are also six *metropolitan counties* of similar status. It is planned to restore some of the historic counties, especially in Wales.

county council /ˌkaʊntɪ ˈkaʊnsl/ (government) The *local authority* of a *county²* (but not a *metropolitan county*) that is responsible for such matters as education, traffic and transport, the *police*, the fire service, social services and libraries. Compare *district council*.

county cricket /ˌkaʊntɪ ˈkrɪkɪt/ (sport and leisure) *Cricket* matches played between teams of different *counties*[1]. There are 17 county teams who play matches over a three- or four-day period, as well as one-day matches. All such games are financially sponsored by a commercial firm.

County Hall /ˌkaʊntɪ ˈhɔːl/ (government) **1** A large building on the banks of the *Thames* in *London*, erected in 1905 to house the offices of the London County Council (LCC). From 1965 to 1986 it was the headquarters of the LCC's successor, the *Greater London* Council (GLC). When the GLC was abolished it was put up for private sale and in 1992 was bought by a Japanese hotel company. **2** (**county hall**) In some towns, the headquarters of the local *county council*.

county school /ˌkaʊntɪ ˈskuːl/ (education) A state school provided and maintained in a *county*[2] by the *LEA*. Compare *voluntary school*.

county town /ˌkaʊntɪ ˈtaʊn/ (geography) The town in a *county*[2] where the headquarters of the *county council* are, the town being regarded as the county 'capital' for purposes of local government and administration.

coursing /ˈkɔːsɪŋ/ (sport and leisure) The hunting of hares with hounds, one of the *blood sports*.

court /kɔːt/ (**1** daily life **2** style **3** law) **1** In street names, a block of flats, such as 'Hastings Court'. **2** An inner courtyard of a *college*[1], especially one at *Cambridge University*. Compare *quadrangle*. **3** A place where law cases are held, such as the *Central Criminal Court*.

court circular /ˌkɔːt ˈsɜːkjʊlə(r)/ (royal family) A daily report of the activities and engagements of the sovereign and members of the *royal family*, as published in a newspaper.

Courtauld Institute (Galleries) /ˈkɔːtəʊld ˌɪnstɪtjuːt (ˌkɔːtəʊld ˌɪnstɪtjuːt ˈgælərɪz)/, **the** (arts) An art gallery in *London* open to the public and famous for its collections of Italian paintings, English and Dutch portraits and impressionist and post-impressionist works. It grew from the paintings left by the industrialist Samuel Courtauld (1876–1947).

Coutts /kuːts/ (finance) A small but exclusive bank with a head office in *London*. Almost all the bank's clients are rich people or members of the aristocracy, and *Queen Elizabeth* has her account there. [founded in 1692 and subsequently named after James Coutts]

Covent Garden /ˌkɒvənt ˈgɑːdn/ (**1** London **2** arts) **1** *London*'s wholesale fruit, flower and vegetable market, formerly in central London but in 1973 moved to new buildings (*New Covent Garden* (*Market*)) south of the *Thames*. In 1980 the restored buildings of the old market were opened as a complex of shops, cafés and promenades, with the former flower market housing the museum of *London Transport*. [formerly 'convent garden', as the market was on the site of the garden of a convent attached to *Westminster Abbey*] **2** The name used for the *Royal Opera House*, which is near the former site of the Covent Garden market in central London.

Cowdray Park /ˌkaʊdreɪ ˈpɑːk/ (sport and leisure) A famous polo ground near Midhurst, West Sussex. Several celebrities have played there, including members of the *royal family* such as the present *Prince of Wales* and, before him, his father, the *Duke of Edinburgh*. [ground is in park of former *country house*, burnt down in 18th century]

Cowes (Week) /ˈkaʊz (wiːk)/ (sport and leisure) An annual sailing and yachting regatta at Cowes, *Isle of Wight*, regarded as one of the most important sporting and social events of the year. Among the many races one of the best known is the Britannia Cup.

Cox's (Orange Pippin) /ˈkɒksɪz (ˌkɒksɪz ˌɒrɪndʒ ˈpɪpɪn)/ **(Coxes, Cox)** (food and drink) **1** A popular variety of eating apple with a sweet, somewhat spicy taste and a greenish-yellow fruit tinged with red. [first propagated in the 19th century by R Cox] **2** A name used for a number of similar varieties of apple.

CPVE (Certificate of Pre-Vocational Education) /ˌsiː piː viː ˈiː/, **the** (education) An examination introduced in 1986 for students who wish to stay on at school for a further year after taking their *GCSE* examination in order to prepare for work or a vocational course but who are not academically suited to take an *A-level* or *AS-level* course.

cracker /ˈkrækə(r)/ (tradition) A *Christmas* decoration placed either on a *Christmas tree* or on a dining table for the *Christmas dinner* or other meal of the season. It consists of a cardboard tube covered with coloured paper. This traditionally contains an explosive strip and a small present (and often a printed joke), as well as a tightly folded paper hat. When pulled apart by two people, one holding each end, the strip explodes ('cracks') and the contents of the cracker are kept by the person holding the half that contains them. Crackers are usually pulled at the start of a meal or party, and the paper hats worn throughout the celebration.

crammer /'kræmə(r)/ (education) A colloquial, rather critical term for a *private school* or institution that prepares students for an examination, especially one that a student has already taken but failed. A more formal and respectable name for such an establishment is a 'tutorial college'. [from the colloquial verb 'to cram', meaning to 'to fill forcibly (with knowledge)']

Cranwell /'krænwel/ (education) A *college²* for officer cadets of the *RAF*, near the village of Cranwell, Lincolnshire. Compare *Dartmouth*, *Sandhurst*.

cream cracker /ˌkriːm 'krækə(r)/ (food and drink) A type of crisp, flaky, unsweetened biscuit, usually eaten with butter and cheese. [from 'cracker', meaning 'biscuit', and the 'cream' or dairy products eaten with it]

cricket /'krɪkɪt/ (sport and leisure) A very popular summer sport which is played between two teams, each of eleven people. They play on a mown grass field at the centre of which is the 'pitch' (playing area). The aim is for one team (the batsmen) to score a large number of runs by hitting the ball 'bowled' (thrown) to them by the other team (the fielders). The fielders try to send the batsmen out of the game as quickly as possible, for example by catching a ball hit by a batsman before it touches the ground. Cricket is usually

cricket

played by men and boys though there are teams of women and girls as well. Players traditionally wear white clothes.

Crisis /ˈkraɪsɪs/ (charities) A charity which offers a home, food and clothing to the growing number of poor and homeless people in large cities such as *London* in the weeks before *Christmas*. It usually takes over some kind of vacant or empty building for the purpose, such as a *church* or a disused factory.

Crockford /ˈkrɒkfəd/ (religion) The short name of 'Crockford's Clerical Directory', the register of clergy in the *Church of England*, published annually. [named after John Crockford, who first published it in 1857]

croft /ˈkrɒft/ (geography) A small piece of arable land or a small farm in the north of *Scotland*, especially one that has been rented from the government. See also *crofter* and compare *smallholding*.

crofter /ˈkrɒftə(r)/ (life and society) The owner or tenant of a *croft* in northern *Scotland*. Most crofters rent their crofts from the government, and use the money granted by the government for the maintenance of the croft to supplement their income from other work such as weaving, fishing and receiving tourists.

crossbencher /ˈkrɒsbentʃə(r)/ (government) In the *Houses of Parliament*, an independent or neutral member, who belongs neither to the government nor to the *Opposition*, and who sits on the 'crossbenches' which are at one end of the chamber at right angles to the main benches of the government and the Opposition (which face each other). Compare *backbencher*, *frontbencher*.

Crown /kraʊn/, **the** (government) **1** A term used to refer to the realm or authority of the sovereign. **2** A term used to refer to the government, with the sovereign being the head of state.

Crown Agent /ˌkraʊn ˈeɪdʒənt/ (government) One of the members of a board appointed by the government to provide commercial, financial and professional services for various overseas governments and organizations, mainly in the public sector. The full official title of the board is 'Crown Agents for Overseas Governments and Administrations'.

crown court /ˌkraʊn ˈkɔːt/ (law) A criminal court that deals with serious offences such as murder, manslaughter, rape and robbery. It is presided over by a judge with a jury. People charged with such offences must first appear before a *magistrates'* court. This then decides whether to commit them to the crown court or not, depending on the nature and circumstances of the offence.

Crown Derby /ˌkraʊn ˈdɑːbɪ/ (style) A type of fine porcelain manufactured in Derby in the 18th and 19th centuries, marked with a crown over the letter 'D' (for 'Derby').

Crown Jewels /ˌkraʊn ˈdʒuːəlz/, **the** (tradition) The jewellery that is used by the sovereign on state occasions. When not in use, it is displayed to the public in the *Tower of London*.

Crown Prosecution Service /ˌkraʊn prɒsɪˈkjuːʃn ˌsɜːvɪs/, **the (CPS, the)** (law) The independent body set up in 1986 to decide whether a criminal prosecution should be brought as a result of investigations by the *police*. The decision to prosecute was previously made by the police themselves. See also *Director of Public Prosecutions*.

Cruft's /krʌfts/ (animal world) The most important annual dog show in *Britain*, held every January at the *National Exhibition Centre*, Birmingham. [first held in *London* by Charles Cruft in 1886]

crumpet /ˈkrʌmpɪt/ (food and drink) A round, light, soft cake full of small holes on the upper side and traditionally toasted, buttered and eaten at teatime, especially in winter. Compare *muffin*.

Crystal Palace /ˌkrɪstl ˈpælɪs/ (1 London 2 sport and leisure) **1** The name (originally a nickname) of a huge glass and iron exhibition hall built in *Hyde Park, London*, for the *Great Exhibition* of 1851, and later moved to south London, where it was destroyed by fire in 1936. **2** A London *football club* with a stadium in south London (originally near the Crystal Palace, but later moved).

cub (scout) /ˌkʌb (ˈskaʊt)/ (sport and leisure) A boy aged 8 to 10 who is a member of the Cub Scouts, the junior branch of the *Scout Association*.

Culloden /kəˈlɒdn/ **(Battle of Culloden, the)** (history) The battle of 1746 in which the Scottish prince Charles Edward Stuart (*Bonnie Prince Charlie* or the *Young Pretender*) and his followers were finally defeated by English troops in the *Forty-Five*. [from Culloden Moor, near Inverness, *Scotland*, where it was fought]

Cunard /kjuːˈnɑːd/ (transport) A large shipping company (in full Cunard Steamship Company) that operates the passenger liner *QE2* and previously operated the 'Queen Mary' (sold in 1967) and the 'Queen Elizabeth' (sold in 1968). Today the company operates passenger ships on regular transatlantic

crossings and on cruises in the Caribbean and
Mediterranean. [founded in 1839 by a Canadian shipowner,
Samuel Cunard (1787–1865)]

Cup /kʌp/, **the** (sport and leisure) **1** A short colloquial title for
the *FA Cup*. **2** A short colloquial title for the *Cup Final*.

Cup Final /ˌkʌp ˈfaɪnl/, **the** (sport and leisure) The final match
of the *FA Cup* contest, played at *Wembley* in *London*.

cup tie /ˈkʌp taɪ/ (sport and leisure) An elimination match
between two teams in a competition for a cup, especially one
in the *FA Cup*.

cuppa /ˈkʌpə/ (food and drink) A colloquial term for a cup of *tea[1]*.

curate /ˈkjʊərət/ (religion) **1** In the *Church of England*, a
clergyman appointed to assist a parish priest such as a *vicar*
or *rector*. **2** In the Church of England, a clergyman appointed
to take charge of a parish in the absence of the parish priest.
As such, his full title is 'curate-in-charge'.

curling

curling /ˈkɜːlɪŋ/ (sport and leisure) A game played on ice,
mainly in *Scotland*, in which heavy stones with handles are
thrown so as to slide across the ice towards a target.

custard /ˈkʌstəd/ (food and drink) A sweet yellow sauce made
of milk and sugar thickened with cornflour and served hot or
cold with *puddings[1,2]*, pies, fruit and similar sweet dishes. It is
also available commercially as a powder to be boiled with milk.

Customs and Excise /ˌkʌstəmz ən ˈeksaɪz/, **the** (government)
The Department of Customs and Excise is the government
department responsible for collecting and accounting for
money from Customs (duty paid on imports and exports) and
Excise (tax paid on goods, such as alcoholic drinks and
tobacco, produced for the home market). This money
includes *VAT*. They are also responsible for controlling
certain imports and exports and for compiling overseas trade
statistics.

Cutty Sark /ˌkʌtɪ ˈsɑːk/, **the** (history) The name of a famous
tea-clipper built in 1869 and now anchored on the *Thames* at
Greenwich where it is open to the public. [named after a witch
in Robert Burns' poem 'Tam o'Shanter', who wore a 'cutty
sark' or 'short shirt']

daffodil /ˈdæfədɪl/ (tradition) A yellow flower that is a symbol of *Wales*. Many Welsh people wear it pinned to their coats on *St David's Day*. See also *leek*, *thistle* and *rose*.

Daily Express /ˌdeɪlɪ ɪkˈspres/, **the** (media) A daily *popular paper* with a current circulation of just under 1.7 million (1970, 3.6 million). Its views generally support those of the *Conservative Party*. It was founded in 1900 and publishes a Saturday supplement, 'Forty-Eight Hours' (referring to the *weekend*).

Daily Mail /ˌdeɪlɪ ˈmeɪl/, **the** (media) A daily *popular paper* with a current circulation of just under 1.7 million (1970, 1.9 million). Its views mainly support those of the *Conservative Party*, though it is read by a wide range of social groups.

Daily Mirror /ˌdeɪlɪ ˈmɪrə(r)/, **the** (media) A daily *popular paper* with a circulation of about 2.8 million (1970, 4.7 million). It is politically left of centre, and is noted for its outspokenness on topical matters. It was founded in 1903.

Daily Sport /ˌdeɪlɪ ˈspɔːt/, **the** (media) A daily *popular paper* chiefly centred on sex and sport, with pictures and stories of gross or unbelievable feats and many advertisements for pornographic videos and telephone sex lines. It was founded in 1988 as a daily version of the weekly *Sunday Sport* and has a current circulation of about 300,000.

Daily Star /ˌdeɪlɪ ˈstɑː(r)/, **the** (media) A daily *popular paper* similar to The *Sun* in format and content. It was founded in 1978 and has a current circulation of about 808,000 (1978, 900,000).

Daily Telegraph /ˌdeɪlɪ ˈtelɪɡrɑːf/, **the** (media) A daily *quality* *paper* with a current circulation of about 1 million (1970, 1.4 million). Its views traditionally support those of the *Conservative Party*, though in recent years it has not been afraid to criticize certain government policies and personalities, including John *Major*. It was founded in 1855 and issues a Saturday colour supplement, 'Telegraph Magazine'.

Daimler /'deɪmlə(r)/ (transport) An expensive make of car built by *Rover*. [named after the original engine designer, the German engineer Gottfried Daimler (1834–1900)]

dalesman /'deɪlzmən/ (geography) **1** An inhabitant of the valleys (dales) of Yorkshire, in particular a farmer there. **2** An inhabitant of the valleys of the *Lake District*.

dame /deɪm/ (tradition) One of the main characters in a *pantomime*—the mother, or an elderly female relative, of the *principal boy*. The part is traditionally played by a male actor.

Dame /deɪm/ (life and society) The title of a woman who has been awarded the *OBE* or one of a number of certain other awards.

Dandy /'dændɪ/**, the** (media) A popular weekly comic for young children, first published in 1937.

Darby and Joan club /ˌdɑːbɪ ən 'dʒəʊn klʌb/ (charities) A social *club* for elderly people, usually run on a voluntary basis by charity workers who organize parties, concerts and outings. [from the name of a loving elderly couple in a ballad by Henry Woodfall (died 1769)]

Dartmoor /'dɑːtmɔː(r)/ (**1** geography **2** law) **1** A bleak region of moors and hills in Devon, through which flows the river Dart. **2** The short name of Dartmoor Prison for men, located at Princetown in the middle of the moors there.

Dartmoor pony /ˌdɑːtmɔː 'pəʊnɪ/ (animal world) A breed of small pony popular as a riding pony for children and originally bred on *Dartmoor¹*.

Dartmouth /'dɑːtməθ/ (education) The short name of the *Britannia Royal Naval College*, at Dartmouth, Devon. Compare *Sandhurst*, *Cranwell*.

darts /dɑːts/ (sport and leisure) An indoor game popular in *pubs* and *working men's clubs*. Short, weighted steel darts with a feathered base are thrown at a circular cork board (dartboard) marked out in numbered sections. The aim is to score a particular number of points, usually 301 or 501.

Datapost /'deɪtəpəʊst/ (commerce) An express delivery service for parcels and packets provided by the *Parcelforce*

darts

department of the *Post Office*. [from 'data' and 'post']

day boy /'deɪ ˌbɔɪ/ (education) A boy who attends a boarding school daily, but who lives at home.

day girl /'deɪ ˌgɜːl/ (education) A girl who attends a boarding school daily, but who lives at home.

day release /ˌdeɪ rɪ'liːs/ (education) The release of employees from their place of work one day a week to attend a *college²* of *further education* with the aim of obtaining a qualification related to their work. Compare *block release*.

D-day /'diː deɪ/ (history) **1** 6 June 1944, the day in the Second World War when Anglo-American troops landed in Normandy to fight German forces occupying mainland Europe. ['D' for 'day'] **2** 15 February 1971, the day when decimal currency was officially introduced in *Britain*. ['D' for 'decimal']

deacon /'diːkən/ (religion) The lowest ordained minister in the *Church of England*, with a minimum age of 23.

deaconess /ˌdiːkə'nes/ (religion) A woman who has been authorized to conduct certain religious services in some *Free Churches* (especially the *Methodist Church* and the *Church of Scotland*) and the *Church of England*. The powers of *Anglican* deaconesses are at present limited, but in 1986 they were officially permitted to conduct marriage services for the first time.

dean /diːn/ (**1, 2** education **3** religion) **1** The administrative head of a *college¹* or faculty in a university. **2** The *fellow¹* of a *college¹* at *Oxford University* or *Cambridge University* who is responsible for student discipline. **3** A senior clergyman in the *Church of England*.

death duty /'deθ ˌdjuːtɪ/ (finance) A term formerly used for what is now officially *inheritance tax*.

death penalty /'deθ ˌpenəltɪ/ see *capital punishment* (law)

debit card /'debɪt kaːd/ (finance) A card issued to bank customers enabling them to buy goods and pay for services by having the cost debited (charged) direct to their bank account, unlike a credit card account which has to be settled monthly. The advantage is that a customer with a debit card will not have to carry a cheque book, and the same card can be used to obtain money from automatic cash dispensers.

Debrett /də'bret/ (life and society) The short title of an annual register of the British aristocracy, in full 'Debrett's Peerage, Baronetage, Knightage and Companionage'. Compare *Burke('s Peerage)*. [first issued in 1802 by John Field Debrett]

Decorated (style) /'dekəreɪtɪd (staɪl)/ (style) A *Gothic (style)* of architecture of the first half of the 14th century, characterized by pointed arches, geometrical tracery in windows, curved wooden roofs and many ornamental decorations in external stonework.

decree absolute /dɪˌkriː 'æbsəluːt/ (law) The final decree in a divorce after which both the man and the woman who used to be married to each other are free to marry someone else. Compare *decree nisi*.

decree nisi /dɪˌkriː 'naɪsaɪ/ (law) A judgement made by a court of law that a divorce will be effective at some specified time in the future (usually six weeks) unless someone shows a good reason why the divorce should not happen. Compare *decree absolute*. ['nisi' from the Latin word meaning 'unless', i.e. 'unless cause is shown to the contrary']

deerstalker (hat) /'dɪəstɔːkə(r) (hæt)/ (clothing) A woollen hat with a peak at the front and the back, and with ear flaps usually tied together on top. Such a hat was traditionally worn by Sherlock *Holmes[1]*. [so called from their use by hunters when stalking deer on foot]

department /dɪ'paːtmənt/ (government) A major branch of the government. Many departments are *ministries[2]* (eg, the Department of Education and Science), and have a *minister[2]* at their head.

Depression /dɪ'preʃn/**, the** (history) The economic slump that occurred in *Britain* in 1929 and at times throughout the 1930s.

deerstalker hat

Deputy Lieutenant /ˌdepjʊtɪ lefˈtenənt/ (government) The deputy of a *Lord-Lieutenant* of a *county*.

Derby /ˈdɑːbɪ/, **the** (sport and leisure) A popular annual horse race for three-year-olds held on the course at *Epsom* Downs. [named after the Earl of Derby who first organized such a race in 1780]

derv /dɜːv/ (transport) A name for diesel oil when used as fuel for road transport. [from the initials *d*iesel *e*ngine *r*oad *v*ehicle]

Derwentwater /ˈdɜːwentˌwɔːtə(r)/ (geography) One of the most beautiful lakes in *England*, in the *Lake District*, where it is surrounded by steep rocks, green hills and mountain peaks. There are a number of small islands in the lake.

Desert Island Discs /ˌdezət ˌaɪlənd ˈdɪsks/ (media) A weekly programme on *Radio 4* in which a well-known personality is interviewed and is invited to choose eight records (discs) that he or she would like to have on a desert island, together with one book (apart from the Bible or *Shakespeare*) and one luxury. The records are played during the interview. The programme was first broadcast in 1942.

detached house /dɪˌtætʃt ˈhaʊs/ (style) A house standing on its own land and not attached to another building. Such houses are generally more expensive to buy than *semi-detached* or *terraced houses*.

detention centre /dɪˈtenʃn ˌsentə(r)/ (law) Until 1988, a centre

detached house

where young male offenders were kept for a period ranging
from three weeks to four months with a strict programme of
work to do. Such offenders are now sent to a *young offender
institution*.

development area /dɪˈveləpmənt ˌeərɪə/ (work) An *assisted* area
in which the government offers incentives to encourage
enterprise and economic growth. Current development areas
include west central *Scotland*, the *metropolitan counties*, northeast and south *Wales*, and west *Cornwall* and the *Scilly Isles*.

Devizes-Westminster race /dɪˌvaɪzɪz ˈwestmɪnstə ˌreɪs/**, the**
(sport and leisure) An annual canoe race held at *Easter* along
the Kennet and Avon Canal and river *Thames* from Devizes,
Wiltshire, to *London*. The length of the course is
approximately 200 km.

devolution /ˌdiːvəˈluːʃn/ (government) The transference of
certain powers from central government in *London* to
Scotland, *Wales* and *Northern Ireland*. Devolution began in
Britain in 1920 when Northern Ireland gained powers in most
areas except foreign affairs and defence. This was suspended
in 1972 after outbreaks of violence between the Protestant
majority in Northern Ireland and the Roman Catholic
minority, and *direct rule* from *Westminster*[2] was imposed
instead. Devolution has also been discussed for Scotland and
Wales, but has not yet been introduced. This is because when
referenda were held in Wales and Scotland in 1979, most

people in Wales did not want devolution of government powers to a regional assembly. In Scotland there was a small majority in favour of a Scottish assembly but so few people voted (only 33% of the voters) that the idea of devolution was abandoned.

Devonshire cream /ˌdevənʃə ˈkriːm/ (food and drink) Another name for *clotted cream*.

dewpond /ˈdjuːpɒnd/ (geography) A small pond, usually man-made, occasionally natural, found in the chalk hills of southern *England*, and never drying up, even in a drought. Many such ponds are very old and it was originally thought that dew or natural condensation kept the ponds wet.

dialling code /ˈdaɪəlɪŋ ˌkəʊd/ (daily life) The number that must be dialled before an individual telephone number in order to make a connection. It is usually the exchange number, but in large cities is the exchange number preceded by a three-figure number. These are currently 071 for central *London*, 081 for the rest of *Greater London*, 021 for Birmingham, 031 for

CHARLES DICKENS'S LEGACY TO ENGLAND.

Charles Dickens

Edinburgh, 041 for *Glasgow*, 051 for Liverpool, 051 for Manchester, and 091 for Newcastle upon Tyne. In written form, the dialling code, or the first part of it, is usually hyphenated to the individual number, for example 0780-52097, where 0780 is the exchange number. A typical London number (that of *Heathrow*) is 081-759 4321.

Diamond Sculls /ˌdaɪəmənd ˈskʌlz/, **the** (sport and leisure) The annual rowing race for sculls (single oarsmen) at the *Henley Regatta*. The race is open to amateurs and is regarded as the most important international sculling contest.

Diana, Princess /daɪˈænə, ˌprɪnses/ (royal family) see *Princess of Wales*

Dickens, Charles /ˈdɪkɪnz, tʃɑːlz/ (people) Charles Dickens (1812-70) is popularly regarded as one of the greatest English novelists. He mocked and denounced the social evils of *Victorian England* as well as showing humour and pathos. His sentimentality and caricature are still widely appreciated, and many of his characters, with their unusual names, have entered popular folklore. Among them are the miser *Scrooge*, the orphan Oliver Twist (who 'asked for more'), the drunken midwife Sarah Gamp, who always carried an old umbrella (so that 'gamp' is now a colloquial word in English for an umbrella) and the pathetic cripple boy Tiny Tim in 'A Christmas Carol' (1843). This last story, with its evocation of a Victorian *Christmas*, is probably still the most popular and best-known work that Dickens produced.

dinner /ˈdɪnə(r)/ (food and drink) The main meal of the day, taken either in the evening or (traditionally, by working people and children) at midday. Compare *lunch*.

dinner dance /ˈdɪnə dɑːns/ (sport and leisure) An evening *dinner* followed by a dance.

dinner jacket /ˈdɪnə ˌdʒækɪt/ (clothing) A man's black jacket with silk lapels, worn, together with black trousers, a white or coloured shirt and a black bow tie, on formal or semi-formal occasions, such as a special *dinner*. See also *black tie*.

dinner lady /ˈdɪnə ˌleɪdɪ/ (education) The colloquial term for a woman who serves *dinners* at midday in a school.

Diplomatic Service /ˌdɪpləˈmætɪk ˌsɜːvɪs/, **the** (government) A department of the *Civil Service* that provides staff for the *Foreign and Commonwealth Office* and for diplomatic and consular posts overseas.

direct debit /ˌdɪrekt ˈdebɪt/ (finance) An order from a customer to a bank or *building society* to make regular payments from his or her account to a particular organization. The order may be for a stated payment or for a variable amount. Compare *standing order*.

direct rule /ˌdɪrekt 'ruːl/ (government) The direct control of law and order in *Northern Ireland* by the British government, instead of locally by the Northern Ireland government, from 1972. See also *Northern Ireland Assembly*.

disability living allowance /ˌdɪsə'bɪlətɪ 'lɪvɪŋ ə,lauəns/ (finance) A government payment made to disabled people who need personal care or help with transport. The payment is free of *income tax*. See also *Motability*.

disc parking /'dɪsk ˌpɑːkɪŋ/ (transport) A system whereby cars may be parked in a public car park or on town streets only if they display a special disc indicating their time of arrival or intended time of departure.

discount house /'dɪskaunt haus/ (finance) A special financial institution that acts as an intermediary between the *Bank of England* and the rest of the banks by dealing in money at a discount of its face value. There are currently nine discount houses in *Britain*.

Discovery /dɪ'skʌvərɪ/, **the** (history) The ship on which Captain Robert Scott made his expeditions to the Antarctic in 1901-4. For many years it was a museum open to the public on the river *Thames* in *London* until it was returned to Dundee in *Scotland* where it was originally built.

Disgusted, Tunbridge Wells /dɪsˌgʌstɪd ˌtʌnbrɪdʒ 'welz/ (life and society) A traditional nickname for an *upper class* or *middle class* person who writes a letter of complaint to the editor of a newspaper, especially when the complaint is on a trivial matter. [from the common pen-name formerly used by such correspondents; Tunbridge Wells is a town in Kent where a number of professional and retired people live]

district council /ˌdɪstrɪkt 'kaunsl/ (government) A *local authority* within a *county*[2] or *metropolitan county* that is responsible for such matters as local planning, housing, roads, environmental regulations and refuse collection. Compare *county council*.

district nurse /ˌdɪstrɪkt 'nɜːs/ (medicine) A trained medical nurse who gives care and treatment to people in their homes or elsewhere outside hospital, and who covers a particular district in the town or the country. Compare *district visitor* and *health visitor*.

district visitor /ˌdɪstrɪkt 'vɪzɪtə(r)/ (religion) A member of the

Church of England who volunteers to visit the sick and needy in a parish.

dividend /ˈdɪvɪdend/ (finance) A payment made regularly from the profits of a company to its shareholders, usually twice a year.

division /dɪˈvɪʒn/ (**1** government **2** sport and leisure) **1** A formal vote in the *House of Commons*, when *MPs* divide into two groups, for the motion ('aye') or against it ('no'), and go to one of two special corridors (division lobbies) to cast their vote. **2** One of four groups into which professional *football clubs* are placed in the *Football League*.

divvy/divi /ˈdɪvɪ/ (finance) A colloquial term for a *dividend*.

DIY /ˌdiː aɪ ˈwaɪ/ (**do-it-yourself**) (daily life) The popular British hobby of making improvements and additions to one's house without the help of professional or skilled workers such as painters, builders and carpenters. The pastime is not only specially satisfying to the home-owner but is cheaper than engaging professional craftsman to do the work. Many special 'DIY shops' sell equipment and materials for DIY work.

D-notice /ˈdiː ˌnəʊtɪs/ (defence) An instruction circulated to the news media by the government advising against the publication of information on a topic regarded as harmful to the defence interests of the country. ['D' for 'defence']

Doctor Who /ˌdɒktə ˈhuː/ (media) A television science-fiction series for children broadcast by the *BBC* since 1963. The central character (Doctor Who of the title) has a 'time machine' (the 'Tardis') in which, with one or more companions, he travels backwards or forwards in time to combat a variety of evil forces and characters.

Dodgem /ˈdɒdʒəm/ (sport and leisure) The trade name of a type of bumper car—a low-powered electrically operated vehicle driven and bumped into similar cars on a special rink at a fairground. [from 'dodge 'em' ('dodge them'), the aim being to bump while dodging the other cars]

dog-collar /ˈdɒgˌkɒlə(r)/ (clothing) A colloquial term for a priest's stiff white collar (officially, 'clerical collar').

dogs /dɒgz/, **the** (sport and leisure) A colloquial term for *greyhound racing*. On a special circular track a mechanical hare is chased by greyhounds, on which bets are placed as in horse racing.

dog's nose /ˈdɒgz nəʊz/ (food and drink) A colloquial name for a mixture of *gin* and beer, popular in the *North Country* as an alcoholic drink.

dole /dəʊl/, **the** (finance) A colloquial term for *unemployment benefit*, especially in the phrase 'on the dole', meaning 'receiving unemployment benefit' or simply 'unemployed'.

Domesday Book /'duːmzdeɪ bʊk/, **the** (history) The records of a survey of the land of *England* made by order of William the *Conqueror* (William I of Normandy) in 1086, and used for tax purposes and as a general reference book of the population, its property, stock, etc. Some of the remoter areas of northern England were not included in the survey. [probably so named as the records were the final ('day of judgement' or 'doomsday') authority for disputes over property]

don /dɒn/ (education) A member of the teaching staff of a university or *college¹*, especially at *Oxford University* or *Cambridge University*.

donkey derby /'dɒŋkɪ ˌdɑːbɪ/ (sport and leisure) A race in which people, especially children, ride donkeys, usually at a *fête*.

donkey jacket /'dɒŋkɪ ˌdʒækɪt/ (clothing) A short, thick, outdoor jacket, often dark blue in colour, worn either by workmen in bad weather or as a fashionable garment.

donor card /'dəʊnə kɑːd/ (medicine) A card carried by a person who has agreed to have parts of their body used for transplant surgery in the event of their death.

doorstep /'dɔːstep/ (food and drink) A colloquial word for a thick slice of bread.

Dorchester /'dɔːtʃɪstə(r)/, **the** (London) A luxury hotel in *Park Lane, London*.

Dorking /'dɔːkɪŋ/ (animal world) A large breed of chicken with silver-grey feathers and short legs. [originally bred at Dorking, Surrey]

double /'dʌbl/ (**1** food and drink **2 ,3** sport and leisure) **1** A double measure of spirits as an alcoholic drink, especially one measured in a *bar¹*. **2** In *darts*, a hit inside the narrow double ring that runs round the outer edge of a dartboard, thus scoring double the number of points in the particular section. **3** In gambling, a bet placed on two horses in different races, the winnings (and stake) from the first bet being placed as the second. See also *autumn double, accumulator*.

double decker /ˌdʌbl 'dekə(r)/ (transport) A bus with two passenger decks, especially a red bus of this type in *London*. At many seaside resorts, double deckers with an open top deck are used in the summer season for tourists who are sight-seeing.

double Gloucester (cheese) /ˌdʌbl ˈɡlɒstə(r) (ˌdʌbl ˌɡlɒstə ˈtʃiːz)/ (food and drink) A kind of smooth, mellow, orange-red cheese, originally made in the Vale of Gloucester. ['double' by contrast with the former 'single Gloucester' cheese, which was thinner and milder and made with less creamy milk]

Doulton (pottery) /ˈdəʊltən (ˌdəʊltən ˈpɒtərɪ)/ (style) A type of stoneware, typically brown and salt-glazed, originally made by Henry Doulton in *London*. The name 'Royal Doulton' is the mark of this and other china products.

Downing Street /ˈdaʊnɪŋ striːt/ (government) **1** A short street in central *London*, off *Whitehall[1]*, where the official homes of the *Prime Minister* (*Number Ten*) and of the *Chancellor of the Exchequer* (Number 11) are. **2** A term used for the British government.

Downs /daʊnz/**, the** (geography) The name of a number of chains of low chalk hills in the south of *England*, in particular the *South Downs*.

DPP /ˌdiː piː ˈpiː/**, the (Director of Public Prosecutions, the)** (law) The official who brings criminal proceedings in special or important cases under the superintendence of the *Attorney General*. He also advises government *departments*, *Chief Constables* and others who are involved in important legal matters.

Dr Watson /ˌdɒktə ˈwɒtsn/ (arts) The doctor who is the companion and assistant of Sherlock *Holmes[1]* in the stories by Arthur Conan Doyle. Dr Watson is the person who tells the stories and whose stupidity shows how brilliant the great detective is. It is said that Dr Watson is a self-mocking portrayal of Conan Doyle himself.

Drabble, Margaret /ˈdræbl, ˈmɑːɡrɪt/ (people) Margaret Drabble (born 1939) has won popularity as a sensitive writer of novels that usually centre on the theme of a woman's progress through life, with its many complexities. The characters are often shown in a situation of stress or emotional trouble, and are faced with important decisions in their lives, such as the choice between a career or a family.

Drain /dreɪn/**, the** (transport) A nickname for the *Waterloo and City Line*, referring to its darkness and dinginess as the oldest railway in the *London Underground* system.

draught beer /ˌdrɑːft ˈbɪə(r)/ (food and drink) A beer stored in a cask or barrel, as distinct from one that is bottled or canned. Such a beer is regarded as purer, and often stronger, by people knowledgeable about the drink. See also *CAMRA*, *real ale*.

dress circle /'dres ˌsɜːkl/, **the** (daily life) The first gallery in a theatre, in which *evening dress* formerly had to be worn.

drive /draɪv/ (**1** sport and leisure **2** style) **1** A game of whist or a session of *bingo*. **2** A private road that leads, usually from a gate, up to a person's house.

driving licence /'draɪvɪŋ ˌlaɪsns/ (transport) A document authorizing a person to drive a car or other motor vehicle. A 'full' licence, issued to a driver on passing a driving test, is valid until the person is 70 years old. A *provisional licence* enables a person to learn to drive. Licences are issued by the *DVLC*. The driving test itself is administered by a special test centre. It lasts about 35 minutes (70 minutes for lorry and bus drivers) and includes questions on the *Highway Code*.

drop scone /'drɒp skɒn/ (food and drink) A *scone* made by dropping a spoonful of batter on to a hot cooking surface. Also known as a 'Scotch pancake'.

Druids /'druːɪdz/, **the** (**1** history **2** life and society) **1** An ancient order of priests in *Britain*, *Ireland* and Gaul in pre-Christian times. **2** One of a number of modern religious societies who aim to revive the ancient order, in particular those who greet the rising of the sun on *Midsummer Day* at *Stonehenge*.

Drury Lane /ˌdrʊərɪ 'leɪn/ (arts) A *London* theatre officially known as the *Theatre Royal* and famous for its musicals. It is London's oldest theatre still in use, founded in 1663. [named after Drury Lane, a street that runs behind it]

dry /draɪ/ (politics) A term used, often half-humorously, for a *Conservative Party* politician who supported the 'hard line' policies of Margaret *Thatcher*, as distinct from a *wet*, who opposed them.

Duchess of York /ˌdʌtʃɪs əv 'jɔːk/, **the** (royal family) The royal title granted Sarah Ferguson (born 1959) as a result of her marriage in 1986 to the *Duke of York*. Nicknamed 'Fergie' by the media, the Duchess soon gained a reputation for her sense of fun and lively behaviour, which some thought inappropriate for a member of the *royal family*. In 1988 she gave birth to her first child, Princess Beatrice, and in 1990 to her second, Princess Eugenie. The marriage became strained, however, and in 1992 the royal couple separated.

duchy /'dʌtʃɪ/ (life and society) The lands or territory held by a duke or duchess. See also *Duchy of Cornwall*, *Duchy of*

Lancaster.

Duchy of Cornwall /ˌdʌtʃɪ əv ˈkɔːnwəl/, **the** (history) The *duchy* established in *Cornwall* in 1337 by King Edward III for his eldest son, Edward the *Black Prince*. Since this time, the duchy has always passed to the eldest son of the sovereign. See *Duke of Cornwall* and compare *Prince of Wales*.

Duchy of Lancaster /ˌdʌtʃɪ əv ˈlæŋkəstə(r)/, **the** (history) The royal estates in Lancashire that have provided an inheritance for the sovereign since 1399. Most of the funds are used for the annual payment from the *Privy Purse*. The inheritance is kept distinct from other royal possessions and is nominally administered by the *Chancellor of the Duchy of Lancaster*.

duffle-coat /ˈdʌfl kəʊt/ (clothing) A short or knee-length outdoor coat, made of strong or heavy wool cloth and usually with a hood. [named after the town Duffel, Belgium, where the cloth for such coats was first made]

Duke of Cornwall /ˌdjuːk əv ˈkɔːnwəl/, **the** (royal family) One of the titles of the eldest son of the sovereign as heir to the throne. See *Duchy of Cornwall* and compare *Prince of Wales*.

Duke of Edinburgh /ˌdjuːk əv ˈedɪnbrə/, **the** (royal family) The principal title held by Prince Philip, the husband of *Queen Elizabeth*, and the one by which he is usually known. Born in 1926, he served in the *Royal Navy* both before and for some years after his marriage in 1947 to the then Princess Elizabeth. He takes a great deal of interest in industry, in the achievements of young people (see *Duke of Edinburgh's Award Scheme*) and in saving rare wild animals from extinction.

Duke of Edinburgh's Award Scheme /ˌdjuːk əv ˌedɪnbrəz əˈwɔːd skiːm/, **the** (education) A scheme by which a range of awards (Bronze, Silver and Gold medals) are made to young people between the ages of 14 – 23 for enterprise, initiative and achievement in such activities as community service, expeditions and the development of personal interests and skills. The scheme was founded by the *Duke of Edinburgh* in 1956, and operates through schools, *local authorities* and youth organizations.

Duke of Windsor /ˌdjuːk əv ˈwɪnzə(r)/, **the** (royal family) The title given to King Edward VIII (1894-1972) after his *Abdication* in 1936.

Duke of York /ˌdjuːk əv ˈjɔːk/, **the** (royal family) The royal title granted Prince Andrew (born 1960), second son of *Queen Elizabeth*, upon his marriage in 1986 to Sarah Ferguson, who became the *Duchess of York*. The title of Duke of York has traditionally been given to the second son of a British *king* or *queen* since 1474, when Edward IV granted it to his son Richard, one of the *Princes in the Tower*. *Henry VIII* was also Duke of York before becoming King.

Dulwich (College) /ˈdʌlɪdʒ (ˌdʌlɪdʒ ˈkɒlɪdʒ)/ (education) A large *public school*[1] for boys in the district of this name in southeast *London*, founded in 1619. It has about 1,400 students.

Dundee cake /dʌnˈdiː keɪk/ (food and drink) A large, round, rich fruit cake containing nuts and spices and decorated with almonds. [first made in Dundee, *Scotland*]

Dunkirk /dʌnˈkɜːk/ (history) The name of the mass evacuation of British troops, and also some French and Belgians, from Dunkirk (Dunkerque), a port in occupied France, in May and June 1940.

Dunlop /ˈdʌnlɒp/ (food and drink) A soft, mild cheese resembling *Cheddar*, originally made at Dunlop, Ayrshire in *Scotland*.

Durham Miners' Gala /ˌdʌrəm ˌmaɪnəz ˈgeɪlə/, **the** (work) An annual parade of miners through the streets of Durham, held on the second Saturday in July, accompanied by brass bands and colourful displays and tableaux. The parade is traditionally led by the leader of the *Labour Party* and the president of the *NUM*. [Note the special pronunciation in this name of 'gala'; compare *gala*]

Dutch barn /ˌdʌtʃ ˈbɑːn/ (style) A tall shed for storing hay or straw on a farm. It has no walls, and is usually made of steel with a curved roof.

duty-free /ˌdjuːtɪ ˈfriː/ (government) A term for goods such as alcoholic drinks and tobacco that can be purchased at a lower price than usual since they carry no *Customs and Excise* duty. The goods are usually obtainable at a special 'duty-free shop' at an airport or on board a ship. The goods themselves are colloquially known as 'duty-frees'.

DVLC /ˌdiː viː el ˈsiː/, **the (Driver and Vehicle Licensing Centre, the)** (transport) A government centre in Swansea, *Wales,* which issues *vehicle licences* and *driving licences*. It is run by the *Ministry*[2] of Transport and holds records of all licensed vehicles and drivers.

EGG & SPOON RACE

each way bet /ˌiːtʃ weɪ ˈbet/ (sport and leisure) A bet placed on a horse both for it to win and to be placed, ie, to come first, second or third.

Ealing comedy /ˌiːlɪŋ ˈkɒmədɪ/ (arts) One of a number of comedy films, produced by the Ealing Studios, west *London*, in the period 1948–50. The films were typically 'English' in character and usually featured a group who rebelled against authority.

Earl Marshal /ˌɜːl ˈmaːʃl/**, the** (life and society) The title of the head of the *College of Arms*, who organizes royal processions and other important state ceremonies.

Earls Court /ˌɜːlz ˈkɔːt/ (London) A large exhibition hall in west central *London*, where several important annual events are held, including the *Royal Tournament*, the *Boat Show* and the *Ideal Home Exhibition*. [named after district here]

Early English /ˌɜːlɪ ˈɪŋglɪʃ/ (style) A *Gothic* (*style*) of architecture flourishing in *England* from the last decade of the 12th century to the end of the 13th century, and characterized by tall, slender, pointed windows with little tracery (open stone work), thick, heavy walls, and the use of columns of stone surrounded by a number of shafts of black marble. Many cathedrals are noted examples of the style, especially those of Salisbury, Wells, Ely and Worcester.

East Anglia /ˌiːst ˈæŋglɪə/ (geography) A historic *Anglo-Saxon* kingdom in the east of *England*, today represented by the counties of Norfolk and Suffolk and parts of Essex and Cambridgeshire. Although still mainly agricultural, East Anglia has been the fastest-growing region of England in both population and employment since the 1960s.

East End /ˌiːst ˈend/**, the** (London) A commercial and residential area of *London* to the east of the *City (of London)*. It was at one time famous for its docks (see *London Docklands*) and notorious for its slums. Today several businesses are based there, among them the newspaper offices at *Wapping*.

EastEnders /ˌiːst ˈendəz/ (media) A popular television 'soap opera' (serial story on the daily lives and relationships of a group of people) broadcast twice a week on *BBC 1* from 1985. The story centres on the lives of several families living in 'Albert Square', an imaginary location in the *East End* of *London*, and deals with topical moral and other issues. It currently has over 13 million viewers, and is the *BBC's* most widely watched programme.

Easter /ˈiːstə(r)/ (religion) For Christians, the most important Christian festival, with its central day a *Sunday* (Easter Day) falling between 22 March and 25 April. Traditionally it is associated with the eating of *Easter eggs*. The season is also closely associated with the coming of spring, and most *churches* are specially decorated with flowers for the services held on Easter Day. Presents, apart from chocolate eggs and *greeting cards*, are rarely exchanged. See also *Easter Monday*.

Easter egg /ˈiːstə eg/ (tradition) An egg eaten symbolically at *Easter* to mark the birth of new life and the coming of the spring. The egg may be that of a hen, with a painted or decorated shell, or, more popularly, one made of chocolate (usually large and hollow and often containing individual chocolates or other sweets).

Easter Monday /ˌiːstə ˈmʌndɪ/ (daily life) The day after *Easter* Day (also called Easter *Sunday*) and a *bank holiday*. It is a traditional date for the start of the summer tourist season.

EC /ˌiː ˈsiː/**, the (European Community, the)** (government) The economic community of 12 European countries which *Britain* joined in 1973. The EC also has certain monetary, social, and political objectives in common. See also *Common Agricultural Policy, Exchange Rate Mechanism, Maastricht Treaty, Single Market*.

Eccles cake /ˈeklz keɪk/ (food and drink) A small round pastry cake containing currants and other dried fruit. [originally made in Eccles, Lancashire (now Greater Manchester)]

Economist /ɪˈkɒnəmɪst/**, the** (media) A weekly political, economic and financial magazine that is influential in business circles. Its views tend to support those of the *Conservative Party*. It was founded in 1843 and has a current circulation of about 480,000 worldwide.

Edgbaston /ˈedʒbəstən/ (sport and leisure) A well-known

cricket ground in Birmingham, where *test match*es have been played since 1902.

Edgehill /ˌedʒ 'hɪl/ **(Battle of Edgehill, the)** (history) The first important battle of the *English Civil War*, in which the Parliamentarians fought the Royalists, but neither side won. It took place near the hill so named in Warwickshire in 1642.

Edinburgh /'edɪnbrə/ (geography) The capital city of *Scotland*, famous for its fine buildings (especially *Edinburgh Castle*) and for the annual *Edinburgh Festival*. It is a popular tourist centre.

Edinburgh Academy /ˌedɪnbrə ə'kædəmɪ/, **The** (education) A Scottish independent (fee-paying) *secondary school* similar to an English *public school[1]*. It was founded in 1824 and has about 580 students.

Edinburgh Castle /ˌedɪnbrə 'kɑːsl/ (history) A famous fortress built on a basalt hill (Castle Rock) in the centre of *Edinburgh*, overlooking *Princes Street* and the streets of the old town. The oldest parts of the building date back to about 1100. The *Edinburgh Military Tattoo* is held annually in the grounds of the castle.

Edinburgh Festival /ˌedɪnbrə 'festəvl/, **the** (arts) An annual festival of music and drama held in August and September at various centres in *Edinburgh*. The festival, first held in 1947, has gained international status and has won a reputation for its inclusion of experimental or 'avant-garde' events (the so-called 'Edinburgh *Fringe*').

Edinburgh Military Tattoo /ˌedɪnbrə ˌmɪlɪtrɪ tə'tuː/, **the** (defence) An annual floodlit military parade held for three weeks in August and September on the parade ground of *Edinburgh Castle*. The event is a popular tourist attraction.

Edinburgh rock /ˌedɪnbrə 'rɒk/ (food and drink) A form of sweet consisting of a short, coloured, brittle stick made from sugar, and tasting of peppermint. It was first manufactured in *Edinburgh* in 1822. ['rock' is a humorous reference to the rock on which *Edinburgh Castle* stands]

egg-and-spoon race /ˌeg ən 'spuːn reɪs/ (sport and leisure) A race in which contestants run a course balancing an egg in a spoon. If a runner's egg falls from the spoon as he is running, he is out of the race. The event is a popular one with children and so often features at *fêtes* and on school sports days.

18 /ˌeɪ'tiːn/ (arts) A category in which a cinema film is placed by the *British Board of Film Classification* to show that no person under the age of 18 will be admitted. The category implies that the film may contain scenes of violence or explicit sex (or both). Compare *12* (under letter T), *15* (under letter F), *PG* and *U*.

Eights /eɪts/ (sport and leisure) Traditional annual rowing races held between teams of eight people representing individual *colleges[1]* of *Oxford University* on the river *Thames* at *Oxford[1]*. The various races are held over a week (Eights Week) at the end of the *academic year* in June, and are accompanied by a number of events such as dances and concerts. Compare *Mays*.

eisteddfod /ˌaɪ 'stedfəd/ (arts) **1** (Eisteddfod) An annual Welsh national bardic (see *bard*) festival of music, literature and drama held alternately in North and South *Wales* during the first week of August. The modern Eisteddfod (Welsh, 'chairing' from the chairing, or seating in a ceremonial chair, of the winning bard) has developed from the gathering of bards held in the 12th century. It is conducted entirely in Welsh and is open to the public. Its formal title is the Royal National Eisteddfod. **2** (Eisteddfod) An international festival of folk-dancing and music held every July at Llangollen, North Wales. The festival has no bardic or literary content and is conducted entirely in English. Its formal title is the International Music Eisteddfod. **3** (Eisteddfod) An annual festival for young people similar to the national bardic festival, held alternately in North and South Wales. Its aim is to encourage the use of the Welsh language. **4** (eisteddfod) A festival of folk-dancing and music held in *England*, resembling the Eisteddfod[2] at Llangollen.

Eleanor Cross /ˌelɪnə 'krɒs/ (history) One of the 12 tall crosses set up by Edward I in memory of his wife, Queen Eleanor of Castile (1246-90). They mark the places where her body rested on its journey from Harby, Nottinghamshire, where she died, to *London*, where she is buried (in *Westminster Abbey*). Only three of the original crosses survive: at Geddington (Northamptonshire), Northampton and Waltham Cross (Hertfordshire). The Eleanor Cross at *Charing Cross[2]* is a modern copy of the original.

electoral register /ɪˌlektərəl 'redʒɪstə(r)/ (politics) An official register of people entitled to vote in a parliamentary election, such as a *by-election* or a *general election*. The register is compiled annually, and comes into force on 15 February following the qualifying date of 10 October. People who will be entitled to vote for the first time on reaching the age of 18 are included with a special note to this effect. The register

gives both the person's full name and his or her address, as
supplied by the voter to the *local authority* the previous year.

eleven /ɪ'levn/ (sport and leisure) A team, consisting of 11
players, for *football* (soccer), hockey or *cricket*.

eleven-plus /ɪˌlevn 'plʌs/, **the** (education) An examination for
entrance to *secondary school* taken by children aged about 11
at the end of their time at *primary school*. It was formerly
widespread, but became mostly obsolete when *comprehensive
schools* were introduced in the late 1960s and early 1970s. It is
now operated only by a few *LEA*s.

elevenses /ɪ'levənzɪz/ (food and drink) A drink or snack (or
both) taken in the middle of the morning at about eleven
o'clock.

Elgar, Edward /'elgɑː(r), 'edwəd/ (people) Edward Elgar
(1857–1934) is generally regarded as the first English
composer of international stature since Purcell in the 17th
century. His own works encouraged a revival of English
music, but his symphonies have been compared to those of
Brahms, and his fine 'Dream of Gerontius' (1900), regarded
by many as his masterpiece, has been likened to the style of
Wagner. Many of Elgar's compositions are popular for their
bold melodies, such as the moving slow theme of the much
loved 'Enigma Variations' (1899) and the patriotic *Land of
Hope and Glory* tune in one of his 'Pomp and Circumstance'
marches (1901–7, 1930). He is thought of as a very 'English'
composer.

Elgin Marbles /ˌelgɪn 'mɑːblz/, **the** (arts) A collection of 5th-
century BC Greek sculptures brought from the Parthenon,
Athens, to *England* in 1803 by Thomas Bruce, seventh Earl of
Elgin, and now displayed in the *British Museum*. Many people
in Greece and some people in *Britain* now believe that the
sculptures should be returned to Greece.

Elizabethan /ɪˌlɪzə'biːθn/ (style) A style of architecture found
in many large houses built in the second half of the 16th
century, in the reign of Queen Elizabeth I, and characterized
by large, square windows, neoclassical towers and turrets,
and elaborate plasterwork in ceilings, as well as the use of
oak-panelling.

Elle /el/ (media) A glossy monthly magazine for women,
aimed in particular at the fashionable and socially aware
reader. It has a current readership of about 250,000 and was
founded in 1985, keeping the name (French for 'she') of its
French original.

Embankment /ɪm'bæŋkmənt/, **the** (London) The short name of the Victoria Embankment, *London*, a street that runs along the north bank of the *Thames*.

Emmerdale /ˌemə'deɪl/ (media) A popular 'soap opera' (series about the lives and relationships of a group of people) broadcast twice a week on *ITV* since 1972. It is centred on the lives of families in a Yorkshire village and is currently watched by about 10 million viewers.

Employment Training /ɪmˌplɔɪmənt 'treɪnɪŋ/ **(ET)** (work) A government training scheme providing a course of 6 to 12 months for young people aged 18 to 25 who have been out of work for more than six months or for older people who have been unemployed for over two years. The course itself is designed to help the person find a suitable job while simultaneously providing experience in an appropriate type of work. Trainees can enter the programme either through a *Restart* interview or by applying at a *jobcentre*.

EN /ˌiː 'en/ **(Enrolled Nurse)** (medicine) A nurse who has successfully completed a two-year training course and who is qualified to give individual nursing care to a hospital patient. Until 1983, the equivalent qualification was that of the *SEN* (State Enrolled Nurse). Compare *RGN*.

Encyclopaedia Britannica /ɪnˌsaɪkləˌpiːdɪə brɪ'tænɪkə/, **the** (education) The oldest and largest English language encyclopaedia, first published in *Scotland* in 1768, but from the 11th edition of 1910–11 produced under American ownership and today having a distinct American tone.

England /'ɪŋglənd/ (geography) The largest and most southerly country in *Britain*, with *Wales* to the west and *Scotland* to the north. The name is properly applied only to this land, not to mainland Britain as a whole (and even less to the *United Kingdom*, which includes *Northern Ireland*). England does, however, contain the capital of the United Kingdom, *London*, where the British government is, together with the headquarters of many national and commercial bodies.

English breakfast /ˌɪŋglɪʃ 'brekfəst/ (food and drink) A traditional full, cooked breakfast with a hot dish (such as *bacon and eggs*) preceded by cereals or *porridge* and followed by *toast* and *marmalade*, the accompanying drink being either tea or coffee. Such breakfasts have in recent years given way to a lighter meal, the so-called *continental breakfast*.

English Chamber Orchestra/ ˌɪŋglɪʃ 'tʃeɪmbər ˌɔːkɪstrə/, **the**

(arts) A noted chamber orchestra founded in 1948 by Arnold Goldsbrough and originally (to 1960) called the Goldsbrough Orchestra.

English Civil War /ˌɪŋglɪʃ ˌsɪvl 'wɔː(r)/, **the** (history) The war between the Cavaliers (supporters of King Charles I) and the Roundheads (supporters of *Parliament*) in the mid-17th century. A series of battles led to the defeat of the king and his supporters and the establishment of the *Commonwealth*[2].

English Heritage /ˌɪŋglɪʃ 'herɪtɪdʒ/ (government) The short name of the Historic Buildings and Monuments Commission for *England*, a government body set up in 1984 to care for *ancient monuments* and historic buildings in England and to encourage the public to visit them. At present English Heritage has about 400 such sites under its care, including such famous structures as *Stonehenge*, Dover Castle and parts of *Hadrian's Wall*.

English National Ballet /ˌɪŋglɪʃ ˌnæʃnəl 'bæleɪ/, **the** (arts) A well-known ballet company performing both classical and modern works, founded in 1950 immediately before the *Festival of Britain*. The Company has no home theatre and most of its performances are held either at major London theatres such as the *Coliseum*, the *Royal Festival Hall* or *Sadler's Wells*, or else at theatres round *Britain* while on tour. Until 1989 the company was known as the London Festival Ballet.

English National Opera /ˌɪŋglɪʃ ˌnæʃnəl 'ɒprə/, **the (ENO, the)** (arts) A well-known opera company founded in 1931 and based in *London*. It was earlier at *Sadler's Wells* and was known as the Sadler's Wells Opera. In 1968 it moved to the *Coliseum (Theatre)* and in 1974 took its present name. It frequently goes on tour to different parts of *England*.

English Nature /ˌɪŋglɪʃ 'neɪtʃə(r)/ (government) The public body set up in 1991 to be responsible for nature conservation in *England*. It sets up *nature reserves*, identifies *sites of special scientific interest*, and advises the government generally on nature conservation.

English setter /ˌɪŋglɪʃ 'setə(r)/ (animal world) A breed of working dog with long, silky coat, usually black and white or brown and white in colour. Compare *Irish setter*. [so-called since, as a gundog, it 'sets' or crouches to mark the position of hunted game]

English-Speaking Union /ˌɪŋglɪʃ ˌspiːkɪŋ 'juːnɪən/, **the (ESU,**

the) (life and society) A body founded in 1918 to strengthen cultural ties between English-speaking countries. [full title, English-Speaking Union of the *Commonwealth[1]*]

English Stage Company /ˌɪŋglɪʃ 'steɪdʒ kʌmpənɪ/**, the** (arts) A theatre company founded in 1956 to present plays by young and experimental writers and to stage contemporary plays from abroad. It is based at the *Royal Court (Theatre)* in *London*.

Enterprise Neptune /ˌentəpraɪz 'neptjuːn/ (life and society) A campaign run by the *National Trust* to acquire attractive stretches of coastline that can be used for public recreation. The Trust now protects 530 miles (853 km) of coastline in *England*, *Wales* and *Northern Ireland*. The *National Trust for Scotland* runs a similar campaign in *Scotland*.

enterprise zone /'entəpraɪz ˌzəʊn/ (work) A special urban area, established by the government since 1981 to bring new life to a region of economic decay. There are now 27 such zones, located in *London*, the *Midlands*, South *Wales*, northern *England*, central *Scotland* and *Northern Ireland*. Firms established in the zones receive special financial support and tax exemptions.

Entryphone /'entrɪfəʊn/ (daily life) The trade name of a special telephone installed at the main entrance to a block of flats or offices, where a visitor can announce his arrival and say who he wishes to see. If he is recognized or expected, the person to whom he speaks unlocks the door by remote control so that the visitor can enter.

Epsom /'epsəm/ (sport and leisure) A famous race-course (in full, Epsom Downs) near Epsom, Surrey where, among other horse races, the *Derby* and the Oaks are run annually.

Equal Opportunities Commission /ˌiːkwəl ɒpə'tjuːnətɪz kəˌmɪʃn/**, the (EOC, the)** (life and society) A government body set up in 1975 (1976 in *Northern Ireland*) to eliminate sex discrimination and promote equal opportunities for men and women in their work and in the services available to them. The Commission has the power to enforce parts of the Sex Discrimination Acts of 1975 and 1986 and the Equal Pay Act of 1970 (as amended in 1984).

Equity /'ekwətɪ/ (work) The trade union to which most actors belong.

ERM / an acronym for *Exchange Rate Mechanism*.

Ermine Street /'ɜːmɪn striːt/ (history) **1** The name of one of the main *Roman roads* in *Britain*, from *London* to York. **2** The name of certain other minor Roman roads or old trackways, mainly in the south of *England*. [named after an old Saxon tribe]

Ernie /ˈɜːnɪ/ (finance) The colloquial name of a special computer unit used by the *Post Office* to select the prize-winning numbers of holders of *Premium Bonds*. [from the initials of *E*lectronic *r*andom *n*umber *i*ndicating *e*quipment, suggested by the man's name Ernie (familiar form of Ernest)]

Eros /ˈɪərɒs/ (London) The colloquial name of the monument to the philanthropist the Earl of Shaftesbury, that stands in the centre of *Piccadilly Circus* in *London*. The monument, formally known as the Shaftesbury Memorial, consists of a fountain topped by a winged archer and his bow, intended to represent the Angel of Christian Charity but popularly taken to be Cupid or Eros. The monument is a traditional meeting place for young people.

Establishment /ɪˈstæblɪʃmənt/**, the** (life and society) A collective term for the top influential sectors of British society, in particular, industrialists and business leaders, the aristocracy (the *peerage*) and the *Church of England*.

estate agent /ɪˈsteɪt ˌeɪdʒənt/ (commerce) A professional firm that deals in the buying and selling of houses, land and other fixed property (though not in *Scotland* where a *solicitor* does all the work that is involved).

estate car /ɪˈsteɪt ˌkɑː(r)/ (transport) A large car designed to carry both passengers and goods (or animals), with a special area behind the seats for the goods and usually with a rear door or doors. Such cars were originally used on farm estates.

Estuary English /ˌestʃʊərɪ ˈɪŋglɪʃ/ (language) A term sometimes used for a type of English that is a blend of *RP* and *cockney*[1]. It originated in *London* and the *Home Counties*, but is now spoken more widely in *England* by some people. [from the estuary of the *Thames* in the original region]

Eton (College) /ˈiːtn (ˌiːtn ˈkɒlɪdʒ)/ (education) One of the oldest and best-known *public schools*[1] for boys, at Windsor, Berkshire, on the river *Thames*. Its students (currently 1,270 in number) are largely from aristocratic and *upper class* families, and many former *prime ministers* of *Britain* were educated there. The school was founded in 1440.

Eton suit /ˌiːtn ˈsuːt/ (clothing) A school uniform, or a suit resembling it, worn at *Eton College* and some other schools. It consists of a black jacket (resembling a morning coat without tails), a black waistcoat and tie, black trousers with narrow stripes, a white shirt and a detachable stiff collar, known as an Eton collar.

E-type /ˈiː taɪp/ (transport) An expensive type of *Jaguar* sports car, especially popular in the 1960s.

Euro-MP /ˌjʊərəʊ em ˈpiː/ (government) A colloquial term for a Member of the European Parliament (MEP), that is, an *MP* who represents his or her party and *constituency* (larger than that for national or local elections) in the European Parliament, as the legislative body of the *EC*. *Britain* has 87 MEPs out of a total of 518. Elections to the European Parliament are held every five years. The first was in 1979, but so far British voters have shown little interest.

Euston /ˈjuːstən/ (transport) A main line railway station and terminus in *London*, from which trains leave for the *Midlands*, northern *England* and *Scotland*.

evening dress /ˈiːvnɪŋ dres/ (clothing) A formal type of dress for a social function held in the evening, such as a special *dinner* or theatre performance. For men, it consists of a black coat with tails, black trousers, white waistcoat, stiff-fronted white shirt, white wing collar and white bow tie. (A more popular alternative for the coat today, however, is the *dinner jacket*, which is usually worn with a black bow tie.) For women, evening dress is usually a floor-length dress often with a low-cut neck.

Evening Standard /ˌiːvnɪŋ ˈstændəd/**, the** (media) *London*'s only evening newspaper, covering both national and international news and local affairs. It is noted for its lively reporting, well-written regular features, and large advertising section. It was founded in 1827 and has a current circulation of about 528,000. It has a monthly colour supplement, 'ES - The Evening Standard Magazine'.

eventing /ɪˈventɪŋ/ (sport and leisure) An equestrian contest that usually includes dressage, cross-country riding and show jumping, and often lasts for three days. See *three-day event*.

Everton /ˈevətən/ (sport and leisure) A Liverpool *football club* with a stadium at *Goodison Park*. [named after the district of Liverpool where it is]

Exchange and Mart /ɪksˌtʃeɪndʒ ən ˈmɑːt/ (media) A weekly magazine consisting entirely of advertisements, enabling readers to buy, sell and exchange almost anything. It was first published in 1868 and has a readership of about 216,000.

Exchange Rate Mechanism /ɪksˈtʃeɪndʒ reɪt ˌmekənɪzəm/**, the (ERM, the)** (finance) The arrangement set up in 1979 to regulate the exchange rates of *EC* currencies by fixing the rates (and limiting their degree of fluctuation) against the ECU (European Currency Unit). *Britain* did not at first participate in the ERM, but the financial markets persuaded John *Major* (then *Chancellor of the Exchequer*) to join it in 1990. However, following upheaval on the same markets, John Major as *Prime Minister* took Britain out of the ERM in 1992, saying that the *pound (sterling)* would not rejoin it until there was a proper review of the way it worked. See also *Maastricht Treaty*, *Single Market*.

Exchange Telegraph Company /ɪksˌtʃeɪndʒ ˈtelɪɡrɑːf ˌkʌmpənɪ/, **the (Extel)** (media) An independent news agency supplying financial and sporting news and, together with the *Press Association*, transmitting racing information by telephone and video terminals.

ex-directory /ˌeks dɪˈrektərɪ/ (daily life) A telephone number that is not listed in the official telephone directory, usually because the person concerned is famous or has private reasons for not wanting people to be able to ring up.

Exmoor pony /ˌeksmɔː ˈpəʊnɪ/ (animal world) A breed of wild pony found on Exmoor, the high, bleak moorland of Somerset and Devon. When tamed, it is used as a riding pony for children.

Express /ɪkˈspres/, **the** (media) The short name of the *Daily Express* newspaper.

Extel /ˈekstel/ (media) The short name of the *Exchange Telegraph Company* Ltd.

F W Woolworth /ˌef ˌdʌblju: ˈwʊlwəθ/ see *Woolworth's* (commerce)

FA /ˌef ˈeɪ/, **the (Football Association, the)** (sport and leisure) The official body that controls professional and amateur football in *Britain*. In *England* 340 football *clubs* are affiliated directly to the English FA and more than 42,000 through regional or district associations. From 1992 22 professional football clubs have been run by the English FA *Premier League*, while the remaining 70 continue with the *Football League*. The FA was founded in 1863.

FA Cup /ˌef eɪ ˈkʌp/, **the** (sport and leisure) One of the main annual competitions of the *football* season, organized on a knock-out basis, with the final match (*Cup Final*) played at *Wembley*. [in full, Football Association Challenge Cup]

Fabian Society /ˈfeɪbɪən səˌsaɪətɪ/, **the** (politics) A political society founded in 1884 and having as its aim the gradual introduction of socialism by democratic means. It was indirectly responsible for the appearance of the *Labour Party*, and has had a number of famous intellectuals and writers among its members, as well as several Labour politicians. Its current membership is about 3,500. [named after the Roman general Fabius Maximus, surnamed Cunctator ('delayer'), famous for his delaying tactics when fighting Hannibal]

Fair Isle /ˈfeər aɪl/ (clothing) A distinctive style of knitting using different colours and designs, particularly for garments such as sweaters and gloves. It was originally developed on Fair Isle, Shetland (see the *Shetlands*).

family allowance /ˌfæməlɪ əˈlaʊəns/ (finance) An alternative name for *child benefit*.

family credit /ˌfæməlɪ ˈkredɪt/ (finance) A government

Fair Isle

payment additional to *child benefit* made to families with low incomes and at least one child. The amount paid depends on the income and on the number and ages of the children.

fancy dress /ˌfænsɪ ˈdres/ (clothing) A costume representing a familiar or historical character, such as a ballerina or *Henry VIII*. Fancy dress may be worn by adults or children at a social gathering of some kind, such as a dance or party.

Farnborough Air Show /ˌfɑːnbrə ˈeə ʃəʊ/, **the** (transport) An important international air show held at the *Royal Aircraft Establishment*, Farnborough, Hampshire, once every two years.

farthing /ˈfɑːðɪŋ/ (tradition) For many years the smallest British coin, worth one quarter of a pre-decimal *penny*. It was taken out of circulation in 1961. [from Old English 'fēorthing', 'fourth (part)']

Fastnet (Race) /ˈfɑːstnet (ˌfɑːstnet ˈreɪs)/, **the** (sport and leisure) An international yachting race held every two years in August, with the course running from Ryde, *Isle of Wight*, to (and round) the Fastnet Rock, off south west *Ireland*, and back to Plymouth, Devon. The total length of the course is 1,085 km. See also *Admiral's Cup*.

Father Christmas /ˌfɑːðə ˈkrɪsməs/ (tradition) An alternative name for *Santa Claus*.

father of the chapel /ˌfɑːðər əv ðə ˈtʃæpl/ (work) The title of the president of a *chapel*[5].

Father of the House /ˌfɑːðər əv ðə ˈhaʊs/ (government) The traditional title of the *MP* (in the *House of Commons*) or *peer* (in the *House of Lords*) who has served the longest as a member.

Father's Day /ˈfɑːðəz ˌdeɪ/ (tradition) The third *Sunday* in June, when presents are traditionally given by children to their father. [based on *Mother's Day*; the tradition was imported to *Britain* in the 20th century from America]

fayre /feə(r)/ (daily life) An alternative name for a *fête*, especially a large or seasonal one, such as a 'spring fayre'. [a fancy (but genuine former) spelling of 'fair']

fellow /ˈfeləʊ/ (1, 2 education 3 life and society) 1 A senior member (often a professor) of a *college*[1]. 2 A member of a college[1] or university engaged in scientific research and usually combining his work with lecturing. 3 An active or senior member of a scientific or learned society, usually by election or nomination (eg, a Fellow of the *Royal Society*). Such a member has the right to put the appropriate letters after his name, for example, John Smith FRGS (Fellow of the Royal Geographical Society).

Fens /fenz/**, the** (geography) A name used for the low, marshy districts of eastern *England*, especially in Cambridgeshire, Lincolnshire and Norfolk. The districts are noted for their many drains and sluices, built to reclaim the land and to guard against flooding. The name (also Fen District) particularly applies to the rich agricultural land bordering the *Wash*.

Ferguson, Sarah /ˈfɜːgəsn, ˈseərə/ (royal family) see *Duchess of York*

Festival Gardens /ˌfestəvl ˈgɑːdnz/**, the** (London) Pleasure gardens added to Battersea Park in southwest *London* at the time of the *Festival of Britain*, and based on the Tivoli Gardens in Copenhagen, Denmark. Amenities include a concert pavilion, restaurants, bars, tea-rooms and an amusement section with a children's zoo.

Festival of Britain /ˌfestəvl əv 'brɪtn/, **the** (history) A large-scale exhibition opened on the site of the *South Bank, London,* in 1951, to mark the centenary of the *Great Exhibition* of 1851 and to demonstrate British economic and technical progress over the intervening hundred years. A number of buildings put up for the Festival remain in permanent use here, among them the *Royal Festival Hall.* Similar festivals were held throughout *Britain* at the same time.

fête /feɪt/ (daily life) An open-air sale of goods, many of them home-made, and usually accompanied by sports contests, children's entertainments and games and a *raffle.* Fêtes are usually held in summer months, especially at *weekends* and on *bank holidays,* and are traditionally designed to raise money for a particular cause, such as a local *church* fund, a charity or a school building fund.

Field /fiːld/, **The** (media) A monthly illustrated magazine devoted to the countryside and rural pursuits, such as natural history, *field sports,* gardening and farming. It was first published in 1853 and has a current circulation of about 36,000.

field sports /'fiːld spɔːts/ (sport and leisure) The three sports which, together with horse-racing, are traditionally associated with the English *gentry*—hunting (after foxes or hares), shooting (wild or reared animals or birds) and fishing. See also *blood sports.* [so called as taking place 'in the field' rather than on a special course]

15 /ˌfɪf'tiːn/ (arts) A category in which a cinema film is placed by the *British Board of Film Classification* to show that no young person under the age of 15 may see it. Compare *12* (under letter T), *18* (under letter E), *PG* and *U.*

fifth form/year /'fɪfθ fɔːm/jɪə(r)/ (education) A class in a *secondary school* in the year in which the students will usually take the *GCSE* examination. Such students will be in their fifth year at the school, having entered at age 11.

Fifth of November /ˌfɪfθ əv nəʊ'vembə(r)/, **the** (history) An alternative name for *Guy Fawkes' Day* (or *Guy Fawkes' Night*), when the failure of the *Gunpowder Plot* (of 5 November 1605) is traditionally celebrated with a bonfire and fireworks.

50 pence (piece) /ˌfɪftɪ 'pens (ˌfɪftɪ ˌpens 'piːs)/ (finance) A seven-sided coin made from a mixture of copper and nickel that looks like silver. It is worth half the value of a *pound (sterling).* It replaced the 10/- (ten *shilling*) note in 1969. See p 472.

finance house /fɪ'næns haʊs/ (finance) A company specializing in lending money, especially to finance hire-purchase agreements.

Financial Times /faɪˌnænʃl 'taɪmz/, **the (FT, the)** (media) A daily national *quality paper* providing the latest financial information, including company news and the movement of stocks and shares. It is read mainly by business people, especially in the *City (of London)*. It was founded in 1888 and since 1893 has been printed on distinctive pink paper. Its current circulation is about 291,000. Overseas editions are printed in Germany, France, the USA and Japan.

financial year /faɪˌnænʃl 'jɪə(r)/, **the** (finance) The annual period ending on 5 April, serving as the *income tax* year, and the period over which the government plans its financial policies, and makes its estimates.

Fingal's Cave /ˌfɪŋglz 'keɪv/ (geography) A large cave on the island of Staffa, in the *Hebrides*, *Scotland*, with six-sided pillars of rock. The same rock formation can be seen at the *Giant's Causeway* in *Northern Ireland*. Fingal's Cave is a popular tourist attraction, although visitors are not now allowed inside the cave because of the danger of falling rock. The cave has been commemorated in the works of a number of poets and musicians, including Keats, Wordsworth, Tennyson and Mendelssohn. ['Fingal' is a shortened form of the name of one of two giants in a folk tale. The tale describes a fight in which the two threw distinctively-shaped rocks at each other]

finishing school /'fɪnɪʃɪŋ skuːl/ (education) A privately run *college*[2], usually residential, where some girls complete their education, with the emphasis more on social graces than academic achievement.

first class /ˌfɜːst 'klɑːs/ (**1** transport **2** commerce **3** education) **1** The more comfortable and more expensive class of seats in a railway train. **2** The higher of two postal rates, usually providing delivery the next day within *Britain*. **3** The highest class of *honours degree*, denoting an outstanding academic performance.

first degree /ˌfɜːst dɪ'griː/ (education) The degree (usually a *BA* or *BSc*) obtained by most students when graduating from university. At *Cambridge*[2], however, the BSc does not exist, while at *Oxford*[2] it is a *higher degree*. In *Scotland* the first degree in arts at three of the four older universities is an *MA*.

first floor /ˌfɜːst 'flɔː(r)/, **the** (daily life) According to the

British system of numbering, the floor above the *ground floor* (which is the bottom or lowest floor).

first past the post /ˌfɜːst pɑːst ðə ˈpəʊst/ (politics) A colloquial phrase (from horse-racing) that describes how the British electoral system works. The candidate given the largest number of individual votes, or the party gaining the largest number of seats subsequently, wins an election. See *voting system*.

first reading /ˌfɜːst ˈriːdɪŋ/ (government) The first stage through which a *bill* must pass in its progress through the *House of Commons* (or *House of Lords*). This is thus the official introduction of the bill. Compare *second reading, third reading*.

first school /ˈfɜːst skuːl/ (education) A type of *primary school* from which the children move to a *middle school* at the age of eight or nine.

fish and chips

fish and chips /ˌfɪʃ ən ˈtʃɪps/ (food and drink) A popular and relatively inexpensive British dish, consisting of plaice or cod fried in batter and served hot with fried, chipped potatoes (known in many restaurants as 'French fries'). The dish is sold in special shops ('fish and chip shops') either to be taken away, wrapped in paper, or if tables are provided, to be eaten in the shop. Some young people buy the chips alone to be eaten as a cheap, filling snack. See also *chippy*.

fish fingers /ˌfɪʃ ˈfɪŋɡəz/ (food and drink) A type of fish dish

popular with children. It consists of short lengths ('fingers')
of fish coated in breadcrumbs or batter.

Fitzwilliam Museum /ˌfɪtsˌwɪljəm mjuːˈzɪəm/, **the** (arts) A
famous museum in *Cambridge¹* founded in 1816. Its
collections of antiquities, paintings and drawings, coins,
ceramics, glass and armour make it one of the most important
in the country. [named after its founder, Viscount
Fitzwilliam]

5 pence (piece) /ˌfaɪv ˈpens (ˌfaɪv pens ˈpiːs)/ (finance) A very
small coin made from a mixture of copper and nickel that
looks like silver. It is worth one-twentieth of the value of a
pound (sterling) and replaces the old *shilling*, which was the
same colour and had the same value. See p 472.

fiver /ˈfaɪvə(r)/ (daily life) A colloquial term for a £5 note.
Compare *tenner*.

fives /faɪvz/ (sport and leisure) A ball game played on a
special court enclosed on three sides, in which two
(occasionally four) players throw the ball from a gloved hand
so that it bounces off the wall, the aim being to force one's
opponent to make a mistake. The game is particularly
associated with *Eton College*, and is played at other *public
schools¹*. [perhaps originally played by two teams of five
players each, or so called with reference to the five fingers of
the hand]

flag day /ˈflæg deɪ/ (charities) A day (usually a Saturday) on
which small paper stickers are sold on the street in aid of a
particular charity, the buyer placing a sum of money in a tin
and wearing the sticker on his or her clothes. [formerly small
paper flags, which were pinned to the clothes, were used]

Flat /flæt/, **the** (sport and leisure) The horse-racing season. [in
full, 'flat racing', as distinct from a steeplechase, which has
jumps]

Fleet Air Arm /ˌfliːt ˈeər ɑːm/, **the** (defence) The branch of the
Royal Navy concerned with aviation, both shore-based and
from aircraft carriers.

Fleet Street /ˈfliːt striːt/ (1 London 2 media) 1 A street in
central *London* where until recently many national
newspapers had their editorial offices. Many newspapers
now have their offices either at *Wapping* or in the London
Docklands. 2 The press and the world of journalism
generally. [from the river Fleet, now running underground
there into the *Thames*]

fly-fishing /ˈflaɪ ˌfɪʃɪŋ/ (sport and leisure) A special type of fishing using man-made flies instead of hooks with live bait (eg worms). There are both 'dry' and 'wet' flies imitating three main types of real fly: midges, mayflies and sedge flies. The man-made flies are successful because real flies form the main diet of trout and salmon as well as other fish. Experienced fly-fishermen have a special knowledge of the different species of fly normally found in a local area.

flying pickets /ˌflaɪɪŋ 'pɪkɪts/ (work) Mobile *pickets* available to travel to support local pickets during a strike. The first such pickets operated in the miners' strike of 1973.

Flying Squad /'flaɪɪŋ skwɒd/**, the** (law) A *department* of the *CID*, comprising a group of expert detectives working from *New Scotland Yard* and concentrating on major criminals. [originally a force of police travelling in a motor van to the scene of a smash-and-grab raid]

folk museum /'fəʊk mjuːˌzɪəm/ (tradition) A museum that exhibits unique or historic items of everyday domestic use, such as period costumes, cooking utensils, tools, etc. There are such museums in a number of towns and *cities*, for example, York (Castle Museum), *Cardiff* (Welsh Folk Museum) and *Cambridge[1]* (Cambridge Folk Museum).

folly /'fɒlɪ/ (style) A group of artificially built ruins, or an extravagantly decorated but useless building, designed to improve the landscape in a particular rural area. Such buildings were first put up in the 18th century to improve the view on the estate of a *country house*. [so called with reference to the folly or foolishness of building a grand structure without thought for the cost]

Fontwell Park /ˌfɒntwel 'pɑːk/ (sport and leisure) A race-course near Bognor Regis, West Sussex.

foolscap /'fuːlskæp/ (daily life) A size of paper (17 x 13$\frac{1}{2}$ *inches*) now replaced by the international A4 size (297 x 210 mm). [originally bearing the watermark of a fool's cap and bells]

foot /fʊt/ (daily life) A measure of length still in common use, in particular for the height of a person, comprising 12 *inches* and equivalent to 30.48 cm. [regarded as the length of a man's foot]

football /'fʊtbɔːl/ see *association football* (sport and leisure) and *rugby football* (sport and leisure)

Football League /ˌfʊtbɔːl 'liːg/**, the** (sport and leisure) The organization which controls the league competition of the 70 professional *football clubs* below the *Premier League* in *England* and *Wales*, divided into three divisions. In *Scotland*, the

Scottish Football League controls the league competition of all 38 Scottish professional clubs, also divided into three divisions.

Footsie /ˈfʊtsɪ/ (finance) A colloquial name for the stocks and shares index introduced in 1984 by the *Stock Exchange*. The index, which operates jointly with the older *FT Index*, records the movements of shares of 100 selected companies, as its full name suggests ('Financial Times-Stock Exchange 100 Index'). [humorous pronunciation of abbreviated title, FT-SE Index]

Foreign and Commonwealth Office /ˌfɒrən ən ˈkɒmənwelθ ˌɒfɪs/, **the (FCO, the)** (government) The government *department* that conducts *Britain*'s relations with countries overseas and which advises the government on all aspects of foreign policy. It is largely staffed by members of the *Diplomatic Service*, and was created in its present form in 1968 from the former Foreign Office and the Commonwealth Office (the latter established in 1964).

Foreign Secretary /ˌfɒrən ˈsekrətrɪ/, **the** (government) The short title of the *Secretary of State* for Foreign and Commonwealth Affairs, otherwise the government *minister²*, and member of the *Cabinet*, who is the head of the *Foreign and Commonwealth Office*.

forest park /ˌfɒrɪst ˈpɑːk/ (geography) An area of forest land administered by the *Forestry Commission*, and having camping and other facilities for the public on the lines of a *national park*. There are 11 such parks at present in *Britain* and nine in *Northern Ireland*.

Forestry Commission /ˈfɒrɪstrɪ kəˌmɪʃn/, **the** (government) The government body which administers national (state-owned) forests in *Britain*. Over half the total forest area in Britain is privately owned, and the Commission awards grants to such owners to encourage effective management of their forest land.

Forth /fɔːθ/, **the** (geography) A Scottish river almost 105 miles (170 km) in length that flows into the North Sea through its well-known large estuary, the Firth of Forth (itself almost 50 miles long), where it is crossed by the two *Forth Bridges*.

Forth Bridge /ˌfɔːθ ˈbrɪdʒ/, **the** (transport) **1** The impressive rail bridge built in 1890 over the estuary of the river *Forth* in *Scotland*, west of *Edinburgh*. The bridge constantly needs painting. Hence the expression 'like the Forth Bridge', used of an apparently unending task. **2** The road bridge, one of the longest suspension bridges in the world, built in 1964 across the same estuary next to the rail bridge. Because of the growing volume of traffic over this bridge, it is planned to build a new and wider bridge nearby.

Fortnum and Mason /ˌfɔːtnəm ən ˈmeɪsn/ (commerce) One of *London*'s leading high-class stores, in *Piccadilly*, famous for its exotic foods. [founded in 1707 by William Fortnum, a footman in the court of Queen Anne, and Hugh Mason, a local shop owner]

Forty-Five /ˌfɔːtɪ ˈfaɪv/, **the** (history) The rising of the Jacobites (supporters of the exiled King James II) led by the Scottish prince Charles Edward Stuart, the *Young Pretender*, in 1745, in an attempt to regain the throne. See also *Culloden*.

Fosse Way /ˌfɒs ˈweɪ/, **the** (history) One of the main *Roman roads* in *Britain*, running from Lincoln to Exeter, Devon. [said to have been named from the 'foss' or ditch that ran next to it]

four-letter word /ˌfɔː letə ˈwɜːd/ (language) A term for a vulgar short word referring to a sexual or excretory organ or function. Many such words are of Germanic origin and today are spelt with four letters. Such words are often called *Anglo-Saxon²*.

fourth estate /ˌfɔːθ ɪˈsteɪt/, **the** (media) A term for the press, seen as influencing a country's politics (like the *House of Lords*, the 'first estate', the *House of Commons*, the 'second estate' and the clergy of the *Church of England*, the 'third estate').

Fowler /ˈfaʊlə(r)/ (language) The short title of 'A Dictionary of Modern English Usage', first published by Henry Fowler (1858–1933) in 1926, and regarded as a standard reference work on the English language.

fox-terrier /ˌfɒks ˈterɪə(r)/ (animal world) A breed of dog originally trained to unearth foxes. There are two varieties in *Britain*: smooth-haired and wire-haired, with colouring usually white with black or light brown markings.

Foyle's /ˈfɔɪlz/ (commerce) *London*'s largest bookshop, in Charing Cross Road, selling both new and second-hand books. The shop has more books on sale than any other bookshop in the world. [named after its original owner, William Alfred Foyle]

Fraud Squad /ˈfrɔːd skwɒd/, **the** (law) A special police branch run jointly by the *Metropolitan Police* and the *City (of London) Police* to investigate company frauds.

Free Churches /ˌfriː ˈtʃɜːtʃɪz/, **the** (religion) A collective name for all non-*Anglican* and non-*Roman Catholic* Christian *churches* in *Britain*, including the *Methodist Church*, the

Baptists, the *United Reformed Church* and the *Church of Scotland*. ['free' as they are not 'established', like the *Church of England*]

free house /ˈfriː haʊs/ (daily life) A *pub* that is free to receive its supplies from a number of brewers and is not tied to a single brewer. Compare *tied house*.

free paper /ˌfriː ˈpeɪpə(r)/ (media) A free weekly local paper that contains mainly advertisements (which pay for the cost of publishing it) but that also has some local news and features. There are currently about 750 such papers in *Britain*.

freedom of the city /ˈfriːdəm (ˌfriːdəm əv ðə ˈsɪti)/, **the** (life and society) An honorary (nominal) privilege awarded to a person who is a famous resident of a *city* (or who was born there), or who has performed particular services for a city. Such a person is usually called a 'freeman'.

Freefone /ˈfriːfəʊn/ (commerce) A special telephone service operated by *BT* enabling a person to make a telephone call free when responding to an advertisement. A Freefone telephone number always begins with the *dialling code* 0800.

Freepost /ˈfriːpəʊst/ (commerce) A special mail delivery service operated by the *Post Office* by which a business customer or member of the public can send a letter to a firm or advertiser free of postal charge, with the addressee paying the postage. Such letters travel by *second class* mail only.

freightliner /ˈfreɪtlaɪnə(r)/ (transport) A type of express goods train with specially designed containers. [from 'freight train' and 'liner' as in 'air liner']

French cricket /ˌfrentʃ ˈkrɪkɪt/ (sport and leisure) A simplified version of *cricket*, popular among some children. The game is played with a single bat and ball, with the batsman using his own legs as a wicket. The game is often played with a tennis racket at the seaside.

fresher /ˈfreʃə(r)/ (education) The name given to first-year students in some universities. [short for 'freshman']

friendly society /ˈfrendli səˌsaɪəti/ (finance) A kind of insurance association, with members' subscriptions providing financial aid in time of need, such as sickness, old age or widowhood.

Friends of the Earth /ˌfrendz əv ði ˈɜːθ/, **the** (politics) A voluntary organization (also a *limited company*) established in 1971 with the aim of conserving the natural resources of the world and discouraging mistreatment of the natural environment. It has 18,000 members worldwide.

Fringe /frɪndʒ/, **the** (arts) The short name of the 'Edinburgh Fringe' at the *Edinburgh Festival*. The term can also apply to any similar festival that has a 'fringe' or unorthodox section.

fringe benefits /'frɪndʒ ˌbenɪfɪts/ (work) Additional benefits or privileges provided with a person's regular salary, such as the use of a car, meals free or at reduced cost or free insurance.

fringe party /'frɪndʒ ˌpɑːtɪ/ (politics) A small political party with extreme or eccentric policies. Two extreme parties are the *National Front* and the *British National Party*. Many fringe parties are eccentric, however. One of the best known is the Monster Raving Loony Party, founded by David 'Screamin' Lord' Sutch (born 1942), a former rock 'n' roll singer. Fringe parties usually enter candidates for a *by-election* or *general election*, the less serious parties doing so simply to add a light note to the formal proceedings. Examples of other fringe parties are the Common Sense Party, the Fancy Dress Party (see *fancy dress*), the Revolutionary Communist Party, the Forward to Mars Party and the Gremloids. There are currently about 70 fringe parties in *Britain*.

front /ˌfrʌnt/, **the** (sport and leisure) The esplanade or promenade (broad public walk) running along the shore in a seaside town.

front bench

front bench /ˌfrʌnt ˈbentʃ/, **the** (government) One of the two front benches or rows of seats in the *House of Commons*, to the right and left of the *Speaker*. They are occupied respectively by *ministers*[2] of the current government and equivalent members of the *Opposition* (in particular, of the *Shadow Cabinet*).

frontbencher /ˌfrʌnt ˈbentʃə(r)/ (government) An *MP* entitled to sit on one of the *front benches* in the *House of Commons*. Compare *backbencher* and see also *crossbencher*.

front room /ˌfrʌnt ˈruːm/ (daily life) The main *ground floor* room of a smallish or modest house, often, of a *terraced house*, used either regularly as a sitting-room for relaxation, or only occasionally for receiving guests and visitors. The room is at the front of the house, usually looking onto a road or street.

FT /ˌef ˈtiː/, **the** (media) A colloquial name for the *Financial Times*. See also *FT Index* and *Footsie*.

FT Index /ˌef ti: ˈɪndeks/, **the** (finance) The daily record of the movement of shares on the *Stock Exchange*, as provided by the *Financial Times*. See also *Footsie*. [in full, Financial Times Industrial Ordinary Share Index]

fudge /fʌdʒ/ (food and drink) A type of soft, creamy sweet, light brown in colour, that is made from sugar, milk, butter and flavouring, and is usually formed into small square lumps.

Fulham /ˈfʊləm/ (sport and leisure) A popular *London football club*, with a stadium in the district of the same name in southwest London.

fun run /ˈfʌn rʌn/ (sport and leisure) A race in which many people take part, often to raise money for charity. The best known is the annual *London* Fun Run held every autumn and organized by the *Sunday Times*. See also *London Marathon*, *sponsored walk*.

Furry Dance /ˈfʌrɪ dɑːns/, **the** (tradition) A traditional massed folk dance held in the streets of Helston, *Cornwall*, on 8 May annually. [origin of name uncertain: perhaps connected with 'fair' or with 'floral']

further education /ˌfɜːðər edʒʊˈkeɪʃn/ (education) A term used to apply to any education after *secondary school*, but not including university work (which is *higher education*). See *CFE*.

GUY FAWKES' NIGHT

G and S /ˌdʒiː ən ˈes/ (arts) A colloquial abbreviation for the *Gilbert and Sullivan operas*.

Gaelic /ˈɡeɪlɪk/ (language) The Celtic language spoken or understood by about 80,000 people in the *Highlands* and western coastal regions of *Scotland* and, in its Irish form, by about 500,000 people in *Ireland*.

Gaelic coffee /ˌɡeɪlɪk ˈkɒfɪ/ (food and drink) A drink, usually served in a glass, consisting of coffee to which cream, sugar and *whisky* have been added. Compare *Irish coffee*.

Gaiety Girls /ˈɡeɪətɪ ɡɜːlz/, **the** (history) The title of chorus girls at the Gaiety Theatre, *London*, popular in the 1890s for their beauty. Many of them married members of the *peerage*.

gala /ˈɡɑːlə/ (sport and leisure) **1** A sporting event in which there are a variety of different contests, such as a swimming gala. **2** An annual fair, march or parade, eg, the *Durham Miners' Gala*.

gallon /ˈɡælən/ (daily life) A measure of capacity for liquids and dry goods (such as corn) equal to 4 quarts or 8 *pints* (=4.546 litres in *UK*, 3.715 litres in USA).

Galloway cattle /ˌɡæləweɪ ˈkætl/ (animal world) A breed of large, hornless cattle with thick black or dark brown coats. [originally bred in the district of Galloway, southwest *Scotland*]

gamekeeper /ˈɡeɪmkiːpə(r)/ (sport and leisure) A person employed to look after wild life and game (ie, animals and birds reared for sport, food or profit) on an estate, normally that owned by a member of the *gentry* in the country.

gamesmanship /ˈɡeɪmzmənʃɪp/ (sport and leisure) A term for the art of winning in a game or sport, or of scoring over one's opponent, by the use of various tricks without, however, breaking the rules. One such way might be to speak to one's opponent as he is about to hit the ball. The term was devised by the writer Stephen Potter (1900–69) for his book (1949) on the subject, whose full title was 'The Theory and Practice of Gamesmanship or the Art of Winning Games Without Actually Cheating'. See *one-upmanship*.

Gang Show /ˈgæŋ ʃəʊ/, **the** (sport and leisure) A variety show staged until 1974 in *London* by the *Scout Association* and now by local *Scout* and *Guide* groups.

ganger /ˈgæŋə(r)/ (work) A colloquial term for the foreman of a gang of manual workers.

gangway /ˈgæŋweɪ/, **the** (government) The cross passage between the seats, about half-way down the chamber of the *House of Commons*. A member sitting 'below the gangway', that is, in that part of the chamber that is further from the *Speaker*, is taken to hold a greater independence of political views than one who sits in the half nearer to him.

garden centre /ˈgɑːdn ˌsentə(r)/ (commerce) A trading centre where equipment, plants, shrubs, bulbs and seeds for the garden are sold.

garden city /ˌgɑːdn ˈsɪtɪ/ (geography) A town laid out with carefully planned parks, gardens and open spaces, and surrounded by a *green belt*, near to an industrial *city*. The first such town was built (1903) at Letchworth, Hertfordshire, north of *London*. Many *new towns* are garden cities.

Garden of England /ˌgɑːdn əv ˈɪŋglənd/, **the** (geography) A nickname for the *county* of Kent, famous for its picturesque orchards and fields of hops. The name is also used, but less often, for the former county of Worcestershire, famous for its fertile farmland and orchards.

garden party /ˈgɑːdn ˌpɑːtɪ/ (life and society) An afternoon *tea* party held on the lawn of a large private house or residence of some kind. Famous garden parties are those held annually (usually in June) by the sovereign at *Buckingham Palace*, to which political, industrial and diplomatic leaders are invited.

garden suburb /ˌgɑːdn ˈsʌbɜːb/ (geography) The suburb of a town or *city* laid out on the same lines as a *garden city*, for example, *Hampstead* Garden Suburb.

garden village /ˌgɑːdn ˈvɪlɪdʒ/ (geography) A new village laid out on the lines of a *garden city*.

Gardeners' World /ˌgɑːdnəz ˈwɜːld/ (media) A popular gardening magazine published by the *BBC* to tie in with its television programme of the same name. It was founded in 1992 and has a current circulation of about 344,000, higher than any other gardening magazine.

Garnett, Alf /'gɑːnɪt, ælf/ (media) The name of a leading character in two *BBC* television comedy series: 'Till Death Us Do Part', broadcast from 1964 to 1974, and 'In Sickness and in Health', shown from 1985 to 1986. Alf Garnett is the *working class* head of a family who openly expresses his views and prejudices about such controversial subjects as race, religion and royalty. In what he says, however, Alf Garnett actually voices the opinions that are held by many people, so that many viewers, while laughing at him and being shocked by him, privately agree with him. The programme titles are familiar quotations from the marriage service in the *Book of Common Prayer*.

Garter /'gɑːtə(r)/, **the** (life and society) A colloquial term for the *Order of the Garter*.

Garter ceremony /'gɑːtə ˌserɪmənɪ/, **the** (life and society) The ceremonial installation of new Knights of the Garter at *St George's Chapel, Windsor*. The route to the Chapel is lined on this occasion by dismounted troopers of the *Household*

gate-leg(ged) table

Cavalry. See also *Order of the Garter*.

gate-leg(ged) table /ˌɡeɪt leɡ(d) ˈteɪbl/ (style) A table with one or two hinged flaps that are supported when in use by a hinged leg pulled out from the centre. [the leg opens and closes like a gate]

Gatwick /ˈɡætwɪk/ (transport) An international airport, the second largest in *Britain* (after *Heathrow*), in west Sussex, 24 miles (39 kilometres) south of *London*.

gaudy /ˈɡɔːdɪ/ (life and society) An annual celebratory dinner held in the *colleges[1]* of *Oxford University* and *Cambridge University* to which former students of particular years are invited. [from Latin 'gaudium', 'joy']

Gay Gordons /ˌɡeɪ ˈɡɔːdnz/, **the** (sport and leisure) A Scottish dance popular in ballroom dancing. The name comes from the nickname of the *Gordon Highlanders*.

gazumping /ɡəˈzʌmpɪŋ/ (commerce) The raising of the price of a house by the seller after a verbal agreement has been made but before the sale has been legally completed. [perhaps from Yiddish 'gezumph', 'to swindle']

GC /ˌdʒiː ˈsiː/, **the (George Cross, the)** (life and society) An award for heroism made primarily to civilians and ranking next after the *VC*. The award, instituted in 1940 by King George VI, is in the form of a silver cross on which a representation of St George and the Dragon is surrounded by the words 'For Gallantry'.

GCHQ /ˌdʒiː siː eɪtʃ ˈkjuː/ **(Government Communications Headquarters, the)** (defence) The government establishment at *Cheltenham*, Gloucestershire, that is the centre for electronic surveillance operations and that monitors broadcasts of all kinds from all over the world. The centre gained notoriety in 1982 when one of its members was jailed for 35 years for spying.

GCSE /ˌdʒiː siː es ˈiː/, **the (General Certificate of Secondary Education, the)** (education) The standard school-leaving examination, usually taken by a student after five years at a *secondary school*. GCSE certificates are awarded for each subject on a seven-point scale, A to G. The first GCSE examinations were introduced in 1988, replacing two different examination courses.

Geffrye Museum /ˈdʒefrɪ mjuːˌzɪəm/, **the** (arts) A museum in east *London* opened in 1914. It currently displays the furniture and domestic equipment of a typical *middle class* English home in all periods from 1600 to 1939. There are also displays of costume and a library. The museum is housed in a building erected originally (1715) as an *almshouse* under a bequest from a *Lord Mayor* of London, Sir Robert Geffrye (died 1704).

General Assembly of the Church of Scotland /ˌdʒenrəl əˌsemblɪ əv ðə ˌtʃɜːtʃ əv ˈskɒtlənd/, **the** (religion) The supreme court or governing body of the *Church of Scotland*. It is composed of ministers, elders and other elected members of the Church.

General Council /ˌdʒenrəl ˈkaʊnsl/, **the** (work) The body elected annually by the *TUC* to represent it between Congresses (the important annual meeting of the TUC) and to carry out Congress decisions. It also watches economic and social developments, provides educational and advisory services to unions, and presents trade union viewpoints to the government. It can also help to solve disputes between unions.

general degree /ˈdʒenrəl dɪˌgriː/ (education) A degree (also known as an ordinary degree or a *pass degree*) obtained in several subjects on a non-specialized course at some universities. Compare *honours degree*.

general election /ˌdʒenrəl ɪˈlekʃn/ (politics) An election held throughout the *United Kingdom* on a particular day to elect a government. Voters cast their votes at a local *polling station* in the *ward* of their particular *constituency* to elect their next *MP*. Compare *by-election*.

general hospital /ˌdʒenrəl ˈhɒspɪtl/ (medicine) A hospital that treats a wide range of patients and diseases and does not restrict itself to any one disease or type of patient.

general practitioner /ˌdʒenrəl prækˈtɪʃənə(r)/ see *GP* (medicine)

General Strike /ˌdʒenrəl ˈstraɪk/, **the** (history) The 'sympathetic' strike of 4–12 May 1926 organized by the *TUC* in support of the miners in their dispute with the coal owners. Although the strike spread to involve workers in the rail, road transport, iron and steel, and building and printing industries, the miners alone stayed on strike for nearly six months.

General Synod /ˌdʒenrəl ˈsɪnəd/, **the** (religion) The central governing body of the *Church of England*. It deals with such matters as education, inter-church relations, recruitment of clergy and the care of church buildings.

gentleman /ˈdʒentlmən/ (life and society) **1** A general term used to refer politely to any man. **2** A man regarded as having the best British characteristics, in particular culture, courtesy and a good education. **3** A man who comes from an aristocratic family, that is, a member of the *gentry*.

gentleman farmer /ˌdʒentlmən 'fɑːmə(r)/ (life and society) **1** A man who runs a farm but does not depend on it for his main income. **2** A man who owns farm land but does not farm it himself.

gentleman-at-arms /ˌdʒentlmən ət 'ɑːmz/ (life and society) A member of one of the two corps forming the dismounted bodyguard of the sovereign (officially the Honourable Corps of Gentlemen-at-Arms), which consists of 40 retired *Army* and *Royal Marines* officers. The other group is the *Yeomen of the Guard*.

gentleman's gentleman /ˌdʒentlmənz 'dʒentlmən/ (life and society) The personal servant of a *gentleman*[3]. An example in literature is Jeeves, a leading character in the novels of P G *Wodehouse*.

Gentlemen-at-Arms /ˌdʒentlmən ət 'ɑːmz/, **the** (life and society) The short name for the Honourable Corps of Gentlemen-at-Arms (see *gentleman-at-arms*).

gentry /'dʒentrɪ/, **the** (life and society) A collective term for members of the aristocracy, individually known as gentlemen and gentlewomen, who rank socially just below the nobility.

Geological Museum /ˌdʒɪə'lɒdʒɪkl mjuːˌzɪəm/, **the** (science and technology) The national museum of earth sciences, in *London*, next to the *Science Museum*. It has a large collection of minerals and fossils, and has the largest geological library in *Britain*. It was founded in 1837.

Geordie /'dʒɔːdɪ/ (geography) **1** The nickname of an inhabitant of Tyneside (northeast *England*), or of a person who comes from there. **2** The English dialect spoken by such a person. [from the dialect version of the name Georgie]

George Cross /ˌdʒɔːdʒ 'krɒs/ see *GC* (life and society)

George Medal /ˌdʒɔːdʒ 'medl/, **the** (life and society) A medal instituted at the same time as the *GC* to be awarded for acts of heroism which are not considered to merit the Cross. The medal has a representation of St George and the Dragon and the words 'The George Medal'.

Georgian /'dʒɔːdʒən/ (history) Relating to one or all the four Kings George I–IV who reigned from 1714 to 1830 or to George V who reigned 1910–36. See also *Georgian poets*, *Georgian (style)*.

Georgian (style) /'dʒɔːdʒən (staɪl)/ (style) A style of

architecture and furniture characteristic of the 18th century. In architecture the main features of the style were dignity and restraint and a special regard for symmetry (see *Regency (style)*). In furniture the designs were typically those of *Chippendale*, *Hepplewhite* and *Sheraton*.

Georgian poets /ˌdʒɔːdʒən ˈpəʊɪts/, **the** (arts) A group of English poets who, in the reign of George V (1910–36), wrote about nature and rural life in the manner of William Wordsworth (1770–1850). Among the main poets in the group were John Masefield (1878–1967), Robert Graves (1895–1985), A E Housman (1859–1936), Harold Monro (1879–1932) and Walter de la Mare (1873–1956).

Giant's Causeway

Giant's Causeway /ˌdʒaɪənts ˈkɔːzweɪ/, **the** (geography) A tourist attraction on the north coast of *Northern Ireland*. It is a headland consisting of several thousand pillars of rock, most of them five- or six-sided. The same rock formation can be seen in *Fingal's Cave*. ['giant' comes from a folk tale that tells of a fight between two giants in which they threw distinctively-shaped rocks at each other]

Gielgud, John /ˈɡiːlɡʊd, dʒɒn/ (people) John Gielgud (born 1904) has shown particular talent as a Shakespearian actor and producer, but has also appeared in non-Shakespearian roles in classic and modern plays. He is famous for his ability to act in very varied roles and for his finely-controlled speaking voice, which he used to great effect in his popular recitations of solo passages from *Shakespeare*. He has appeared in many cinema and television films.

gift token /'gɪft ˌtəʊkən/ (commerce) A voucher for a fixed amount bought in a shop and presented as a gift to a person who is then able to select goods to the value of the token in that same shop or an equivalent branch (where the shop is a chain store). The token looks like a *greetings card*. Some shops make a small charge for the card, while others charge only the value of the token. Compare *book token*.

Gilbert and Sullivan operas /ˌgɪlbət ən 'sʌlɪvn ˌɒprəz/ (arts) Popular comic operettas by the composer Sir Arthur Seymour Sullivan (1842–1900) and librettist Sir William Schwenck Gilbert (1836–1911). The operettas, which contain elements of satire, were originally staged (1875–1896) at the *Savoy* (*Theatre*), *London*, and have continued to attract a small but enthusiastic following. Among the best known are 'HMS Pinafore' (1878), 'The Pirates of Penzance' (1879) and 'The Mikado' (1885).

gill /dʒɪl/ (daily life) A unit of liquid measure equal to one quarter of a *pint* (= 142 millilitres).

gillie /'gɪlɪ/ (sport and leisure) In *Scotland*, an attendant or guide for a person who is hunting or fishing. [from Scottish *Gaelic* 'gille', 'servant']

gilt-edged securities /ˌgɪlt edʒd sɪ'kjʊərətɪz/ (finance) Stocks, usually those issued by the government, that are almost certain to produce interest and can be redeemed (repaid) at face value at almost any time. Such stocks originally had gilt edges.

gin /dʒɪn/ (food and drink) A spirit distilled from grain or malt and flavoured with juniper berries. It is always drunk diluted either with fruit juice or in the form of a cocktail (see *gin and tonic*).

gin and tonic /ˌdʒɪn ən 'tɒnɪk/ (food and drink) A popular drink of *gin* and tonic water, usually with a slice of lemon and chunk of ice added. It is sometimes called 'a g and t'.

ginger biscuit /ˌdʒɪndʒə 'bɪskɪt/ (food and drink) A hard round biscuit flavoured with ginger and usually sprinkled with sugar.

ginger group /'dʒɪndʒə gruːp/ (life and society) A group within a political or other organization that aims to 'activate' its parent body, especially when the latter shows little sign of decisive action. [from colloquial 'ginger' = 'liveliness', 'vigour', from the hot, spicy taste of ginger]

Gingerbread /'dʒɪndʒəbred/ (charities) A charity organization providing support and advice to single-parent families, expecially on a 'self-help' basis. It was founded in 1970 and has about 400 branches in *England* and *Wales*. [name is pun on cake so called, with 'ginger' in colloquial sense of 'enliven', 'make active'; and 'bread' in slang sense 'money']

Girl Friday /ˌgɜːl 'fraɪdɪ/ (work) A term for a girl or woman who is a *PA* or secretary, either in a business organization or privately. [from Man Friday, Robinson Crusoe's servant in the novel (1719) by Daniel Defoe]

Girl Guide /ˌgɜːl 'gaɪd/ (sport and leisure) A term still in popular use for a member of the *Guides Association* (now officially a *Guide*).

giro /'dʒaɪrəʊ/ (finance) **1** A system of transferring money between one bank and another ('bank giro credit'), introduced when the *Post Office* created its National *Girobank* in 1968. **2** A short name for the National Girobank. **3** A short name for a *giro cheque*.

Girobank /'dʒaɪrəʊbæŋk/ (finance) One of the major *clearing banks*, established in 1968 and formerly a subsidiary of the *Post Office*, through which it continues to operate. It was privatized in 1990 when it was bought by a *building society*.

giro cheque /'dʒaɪərəʊ ˌtʃek/ (finance) A payment of *unemployment benefit* or *income support* made through the *giro*[1] system by a cheque which can be cashed at a post office. Such cheques are sent out fortnightly.

Glamis Castle /ˌglɑːmz 'kɑːsl/ (royal family) A picturesque 17th-century castle in *Scotland*, north of Dundee, which was the Scottish family home of *Queen Elizabeth, the Queen Mother* before her marriage.

Glasgow /'glɑːzgəʊ/ (geography) An important industrial and commercial city in *Scotland* and a famous port on the *Clyde*. Its principal industries are ship building and heavy engineering. It is the third largest city in *Britain*.

Glaswegian /glæz'wiːdʒən/ (geography) A native or inhabitant of *Glasgow*.

Glencoe Massacre /glen'kəʊ (ˌglenkəʊ 'mæsəkə(r))/**, the** (history) A massacre which took place in 1692 in a valley in west *Scotland* where the Scottish *clan* Campbell, assisted by English troops, massacred the clan Macdonald. [from the name of the valley]

glengarry /glen'gærɪ/ (clothing) A brimless Scottish woollen cap, usually with ribbons hanging at the back. [named after Glen Garry, a valley in the *Highlands*]

Globe (Theatre) /gləʊb (ˌgləʊb 'θɪətə(r))/, **the** (1 history 2 arts)
1 A famous theatre built in 1599 on the south bank of the
Thames, London, in which *Shakespeare*'s greatest plays were
first performed. It was burnt down in 1613, rebuilt in 1614,
and remained in use until 1644 when it was demolished to
make space for new houses. In 1988 the American actor and
director Sam Wanamaker was given permission to build a
copy of the original theatre on the site. Six of its 20 sections
were in place by late 1993. 2 A theatre in *Shaftesbury Avenue*,
London, staging mainly light comedies and musicals. It
opened in 1906.

Glorious Goodwood /ˌglɔːrɪəs 'gʊdwʊd/ (sport and leisure) A
nickname of the racecourse at *Goodwood*, West Sussex,
famous for its attractive setting and for the excellence of its
turf. The name is also used of the horse races themselves,
especially those held annually in 'Goodwood Week' (July/
August).

Glorious Twelfth /ˌglɔːrɪəs 'twelfθ/, **the** (1 history 2 sport and
leisure) 1 12 July 1690, the day (actually 1 July in the old style
calendar, and 11 July in the new style) when the Battle of the
Boyne took place in *Ireland*. The date 12 July is celebrated
annually in modern *Northern Ireland* by the Protestants to
mark their victory over the Catholics in the Battle. 2 A name
for 12 August, when *grouse shooting* begins annually.

Gloucester /'glɒstə(r)/ (geography) The county town of
Gloucestershire, whose cathedral is a fine example of
Perpendicular (style) architecture, with parts in the older
Norman style.

Glover, Jane /'glʌvə(r), dʒeɪn/ (people) Jane Glover (born
1949) is one of *Britain*'s leading conductors. She became
musical director of the London Choral Society in 1983 and
was artistic director of the *London Mozart Players* from 1984 to
1991. She was appointed principal conductor of the
Huddersfield Choral Society in 1989 and a governor of the
BBC in 1991. Jane Glover is a regular broadcaster on
television and radio, and is noted especially for her
conducting of choral and operatic works.

GLR /ˌdʒiː 'el ˌɑːr/ **(Greater London Radio)** (media) A *BBC*
local radio station opened in 1988 to transmit to *Greater*
London. The station arose out of the former BBC Radio
London. Unlike many local radio stations, it aims to
broadcast both pop and classical music, and to include a
number of talk programmes.

glue-sniffing /ˈgluːsnɪfɪŋ/ (life and society) The practice, sometimes fatal, of inhaling the fumes of certain types of glue and other substances in order to achieve a hallucinatory effect. The practice was adopted by some young people in the 1970s, and became more widespread in the 1980s.

Glyndebourne /ˈglaɪndbɔːn/ (arts) An opera festival held every summer in an opera house in the grounds of a country house near Lewes, East Sussex. The festival was inaugurated by John Christie, owner of the house, in 1934 and specializes in operas by Mozart and Richard Strauss.

GMB /ˌdʒiː em ˈbiː/, **the (General, Municipal and Boilermakers Union, the)** (work) A large trade union of about 860,000 members, formed in 1989 on the amalgamation of two former unions. Its members come from a wide range of jobs. [initials of former full official name: *General, Municipal, Boilermakers and Allied Trades Union*]

GMT /ˌdʒiː em ˈtiː/ **(Greenwich Mean Time)** (geography) The local time of the 0° meridian that passes through *Greenwich*, and thus the standard time for *Britain* and a basis for other time zones in the world.

GMTV /ˌdʒiː em tiː ˈviː/ (media) The main *breakfast television* company of the *ITC*, based in *London* and broadcasting daily on *ITV* from 6.00 to 8.50 am. [initials of 'Good Morning Television']

gnome

gnome /nəʊm/ (style) A small statue or figure of a gnome, sometimes placed in a front garden as a decoration.

gobstopper /ˈɡɒbstɒpə(r)/ (food and drink) A large, hard, round sweet gradually changing in colour as it is sucked. [from 'gob', a slang term for 'mouth']

God Save the Queen /ˌɡɒd seɪv ðə ˈkwiːn/ (life and society) The title of the British *national anthem* (in fact the final words of the first verse). In the reign of a king the word 'Queen' changes to 'King'. It is not known who wrote the text of the anthem, but it may have been established in its present form some time in the 18th century.

Gog Magog Hills /ˌɡɒɡ məɡɒɡ ˈhɪlz/, **the** (geography) Low hills near *Cambridge¹* where there is a golf course. The hills are a favourite place for *undergraduates* of *Cambridge University*. The name, which also exists in the form Gogmagogs, is said to derive from two local legendary giants. The hills are also known colloquially as the Gogs.

Gold Cup Day /ˌɡəʊld ˈkʌp deɪ/ (sport and leisure) The most important day of the horse races at *Ascot*, when the prize of the Ascot Gold Cup is competed for. The prize was established in 1807.

Gold Stick /ˌɡəʊld ˈstɪk/ (life and society) **1** The gilt rod carried as a badge of office before the sovereign by the colonel of the *Life Guards* or the captain of the *Gentlemen-at-Arms*. **2** The title of the colonel himself when performing this duty.

Golden Age /ˌɡəʊldən ˈeɪdʒ/, **the** (history) A term used for the reign of Queen Elizabeth I, from 1558 to 1603. This was a period of marked economic progress and of the flowering of the arts, both largely resulting from Elizabeth's encouragement and inspiration.

golden handshake /ˌɡəʊldən ˈhændʃeɪk/ (work) A colloquial term for a substantial sum of money paid to an employee, often a director or other executive, either on his retirement in recognition of his work, or on his dismissal by way of compensation.

Golden Hind /ˌɡəʊldən ˈhaɪnd/, **the** (1 history 2 transport) **1** The name of the ship in which Sir Francis Drake (?1540–96) sailed round the world (1577–80). **2** The name of a daily express train from *London* to Plymouth. (Francis Drake returned to Plymouth at the end of his voyage and was made *mayor* of Plymouth the following year.)

Golding, William /ˌɡəʊldɪŋ, 'wɪlɪəm/ (people) William Golding (1911-93) gained instant popularity as a writer with his novel 'Lord of the Flies' (1954), depicting the gradual disintegration of human values as experienced by a group of schoolboys stranded on a desert island after a plane crash. Many saw the book as an allegory of contemporary human society. Several of Golding's novels have cruelty as a theme, and are at least partly based on his own life as a teacher and naval officer. William Golding was awarded the Nobel Prize for Literature in 1983 and he was knighted in 1988.

Goldsmiths' Company /'ɡəʊldsmɪθs ˌkʌmpənɪ/, **the** (tradition) One of the oldest *livery companies*, founded in 1327 and the fifth in precedence. Its members, originally goldsmiths, still regulate the manufacture and sale of gold and silver articles.

Goldsmiths' Hall /ˌɡəʊldsmɪθs 'hɔːl/ (London) The building in the *City* (*of London*) where the *Goldsmiths' Company* is based. It contains a valuable collection of portraits and goldware.

Good Friday /ˌɡʊd 'fraɪdɪ/ (religion) The Friday before *Easter* when the Christian *church* marks the Crucifixion of Christ. In *Britain* it is a *bank holiday* and a day when traditionally *hot cross buns* are eaten.

Good Housekeeping /ˌɡʊd 'haʊskiːpɪŋ/ (media) A monthly glossy magazine for women, containing a much wider range of material than its name suggests. It was founded in 1922 and has a current circulation of about 391,000.

Good King Wenceslas /ˌɡʊd kɪŋ 'wensəslæs/ (tradition) The title, and opening words, of a well-known *Christmas* carol (see *carol service*), particularly popular among children. [the carol is of 19th-century origin, but has the 10th-century Bohemian martyr prince Wenceslas as its subject]

Goodison Park /ˌɡʊdɪsn 'pɑːk/ (sport and leisure) The stadium of the *football club Everton* in Liverpool. [from the name of a nearby park]

goodwill /ˌɡʊd'wɪl/ (commerce) The term for an intangible asset, such as a good reputation or favourable customer connections, taken into account in assessing the value of a deal, particularly the sale of a business.

Goodwin Sands /ˌɡʊdwɪn 'sændz/, **the** (geography) A dangerous stretch of sand banks at the entrance to the Strait of Dover. [traditionally said to have been an island, belonging to an earl named Godwine, that was washed away by the sea in 1097]

Goodwood /'gʊdwʊd/ (sport and leisure) A fashionable race course near Chichester, West Sussex. See also *Glorious Goodwood*. [from the house and park near which it is]

Goons /guːnz/, **the** (media) The name adopted by a group of radio comedians for their programme 'The Goon Show' in the 1950s. Their humour was a blend of the witty and the near-absurd. The comedians were: Michael Bentine (born 1922), Spike Milligan (born 1918), Harry Secombe (born 1921) and Peter Sellers (1925–80). [name allegedly based on that of a cartoon character]

Goose Fair /ˌguːs 'feə(r)/, **the** (tradition) An annual fair held in Nottingham, originally one at which geese were sold. The fair takes place on the first Thursday, Friday and Saturday in October.

Gorbals /'gɔːblz/, **the** (geography) A southern suburb of *Glasgow*, once notorious for its slums.

Gordon Highlanders /ˌgɔːdn 'haɪləndəz/, **the** (defence) A well-known Scottish army regiment. It was formed in 1881 when the 92nd and 75th regiments were combined, but was originally raised in 1794 by the 5th Duke of Gordon.

Gordonstoun (School) /'gɔːdnstən (ˌgɔːdnstən 'skuːl)/ (education) A *public school*[1] near the coast in northeast *Scotland*. It was founded in 1934 by the German educationalist Kurt Hahn (1886–1974) with the aim of developing a pupil's all-round capabilities, both physical and mental. The school, currently with 470 students, has been attended by several members of the *royal family*, including the *Duke of Edinburgh* (Prince Philip) and his sons the *Prince of Wales* (Prince Charles) and the *Duke of York* (Prince Andrew). Kurt Hahn also founded the *Outward Bound* (*Trust*).

go-slow /ˌgəʊ'sləʊ/ (work) A deliberate slowing of the work rate or rate of production by a labour force as a tactic in an industrial dispute. Compare *work-to-rule*.

gossip column /'gɒsɪp ˌkɒləm/ (media) A regular feature in a newspaper (especially a *popular paper*) or magazine in which the latest news and rumours about people in the public eye are given.

Gothic novel /ˌgɒθɪk 'nɒvl/ (arts) A mock-romantic horror story, traditionally set in a castle built in the *Gothic (style)*, popularized in the 18th century by the novelist Horace Walpole (1717–97), notably in his novel 'The Castle of Otranto' (1764).

Gothic Revival

Gothic Revival /ˌɡɒθɪk rɪˈvaɪvl/**, the** (style) The revival (1750)
of *Gothic (style)* architecture in *England*. A typical example of
the style are the *Houses of Parliament, London.*

Gothic (style) /ˈɡɒθɪk (staɪl)/ (style) An architectural style in
which pointed arches, soaring lines and height predominate.
In *Britain* it is typified by the *Early English, Decorated* and
*Perpendicular (style*s), notably in *churches* and cathedrals.

government health warning /ˌɡʌvənmənt ˈhelθ ˌwɔːnɪŋ/
(medicine) An official warning about the danger to health of
smoking, printed by law on all cigarette packets and
advertisements. The warning appears in different forms,
such as 'Smoking can cause fatal diseases' or 'Smoking when
pregnant can injure your baby and cause premature birth'.
Cigarette advertising is banned on television and radio.

governor /ˈɡʌvənə(r)/ (**1** life and society **2** education **3** law)
1 The official title of the head of certain establishments, for
example, the Governor of the *Bank of England*. **2** A member of
a governing body of a university, *college[1]* or school. **3** The
title of the head of a prison.

gown /ɡaʊn/ (**1** clothing **2** education) **1** The loose top garment
worn as part of the official dress of certain people, such as a
mayor, a judge or the students and staff of a university or
school. **2** A collective term for the students of a university, as

opposed to the inhabitants of the town where the university is located. See *town and gown*.

GP /ˌdʒiː 'piː/ **(general practitioner)** (medicine) A doctor who is not a specialist but who has a medical practice (a 'general practice') in which he treats all illnesses. He is also sometimes known as a 'family doctor', and often works as a member of a *group practice*.

GPO /ˌdʒiː piː 'əʊ/, **the (General Post Office, the)** (commerce) The official title of the *Post Office* before 1969.

GQ /ˌdʒiː 'kjuː/ (media) A monthly glossy magazine for the successful and stylish young man, with articles and features on fashion, sex life, money and male celebrities from sports stars to film actors. It was founded in 1988. [abbreviation of its official title, 'Gentlemen's Quarterly']

grace /ɡreɪs/ (religion) A short, usually formal, prayer said before or after a meal, especially in a school or a religious community. Many formal dinners often begin and end with grace, which is said by a clergyman, if one is there, or some other senior person. In some older establishments, such as university *colleges[1]* and *public schools[1]*, grace is still said in Latin. A typical English grace runs: 'Bless us, O Lord, and these thy gifts, for Jesus Christ's sake. Amen.'

Grace and Favour residence /ˌɡreɪs ən 'feɪvə resɪdəns/ (life and society) A house or flat owned by the sovereign and granted free of rent to a person to whom the sovereign wishes to show gratitude. Among such residences are those at *Windsor Castle*, *Hampton Court* and *Kensington Palace*.

graduate /'ɡrædʒʊət/ (education) A person who holds a university degree, normally having attended a university course and passed the final examination.

graduate student /'ɡrædʒʊət ˌstjuːdənt/ (education) An alternative term for a *postgraduate*.

grammar school /'ɡræmə skuːl/ (education) **1** A dated or colloquial term for a *public school[1]*, especially one that still has the word 'Grammar' in its name, such as Bristol Grammar School. **2** A state *secondary school* offering a more academic education than a *comprehensive school*. There are now very few schools of this type.

Gramophone /'ɡræməfəʊn/ (media) A monthly magazine almost entirely devoted to reviews of the latest recordings of classical music. It was founded in 1923, and has a current circulation of about 72,000.

Grampian TV /'ɡræmpɪən tiː ˌviː/ (media) One of the 15 regional television companies of the *ITC*, based in Aberdeen and broadcasting to northeast *Scotland*. [named after the *Grampians* in that region]

Grampians /ˈgræmpɪənz/, **the** (geography) A range of mountains in the *Highlands* of central *Scotland* that includes the *Cairngorms* and is popular with mountain climbers and hill walkers. Many of the high moors in the Grampians are used for *grouse shooting* at the appropriate time of year.

Granada TV /grəˈnɑːdə tiː ˌviː/ (media) One of the 15 regional television companies of the *ITC*, based in Manchester and broadcasting to the surrounding region. [named after the Granada Group that founded it]

Grand National /ˌgrænd ˈnæʃnəl/, **the** (sport and leisure) The most important steeplechase in *Britain*, held annually in the spring at the *Aintree* race course near Liverpool. It was instituted in 1839 and given its present name in 1847. See also *Becher's Brook*, *Valentine's Brook*.

Grand Old Man /ˌgrænd əʊld ˈmæn/ (life and society) A title, serious or humorous, for any person who has given long service in some activity. It was originally a nickname of William Ewart Gladstone (1809–98) who was four times *Prime Minister*.

Grand Union Canal /ˌgrænd ˌjuːnɪən kəˈnæl/, **the** (transport) The longest canal in *Britain*, linking *London* with Birmingham and extending for 240 miles (385 km).

Grandstand /ˈgrændstænd/ (media) A weekly television programme broadcast by *BBC 1* on Saturdays (and occasionally on *Sundays* and *bank holidays*). It usually consists of live transmissions of important sports events. The programme was first broadcast in 1958.

Granite City /ˌgrænɪt ˈsɪtɪ/, **the** (geography) A nickname of Aberdeen, *Scotland*, since many of its buildings are made of local granite, a silver-grey or pink stone.

granny flat /ˈgrænɪ ˌflæt/ (daily life) A flat built onto a house, or made inside it, for an elderly relative (not necessarily a grandmother).

Granny Smith /ˌgrænɪ ˈsmɪθ/ (food and drink) A common variety of large, green apple, suitable for cooking or eating raw. Such apples are now imported to *Britain* from several countries, but the variety originally came from Australia, where it was named after Maria Ann ('Granny') Smith, the gardener who introduced it as a new type in the 19th century.

grant-maintained school /ˌgrɑːnt meɪnˈteɪnd ˌskuːl/ (education) A state *secondary school* or large *primary school* in

England or *Wales* that is funded by a direct grant from the government, rather than by its *LEA*. Such schools are run entirely by their *governors*[2] and are free to alter their particular type. A successful grant-aided *comprehensive school* could thus turn itself into a *grammar school*. Compare *self-governing school*.

Granta /ˈɡrɑːntə/ (geography) The local name of the river Cam as it flows through *Cambridge*[1]. Compare *Isis*.

Grasmere /ˈɡrɑːsmɪə(r)/ (geography) A picturesque village in the *Lake District* where the poet William Wordsworth (1770–1850) lived for much of his life and where the *Lake Poets* used to meet.

gravy /ˈɡreɪvɪ/ (food and drink) A type of hot sauce made from the juice of meat that is added to meat dishes to make them more tasty. It is usually poured from a small jug called a 'gravy boat'. See also *Sunday roast*.

Gray's 'Elegy' /ˌɡreɪz ˈelədʒɪ/ (arts) A famous and much quoted poem by Thomas Gray (1716–71). The poem appeared in 1751 and has the full title 'Elegy Written in a Country Churchyard'. The churchyard is traditionally believed to be that of Stoke Poges, Buckinghamshire.

Gray's Inn /ˌɡreɪz ˈɪn/ (law) The most recent of the *Inns of Court*, named after the 14th-century family de Gray, who owned the land on which it was built.

Great Britain /ˌɡreɪt ˈbrɪtn/ (geography) The largest island of the *British Isles* and consisting of *England*, *Scotland* and *Wales*. It is often used (incorrectly) to include *Northern Ireland* which is (correctly) part of the *United Kingdom* of Great Britain and Northern Ireland. See map on p 466.

Great Exhibition /ˌɡreɪt eksɪˈbɪʃn/, **the** (history) The first international trade fair held in *London* at the *Crystal Palace*[1] in 1851.

Great Fire (of London) /ˌɡreɪt ˈfaɪə(r) (ˌɡreɪt faɪər əv ˈlʌndən)/, **the** (history) A fire which destroyed more than half the city of *London*, including the old *St Paul's Cathedral*, in 1666.

Great Glen /ˌɡreɪt ˈɡlen/, **the** (geography) The name of a long valley, also called Glen More, that runs northeast to southwest across the whole of the north of *Scotland* and that includes *Loch Ness*.

Great North Road /ˌɡreɪt nɔːθ ˈrəʊd/, **the** (transport) The name of the old trunk road from *London* to *Edinburgh* in *Scotland*, today mainly followed by the A1 (see *A-road*) and in a few places by the *M1* (see *motorway*).

Great Ormond Street /ˌɡreɪt ˈɔːmənd striːt/ (medicine) The street in *London* where there is a famous hospital for children, known either as the Great Ormond Street Hospital or the Hospital for Sick Children.

Great Paul /ˌgreɪt ˈpɔːl/ (London) The name of the largest bell in *Britain*, in *St Paul's Cathedral, London*. It weighs 16 tons (17,000 kilograms).

Great Plague (of London) /ˌgreɪt ˈpleɪg (ˌgreɪt pleɪg əv ˈlʌndən)/, **the** (history) An epidemic of bubonic plague in *London* in 1664–5, when more than 70,000 people died, out of an estimated population of 460,000.

Great Seal /ˌgreɪt ˈsiːl/, **the** (government) The state seal of the *United Kingdom* used on documents of the greatest importance and kept in the office of the *Lord Chancellor*.

Great Tom /ˌgreɪt ˈtɒm/ (tradition) The name of the bell over the gate at Christ Church, *Oxford*[1], still traditionally rung 101 times each evening at 9.05. Its original use was to summon students out in the town to return to the *college*[1] at night, 101 being the number of students in residence. [from Tom, a traditional name for a large bell]

Great Train Robbery /ˌgreɪt ˈtreɪn ˌrɒbərɪ/, **the** (history) The name used for the robbery of a mail train in Buckinghamshire in 1963. The train was travelling from *Scotland* to *London* and over £2 million in bank notes were stolen from it.

Greater London /ˌgreɪtə ˈlʌndən/ (London) **1** The name first used in 1882 for the district of *London* controlled by the *Metropolitan Police*. **2** The name of the local government area set up in 1964 to include the *City (of London)*, the historic *county*[1] of *London* (created in 1888 but not including the City), almost the whole of the county[1] of Middlesex, and parts of other counties. The present Greater London is divided into 32 *boroughs*[2]. Its area is 610 square miles (1,580 square kilometres) and its population is currently about 6.4 million.

Greats /greɪts/ (education) A colloquial term for the final examination at *Oxford University* in Literae Humaniores, the study of Latin and Greek language, literature, history and philosophy.

green belt /ˈgriːn belt/ (geography) A zone of farmland, parks or woodland surrounding a town, especially a *new town*, planned with a view to preventing unnecessary urban development.

green card /ˌgriːn ˈkɑːd/ (transport) A special document certifying that a vehicle such as a car has been insured for travel abroad. [document is green in colour]

Green Cross Code /ˌgriːn krɒs ˈkəʊd/, **the** (daily life) A set of road safety rules for children, first published in 1971. ['Green' for the colour's connotations of safety, 'Cross' to suggest 'crossing the road', 'Code' to suggest the *Highway Code*]

Green Jackets /ˈgriːn ˌdʒækɪts/, **the** (defence) The short form of the name of the *Army* regiment known in full as the Royal Green Jackets, formed in 1866.

Green Line bus /ˌgriːn laɪn ˈbʌs/ (transport) One of the green buses operated by *London Transport* to serve the area round *London* to a radius of about 40 miles (64 kilometres).

green paper /ˌgriːn ˈpeɪpə(r)/ (government) A *command paper* setting out proposals for future government policy to be discussed in *Parliament*. [from the colour of the cover]

Green Park /ˌgriːn ˈpɑːk/ (London) A park in *London* extending along the south side of *Piccadilly*. Traditionally no flowers are grown there. [named for its green grass and trees]

Green Party /ˈgriːn ˌpɑːtɪ/, **the** (politics) A political party founded in 1973 (as the Ecology Party) with the aim of solving environmental problems. In 1985 it adopted its present name and rapidly gained public support until 1990, since when its popularity has fallen. It now has about 9,700 members, half its 1990 number. It has no *MPs* in the *House of Commons*.

green wellies /ˌgriːn ˈwelɪz/ (clothing) A colloquial name for the green-coloured *wellington boots* worn by some *upper class* and *upper middle class* people, typically, *Sloane Rangers*, especially when in the country or attending an outdoor sporting event.

Greene, Graham /ˈgriːn, ˈgreɪəm/ (people) Graham Greene (1904–91) gained an international reputation for his novels and plays, many of which deal with exciting or 'moral' subjects, often interwoven with a religious theme. Some of his works he himself classified as 'entertainments', such as 'Brighton Rock' (1938) and 'The Third Man' (1950), the latter written specially for the cinema. He was also well known for his books on travel.

Greensleeves /ˈgriːnsliːvz/ (arts) A popular old love song known from the 16th century and twice mentioned by *Shakespeare*. The song tells of a 'Lady Greensleeves'. It is popularly believed *Henry VIII* wrote the music and the words, though this is not certain.

Greenwich /ˈgrenɪdʒ/ (geography) A southern suburb of

London, where the *Royal Greenwich Observatory* was until it moved to Herstmonceux in 1958. The 0° meridian that indicates where *GMT* is measured passes through this part of London.

Greenwich Park /ˌɡrenɪdʒ ˈpɑːk/ (geography) A large park in *Greenwich* through which passes the 0° meridian that gives *GMT*. From the hill in the centre of the park there is a fine panoramic view of southeast *London*.

greetings card /ˈɡriːtɪŋz kɑːd/ (life and society) A decorative card, usually folded in two, with an illustration and wording on the outside and with wording or blank in the middle, sent to greet a person on a special occasion such as *Christmas*, a birthday or the announcement of an engagement to be married.

Grenadier Guards /ˌɡrenədɪə ˈɡɑːdz/, **the** (defence) The senior regiment of the *Army* in the *Guards Division* of infantry. It was raised in 1685.

Gretna Green /ˌɡretnə ˈɡriːn/ (tradition) A village in southern *Scotland*, on the border with *England*. Here there is a famous smithy where eloping couples from England could be married by the blacksmith without the usual legal formalities. This tradition operated from 1754 until 1940 when such marriages were declared illegal.

Greyfriars /ˈɡreɪfraɪəz/ (education) An imaginary boys' *public school*[1] that was the setting for a famous series of school stories with *Billy Bunter* as their hero.

greyhound /ˈɡreɪhaʊnd/ (animal world) A tall slender fast-moving breed of hunting dog traditionally used in *greyhound racing*. Greyhounds are not necessarily grey in colour: 'grey' comes from an old word for bitch.

Greyhound Derby /ˌɡreɪhaʊnd ˈdɑːbɪ/, **the** (sport and leisure) An important annual event in *greyhound racing*, held at the *White City* stadium in *London*. It was first run in 1927.

greyhound racing /ˈɡreɪhaʊnd ˌreɪsɪŋ/ (sport and leisure) A popular type of gambling sport in which bets are placed on *greyhounds* racing round a track after a mechanical hare. There are 89 tracks in *Britain*, each licensed by a *local authority*.

griddle cake /ˈɡrɪdl ˌkeɪk/ (food and drink) An alternative name for a *drop scone*.

Grosvenor House /ˌɡrəʊvnə ˈhaʊs/ (London) The name (in full Grosvenor House Hotel) of a fashionable hotel in *Park Lane, London*.

Grosvenor Square /ˌɡrəʊvnə ˈskweə(r)/ (London) A large square in central *London* where the United States Embassy and other diplomatic offices are. See *Little America*.

ground floor /ˌɡraʊnd ˈflɔː(r)/, **the** (daily life) The bottom floor in a building, corresponding in many other countries to the *first floor*. The first floor in *Britain* is the one above the ground level.

ground rent /ˈɡraʊnd rent/ (finance) A rent, traditionally running for 99 years, payable for the lease of a building, in particular a home.

groundsman /ˈɡraʊndzmən/ (sport and leisure) A man responsible for the upkeep of a sports ground or field and for preparing the area of play before a game or match.

group practice /ˌɡruːp ˈpræktɪs/ (medicine) A medical practice in which several *GP*s see their patients in a surgery or clinic shared by all the doctors working there.

grouse shooting /ˈɡraʊs ˌʃuːtɪŋ/ (sport and leisure) A type of shooting popular among the aristocracy, particularly in *Scotland* where there are many moors where grouse live. The sport is restricted to the period 12 August (see *Glorious Twelfth*[2]) to 10 December.

GT /ˌdʒiː ˈtiː/ **(gran turismo)** (transport) The name given to some models of sports car, usually ones capable of high speeds. The term is Italian for 'great touring'.

Guardian /ˈɡɑːdɪən/, **The** (media) A daily *quality paper* tending to left-wing views and noted for its crusading campaigns in such areas as education, racial and sexual equality, and protection of the environment. It was founded in 1821 in Manchester and until 1961 was known as 'The Manchester Guardian'. Its current circulation is about 418,000 (1970 – 293,000).

Guards /ɡɑːdz/, **the** (defence) A general name for any or all of the regiments in the *Guards Division* of the *Army*, and for the *Life Guards* and the *Blues and Royals* in the *Household Cavalry*.

Guards Division /ˈɡɑːdz dɪˌvɪʒn/, **the** (defence) The infantry division of the *Army* that comprises the *Grenadier Guards, Coldstream Guards, Scots Guards, Irish Guards* and *Welsh Guards*. These are the most famous regiments in the Army.

guardsman /ˈɡɑːdzmən/ (defence) A member of any regiment of the *Guards*.

guernsey /ˈɡɜːnzɪ/ (clothing) A thick dark-blue woollen sweater, originally as worn by sailors on Guernsey, in the *Channel Islands*. Compare *jersey*[2].

Guernsey (cow) /ˈɡɜːnzɪ (ˌɡɜːnzɪ ˈkaʊ)/ (animal world) A breed of dairy cattle, larger than the *Jersey* (cow), producing high-quality creamy milk. Such a cow is usually fawn in colour, occasionally with white markings. Guernsey cows originally came from the island of Guernsey, in the *Channel Islands*; today they are usually found chiefly in the south of *England*, especially *Cornwall*.

guest house /ˈɡesthaʊs/ (daily life) A modest hotel or boarding house, often a private house, offering accommodation to business travellers or holiday makers.

Guide /ɡaɪd/ (sport and leisure) A girl aged 10 to 15 who is a member of the *Guides Association*.

guide dog /ˈɡaɪd dɒɡ/ (animal world) A dog specially trained to lead a blind person. Such dogs are trained by the Guide Dogs for the Blind Association, a charity founded in 1933.

Guider /ˈɡaɪdə/ (sport and leisure) An adult helper in the *Guides Association*.

Guides Association /ˈɡaɪdz əsəʊsɪˌeɪʃn/, **the** (sport and leisure) An organization for girls founded (as the Girl Guides Association) in 1910 as an equivalent to the Boy Scouts (now the *Scout Association*). Its members are divided into four

guide dog

groups, which from the youngest up are the *Rainbows*, the *Brownies*, the *Guides* and the *Rangers*. It currently has about 750,000 members.

guildhall /ˈgɪldhɔːl/ (tradition) The title of a *town hall* in a number of towns and *cities*. Originally it was the hall belonging to a medieval guild or corporation.

Guildhall /ˈgɪldhɔːl/, **the** (London) The ancient building that serves as the *town hall* for the *City* (*of London*), famous for its large banqueting hall in which official receptions are held on specially important occasions. The Guildhall also contains a library and picture gallery. It was built originally in 1411, with parts rebuilt in 1788.

Guildhall School of Music (and Drama) /ˌgɪldhɔːl ˌskuːl əv ˈmjuːzɪk (ˌgɪldhɔːl ˌskuːl əv ˌmjuːzɪk ən ˈdrɑːmə)/, **the** (education) A private *college*[2] in *London*, teaching music, stagecraft and the dramatic arts. It was founded in 1880. [from its nearness to the *Guildhall*]

guillotine /ˈgɪlətiːn/ (government) A term for a procedure whereby a *bill* that is going through one of the *Houses of Parliament* is divided into 'compartments', groups of which must be completely dealt with in a day. An alternative term for the procedure is 'closure by compartment'. [after the instrument used for execution by beheading]

guinea /ˈgɪnɪ/ (**1** history **2** finance) **1** A gold coin originally worth one *pound (sterling)*, later worth 21 *shillings*, that was withdrawn from circulation in 1813. **2** A monetary unit of 21 shillings (since 1971, £1.05) used for calculating professional fees and charges although now only rarely. [coin was originally made from gold imported from Guinea]

Guinness /ˈgɪnɪs/ (food and drink) The brand name of a type of strong dark beer (correctly known as *stout*) manufactured by Arthur Guinness Son & Co. Ltd.

Guinness, Alec /ˈgɪnɪs, ˈælɪk/ (people) Alec Guinness (born 1914) gained an early reputation as a gifted and versatile actor of stage and screen, with his film roles including popular characters in the *Ealing comedies*. He is best known for his characteristically 'underplayed' performances, making each role a distinctive and memorable one. He was knighted in 1959.

Guinness Book of Records /ˌgɪnɪs bʊk əv ˈrekɔːdz/, **the** (media) An annual reference book published by Guinness Superlatives Ltd., a subsidiary company of the firm that manufactures *Guinness*. The book publishes the records that have been broken or achieved in a wide range of activities on a worldwide basis. It was first published in 1955.

gum boots /ˈɡʌm buːts/ (clothing) Another name for *wellington boots*.

gun dog /ˈɡʌn dɒɡ/ (sport and leisure) A dog trained to help a shooting party by searching out or retrieving birds and animals.

Gunnell, Sally /ˈɡʌnl, ˈsælɪ/ (sport and leisure) Sally Gunnell (born 1966) is a leading British athlete. In 1988 she was the first *Briton*[1] to compete in the Olympic Games in the 100-metre hurdles, 400-metre hurdles and 4 x 400-metre relay. After further successes, she won a gold medal in the women's 400-metre hurdles in the 1992 Olympics, for which she was voted Sportswoman of the Year, and in 1993 she broke the world record in this same event when she became world champion.

Gunpowder Plot /ˈɡʌnpaʊdə plɒt/, **the** (history) The name of a plot in 1605 when on 5 November Roman Catholics planned to assassinate King James I at the *State Opening of Parliament* by exploding barrels of gunpowder in the vaults of the *Houses of Parliament*. One of the conspirators was Guy Fawkes (see *Guy Fawkes' Night*).

gutter press /ˈɡʌtə pres/, **the** (media) A colloquial term for those *popular papers*, and similar periodicals, that seek sensationalism by means of *gossip columns*, detailed reports of disasters and scandals and erotic features and photographs.

guy /ɡaɪ/ (tradition) A crude model of a human figure, representing Guy Fawkes, made by stuffing old clothes with straw, paper, leaves, etc., and burnt on top of a bonfire on *Guy Fawkes' Night*. Such a model may also be carried or displayed by children in the days before Guy Fawkes' Night with the aim of collecting money.

Guy Fawkes' Day /ˈɡaɪ fɔːks deɪ/ (tradition) An alternative name for *Guy Fawkes' Night*.

Guy Fawkes' Night /ˈɡaɪ fɔːks naɪt/ (tradition) A popular celebration annually on the evening of 5 November, the day of the original *Gunpowder Plot*. A bonfire is lit to burn a *guy* and a firework display is arranged. The occasion is usually accompanied by a supper or barbecue and is held both publicly in parks and recreation fields and privately in the gardens of houses. The historic significance of the event has long been ignored. [Guy Fawkes (1570–1606) was one of the

Roman Catholic conspirators in the Gunpowder Plot; under torture he revealed the names of the other conspirators and was convicted and executed]

Guy's Hospital /ˌgaɪz ˈhɒspɪtl/ (medicine) A leading *teaching hospital* in *London*. It was founded in 1721 by Thomas Guy (?1645–1724), a book dealer and philanthropist. The hospital is colloquially known as 'Guy's'.

gymkhana /dʒɪmˈkɑːnə/ (sport and leisure) A popular sporting event for children in which horses and ponies and their riders display their skills in various races and contests. [from a Hindi word meaning 'ball house', later associated with 'gymnasium']

gyp /dʒɪp/ (tradition) A colloquial term used especially at *Cambridge University* and Durham University for a *college[1]* servant. [perhaps from an old word 'gippo' originally meaning a man's short tunic as worn by a servant]

habeas corpus /ˌheɪbɪəs ˈkɔːpəs/ (law) A writ (legal order) ordering a person who is in custody or prison to be brought before a *court³* or judge so that the court can decide whether the person was legally imprisoned or not. [from the opening words of the Latin writ, 'habeas corpus' ('ad subjiciendum'), 'you should have the body (brought before the judge)']

hackney carriage /ˈhæknɪ ˌkærɪdʒ/ (transport) A term used to apply to a taxi that has been officially licensed to carry fare-paying passengers. [originally used of a carriage drawn by a 'hackney', a type of horse used in harness]

Hadrian's Wall /ˌheɪdrɪənz ˈwɔːl/ (history) An ancient wall built by order of the Roman emperor Hadrian in the 2nd century AD to defend the northern border of *England* against attacks by Celtic tribes. The wall, which is about 120 km long, crossed England from the river Tyne in the east to the Solway Firth in the west. Long sections of the wall remain today and are a popular tourist attraction. Compare *Antonine Wall*.

haggis /ˈhægɪs/ (food and drink) A traditional Scottish dish made from sheep's or calf's offal (edible internal organs), suet, oatmeal and onions, and boiled in a bag. The bag was originally made from a sheep's stomach but is now made from a synthetic substance. See also *Burns' Night*.

halfpenny /ˈheɪpnɪ/ (finance) A small bronze coin worth half a *penny* (pre-decimal or decimal, see *D-day²*). The decimal halfpenny was withdrawn from circulation in 1985.

half-term /haːʃ ˈtɜːm/ (education) A short holiday or break, often a week long, in the middle of a school *term*.

hall /hɔːl/ (**1** life and society **2, 3, 4, 5** education) **1** The name often given to *country houses* in many parts of the country, especially the *Midlands* and north of *England*. **2** The name of some *colleges¹* in a university, such as Trinity Hall, *Cambridge²*. **3** The short title of a *hall of residence*. **4** The dining room in a *college¹*. **5** An assembly room in a school.

hall of residence /ˌhɔːl əv ˈrezɪdəns/ (education) A term used in some *colleges¹* and universities for a student hostel.

Hallé (Orchestra) /ˈhæleɪ (ˌɔːkɪstrə)/, **the** (arts) A leading British symphony orchestra, founded by Charles Hallé in Manchester in 1857.

Hallowe'en /ˌhæləʊˈiːn/ (tradition) A name for 31 October, the eve of All Saints Day, when according to an old tradition girls would use certain 'magic' rites to foresee who they would marry. Today the day is usually marked by costume or fancy-dress parties, and is a popular occasion with young people and children. [from an alternative name for All Saints Day, 'All Hallows', and 'even' ('eve')]

Hampden Park /ˌhæmdən ˈpɑːk/ (sport and leisure) A *football* stadium in *Glasgow, Scotland*, where a number of international football matches are played, as well as the annual Scottish Cup Final (the equivalent of the English *Cup Final*).

Hampden roar /ˌhæmdən ˈrɔː(r)/, **the** (sport and leisure) The loud massed cheering and chanting at *Hampden Park* during *football* matches, and in particular during the Scottish Cup Final.

Hampstead /ˈhæmpstɪd/ (London) A fashionable residential district of northwest *London*, in places still keeping the character of a picturesque village, which it originally was. In the 20th century it came to be associated with left-wing intellectualism and the unorthodox life-style of some of its residents.

Hampton Court /ˌhæmptən ˈkɔːt/ (history) A great palace with gardens on the banks of the *Thames*, west of *London*, and one of the finest historical monuments in *Britain*. The palace was first built by Cardinal Wolsey in the early 16th century, and was later enlarged and improved by *Henry VIII* and a number of famous architects and sculptors. The palace gardens contain a well-known maze. [in full Hampton Court Palace, named after the village of Hampton there]

Hansard /ˈhænsɑːd/ (government) The short title of the daily publication that gives a word-for-word report of proceedings in the *House of Commons* (properly the Official Report of Parliamentary Debates). [named after Luke Hansard, who first printed the journals of the House of Commons in 1774]

happy hour /ˈhæpɪ aʊə(r)/ (daily life) A time (usually in the early evening, and not necessarily an hour) when alcoholic drinks are sold at reduced prices in a *bar¹*, *club* or other establishment.

hare and hounds /ˌheər ən ˈhaʊndz/ (sport and leisure) A children's game in which one group of players tries to find and capture the other group. The chased group ('hares') leaves a trail of some kind for the chasers ('hounds') to follow.

Harefield Hospital /ˌheəfiːld ˈhospɪtl/ (medicine) A hospital in west *London* that has specialized in heart transplant operations since the early 1980s. Compare *Papworth Hospital.* [named after district]

Harley Street /ˈhɑːlɪ striːt/ (medicine) A street in central *London* famous for its many private medical specialists and consultants.

Harris tweed /ˌhærɪs ˈtwiːd/ (clothing) The name of a type of tweed (thick woollen cloth) used for men's suits and other clothing, made on the Scottish island of Harris, Outer *Hebrides.*

Harrods /ˈhærədz/ (commerce) A fashionable *London* department store, one of the largest in Europe. The store, in *Knightsbridge*, claims to be able to supply any article and provide any service. Henry Harrod owned a small grocer's shop on the same site in the 1840s, and, in 1861, his son Charles turned it into a shop selling many different kinds of articles.

Harrogate /ˈhærəgɪt/ (geography) A fashionable resort in North Yorkshire, famous as a trade fair and *conference centre*, and for its annual International Festival of the Arts and Sciences.

Harrow (School) /ˈhærəʊ (ˌhærəʊ ˈskuːl)/ (education) A leading *public school¹* for boys, in the *Greater London borough²* of the same name. It was founded in 1571 and has 775 students.

harvest festival /ˌhɑːvɪst ˈfestəvl/ (religion) A special annual *church* service held in the autumn to give thanks for the gathering in of the harvest. On the day of the service, the church is usually decorated with fruit, vegetables, loaves of bread and other produce.

Harwell /ˈhɑːwel/ (science and technology) A short name used for the Atomic Energy Research Establishment, the chief nuclear energy research establishment of the *United Kingdom Atomic Energy Authority*, near the village of this name in Oxfordshire.

Hastings /'heɪstɪŋz/ (geography) A popular seaside resort in East Sussex, and one of the *Cinque Ports*, where a well-known annual international chess contest is held. See also *Hastings, (Battle of)*.

Hastings /'heɪstɪŋz/ (**Battle of Hastings, the**) (history) A famous battle in English history, in which William the *Conqueror* defeated the Anglo-Saxon King Harold near Hastings in 1066, thus beginning the *Norman Conquest* of *Britain*.

hat trick /'hæt trɪk/ (sport and leisure) The scoring of three goals in *football* or hockey by the same player, or the dismissing of three batsmen in *cricket* by the same bowler. [from the special hat formerly awarded a player for this achievement]

hatches, matches and dispatches /ˌhætʃɪz, ˌmætʃɪz ən dɪ'spætʃɪz/ (daily life) A semi-humorous term for the advertisements in the *personal columns* of a newspaper that announce, respectively, births, marriages and deaths.

Haymarket (Theatre) /'heɪmɑːkɪt (ˌheɪmɑːkɪt 'θɪətə(r))/, **the** (arts) A famous *London* theatre built in 1820 in the Haymarket (where *Her Majesty's Theatre* is also), and officially named the 'Theatre Royal, Haymarket'.

Hayward Gallery /ˌheɪwəd 'gæləri/, **the** (arts) An art gallery opened in 1968 on the *South Bank, London*, where special exhibitions are held. The Gallery also has open air sculpture displays. [named after Isaac Hayward, leader of the London County Council from 1947 to 1965]

H-blocks /'eɪtʃ blɒks/, **the** (law) The main prison blocks of the *Maze Prison*, near *Belfast*, which are built in the form of a letter 'H'.

Head of the River Race /ˌhed əv ðə 'rɪvə reɪs/, **the** (sport and leisure) An annual race between the eights of various rowing *clubs* held on the river *Thames* in *London* over the same course as that followed by the crews of the *Boat Race*, but in the opposite direction.

health centre /'helθ ˌsentə(r)/ (medicine) A centre for medical and administrative health welfare work, where a *group practice* is operated.

health visitor /'helθ ˌvɪzɪtə(r)/ (medicine) A medical worker who visits families needing preventive care and health education, especially those with young children and babies. She is appointed by the local health authority and works closely with *GP*s and *district nurses*.

Heart of Midlothian /ˌhɑːt əv mɪdˈləʊðɪən/ (sport and leisure)
A Scottish *football club* founded in 1875, with a stadium in
Edinburgh. [probably named after the Edinburgh prison that
also gave its name to a novel by Walter Scott]

Heart of Oak /ˌhɑːt əv ˈəʊk/ (tradition) A well-known sailors'
song and march, written in 1770 by the English actor David
Garrick (1771–79). [title of the song, which contains the lines,

Heath Robinson: *Testing Artificial Teeth*

'Heart of oak are our ships, Heart of oak are our men']

Hearts /hɑːts/ (sport and leisure) The short name of *Heart of Midlothian football club*.

Heath, Edward /'hiːθ, 'edwəd/ (people) Edward Heath (born 1916) is a prominent member of the *Conservative Party* who was *Prime Minister* from 1970 to 1974 and who negotiated *Britain*'s entry into the *EC* in 1973. As a *backbencher* in the *House of Commons*, he has not always been happy about EC policies pursued by his successors.

Heath Robinson /ˌhiːθ 'rɒbɪnsən/ (daily life) A term used to refer to a machine or contrivance that is absurdly complex for the simple task it is supposed to perform. [from William Heath Robinson (1872–1944), the cartoonist and illustrator who drew such mechanical contrivances]

heather mixture /'heðə ˌmɪkstʃə(r)/ (clothing) A woollen cloth of mixed colours speckled like heather (ie, with mixed threads of green, purple and brown).

Heathrow /ˌhiːθ 'rəʊ/ (transport) *Britain*'s largest international airport, west of *London* and linked with the capital by the Underground (see *London Underground*). It was opened in 1946 and is officially known as *London Airport*.

heavies /'hevɪz/, **the** (media) A colloquial term for the *quality papers*.

Hebrides /'hebrədiːz/, **the** (geography) A group of islands off the northwest coast of *Scotland*, divided into the Outer Hebrides and Inner Hebrides. The main islands of the Outer Hebrides are Lewis and Harris (the northern and southern parts of the same island), North Uist and South Uist. In the Inner Hebrides the largest islands are Skye, Mull, Jura and Islay. All the islands are popular with tourists seeking a remote summer holiday in *Britain*.

Hello! /hə'ləʊ/ (media) A popular weekly magazine for women, with features and gossip on celebrities and members of the *royal family*. It was first published in 1988 as an English version of the Spanish magazine 'Hola!' and has a current circulation of about 444,000.

Help the Aged /ˌhelp ðɪ 'eɪdʒɪd/ (charities) A charity that aims to provide financial and material aid for poor and disadvantaged elderly people, both in the *United Kingdom* and overseas.

hen night /'hen naɪt/ (life and society) An evening dinner party, entertainment, or 'night out' for women only. Compare *stag night*. [from 'hen' as a female bird]

Henley Regatta /ˌhenlɪ rɪ'gætə/ (sport and leisure) An

important international rowing contest (officially Henley Royal Regatta) held annually over five days in late June and early July on the river *Thames* at Henley, Oxfordshire. The Regatta was established in 1834 and by the end of the 19th century had become, as it still is, a very fashionable event.

Henry VIII /ˌhenrɪ ðɪ 'eɪtθ/ (people) The king of *England* (1491–1547) who rejected the belief that the Pope was head of the Church and had himself declared to be the supreme head of the Church in England. Today he is often more popularly remembered for his six wives. He divorced two of his wives and had two others executed.

Hepplewhite /'heplwaɪt/ (style) A style of elegant and graceful wooden furniture, with distinctive heart-shaped chair-backs, designed in the 18th century by George Hepplewhite. Compare *Chippendale* and *Sheraton*.

* **Her Majesty** /hɜː 'mædʒəstɪ/ **(HM)** (royal family) The title used when referring to the sovereign as *queen*, in full, 'Her Majesty the Queen'.

* **Her Majesty's Theatre** /hɜː ˌmædʒəstɪz 'θɪətə(r)/ (arts) A leading *London* theatre in the Haymarket. It opened in 1705 as the Queen's Theatre, was renamed the King's Theatre in 1714, and Her Majesty's Theatre, in honour of *Queen Victoria*, in 1837. Since then it has traditionally changed 'Her' to 'His' in the reign of a king (eg, during the years 1902 to 1952).

hereditary peer /hɪˌredɪtrɪ 'pɪə(r)/ see *peer¹* (life and society)

Hereford (cow) /'herɪfəd (ˌherɪfəd 'kaʊ)/ (animal world) One of the most common breeds of beef cattle, usually brown with a white head. [originally bred in Herefordshire]

Heriot-Watt University /ˌherɪət ˌwɒt juːnɪ'vɜːsətɪ/ (education) A university in *Edinburgh, Scotland,* founded in 1966. [originally the Heriot-Watt Institution and School of Arts; named after the jeweller and educational benefactor George Heriot (1563–1624) and the engineer and inventor James Watt (1736–1819)]

heritage coast /'herɪtɪdʒ kəʊst/ (geography) A stretch of undeveloped coast defined by the *Countryside Commission* in *England* and its equivalents in *Scotland* and *Wales* as deserving protection. There are currently 44 such coasts, with a total length of 937 miles (1,508 kilometres). See also *Enterprise Neptune*.

Heseltine, Michael /'hesltaɪn, 'maɪkl/ (people) Michael

---

* In the reign of a king, 'Her' in these titles changes to 'His'.

Heseltine (born 1933) is a leading member of the *Conservative Party* who has long had an ambition to become *Prime Minister*. He began his career as an *MP* in 1966, and was a junior *minister*[2] under Edward *Heath* in the 1970s. In 1983 he was appointed *Secretary of State* for Defence. He resigned from this post in 1986, however, because of a dispute about the future of the Westland Helicopter Company. In 1990 Michael Heseltine challenged Margaret *Thatcher* for the leadership of the Conservative Party. He was unsuccessful, but the voting figures showed that Mrs Thatcher was losing support and she resigned as Prime Minister. In 1992, under John *Major*, Michael Heseltine was appointed *President of the Board of Trade* and Secretary of State for Trade and Industry. Michael Heseltine has always supported *Britain*'s full involvement in the *EC*.

HGV /ˌeɪtʃ dʒiː ˈviː/ **(heavy goods vehicle)** (transport) **1** A large or heavy lorry (truck) or commercial vehicle, whose driver must possess a special driving licence. **2** The licence itself, obtained by passing a special driving test.

Hibernian /hɪˈbɜːnɪən/ **(Hibs)** (sport and leisure) A Scottish *football club* founded in 1875, with a stadium in *Edinburgh*. [from Hibernia, the Roman name for *Ireland*, as club was founded by an Irishman]

High Church /ˌhaɪ ˈtʃɜːtʃ/ (religion) A member of the *Church of England* who attaches much importance to the authority of the priesthood, the spiritual power of the sacraments, and the observance of ritual. Compare *Low Church* and *Anglo-Catholic*.

High Commissioner /ˌhaɪ kəˈmɪʃənə(r)/ (government) The senior diplomatic representative of one *Commonwealth*[1] country in another, corresponding to an ambassador.

High Court (of Justice) /ˌhaɪ ˈkɔːt (ˌhaɪ kɔːt əv ˈdʒʌstɪs)/, **the** (law) A part of the *Supreme Court* that covers all civil cases and some criminal ones. It is divided into the *Chancery*[1] Division, the *Queen's Bench Division*, and the Family Division (the latter being concerned with all jurisdiction affecting the family, such as adoption and guardianship). The High Court has 80 or so judges who are attached to a particular division within it. Each judge sits alone (without a *jury*) when first hearing a case.

high school /ˈhaɪ skuːl/ (education) A term used for some *grammar schools* for boys and in particular for many *secondary schools* for girls. (Almost all the 24 girls' *public schools*[1] operated by the Girls' Public Day School Trust have 'High School' as part of their name.)

High Street /ˈhaɪ striːt/ (daily life) The name of one of the central streets, with many shops, in a town or *city*. The High Street was originally the most important street; today it may be considerably shorter and (because of traffic restrictions) quieter than many other streets in a town. ['High' in the sense of 'main' or 'chief']

high tea /ˌhaɪ ˈtiː/ (food and drink) An early evening meal similar to a light supper, usually with a cooked dish or sandwiches, and accompanied by a pot of tea. The meal is particularly popular in the north of *England* and in *Scotland*.

higher degree /ˌhaɪə dɪˈɡriː/ (education) A more advanced degree than a *first degree*, such as an *MA*, or a doctoral degree such as a Doctor of Philosophy (PhD).

higher education /ˌhaɪər edʒʊˈkeɪʃn/ (education) Education at a university or *polytechnic*, at degree level or higher, as distinct from *further education*.

Highland fling /ˌhaɪlənd ˈflɪŋ/, **the** (sport and leisure) A kind of energetic Scottish reel (dance), typically one danced by a *highlander*[1]. The reel is danced by one person alone. [said to be named from the lively actions of the dance, when the arms are flung in the air]

Highland games /ˌhaɪlənd ˈɡeɪmz/, **the** (sport and leisure) An alternative name for a *Highland Gathering*.

Highland Gathering /ˌhaɪlənd ˈɡæðərɪŋ/ (sport and leisure) A traditional annual festival of Scottish sports and music held at a centre in the *Highlands*. The best known is the *Braemar Gathering*, first held in 1832, but other Gatherings (or Games) are also held at Aboyne, Lonach, Blackford, Alloa, Markinch, Leslie, etc, even though not all of these places are in the Highlands.

highlander /ˈhaɪləndə(r)/ (1 geography 2 defence) 1 A native of the *Highlands* of *Scotland*. 2 A soldier in a Scottish Highland Regiment, such as the Royal Highland Fusiliers or the *Gordon Highlanders*.

Highlands /ˈhaɪləndz/, **the** (geography) A mountainous region of northern *Scotland*, in particular the area north of the *Grampians*, famous for its *Gaelic* speakers.

Highlands and Islands /ˌhaɪləndz ən ˈaɪləndz/, **the** (geography) 1 The administrative region of northern *Scotland* that comprises the *Highlands* and the islands of the Inner *Hebrides*. 2 A general term for the whole of northern Scotland including the mainland Highlands and the major island groups, the Hebrides, the *Orkneys* and the *Shetlands*.

Highway Code /ˌhaɪweɪ ˈkəʊd/**, the** (transport) A government publication setting out the main rules and regulations applying to road users, whether pedestrians, riders or drivers. It was first published in 1931.

Hilton /ˈhɪltən/**, the** (London) An American-style modern multi-storey hotel in *Park Lane, London*, owned by Hilton International UK. There are also Hilton hotels elsewhere in *Britain*. [in full, Hilton International London Hotel, named after the American parent company founded by Conrad Hilton (1887–1979) in 1919]

hippie /ˈhɪpɪ/ (life and society) **1** In a general sense: an unconventionally dressed young person, especially one who rejected the accepted values and morals of society in the 1960s, and took drugs; **2** In a specific sense: a member of the group of travelling people (styling themselves the 'peace convoy') who gather annually at or near *Stonehenge* on *Midsummer Day*.

Hippodrome /ˈhɪpədrəʊm/**, the** (London) A fashionable restaurant in *Leicester Square, London*, famous for its nightly floor show and for its international stars.

* **HMG** /ˌeɪtʃ em ˈdʒiː/ **(Her Majesty's Government)** (government) An abbreviation for the official title of the government of the day.

* **HMS** /ˌeɪtʃ em ˈes/ **(Her Majesty's Ship)** (defence) The official designation of all *Royal Navy* ships, followed by the name of the ship, as in 'HMS Invincible'. The designation is also used for various naval training establishments in *Britain* itself.

* **HMSO** /ˌeɪtʃ em es ˈəʊ/ **(Her Majesty's Stationery Office)** (government) The government publishing house, founded in 1786. It publishes only material sponsored by *Parliament*, government *departments* and other official bodies. Most of its wide-ranging books and booklets are informational, and include school textbooks, guidebooks, year books and naval and military publications.

HMV /ˌeɪtʃ em ˈviː/ **(His Master's Voice)** (commerce) A well-known gramophone record company, with the name now used as a record label by EMI Records Ltd. The label shows a dog listening to an old-style gramophone.

Hockney, David /ˈhɒknɪ, ˈdeɪvɪd/ (people) David Hockney

---

* In the reign of a king, 'Her' in these titles changes to 'His'.

(born 1937) has for many years been one of the leading 'cult' artists in *Britain*, and has become well known for his imaginative and witty paintings. Many of his pictures show isolated or solitary subjects, such as a single vase of yellow tulips or a lone nude boy in a swimming pool. Hockney's own personal appearance has itself become as distinctive as his paintings, with his bleached hair, round spectacles and odd-coloured socks.

Hogmanay /'hɒgməneɪ/ (tradition) A name used in *Scotland* for *New Year's Eve* (31 December), and in particular for the traditional annual celebration held on that day. [said to be derived from an old French dialect word meaning 'a gift at the New Year']

holding company /'həʊldɪŋ ˌkʌmpənɪ/ (finance) A company having controlling shareholdings in other companies.

Holloway (Prison) /'hɒləweɪ (ˌhɒləweɪ 'prɪzn)/ (law) A large prison for women, in north *London*. [named after district where it is]

holly /'hɒlɪ/ (tradition) A tree with bright red berries and shiny, dark green, prickly leaves. In *Britain* the tree is associated with *Christmas*, and small pieces of holly are often used for decoration in houses and *churches*. A piece of holly, too, is often used to decorate the top of a *Christmas pudding*. At Christmas time pictures of holly are used on greetings cards and in advertisements. Holly is mentioned in the words of several Christmas carols. Some people believe that it is unlucky to bring holly into a house before *Christmas Eve*.

Holmes, Sherlock /'həʊmz ˌ'ʃɜːlɒk/ (1 arts 2 London) 1 The famous detective in the stories by Arthur Conan Doyle (1859–1930). 2 A popular *pub* in central *London*, containing a reconstruction of Sherlock Holmes's fictional residence in *Baker Street*.

Holy Island /'həʊlɪ ˌaɪlənd/ (geography) An island off the coast of northeast *England*, famous as one of the earliest Christian communities in England. It is also known as Lindisfarne, and has a small resident population.

Holy Loch /ˌhəʊlɪ 'lɒk/ (defence) An inlet of the river *Clyde*, *Scotland*, used as a base (since 1961) for American nuclear submarines.

Holyrood House /ˌhɒlɪruːd 'haʊs/ (royal family) A large mansion (properly, the Palace of Holyrood House) in *Edinburgh*, *Scotland*, used as a residence by members of the *royal family* when visiting Scotland. The house, which stands in a park beside a ruined abbey, was built in the early 16th century. [house was named after abbey, itself dedicated to the 'Holy Rood', or cross of Christ]

Home Counties /ˌhəʊm ˈkaʊntɪz/**, the** (geography) A general name for the *counties* surrounding *London*, especially Essex, Kent, and Surrey, and also including the former county of Middlesex (now mostly in *Greater London*).

Home Guard /ˌhəʊm ˈgɑːd/**, the** (history) A part-time army defence force recruited in the Second World War to fight a possible German invasion of *Britain*. Enlistment was at first voluntary, but later (for younger men) compulsory. Although disbanded in 1945, the Home Guard was again formed for the period 1951–6. [originally called Local Defence Volunteers; name changed to Home Guard by Winston *Churchill* in 1940]

home help /ˌhəʊm ˈhelp/ (daily life) A person appointed by a *local authority* to provide practical assistance in the home for disadvantaged people such as the sick, the disabled and the elderly.

Home Office /ˈhəʊm ˌɒfɪs/**, the** (government) The government *department* responsible for internal affairs in *Britain*, in particular the administration of law and order, immigration, community and race relations, broadcasting and the conduct of political elections.

Home Rule /ˌhəʊm ˈruːl/ (politics) The self-government of *Ireland*, unsuccessfully campaigned for by Irish nationalists from the 1870s to the 1920s, when the cause was taken up in a new form by *Sinn Féin* and the *IRA* after the creation of *Northern Ireland* and the Republic of Ireland. The Home Rule campaign might have succeeded in the early 1900s if it had not been for the First World War and the constant opposition of the *Ulster* Unionists. See *Ulster Democratic Unionist Party*, *Ulster Unionist Party*.

Home Secretary /ˌhəʊm ˈsekrətrɪ/**, the** (government) The minister responsible for the *Home Office* (in full *Secretary of State* for the Home Department).

Home, Sweet Home /ˌhəʊm swiːt ˈhəʊm/ (tradition) The title of a popular song of 1823 (by J H Payne) used to express an Englishman's traditional love of his home.

Honourable /ˈɒnərəbl/**, the (Hon, the)** (life and society) A courtesy title placed before the names of various members of the *peerage*, including the children of viscounts and barons and the younger sons of earls, for example 'The Honourable William Fraser' ('The Hon. William Fraser'). The title is also

hopscotch

used in the *House of Commons* by one *MP* when speaking of another, as 'the honourable member for Swindon' or 'my honourable friend'.

honours degree /'ɒnəz dɪˌgriː/ (education) A *first degree* at a university obtained with distinction, with the student obtaining a 'class I', 'class II' or 'class III' degree, as distinct from a *pass degree*.

Hooray Henry /ˌhuːreɪ 'henrɪ/ (life and society) A term used for a male *Sloane Ranger*, especially someone who has a loud voice or is unusually jolly. The female equivalent is sometimes known as a 'Hooray Henrietta'.

hopscotch /'hɒpskɒtʃ/ (sport and leisure) A game popular among young children. A player throws a stone or other small object into one of a number of squares chalked or scratched on the ground in a particular arrangement, and then hops to it through the other squares to pick it up. [from 'hop' and 'scotch', the latter word meaning 'trace (a line)']

hornpipe /'hɔːnpaɪp/ (sport and leisure) A lively traditional sailors' dance, performed by one person, originally to a hornpipe (an old instrument like a clarinet) but today to any solo instrument.

Horse Guards /'hɔːs gɑːdz/, **the** (**1** defence **2** London) **1** A cavalry regiment of the *Army* which, together with the *Life Guards*, forms the *Household Cavalry* (today as part of the *Blues and Royals*). **2** The building in *Whitehall[1]*, *London*, where the daily *Changing of the Guard* by the mounted guards of the Household Cavalry is a popular tourist attraction. See also *Horse Guards Parade*.

Horse Guards Parade /ˌhɔːs ˈgɑːdz pəˈreɪd/ (London) A parade-ground behind the *Horse Guards[2]* where the annual ceremony of *Trooping the Colour* takes place on the sovereign's *Official Birthday*.

Horse of the Year Show /ˌhɔːs əv ðə ˈjɪə ˈʃəʊ/, **the** (sport and leisure) An annual show-jumping contest held in October, usually at *Wembley*, *London*. The contest, which decides the leading show jumpers of the year, was first held in 1949.

hospice /ˈhɒspɪs/ (medicine) A hospital or home for the care of the terminally ill.

hot cross bun /ˌhɒt krɒs ˈbʌn/ (food and drink) A bun containing currants or candied peel, marked on top with a cross and traditionally eaten hot (toasted) with butter on *Good Friday*.

hotpot /ˈhɒtpɒt/ (food and drink) A hot dish especially popular in the north of *England*, consisting of a stew or casserole of meat (less often, fish) cooked with sliced potatoes. A common version is the Lancashire hotpot.

house /haʊs/ (education) In a school such as a *preparatory school* or *public school[1]*, a building where a group of pupils lives. Each group of pupils is seen as having a distinctive group identity especially in competitions within the school. The term 'house' is also used in some day schools for such a group of pupils.

House /haʊs/, **the** (1 government 2 finance) **1** A short name for the *House of Commons* (less often, the *House of Lords*). **2** A short name for the *Stock Exchange* in *London*.

House of Commons /ˌhaʊs əv ˈkɒmənz/, **the** (government) The lower house of the British *Parliament*, consisting of 651 elected *MP*s: 524 for *England*, 38 for *Wales*, 72 for *Scotland* and 17 for *Northern Ireland*. The main purpose of the House of Commons is to make the laws of the land by passing various *Acts (of Parliament)*, as well as to discuss current political issues. The House sits for five days each week. Each 'sitting' starts in the afternoon and may go on throughout the night. The House sits for about 168 days in the year and has a maximum term of five years, at the end of which a *general election* must be held. Compare *House of Lords*.

House of Lords /ˌhaʊs əv 'lɔːdz/, **the** (government) The upper house of the British *Parliament*, consisting of nearly 1,200 non-elected members (*Lords Spiritual* and *Lords Temporal*). Its work is largely complementary to that of the *House of Commons* and includes examining and revising *bills* from the Commons, and discussing important matters which the Commons cannot find time to debate. It also acts in a legal capacity as a final court of appeal (see *Law Lords*). The House usually sits for four days a week (on average, 150 days in the year) and has an average daily attendance of about 320 *peers*.

Household Cavalry /ˌhaʊshəʊld 'kævlrɪ/, **the** (defence) A section of the *Army*, comprising the two regiments of the *Life Guards* and the *Blues and Royals*, that among other duties attends the sovereign and carries out special ceremonial functions in *London*. See also *Horse Guards*.

Household Troops /ˌhaʊshəʊld 'truːps/, **the** (defence) A general term for the cavalry regiments of the *Army* (the *Household Cavalry*) who with the five infantry regiments of the *Guards Division* carry out special escort and guard duties for the sovereign.

housemaster /'haʊsˌmɑːstə(r)/ (education) A teacher in charge of a *house*, especially in a boys' boarding school.

housemistress /'haʊsˌmɪstrɪs/ (education) A teacher in charge of a *house*, especially in a girls' boarding school.

Houses of Parliament /ˌhaʊzɪz əv 'pɑːləmənt/, **the** (government) The buildings in *London* in which the *House of Commons* and the *House of Lords* assemble. The modern buildings stand on the site of the Royal *Palace of Westminster*[1], which was built by Edward the Confessor in the 14th century. The Palace was very badly damaged by fire in 1834 and all that could be saved was *Westminster Hall*. The present Houses of Parliament were built on the site between 1840 and 1867 from designs by Sir Charles Barry and Augustus Pugin. The House of Commons was bombed during the Second World War but was completely rebuilt by 1950.

housing association /'haʊzɪŋ əsəʊsɪˌeɪʃn/ (finance) A local organization that provides rented homes for poorer families and in particular for elderly, disabled and single people. It also shares ownership of a house with people who cannot afford to buy a house without considerable financial help.

housing benefit /'haʊzɪŋ ˌbenɪfɪt/ (finance) A state payment made to a person with a low income, whether employed or

housing estate

not, who finds it difficult to pay his or her rent or *rates*. The amount varies depending on the person's family status and actual income.

housing estate /ˈhaʊzɪŋ ɪˌsteɪt/ (daily life) A planned area of housing, either of private houses or *council houses*, usually having its own shops and other amenities.

hovercraft /ˈhɒvəkrɑːft/ (transport) A type of vehicle that crosses water on a 'cushion' of air. Hovercraft are used on some routes across the English Channel between *England* and France.

hoverport /ˈhɒvəpɔːt/ (transport) A port, such as Folkestone in Kent, from which *hovercraft* travel on a regular passenger route.

Hoverspeed /ˈhɒvəspiːd/ (transport) A passenger company operating a *hovercraft* service across the English Channel between Folkestone in *England* and Boulogne in France.

HTV /ˌeɪtʃ tiː ˈviː/ (media) One of the 15 regional television companies of the *ITC*, based in *Cardiff* and transmitting to *Wales* and western *England*. [an abbreviation of Harlech Television, so named for the company's founder, Lord Harlech (1918–85)]

Hughes, Ted /ˈhjuːz, ted/ (people) The poet Ted Hughes (born 1930) was appointed *Poet Laureate* in 1984. He is best known for his original and inventive poems on the cruelty of the animal world. The underlying theme of his writing is that civilized society has lost much of the vitality and strength of its origins.

Hume, Basil /ˈhjuːm, ˈbæzl/ (people) Basil Hume (born 1923)

Humpty Dumpty

was elected Archbishop of Westminster (see *Westminster Cathedral*), and so head of the *Roman Catholic Church* in Britain, in 1976. Cardinal Hume has become well known for his desire to reconcile opposed parties within the Church and is admired by many for not being afraid to speak out against what he regards as wrong.

Humpty Dumpty /ˌhʌmptɪ ˈdʌmptɪ/ (tradition) An egg-shaped character in a popular nursery rhyme, who also features in Lewis *Carroll*'s 'Through the Looking Glass' (1872). The name is used figuratively for a person or thing that cannot be restored or mended once overthrown, since in the nursery rhyme Humpty Dumpty 'had a great fall' and 'all the king's horses and all the king's men/Couldn't put Humpty together again'.

hundred /ˈhʌndrəd/ (history) A former division of a *county* in *England*, having its own court and supposed to contain a hundred families. Hundreds had become established administrative units by the 10th century, and existed, though with less importance, down to the 20th century. Compare *Chiltern Hundreds*.

hundreds and thousands /ˌhʌndrədz ən ˈθaʊzndz/ (food and drink) Tiny pieces of coloured sugar, used for decorating cakes and sweets.

hunt /hʌnt/ (sport and leisure) A *club* or association of men and women who hunt animals on horseback or, less frequently, on foot. The traditionally established hunts are those that hunt foxes on horseback, using packs of hounds, with the members of the hunt wearing a special uniform (often, scarlet coats, but also green, and other colours) and having a base in a particular *county* or district. Hunting is a sport followed mainly by the *gentry*, as well as by large landowners and *gentlemen farmers*, and has in recent years come increasingly under attack from movements such as the *League Against Cruel Sports*. Animals hunted, apart from the fox, are the deer, the hare, the otter and the badger. See also *blood sports, field sports, master of foxhounds*.

hunt the thimble /ˌhʌnt ðə ˈθɪmbl/ (sport and leisure) A children's game in which players in turn try to find a thimble (or other object) hidden in an unlikely place.

Hurlingham /ˈhɜːlɪŋəm/, **the** (sport and leisure) **1** The short name of the Hurlingham Polo Association, the governing body of polo in *Britain*, founded in 1886 and with its headquarters near *Cowdray Park*. [named after the Hurlingham[2], where originally formed] **2** The short name of the Hurlingham Club, *London*, formerly a *club* for polo players, but now for players of many other sports, including tennis, *squash* and croquet. [formed at Hurlingham House]

Hyde Park /ˌhaɪd ˈpɑːk/ (London) *London*'s best-known public park, extending (with neighbouring *Kensington Gardens*) to an area of 615 acres (249 hectares). It includes the *Serpentine, Speakers' Corner* and *Rotten Row*, and has become a centre for massed meetings and demonstrations. It was first open to the public in 1635, and the *Great Exhibition* was held there in 1851. [name said to derive from 'hide', a former area of land]

Hyde Park Corner /ˌhaɪd pɑːk ˈkɔːnə(r)/ (London) A road junction at the southeast corner of *Hyde Park, London*, regarded as one of the busiest and noisiest in *Britain*.

Hymns Ancient and Modern /ˌhɪmz ˌeɪnʃənt ən ˈmɒdn/ (**Hymns A and M**) (religion) A well-known collection of hymns used by the *Church of England* and first published in 1861.

INTER-CITY TRAIN

Ibrox Park /ˌaɪbrɒks ˈpɑːk/ (sport and leisure) The stadium in *Glasgow, Scotland*, of *Rangers football club*.

ICI /ˌaɪ siː ˈaɪ/ **(Imperial Chemical Industries)** (science and technology) The largest chemical concern in *Britain*, formed in 1926 from four other chemical companies. Among the group's principal products are pharmaceuticals, paints, plastics and petrochemicals.

Ideal Home Exhibition /ˌaɪdɪəl ˈhəʊm eksɪˌbɪʃn/, **the** (commerce) An annual exhibition of house interiors, furniture, and a wide range of household items, sponsored by the *Daily Mail* and held in spring at *Earls Court, London*.

Illustrated London News /ˌɪləstreɪtɪd ˌlʌndən ˈnjuːz/, **the** (media) A quality magazine published six times a year with high-class photographs illustrating topical and cultural news and events in *London* and the rest of *Britain*. Its current circulation is about 54,000.

ILR /ˌaɪ el ˈɑː(r)/ **(Independent Local Radio)** (media) The network of independent radio companies that operate under licence to the *Radio Authority*. There are currently over 100 ILR stations. Compare *IRN*.

immigration /ˌɪmɪˈɡreɪʃn/ (law) Immigration to *Britain* is controlled by special rules. Foreign citizens normally need permission to enter and remain in Britain, and some must obtain a visa first. Permission need not be obtained by British or *Commonwealth* citizens or by people from *EC* countries.

Imperial War Museum /ɪmˌpɪərɪəl ˈwɔː mjuːˌzɪəm/, **the** (defence) A military museum in *London*, founded in 1917. It illustrates all aspects of the two world wars and other military operations in which *Britain* and the *Commonwealth* have been involved since 1914.

In Britain /ˌɪn ˌbrɪtn/ (media) The monthly magazine of the *BTA*, with features for overseas readers and visitors to *Britain*, recommending things to do and places to see. The magazine, which is illustrated with high-quality colour photographs, has a current readership of around 100,000. It was first published in 1930.

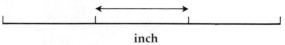

inch

inch /ɪntʃ/ (daily life) A measure of length still in common use, together with the *foot*, for a person's height and certain other regular measurements. There are twelve inches in a foot, with one inch equal to 2.54 cm.

Income Bonds /ˈɪŋkʌm bɒndz/ (finance) A government savings scheme designed for people who are able to invest a large amount as a lump sum and obtain a monthly income from it as interest without deduction of *income tax*.

income support /ˈɪŋkʌm səˌpɔːt/ (finance) A special government payment for people who do not have much money to live on, such as the unemployed, *OAP*s, single parents, people too sick to work, and those working part-time. See also *Social Fund*.

income tax /ˈɪŋkʌm ˌtæks/ (finance) The tax on a person's annual income, or on the money a person receives from investments in a year. At present the rate of tax is 20% on the first £2,500 of taxable income, 25% on income above this up to £23,700, and 40% on income higher than this. See also *Inland Revenue*, *PAYE*.

Independent /ˌɪndɪˈpendənt/**, The** (media) A daily *quality paper* with a tendency to left-wing views and with the highest proportion of *Liberal Democrats* among its readers. It is aimed at professional people, and is noted for its well-written features on arts and media subjects. It was founded in 1986 and has a current readership of about 376,000 (1987 – 292,000).

Independent on Sunday /ˌɪndɪˈpendənt ɒn ˈsʌndɪ/**, The** (media) A Sunday *quality paper* that is a sister publication to the *Independent*. It was first published in 1990 and has a current readership of about 365,000 (1990 – 362,000).

independent school /ɪndɪˈpendənt skuːl/ (education) A fee-paying school, usually a *public school*[1] or *preparatory school*, that operates outside the state system. Many such schools are long established and have gained a reputation for their high standards; however, only approximately 7% of all school children attend independent schools. See also *private school*.

industrial action /ɪnˌdʌstrɪəl 'ækʃn/ (work) A term used for a strike or an industrial protest of some kind, such as a *go-slow* or *work-to-rule*.

industrial council /ɪnˌdʌstrɪəl 'kaʊnsl/ (work) A general name for a *Whitley council*.

industrial estate /ɪn'dʌstrɪəl ɪˌsteɪt/ (work) An area of a town, usually on the outskirts, set aside for factories or the commercial premises of various firms.

Industrial Revolution /ɪnˌdʌstrɪəl revə'lu:ʃn/, **the** (history) The great economic and social change that took place in *Britain* starting in the second half of the 18th century. Agricultural and home-based trades and industries gradually gave way to factory-based industries with complex machinery. As a result, many people who had previously been employed in agriculture moved to towns and *cities*. Britain was the first country to become industrialized in this way.

infant school /'ɪnfənt sku:l/ (education) A school for very young children from the age of five, when compulsory education begins, to seven. See also *first school*.

inheritance tax /ɪn'herɪtəns tæks/ (finance) A special tax charged on amounts higher than £150,000 left in a will. No tax is charged on amounts lower than this.

Inland Revenue /ˌɪnlənd 'revənju:/, **the** (finance) The government *department* (in full, Board of Inland Revenue) that administers the tax laws and is responsible for collecting *income tax* from employees. See also *PAYE*.

in-laws /'ɪn lɔ:z/, **the** (life and society) A colloquial term for the close relatives of a person's wife or husband. [short for 'mother-in-law', 'brother-in-law', etc]

inn /ɪn/ (daily life) An alternative term for a *pub* or (usually small) hotel, often occurring in the name of the house, as the 'New Inn', the 'Market Inn'. The term suggests an old or historic building with 'character'.

inn sign /'ɪn saɪn/ (daily life) A painted signboard outside a *pub* illustrating its name.

inner city /ˌɪnə 'sɪtɪ/ (geography) The older central area of certain large towns and *cities*, especially ones with high unemployment, a rootless, often immigrant population, and decaying or derelict houses and buildings. The economic decline in such places occurred when industry moved out of city centres from the 1970s. In recent years the government has devoted much attention to the improvement ('urban regeneration') of inner cities, mainly by reconstruction programmes. Several inner cities were designated as appropriate sites for a *National Garden Festival*. From the early 1980s many inner cities have been areas of physical conflict between the police and local residents. See also *City Action Team, London Docklands, Task Force, Urban Development Corporation, Urban Programme*.

Inner Temple /ˌɪnə ˈtempl/, **the** (law) The oldest and best known of the *Inns of Court*. See also *Temple[1]*.

Inns of Court /ˌɪnz əv ˈkɔːt/, **the** (law) The four societies, and their buildings, to one or other of which all *barristers* and judges belong. The societies (*Lincoln's Inn, Inner Temple, Middle Temple, Gray's Inn*) are in central *London* and have been in existence at least since the 14th century. Today their buildings are largely used as offices (*chambers[1]*) where about 2,000 barristers practise, although there are also flats there where people live.

INR /ˌaɪ en ˈɑːr/ (**independent national radio**) (media) The independent radio companies that broadcast nationwide under licence to the *Radio Authority*. The first INR station was *Classic FM*. Others are planned.

Institute of Directors /ˌɪnstɪtjuːt əv dɪˈrektəz/, **the** (work) One of the largest organizations for businessmen, founded in 1903. Its members are mainly company directors, *stockbrokers* and lawyers.

insurance broker /ɪnˈʃɔːrəns brəʊkə(r)/ (finance) An agent who arranges various types of insurance for other people and who charges commission for doing this.

InterCity /ˌɪntəˈsɪti / (transport) One of the five business sectors of *BR*, operating fast passenger trains between major towns and *cities* in *Britain*. About half the trains on such routes are the 'InterCity 125' expresses, so called as they can travel at 125 miles an hour (201 km an hour). They run from *London* to the west of *England* and *Wales*, to the East *Midlands*, and on routes through the West Midlands linking the south of the country with the north, including *Scotland*.

intermediate area /ˌɪntəˈmiːdiət ˌeəriə/ (work) An *assisted area* where the government actively encourages industrial growth and investment, although less urgently than in a *development area*. The main intermediate areas are northwest and southwest *Scotland*, northeast and north central *England*, the region round Birmingham, south *Wales*, and parts of the *West Country*, especially north and east *Cornwall* and round Plymouth in Devon.

internment /ɪn'tɜ:nmənt/ (law) The imprisonment of suspected terrorists in *Northern Ireland* as a means of controlling the activities of the *IRA*. Internment was in force in the early 1970s, but was abandoned in 1975. In recent years, however, the government has considered the reintroduction of internment to counter the increasing acts of terrorism and violence carried out by the IRA.

invalidity benefit /ˌɪnvə'lɪdətɪ ˌbenɪfɪt/ (finance) The state payment made to people who are unable to work after more than 28 weeks of sickness. A person who is sick for less than 28 weeks can claim *sickness benefit* and is entitled to *statutory sick pay*.

Inverness /ˌɪnvə'nes/ (geography) A town in northern *Scotland* that is a popular tourist centre and 'capital' of the *Highlands*.

investment trust /ɪn'vestmənt trʌst/ (finance) A company that invests its shareholders' money, and pays them a dividend out of its income and profits. See also *PEP*.

Iona /aɪ'əʊnə/ (geography) A small, historic island off the west coast of *Scotland*, close to Mull in the *Hebrides*. It has many important early Christian monuments, and several Scottish, Irish and Norwegian kings of this period are buried here. The island is popular with tourists in the summer.

IOU /ˌaɪ əʊ 'ju:/ (finance) A note of a debt given by a borrower to a person who has lent him a sum of money. [pronunciation of 'I owe you']

IRA /ˌaɪ ɑ:r 'eɪ/, **the (Irish Republican Army, the)** (politics) A militant organization of Irish nationalists aiming to establish a united *Ireland* by campaigns of violence and terror. They have been increasingly active in *Britain* since the *Troubles* began in 1968, and have carried out destructive bomb attacks in *London* and other cities. In *Northern Ireland* their victims include 27 prison officers, killed between 1974 and 1989 in revenge for the alleged mistreatment of IRA prisoners in the *Maze (Prison)*. In recent years IRA members have themselves been the victims of attacks by such Protestant groups as the *Ulster Defence Association* and *Ulster Volunteer Force*.

Ireland /'aɪələnd/ (geography) The most westerly country of the *British Isles*, separated from mainland *Britain* by St George's Channel and the Irish Sea. The name Ireland can be used to apply to the island as a geographical entity, but is normally used to mean the Republic of Ireland, as distinct from *Northern Ireland*, which is part of the *United Kingdom*.

Irish coffee /ˌaɪərɪʃ ˈkɒfɪ/ (food and drink) An alcoholic drink consisting of a mixture of Irish *whiskey* with coffee, sugar and cream. Compare *Gaelic coffee*.

Irish Guards /ˌaɪərɪʃ ˈgɑːdz/, **the** (defence) The fourth oldest regiment of the *Guards Division* of the *Army* formed in 1900.

Irish Republican Army /ˌaɪərɪʃ rɪˌpʌblɪkən ˈɑːmɪ/ see *IRA* (politics)

Irish setter /ˌaɪərɪʃ ˈsetə(r)/ (animal world) A breed of working dog with smooth, silky coat, always chestnut in colour. Compare *English setter*.

Irish stew /ˌaɪərɪʃ ˈstjuː/ (food and drink) A stew of mutton (less often, lamb or beef), onions and potatoes. [said to have been originally a meatless stew, as the only kind that Irish peasants could afford]

IRN /ˌaɪ ɑːr ˈen/ **(Independent Radio News)** (media) A national and international news service for all *ILR* stations provided by *LNR*.

Isis /ˈaɪsɪs/ (geography) The name of the river *Thames* as it flows through *Oxford*[1]. Compare *Granta*.

Isle of Man /ˌaɪl əv ˈmæn/, **the** (geography) An island of the *British Isles* between *England* and *Northern Ireland*, in the Irish Sea. The Isle of Man is not part of the *United Kingdom*, but is a self-governing crown dependency, with the monarch represented by a lieutenant-governor. It thus has its own parliament (the *Tynwald*), and its own system of local administration, with its own law courts. It is popular with tourists from *Britain* and some Britons go there to live, partly because of its low tax rate. It is famous for the annual *TT* motorcycle races held there. See also *Manx*, and compare *Channel Islands*.

Isle of Wight /ˌaɪl əv ˈwaɪt/, **the** (geography) An island off the south coast of *England*, and an English *county* in its own right. It is popular with tourists and has a sunny climate and mostly mild weather. It is well known for its many seaside resorts, at one of which *Cowes Week* is held.

I-spy /ˌaɪ ˈspaɪ/ (sport and leisure) A children's guessing game. One player names the first letter of an object he can see (with the rhyming formula, 'I spy, with my little eye, something beginning with P'), and the others have to guess what the object is.

i t a /ˌaɪ tiː ˈeɪ/, **the (Initial Teaching Alphabet, the)**

(language) A special alphabet of 44 characters, sometimes used for teaching children to read. Each character corresponds to a sound in the English language.

ITC /ˌaɪ tiː ˈsiː/ **, the (Independent Television Commission, the)** (media) The body set up in 1991 to license and regulate all *ITV* broadcasting in *Britain*. Compare *Radio Authority*.

ITN /ˌaɪ tiː ˈen/ **(Independent Television News)** (media) A company based in *London* that provides a common news service for the *ITV* stations licensed by the *ITC*.

It's a Long Way to Tipperary /ɪts ə ˌlɒŋ weɪ tə tɪpəˈreəri/ (tradition) A popular marching song, originally composed in 1912, and sung by troops embarking for France in the First World War. [referring to the girl left behind in Tipperary, *Ireland*]

ITV /ˌaɪ tiː ˈviː/ **(Independent Television)** (media) A general term for the television programmes transmitted by the regional and *breakfast television* companies that are licensed by the *ITC*.

Jack Russell (terrier) /ˌdʒæk ˈrʌsl (ˌdʒæk ˌrʌsl ˈterɪə(r))/ (animal world) One of a number of breeds of small terrier. The original breed, introduced by John Russell, a 19th-century clergyman, is now extinct. [from Jack, a familiar form of the name John]

Jack the Giant-Killer /ˌdʒæk ðə ˈdʒaɪənt ˌkɪlə(r)/ (tradition) The legendary Cornish hero of a tale of *King Arthur*. He had a cap that made him invisible, seven-league boots and a magic sword, and went round the country killing troublesome giants.

Jack the Ripper /ˌdʒæk ðə ˈrɪpə(r)/ (history) The nickname given to the undiscovered murderer of at least seven women in *London* in 1888. See also *Yorkshire Ripper*. ['ripper' meaning 'cutter': all the victims had their throats cut]

Jack-in-the-box /ˈdʒæk ɪn ðə ˌbɒks/ (tradition) A toy consisting of a box containing a doll that springs out when the box is opened.

Jacobean /ˌdʒækəˈbɪən/ (style) **1** A furniture style of the 17th century, characterized by the use of dark oak with rich carving, particularly in wooden armchairs with high backs and straight seats and arms. **2** An architectural style of the same period, characterized by its straight lines and symmetry and similar to the *Elizabethan* style but with curved arches. **3** A literary period when many famous writers were active, especially dramatists such as *Shakespeare* and poets such as John Donne. The *King James Bible* was published during the period. [found in the reign of James I (1603–25) whose Latin name was 'Jacobus']

Jaguar /ˈdʒægjʊə(r)/ (transport) An expensive make of car first produced in the 1930s, and colloquially known as a 'Jag'.

jamboree /ˌdʒæmbə'riː/ (sport and leisure) **1** A large rally of *Scouts* or *Girl Guides*. **2** A slightly dated term for a party or large gathering.

Jazz FM /ˌdʒæz ef 'em/ (media) An *ILR* station in *London* that broadcasts mainly soul and blues music in the daytime, but jazz at night. It opened in 1990. ['FM' for 'frequency modulation' as an enhanced method of radio transmission]

jelly /'dʒelɪ/ (food and drink) A dessert or *pudding*² popular with young children. It is soft and transparent, and set in gelatine, and has a particular fruit flavour, such as orange or blackcurrant. It is eaten cold and usually covered with a sweet sauce such as *custard* or ice-cream.

jersey /'dʒɜːzɪ/ (clothing) **1** A warm knitted long-sleeved garment, originally woollen but now often of man-made fibre, for the upper part of the body. **2** A fine machine-knitted fabric (of wool, cotton, nylon, etc) used for clothing. [from the sweaters traditionally worn by the fishermen of Jersey, *Channel Islands*; compare *guernsey*]

Jersey (cow) /'dʒɜːzɪ (ˌdʒɜːzɪ 'kaʊ)/ (animal world) A breed of dairy cow with dark red or light brown colouring, famous for its rich milk. [originally bred in Jersey, *Channel Islands*]

Jerusalem /dʒə'ruːsələm/ (tradition) The title of a hymn with words by William Blake (1757–1827) traditionally sung at the end of a meeting by members of the *WI*. [from the reference in the hymn to building 'Jerusalem in England's green and pleasant land']

Jerusalem Bible /dʒəˌruːsələm 'baɪbl/**, the** (religion) A translation of the Bible into modern English by Roman Catholic scholars, first published in 1966. [translated in Jerusalem]

Jiffybag /'dʒɪfɪ ˌbæg/ (daily life) The trade name of a type of padded envelope used for sending books and other articles through the post. [from 'jiffy', a colloquial term for 'moment', 'instant': the envelopes are designed to pack articles 'in a jiffy']

Jobcentre /'dʒɒbˌsentə(r)/ (work) A local government office in a town where notices of job vacancies are on display and where a person wanting advice about a job can consult an employment adviser.

Jobclub /'dʒɒbklʌb/ (work) A local government centre for the unemployed, where people are given training and advice in applying for a job and provided with free facilities such as stationery, stamps, telephones and typewriters. Many Jobclubs are in *Jobcentres*.

jobs for the boys /ˌdʒɒbz fə ðə ˈbɔɪz/ (work) A term used to describe jobs or posts given to a person's close friends or associates.

Jock /dʒɒk/ (tradition) A colloquial name for a Scotsman, especially a soldier in the *Scots Guards*. [Scottish form of 'Jack', itself a general name for a man]

Jockey Club /ˈdʒɒkɪ ˌklʌb/, **the** (sport and leisure) The governing body of horse-racing, founded in the 1750s.

jodhpurs /ˈdʒɒdpəz/ (clothing) A type of riding breeches worn by men and women, loose-fitting round the hips and tight-fitting from the thighs down to the ankles.

Jodrell Bank /ˌdʒɒdrəl ˈbæŋk/ (science and technology) The astronomical laboratory near Macclesfield, Cheshire, that is officially called the Nuffield Radio Astronomy Laboratories of Manchester University. It is famous for its giant radio telescope, which was first used in 1957. The Observatory itself was founded in 1947. [local name for land on which the laboratory was built]

John Bull /ˌdʒɒn ˈbʊl/ (tradition) A personification of *England* or the English, originally represented (in a political satire of 1712 by John Arbuthnot) as a bluff, kind-hearted, bull-headed farmer.

John, Elton /ˈdʒɒn, ˈeltən/ (people) Elton John (born 1947), whose original name was Reginald Dwight, is one of the best-known pop musicians, and has gained international status for his songwriting and piano-playing and singing. He originally gained fame through his lively performances and outrageous costumes, including outsized spectacles, but in recent times has adopted a more conventional image.

John o'Groats /ˌdʒɒn əˈɡrəʊts/ (geography) A village in the extreme northeast of the Scottish mainland, traditionally regarded as the northernmost point of mainland *Britain* (compare *Land's End*). [said to be named after a Dutchman, Jan de Groot, who built a house there in the late 15th century]

Joneses /ˈdʒəʊnzɪz/, **the** (life and society) A term used to refer to one's neighbours in the phrase, 'to keep up with the Joneses', meaning 'to be (seen to be) socially and materially equal to one's neighbours'. [Jones is one of the most common British surnames; the phrase originated in an American comic strip cartoon before the First World War]

Jorvik Viking Centre /ˌjɔːvɪk ˈvaɪkɪŋ ˌsentə(r)/, **the** (history) A special archaeological and historical museum opened at York in 1984 to illustrate the city's Viking heritage. York was captured by the Vikings in the 9th century and became the capital of their British kingdom of Jorvik. [name is early form of modern 'York']

JP /ˌdʒeɪ 'piː/ **(Justice of the Peace)** (law) An unpaid *magistrate* appointed by the *Lord Chancellor* to 'keep the peace' in a particular area, or deal with minor criminal offences (without a *jury*) in a court of law.

jugged hare /ˌdʒʌgd 'heə(r)/ (food and drink) A stew of hare cooked in an earthenware pot or casserole, usually with wine and seasoning, and served with red currant sauce. [special use of 'jug']

juggernaut /'dʒʌgənɔːt/ (transport) A word for any large, heavy lorry or truck, especially one driven along narrow roads or through a town and threatening other road users or local residents. [from the Hindi name, meaning 'lord of the world', of the god Vishnu, whose idol was pulled through the town of Puri, India, on a gigantic chariot, with worshippers throwing themselves under the chariot's wheels as a form of self-sacrifice]

jumble sale /'dʒʌmbl ˌseɪl/ (daily life) A sale of varied, cheap, secondhand goods or home-made wares, with the profit usually going to a charity.

jury /'dʒʊərɪ/ (law) A group of twelve people sworn to deliver a verdict ('guilty' or 'not guilty') according to the evidence put before them in a criminal case in a *court³* of law. Normally, their verdict is a unanimous one; but it may also be a majority verdict, provided that there are not more than two people who disagree. If agreement cannot be reached, there must be a retrial.

Just Seventeen /'dʒʌst ˌsevn'tiːn/ (media) A weekly magazine for teenage girls, with a wide range of features and stories and a popular 'problem page' of readers' letters. It was first published in 1983 and has a current circulation of about 205,000.

KEW GARDENS

Kelly's (Directories) /ˈkelɪz (ˌkelɪz daɪˈrektərɪz)/ (media) A series of *county* and town directories of *England* giving commercial and private addresses, details of local authorities and postal information. They were first published in 1799.

Kempton Park /ˌkemptən ˈpɑːk/ (sport and leisure) A race course in Surrey near Sunbury, southwest *London*. [named after park there]

Kennel Club /ˈkenl ˌklʌb/, **the** (animal world) The leading organization for dog breeders and showers, founded in 1873. Its headquarters are in *London*.

Kensington /ˈkenzɪŋtən/ (London) A fashionable district of southwest central *London*, famous for its high-class shops and stores, its luxury homes and its foreign embassies.

Kensington Gardens /ˌkenzɪŋtən ˈgɑːdnz/ (London) A park extending to the west of *Hyde Park*, and originally the private gardens of *Kensington Palace*. The Gardens are famous for the *Round Pond*, and for the statue of *Peter Pan*[3].

Kensington Palace /ˌkenzɪŋtən ˈpælɪs/ (London) A royal palace in *Kensington, London*, originally known as Nottingham House (as the home of the Earl of Nottingham) but bought in 1689 by King William III and from then until 1760 the main private residence of the sovereign. *Queen Victoria* was born there in 1819, and Queen Mary, wife of George V, in 1867. Today part of the building is still occupied by relations of the *royal family* and certain aristocratic pensioners. The *London Museum* was there until 1976. See *Museum of London*.

Kentishman /ˌkentɪʃmən/ (geography) A traditional name for a native of west Kent (strictly, one born west of the river Medway). Compare *Man of Kent*.

Kenwood /ˈkenwʊd/ (London) A fine mansion house, open to the public, in *Hampstead*, northwest *London*. The house is

famous for its art collection and for its park, in which open air
concerts are held in the summer.

Kew Gardens /ˌkjuː ˈgɑːdnz/ (London) The name usually used
for the Royal Botanical Gardens which are beside the river
Thames at Kew in west *London*. The Gardens are mainly a
centre for botanical research, but are open to the public and
are famous for their hothouses, landscaped park, lake and
water garden and their interesting buildings.

Kidderminster (carpet) /ˈkɪdəmɪnstə(r) (ˌkɪdəmɪnstə ˈkɑːpɪt)/
(style) A type of reversible carpet made from wool fibres that
are dyed before they are spun into yarn. [as originally
manufactured at Kidderminster, in the county of Hereford
and Worcester]

kilt

kilt /kɪlt/ (clothing) Part of the traditional dress of a
Scotsman: a heavy pleated woollen skirt, usually of *tartan*[1], in
front of which is worn a *sporran*. The kilt is part of the
uniform of a *highlander*[2].

kindergarten /ˈkɪndəgɑːtn/ (education) An alternative term for
a *nursery school*, especially a private one.

king /kɪŋ/ (royal family) The title of a male sovereign. The last
king of the *United Kingdom* was George VI (reigned 1936–52).
Compare *queen*.

King Arthur /ˌkɪŋ ˈɑːθə(r)/ (people) King Arthur is a half-legendary, half-historical king of *Britain* and the hero of several tales of medieval romance, the so-called 'Arthurian cycle' with the famous *Knights of the Round Table* and the magician Merlin. The historical King Arthur may have been a Briton who fought against the invading Anglo-Saxons in the 5th century. His 'kingdom' is traditionally set in the *West Country*, with his 'capital' in the Somerset town of Glastonbury. Stories about King Arthur and his knights have been constantly told for many centuries. The name of King Arthur is still preserved in popular affection as that of a national hero and king.

King Charles spaniel /ˌkɪŋ tʃɑːlz ˈspænjəl/ (animal world) One of four breeds of toy spaniel (King Charles, Tricolour, Ruby, Blenheim). The King Charles has a black coat with bright tan markings. [the breed was popularized by King Charles II]

King James Bible /ˌkɪŋ dʒeɪmz ˈbaɪbl/**, the** (religion) An alternative name for the *Authorized Version* of the Bible, whose translation was authorized by King James I.

King's College Hospital /ˌkɪŋz ˌkɒlɪdʒ ˈhɒspɪtl/ (medicine) A teaching hospital in south *London* that was originally part of King's *College[1]*, which itself is part of *London University*.

King's Cross /ˌkɪŋz ˈkrɒs/ (transport) **1** A main line railway station and terminus in north central *London*, from which trains leave for northern *England* and *Scotland*. **2** An Underground station here. [named after a nearby crossroads where a statue of King George IV stood from 1833 to 1848]

King's School /ˌkɪŋz ˈskuːl/ (education) The name of certain *public schools[1]*, especially former *cathedral schools* that were reorganized by King *Henry VIII* during the Reformation. Some of the schools are still in *cathedral cities*, including those of *Canterbury*, Chester, and Worcester.

kipper /ˈkɪpə(r)/ (food and drink) A type of fish that has been specially prepared as a popular dish. The fish, usually a herring, is first cleaned and split, then salted and dried in smoke before being cooked. Kippers are eaten for either breakfast or supper.

kirk /kɜːk/**, the** (religion) **1** A word sometimes used for a Scottish *church*, especially one belonging to the *Church of Scotland*. **2** A colloquial term sometimes used for the Church of Scotland itself, especially by people who do not belong to it.

Kiss 100 FM /ˌkɪs wʌn ˈhʌndrəd ef ˌem/ (media) An *ILR* station based in *London* that broadcasts non-stop dance music of all

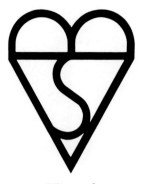

Kitemark

types. It officially opened in 1990 but had already operated as an illegal 'pirate' before this. ['kiss' for a dancing couple; '100 FM' for the station's frequency]

Kitemark /ˈkaɪtmɑːk/ (daily life) An official mark, representing a stylized toy kite, on products that conform to the standards set by the *BSI*. [mark is formed as monogram of letters BSI enclosed in a triangle]

knees-up /ˈniːz ʌp/ (daily life) A colloquial term for a (lively) party or gathering. [from the opening words of the popular song of the 1930s, 'Knees up, Mother Brown!']

Knights of the Round Table /ˌnaɪts əv ðə ˌraʊnd ˈteɪbl/, **the** (tradition) The legendary group of knights, 150 in number, created by *King Arthur*. Among the best known are Sir Lancelot, Sir Galahad, Sir Gawain and Sir Tristram. See also *Round Table*.

Knightsbridge /ˈnaɪtsbrɪdʒ/ (London) A fashionable district in *London*'s *West End*, well known for its high-class shops and in particular for its jewellers' shops and antique shops.

Labour Party /'leɪbə ˌpɑːtɪ/, **the** (politics) One of the two largest political parties in *Britain* (together with the *Conservative Party*). It claims to represent the interests of the *working class* (ie, labour) as against the interests of the employers (who represent capital). It grew up at the end of the 19th century, first taking the name Labour Party in 1906. It draws most of its support from highly urban and industrialized areas, particularly in the *Midlands* and *North* (*Country*), and, as well as being the main party for working class people, it is also supported by a significant number of *middle class* people, especially intellectuals. Its policies were formerly closely linked with those of the trade union movement (see *TUC*). It has not been in power, however, since 1979.

Ladies' Day /'leɪdɪz ˌdeɪ/ (sport and leisure) The second day of *Royal Ascot*, when ladies wear their finest fashions and show off their most original hats.

lady /'leɪdɪ/ (life and society) **1** A general term used to refer to any woman, and now much more acceptable than 'woman' which many people think is less polite. 'Lady' is often used with another word to describe a particular job, for example, *dinner lady* and *lollipop lady*. **2** A woman regarded as possessing the best British characteristics, in particular culture, courtesy and consideration for the needs of others. Compare *gentleman*[2]. **3** (Lady) A title of honour borne by various classes of women of the *peerage*. **4** A woman who comes from an *upper class* or aristocratic family, whether officially having the title 'Lady' or not.

Lady Chapel /'leɪdɪ ˌtʃæpl/ (religion) In most cathedrals and some large *churches*, a *chapel[1]* dedicated to the Virgin Mary, usually situated behind the high altar.

Lady Day /'leɪdɪ ˌdeɪ/ (religion) 25 March, the day of the feast of the Annunciation of the Virgin Mary, celebrated in many *Anglican* and all *Roman Catholic Churches* with a special service. It is not a *bank holiday*.

lady-in-waiting /ˌleɪdɪ ɪn 'weɪtɪŋ/ (royal family) A woman, often a member of the *gentry*, appointed to be a personal attendant to the sovereign or to some other member of the *royal family*.

lager lout /'lɑːgə laʊt/ (life and society) A colloquial term for a young person who, under the influence of drink, engages in fights and causes destruction to property. In the 1980s the term came to be used particularly for rowdy spectators at a football match, or people travelling to one.

laird /leəd/ (life and society) The title of a landowner in *Scotland*. [form of 'lord']

Lake District /'leɪk ˌdɪstrɪkt/**, the** (geography) A picturesque district of northwest *England* in Cumbria, popular with tourists and famous for its lakes and mountain peaks. It is a *national park*.

Lake Poets /ˌleɪk 'pəʊɪts/**, the** (arts) The name used for the poets William Wordsworth, Samuel Taylor Coleridge and Robert Southey, who lived in the *Lake District* in the 19th century and drew inspiration for much of their poetry from the scenery there.

Lake School /'leɪk skuːl/**, the** (arts) A collective term for the *Lake Poets*.

Lambeth Conference /ˌlæmbəθ 'kɒnfərəns/**, the** (religion) A conference of bishops of the *Church of England* held every ten years (since 1867) at *Lambeth Palace, London*.

Lambeth Palace /ˌlæmbəθ 'pælɪs/ (religion) The *London* residence of the *Archbishop of Canterbury*, in the district of Lambeth, south of the *Thames*.

Lambeth walk /ˌlæmbəθ 'wɔːk/**, the** (tradition) A popular *cockney[2]* dance, traditionally performed on a street with all the dancers in line. It was specially popular in the 1930s. It is also the name of a song. [named after Lambeth Walk, a street in Lambeth, south *London*]

Lancashire (cheese) /'læŋkəʃə(r) (ˌlæŋkəʃə 'tʃiːz)/ (food and drink) A type of crumbly, white cheese usually with a mild and creamy flavour. [originally from Lancashire]

Lancaster House /ˌlæŋkəstə 'haʊs/ (government) A grand

house in central *London* used mainly for government conferences. It was built in 1825 for the Duke of York (as York House) but was bought in 1912 by Sir William Lever (later Lord Leverhulme) who changed its name to that of the county where he grew up and presented it to the nation. The *London Museum* was housed in it until 1946.

Lancet /'lɑːnsɪt/, **The** (medicine) A weekly journal for doctors and members of the medical profession. It was first published in 1823 and its current circulation is about 27,000.

Land of Hope and Glory /ˌlænd əv ˌhəʊp ən 'glɔːrɪ/ (tradition) A popular patriotic song, originally glorifying the *British Empire* when first sung in 1902 (words by A C Benson (1862–1925), music by Edward *Elgar* (1857–1934)), but still sung on special occasions, and traditionally performed at the *Last Night of the Proms*.

Land of my Fathers /ˌlænd əv maɪ 'fɑːðəz/ (tradition) The (unofficial) national anthem of the Welsh, first published in 1860. [Welsh, 'Hen Wlad fy Nhadau']

landlady /'lændleɪdɪ/ (daily life) A woman who owns or runs a boarding house or lodgings, or who rents out a *bedsit(ter)*.

Land's End /ˌlændz 'end/ (geography) The extreme southwest point of *England*, in *Cornwall*, and a popular tourist attraction. The total length of *Britain* is traditionally expressed as 'from Land's End to *John o'Groats'*, a distance of 603 miles (970.4 km) in a straight line, or 900 miles (1448.4 km) by road.

landslide (victory) /'lændslaɪd (ˌlændslaɪd 'vɪktərɪ)/ (politics) In an election, especially a *general election*, either a massive change of votes from one party to another, or a considerably increased majority for a party already in power.

lardy cake /'lɑːdɪ keɪk/ (food and drink) A rich, sweet cake or loaf made of bread dough, with lard, dried fruit and other ingredients. The cake is traditionally found in the south of *England*.

Larkin, Philip /'lɑːkɪn, 'fɪlɪp/ (people) Philip Larkin (1922–85) was a poet and novelist who gained a keen 'cult' following for his verse, in which he skilfully combined everyday colloquial speech with distinctively poetic language and metre. Much of his output, which was not large, had death and the brevity of life as its overall theme. Probably his best-known collection of poems was 'High Windows' (1974). His considerable popularity, especially among young people, was doubtless due to the fact that he could express what many people feel but are unable to put into words.

Last Night of the Proms /ˌlɑːst ˌnaɪt əv ðə ˈprɒmz/, **the**
(arts) The final performance of the annual *Promenade
Concerts*, when the audience is traditionally very lively (eg,
waving flags and banners, joining in the chorus of the songs)
and when favourite musical compositions are usually
performed, among them a version of the *hornpipe* and the
accompanied song *Land of Hope and Glory*. At the end of the
performance, the conductor usually makes a speech to the
promenaders.

latchkey child /ˈlætʃkiː tʃaɪld/ (life and society) A child who
returns from school to let himself in with his own key to an
empty house or flat, since his parents are both out at work.

Law Lords /ˈlɔː lɔːdz/, **the** (law) *Peers* in the *House of Lords*
who sit as the highest *court*[3] of appeal in *England*. They
include the *Lord Chancellor* and any peers who have held
high judicial office or have themselves been Lord Chancellor.
See *peer*[3].

Law Society /ˈlɔː səˌsaɪətɪ/, **the** (law) The professional body,
founded in 1825, that registers *solicitors* and investigates
complaints about the conduct of any solicitor.

Laxton's Superb /ˌlækstənz suːˈpɜːb/ (food and drink) A
variety of late eating apple with large, red-skinned fruit.
[after the firm of Laxton Brothers, who first bred it in the
1920s]

lay reader /ˈleɪ ˌriːdə(r)/ (religion) A person who, although not
a member of the clergy, has been authorized to conduct
certain religious services in a *church*.

L-driver /ˈel ˌdraɪvə(r)/ (transport) A person who is learning to
drive a road vehicle such as a car or motor-cycle. See also *L-
plates*. ['L' for 'learner']

LEA /ˌel iː ˈeɪ/ **(local education authority)** (education) The
local government body that is responsible for the state
schools in a district, as well as *further education*, and that
engages teachers, maintains school buildings and supplies
school equipment and materials.

Leader of the House /ˌliːdər əv ðə ˈhaʊs/, **the** (government)
1 In the *House of Commons*, an *MP* chosen from the political
party with the highest number of seats. He is given the
responsibility of planning and supervising the government's
legislative programme and of arranging the business of the
House. In particular, he advises when any difficulty arises. It
is not an official government post so he receives no special
salary. **2** In the *House of Lords*, the chief spokesman for the

government, with functions similar to those of the Leader of the House of Commons.

Leader of the Opposition /ˌliːdər əv ði ɒpəˈzɪʃn/, **the** (government) The leader of the main opposing party in the *House of Commons* who, if his party wins the next *general election*, will become *Prime Minister*. See also *Shadow Cabinet*.

League Against Cruel Sports /ˌliːg əˌgenst ˌkrʊəl ˈspɔːts/, **the** (sport and leisure) An organization actively campaigning for the abolition of all *blood sports*. The group was founded in 1924 and in recent years has become increasingly militant, with a current membership of about 20,000.

leap year /ˈliːp jɪə(r)/ (tradition) A calendar year that has 366 days instead of the usual 365 days. This happens every fourth year. According to popular tradition, a woman has the right to ask a man to marry her (instead of the other way round, which is more usual) on the 'extra' day, 29 February.

leek /liːk/ (tradition) The vegetable that is the national emblem of *Wales*. See *daffodil*.

legal aid /ˌliːgl ˈeɪd/ (law) Financial help for people who cannot afford the full cost of legal proceedings, such as the services of a *solicitor*.

Leicester Square /ˌlestə ˈskweə(r)/ (London) A square in central *London* where, round a public garden, there are several cinemas, theatres and restaurants. [from the former residence there of the Earl of Leicester in the 17th century]

leisure centre /ˈleʒə ˌsentə/ (sport and leisure) A building with various recreational facilities, such as a sports hall, swimming pool, rooms for meetings, cafés, library and the like. Most leisure centres are at their busiest in the evenings and at the *weekend*, when people are not at work. They are also popular with schoolchildren and students in holiday periods.

Lent /lent/ (religion) The most solemn period of the Christian year. It lasts for 40 days from *Ash Wednesday* to the day before *Easter*, with its climax in Holy Week (the week before Easter) which includes *Palm Sunday, Maundy Thursday* and *Good Friday*. Traditionally, people did not eat meat or other rich food during Lent. Today, very few Christians follow the tradition strictly, preferring to make a smaller sacrifice, such as not eating sweets, or giving up some minor luxury.

Lib Dems /lɪb ˈdemz/, **the** (politics) A short colloquial name for the *Liberal Democrats*.

Liberal Democrats /ˌlɪbərəl ˈdeməkræts/, **the** (politics) The third major political party in *Britain* after the *Conservative Party* and *Labour Party*. It is the youngest of the three, and has its origins in the *SDP*, founded in 1981 by four right-wing members of the Labour Party. The SDP immediately formed an alliance with the *Liberal Party*, merged with it in 1988, and in 1989 adopted its present name. The party's main aim is to offer a 'realistic' alternative to the two main parties. It has gained increasing public support in recent years, and has won a number of *by-elections*. Its leader is Paddy *Ashdown*.

Liberal Party /'lɪbərəl ˌpɑːtɪ/, **the** (politics) The former third major party in *Britain*, after the *Conservative Party* and *Labour Party*. It arose in the 19th century as a left-wing party, representing the interests of commerce and industry. Its considerable influence declined with the formation of the Labour Party in the early 20th century, and it gradually lost public support. In 1981 it joined forces with the new *SDP*, and merged with it in 1988 to form the Social and Liberal Democrats (SLD), now the *Liberal Democrats*.

Liberty's /'lɪbətɪz/ (commerce) A large store in *Regent Street, London*, founded in 1875 by Arthur Liberty. The store is famous for the distinctive design of its fabrics.

licensing hours /'laɪsnsɪŋ ˌaʊəz/ (daily life) The hours when *pubs* are open for the sale of alcoholic drink. The hours vary from one part of the country to another, but are on average 11.30 am to 2.30 pm and 6.00 pm to 10.30 pm. In 1988, however, a law was passed allowing pubs to stay open all day, from 11.00 am to 11.00 pm.

Life Guards /'laɪf gɑːdz/, **the** (defence) The premier regiment of the British *Army*, together with the *Blues and Royals*. They were first formed in 1656 and are now part of the *Household Cavalry*.

life peer /ˌlaɪf 'pɪə(r)/ see *peer*² (life and society)

light ale /ˌlaɪt 'eɪl/ (food and drink) A general term for a light-coloured beer. Compare *bitter*.

lighting-up time /ˌlaɪtɪŋ-'ʌp taɪm/ (daily life) The time in the evening when drivers of motor vehicles must turn their lights on. Officially, this is half an hour after sunset.

Lilliburlero/Lillibullero /ˌlɪlɪbə'leərəʊ/ (arts) The signature tune of the *BBC World Service*, once attributed to Purcell but now known to have existed earlier (in the 16th century). The word itself is part of a meaningless refrain in a 17th-century political ballad mocking the Irish Roman Catholic supporters of James II.

limerick /'lɪmərɪk/ (language) A short poem, usually about something funny or improbable. It is always five lines long and has a characteristic rhyming scheme. Limericks have been popular since the end of the 19th century and in modern times have often been indecent or vulgar. Some of the best-known limericks were written by Edward Lear (1812–1888), including this one:

'There was an old man with a beard,
  Who said, "It is just as I feared—
      Two owls and a hen
      Four larks and a wren
  Have all built their nests in my beard!" '

limited company /ˌlɪmɪtɪd 'kʌmpənɪ/ (finance) A company owned by the individuals and organizations who have bought shares in it, in particular a public limited company (see *PLC*). If the company gets into debt, the amount that the shareholder will be called on to pay is limited by law, and will be related to the amount of shares the shareholder has. See also *Ltd*.

Lincoln's Inn /ˌlɪŋkənz 'ɪn/ (law) One of the four *Inns of Court* in *London*. [named after the original owner of the inn there, Thomas de Lincoln]

lion /'laɪən/ (tradition) The lion, the 'king of beasts', has been used as a symbol of national strength and of the British monarchy for many centuries.

Lions Club /'laɪənz klʌb/ (charities) A local branch of an international association (in full, International Association of Lions Clubs) devoted to community service work. There are currently 801 branches in *Britain*, with a total membership of about 20,000. The Association was founded in 1917.

liquorice allsorts /ˌlɪkərɪs 'ɔːlsɔːts/ (food and drink) A type of confectionery consisting of black and white or brightly coloured sweets containing liquorice. ['all sorts' for the different colours and shapes of the sweets]

listed building /ˌlɪstɪd 'bɪldɪŋ/ (history) A building officially listed as being of architectural or historic interest, and thus one that cannot be pulled down or altered without the approval of the *local authority*.

Little America /ˌlɪtl ə'merɪkə/ (London) A nickname for *Grosvenor Square, London*, where the American Embassy is located.

Lively, Penelope /'laɪvlɪ, pə'neləpɪ/ (people) Penelope Lively (born 1933) is the author who won the *Booker prize* in 1987.

She is one of *Britain*'s leading novelists and short story writers, and has written several books for children. The winning novel, her seventh, was entitled 'Moon Tiger' and is a love story set in wartime Cairo. Penelope Lively was born in Cairo and spent the first 13 years of her life there. Some people felt that the prize should have gone to a writer who was less obviously *middle class* and who was more adventurous and original in their writing.

Liver bird /'laɪvə bɜ:d/ (tradition) A name for an inhabitant of Liverpool. [from a mythical bird invented in the 17th century to explain the origin of the name Liverpool, and now adopted as the *city*'s emblem]

Liverpool Football Club /ˌlɪvəpu:l 'fʊtbɔ:l klʌb/ **(Liverpool FC)** (sport and leisure) A popular and successful *football club*, founded in 1892, and having a ground at *Anfield Road*, Liverpool. They have been *Football League* champions many times this century, and have several times been *FA Cup* winners and European Champions.

Liverpool Street /'lɪvəpu:l stri:t/ (transport) **1** A main line railway station and terminus in east London, from which trains depart for *East Anglia*. **2** An Underground station here. [street named in honour of Lord Liverpool, a 19th-century *Prime Minister*]

Liverpudlian /ˌlɪvə'pʌdlɪən/ (geography) A native or resident of Liverpool. ['pool' of Liverpool humorously altered to 'puddle']

livery company /'lɪvərɪ ˌkʌmpənɪ/ (tradition) One of the 83 guilds of the *City (of London)*. Such guilds are mostly descended from medieval associations of craftsmen (goldsmiths, tailors, basketmakers, etc) and today not only maintain associations with their craft or trade but make grants to education and charity. [named for their 'livery' or special uniform worn on ceremonial occasions]

living room /'lɪvɪŋ ˌru:m/ (daily life) The main *ground floor* room in a house used for relaxation and for entertaining guests. Compare *front room*.

Lloyd's /lɔɪdz/ (finance) An association of *London underwriters* established in 1688. It was originally mainly concerned with marine insurance and the publication of shipping news, but today deals in a wide range of insurance policies as well as issuing a daily bulletin ('Lloyd's List') of shipping information. [named after Edward Lloyd, in whose coffee house the underwriters originally carried on their business]

Lloyds (Bank) /lɔɪdz ('bæŋk)/ (finance) One of the five main English banks, founded in 1865 and with branches in most towns and *cities*. It was first established under the name of Taylor and Lloyd, and adopted its present name in 1889.

Lloyd's Register /ˌlɔɪdz 'redʒɪstə(r)/ (transport) A society formed in 1760 to classify ships. Today it is managed by a large committee of shipowners, shipbuilders and *underwriters*, and publishes 'Lloyd's Register Book', with details of all sea-going vessels and 'Lloyd's Register of Yachts'. [named after the coffee house where *Lloyd's* originated]

Lloyd Webber, Andrew /lɔɪd 'webə(r), 'ændru:/(people) Andrew Lloyd Webber (born 1948) is one of the most popular and successful writers of musicals in the present century. He rose to instant fame in 1969 with the rock opera 'Jesus Christ Superstar', written with Tim Rice. Recent box office hits, some also written with Rice, include 'Evita' (1978), 'Cats' (1981), 'The Phantom of the Opera' (1986), 'Aspects of Love' (1989) and 'Sunset Boulevard' (1993). Andrew Lloyd Webber was knighted in 1992.

LNR /ˌel en 'aːr/ **(London News Radio)** (media) An *ILR* station based in *London* that in 1993 took over from LBC (London Broadcasting Company), *Britain*'s first ILR station, founded in 1973. It broadcasts news reports round the clock, with updates every 20 minutes.

local /'ləʊkl/ (daily life) A familiar name for a *pub*, especially one regularly visited by a person since it is close to his home or place of work.

local authority /ˌləʊkl ɔː'θɒrətɪ/ (government) A body elected for the local government of a district such as a town or *county*[2], as distinct from a national government body. Examples of local authorities are a *county council, town council* or *district council*.

local call /ˌləʊkl 'kɔːl/ (daily life) A telephone call in a local area, officially over a distance less than 35 miles (56 kilometres). A local call is cheaper than a *national call*, which is over a greater distance. The *dialling code* 0345 is used for calls anywhere in *Britain* that, by special arrangement with *BT*, are charged only at the rate of a local call.

Local Government Commission /ˌləʊkl 'gʌvənmənt kaˌmɪʃn/, **the** (government) A government body set up in 1992 to review the system of *local Government* in *England*.

local radio /ˌləʊkl 'reɪdɪəʊ/ (media) A local radio station operated either by the *BBC* or by the *Radio Authority*. The latter are collectively known as *ILR*. See also *INR*.

Loch Lomond /ˌlɒk ˈləʊmənd/ (geography) The largest lake in *Britain*, northwest of *Glasgow* in south central *Scotland*. Its attractive setting among green hills and wooded mountains make it popular with tourists, who also like to visit the nature reserve at its southeast corner. 'Loch' is the Scottish word for 'lake'.

Loch Ness /ˌlɒk ˈnes/ (geography) Probably *Britain*'s best known lake, because of the *Loch Ness monster* which may live in the deep water. It is a long lake in northern *Scotland*, where it forms part of the *Caledonian Canal*. It extends for 23 miles (36 km), and in places is over 700 feet (213 metres) in depth. 'Loch' is the Scottish word for 'lake'.

Loch Ness Monster /ˌlɒk nes ˈmɒnstə(r)/**, the** (tradition) A large prehistoric creature said to be living in the deep waters of *Loch Ness, Scotland*, but as yet, in spite of various 'sightings', not scientifically proved to exist. See also *Nessie*.

locum /ˈləʊkəm/ (medicine) A doctor or clergyman who stands in temporarily in the absence of the regular doctor (clergyman). [short for Latin 'locum tenens', 'holding the place']

lodge /lɒdʒ/ (**1** daily life **2, 3** education) **1** A small house at the entrance of the *drive²* to a *country house*, usually occupied by a *gamekeeper* or gardener. **2** The residence of the head of a *college¹* at *Cambridge University*. **3** An office for porters or other domestic staff at the entrance to a college¹ or university.

lollipop lady

lollipop /'lɒlɪpɒp/ (food and drink) A large boiled sweet or toffee stuck on a short stick to be sucked.

lollipop lady/man /'lɒlɪpɒp ˌleɪdɪ/mæn/ (daily life) A woman or man employed by a *local authority* to help children across a busy street on their way to or from school. She or he carries a pole with a disc on the end (resembling a *lollipop*) and holds it up as a sign to stop traffic.

Lombard Street /'lɒmbɑːd striːt/ (finance) **1** A street in the *City (of London)* traditionally associated with banking. **2** The *London* money market in general. [named after the money-dealers from Lombardy, Italy, who came here in medieval times]

London /'lʌndən/ (London) The capital of *Britain* and its largest city, with a current population of 6.7 million. The *Houses of Parliament* are there, as is the Queen's (see *Queen Elizabeth*) most important residence, *Buckingham Palace*. London stands on the river *Thames* and is an important port. The *London Docklands* are in the *East End* while the *West End* is famous for its theatres (eg, the *Palladium*) and shops (eg, *Harrods*). The *City (of London)* is one of the most important financial centres in the world. There are many historic buildings in London (eg, the *Tower of London*), as well as famous art galleries, concert halls and opera houses (eg, the *National Gallery*, the *Royal Festival Hall* and the *Royal Opera House*). There are several large and attractive public parks within the city (see *royal parks*). Administratively London consists of the City and 32 *boroughs*[2].

London Airport /ˌlʌndən 'eəpɔːt/ (transport) The official name of *Heathrow*.

London Bridge /ˌlʌndən 'brɪdʒ/ (transport) **1** Until 1747 the only bridge across the *Thames* in *London*. It was rebuilt and reopened in 1831, but in 1968 it was dismantled and sold to an American millionaire who reassembled it in the United States. (It is said he believed he was buying *Tower Bridge*.) The present bridge was built in 1973. **2** An *Underground* railway station south of the bridge.

London Docklands /ˌlʌndən 'dɒklændz/, **the** (London) A modern development in the *East End* of *London*, arising when the last of the docks closed in the early 1980s, with the transferral of the main docking and shipping facilities to Tilbury, some 26 miles (41 km) east of London. The former site of the docks has become a select residential area, with new buildings erected to house financial and other professional concerns. An extension of the *London Underground* has been created by the construction of a light railway from the *City of London*, and the London City Airport opened in 1987. The whole project is in the hands of the London Docklands Development Corporation, set up in 1981.

London Gazette /ˌlʌndən gəˈzet/, **the** (government) The bulletin of the British government, publishing mainly official announcements and legal advertisements, but also armed forces promotions and the *New Year Honours* and *Birthday Honours*. It first appeared (as the 'Oxford Gazette') in 1665, and today is published four times a week (including *bank holidays*).

London Institute /ˌlʌndən ˈɪnstɪtjuːt/, **the** (London) An art and design *college*[2] in *London* formed in 1986 from the merger of four leading art schools (Camberwell, Central, Chelsea and St Martin's) with other colleges.

London Library /ˌlʌndən ˈlaɪbrərɪ/, **the** (arts) *Britain*'s largest private subscription library, in central *London*. It was founded in 1841 and currently contains nearly one million books on all subjects except medical, legal and scientific.

London Marathon /ˌlʌndən ˈmærəθn/, **the** (sport and leisure) An annual running race held since 1981 in *London* in the spring or early summer. The race, which is commercially sponsored, extends over a distance of 26 miles (42 km), the same as that of the Olympic Marathon. The course starts at *Greenwich*, then crosses the *Thames* to pass through the *East End* and finish at *Westminster Bridge*. (In 1994 the finish was moved to *St James's Palace* because the bridge was closed for repairs.) The race is open to anyone, and many of the thousands of people who take part use it to raise money for charity, as in a *sponsored walk*.

London Mozart Players /ˌlʌndən ˈməʊtsɑːt ˌpleɪəz/, **the** (arts) A leading chamber orchestra, performing mainly the works of Mozart and Haydn.

London Museum /ˌlʌndən mjuːˈzɪəm/, **the** (London) The name of the *Museum of London* before it was reorganized and expanded in 1976.

London Philharmonic Orchestra /ˌlʌndən ˌfɪlɑːmɒnɪk ˈɔːkɪstrə/, **the (LPO, the)** (arts) A leading British symphony orchestra, founded in 1932.

London Symphony Orchestra /ˌlʌndən ˈsɪmfənɪ ˌɔːkɪstrə/, **the (LSO, the)** (arts) A leading symphony orchestra founded in 1904. It is based at the *Barbican*.

London Tourist Board /ˌlʌndən ˈtʊərɪst bɔːd/, **the (LTB, the)** (London) A service set up in *London* in 1963 to provide information for tourists visiting both London and *Britain* in general.

London Transport /ˌlʌndən ˈtrænspɔːt/ (transport) The state body that runs public transport in *London*. Its two main branches are London Underground *Ltd*, which operates the *London Underground*, and London Buses Ltd, which manages London's buses.

London Underground /ˌlʌndən ˈʌndəgraʊnd/, **the** (transport) The most important underground railway in *Britain*, evolving in *London* in the 19th century and now providing a network of lines (not all of them underground) in *Greater London* and parts of the surrounding area. There are eleven lines, most with stations at points where lines intersect, so that passengers can change from one line to another. The eleven are: the Bakerloo Line, the Central Line, the Circle Line, the District Line, the East London Line, the Hammersmith and City Line, the Jubilee Line, the Metropolitan Line, the Northern Line, the Piccadilly Line and the Victoria Line. A special service operates on the *Waterloo and City Line*. The Docklands Light Railway in the *London Docklands* also links up with the Underground. Apart from the Waterloo and City Line, which is operated by *BR*, the Underground is run by London Underground *Ltd*, a subsidiary of *London Transport*.

London University /ˌlʌndən juːnɪˈvɜːsətɪ/ (education) One of the largest universities in *Britain*, founded in *London* in 1836. It has over 50 independent *colleges*[1], including a number of language institutes and several medical schools, the latter mostly for *postgraduates* (when they are known as 'institutes'). It has about 51,000 'internal' students, who attend locally, and about 25,000 'external' students, who study through a *correspondence course*.

London Zoo /ˌlʌndən ˈzuː/, **the** (London) The short name of the Zoological Gardens, *Britain*'s best-known zoo, opened in *Regent's Park, London*, in 1826 by the Zoological Society of London.

Londonderry Air /ˌlʌndəndərɪ ˈeə(r)/, **the** (arts) A popular Irish folk tune, first published in 1885 and since then arranged and recorded in a variety of ways, by various instruments. The tune is popular as much for its slow, haunting melody as for its words.

Long Man of Wilmington /ˌlɒŋ mæn əv ˈwɪlmɪŋtən/, **the**
(history) An ancient landmark near the village of
Wilmington, East Sussex, consisting of the giant outline of a
man, holding an upright stick in each hand, cut out of the turf
on a chalk hill. The origin of the figure is unknown.

long vacation /ˌlɒŋ vəˈkeɪʃn/ (education) The summer vacation
at a university, which usually extends for at least three
months, from July to September.

Lonsdale Belt /ˌlɒnzdeɪl ˈbelt/, **the** (sport and leisure) The
highest award in professional boxing, a richly decorated belt
awarded to a British champion, and kept by him if won three
times running. [originally given by the Earl of Lonsdale in 1909]

lord /lɔːd/ (**1** government **2** religion **3** law) **1** A *peer* who is a
member of the *House of Lords*. **2** The title of a bishop,
especially if a member of the House of Lords. **3** The title of
certain senior judges.

Lord Chamberlain /ˌlɔːd ˈtʃeɪmbəlɪn/, **the** (life and society) The
chief official of the royal household. He is responsible for all
royal ceremonial, except important state functions, which are
arranged by the *Earl Marshal*.

Lord Chancellor /ˌlɔːd ˈtʃɑːnsələ(r)/, **the** (government) The
title (in full, Lord High Chancellor) of the chief legal officer in
England. He is a member of the *Cabinet* and of the *Privy
Council* and he is the *Speaker*[2] of the *House of Lords* (where he
sits on the *woolsack*).

Lord Chief Justice /ˌlɔːd tʃiːf ˈdʒʌstɪs/, **the** (law) The title of the
judge who presides over the *Queen's Bench Division* in the
High Court of Justice. He ranks next after the *Lord Chancellor*
and is a *peer*.

Lord High Chancellor /ˌlɔːd haɪ ˈtʃɑːnsələ(r)/ see *Lord
Chancellor* (government)

Lord Lieutenant /ˌlɔːd lefˈtenənt/, **the** (government) The
representative of the sovereign in a *county*. The title was
created in the 16th century, and originally carried many
responsibilities. Today the position is mainly ceremonial,
although the holder does make recommendations for
appointments as a *JP*. The title is an honorary one and the
holder (who can be a woman) is not necessarily a *peer*.

Lord Mayor /ˌlɔːd ˈmeə(r)/, **the** (government) The title given
to the *mayor* of *London* and of certain other large *cities*. It can
be borne by a man or woman (see *mayoress*).

Lord Mayor's Banquet /ˌlɔːd meəz ˈbæŋkwɪt/, **the** (London) An
annual ceremonial dinner held in the *Guildhall, London*, after

the election of a new *Lord Mayor* of London. The *Prime Minister* traditionally makes an important speech at the dinner.

Lord Mayor's Show /ˌlɔːd meəz ˈʃəʊ/, **the** (London) A ceremony held each year on the second Saturday in November, when the newly elected *Lord Mayor* of *London* rides in a horse-drawn carriage through the streets of London to be presented to the *Lord Chief Justice* at the Royal Courts of Justice. His carriage is accompanied by a procession of other vehicles, arranged to make a colourful display on a particular theme chosen personally by the Lord Mayor. In 1981, for example, the theme was 'Transport'.

Lord President of the Council /ˌlɔːd ˌprezɪdənt əv ðə ˈkaʊnsl/, **the** (government) The title of the peer who presides at meetings of the *Privy Council*. He is responsible for presenting the business of the Council to the sovereign, and is also *Leader of the House*[1] of Commons and a member of the *Cabinet*.

Lord Privy Seal /ˌlɔːd ˌprɪvɪ ˈsiːl/, **the** (government) The senior member of the *Cabinet* without any special duties. He is usually, however, the *Leader of the House*[2] of Lords, and until 1884 had the special responsibility of keeping the *Privy Seal*.

Lord Provost /ˌlɔːd ˈprɒvəst/, **the** (government) The title of the provost (equivalent to the English *mayor*) of five Scottish cities: Aberdeen, Dundee, *Edinburgh, Glasgow* and Perth.

Lord's /lɔːdz/ (sport and leisure) A famous cricket ground in north *London*, the headquarters of the *MCC*. [named in honour of Thomas Lord, who bought the ground for this Club in 1814]

Lord's Day Observance Society /ˌlɔːdz ˌdeɪ əbˈzɜːvəns səˌsaɪətɪ/, **the** (life and society) A society founded in 1831 to promote the religious observance of *Sunday* ('the Lord's Day') as the Christian Sabbath. The Society today is most active in campaigning against the introduction of laws that permit commercial or sporting activities on Sundays.

Lords Spiritual /ˌlɔːdz ˈspɪrɪtʃʊəl/, **the** (government) A collective term for those bishops in the *Church of England* who are members of the *House of Lords*. Compare *Lords Temporal*.

Lord's Taverners /ˌlɔːdz ˈtævənəz/, **the** (sport and leisure) A *cricket* team consisting of stage personalities who take part in matches at *Lord*'s and elsewhere in order to raise money for charity. [named after the Tavern, the *club* at Lord's where the team was first planned in 1950]

Lords Temporal /ˌlɔːdz ˈtempərəl/, **the** (government) A collective name for all those *peers* in the *House of Lords* who are not *Lords Spiritual*.

Lough Neagh /ˌlɒk ˈneɪ/ (geography) The largest lake in the *British Isles*, in *Northern Ireland* west of *Belfast*. It is popular with yachtsmen and walkers. 'Lough' is the Irish word for 'lake'.

lounge bar /ˈlaʊndʒ bɑː(r)/ (daily life) A *bar¹* in a *pub*, hotel or restaurant, which is more comfortable than a *public bar*, and where the drinks are more expensive.

Low Church /ˌləʊ ˈtʃɜːtʃ/ (religion) A member of the *Church of England* who attaches greater importance to the literal interpretation of the Bible and to evangelism generally than to ritual or the value of the sacraments. Compare *High Church*.

Low Sunday /ˈləʊ ˌsʌndɪ/ (religion) The *Sunday* after *Easter*.

lower class /ˌləʊə ˈklɑːs/ (life and society) The sector of society that has the lowest position in the social scale. The term is in many ways similar to *working class* and is regarded by many, because of its implication of inferiority, as critical or patronizing. Compare *middle class, upper class*.

lower middle class /ˌləʊə ˈmɪdl klɑːs/ (life and society) The sector of society that is midway between *lower class* and *middle class* and that is usually considered to be made up of shopkeepers, minor *civil servants*, etc.

lower school /ˈləʊə skuːl/ (education) A term occasionally used for the junior classes of a *secondary school*. Today such classes are often organized as a *middle school*.

Lowlands /ˈləʊləndz/, **the** (geography) The relatively flat region of central *Scotland*, in the valleys of the *Clyde* and the *Forth*, as distinct from the *Highlands* to the north.

loyal toast /ˌlɔɪəl ˈtəʊst/ (tradition) A toast to the sovereign proposed at the end of an official *dinner* or banquet. Traditionally, diners are not permitted to smoke until the toast has been drunk.

Loyalists /ˈlɔɪəlɪsts/, **the** (politics) The Protestants in *Northern Ireland* who wish *Ulster* to retain her links with *Britain*.

L-plates /ˈel pleɪts/ (transport) The metal or plastic plates attached to the front and rear of a vehicle driven by an *L-driver*. The plates are square in shape and contain a red letter 'L' on a white background.

LSE /ˌel es ˈiː/, **the (London School of Economics, the)**

L-plates

(education) A branch of *London University* founded in 1895 (full name, London School of Economic and Political Science). It provides degree courses in arts, law, science (anthropology and geography) and economics. In the 1960s and 1970s it gained a reputation for the radical views of its staff and students.

Ltd /'lɪmɪtɪd/ **(Limited)** (finance) An abbreviation following the name of a firm or company to show that it is a *private limited company*, not a public limited company (which has the letters *PLC* after its name).

lucky dip /ˌlʌkɪ 'dɪp/ (sport and leisure) A box or container of some kind holding small prizes, buried in sawdust or something similar, to be searched for by children. The game is a common attraction at a *fête*. See also *Santa Claus*.

ludo /'luːdəʊ/ (sport and leisure) A board game in which players move counters over the squares of a straight course by throwing a dice. The player who reaches the centre of the board first is the winner. [Latin, 'I play']

lump /lʌmp/**, the** (work) A colloquial term for workers in the construction trade, especially with reference to their non-payment of *income tax* and *national insurance*. [such workers are paid a 'lump sum', that is, in cash with no deductions]

lunch /lʌntʃ/ (food and drink) A midday meal, usually eaten between 12.00 and 2.00. For those who have supper in the evening, it will usually be the main meal of the day; for those who have dinner in the evening as their main meal, it will usually be a light meal. See also *dinner* as an alternative name for lunch.

luncheon /ˈlʌntʃən/ (food and drink) A formal name for *lunch*, especially as printed on an invitation card, a menu, etc.

Luncheon Voucher /ˈlʌntʃən ˌvaʊtʃə(r)/ **(LV)** (commerce) A voucher worth a particular sum of money that can be exchanged for a *lunch* or for food in a café, restaurant, snack bar, etc by the employee to whom it has been issued.

Lutine bell /ˌluːtiːn ˈbel/, **the** (tradition) A bell in the building of *Lloyd's, London*, rung before the announcement of the loss of a ship. The bell is the ship's bell of the French frigate 'Lutine' sunk in 1799: the vessel was insured with Lloyd's for the sum of half a million *pounds* (*sterling*).

LWT /ˌel ˌdʌblju: ˈtiː/ **(London Weekend Television)** (media) One of the 15 regional television companies of the *ITC*, based in *London* but broadcasting only at the *weekend*. In the week, London's *ITV* station is *Carlton TV*.

Lyonesse /ˌlaɪəˈnes/ (tradition) In the stories about *King Arthur*, the mythical country that was the birthplace of Sir Tristram, one of the *Knights of the Round Table*. It was said to have been somewhere in southwest *England* and to have been covered by the sea (perhaps between *Land's End* and the *Scilly Isles*).

MA /ˌem ˈeɪ/ **(Master of Arts)** (education) **1** The commonest type of *higher degree* awarded by an English university, usually for studying a non-scientific subject. Unusually, *Oxford University* awards an MA to anyone who has an *Oxford*² *BA* degree, who has been a member of the university for at least 21 terms and who pays £5. Similarly, *Cambridge University* awards an MA degree to anyone who has had a *Cambridge*² BA degree for at least two years and who requests it (no fee is paid). **2** A *first degree* (equivalent to an English BA) awarded at the Scottish Universities.

ma'am /mæm/ (life and society) A title of respect used to speak to a female member of the *royal family* and certain other women of rank. [conventional abbreviation of *madam*]

Maastricht Treaty /ˌmɑːstrɪkt ˈtriːtɪ/, **the** (government) The treaty of 1992 that committed the countries of the *EC* to closer union, sharing joint economic and monetary policies in a *Single Market*. The treaty was not popular in some countries, and Denmark rejected it. *Britain* also had doubts, and opposition from some *MPs* caused a split in the *Conservative Party* and lost John *Major* much support, especially when he said that Britain would not ratify the treaty until Denmark accepted it. It did so, and Britain then followed in 1993.

madam /ˈmædəm/ (life and society) A polite way of addressing a woman, especially when the speaker does not know her well enough to use her name or wants to show a formal, respectful relationship. Compare *sir*.

Madame Tussaud's /ˌmædəm təˈsɔːdz/ (London) A famous waxworks museum in *London*, opened in 1835 by Marie Tussaud (1760–1850). The museum contains wax figures of famous and notorious characters in both history and contemporary life, and is also noted for its displays of particularly gruesome events in the *Chamber of Horrors*.

Madeira cake /mə'dɪərə keɪk/ (food and drink) A kind of rich sponge case, round in shape and decorated with lemon peel. [formerly eaten with Madeira wine]

Magic Circle /ˌmædʒɪk 'sɜːkl/, **the** (arts) A professional association of conjurors and illusionists, founded in 1905. Its *London* headquarters possess a museum and a library of publications on magic and conjuring. Its current membership is about 1,500.

magistrate /'mædʒɪstreɪt/ (law) A general term used for a minor legal officer, in particular a *JP* in *England*.

Magna Carta /ˌmægnə 'kɑːtə/ (history) **1** The charter granted by King John in 1215, which recognized the rights and privileges of the barons, the *church* and the freemen, and which is traditionally regarded as the basis of English liberties. [Latin, 'Great Charter'] **2** An original copy of this charter, especially the ones in Lincoln Cathedral and Salisbury Cathedral and the two copies in the *British Museum*.

maiden speech /ˌmeɪdn 'spiːtʃ/ (government) The first speech of an *MP* in the *House of Commons*, or of a *peer* in the *House of Lords*.

Mail /meɪl/, **the** (media) The short name of the *Daily Mail* newspaper.

Mail on Sunday /ˌmeɪl ɒn 'sʌndɪ/, **The** (media) A Sunday *popular paper* first published in 1982 and controlled by the same company that owns the *Daily Mail*. The paper is noted for its many topical news features and articles, many of them 'scoops'. Its current circulation is about 1.9 million (1983 – 1.3 million). It is accompanied by a colour magazine, 'You'.

Major, John /'meɪdʒə, dʒɒn/ (people) John Major (born 1943) was elected leader of the *Conservative Party*, and so *Prime Minister*, in 1990, having previously been (for a few months each) *Foreign Secretary* and *Chancellor of the Exchequer*. To the surprise of many, he led his party to victory in the *general election* of 1992, but since then has been criticized for his poor political judgment, especially in his handling of the *Exchange Rate Mechanism* and *Maastricht Treaty*, and in public opinion polls he has been voted the most unpopular Prime Minister for many years.

Mallory Park /ˌmælərɪ 'pɑːk/ (sport and leisure) A motor-cycle and motor-car racing circuit near Hinckley, Leicestershire, where international motor-cycle races are held.

Malvern Festival /ˌmɔːlvən ˈfestəvl/, **the** (arts) An annual drama festival held in August at Great Malvern, Hereford and Worcester.

Man Alive /ˌmæn əˈlaɪv/ (media) A weekly television series of programmes about various people's professions and special vocations, broadcast at irregular intervals on *BBC 2* since 1965.

Man of Kent /ˌmæn əv ˈkent/ (geography) A traditional name for someone born in east Kent (strictly, one born east of the river Medway). Compare *Kentishman*.

Manchester City /ˌmæntʃɪstə ˈsɪtɪ/ (sport and leisure) A popular *football club* founded in 1887 (originally as Ardwick Football Club) with a stadium in south Manchester.

Manchester United /ˌmæntʃɪstə juːˈnaɪtɪd/ (sport and leisure) A leading English *football club* founded in 1878 with a stadium in southwest Manchester near *Old Trafford*.

Mancunian /mænˈkjuːnɪən/ (geography) A native or inhabitant of Manchester. [from the supposed medieval Latin name of Manchester, 'Mancunium', actually 'Mamucium']

Mandy/Judy /ˈmændɪ ˈdʒuːdɪ/ (media) A weekly picture-story magazine for schoolgirls, first published in 1967. It was originally called 'Mandy', but merged with another comic, 'Judy', to give its present name.

Mansion House /ˈmænʃn ˌhaʊs/, **the** (1 London 2 transport) **1** The official residence of the *Lord Mayor* of *London*, with a large banqueting hall (the so-called Egyptian Hall) where official banquets and receptions are held. The house was built in the mid-18th century. **2** An Underground railway station nearby. See *London Underground*.

Manx /mæŋks/ (language) A former Celtic language of the *Isle of Man*, not now used for everyday speech except by a few enthusiasts.

Manx cat /ˌmæŋks ˈkæt/ (animal world) A breed of tailless cat, believed to have originated on the *Isle of Man*.

Mappin Terraces /ˌmæpɪn ˈterəsɪz/, **the** (animal world) An enclosure of man-made cliffs and caves in the *London Zoo*, where polar bears and mountain sheep, among other animals, are housed. [named after the benefactor, Jonathan Mappin, who gave money for the Terraces to be opened in 1914]

Marble Arch /ˌmɑːbl ˈɑːtʃ/ (London) A triumphal arch in *London* originally built in 1828 to form the main entrance to *Buckingham Palace*. It was found to be too narrow for the royal carriage, so was re-erected on its present site, northeast of

Hyde Park, in 1851, where it served for some years as a gateway to the Park.

Margaret, Princess /'mɑːɡrɪt ˌprɪnses/ (royal family) Princess Margaret (born 1930) is the sister of *Queen Elizabeth*. In 1960 she married Anthony Armstrong-Jones, later Lord Snowdon, but they separated in 1976 and were divorced in 1978. There were two children of the marriage: David, Viscount Linley (born 1961) and Lady Sarah Armstrong-Jones (born 1964). Princess Margaret is noted for her enjoyment of social life but she has also many charity interests.

marginal constituency /ˌmɑːdʒɪnl kənˈstɪtjʊənsɪ/ (politics) A *constituency* whose *MP* was elected by a narrow majority in a *by-election* or *general election*.

marginal seat /ˌmɑːdʒɪnl ˈsiːt/ see *marginal constituency* (politics) and *seat* (politics)

market day /'mɑːkɪt deɪ/ (daily life) A day, once weekly or twice weekly, when a market is held in a *market town*.

market garden /ˌmɑːkɪt ˈɡɑːdn/ (commerce) A special garden where fruit and vegetables are grown for sale.

market town /'mɑːkɪt taʊn/ (geography) A town, especially one in a rural area, that holds a regular market on a *market day*. The market consists of individual stalls selling agricultural produce and cheap manufactured goods (often, clothes and domestic products), and is usually held on a central square or along central streets.

market-maker /'mɑːkɪt ˌmeɪkə(r)/ (finance) A member of the *Stock Exchange* who buys and sells shares not only for clients (the former work of a *stockbroker*) but for other members as well (formerly the work of a 'stockjobber'). The term came into use after 1986, when the Stock Exchange was reorganized.

Marks & Spencer /ˌmɑːks ən ˈspensə(r)/ (commerce) A chain store selling high-quality clothing and food products, founded in 1884 by Michael Marks (who took Thomas Spencer into partnership in 1894). The store is known colloquially as 'Marks and Sparks' or simply 'M and S'.

Marlborough (College) /'mɔːlbrə (ˌmɔːlbrə ˈkɒlɪdʒ)/ (education) A leading *public school*[1], founded in 1843 in Marlborough, Wiltshire, and having about 875 students.

Marlborough House /ˌmɔːlbrə ˈhaʊs/ (London) A large house in *Pall Mall*, *London*, built in the early 18th century for the Duchess of Marlborough and serving until 1953 as a residence for members of the *royal family*. In 1962 it became a

214

centre for conferences of the heads of countries to the *Commonwealth[1]*.

marmalade /'mɑːmǝleɪd/ (food and drink) A type of jam made from the pulp and peel of oranges, or other citrus fruits, and usually eaten at breakfast, spread on buttered bread, rolls or *toast*.

Marplan /'mɑːplæn/ (media) An organization that conducts public opinion polls, founded in 1959. It publishes its results in *quality papers*, mostly the *Financial Times* and the *Guardian*. [abbreviation of '*mar*ket research *plan*']

Martello tower /mɑːˌtelǝʊ 'taʊǝ(r)/ (history) A type of small circular tower by the sea. Such towers were originally built in *Britain* in about 1803 for coastal defence against a possible invasion by Napoleon's forces, and they can still be found in southeast *England*. [named after Mortella Point, Corsica, where the British navy captured a similar tower in 1794]

Marylebone /'mærǝlǝbǝn/ (transport) **1** A main line *London* railway station, and a terminus of the Western Region of *BR* (for trains from Banbury, Oxfordshire and Aylesbury, Buckinghamshire). **2** An Underground railway station there. See *London Underground*.

master /'mɑːstǝ(r)/ (education) **1** A short title of a person holding an *MA* degree, or some other *higher degree*. **2** The title of the head of some *colleges[1]*, in particular those of *Cambridge University*.

Master /'mɑːstǝ(r)/ (life and society) A written, and occasionally spoken, form of address for a boy, placed before his first name (eg, Master Peter Jones). The usage is becoming increasingly old-fashioned.

master of foxhounds /ˌmɑːstǝr ǝv 'fɒkshaʊndz/ (**MFH**) (sport and leisure) A man or woman in charge of a pack of foxhounds, as used for a *hunt*, and responsible for various administrative duties in connection with the hunt.

master of hounds /ˌmɑːstǝr ǝv 'haʊndz/ (sport and leisure) A short term for a *master of foxhounds*, or a term used when the hounds are not foxhounds.

Master of the Horse /ˌmɑːstǝr ǝv ðǝ 'hɔːs/**, the** (royal family) An official responsible for the personal safety of the sovereign. At the ceremony of *Trooping the Colour* he rides immediately behind the sovereign, and when the sovereign is in procession to the *State Opening of Parliament*, or on any other occasion, he rides in the next carriage.

Master of the Queen's Music /ˌmɑːstǝr ǝv ðǝ ˌkwiːnz 'mjuːzɪk/**,**

the (royal family) The title of the musician, usually a well-known composer, appointed to attend members of the *royal family* on musical occasions such as special concerts, to organize the music for coronations, royal weddings and similar state occasions, and to compose music for such occasions. The post is an honorary one, and when the sovereign is a *king* changes in title to 'Master of the King's Music'. ['Music' in the title was until recently traditionally spelt 'Musick']

Master of the Rolls /ˌmɑːstər əv ðə ˈrəʊlz/, **the** (law) The senior civil judge in *England*. He presides over the Court of Appeal in the *Supreme Court of Judicature*, is keeper of the records at the *Public Record Office*, and is a member of the *Privy Council*. He ranks third in importance after the *Lord Chancellor* and the *Lord Chief Justice*.

Mastermind /ˈmɑːstəmaɪnd/ (media) A weekly television quiz programme which has been broadcast on *BBC 1* since 1971. Contestants answer both specialized questions (on a subject of their own choice) and general questions, with the winner proceeding to further rounds, until the final contestant, with the highest score, wins the title of 'Mastermind' for the year.

maternity allowance /məˈtɜːnɪtɪ əˈlaʊəns/ (finance) The state payment made to a pregnant woman who does not qualify for *maternity pay* for some reason, for example, if she is self-employed or has just changed her job. The current rate of maternity allowance is £42.25 a week.

maternity pay /məˈtɜːnɪtɪ ˌpeɪ/ (finance) The money paid for 18 weeks by an employer to a woman who leaves work to have a baby. If a woman has been working for the same employer for at least two years, she is entitled to 90% of her pay for the first six weeks she is absent, and to a lower rate for the remaining 12 weeks. If she has been employed for between six months and two years, she receives payment for the 18 weeks at the lower rate.

matron /ˈmeɪtrən/ (medicine) **1** The head of the nursing staff and medical facilities in a school or other residential institution such as a *rest home*. **2** The title (now no longer official) of the administrative head of the nursing staff in a hospital.

mature student /məˌtjʊə ˈstjuːdənt/ (education) An adult student, in particular one entering a university having worked for some years after leaving school, or enrolling on an *adult education* course.

Maundy money

Maundy money /ˈmɔːndɪ ˌmʌnɪ/ (tradition) Coins specially
minted for presentation by the sovereign to selected elderly
people on *Maundy Thursday*. Currently there are four such
coins, value 4p, 3p, 2p and 1p.

Maundy Thursday /ˌmɔːndɪ ˈθɜːzdɪ/ (tradition) The Thursday
before *Easter*, when in a selected *cathedral city* the sovereign
traditionally presents small purses of *Maundy money* to
specially chosen men and women, the number of each being
the same as the sovereign's age in years. Originally the
sovereign also washed the feet of the old people, in memory
of the washing of the disciples' feet by Christ.

May Day /ˈmeɪ deɪ/ (tradition) 1 May, traditionally a
celebration of the arrival of spring, when *fêtes*, *fayres* and
other outdoor events are held, and at which a *May Queen*
may be elected. May Day, or the first working day after it, has
been an official *bank holiday* since 1978.

May Queen /ˈmeɪ kwiːn/ (tradition) A girl or young woman in
a town or neighbourhood elected as the prettiest for a local
May Day parade. She is sometimes crowned with a garland of
flowers and is driven through the streets with two or more
younger girls as attendants, like a bride and her bridesmaids
at a wedding.

Mayfair /'meɪfeə(r)/ (London) A fashionable and expensive area of *London*'s *West End*, containing a number of high-class hotels, restaurants and shops. It extends over the area bounded by *Oxford Street* (to the north), *Regent Street* (east), *Piccadilly* (south) and *Park Lane* (west), and was formerly the site of an annual summer fair.

mayor /meə(r)/ (government) In *England* and *Wales*, the chief municipal officer of a town or *city*, and especially a *borough*[1]. He is the chairman of the council and carries out a number of honorary functions such as entertaining an important guest, opening a new building and attending special *church* services. He is formally addressed as 'The Worshipful (the Mayor of . . .)' (in a city, 'The Right Worshipful'), and his wife is known as the *mayoress*. A mayor may be a woman, in which case she is still (usually) called 'mayor'. In *Scotland* the function of a mayor is carried out by a *provost*. See also *Lord Mayor*.

mayoress /meə'res/ (life and society) The wife (or other official female companion, such as the daughter) of a *mayor*. She usually accompanies the mayor on his official engagements, but she is not formally addressed as 'The Worshipful'. The word is also occasionally used for a female mayor.

maypole /'meɪpəʊl/ (tradition) A tall pole fixed upright in the ground and traditionally danced round on *May Day*, each dancer holding a ribbon attached to the top of the pole.

Mays /meɪz/, **the** (1 education 2 sport and leisure) 1 The final examinations at *Cambridge University*, held in May. 2 The rowing races held after these examinations, originally in May but now in June. Compare *Eights*.

Maze (Prison) /meɪz ('prɪzn)/, **the** (law) A prison south of *Belfast*, *Northern Ireland*, where members of various terrorist organizations have been held since the *Troubles* began in 1968. There have been several riots in the prison, and in 1981 eight members of the *IRA* imprisoned there starved themselves to death. [name is a corruption of Irish 'An Mhaigh', meaning 'the plain']

MCC /ˌem si: 'si:/, **the (Marylebone Cricket Club, the)** (sport and leisure) *Britain*'s leading professional *cricket club*, and until 1969 the governing body of cricket (now controlled by the Cricket Council). It was founded in 1787 in the village of Marylebone, northwest of *London* (now a district of London), and has its home ground at *Lord*'s.

McNaughten Rules /mək̩nɔ:tn 'ru:lz/, **the** (law) A set of rules stating that a person can be said to have been insane when committing a crime only if he can prove that he did not know what he was doing, or that he did not realize that what he was doing was wrong. The rules date from the case of *Regina* v. McNaughten in 1843. (Also spelt as McNaghten Rules.)

meals on wheels /̩mi:lz ɒn 'wi:lz/ (daily life) A system organized by the *WRVS* to deliver hot meals by car to old people and invalids. Some *local authorities* organize this sort of system as well.

Meccano /mə'kɑ:nəʊ/ (daily life) The trade name of a construction kit for children (or adults) consisting of miniature metal or plastic parts (rods, wheels, etc) from which a working model can be made.

Medical Research Council /̩medɪkl rɪ'sɜ:tʃ ̩kaʊnsl/, **the (MRC, the)** (medicine) The main government agency for the promotion of medical and biological research. It was founded in 1920 and currently has 46 research units, mostly in universities and hospitals.

Melba toast /̩melbə 'təʊst/ (food and drink) A type of very thin, crisp toast. [said to have been a favourite of Dame Nellie Melba (1861–1931), the Australian opera singer]

Melody Maker /'melədɪ ̩meɪkə(r)/ **(MM, the)** (media) A weekly pop and rock music magazine, regarded as a rival to *NME*. It was founded in 1926 and has a current circulation of about 71,900.

Melton Mowbray pie /̩meltən ̩məʊbreɪ 'paɪ/ (food and drink) A high-quality type of pork pie, originally manufactured in Melton Mowbray, Leicestershire.

Men of Harlech /̩men əv 'hɑ:lek/ (tradition) An old Welsh marching song, originally sung by soldiers marching into battle. [properly, Welsh 'Rhyfelgyrch Gwŷr Harlech', 'Campaign of the men of Harlech'; Harlech is an ancient coastal town with a castle in northwest *Wales*]

Men of the Trees /̩men əv ðə 'tri:z/, **the** (life and society) An organization founded in 1924 to campaign for the appreciation of trees as a part of the ecological environment and to encourage their planting and protection. The association has about 3,000 members.

MENCAP /'meŋkæp/ (charities) A charity organization that provides a range of services for the mentally handicapped. It was founded in 1946 and currently has about 55,000 members. [an abbreviation of '*mentally handicapped*']

Mensa /'mensə/ (life and society) A social organization (now international) whose members are able to score, in an intelligence test, a result higher than 98% of people in general. The British society was founded in 1946 and has a membership of about 18,000. [Latin, 'table': the organization operates on the principle of a 'round table', with all members having equal status]

merchant bank /ˌmɜːtʃənt 'bæŋk/ (finance) A special kind of bank whose functions include financing the transit of goods and providing financial and commercial advice to business.

Mercury /'mɜːkjʊrɪ/ (commerce) A private telecommunications company formed in 1983 to compete with *British Telecom* (now *BT*). [short form of full name, Mercury Communications *Ltd*, itself named after Mercury, the messenger of the gods in Roman mythology]

Meridian /məˈrɪdɪən/ (media) One of the 15 regional television companies of the *ITC*, based in *London* and broadcasting to southern and southeast *England*. [from 'meridian' in sense 'south']

Merlin /'mɜːlɪn/ (tradition) In the stories about *King Arthur*, a famous wizard and Arthur's adviser.

Mermaid Theatre /ˌmɜːmeɪd 'θɪətə(r)/, **the** (arts) A *London* theatre, opened in 1959, that originally staged mainly classic productions but today covers a wide repertoire of modern and traditional plays. [named after the Mermaid Tavern where writers met in the time of *Shakespeare*]

Merry England /ˌmerɪ 'ɪŋglənd/ (tradition) A traditional concept of 'good old England', in particular the *England* of *Elizabethan* times (the 16th century), when life is imagined to have been generally pleasant and the national mood one of optimism. ['merry', now meaning 'cheerful', 'jolly', meant 'pleasant' in the 16th century]

Merry Monarch /ˌmerɪ 'mɒnək/, **the** (history) A nickname of Charles II (1630–85), mainly on account of his many mistresses (including the famous actress and seller of oranges, Nell Gwyn) and his extravagant way of life.

Mersey sound /ˌmɜːzɪ 'saʊnd/, **the** (arts) The characteristic pop music of the *Beatles* and other groups performing in Liverpool (on the river Mersey) in the 1960s.

Messrs /'mesəz/ (life and society) The plural of Mr, used in particular for the names of firms, as 'Messrs J Smith & Sons'. [contraction of 'Messieurs', of French origin]

Methodist /'meθədɪst/ (religion) A member of the *Methodist Church*.

Methodist Church /ˌmeθədɪst ˈtʃɜːtʃ/ (religion) The largest of
the *Free Churches*, founded in 1739 within the *Church of
England* by the preacher John Wesley (1703–91) as an
evangelical revivalist movement, but becoming a separate
body in 1795. The present Church is based on a union in 1932
of most of the different Methodist bodies that had developed
by then. It currently has about 430,000 adult full members
and a community of more than 1.3 million.

Metro /ˈmetrəʊ/, **the** (transport) The urban electric railway
that operates on Tyneside, northeast *England*, to link
Newcastle upon Tyne with surrounding towns such as
Gateshead, Wallsend, Whitley Bay and South Shields. The
service, with full name Tyne and Wear Metro, opened in 1980
and now has 42 stations. Trains run every 10 minutes on four
lines: Greenline, Redline, Yellowline and Blueline. Compare
Metrolink.

Metrolink /ˈmetrəʊˌlɪŋk/ (transport) The private electric
railway that links Manchester's main railway stations and
provides an improved public transport service to the nearby
towns of Altrincham and Bury. The railway, with full name
Manchester Metrolink, opened in 1992. Compare *Metro*.

metropolitan county /ˌmetrəˈpɒlɪtən ˈkaʊntɪ/ (geography) One
of the six conurbations outside *London* named as *counties*[2] in
the reorganization of local government boundaries in *England*
in 1974. The six are: Greater Manchester, Merseyside (centred
on Liverpool), South Yorkshire (centred on Sheffield), Tyne
and Wear (centred on Newcastle upon Tyne and Sunderland),
West *Midlands* (centred on Birmingham and Coventry) and
West Yorkshire (centred on Bradford, Leeds and Wakefield).
Metropolitan counties do not have *county councils* but *district
councils* instead.

Metropolitan Police /ˌmetrəˈpɒlɪtən pəˈliːs/, **the** (law) The
police force responsible for *Greater London*[2] and small parts of
surrounding *counties*[2]. The Metropolitan Police is not
responsible for the *City (of London)*, however, as this has its
own force, the City of London Police. The Metropolitan Police
was founded in 1827.

M4 /ˌem ˈfɔː(r)/ see *motorway* (transport)

MG /ˌem ˈdʒiː/ (transport) The name of a make of popular
sports car, originally produced in the 1920s by the firm of
Morris Garages, at *Oxford*[1].

Michaelmas /ˈmɪklməs/ (tradition) 29 September, and a
quarter day. In the *Church of England* and the *Roman Catholic*

Church, the day is celebrated as that of St Michael and All
Angels. The name is still used for the academic term that
starts about this time in some schools and universities. A
traditional dish for Michaelmas Day was roast goose. The day
is not a *bank holiday*.

middle class /ˌmɪdl ˈklɑːs/ (life and society) A social class not
clearly defined but generally regarded as above *lower class*
and below *upper class*. To this class belong a wide range of
businessmen and professional people, although the term is
frequently used in a critical sense to mean 'bourgeois',
'materialistic', 'petty-minded'.

Middle England /mɪdl ˈɪŋglənd/ (geography) A touristic name
for the *Midlands*.

middle school /ˈmɪdl skuːl/ (education) **1** A *state school* for
pupils aged between nine and 12, 13, or 14 after which they
move on to a senior *comprehensive school*. See also *first
school*. **2** The fourth and fifth years in some *secondary schools*,
when students are preparing for the *GCSE* examination.
['middle' since between the junior or *lower school* and senior
or *upper school*]

Middle Temple /ˌmɪdl ˈtempl/, **the** (law) One of the four *Inns
of Court* in *London*. [so named as between the *Inner Temple*
and a site known as the 'Outer Temple']

Middlesex Hospital /ˌmɪdlseks ˈhɒspɪtl/, **the** (medicine) A
teaching hospital in *London*, founded in 1745. [named after the
county[1] of Middlesex in which London was situated until the
separate County of London was formed in 1888]

midibus /ˈmɪdɪbʌs/ (transport) A small bus, seating about 25
passengers, that operates in some towns and *cities*.
Such buses can operate more economically than standard
buses, especially *double deckers*, and also travel faster.
Midibuses were introduced to central *London* in 1986. [such a
bus is *mid*way in size between an ordinary bus and a
mini*bus*]

Midland (Bank) /ˈmɪdlənd (ˌmɪdlənd ˈbæŋk)/, **the** (finance)
One of the five main English banks, with branches in many
towns and *cities*. [founded in 1836 as the Birmingham and
Midland Bank; see *Midlands*]

Midlands /ˈmɪdləndz/, **the** (geography) The central *counties* of
England, with their many manufacturing industries. The
region is usually thought of as extending from the
metropolitan county of West Midlands to what is generally
known as the East Midlands, a group name for the counties of

Derbyshire, Leicestershire, Northamptonshire and Nottinghamshire.

Midsummer Day /ˌmɪdsʌmə ˈdeɪ/ (tradition) 24 June, and a *quarter day*. In the *Church of England*, the day is celebrated as that of St John the Baptist. At dawn on this day *Druids*[2] greet the sunrise at *Stonehenge*.

MI5 /ˌem aɪ ˈfaɪv/ (defence) The former name, still often used unofficially, of the security service of the British government which deals with counter-intelligence. Compare *MI6*. [initials of 'Military Intelligence', section five]

mild /maɪld/ (food and drink) A kind of beer that is darker in colour than *bitter* and contains fewer hops.

Milk Marque /ˈmɪlk mɑːk/ (commerce) The independent body that controls the supply and marketing of milk in *Britain*.

Milk Race /ˈmɪlk reɪs/, **the** (sport and leisure) An annual international cycle race for amateurs on a road course of over 1,000 miles (1,600 kilometres) round *Britain*. It was first held in 1951 as the 'Tour of Britain', still its official name today. Its present name refers to its sponsors, *Milk Marque*.

milkman /ˈmɪlkmən/ (daily life) A man who delivers bottled milk every day, including *bank holidays* (in most regions of *Britain*), to private houses and business premises such as shops and offices. He makes his deliveries in the early

milkman

morning, often so that the milk is fresh for breakfast, and, although in rural areas he uses conventional transport such as a van, in towns and *cities* he makes deliveries mostly by means of a 'milk float', a small electrically-powered vehicle. The customer normally pays for the milk each week.

Millbank /'mɪlbæŋk/ (London) An embankment on the north bank of the *Thames, London*, on which are situated the *Tate Gallery* and the *Millbank Tower*. [named after a former watermill on the bank there]

Millbank Tower /ˌmɪlbæŋk 'taʊə(r)/, **the** (London) A modern tower block, 34 storeys high, on *Millbank, London*, built in 1963 and currently occupied by the offices of various commercial companies, in particular the engineering firm of Vickers, for whom it was originally designed.

Millionaires' Row /ˌmɪljəneəz 'rəʊ/ (London) A nickname for the street of Kensington Palace Gardens, *London*, famous for its houses belonging to rich people.

Milton, John /'mɪltən, dʒɒn/ (people) John Milton (1608–74) is best known for his great poem 'Paradise Lost' (1667), written when he had already gone blind. It is based on the Old Testament theme of man's disobedience in the Garden of Eden, with Satan as the main character. Milton's two other best-known works are 'Paradise Regained' (1671) and 'Samson Agonistes' (1671). Milton has had his imitators in more recent times, but none has matched the rich style and heroic characterization of his greatest epic poem.

mince pie /ˌmɪns 'paɪ/ (food and drink) A small round pastry pie filled with *mincemeat¹*, and traditionally eaten at *Christmas*.

mincemeat /'mɪnsmiːt/ (food and drink) **1** A rich mixture of dried fruit, spices and other ingredients used for making *mince pies*. **2** Minced meat.

MIND /maɪnd/ (charities) A charitable organization founded in 1946 to promote the mental health and welfare of people who are mentally ill. Its official title is the National Association for Mental Health, but with the aim of publicizing its objectives it adopted the name MIND after a campaign in 1971.

Mini /'mɪnɪ/ (transport) The name of a series of small cars manufactured by *Rover* since the 1960s, when they were particularly popular among young people.

minister /'mɪnɪstə(r)/ (**1** religion **2, 3, 4** government) **1** A clergyman in any one of the *Free Churches*. **2** The head of a government *department*. Most of these are formally called *Secretaries of State*. **3** A minister of state who is a government minister appointed to help a Secretary of State (see *minister²*) with the work of his department. **4** A non-departmental office-holder in the government, such as the *Chancellor of the Duchy of Lancaster* or the *Paymaster General*.

ministry /'mɪnɪstrɪ/ (government) **1** A collective term for all the *ministers²,³,⁴* in a government. **2** A government *department* headed by a minister² or a *Secretary of State*. **3** The building where such a department operates.

minor /'maɪnə(r)/ (law) For legal purposes, a young person under the age of 18.

minster /'mɪnstə(r)/ (religion) A name used for certain cathedrals and large *churches*, especially ones originally part of a monastery. Among the best known are York Minster and Beverley Minster (Humberside).

Minton /'mɪntən/ (style) A fine-quality chinaware manufactured in Stoke-on-Trent, Staffordshire, since 1798. [first produced by the potter Thomas Minton (1765-1836)]

MIRAS /'maɪræs/ (finance) A special scheme that allows a person making payments for a *mortgage* to a *building society* or other financial body to deduct and keep the amount of *income tax* due on the interest payable on the money loaned. [abbreviation of 'Mortgage Interest Relief At Source']

Mirror /'mɪrə(r)/ see *Daily Mirror* (media)

MI6 /ˌem aɪ 'sɪks/ (defence) The former name, still popularly used, of the intelligence and espionage agency of the British government. Compare *MI5*.

Miss /mɪs/ (life and society) **1** A title normally used, in speech and writing, for an unmarried woman or girl, placed either before the first name (as 'Miss Jane Brown') or before the surname ('Miss Brown'). **2** A title sometimes used by the media for a professional married woman, such as a writer, actress or sportswoman, who has retained her maiden name for her public role. See also *Ms*. **3** A form of address sometimes used by schoolchildren to a female teacher and, less often, by a customer to attract the attention of a female assistant in a shop, café, etc.

M'lud /mə'lʌd/ (law) A conventional written formula used to represent the pronunciation of *'My Lord'* when addressing a judge in a court of law. See *lord³*.

mock turtle soup /ˌmɒk ˌtɜːtl ˈsuːp/ (food and drink) A kind of imitation turtle soup made from a calf's head.

mod /mɒd/, **the** (arts) An annual meeting in the *Highlands* of *Scotland* with musical and literary contests in which *Gaelic*, not English, is the language used. [Gaelic, 'assembly']

Mods /mɒdz/, **the** (life and society) **1** A name for teenagers who in the 1960s aimed to rival the *Rockers*. Mods were neatly dressed, with short hair, and drove motor scooters. There were frequent fights between the two groups, especially on *bank holidays* at seaside resorts such as *Brighton*. **2** A name for teenagers and young adults who go on motorcycles to seaside resorts as the earlier Mods had done. They do not usually fight with rival groups, since there are now no Rockers, but they do sometimes fight with other young people who live locally or are on holiday there. [short for 'modern']

Mods /mɒdz/ (education) The first *honours degree* at *Oxford University*, held in classics and some other subjects, with the final examination being *Greats*. [short for 'Moderations', since the examiners are officially known as Moderators]

M1 /ˌem ˈwʌn/ see *motorway* (transport)

Monopolies and Mergers Commission /məˌnɒpəliz ənd ˈmɜːdʒəz kəˈmɪʃn/, **the** **(MMC, the)** (government) An independent body established in 1948 to investigate and report on any monopoly or company merger that could unreasonably prevent competition. In 1993, for example, it recommended that *British Gas*, which has a monopoly on gas supplies in *Britain*, should allow private gas companies to compete.

Montagu Motor Museum /ˌmɒntəgjuː ˈməʊtə mjuːˌzɪəm/, **the** (transport) A private museum of old motor-cars (especially *veteran cars* and *vintage cars*) in the grounds of Palace House, *Beaulieu*, Hampshire, a *country house* that is the home of Lord Montagu (born 1936). The museum, formally known as the National Motor Museum, was founded by Lord Montagu in 1952 in memory of his father, an early motor-car enthusiast.

Monument /ˈmɒnjʊmənt/, **the** (London) A stone column in east central *London* commemorating the *Great Fire* of 1666. The column was built in 1671–7, and is 202 feet (61.5 metres) high—popularly regarded as the exact distance of the column from the baker's shop where the Great Fire started.

Moonraker /ˈmuːnreɪkə(r)/ (tradition) A nickname for a native or inhabitant of the *county* of Wiltshire. According to an old tale, some Wiltshiremen, who had smuggled casks of brandy into the county, were caught one evening by a customs officer just as they were trying to rake the casks out of the pond where they had hidden them. When asked what they were doing, they replied that they were 'raking for the moon', whose reflection they could see in the water. The customs officer, pitying such apparent stupidity, passed on, leaving the quick-thinking men with their brandy.

Moor /mɔː(r)/, **the** (law) A colloquial name for *Dartmoor*[2].

Moor Park /ˌmɔː ˈpɑːk/ (sport and leisure) A well-known golf course near Rickmansworth, Hertfordshire.

MORI /ˈmɒrɪ/ (life and society) An organization that conducts public opinion polls, established in 1969 as a joint Anglo-American enterprise. [initials of *M*arket and *O*pinion *R*esearch *I*nternational]

morning coat /ˈmɔːnɪŋ kəʊt/ (clothing) A type of frock coat with broad, rounded tails, forming part of *morning dress*.

morning dress /ˈmɔːnɪŋ dres/ (clothing) A formal type of dress for men, consisting of *morning coat*, dark grey trousers and (usually) grey top hat. It is worn for formal occasions in the early part of the day, as distinct from *evening dress*.

Morning Star /ˌmɔːnɪŋ ˈstɑː(r)/, **the** (media) A daily *popular paper* that formerly supported the Communist Party, who founded it in 1930. Until 1966 it was called the 'Daily Worker'. Its current circulation is about 7,000 (1972 - 48,750).

morris dance

morris dance /'mɒrɪs dɑːns/ (sport and leisure) An old English folk dance usually performed by a group of men wearing a distinctive costume which includes knee-straps covered in small bells. [according to some, 'morris' denotes the Moorish origin of the dance]

Morris, Desmond /'mɒrɪs, 'dezmənd/ (people) Desmond Morris (born 1928) is a prolific writer on anthropology and zoology, and especially on the behaviour of human beings and animals. Among his many popular books on the subject are 'The Naked Ape' (1967), about man as a 'human animal', 'Manwatching' (1977), about human behaviour, and later 'Watching' books, such as 'Bodywatching' (1985), a 'field-guide to the human species', 'Catwatching' (1986) and others.

mortarboard /'mɔːtəbɔːd/ (education) A black academic *cap*[5] with a tassel on top, worn by the students and members of the teaching staff of some universities and schools. [cap has flat, square top resembling the square board used by builders for carrying mortar]

mortgage /'mɔːgɪdʒ/ (finance) An agreement by which a person can buy a house by means of a loan from a *building society* or other source. The buyer must pay back the loan in instalments, usually monthly. If he fails to do this, the loaner can legally claim the house. [Old French, 'dead pledge']

Moss Bros /'mɒs brɒs/ (clothing) A firm with branches in several towns and *cities* where men's clothes, in particular *evening dress* and *morning dress*, can be bought or hired. The firm was founded in 1881. [abbreviation for 'Moss Brothers']

mortarboard

MOT (test) /ˌem əʊ 'tiː (test)/, **the (Ministry of Transport test)** (transport). The popular name for the annual test of a motor vehicle to make sure that it is working properly and will run safely on the road. In *Great Britain* private cars and light vans which are three or more years old must be tested (at private garages authorized to do the test); in *Northern Ireland* private cars five or more years old must be tested (at official vehicle inspection centres). Heavy goods vehicles (see *HGV*[1]) are also subject to annual tests at special testing stations.

Motability /ˌməʊtə'bɪlətɪ/ (transport) An independent organization that provides special motor vehicles for disabled drivers and passengers. The drivers pay for the vehicle with payments from their *disability living allowance*. [blend of '*mot*or' and 'dis*ability*']

Mothering Sunday /'mʌðərɪŋ ˌsʌndɪ/ (tradition) The fourth *Sunday* in *Lent*, when people traditionally give or send cards and presents to their mothers. The day was originally a *church* festival observed mainly by children. Today it is popularly kept by everyone and is usually called *Mother's Day*.

Mother's Day /'mʌðəz deɪ/ (tradition) The popular name for *Mothering Sunday*.

Motor Show /'məʊtə ʃəʊ/, **the** (transport) An international exhibition of the latest motor car models, held every two years at the *National Exhibition Centre*, Birmingham.

Motorail /'məʊtəreɪl/ (transport) A service operated by *BR* to transport motor-cars and their passengers on special trains over certain long-distance routes (mainly from the south of *England* to *Scotland*). [blend of 'motor' and 'rail']

motorway /'məʊtəweɪ/ (transport) A main road for fast-

motorway

moving traffic, usually with two or three lanes in each
direction, and running between large *cities*. Motorways
usually have the same number as the *A-road* that they
duplicate or replace. The *M1*, for example, runs north from
London to Leeds, and the *M4* runs west to Bristol and south
Wales. A well-known motorway is the *M25* (the London
Orbital Motorway), which encircles *Greater London* and is
notorious for its traffic jams. Most motorways are gradually
being extended or widened. See also *service area, slip road*.

Mount Pleasant /ˌmaʊnt 'pleznt/ (commerce) The name of the
Post Office's main sorting office, in *London*, and one of the
largest of its kind in the world. [original site was given name
humorously, referring to former large mound of refuse and
cinders at the end of a lane there]

MP /ˌem 'piː/ **(Member of Parliament)** (government) A
member of the *House of Commons* elected by the voters of his
constituency to represent them in *Parliament* and to pursue the
policies of his particular political party.

Mr /'mɪstə(r)/ (life and society) **1** A title used in spoken and
written form of a man, either before the first name (as 'Mr
James Green') or before the surname ('Mr Green'). **2** A form
of address used in the same way. **3** A form of address
conventionally used, normally before the surname alone, for
a senior warrant officer in the *Royal Navy*, for the officers of a
merchant ship (except the captain), for a surgeon, and for the
holders of certain posts in authority (as 'Mr Chairman', 'Mr
Speaker'). **4** A form of address occasionally used alone,
especially by a child to a man or a younger man to an older
(although such usage is considered over-familiar). In this use
it is always written 'Mister'.

MRP /ˌem ɑː 'piː/ **(manufacturer's recommended price)**
(commerce) The retail price of an article recommended by its
manufacturer. Such prices are usually quoted when the goods
are actually sold at a lower price in a sale or by a mail order
company, for example 'garden furniture set £39.99 (MRP
£59.99)'.

Mrs /'mɪsɪz/ (life and society) **1** A title used in spoken and
written form of married women, either before the first name
('Mrs Anne Hodgson') or before the surname ('Mrs
Hodgson'). **2** A form of address used the same way. **3** A form
of address occasionally used alone, especially familiarly or
jokingly (and usually written as 'Missis'). [in origin an
abbreviation of 'mistress']

Mrs Beeton /ˌmɪsɪz ˈbiːtn/ (food and drink) The short name of a popular cookery book, still published, which originally appeared in 1861 as 'The Book of Household Management', by Mrs Isabella Beeton (1836–65).

Ms /məz/ (life and society) A title in use in *Britain* from the 1970s (although earlier in the United States) for a woman regardless of her marital status, largely in order to avoid the use of *Miss¹* (unmarried) or *Mrs¹* (married). The title is by no means universally accepted, and many women prefer either the older titles or no title at all. [artificially devised to be an abbreviation of both 'Miss' and 'Mrs']

MSF /ˌem es ˈef/, **the (Manufacturing, Science and Finance Union, the)** (work) A trade union formed in 1988 as the result of a merger between two earlier unions. It currently has about 653,000 members working in a wide range of managerial, professional and technical areas.

M25 /ˌem ˌtwentɪ ˈfaɪv/ see *motorway* (transport)

muffin /ˈmʌfɪn/ (food and drink) A thick round yeast cake somewhat resembling a large *crumpet* (although not as porous), and also served toasted and spread with butter.

Murder Squad /ˈmɜːdə skwɒd/, **the** (law) A colloquial name for the *CID*, the detective branch of the police force. [based on *Fraud Squad*]

Murdoch, Iris /ˈmɜːdɒk, ˈaɪərɪs/ (people) Iris Murdoch (born 1919) is a novelist who has gained an international reputation for her so-called 'psychological detective stories', in which *middle class* and *upper class* characters are involved in a series of unusual or even bizarre incidents. Underneath the main plots, however, the novels usually have a philosophical basis that deals with such matters as the nature of religion and the contrast between good and evil, as well as illustrating different types of sexuality. Iris Murdoch was awarded the title *Dame* in 1987.

Murdoch, Rupert /ˈmɜːdɒk, ˈruːpət/ (people) Rupert Murdoch (born 1931) is an Australian who became a prominent journalist and newspaper owner. In the late 1960s he bought the *News of the World* and The *Sun,* and a few years later also acquired The *Times* and the *Sunday Times.* At the time, all four papers except the 'News of the World' were selling at a loss. Under Murdoch their sales recovered. In 1987 Rupert Murdoch bought a fifth newspaper, *Today,* and in 1989 his satellite television company *Sky Television* came into operation.

Murrayfield /ˈmʌrɪfiːld/ (sport and leisure) The ground of the Scottish *Rugby Union* in *Edinburgh*.

Museum of London /mjuːˌzɪəm əv ˈlʌndən/, **the** (London) A museum of the history of *London* from prehistoric times to the present day, opened in the *City (of London)* in 1976 as an amalgamation of the former Guildhall Museum (on the site of the present *Barbican*) and the *London Museum*.

Museum of Mankind /mjuːˌzɪəm əv mænˈkaɪnd/, **the** (arts) A museum illustrating the life and culture of the native-peoples of Africa, America and the Pacific. Until 1970 it was housed in the *British Museum*, where it was officially the Ethnological Department. Because of lack of space it was then moved to its present site near the *Royal Academy*, and was renamed.

Museum of the Moving Image /mjuːˌzɪəm əv ðə ˌmuːvɪŋ ˈɪmɪdʒ/, **the (MOMI)** (London) A museum opened on the *South Bank*, *London*, in 1988. It contains exhibitions of 'moving images' from early historic times to the present, ranging from ancient shadow displays to modern television and video, including images produced by optic fibres and lasers.

mushy peas /ˌmʌʃɪ ˈpiːz/ (food and drink) Peas that are cooked until they are soft and pulpy, whether in the home or commercially. Mushy peas are a favourite with many children.

musical chairs /ˌmjuːzɪkl ˈtʃeəz/ (sport and leisure) A popular children's game. While music is played children run round a group of chairs placed back to back and numbering one fewer than the number of players. When the music suddenly stops, the children race to sit down on the chairs, the last player being out of the game, since he has no chair to sit on. The number of chairs is then progressively reduced by one until only one chair is left. The winner is the first of the two remaining players to sit on this chair when the music finally stops.

Muzak /ˈmjuːzæk/ (commerce) The trade name of a system of background music relayed to restaurants, shops, clubs and other public buildings. The term is also used as a general name for any recorded light music played in shops, restaurants, *pubs* or factories.

My Lady /maɪ ˈleɪdɪ/ (life and society) A form of address used to a woman who bears the official title of *Lady³*. Compare *My Lord*.

My Lord /maɪ ˈlɔːd/ (life and society) A form of address used to a man who bears the official title of *Lord*[1,2,3]. See also *M'lud*.

mystery tour /ˈmɪstəri ˌtʊə(r)/ (transport) A commercially organized coach tour to a destination known only to the driver. Such tours are popular at seaside resorts.

NAAFI /'næfɪ/ (defence) One of a number of canteens and shops providing services for the armed forces both in *Britain* and overseas. [abbreviation of *N*avy, *A*rmy and *A*ir Force *I*nstitutes]

Naffy /'næfɪ/ (defence) A colloquial spelling for a *NAAFI* or the organization that runs them.

nanny /'nænɪ/ (life and society) A woman employed by a professional or *upper class* family to look after one or more young children in the family. She will often live with the family, accompany them on holidays and visits abroad, and frequently becomes a firm family friend. Formerly, nannies were sometimes even called by the family surname instead of their own, for example, 'Nanny Simpson'. Compare *childminder*. See also *Norland nurse*.

National /'næʃnəl/, **the** (sport and leisure) A short title for the *Grand National*.

national anthem /ˌnæʃnəl 'ænθəm/ see *God Save the Queen* (life and society)

national call /'næʃnəl kɔːl/ (commerce) The official name for a telephone call over a distance greater than 35 miles (56 kilometres). Compare *local call*.

National Coal Board /ˌnæʃnəl 'kəʊl bɔːd/ see *British Coal* (work)

National Council for Civil Liberties /ˌnæʃnəl ˌkaʊnsl fə ˌsɪvl 'lɪbətɪz/, **the (NCCL, the)** (life and society) A voluntary body founded in 1934 to promote the rights of the individual citizen and to oppose discrimination of all kinds and the abuse of power. Some people have recently criticized it because they feel it is becoming too openly political.

National Curriculum /ˌnæʃnəl kəˈrɪkjʊləm/, **the** (education) The common course of study in *state schools* in

England and *Wales*, introduced from 1989. The course concentrates on the three central ('core') subjects of English, mathematics and science, and the seven basic ('foundation') subjects of history, geography, technology, music, art, physical education and, at *secondary school* level, a foreign language. For each subject there are attainment targets, and there are assessments and tests for pupils aged 7, 11 and 14, with the *GCSE* the main form of assessment for those aged 16.

National Debt /ˌnæʃnəl ˈdet/, **the** (finance) The amount of money borrowed each year by the government from the public to meet its requirements for spending. Most of the money is borrowed as either long-term or short-term loans in the form of *gilt-edged securities*. The National Debt first featured in the economy in 1694, when the *Bank of England* was founded. It was then £49 million. The amount has gradually risen ever since, so that in 1903 it was £798 million and in 1991 £198,700 million.

National Exhibition Centre /ˌnæʃnəl eksɪˈbɪʃn ˌsentə(r)/, **the (NEC, the)** (commerce) A large exhibition complex east of Birmingham, opened in 1976 to house many major exhibitions, including some, such as the *Motor Show*, that were previously held only in *London*.

National Farmers Union /ˌnæʃnəl ˈfɑːməz ˌjuːnɪən/, **the (NFU, the)** (work) An association (not a trades union) to which farmers belong. It was founded in 1908 and has the aim of giving practical advice and support to farmers, especially in particular fields such as poultry farming, beekeeping and fish farming. There is a separate NFU for *Scotland* (National Farmers Union of Scotland). The NFU in *England* and *Wales* has at present about 110,000 members.

National Film Theatre /ˌnæʃnəl ˈfɪlm ˌθɪətə(r)/, **the (NFT, the)** (arts) A cinema theatre founded in 1951 on the *South Bank* complex, *London*, as an extension of the *British Film Institute*. It runs a daily showing of important or historic films of all kinds and nationalities in two auditoriums, and holds the annual London Film Festival.

National Front /ˌnæʃnəl ˈfrʌnt/, **the (NF, the)** (politics) A small extreme right-wing political party founded in 1966 and campaigning, among other radical policies, for the expulsion of coloured immigrants from *Britain*, and for the introduction of *corporal punishment* and *capital punishment* for certain criminal offences.

National Gallery /ˌnæʃnəl ˈgælərɪ/, **the** (arts) One of *London*'s best-known art galleries, in *Trafalgar Square*. It was founded in 1824 and houses one of the most important collections of Italian art outside Italy. An extension known as the Sainsbury Wing was opened next to the existing building in 1991.

National Garden Festival /ˌnæʃnəl ˈgɑːdn ˌfestəvl/ (daily life) A special large-scale 'garden show' held in an *inner city* area every two years from 1984 with the aim of improving the area. The first was in Liverpool. Subsequent festivals were held in Stoke-on-Trent in 1986, *Glasgow* in 1988, Gateshead in 1990, and Ebbw Vale, south *Wales*, in 1992. The festivals were then discontinued.

national grid /ˌnæʃnəl ˈgrɪd/, **the** (geography) **1** The national network of transmission lines, pipes, etc that distributes electricity, gas and water (or any of these individually) throughout *Britain*. See also *National Grid Company*. **2** The network of horizontal and vertical lines on *Ordnance Survey* maps that serves to locate places on the maps. The origin of the grid lies to the west of the *Scilly Isles* at a point whose true co-ordinates are 2°W, 49°N.

National Grid Company /ˌnæʃnəl ˈgrɪd ˌkʌmpənɪ/, **the (NGC, the)** (commerce) The independent company responsible for the transmission of electricity through the *national grid[1]* in *England* and *Wales*. It owns two pumped storage stations in north Wales.

national insurance /ˌnæʃnəl ɪnˈʃɔːrəns/ (finance) A system of compulsory contributions by employees and employers to provide state financial assistance in sickness, retirement, unemployment and certain other cases.

National Lottery /ˌnæʃnəl ˈlɒtərɪ/, **the** (charities) The national lottery that the government plans to introduce in 1994. Income from the lottery will help fund sport, the arts, the conservation of 'heritage' (historic buildings and the natural environment) and various charities.

national park /ˌnæʃnəl ˈpɑːk/ (geography) One of the 10 large rural areas designated by the *Countryside Commission* in *England* and the *Countryside Council for Wales* in *Wales* as deserving both protection and the provision of amenities for the public. They are 'national' in the sense that they are of value to the nation as a whole, but their land is almost entirely privately owned. Each park has its own local authority. The *Broads* are not a national park as such but have an equivalent status and their own local authority.

National Physical Laboratory /ˌnæʃnəl ˈfɪzɪkl ləˌbɒrətrɪ/, **the (NPL, the)** (science and technology) The research station of the *Department* of Trade and Industry, based mainly at Teddington, *Greater London*, where it is the national standards laboratory of the *United Kingdom*. Its work includes establishing internationally acceptable basic standards of measurement, and research in mathematics and computer usage and in marine and offshore technology.

National Portrait Gallery /ˌnæʃnəl ˈpɔːtreɪt ˌgælərɪ/, **the** (arts) *Britain*'s leading art gallery of portraits of famous people in British history. It is next to the *National Gallery* in *London*. It was founded in 1856, and contains over 8,000 original portraits and more than 500,000 photographs.

National Power /ˌnæʃnəl ˈpaʊə(r)/ (commerce) The larger of the two independent companies, founded in 1991, that generated electricity in England and *Wales*. The other is *PowerGen*. Both companies are fuelled by coal and (to a much lesser extent) oil, unlike *Nuclear Electric*. National Power currently owns 35 power stations.

National Railway Museum /ˌnæʃnəl ˈreɪlweɪ mjuːˌzɪəm/, **the** (transport) A museum of railway relics, locomotives and rolling stock opened in York in 1975 as a department of the *Science Museum, London*.

National Rivers Authority /ˌnæʃnəl ˈrɪvəz ɔːˌθɒrətɪ/, **the (NRA, the)** (government) The government body that regulates the environment of rivers, lakes, reservoirs and coastal waters in *England* and *Wales*. It oversees the volume or flow of water, controls pollution, provides defences against flooding, protects fishing, and monitors conservation and navigation generally.

National Savings Bank /ˌnæʃnəl ˈseɪvɪŋz bæŋk/, **the (NSB, the)** (finance) A savings bank operated by the *Post Office* and offering a wide range of investment schemes, among them *National Savings Certificates* and *Premium Bonds*.

National Savings Certificates /ˌnæʃnəl ˈseɪvɪŋz səˌtɪfɪkəts/ (finance) Certificates, offered for sale by the *Post Office* through the *National Savings Bank*, that give an increasing rate of interest to the purchaser until they are sold back, usually after a fixed number of years. No *income tax* is payable on the interest of the certificates, which were first issued in 1916 to raise money for the First World War. There is a fixed upper limit to the number of certificates an individual may hold.

national scenic area /ˌnæʃnəl ˈsiːnɪk eərɪə/ (geography) The
equivalent in *Scotland* of a *national park* in *England* and *Wales*.
At present there are 40 such areas, amounting to 13 per cent
of the country.

national service /ˌnæʃnəl ˈsɜːvɪs/ (history) A compulsory
period of service in the armed forces introduced during the
Second World War (for men aged 18 to 41), from 1948 to 1951
(for 21 months for men aged 19 to 25), and from 1951 to 1960
(for two years for men aged 18½ to 25).

national trail /ˌnæʃnəl ˈtreɪl/ (sport and leisure) An official
long-distance route for walkers across countryside in *England*
and *Wales*. Of the present 10 trails, one of the best-known,
and one of the longest, is the *Pennine Way*.

National Trust /ˌnæʃnəl ˈtrʌst/, **the (NT, the)** (life and
society) A charitable organization founded in 1895 to protect
and preserve historic buildings and countryside areas of
natural beauty in *England* and *Wales*. It currently owns over
300 *country houses* and other buildings, and has a
membership of more than 2 million. [full title, National Trust
for Places of Historic Interest or Natural Beauty]

National Trust for Scotland /ˌnæʃnəl ˌtrʌst fə ˈskɒtlənd/, **the
(NTS, the)** (life and society) The equivalent body in *Scotland*
to the *National Trust* in *England* and *Wales*.

National Westminster (Bank) /ˌnæʃnəl ˈwestmɪnstə(r) (ˌnæʃnəl
ˌwestmɪnstə ˈbæŋk)/, **the** (finance) One of the five main banks
in *England*, with branches in many towns and cities. It was
formed in 1968 as the result of a merger between the National
Provincial Bank and the Westminster Bank. The Bank
introduced the *Access* credit card in 1972, in association with
Lloyds (Bank) and the *Midland (Bank)*.

National Youth Orchestra /ˌnæʃnəl ˈjuːθ ˌɔːkɪstrə/, **the (NYO,
the)** (arts) The leading orchestra of young professional
musicians and music students in *Britain*, organized through a
system of local youth orchestras.

National Youth Theatre /ˌnæʃnəl ˈjuːθ ˌθɪətə(r)/, **the** (arts) A
company of young professional stage actors based at the
Shaw Theatre in northwest *London*.

nationalized industries /ˌnæʃnəlaɪzd ˈɪndəstrɪz/, **the**
(commerce) Nationalized (state-owned) industries in *Britain*
were mostly created after 1945 by the *Labour Party*. Under the
Conservative Party, in power from 1979, most of them were
privatized, however. There are currently four remaining
major nationalized industries: *British Coal, BR,* the *Post Office*

238

and *London Transport*. There are plans to privatize almost all of these in turn. Former nationalized industries privatized since 1980 include *BAe*, *British Airways*, *British Gas*, *British Steel*, *BT*, and the various water and electricity companies.

nativity play

nativity play /nə'tɪvətɪ pleɪ/ (tradition) A play performed by young children, usually before *Christmas*, showing the biblical story of the birth of Jesus Christ.

NATO /'neɪtəʊ/ (defence) The basic purpose of NATO, as established in 1952, is to enable its member countries to maintain peace with freedom by persuading any potential enemy that the use of force will cause the countries who are members to fight back in self-defence. At the same time, NATO countries are continuously negotiating to reduce the level of nuclear and conventional arms. The defence policy of *Britain* is based on that of NATO and is fully committed to it. [abbreviation of 'North Atlantic Treaty Organization']

Natural History Museum /ˌnætʃrəl 'hɪstrɪ mjuːˌzɪəm/, **the** (education) *London*'s leading natural history museum. It houses five major departments (zoology, entomology, palaeontology with anthropology, botany and mineralogy), and has an extensive educational programme. It was founded as part of the *British Museum*, although housed separately since 1862. [official title British Museum (Natural History), although separated administratively from the Museum in 1963]

naturalization /ˌnaetʃrələɪ'zeɪʃn/ (law) A foreign person may apply for British nationality if he or she has lived in *Britain* for five years, can speak English (or Welsh or Scottish *Gaelic*) reasonably well, and intends to go on living in Britain. The non-British wife or husband of a British citizen need have lived in Britain for only three years, and need not be able to speak English. Naturalization is ultimately at the discretion of the *Home Secretary*.

Nature /'neɪtʃə(r)/ (media) A weekly scientific magazine first published in 1879 and having a current circulation of about 51,000.

nature reserve /'neɪtʃə rɪˌzɜːv/ (geography) An area of special botanical or zoological interest, especially one containing a rare species, that is carefully protected and preserved in its natural state. There are at present 245 national reserves of this type in *Britain*. The first marine nature reserve was designated in 1986 as the island of Lundy, off the coast of southwest England. Further local nature reserves have been set aside by *local authorities*.

NatWest /ˌnæt'west/, **the** (finance) A popular abbreviation of the name of the *National Westminster Bank*.

naughty postcard /ˌnɔːtɪ 'pəʊstkɑːd/ (daily life) A picture postcard traditionally sold at seaside resorts and showing a brightly coloured illustration with an amusing 'naughty' (usually punning) caption. ['naughty' in the sense, 'mildly indecent']

NCP /ˌen siː 'piː/ **(National Car Parks)** (commerce) A *London*-based commercial company that operates many paying car parks throughout *Britain*.

Neighbourhood Watch /ˌneɪbəhʊd 'wɒtʃ/ (daily life) A scheme by which the residents of a particular district form a voluntary association to prevent crime and assist the police by keeping watch on each other's houses and property. If a member of the scheme sees anything suspicious, he reports it to the police. There are currently about 92,000 such schemes in operation in *England* and *Wales*. Some people are critical of the scheme, feeling that it allows their neighbours to pry into their private affairs.

Neighbours /'neɪbəz/ (media) A popular 'soap opera' (melodramatic series about a family and its friends) screened twice daily five times a week on *BBC 1* since 1986. The series, which is Australian in origin, is particularly popular with young viewers, and deals with the lives and loves of people living on Ramsay Street, in the fictional Melbourne suburb of

Erinsborough. It currently has a regular viewing audience of about 8 million.

Nelson's Column /ˌnelsnz ˈkɒləm/ (London) A tall column nearly 185 feet (44 m) high in *Trafalgar Square, London,* with a statue of Admiral Nelson (1758–1805). It was erected there in 1840–3 with Trafalgar Square itself planned as a memorial to Nelson. The Column is also famous for the bronze lions by the sculptor, Landseer, added at its base in 1867.

Nessie /ˈnesɪ/ (tradition) A popular nickname for the *Loch Ness Monster.*

Network SouthEast /ˌnetwɜːk saʊθˈiːst/ (transport) One of the five business sectors of *BR,* operating passenger services in southern and southeast *England,* in the region round *London.* In this region passengers are able to travel at a reduced rate on purchase of an annual 'Network Card', a type of *railcard.* The region is more extensive than its name suggests, and includes towns as far north of London as *Oxford[1]* and *Cambridge[1]* and as far west as Southampton and Exeter.

New Commonwealth /ˌnjuː ˈkɒmənwelθ/, **the** (geography) A term sometimes used for all *Commonwealth[1]* countries apart from the older countries of Canada, Australia and New Zealand.

New Covent Garden (Market) /ˌnjuː ˌkɒvənt ˈɡɑːdn (ˌnjuː ˌkɒvənt ˌɡɑːdn ˈmɑːkɪt)/ (London) The present official name of *Covent Garden[1]* since its move to its new premises in 1973.

New Forest pony /ˌnjuː fɒrɪst ˈpəʊnɪ/ (animal world) A breed of pony living in semi-wild conditions in the New Forest, Hampshire. When tamed, such ponies are popular as safe mounts for children, since they have already become used to motor traffic on roads running through the Forest.

New Sadler's Wells Opera /ˌnjuː ˌsædləz ˌwelz ˈɒprə/, **the** (arts) An opera company founded in 1982 and giving performances of light operas at *Sadler's Wells (Theatre), London.*

New Scientist /ˌnjuː ˈsaɪəntɪst/, **the** (media) A weekly magazine on latest developments in science and technology. It was first published in 1956 and has a current circulation of about 102,000.

New Scotland Yard /ˌnjuː skɒtlənd ˈjɑːd/ (law) The headquarters of the *London Metropolitan Police,* housing the *Flying Squad,* the *Murder Squad* (see *CID*), the Criminal Record Office and the Traffic Control Department. The original headquarters was at *Scotland Yard,* off *Whitehall[1],* and the name became New Scotland Yard when the headquarters moved first to a site by the *Thames* in 1890, then to its present building in *Westminster[1]* in 1966.

New Statesman and Society /ˌnju: ˌsteɪtsmən ən sə'saɪətɪ/ (media) A weekly magazine of left-wing political and sociological interest, formed in 1988 as the merger of two earlier magazines, 'New Society' and 'New Statesman'. Its current circulation is about 37,000.

new town /'nju: taʊn/ (geography) A planned town built since 1900 by the government with the aim of encouraging the move of industry and population from crowded cities to new areas. The term particularly applies to the 32 new towns named as such since 1946 (21 in *England*, two in *Wales*, five in *Scotland*, four in *Northern Ireland*).

New Year Honours /ˌnju: jɪər 'ɒnəz/, **the** (life and society) The announcement of honorary titles, orders and medals awarded annually by the sovereign on *New Year's Day*. Compare *Birthday Honours*.

New Year's Day /ˌnju: jɪəz 'deɪ/ (tradition) 1 January, and a *bank holiday* (held on the Monday following if the day falls on a Saturday or *Sunday*). The holiday is not marked with any particular custom in *Britain*, largely because it comes so soon after *Christmas*. Compare *New Year's Eve*.

New Year's Eve /ˌnju: jɪəz 'i:v/ (tradition) 31 December, when traditionally parties and dances are held and when, in *Scotland*, *Hogmanay* is celebrated. In many large towns and *cities* there is a public gathering to 'see the New Year in', the largest and liveliest usually being held in *Trafalgar Square*, *London*. The day is not a *bank holiday*.

Newmarket /'nju:mɑːkɪt/ (geography) A town in Suffolk that has long been associated with horse-racing, where there is a famous racecourse. The *Jockey Club* also has its premises there. In 1983 the National Horseracing Museum was opened at Newmarket.

News At Ten /ˌnju:z ət 'ten/ (media) A nightly television news programme broadcast at 10.00 by *ITN* since 1964. Compare *Nine O'Clock News*.

News of the World /ˌnju:z əv ðə 'wɜːld/, **The** (media) A *Sunday popular paper* with a strong 'human interest', reporting scandals and criminal cases in detail and publishing features on famous people and those in the news. It was founded in 1843 and has a current circulation of about 4.7 million (1972 – 6 million), higher than any other paper. It has a colour supplement, 'Sunday Magazine', mainly devoted to features on popular celebrities.

NFU /ˌen ef ˈjuː/ see *National Farmers Union* (work)

NHS /ˌen eɪtʃ ˈes/, **the (National Health Service, the)** (medicine) The system of national medical services throughout *Britain* that is largely financed by taxation, and that enables people, especially the young, the elderly and the needy, to obtain medical prescriptions and hospital and other treatment either free of charge or at reduced cost. The service was established in 1948. In 1988 the government began a radical review of the way the NHS was run and in particular the way it was financed.

Nightrider /ˈnaɪt ˌraɪdə(r)/, **the** (transport) Two express trains running nightly without sleeping cars. One goes from *London* to *Glasgow* and the other from London to Aberdeen.

999 /ˌnaɪn naɪn ˈnaɪn/ **nine-nine-nine** (daily life) The emergency telephone number to be called if the fire brigade, the police, or an ambulance are needed.

Nine O'Clock News /ˌnaɪn əklɒk ˈnjuːz/, **the** (media) **1** A nightly television news programme broadcast at 9.00 by *BBC 1* since 1970. **2** The nightly radio news broadcast made at this time by the *BBC* from 1927 to 1960.

nineteenth hole /ˌnaɪntiːnθ ˈhəʊl/, **the** (sport and leisure) A humorous name among golf players for the *bar¹* in the clubhouse, to which players go after playing the eighteenth (and final) hole on the course.

nine-to-five-job /ˌnaɪn tə ˈfaɪv dʒɒb/ (work) In many offices, a standard working day of eight hours, from 9.00 am to 5.00 pm.

Ninian Park /ˌnɪnɪən ˈpɑːk/ (sport and leisure) The stadium of *Cardiff City football club*, in west *Cardiff*. [after park there]

NME /ˌen ˌem ˈiː/, **the (New Musical Express, the)** (media) A weekly magazine about British and American rock music and personalities. It was founded in 1952, and has one of the highest circulations of all popular music periodicals, currently around 115,000.

Nonconformists /ˌnɒnkənˈfɔːmɪsts/ (religion) The members of any Protestant church except the *Church of England*, including the *Methodists*, the *Baptists*, the *United Reformed Church* and the *Church of Scotland*. Compare *Free Churches*. [so called because they do not conform to the established *church*, ie, the Church of England]

non-U /ˌnɒn ˈjuː/ (life and society) A somewhat dated term used half-humorously for a word or action that is socially unacceptable, for example, saying 'toilet' instead of 'lavatory', or tucking a serviette (also regarded as a non-U word) into one's collar when dining.

Norfolk Broads /ˌnɔːfək 'brɔːdz/**, the** (geography) Another name for the *Broads,* specifically the ones in Norfolk.

Norland nurse /ˌnɔːlənd 'nɜːs/ (life and society) A nurse who has been professionally trained at the Norland Nursery Training College in Berkshire to work with young children. She may work in a school, such as a *nursery school* or *primary school,* a children's hospital or clinic, in a day or residential nursery, or as a *nanny* with a private family. [establishment, originally the Norland Institute, is named after Norland Place, west *London,* where it was founded in 1892]

Norman /'nɔːmən/ (style) The Romanesque style of architecture found mainly in *Britain,* especially in *churches* and castles from the time of the *Norman Conquest* to the 12th century. It is characterized chiefly by rounded arches, round pillars, square towers and massive stone walls.

Norman Conquest /ˌnɔːmən 'kɒŋkwest/**, the** (history) The invasion and settlement of *England* by the Normans, led by William the *Conqueror* after the Battle of *Hastings* in 1066.

North (Country) /'nɔːθ (ˌkʌntrɪ)/**, the** (geography) The northern part of *England,* whose inhabitants are popularly well known for their friendliness, directness and shrewdness, especially in business, as distinct from the more reserved and elusive character of those who live in the south.

north of Watford /ˌnɔːθ əv 'wɒtfəd/ (daily life) A semi-serious nickname for that part of *England* that lies to the north of Watford, a town just outside *London.* Some people think that anywhere in this area is 'provincial' and lacks the culture of the *Home Counties* and London itself.

North Sea gas /ˌnɔːθ siː 'gæs/ (science and technology) Natural gas obtained from gas fields beneath the North Sea, mainly off the coast of East Anglia and off the east coast of *Scotland. Britain's* gas supply was formerly produced from coal, but natural gas from the North Sea is now the sole source of all the country's gas (since the late 1960s).

North Sea oil /ˌnɔːθ siː 'ɔɪl/ (science and technology) Crude oil obtained from oil fields beneath the North Sea, mainly off the east coast of *Scotland* and the northeast coast of *England. Britain* formerly imported almost all its oil supplies, but from the mid-1970s itself became an oil producer.

North/South divide /ˌnɔːθ ˌsaʊθ dɪˈvaɪd/, **the** (geography) The marked difference that evolved in the late 1980s between the *North* of *England* and the South. The North was shown to have higher unemployment, a greater crime rate, and lower standards of living which resulted in cheaper houses. The South was shown to have less unemployment, less crime, higher standards of living, but more expensive houses. Compare the *North (Country)*.

Northern Ireland /ˌnɔːðən ˈaɪələnd/ (geography) Before the early 20th century, Northern Ireland was part of *Ireland* as a whole, having developed in the middle ages as the Kingdom of *Ulster*, later the Province of Ulster. After many English and Scots people settled there in the 16th century, Northern Ireland became mainly Protestant, unlike the rest of Ireland which remained, as before, mainly Roman Catholic. By the terms of an Anglo-Irish treaty of 1921, Northern Ireland was granted its own parliament in which a Protestant government was formed after successive elections. Roman Catholics, who were excluded from political office, came increasingly to resent the continuing Protestant domination, and, as a result, a vigorous civil rights movement emerged in the late 1960s. The sectarian (Catholic against Protestant) disturbances which followed were exploited by extremists of both faiths, and in particular by the Provisional *IRA* (which broke away from the Official IRA in 1970). Therefore, British troops were sent to Northern Ireland in 1969 to help to keep the peace. As the Northern Ireland government was unable to introduce satisfactory reforms, the British government imposed *direct rule* (of Northern Ireland from *Westminster*[2]) in 1972. Since then, in spite of the efforts of the British government, the police force in Northern Ireland and the British *Army* units there, violence and terrorism has continued, with the IRA also taking its campaign of violence to mainland *Britain* (especially *London* and British military bases). The unrest did not noticeably decrease in 1985 when the *Anglo-Irish Agreement* was made between the Republic of Ireland and the British Government to give the republic a special consultative role in the governing of Northern Ireland. It was hoped that this would lead to a more effective campaign against the activities of the IRA. Many Protestants in Northern Ireland, however, regarded the agreement as an act of treason on the part of the British government, and bitterly opposed it. See also *Northern Ireland Assembly*, *Troubles*.

Northern Ireland Assembly /ˌnɔːðən ˌaɪələnd əˈsemblɪ/, **the**
(government) The elected assembly that was restored in
Northern Ireland from 1982 to 1986. In the latter year, *Unionist
Party* members, who had a majority in the Assembly, decided
not to implement its functions as a protest against the *Anglo-
Irish Agreement* (see *Northern Ireland*), so that the British
government decided it should be dissolved. At the same
time, the government expressed the hope that a future
Assembly would one day be reformed.

Norwich City /ˌnɒrɪdʒ ˈsɪtɪ/ (sport and leisure) The
professional *football club* of Norwich, Norfolk, with its own
stadium in the *city*. It was founded in 1905.

Norwich School /ˈnɒrɪdʒ skuːl/, **the** (arts) A group of early
19th-century painters, led by John Crome (1768–1821), who
were based in Norwich, Norfolk, and represented *England*'s
most distinctive regional school of painting. Followers of the
group found most of their subjects in the countryside of
Norfolk and *East Anglia* with their style in turn influenced by
Dutch 17th-century painters.

not proven /ˌnɒt ˈpruːvn/ (law) In *Scotland*, the verdict given
by a *jury* when the evidence presented in *court*[3] neither
proves nor disproves the case against the person accused.
The verdicts 'guilty' and 'not guilty' are also used in Scotland,
as well as in *England*, *Wales* and *Northern Ireland*. 'Not
proven' is used only in Scotland.

Notting Hill Carnival /ˌnɒtɪŋ hɪl ˈkaːnɪvl/, **the** (life and
society) An annual West Indian carnival held since 1966 on
the *Summer Bank Holiday* in the streets of Notting Hill, west
London, where there is a large black immigrant population.
Some Carnivals have been spoiled by clashes between whites
and blacks and between participants and the police.

NSPCA /ˌen es ˌpiː siː ˈeɪ/, **the (National Society for the
Prevention of Cruelty to Animals, the)** (charities) The
former name of the *RSPCA*.

NSPCC /ˌen es ˌpiː siː ˈsiː/, **the (National Society for the
Prevention of Cruelty to Children, the)** (charities) A
voluntary organization founded in 1884 to prevent the ill-
treatment of children, in private or in public, and the
corruption of their morals. The Society currently has about
50,000 voluntary workers who investigate reported cases of
cruelty or neglect.

nuclear-free zone /ˌnjuːklɪə friː ˈzəʊn/ (science and
technology) An area or district in a town or *city* in which the

local authority has banned the use, storage or transportation of nuclear materials. Such zones exist in Lambeth and Camden, *London*, as well as in Manchester and Leicester. The local authority setting up such zones is often under the control of the *Labour Party*.

Nuclear Power /ˌnjuːklɪə ˈpaʊə(r)/ (commerce) One of the three companies, founded in 1991, that generate electricity in *England* and *Wales*. It uses nuclear power, unlike the other two, *National Power* and *PowerGen*, which use coal and (to a much lesser extent) oil. Nuclear Power currently owns 12 power stations.

nuclear power /ˌnjuːklɪə ˈpaʊə(r)/ (science and technology) Nuclear power has been developed in *Britain* for many years, and in 1956 the country's first large-scale nuclear power station at Calder Hall (now part of *Sellafield*) first supplied electricity to the *national grid*[1]. There are currently 14 nuclear power stations in operation: seven Magnox stations and seven Advanced Gas-cooled Reactor stations (AGRs). ('Magnox' refers to the magnesium-based alloy from which the fuel containers are made, and is an abbreviation of '*mag*nesium *no* oxidation'.) See also *British Nuclear Fuels*, *Sizewell*.

NUJ /ˌen juː ˈdʒeɪ/, **the (National Union of Journalists, the)** (work) The leading trade union for journalists, with a current membership of about 30,000.

NUM /ˌen juː ˈem/, **the (National Union of Mineworkers, the)** (work) An influential trade union for coal miners, formed in 1945. The NUM was long under radical leadership, and gained a reputation for 'militancy'. Its current membership is about 44,000. Compare *Union of Democratic Mineworkers*.

Number Ten/No 10 /ˌnʌmbə ˈten/ (government) The official residence of the *Prime Minister* in *Downing Street*, *London*.

nursery rhyme /ˈnɜːsərɪ raɪm/ (tradition) A short traditional verse or song popular with children. Many such rhymes have a historic or satirical background, the meaning of which is mostly lost today.

nursery school /ˈnɜːsərɪ skuːl/ (education) A school for very young children, usually three or four years old (before compulsory education, which begins at the age of five).

nursery stakes /ˈnɜːsərɪ steɪks/, **the** (sport and leisure) A race for two-year-old horses.

nursing home /ˈnɜːsɪŋ həʊm/ (medical) A private hospital or home usually for old people or invalids.

NUS /ˌen juː ˈes/**, the (National Union of Students, the)**
(education) A voluntary organization for students in *further
education* and *higher education*, founded in 1922, and
operating through local branches in *colleges*[1,2] and
universities. It promotes the educational, social and general

Number Ten/No 10

interests of students, and currently has a membership of
approximately 1.2 million.
NUT /ˌen juː ˈtiː/**, the (National Union of Teachers, the)**
(education) The largest professional organization for
teachers in *England* and *Wales*, with members in both *state
schools* and *independent schools*. It aims to improve the

professional status of teachers and to promote realistic
educational programmes for schoolchildren. The NUT was
founded in 1870 and has a current membership of about
214,000.

THE OVAL

O Come, All Ye Faithful /əʊ ˌkʌm ɔːl jiː ˈfeɪθfl/ (tradition) The title, and opening words, of a popular *Christmas* carol, often sung as the final hymn in a *carol service*. [19th-century English translation of Latin hymn, 'Adeste, fideles']

Oak Apple Day /ˈəʊk æpl ˌdeɪ/ (history) 29 May, the anniversary of the *Restoration* (1660), commemorating the oak tree in which Charles II hid after his defeat in the Battle of Worcester (1651). People formerly wore oak apples or oak leaves on Oak Apple Day.

OAP /ˌəʊ eɪ ˈpiː/ **(old age pensioner)** (life and society) A retired man or woman of pensionable age (see *old age pension*). Such pensioners are entitled to certain services at reduced rates, for example, rail travel at a reduced rate (if the ticket-holder has a *railcard*), cheaper admission fees to cinemas, exhibitions, etc and in some cases free goods or services, such as free bus travel in some areas and also free medical services. See *NHS*, also *bus pass*, *meals on wheels*, *Senior Citizen*.

oatcake /ˈəʊtkeɪk/ (food and drink) A type of thin, brittle cake or biscuit of oatmeal, popular in *Scotland*.

OBE /ˌəʊ biː ˈiː/, **the (Order of the British Empire, the)** (life and society) One of the most common British orders, instituted in 1917 and awarded to both men and women for services to their country, and originally to the *British Empire*. [in full, 'Officer of the Order of the British Empire']

Observer /əbˈzɜːvə(r)/, **The** (media) A *Sunday quality paper* with the same ownership and 'left of centre' political orientation as the *Guardian*. It is noted for its informed, detailed reporting and its original features. It has a colour supplement, 'Observer Magazine'. It is the oldest national newspaper in *Britain*, first published in 1791, and has a current circulation of about 540,000 (1970 – 847,000).

Offa's Dyke /ˌɒfəz 'daɪk/ (history) A long, ancient earthwork extending (with some gaps) from north *Wales* to south. It was built in the 8th century by Offa, King of Mercia (died 796), as a boundary between the English (to the east) and the Welsh (to the west), and today still more or less follows the modern border between the two countries.

Offer /'ɒfə(r)/ (commerce) The short name of the Office of Electricity Regulation, a body set up in 1989, when the electricity industry in *Britain* began to be privatized, to ensure that the various companies operate correctly and to protect the interests of consumers.

Office of Fair Trading /ˌɒfɪs əv ˌfeə 'treɪdɪŋ/, **the** (commerce) The government *department* that administers the *Trade Descriptions Act* and all later similar acts, and that constantly keeps commercial activities and advertising in *Britain* under review. The department arose from the appointment in 1973 of a Director of Fair Trading.

office party /ˌɒfɪs 'pɑːtɪ/ (daily life) A party, especially one on or just before *Christmas Eve*, held in the office of a commercial or government organization. Alcoholic drinks are usually served, and the normal formality of the workplace changes to a much more relaxed atmosphere. The usual business relationship between employers and employees is deliberately ignored. The office party has thus become a suitable subject for a number of jokes and tales of amorous indiscretions.

Official Birthday /əˌfɪʃl 'bɜːθdeɪ/, **the** (royal family) The official birthday of the sovereign, at present the second Saturday in June. It is marked by *Trooping the Colour* and by the announcement of the *Birthday Honours*. The day is not the sovereign's true birthday, and is not a *bank holiday*, although many *civil servants* are given a day off.

off-licence /'ɒf laɪsns/ (commerce) A shop licensed to sell alcoholic drink (to people aged 18 and over) to be drunk off its premises, as distinct from a *pub*, *bar¹* or restaurant, where such drink is drunk on the premises.

Ofgas /'ɒfgæs/ (commerce) The short name of the Office of Gas Supply, a body set up in 1986, when *British Gas* was privatized, whose aim is to ensure that the company operates correctly as a public gas supplier and to protect the interests of consumers.

Oftel /'ɒftel/ (commerce) The short name of the Office of Telecommunications, a body set up in 1984, when *British*

Telecom (now *BT*) was privatized, to monitor the telecommunications industry in *Britain* and to protect the interests of telephone users. Oftel is currently introducing a new national telephone numbering scheme.

Ofwat /'ɒfwɒt/ (commerce) The short name of the Office of Water Services, a body set up in 1989, when the water industry was privatized, to ensure that the various companies operate correctly and to protect the interests of consumers.

old age pension /ˌəʊld eɪdʒ 'penʃn/, **the** (finance) The state pension which all men get when they retire at the age of 65. A woman who has worked gets a pension when she retires at 60. A woman who has not had paid employment can get a pension herself but usually her husband gets a joint pension for them both. The money is raised from the *national insurance* contributions paid during the person's working life.

Old Bailey /ˌəʊld 'beɪlɪ/, **the** (law) The popular name of the *Central Criminal Court*, in *London*. [after the street where it is situated, itself named after an 'old bailey', or former outer castle wall there]

old boy /'əʊld bɔɪ/ (education) A former student of a *secondary school*, especially a *public school*[1]. He may well belong to a society or association of former students run by the school, and thus keep in touch with its progress. See also *old boy network*, *old school tie*.

old boy network /ˌəʊld 'bɔɪ ˌnetwɜːk/ (life and society) An informal 'closed' community of *old boys*, including former university students, used by one individual to gain status in a job or other situation by means of the influence of one or more of the others in the network.

Old Contemptibles /əʊld kən'temptəblz/, **the** (history) A nickname for the survivors of the British Expeditionary Force who fought with the French and Belgians against the Germans in the First World War. After the war, the men held regular annual parades, the last of which took place in 1974. [name said, on doubtful authority, to have come from an order issued by the German Emperor, referring to the British force as a 'contemptible little army'; as used by the veterans, the term lost its critical sense]

Old English sheepdog /ˌəʊld ɪŋglɪʃ 'ʃiːpdɒg/ (animal world) A breed of sheepdog formerly used as a working dog by shepherds in southern *England* and *Wales*, but now mostly kept as a domestic pet. It is distinguished by its long grey and white hair, which traditionally falls over its eyes.

old girl /ˈəʊld gɜːl/ (education) A former female student of a *secondary school*, especially a *public school*[1] (whether for girls only or not). She may well belong to an association of past students, in the same way as an *old boy*.

Old Lady of Threadneedle Street /ˌəʊld ˌleɪdɪ əv θredˈniːdl striːt/, **the** (finance) A nickname for the *Bank of England*, which is in the street of this name. The Bank was itself nicknamed the 'Old Lady' in the late 18th century. [street name said to be a corruption of 'three needles', from the signboard of a Needlemakers' Company there showing three needles]

Old Moore's Almanack /ˌəʊld mɔːz ˈɔːlmənæk/ (media) A popular annual publication which claims to forecast important events for the particular year. The periodical takes its title from the almanac published in 1699 by the physician and astrologer Francis Moore (1657–1715), which predicted the weather as a commercial promotion for the pills he manufactured.

old school tie /ˌəʊld skuːl ˈtaɪ/ (education) A distinctive (often striped or crested) tie worn by an *old boy* as a member of an association of former students. The tie is regarded as typifying the attitudes and values held, or thought to be held, by *public school*[1] students, in particular loyalty, superiority, snobbishness and sportsmanship.

Old Trafford /ˌəʊld ˈtræfəd/ (sport and leisure) A well-known *football* stadium and cricket ground in southwest Manchester. The stadium is the home ground of *Manchester United*, and the cricket ground is used for *test matches* and other important matches. [named after the district]

Old Vic /ˌəʊld ˈvɪk/, **the** (arts) A well-known *London* theatre opened in 1818, originally as the Royal Coburg, but in 1833 renamed the Royal Victoria Theatre in honour of the 14-year-old Princess (later *Queen*) *Victoria*. From 1963 to 1976 the theatre was the home of the *National Theatre* (now the *Royal National Theatre*), and from 1976 to 1982 the *Young Vic* was based there. [name arose as a friendly nickname]

Olivier, Laurence /əˈlɪvɪeɪ, ˈlɒrəns/ (people) Laurence Olivier (1907–1989) was regarded as one of the finest stage and film actors of his generation, as well as being a prominent theatre manager and producer. He joined the *Old Vic* in 1935 and was appointed the first director of the *Royal National Theatre* in 1961, where the largest of the auditoriums was named in his honour. As an actor, he was much admired for the range and expressiveness of his performances. He was made a knight in 1947 and was created a *life peer* in 1970.

Olympia /ə'lɪmpɪə/ (commerce) A large exhibition complex in west *London*, opened in 1886. A number of well-known annual events were formerly held there, and it is still the centre for the London International Book Fair.

ombudsman /'ɒmbʊdzmən/, **the** (government) The popular name for the *Parliamentary Commissioner*, a state-appointed official who investigates complaints referred to him by *MP*s from members of the public who claim to have been unfairly or wrongly treated by a government *department*. Since 1972 the ombudsman has also held the post of Health Service Commissioner, and in his role investigates complaints against the *NHS* authorities. [Swedish, 'commissioner'; Sweden was the first country to appoint such an official]

one-upmanship /ˌwʌn 'ʌpmənʃɪp/ (life and society) A semi-humorous term used to define the 'art' of gaining an advantage, usually by cunning or bluff, over others, especially with reference to social or intellectual superiority. The term was invented by the writer Stephen Potter for his book of that name (1952). Compare *gamesmanship*. [from 'one up', in sense 'one point higher', 'one point ahead']

Open College /'əʊpən ˌkɒlɪdʒ/, **the** (education) A government-sponsored series of educational courses on television and radio, introduced in 1987. The courses are designed to provide both basic and specialist training for people who otherwise might not be able to afford it. The Open College's television programmes are broadcast by *Channel 4*. Compare *Open University*.

open day /'əʊpən deɪ/ (daily life) A day when members of the public are admitted to a normally private or professional establishment such as a school, factory or military base. On such an occasion special displays, tours and exhibits are usually arranged to explain the operation and aims of the establishment and to serve as good publicity for it.

open shop /ˌəʊpən 'ʃɒp/ (work) An arrangement in a factory or other place of employment by which employees can work whether or not they belong to a trade union. Compare *closed shop*.

Open University /ˌəʊpən juːnɪ'vɜːsɪtɪ/, **the (OU, the)** (education) A non-residential university for *mature students* founded in 1969 in the *new town* of Milton Keynes, Buckinghamshire. Students do not need to have formal

qualifications to enrol. Study is mainly by means of a
correspondence course linked to special programmes on *BBC*
television and radio, but for some courses students are
required to attend a short *summer school* held in one of the
traditional universities. The *first degree* awarded by the OU is
based on a system of credits for each subject and is called a
'*BA* (Open)'. The OU currently has about 80,000 students.
Compare *Open College*. [so named because the university is
'open' to all]

Opposition /ˌɒpəˈzɪʃn/, **the** (government) The major political
party (in *Britain* at present, either the *Conservative Party* or
Labour Party) that is opposed to the government of the day,
and whose *MPs* sit opposite (facing) the government benches
in the *House of Commons*. See also *Leader of the Opposition*,
Shadow Cabinet. [officially known as Her Majesty's Loyal
Opposition]

orange badge /ˈɒrɪndʒ bædʒ/ (transport) A badge displayed in
the windscreen of a car to show that the owner is officially
registered as a disabled driver, and so has the right to stop
and park in places where most drivers are not allowed to. The
badge is orange in colour and has a picture of a wheelchair
with the wording 'The holder of this badge has considerable
difficulty in walking or is blind'. ('Blind' means 'officially
registered as a blind person', who despite having imperfect
vision, can still see well enough to drive a car.)

Orangemen /ˈɒrɪndʒmən/ (politics) Members of the Orange
Society, an Irish political society aiming to preserve
Protestantism, especially in *Northern Ireland*, and thus to gain
supremacy over Roman Catholics and Irish nationalists. The
Society was founded in 1795, and took its name from King
William III of Orange (1650–1702) who defeated James II and
his Catholic supporters at the Battle of the *Boyne* (1690). The
Orangemen still hold an annual parade in Northern Ireland
cities on the anniversary of the Battle (12 July). See also
Apprentice Boys' Parade.

oranges and lemons /ˌɒrɪndʒɪz ən ˈlemənz/ (tradition) A game
popular among young children in which two players (an
'orange' and a 'lemon') form an arch by joining hands and,
singing a *nursery rhyme*, suddenly trap one of the other
players in their arms as he runs under the arch, the trapping
occurring when the two singers have reached the word 'chop'
(repeated) at the end of the rhyme. The nursery rhyme,
whose opening words are 'Oranges and lemons', is said to

have a historic origin and to refer to executions in *London*.

order in council /ˌɔːdər ɪn ˈkaʊnsl/ (government) An order made in theory by the sovereign with the advice of the *Privy Council*, but in practice a decree of the *Cabinet*.

Order of Merit /ˌɔːdər əv ˈmerɪt/, **the (OM, the)** (life and society) An order given to both civilians and military personnel who are outstanding in any field. It was instituted in 1902 and is limited in number to 24 men and women.

Order of the Bath /ˌɔːdər əv ðə ˈbɑːθ/, **the** (life and society) One of the highest orders of knighthood, in three classes, each divided into two divisions, military and civil. The order was traditionally founded in 1399, and originally admission to it was characterized by a ritual bathing, among other ceremonies. Women became eligible for the order in 1971. [full title, 'The Most Honourable Order of the Bath']

Order of the Garter /ˌɔːdər əv ðə ˈgɑːtə(r)/, **the** (life and society) The highest order of knighthood, together with the *Order of the Thistle*. According to tradition, the Order was founded in 1348 by King Edward III, who is said to have picked up a garter dropped by the Countess of Salisbury at a court festival and gallantly tied it round his own knee, saying, 'Honi soit qui mal y pense' ('Shame on him who thinks evil of it'), words which today form the motto of the Order. The Order holds its special services in *St George's Chapel, Windsor Castle*. A Knight of the Order places the initials KG after his name. [full title, 'The Most Noble Order of the Garter']

Order of the Thistle /ˌɔːdər əv ðə ˈθɪsl/, **the** (life and society) The highest order of knighthood, together with the *Order of the Garter*. It was founded in 1687, and is mainly given to Scottish noblemen (limited to 16 in number), hence its name (see *thistle*). A Knight of the Order places the initials KT after his name. [full title, 'The Most Ancient and Most Noble Order of the Thistle']

order paper /ˈɔːdə ˌpeɪpə(r)/ (government) A publication listing the order in which business is to be conducted in the *House of Commons*.

ordinary shares /ˌɔːdənrɪ ˈʃeəz/ (finance) Shares issued by a company and entitling their holders to a share of the company's profits after the payment of a dividend of *preference shares* to other holders.

Ordnance Survey /ˌɔːdnəns ˈsɜːveɪ/, **the** (geography) The official government map-making body, founded in 1791 to map southern England when a French invasion was feared. It became well known for its 'inch to a mile' maps of *Britain*, first published in the mid-19th century. From the early 1970s these were superseded by the metric '2 cm to 1 km' maps, on a slightly larger scale.

Orkneys /'ɔːknɪz/, **the** (geography) A sizeable group of islands lying to the north of mainland *Scotland* with Mainland their largest island. The islands are rich in Scandinavian remains and are popular with tourists. Compare the *Shetlands*.

other place /ˌʌðə 'pleɪs/, **the** (tradition) A semi-serious name for *Cambridge*[1,2] by someone in or at *Oxford*[1,2], or for Oxford[1,2] by someone in or at Cambridge[1,2]. Compare *another place*.

Oulton Park /ˌəʊltən 'pɑːk/ (sport and leisure) A motor-racing track east of Chester, Cheshire. [originally the park of Oulton Hall, a country house there]

Outward Bound Trust /ˌaʊtwəd 'baʊnd 'trʌst/, **the** (education) An organization that arranges outdoor enterprises for young people, including sailing, canoeing, rock climbing and orienteering. The Trust was formed in 1946 by the head of *Gordonstoun School*. [from 'outward bound', term used of a ship leaving port for a particular destination]

Oval /'əʊvl/, **the** (sport and leisure) A well-known *cricket* ground in southeast *London*, officially the home ground of the Surrey County Cricket Club. [from its shape]

Owen, David /'əʊɪn, 'deɪvɪd/ (people) David Owen (born 1938) began his political career as an *MP* in the *Labour Party*. In 1981 he resigned from the Party and with three colleagues founded the *SDP*, becoming its leader in 1983. He did not support the merger of the SDP with the *Liberal Party* in 1988, however, and made an unsuccessful attempt to preserve the SDP in a 'breakaway' form. In 1992, as a *life peer*, David Owen was appointed chief mediator to the *EC*.

Oxbridge /'ɒksbrɪdʒ/ (education) A colloquial term for the universities of *Oxford*[2] and *Cambridge*[2], jointly regarded as being academically superior to other universities and as enjoying and giving special privilege and prestige.

Oxfam/OXFAM /'ɒksfæm/ (charities) A well-known charity providing practical relief in developing countries, founded in *Oxford*[1] in 1942 and still having its head office there. It runs many shops in towns round *Britain* in which second-hand goods, as well as goods specially made in developing countries, are sold, to raise funds for its work. [abbreviation of *Ox*ford Committee for *Fam*ine Relief]

Oxford /ˈɒksfəd/ **(1** geography **2** education) **1** A historic city in Oxfordshire, and its *county town*, famed for its university and its fine medieval architecture. It is a major tourist centre. **2** A short name for *Oxford University*. Compare *Cambridge²*.

Oxford accent /ˌɒksfəd ˈæksent/ (language) As popularly used, an informal name for *RP*. However, some people use it as a name for an exaggerated form of RP that is traditionally believed to be associated with *Oxford University*.

Oxford blue /ˌɒksfəd ˈbluː/ **(1** daily life **2** sport and leisure) **1** A dark blue colour. Compare *Cambridge blue¹*. **2** A *blue³* at *Oxford University*.

Oxford English Dictionary /ˌɒksfəd ˌɪŋglɪʃ ˈdɪkʃənrɪ/, **(the OED, the)** (language) One of the most famous dictionaries of the English language, highly reputed for its authoritativeness and comprehensiveness, both in the meanings of words and phrases and in their origins. It was first published (in part) in 1884, with its 12th and final volume appearing in 1928. Supplementary volumes were published in 1933 (a single volume) and between 1972 and 1986 (four new volumes). In 1989 the complete dictionary was published in a new second edition. Smaller abridged and adapted editions of it have since been published as the 'Shorter Oxford English Dictionary', 'Concise Oxford Dictionary', 'Pocket Oxford Dictionary' and 'Little Oxford Dictionary', as well as several special editions for schools and students of English. ['Oxford' because it is published by *Oxford University* Press]

Oxford Group /ˈɒksfəd gruːp/, **the** (life and society) The original name of the worldwide movement for moral and spiritual renewal now known as Moral Rearmament. This was founded in *Oxford¹* in 1921.

Oxford Movement /ˈɒksfəd ˌmuːvmənt/, **the** (religion) A movement towards *High Church* doctrine and practice in the *Church of England*, begun in *Oxford¹* in 1833.

Oxford Street /ˈɒksfəd striːt/ (London) One of *London*'s most popular shopping streets, especially known for its department stores and varied clothing shops. [originally the road out of London leading to *Oxford¹*]

Oxford University /ˌɒksfəd juːnɪˈvɜːsətɪ/ (education) One of the two oldest and most famous universities in *England*, the other being *Cambridge University*. It was founded in the 12th century. There are at present 35 colleges: two are for women only, and the rest take both men and women. Among the best known are: Christ Church, founded in 1546, with its large front *quadrangle* and its famous *chapel[2]* (which is also Oxford Cathedral); Magdalen College, founded in 1458, with its tall bell-tower in the *Perpendicular (style)* (on which the chapel *choir* sings at dawn on *May Day*); All Souls College, founded in 1437, which is unique in having no *undergraduates* but only *fellows[2]*; and New College, founded in 1379, with its fine chapel and well-known choir. There are at present nearly 14,000 students in residence, of whom over a third are women. The city of *Oxford[1]*, although considerably more industrialized than *Cambridge[1]*, is popular with tourists because of the University's many beautiful medieval buildings. See also *Ashmolean Museum, Blackwell's, Bodleian Library, Eights, Greats, Radcliffe Camera, Sheldonian Theatre*.

oyez /əʊˈjez/ (tradition) The traditional cry used by a *town crier[1]*, and called three times to attract the attention of his hearers before he makes his announcement. [from Old French, 'hear!']

PANDA CAR

P & O /ˌpiː ən ˈəʊ/ **(Peninsular and Oriental (Steam Navigation Company), the** (transport) A famous shipping company, one of the largest in the world, founded in 1837, originally as a mail shipping route to the Iberian peninsula. It received its present name when its contract was extended to Egypt (the 'Orient') in 1840. Today it is the world's largest cruise operator.

PA /ˌpiː ˈeɪ/ **(personal assistant)** (work) A woman (less often, a man) who assists a businessman, writer, etc in his work. She acts as secretary, receives clients and visitors, deals with telephone calls, keeps his engagement diary, and generally ensures the smooth running of her employer's office or daily routine. Compare *girl Friday*.

Pacer /ˈpeɪsə(r)/ (transport) A new type of diesel train introduced by *BR* in the mid-1980s for travel on country branch lines and on local urban routes. A Pacer is a smaller and slower train than a *Sprinter*. [both names are borrowed from horseracing: a pacer is a horse that trots at an even rate, while a sprinter is one that runs fast over short distances]

Paddington /ˈpædɪŋtən/ (transport) **1** A main line railway station in west *London*, from which trains run to the West Country. **2** An Underground railway station there. See *London Underground*.

Paddy /ˈpædɪ/ (tradition) An informal, often derogatory, name for an Irishman. [from St Patrick, the patron saint of *Ireland* and the common Irish forename Patrick]

page three /ˌpeɪdʒ ˈθriː/ (media) A newspaper page with a large photograph of a nude or semi-nude young woman, especially one with a prominent figure. Such photographs originally appeared on page 3 of *The Sun* in the late 1960s.

Other *tabloids* followed its example, but printed the photograph on different pages. 'Page three girl' is now used to describe any nude photographic model.

Paisley, Ian /'peɪzlɪ, 'iːən/ (people) Ian Paisley (born 1926) is a moderator (leader) of the Free Presbyterian Church of Ulster in *Northern Ireland* and a prominent member of the Protestant community. As a politician he has been a vigorous campaigner against any possible union of Northern Ireland with the Republic of *Ireland* and a staunch supporter of *Ulster* (ie, Northern Ireland) remaining part of the *United Kingdom*. In 1970 he was elected as Protestant Unionist *MP* and in 1974 became leader of the *Ulster Democratic Unionist Party*. In 1985 he resigned his *seat* in protest at the *Anglo-Irish Agreement*, but regained it in the 1986 *by-election*.

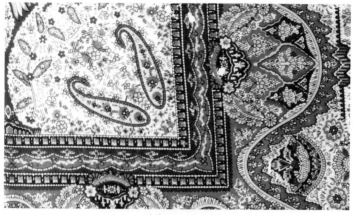

paisley pattern

paisley pattern /'peɪzlɪ ˌpætn/ (style) A distinctive abstract coloured pattern resembling an elaborate curving teardrop or tree cone, today found on the fabric used for a variety of clothes such as dresses and ties, but originally found on the *paisley shawl*.

paisley shawl /ˌpeɪzlɪ 'ʃɔːl/ (clothing) Properly, a shawl of soft, fine wool printed with a *paisley pattern*, originally made in Paisley, *Scotland*, in the 19th century.

Paisleyites /'peɪzlɪaɪts/ (politics) A term for followers or supporters of Ian *Paisley*.

Palace /'pælɪs/, **the** (royal family) A colloquial term for *Buckingham Palace*.

Palace of Westminster /ˌpælɪs əv ˈwestmɪnstə(r)/, **the**
(1 London 2 government) **1** A former royal palace in *London*
(now officially known as the Old Palace of Westminster) on
the site of which the present *Houses of Parliament* stand. The
palace was largely destroyed by fire in the early 19th century,
and the best known surviving part today is *Westminster
Hall*. **2** The official name (in full, New Palace of Westminster)
of the *Houses of Parliament*.

Pall Mall /ˌpæl ˈmæl/ (London) A street in central *London*,
noted for its many *clubs*. [where pall-mall was formerly
played, a now obsolete game in which a ball (Italian 'palla')
was driven along an alley by a mallet (Italian 'maglio')]

Palladium /pəˈleɪdɪəm/, **the** (arts) A well-known *London*
musical and variety theatre (also known as the London
Palladium). [name apparently derived from the Palladium, or
statue of Pallas Athene, in classical mythology, by confusion,
or false association, with the Colosseum, the great
amphitheatre in Rome]

Palm Sunday /ˌpɑːm ˈsʌndɪ/ (religion) In the Christian *church*,
the *Sunday* before *Easter*. In some *Church of England* churches
and in the *Roman Catholic Church* small crosses made of palm
leaves are given to members of the congregation. [from the
Bible story in which palm branches were thrown on the
ground in front of Christ as he entered Jerusalem]

Pancake Day /ˈpæŋkeɪk deɪ/ (tradition) A popular name for
Shrove Tuesday.

pancake race /ˈpæŋkeɪk reɪs/ (tradition) A traditional annual
race on *Shrove Tuesday*, in which (usually) women run with
pancakes. Each runner has a pancake in a pan. As she runs,
she tosses the pancake up and over in the air and catches it
again in the pan. The annual pancake race at Olney,
Buckinghamshire, is a popular tourist attraction, and has
been run since the 15th century. See also *tossing the pancake*.

pancakes /ˈpæŋkeɪks/ (food and drink) Cakes traditionally
eaten on *Shrove Tuesday*. They are thin and flat and made
from eggs, flour and milk, fried on both sides in fat in a pan
and usually served as a dessert, rolled and sprinkled with
lemon juice and sugar.

panda car /ˈpændə kɑː(r)/ (law) A former name for a police car,
especially a blue and white or black and white one. [it was
imagined to look like the black and white stripes of a panda]

Panorama /ˌpænəˈrɑːmə/ (media) A weekly socio-political
documentary television programme on *BBC 1*, devoted to

pancake race

topical subjects or current controversial matters, at home and abroad. It was first broadcast in 1953.

pantomime /'pæntəmaɪm/ (tradition) A type of musical play given annually at *Christmas* in theatres and elsewhere by professionals and amateurs. It has a traditional 'fairy tale' story (eg, 'Babes in the Wood', 'Cinderella') and is usually very lively and colourful with music and songs (in which the audience join) and dancing. Traditionally a man plays the *dame*, the older female, often the hero's mother, while the hero or *principal boy* is played by a young woman. Pantomimes are particularly popular with children, and a visit to one is one of the traditional treats of the Christmas season.

paperboy/papergirl /'peɪpəbɔɪ/'peɪpəgɜːl/ (daily life) A schoolboy or schoolgirl who delivers newspapers and magazines daily to private houses and commercial premises such as offices and shops. The customer orders his papers through a newsagent, and pays his bills there, usually on a weekly basis, with the newsagent often making a special extra charge for the delivery. The paperboy or papergirl makes the delivery in the early morning, before going to school. He or she normally has to sort and 'mark up' (indicate the address on) the papers before beginning the round. The boy or girl is paid a small sum of money for this work.

Papworth Hospital /ˌpæpwəθ ˈhɒspɪtl/ (medicine) A hospital near *Cambridge[1]* that has specialized in heart transplant operations since the early 1980s. Compare *Harefield Hospital*. [named after village]

Parcelforce /ˈpɑːslˌfɔːs/ (commerce) The department of the *Post Office* that handles the despatch and delivery of parcels, including by *Datapost*. There are plans to privatize Parcelforce. See also *Royal Mail*.

parish church /ˌpærɪʃ ˈtʃɜːtʃ/ (religion) The *church* of a parish (church district) attended by churchgoers living in the parish (or in a neighbouring parish). In a village the parish church will often be the only one; in a town it will usually be one of several.

parish council /ˌpærɪʃ ˈkaʊnsl/ (government) In *England* and, formerly, *Wales*, the smallest body involved in local government in rural areas.

parish magazine /ˌpærɪʃ mæɡəˈziːn/ (religion) A regular (usually monthly) magazine published by the priest and *PCC* of a *parish church*, for members of the congregation. It contains a letter from the *vicar* or *rector[1]*, a timetable of *church* services, announcements of births, baptisms, marriages and deaths, reports by members of the *parish council* and articles of topical, social or religious interest.

parish register /ˌpærɪʃ ˈredʒɪstə(r)/ (religion) A book in which the baptisms, marriages and burials in a particular parish are recorded.

parish warden /ˌpærɪʃ ˈwɔːdn/ (law) A member of a village parish appointed to help the *police* by reporting cases of actual or suspected crime. Parish wardens were introduced in 1993 to some rural areas of *England* where there is no regular police patrol. The wardens work in consultation with *Neighbourhood Watch* members and with the local *parish council*.

Park Lane /ˌpɑːk ˈleɪn/ (London) A street in central *London* bordering the eastern side of *Hyde Park* and long famous for its wealth and fine buildings. It is one of the borders of *Mayfair*.

Parkhurst (prison) /ˈpɑːkhɜːst (ˌpɑːkhɜːst ˈprɪzn)/ (law) A prison on the *Isle of Wight* for men serving long sentences. It is noted for its severe regime. [name of village and former forest ('hurst') there]

parking ticket /ˈpɑːkɪŋ ˌtɪkɪt/ (transport) A notice left on an incorrectly parked car by a *traffic warden*, informing the car owner that he must pay a fine or be summoned to a *court*[3] of law.

Parkinson's law /'pɑːkɪnsnz lɔː/ (work) A humorous law, expressed as a law of economics, saying that in official employment, such as the *Civil Service*, work expands to fill the time available for its completion. [formulated by C Northcote Parkinson (born 1909), in a book of the same name published in 1958]

Parkway /'pɑːkweɪ/ (transport) In the names of some railway stations, a word indicating that the station has a large carpark for the use of commuters from the particular town or *city*. Such stations are thus out of the town centre, or even in the country. Examples are Bristol Parkway, serving Bristol, and Didcot Parkway, serving Didcot (Oxfordshire).

Parliament /'pɑːləmənt/ (government) The most important law-making body of the British people consisting of the *House of Commons*, the *House of Lords* and the sovereign (ie, *king* or *queen*).

Parliamentary Commissioner /ˌpɑːləmentrɪ kəˈmɪʃənə(r)/, **the** (government) The official name of the *ombudsman*.

parliamentary private secretary /ˌpɑːləmentrɪ ˌpraɪvɪt 'sekrətrɪ/ **(PPS)** (government) An *MP* (a *backbencher*) who is appointed by a *minister*[3] to help him in his contacts with other backbenchers, and who generally acts as his personal secretary and adviser. Compare *parliamentary secretary*.

parliamentary secretary /ˌpɑːləmentrɪ 'sekrətrɪ/ (government) An *MP* appointed, usually as a junior *minister*[2], to act as a deputy for a senior minister who is not a *Secretary of State*. He shares in his senior's parliamentary and departmental duties and may be given special areas of responsibility in the *department*. Compare *parliamentary under-secretary of state*, *parliamentary private secretary*.

parliamentary under-secretary of state /ˌpɑːləmentrɪ ˌʌndə sekrətrɪ əv 'steɪt/ (government) The equivalent of a *parliamentary secretary* when the senior *minister*[2] is a *Secretary of State*.

party political broadcast /ˌpɑːtɪ pəˈlɪtɪkl ˌbrɔːdkɑːst/ (politics) A short television or radio broadcast made by a political party to promote its policies, especially just before a *general election*.

parson /'pɑːsn/ (religion) **1** A term either for the priest in charge of a parish or for any clergyman. **2** A form of address occasionally used to a clergyman.

pass (degree) /'pɑːs (dɪˌgriː)/ (education) A *college*[1] or

university final examination passed satisfactorily but not at
such a high standard as that of an *honours degree*.

Passion Sunday /ˌpæʃn ˈsʌndɪ/ (religion) The second *Sunday*
before *Easter* (the fifth Sunday in Lent), when the solemn
preparation for Easter begins in the Christian *church*. The day
is marked with special prayers and hymns.

Patent Office /ˈpætnt ˌɒfɪs/, **the** (government) The government
department responsible for issuing patents to firms and
organizations and individual inventors.

patrial /ˈpeɪtrɪəl/ (law) An official term used from the 1970s for
a citizen of the *United Kingdom*, or of a British colony, or the
Commonwealth[1], who has a legal right to enter and stay in
Britain because either he, or his father or his father's father,
was born there. [Latin, 'patria', 'fatherland']

Patten, Chris /ˈpætn, krɪs/ (people) Chris Patten (born 1944) is
a former chairman of the *Conservative Party* who did much to
help the Conservatives win the *general election* of 1992,
although he himself was the only *minister*[2] in the *Cabinet* to
lose his *seat* (to the *Liberal Democrats*). In compensation, John
Major appointed him to the post of governor of Hong Kong.
As governor, Chris Patten proposed a number of reforms that
upset many local people and angered the Chinese, who are
due to reclaim control of Hong Kong in 1997.

Paul Jones /ˌpɔːl ˈdʒəʊnz/ (sport and leisure) An old-time
dance which begins with the women dancing round in an
inner circle, the men circling the opposite way. When the
music stops, a dancer's partner for the coming dance is the
person opposite him or her. The Paul Jones always has the
same music, but the intervening dances vary, and can be a
waltz, quickstep, etc. [said to be named after the 18th-century
Scottish naval adventurer John Paul Jones, who captured
many pirate ships]

pay packet /ˈpeɪ ˌpækɪt/ (finance) A person's weekly pay,
received in cash (usually on Fridays) in a small envelope or
packet, together with a statement of any deductions, for
example for *income tax* or *national insurance*. Many *working
class* people do not have bank accounts, and prefer to receive
their pay in this way, rather than by cheque.

pavement artist /ˈpeɪvmənt ˌɑːtɪst/ (daily life) A person who
attempts to earn money by drawing pictures (usually in
coloured chalks) on the pavements, especially in *London*.

PAYE /ˌpiː eɪ waɪ ˈiː/ **(Pay As You Earn)** (finance) A state
scheme by which an employee's *income tax* is deducted direct

from his pay by his employer, who in turn sends the money to the *Inland Revenue*.

paying guest /ˌpeɪɪŋ 'gest/ **(PG)** (daily life) A person who lives as a lodger in a private house, paying rent to the owner of the house.

Paymaster General /ˌpeɪmɑːstə 'dʒenrəl/, **the** (government) The government *minister*[4] who acts as a banker for *departments* other than the *Inland Revenue* and Customs and Excise, and who is responsible for the payment of many public service pensions, including those of *civil servants*, teachers, members of the *NHS* and the armed forces.

payphone /'peɪfəʊn/ (commerce) A public telephone that is operated either by coins or by a *phonecard*.

PCC /ˌpiː siː 'siː/ **(parochial church council)** (religion) The administrative body of a *parish church*, usually consisting of responsible members of the *church*'s congregation. Most of the members are elected to the council by members of the parish.

PDSA /ˌpiː diː es 'eɪ/, **the (People's Dispensary for Sick Animals, the)** (charities) A voluntary organization, founded in 1917, that provides free veterinary treatment for animals, and through leaflets and films promotes the correct care of domestic pets.

pearly king/queen

Peak District /'pi:k ˌdɪstrɪkt/, **the** (geography) A picturesque region of north central *England*, with hills, valleys, moorlands and caves. The area, popular for the climbing, walking and pot-holing it offers, is a *national park*. The region is mainly in north Derbyshire but also extends into parts of surrounding counties. [named not only for its hill peaks but for the summit of High Peak, 603 m high]

pearly king/queen /ˌpɜːlɪ 'kɪŋ/'kwi:n/ (London) A *London* market trader who on special occasions wears a traditional suit of dark clothes covered with pearl buttons. The pearly king or queen is the man or woman whose clothes have the most lavish design of pearl buttons.

pease pudding /ˌpi:z 'pʊdɪŋ/ (food and drink) A savoury dish of boiled peas with ham or pork.

pebble dash /'pebl dæʃ/ (style) A kind of finish on the exterior walls of some houses, consisting of small stones set in plaster. [originally pebbles were dashed (thrown) against wet plaster to form the wall covering]

peer /pɪə(r)/ (life and society) **1** (hereditary peer) A titled member of the aristocracy (see p 470) who has the right to speak and vote in the *House of Lords* provided he is 21 or older. When a peer dies, the title is inherited by his closest male relation, usually his son. Occasionally, a woman can inherit a title. Since 1963 a peer has had the right to renounce his title during his lifetime, although this does not prevent that peer's heir from inheriting the title in the ordinary way. Most hereditary peers are men. Women peers are called 'lady peers' or, sometimes, 'peeresses'. **2** (life peer) A person who is given a title during his or her lifetime, usually as a reward for public service. Life peers have the right to speak and vote in the House of Lords. Women life peers are addressed in the same way as a hereditary peer. A small number of peers have the right to sit in the House of Lords because of the office they hold. Amongst them are some bishops of the *Church of England* (eg, the *Archbishop of Canterbury* and the *Archbishop of York*) and the *Law Lords* (eg, the *Lord Chancellor*).

peerage /'pɪərɪdʒ/ (life and society) A collective term for all the *peer*s or their titles in their different ranks (see p 470). There are technically five separate peerages in *Britain*: of *England*, *Scotland, Ireland, Great Britain* (since 1707); and the *United Kingdom* (since 1801). Peers of Ireland are not entitled to sit in the *House of Lords* unless they also hold one of the non-Irish titles.

peeress /ˈpɪərəs/ (life and society) **1** A woman who holds an hereditary or a life peerage in her own right (usually called 'lady peer'). **2** The widely-used term for the wife or widow of a *peer¹* (though a peeress is officially only a woman who holds a title in her own right). She may not sit or vote in the *House of Lords*.

pelican crossing /ˌpelɪkən ˈkrɒsɪŋ/ (transport) A type of road crossing for the use of pedestrians. It is marked with black and white stripes or rows of metal studs, and has traffic lights that can be set to stop traffic by people who wish to cross. Compare *zebra crossing* and see *Belisha beacon*. [based on '*pe*destrian *li*ght *con*trolled crossing' assimilated to 'pelican']

penal system /ˈpiːnl ˌsɪstəm/ (law) *Britain*'s penal system is basically divided into non-custodial (without imprisonment) and custodial (with imprisonment). Non-custodial sentences take the form of fines, probation (going free but living under supervision) and absolute discharge (going free with no conditions of any kind). Custodial sentences, for more serious crimes, order imprisonment for any stated period, ranging from a few days to life. Most prisoners serving sentences of more than 18 months become eligible for release on parole after completing one third of their sentence or 12 months, whichever is the longer, and even prisoners serving life sentences are eligible for release on licence, after consideration by the *Home Secretary* or the *Secretary of State* for *Scotland* in the case of Scottish prisoners.

Penalty Fare /ˈpenltɪ feə(r)/ (transport) A charge (currently £10) imposed on a person travelling without a ticket in the *Network SouthEast* region of *BR*.

penalty points /ˈpenltɪ pɔɪnts/ (law) A government system for controlling road safety and the correct behaviour of car drivers when on the road. For certain driving offences, a particular number of points is indicated on the driver's licence. For example, the penalty for speeding is three points, and for not stopping after an accident, from five to nine points. When the points amount to a particular total (currently 12) the driver is automatically disqualified from driving for a set period.

Penguin /ˈpeŋgwɪn/ (arts) A paperback book published by Penguin Books, founded in 1935. The firm was the first to publish good books in paperback form at a price that anyone could afford.

Pennine Way /ˌpenaɪn ˈweɪ/, **the** (geography) A *national trail* extending for some 250 miles (400 km) along the *Pennines*, opened in 1965. It begins just west of Sheffield, in north Derbyshire, and runs north to a point just north of the Cheviot Hills, in southern *Scotland*. On its route, it passes through three *national parks*, including the *Peak District*.

Pennines /'penaɪnz/, **the** (geography) *England*'s main mountain chain, extending southwards from Northumberland to the middle of Derbyshire and the north part of Staffordshire. The so-called 'backbone of England' is really more a series of uplands. The highest point of the Pennines is Cross Fell (2,930 feet (893 m)). See also *Pennine Way*.

penny /'penɪ/ (finance) A low-value bronze coin worth (since

penny-farthing

1971) one-hundredth of a *pound (sterling)*. Before 1971 (when it was made of copper) it had a value of one-twelfth of a *shilling*, or one two-hundred-and-fortieth of a pound. (The plural of 'penny' is 'pennies' to refer to individual coins, 'pence' to refer to a total sum of money, as 5p (five pence).) See p 472.

Penny Black /ˌpenɪ ˈblæk/ (history) The first British postage stamp, and also the first adhesive stamp in general use. It was issued in 1840 and has a profile of *Queen Victoria* on a dark background. It is not the rarest British stamp but is still highly valued today by many collectors.

penny-farthing /ˌpenɪ ˈfɑːðɪŋ/ (transport) An early type of bicycle with a very large front wheel (resembling an old *penny*) and a very small rear one (resembling a *farthing*). The pedals were fastened to the front wheel.

Pentonville (prison) /ˈpentənvɪl (ˌpentənvɪl ˈprɪzn)/ (law) A large prison for men, opened in 1842 in north *London*. [named after district]

People /ˈpiːpl/, **The** (media) A *Sunday popular paper* noted for its 'human interest' stories and features as well as its coverage of sport. It was first published in 1881 and has a current circulation of about 2.1 million (1972, as 'The Sunday People' – 4.6 million).

PEP (Personal Equity Plan) /ˌpiː iː ˈpiː/pep/ (finance) A government savings scheme that is free of *income tax* and *capital gains tax*. At least half the amount invested must consist of shares in a selection of British or *EC* companies, usually through a *unit trust* or *investment trust*. The maximum investment in a *financial year* is at present £6,000, although a further £3,000 can be invested as shares in a single company.

Perpendicular (style) /ˌpɜːpənˈdɪkjʊlə(r) (staɪl)/ (style) A *Gothic (style)* of architecture of the 14th and 15th centuries, characterized chiefly by large windows with vertical lines of tracery and fan vaulting. Examples of the style are the *chapel*[2] of King's College, *Cambridge*[2], *St George's Chapel* at *Windsor Castle* and several of the older *colleges*[1] at *Oxford*[2] and Cambridge[2].

personal column /ˈpɜːsənl ˌkɒləm/ (media) A column of advertisements in a newspaper or magazine, where people can make personal announcements, send private messages and make requests for friends or companions, etc.

Peter Pan /ˌpiːtə ˈpæn/ (**1** arts **2** life and society **3** London) **1** The boy hero of the play of the same name by J M Barrie, first staged in 1904 ('the boy who wouldn't grow up'). **2** A boyish, youthful or immature man. **3** A statue of Peter Pan[1] in *Kensington Gardens, London*, erected in 1912.

Peter Pan collar /ˌpiːtə pæn ˈkɒlə(r)/ (clothing) A close-fitting collar on a girl's or woman's dress, with rounded ends at the front. [so worn by *Peter Pan[1]*]

Petticoat Lane /ˌpetɪkəʊt ˈleɪn/ (London) A street in *London*'s *East End* where a weekly market is held on *Sunday* mornings. The market is famous for the variety of goods on sale there. Formerly these were mainly clothes (including petticoats), hence the name of the street, which is officially Middlesex Street.

PG /ˌpiː ˈdʒiː/ (arts) A category in which a cinema film is placed by the *British Board of Film Classification* to indicate that it contains some scenes which may be unsuitable for children. Compare *12* (under letter T), *18* (under E) and *U*. [abbreviation of 'parental guidance']

PGCE /ˌpiː dʒiː siː ˈiː/ **(Postgraduate Certificate of Education)** (education) A teaching qualification awarded to a *graduate* after a one-year course. Students must have studied the subject they intend to teach for at least two years at university level before doing the course. Compare *BEd*.

Philharmonia Orchestra /ˌfɪlɑːməʊnɪə ˈɔːkɪstrə/, **the** (arts) A leading *London* symphony orchestra founded in 1945 and until 1977 called the New Philharmonia Orchestra.

Philip, Prince /ˈfɪlɪp, prɪns/ see *Duke of Edinburgh* (royal family)

phonecard /ˈfəʊnkɑːd/ (commerce) A special plastic card designed for use with a *payphone* or *cardphone*. The cards are sold by post offices and shops such as newsagents and supermarkets at values of £2, £4, £10 and £20. Each phonecard unit is the equivalent of a *10 pence piece* in a payphone.

Piccadilly /ˌpɪkəˈdɪlɪ/ (London) A central shopping street in *London*, with a wide variety of shops, stores, hotels, tourist offices and showrooms. [said to be named after the 'piccadills' or fancy collars sold there formerly]

Piccadilly Circus /ˌpɪkədɪlɪ ˈsɜːkəs/ (**1, 2** transport **3** language) **1** A well-known road junction in central *London* where a number of famous streets meet, including *Piccadilly*, *Regent Street* and *Shaftesbury Avenue*. The junction is famous for its brightly lit neon advertisements at night. In the centre of the junction stands the memorial popularly known as *Eros*. **2** An Underground railway station there. See *London Underground*.

3 A humorous name for any crowded or busy place, such as a *High Street*, a public swimming pool in summer or a noisy *playground*.

pickets /'pɪkɪts/ (work) A group of workers stationed outside a workplace such as a factory or a coalmine during a strike or other dispute. Usually their aim is to prevent or dissuade employees or clients from entering, or commercial suppliers from delivering goods. Pickets frequently display placards showing the name of the trade union, and stating their demands. See also *flying pickets, secondary picketing*.

pidgin English /ˌpɪdʒɪn 'ɪŋglɪʃ/ (language) **1** A language made up of elements of English and some other foreign language, especially Chinese or Japanese, originally developing as a means of verbal communication when trading. **2** Loosely, any kind of English spoken with the elements of another language, whether for genuine communication or for comic effect. [Chinese pronunciation of English word 'business']

pig in the middle /ˌpɪg ɪn ðə 'mɪdl/ (sport and leisure) A children's game in which one player, in between two others, tries to catch a ball that they throw to each other past him. When he succeeds (in catching the ball), he changes places with the player who threw it.

piggy bank /'pɪgɪ bæŋk/ (daily life) A child's money-box in the shape of a pig, with a slot in the top (the back of the pig) for the coins. [apparently from 'pig' or 'piggin', an old word for a pot or jar, not related to 'pig' the animal]

Pilgrims' Way /ˌpɪlgrɪmz 'weɪ/, **the** (geography) A track running from Winchester, Hampshire, to *Canterbury*, Kent, today used as a footpath but believed by some to have formerly been the route of medieval pilgrims travelling to the shrine of Thomas à Becket (1118-70) in Canterbury Cathedral.

Pimms /pɪmz/ (food and drink) A fashionable alcoholic drink with a spirit base, drunk either neat or as a 'cup' to make a 'long' drink. The best-known variety is 'Pimm's Number One Cup', which is based on *gin*, although there are five other types, with No 2 based on *whisky*, No 3 on brandy, No 4 on rum, No 5 on rye and No 6 on vodka. [proprietary name, after James Pimm, the *London* restaurant proprietor who created the drink in the 19th century]

Pinewood Studios /ˌpaɪnwʊd 'stjuːdɪəʊz/, **the** (arts) A large film studio near Slough, Buckinghamshire, opened in 1936, and now owned by the Rank Organization.

pinstripe suit /ˌpɪnstraɪp ˈsuːt/ (clothing) A formal or business suit for men made of dark cloth with very narrow contrasting stripes.

pint /paɪnt/ (daily life) A liquid measure equal to 0.568 litres, still used for selling milk and beer.

pinta /ˈpaɪntə/ (food and drink) A colloquial word for a *pint* of milk. [corruption of 'pint of']

Pinter, Harold /ˈpɪntə(r), ˈhærəld/ (people) Harold Pinter (born 1930) is regarded by many as *Britain*'s greatest living playwright. The characters in his plays are usually ordinary or unimportant people, and they often speak in a way that reflects the random nature of everyday conversation, with its sudden changes of subject and hesitations. At the same time, many of Pinter's plays show the world as a place of hidden menace and despair. His best known play is probably 'The Caretaker' (1960), in which the three main characters, one of whom is a tramp, find it hard to communicate with one another. More recently he has written short plays about political oppression. In 1993 'Moonlight' was his first full-length play for 18 years. The adjective 'Pinteresque' has come to mean 'unnervingly quiet', 'obscurely menacing'.

pips /pɪps/**, the** (media) The radio time signal broadcast on the hour by the *BBC*, consisting of five short high-pitched sounds ('pips') and a final longer one. Time is measured from the end of the sixth pip.

plaid /plæd/ (clothing) A long piece of cloth with a *tartan[1]* pattern, worn over the shoulder as part of the traditional dress of a Scotsman, especially a *highlander[1]*.

Plaid Cymru /ˌplaɪd ˈkʌmrɪ/ (politics) A Welsh nationalist party founded in 1925 and campaigning for the separation of *Wales* from the *United Kingdom* in order to preserve the country's culture, language and economic life. [Welsh, 'party of Wales']

planning permission /ˈplænɪŋ pəˌmɪʃn/ (law) The necessary permission that must be obtained from a *local authority* by a person planning to make alterations to his building.

playground /ˈpleɪɡraʊnd/ (daily life) An outdoor court or yard at a school for children to play in when they are not in class or otherwise occupied. Some playgrounds have painted markings for popular children's games such as *hopscotch*.

playgroup /ˈpleɪ ɡruːp/ (education) A regular organized gathering of pre-school age children, often supervised by the mother of one of them, in which the children play games and are guided in other activities for a morning or afternoon.

playschool /'pleɪ skuːl/ (education) Another name for a *playgroup* or *nursery school*.

PLC/Plc/plc /ˌpiː el 'siː/ **(public limited company)** (finance) A commercial, usually large, company, whose shares can be bought and sold by the public on the *Stock Exchange*. Such companies must be registered under the Companies Act of 1980 and must place the words 'public limited company' or its abbreviation after their name. Compare *private limited company*.

ploughman's lunch /ˌplaʊmənz 'lʌntʃ/ (food and drink) A snack *lunch* of cheese, bread and butter, usually accompanied by tomatoes, lettuce, celery, or other salad and pickles. Such a meal has been popular in *pubs* as a midday snack since the early 1970s. [suggesting the midday meal that ploughmen used to have in the field]

plum pudding /ˌplʌm 'pʊdɪŋ/ (food and drink) A traditional rich, dark-coloured steamed or boiled pudding made with flour, suet and eggs, and containing raisins, currants, or other dried fruit (but not plums), spices and often alcohol. Compare *Christmas pudding*. [from 'plum' in former and now special sense of 'raisin', 'dried fruit', since raisins were used instead of dried plums in puddings]

plus-fours /ˌplʌs 'fɔːz/ (clothing) A kind of loose, baggy breeches (strictly knickerbockers) coming down to below the knee, that used to be worn by golfers (from the 1920s) and are still worn by some men. [so named from the extra four inches of cloth needed for the distinctive 'overhang' over the knee]

Plymouth Brethren /ˌplɪməθ 'breðrɪn/, **the** (religion) A puritanical religious sect founded in Dublin in about 1825, largely as a reaction against *High Church* principles. Members of the sect aim at strict piety, regard the Bible as infallible and reject a formal ordained priesthood. [from one of the first congregations, established at Plymouth, Devon, in 1831]

Poet Laureate /ˌpəʊɪt 'lɒrɪət/, **the** (arts) The title of the poet appointed for life as an officer of the royal household. He usually produces verse for formal or state occasions such as a coronation or state funeral, but is not obliged to do so. The first Poet Laureate is usually regarded as Ben Jonson (in 1616). The present Poet Laureate is Ted *Hughes*. [from the laurel crown or wreath originally awarded as a sign of honour]

Poets' Corner /ˌpəʊɪts 'kɔːnə(r)/ (arts) An area of *Westminster*

Abbey where several famous poets and writers are buried, or where monuments to them are raised. Among those buried here are Chaucer (1340–1400), Browning (1812–89), Tennyson (1809–92), *Dickens* (1812–70), Hardy (1840–1928) and Kipling (1865–1936).

point-to-point /ˌpɔɪnt tə ˈpɔɪnt/ (sport and leisure) A horse race over fences (steeplechase) organized by a *hunt* or other local group, and usually restricted to amateurs riding horses that they have ridden regularly in the hunt. [originally run over the countryside, not on a course, from one point to another]

police /pəˈliːs/ (law) The police force of *Britain* is relatively small in relation to the population, with about one policeman or policewoman to every 400 people. At present there are 52 regional police forces, each headed by a *Chief Constable*, with *London* looked after by the *Metropolitan Police* (with its headquarters at *New Scotland Yard*) and the *City (of London)* force. The British police are normally not armed, but policemen do carry a truncheon (a short thick club). Their duties range from everyday tasks such as protecting people and property, patrolling roads and streets (see *bobby*) and controlling traffic, to preventing crime and improving relations with ethnic minorities. See also *CID, Fraud Squad, Vice Squad, special constable*.

polling booth /ˈpəʊlɪŋ buːð/ (politics) One of a number of enclosed compartments in a *polling station* where an elector marks his vote on the *ballot paper* in an election such as a *by-election* or *general election*.

polling day /ˈpəʊlɪŋ deɪ/ (politics) A day appointed for electors to cast their votes (at *polling stations*) in an election such as a *by-election* or *general election*. The day is always a Thursday, as this allows the maximum number of days in the final week of the electoral campaign. (The results of the election are declared on Friday, the last day of the working week.)

polling station /ˈpəʊlɪŋ ˌsteɪʃn/ (politics) A building, often a public hall or a school, where electors vote on *polling day*. In a *by-election* or *general election*, polling stations are usually open from 7 am to 10 pm.

polls /pəʊlz/, **the** (politics) A collective term for the *polling stations* in an election.

polytechnic /ˌpɒlɪ ˈteknɪk/ (education) A *college²* that offered a wide range of courses at *further education* or *higher education* level, with some courses leading to a degree. By 1993 all polytechnics had become universities, with some changing their name to avoid confusion with existing universities. Thus Leicester Polytechnic became De Montfort University (named after Simon de Montfort, Earl of Leicester, who ruled *England* in the 13th century), to avoid confusion with Leicester University.

Pony Club /ˈpəʊnɪ klʌb/, **the** (sport and leisure) A *club* for young pony riders, holding a wide range of meetings, shows and contests. It was founded in 1929, and has a current membership of about 35,000 members.

pony-trekking /ˈpəʊnɪ ˌtrekɪŋ/ (sport and leisure) A type of holiday activity in which ponies are ridden cross-country, especially over rough country such as moorland and hill country. The sport became popular from the 1970s.

pools /puːlz/, **the** (sport and leisure) A weekly gambling contest, organized by various firms throughout the country, in which bets are placed on the results of *football* matches. The contest is conducted mainly by predicted results being sent on a special form ('pools coupon') through the post, although some firms also arrange for collectors to call for the forms at people's private houses. [also called 'football pools': 'pool' in sense of 'combined stake']

Poppy Day /ˈpɒpɪ deɪ/ (tradition) A popular name for *Remembrance Sunday*, when people wear an artificial poppy in memory of those who fell in the two world wars. The poppies represent those that grew in the cornfields of Flanders in the First World War, and symbolize the soldiers who died in that war (and now, also, the Second World War). They are made by ex-servicemen and are sold by representatives of the *Royal British Legion*, who gain much of their income from the proceeds.

popular paper /ˌpɒpjʊlə ˈpeɪpə(r)/ (media) A daily or *Sunday* newspaper with a style and content aimed at the undemanding reader. Most popular papers are *tabloids*, and contain short news reports and a large number of photographs, as well as cartoons, competitions, readers' letters, and a section on sport. There are often features of 'human interest' about people in the public eye, such as celebrities and members of the *royal family*. The style of English is often colloquial, especially in the headlines, which are big and bold. Daily popular papers are the *Daily Express*, the *Daily Mail*, the *Daily Mirror*, the *Daily Star*, the *Morning Star*, The *Sun* and *Today*. Sunday popular papers are the *News* *of the World*, the *Sunday Express*, the *Sunday Mirror*, the *Sunday Sport*, The *Mail on Sunday* and The *People*.

pork-pie hat /ˌpɔːk paɪ ˈhæt/ (clothing) A man's hat with a round, flat crown and a brim that can be turned down as well as up. [from its resemblance to the top layer of pastry crust on a pork pie]

porridge /ˈpɒrɪdʒ/ (food and drink) A once standard dish in an *English breakfast*—oatmeal cooked in water or milk until as thick as required. It is eaten hot with a spoon, usually with sugar (or salt) and milk (or cream) added on top. The dish is traditionally popular in *Scotland*, but in *England* has largely been replaced by other prepared cereals that do not need cooking.

Port of London Authority /ˌpɔːt əv ˈlʌndən ɔːˌθɒrətɪ/, **the (PLA, the)** (transport) The independent (non-governmental) body that operates the port and docks of *London*. The Authority is technically a public trust, and similar trusts control other major ports in *Britain*, although many are also operated as nationalized (state-owned) bodies or are managed by a *local authority*. The PLA covers the tidal portion of the Thames from Teddington, west of London, to the seaward limit. Most of its activity is now at Tilbury, Essex, where it owns the dock.

Portakabin /ˈpɔːtəˌkæbɪn/ (daily life) The trade name of a type of small portable building of oblong shape, typically used for an office on a building site, an extra classroom in a school, or an extension to a factory. [from '*porta*ble *cabin*']

Portobello Road /ˌpɔːtəbeləʊ ˈrəʊd/ (London) A street in west *London* famous for its daily market, especially the one held on Saturday. The market is famous for its variety, but its greatest attractions are its antiques, boutique clothes, *Victoriana* and 'junk' (discarded or second-hand objects, some occasionally found to be valuable). [street named after former farm there, named in turn after British capture of Portobello, Panama, in 1739]

Porton Down /ˌpɔːtn ˈdaʊn/ (science and technology) The short name of the Centre for Applied Microbiology and Research, which has its laboratories at Porton, northeast of Salisbury, Wiltshire. The Centre has been the subject of public protest in recent years, both for its work in connection with biological and chemical warfare and for its use of live animals for scientific research. The Centre is a state-owned body.

Post Office /ˈpəʊst ˌɒfɪs/, **the (PO, the)** (commerce) The public corporation that has long had a monopoly in the handling of mail in *Britain*. It operates in three separate departments: *Royal Mail*, *Parcelforce* and *Post Office Counters*.

Post Office Counters /ˌpəʊst ˌɒfɪs ˈkaʊntəz/ (finance) The department of the *Post Office* that operates in the post office itself, receiving letters and parcels, selling stamps, and acting as agent for a number of government and *local authority* services, as well as for *Girobank*.

postal district /ˈpəʊstl ˌdɪstrɪkt/ (geography) The district of a large town or *city* for postal delivery, usually given as a combination of letters and figures, for example, (in *London*) EC3 ('east central district number three'), N4 ('north four'). All postal districts have now become part of a *postcode*.

postal order /ˈpəʊstl ˌɔːdə(r)/ (finance) A printed order to pay a named person or company a stated sum of money, bought at a post office. Postal orders are mostly for small amounts and are chiefly used by people who do not have a bank account (and therefore cannot send a cheque). At present they are issued in values of 50p to £20. A fee for each order is also charged, depending on the amount.

postal vote /ˈpəʊstl vəʊt/ (politics) A vote sent by post in a *by-election* or *general election* by a voter who has to be away from his *constituency* on *polling day*. Compare *proxy vote*.

postbus /ˈpəʊstbʌs/ (transport) A *Post Office* minibus transporting both mail and passengers in some rural areas.

postcode /ˈpəʊstkəʊd/ (daily life) A combination of letters and figures forming the final item in a postal address and used by the *Post Office* to sort and deliver mail. In *Britain* the postcode is written in two halves: the first group gives the initials of the town or *city* where the area head post office is situated, plus the number of the district in that area; the second half gives the *postman*'s delivery area or 'walk' in the form of a figure and letter combination. Thus the postcode for the Oxford University Press is OX2 6DP, with 'OX' standing for 'Oxford' and '2' the district of Oxford in which the Press is located. In London, the first part of the postcode is based on the *postal district*. All addresses in Britain officially have a postcode, but some people prefer not to use it in their address.

postgraduate /ˌpəʊst ˈgrædʒʊət/ (education) A student who has completed a university course and who is continuing to study for a more advanced qualification such as a *higher degree*. See also *graduate student*.

postman /ˈpəʊstmən/ (daily life) An employee of the *Post Office* who delivers mail daily (except on *Sunday*) to private and public buildings. In towns he usually makes his deliveries on foot or by bicycle; in rural areas he will deliver the post by van. There are normally three deliveries a day, two of letters and one of parcels. The first, main delivery is usually in the early morning, and the second in the late morning. Parcels are normally delivered in the morning. On Saturdays there is only one delivery of letters (and one of parcels). There are no deliveries on *bank holidays*. In a few isolated or remote areas the postman will also collect mail from private addresses as well as deliver it.

postman's knock /ˌpəʊstmənz ˈnɒk/ (sport and leisure) A children's game (or, on occasions, adults' game) in which one of the players goes outside and knocks on the door of the room where the other players are as a 'postman' delivering a 'letter' which has to be 'paid for' with a kiss.

Potter, Dennis /ˈpɒtə(r), ˈdenɪs/ (people) Dennis Potter (1935-94) was one of the most gifted television dramatists of recent years. His varied output was to some extent autobiographical, reflecting his own childhood in the Forest of Dean and the crippling illness from which he suffered for some time. Recurring themes in his plays are patriotism, loyalty, the artist's relationship with his work, the legacy of Christianity and popular music of the 1930s. One of his best and most rewarding plays is 'The Singing Detective', broadcast by the *BBC* as a six-part serial in 1986. This deals with the whole range of human experience, from birth and death, sickness and health, to the many joys and cares, mysteries and insights, that make up our daily lives.

Potteries /ˈpɒtərɪz/, **the** (geography) A name for the six towns of Burslem, Hanley, Longton, Fenton, Tunstall and Stoke-on-Trent, Staffordshire (the first five officially became part of Stoke-on-Trent in 1910). The area has long been famous for its china and earthenware industries.

pound (sterling) /paʊnd (ˈstɜːlɪŋ)/ (finance) The basic unit of British currency, divided into 100 pence (see *penny*) and in circulation as a coin since 1983. Its written symbol, placed before the number of pounds, is £, as £5 ('five pounds'). In colloquial speech, most people do not add a plural 's' to 'pound', especially when an amount in pence follows. For £5.50 they would thus say 'five pound fifty'. Pound notes were in circulation until 1988. See p 472.

PowerGen /ˈpəʊədʒen/ (commerce) The smaller of the two independent companies, founded in 1991, that generate electricity in *England* and *Wales*. The other is *National Power*. Both companies are fuelled by coal and (to a much lesser extent) oil, unlike *Nuclear Electric*. PowerGen currently owns 19 power stations and also sponsors the *BBC* television weather forecasts. [from *'power'* and *'ge*nerate']

PPP /ˌpiː piː ˈpiː/ **(Private Patients Plan)** (medicine) An insurance organization similar to *BUPA* by which financial cover can be provided for private medical treatment outside the *NHS* for regular subscribers.

prefect /ˈpriːfekt/ (education) In some schools, a senior boy or girl in a position of authority, for example, in charge of discipline and daily routine in a class.

preference shares /ˈprefrəns ʃeəz/ (finance) Shares that entitle their holders to preference (priority) when *dividends* are paid. The rate of the dividend, however, is usually lower than that of *ordinary shares*.

Premier League /ˌpremɪə ˈliːg/**, the** (sport and leisure) The leading 22 football *clubs* in *England*, run since 1992 by the English *FA*. Compare *Football League* and see also *Premiership*.

Premiership /ˈpremɪəʃɪp/**, the** (sport and leisure) The weekly results, with cumulative points, of football matches played in *England* by the *Premier League*.

Premium (Savings) Bonds /ˈpriːmɪəm bɒndz (ˌpriːmɪəm ˈseɪvɪŋz bɒndz)/ (finance) Bonds (certificates of a loan) issued by the *Treasury* since 1956 for sale to members of the public. Many bonds pay interest to the lender, but Premium Bonds, instead of earning interest, enter a monthly or weekly draw for cash prizes. They are bought at a post office. See *Ernie*.

prep school /ˈprep skuːl/ (education) A colloquial abbreviation for a *preparatory school*.

preparatory school /prɪˈpærətrɪ skuːl/ (education) An independent (fee-paying) school for children aged (usually) 7 to 13. Many are boarding schools and for boys only (aged 7–13) or girls only (7–11) and some form a junior department of a *public school*[1]. Most pupils go on from a preparatory school to a public school by taking the *Common Entrance* examination. [providing education 'preparatory' to a public school]

pre-preparatory school /ˌpriː prɪˈpærətrɪ skuːl/ (education) An independent school that prepares children aged 5 to 7 for entry to a *preparatory school*.

Pre-Raphaelites /ˌpriːˈræfəlaɪts/, **the** (arts) A group of painters (full name, the Pre-Raphaelite Brotherhood) founded in 1848 with the aim of restoring to painting the vivid colours, attention to detail, and naturalistic subjects that they regarded as typical (and best) of the early Italian Renaissance masters, who were painting before Raphael. Many of the group chose biblical and romantic subjects for their themes. Among leading members were Dante Gabriel Rossetti (1828–82), Holman Hunt (1827–1910), John Millais (1829–96) and Edward Burne-Jones (1833–98).

presbytery /ˈprezbɪtrɪ/ (religion) **1** In some *Church of England churches* and cathedrals, the name used for the area where the main altar is. **2** In the *Roman Catholic Church*, the residence of a priest. **3** In a Presbyterian church, a local church court of *ministers[1]* and elders.

pre-school playgroup /ˌpriːskuːl ˈpleɪgruːp/ (education) An alternative name for a *playgroup*.

prescription /prɪˈskrɪpʃn/ (medicine) A written order made by a doctor or dentist for a patient's medicines or medical appliances. The patient usually takes the prescription to a chemist (known as a 'dispensing chemist'), where it is prepared according to its directions. There is a charge for the *NHS* dispensing of a prescription (currently £4.25), but many people pay no charge, including children under 16, pregnant women, *OAPs*, and patients suffering from certain permanent conditions. Private (non-NHS) patients pay the actual cost of any medicine or appliance prescribed for them.

President of the Board of Trade /ˈprezɪdənt əv ðə ˌbɔːd əv ˈtreɪd/, **the** (government) The head of the Board of Trade, the section of the *Department* of Trade and Industry that promotes export trade. The title is held by the *Secretary of State* for this Department.

presiding officer /prɪˌzaɪdɪŋ ˈɒfɪsə(r)/ (politics) A person appointed to be in charge of a *polling station* during a *by-election* or *general election*.

Press Association /ˈpres əsəʊsɪˌeɪʃn/, **the (PA, the)** (media) A leading British news agency, founded in 1868 and providing a full service of home news to national and regional newspapers, the *BBC, ITN* and other subscribers.

Press Council /ˈpres ˌkaʊnsl/, **the** (media) An independent organization founded by the press in 1953 with the aim of preserving the traditional freedom of the British press. It judges complaints made by members of the public about the behaviour of newspapers and magazines and obliges the press to publish the results of its findings, even in a newspaper that itself has been found guilty of unprofessional conduct.

Prestel /'prestel/ (media) The videotext service of *BT*, transmitting information over the telephone to a computer, an electronic terminal, or a specially adapted television. [apparently a blend of '*press*' or '*presto*' and '*tele*phone']

Prestwick /'prestwɪk/ (transport) An international airport near Prestwick, southwest *Scotland.*

Prevention of Terrorism Act /prɪˌvenʃn əv 'terərɪzəm ækt/, **the** (law) An act that came into force in 1984. It gives the police and other authorities the power to refuse admission to *Britain* to any person who is known to have a connection with terrorism in *Northern Ireland.* In addition, the law allows the police to arrest people suspected of being involved in terrorism of any kind, whether in Northern Ireland or some other country, and to hold them for 48 hours.

Prima /'priːmə/ (media) A popular monthly magazine for 'practical women', first published in 1986. It has a current circulation of about 723,000.

primary school /'praɪmərɪ skuːl/ (education) A junior *state school* for children aged (usually) 5 to 11, after which they pass to a *secondary school.* Some children in this age group, however, attend a *first school* or *middle school.*

primate /'praɪmeɪt/ (religion) An alternative title for an archbishop. See *Primate of All England, Primate of England.*

Primate of All England /ˌpraɪmeɪt əv ɔːl 'ɪŋglənd/, **the** (religion) The official title of the *Archbishop of Canterbury.* Compare *Primate of England.*

Primate of England /ˌpraɪmeɪt əv 'ɪŋglənd/, **the** (religion) The official title of the *Archbishop of York.* Compare *Primate of All England.*

Prime Minister /ˌpraɪm 'mɪnɪstə(r)/, **the (PM, the)** (government) The head of the government, who presides over the *Cabinet* and gives posts to *ministers*[2]. The Prime Minister sits in the *House of Commons* and, among other responsibilities, recommends a number of appointments to the sovereign, including senior clergy in the *Church of England* and high legal offices such as the *Lord Chief Justice, Privy Councillors, Lords-Lieutenant* and the *Poet Laureate.* He or she is also, by tradition, Minister for the *Civil Service.* ['Prime' as the first or chief minister of state]

Primrose League /ˌprɪmrəʊz 'liːg/, **the** (politics) An
organization for promoting *Conservative Party* principles,
founded in 1883 in memory of Benjamin Disraeli (1804–81), a
Conservative British *Prime Minister*. The aims of the League
are 'the maintenance of religion, of the constitution of the
realm, and of the unity of the British *Commonwealth*[1] and
Empire'. In the early 1970s it still had over two million
members. [named after what was said to be Disraeli's
favourite flower]

prince /prɪns/ (royal family) The title of the sons of the
sovereign, of the sons of his or her sons and of the husband
of a *queen*. It is used together with the prince's name, as in
'Prince Charles', 'Prince William'. See also *Prince of Wales*.

Prince Consort /ˌprɪns 'kɒnsɔːt/ (history) The title of the
husband of a reigning *queen*. The title is not automatic, and is
specifically conferred by the queen. It was last used for *Prince*
Albert (1819–61), the husband of *Queen Victoria*.

Prince of Wales /ˌprɪns əv 'weɪlz/, **the** (royal family) The title
traditionally given to the sovereign's eldest son, as the heir to
the throne. The present Prince of Wales is Prince Charles
(born 1948), eldest son of *Queen Elizabeth*. He is one of the
more popular members of the *royal family*, and is noted for
his interest in such matters as architectural design, violence
in films, and the standard of English teaching in schools. In
1981 he married Lady Diana Spencer, now the *Princess of*
Wales. The marriage became strained, however, and in 1992
the royal couple announced their intention to separate.

Prince Regent /ˌprɪns 'riːdʒənt/, **the** (history) The title of King
George IV as regent (ruler) of *Great Britain* and *Ireland* while
his father, George III, was insane, from 1811–20. *Regent Street*
in *London*, is named after him.

Princes in the Tower /ˌprɪnsɪz ɪn ðə 'taʊə(r)/, **the** (history) A
popular name for the boy king Edward V (1470–83) and his
younger brother Richard, Duke of York (1472–83), both
(perhaps) murdered in the *Tower of London*, allegedly by
order of their uncle, the Duke of Gloucester, so that he could
succeed to the throne as Richard III (1452–85).

Princes Street /'prɪnsɪz striːt/ (geography) A central street of
Edinburgh, *Scotland*, with fashionable shops and restaurants,
and with gardens running along its south side. In the
gardens are a memorial to the Scottish author Sir Walter Scott
and a famous floral clock. [named after the princes who were
the sons of George III (1738–1820)]

princess /prɪn'ses/ (royal family) The title of the daughters of
the sovereign and of the daughters of his or her sons. It is
used together with the princess's name, as in 'Princess Anne'.
Princess of Wales /ˌprɪnses əv 'weɪlz/, **the** (royal family) The
title traditionally given to the wife of the *Prince of Wales*. The
present Princess of Wales, formerly Lady Diana Spencer
(born 1961), married Prince Charles in 1981. Her natural
charm, beauty and shyness won her the admiration of many,
and the royal wedding was one of the great events of the
year. In 1982 the Princess gave birth to her first child, Prince
William, and in 1984 to her second, Prince Henry (usually
known as Prince Harry). In 1992 the royal couple announced
their intention to separate, however.

principal boy

Princess Royal /ˌprɪnses ˈrɔɪəl/, **the** (royal family) A title of honour awarded to the eldest daughter of a British *king* or *queen*. In 1987 *Queen Elizabeth* awarded the title to her only daughter, Princess Anne. (The previous Princess Royal had died in 1965.) Princess Anne (born 1950) is well-known for her interest in horses and racing, as well as for her active support for a number of charities. In 1973 she married Captain Mark Phillips, who shared her riding interests, but separated from him in 1989 and divorced him in 1992, when she married a *Royal Navy* officer, Commander Tim Laurence. There are two children of her first marriage; Peter Phillips (born 1977) and Zara Phillips (born 1981).

principal boy /ˌprɪnsəpl ˈbɔɪ/ (tradition) The young 'hero' in a *pantomime*, traditionally played by a female actor. In 'Cinderella' the part is that of Prince Charming; in 'Jack and the Beanstalk', that of Jack; in 'Aladdin and his Wonderful Lamp', that of Aladdin; in 'Dick Whittington', that of Dick.

Printing House Square /ˌprɪntɪŋ haʊs ˈskweə(r)/ (media) **1** A square south of *Fleet Street[1]*, *London* where the royal printers had their premises in the 17th century, and where the offices of The *Times* were from its foundation in 1785. In 1986 The Times then made a second move to new premises in *Wapping*. **2** A nickname of 'The Times', or of its London offices.

prison visitor /ˌprɪzn ˈvɪzɪtə(r)/ (law) A person who visits people in prison as a voluntary service.

private bar /ˌpraɪvɪt ˈbɑː(r)/ (daily life) An additional *bar[1]* in a *pub*, similar to a *lounge bar*.

private bill /ˌpraɪvɪt ˈbɪl/ (government) A bill presented to *Parliament* on behalf of a private individual or group of people (eg, the shareholders of a company), as distinct from a *public bill*. Compare also *private member's bill*.

private company /ˌpraɪvɪt ˈkʌmpənɪ/ see *private limited company* (finance)

Private Eye /ˌpraɪvɪt ˈaɪ/ (media) A fortnightly satirical magazine, first published in 1962. It aims to expose scandals and corrupt practices, especially those involving people in positions of authority, such as political or business leaders. As a result of its accusations, it has been sued for libel several times. Its current circulation is about 197,000. [from the nickname for a private detective]

private hotel /ˌpraɪvɪt həʊˈtel/ (daily life) A hotel where the owner has the right to refuse admission to a guest, especially one who arrives without having previously booked.

private income /ˌpraɪvɪt ˈɪŋkʌm/ (finance) Income not from regular work but from other sources, such as investment or gambling.

private limited company /ˌpraɪvɪt ˌlɪmɪtɪd ˈkʌmpənɪ/ (finance) A commercial, often small, company, that is legally defined as any company that is not a public limited company (see *PLC*), and so is one that cannot offer shares to the public. Such companies are in the majority, and the distinction between the two types was introduced with the passing of the Companies Act of 1980. A private limited company usually puts the abbreviation 'Ltd' (Limited) after its name to indicate that it is legally a *limited company*.

private means /ˌpraɪvɪt ˈmiːnz/ (finance) An alternative term for *private income*.

private member /ˌpraɪvɪt ˈmembə(r)/ (government) An *MP* who is not a member of the government (ie, a *minister*[2]) or of the *Shadow Cabinet*.

private member's bill /ˌpraɪvɪt ˈmembəz bɪl/ (government) A *public bill* introduced in the *House of Commons* by a *private member*. Compare also *private bill*.

private patient /ˌpraɪvɪt ˈpeɪʃnt/ (medicine) A patient who pays for his medical treatment and does not receive it through the *NHS*. Most private patients subscribe to a special insurance scheme operated by a *provident society* or *friendly society* such as *BUPA* or *PPP*.

private practice /ˌpraɪvɪt ˈpræktɪs/ (medicine) A doctor's practice where *private patients* are treated.

private road /ˌpraɪvɪt ˈrəʊd/ (transport) A road running over private property, such as the estate of a *country house*. It is usually open to the public but may be closed. Private roads must be closed to the public at least once a year in order to remain private.

private school /ˌpraɪvɪt ˈskuːl/ (education) An *independent* (fee-paying) *school* such as a *preparatory school*, as distinct from a *state* (non-fee-paying) *school*. The finances of such schools are often controlled by a charitable trust. Most *public schools*[1] are in fact private schools, although the term is not generally used in order to avoid confusion.

private treaty /ˌpraɪvɪt ˈtriːtɪ/ (law) An arrangement by which the price of a house to be sold is agreed directly between seller and buyer, not through an *estate agent*.

Privy Council /ˌprɪvɪ ˈkaʊnsl/, **the** (government) The private council of the sovereign. Its main function today is to advise the sovereign to approve certain government decrees (so-called *orders in council*) and to issue royal proclamations. All *Cabinet ministers*[2,4] are members of the Privy Council, as are eminent people in *Commonwealth*[1] countries, as appointed by the sovereign. At present there are about 400 *Privy Councillors*. A full meeting of the Council is called only when a sovereign dies or announces his or her intention to marry.

Privy Councillor/Counsellor /ˌprɪvɪ ˈkaʊnsələ(r)/ (government) A member of the *Privy Council*.

Privy Purse /ˌprɪvɪ ˈpɜːs/, **the** (royal family) An annual payment made by *Parliament* to the *Queen* for her private expenses as sovereign. The money for the payment comes mainly from the *Duchy of Lancaster*. As a private individual, the Queen makes her payments from her own resources.

Privy Seal /ˌprɪvɪ ˈsiːl/, **the** (government) A seal fastened on certain royal documents that are not important enough for the *Great Seal*, or on documents that later receive the Great Seal.

probate /ˈprəʊbeɪt/ (law) The process of officially proving that a will is genuine, and that what it says is valid. This process is carried out in the *High Court of Justice*.

probation /prəˈbeɪʃn/ (law) A scheme whereby a criminal offender is placed under the supervision of a *probation officer* for a period of between six months and three years. The aim is to rehabilitate the offender by allowing him to lead a normal life rather than be put in prison. An offender being supervised in this way is said to be 'on probation'.

probation officer /prəˈbeɪʃn ˌɒfɪsə(r)/ (law) An officer appointed by a court to supervise, advise and befriend a *probationer*[2].

probationer /prəˈbeɪʃənə(r)/ (**1** work **2** law) **1** Someone who is training to do a particular job, for example, a trainee teacher. **2** A criminal offender who is on *probation*.

proctor /ˈprɒktə(r)/ (education) A *don* or member of the teaching staff appointed at some universities to supervise examinations, enforce discipline, and carry out other administrative duties.

procurator fiscal /ˌprɒkjʊreɪtə ˈfɪskl/ (law) In *Scotland*, an officer of a *sheriff*[2] court who acts as a public prosecutor, and who carries out the duties that a *coroner* would carry out in *England*.

Promenade Concerts /ˌprɒməˈnɑːd ˌkɒnsəts/, **the** (arts) An annual series of summer concerts sponsored by the *BBC* and held at the *Albert Hall, London.* The Concerts are particularly popular with younger music-lovers, many of whom stand (as *promenaders*) in the arena in front of the orchestra and fill the Hall on the *Last Night of the Proms.* The Concerts were first held in 1895, originally in the Queen's Hall (a building destroyed in 1941). The programmes are always of classical music but have become more adventurous and original in recent years. ['Promenade' since originally members of the audience 'promenaded' or walked about during the concert, whereas they now stand or sit]

promenader /ˌprɒməˈnɑːdə(r)/ (arts) A person, especially a young concert-goer, who attends *Promenade Concerts* and who stands in the arena (floor of the hall) during the performance.

Proms /prɒmz/, **the** (arts) A colloquial abbreviation for the *Promenade Concerts.*

proportional representation /prəˌpɔːʃənl ˌreprɪzenˈteɪʃn/ (politics) The system whereby a political party secures seats in an election in proportion to the actual numbers of people that voted for it. Proportional representation is not used in British political elections. In recent years there has been a growing demand for some form of this system, but so far neither the *Conservative Party* nor the *Labour Party* has been willing to commit itself to it. See also *voting system.*

prorogation /ˌprəʊrəˈɡeɪʃn/ (government) The act by which the sovereign ends a session of *Parliament*, usually when a *general election* is announced. The *House of Commons* closes completely, but the *House of Lords* may sit when prorogued, in order to hear legal appeals.

Protectorate /prəˈtektərət/, **the** (history) The period of the *Commonwealth*², from 1653 to 1659, when *England* was governed by Oliver Cromwell and, after him, by his son Richard, both of whom had the title 'Lord Protector'.

provident society /ˈprɒvɪdənt səˌsaɪətɪ/ (finance) Another name for a *friendly society.*

provisional licence /prəˌvɪʒənl ˈlaɪsns/ (transport) A licence granted provisionally to the driver of a motor vehicle while he is learning to drive (ie, as an *L-driver*).

Provisionals /prəˈvɪʒənlz/, **the** (politics) The faction of *Sinn Féin* and the *IRA* that has existed since 1969 when the split into the 'Official' and the 'Provisional' IRA was made. The

Provisionals (or 'Provos') follow a policy of terrorism in their aim of achieving a united *Ireland*.

provost /'prɒvəst/ (**1** education **2, 3** religion) **1** The title of the head of some *colleges¹* and schools. **2** A senior official of a cathedral in the *Church of England*, especially one of the newer ones. **3** The head of a cathedral chapter in the *Roman Catholic Church* in *England*.

proxy vote /'prɒksɪ vəʊt/ (politics) A vote at an election, such as a *by-election* or a *general election*, that is made by a person on behalf of a voter when that voter is unable to go to the *polling station* for some reason (eg, disability or long-term illness). Official permission must be given before a proxy vote can be used. Compare *postal vote*.

PSBR /ˌpiː es biː 'ɑː(r)/ (**public sector borrowing requirement**) (finance) The money that the government borrows to supplement what it receives through tax revenue and other sources. It obtains it by selling government stock and securities and by encouraging various forms of national savings. PSBR was gradually reduced by the *Conservative Party* down to 1988, when it was actually negative. It has since increased, however, so that for the *financial year* 1993–94 it was estimated to be £32,000 million.

PTA /ˌpiː tiː 'eɪ/ (**parent-teacher association**) (education) An association organized by an individual school to enable parents of children at the school and their teachers to meet and discuss the school's policies and the children's progress. Most schools have a PTA meeting at the school once a *term¹*.

pub /pʌb/ (**public house**) (daily life) An establishment where alcoholic (and non-alcoholic) drinks and, usually, snacks or meals are sold. The pub is a traditional feature of almost all towns and villages, and is often a building of 'character' or even historic interest (see *inn*). For many people, it is a kind of *club*, where one can relax, talk with friends, listen to music, play games (such as *darts* or *bar billiards*) and enjoy drinking and eating. Most pubs are open twice daily or all day (see *licensing hours*), and many have a garden where food and drink can be consumed in the summer (see *beer garden*). Inside the building, there is often both a *public bar* and a *lounge bar*, and possibly also a *saloon bar* and a *private bar*. There may also be a separate restaurant or dining area. Children under 16 are not admitted to a pub, although they may sit outside with adults in the garden. As a rule, most pubs are owned by a particular brewery (see *tied house*), but some are not (see *free house*). Some of the larger or better furnished pubs also provide overnight accommodation, and thus are like small hotels. All pubs have distinctive names (see *inn sign*), many of which reflect their historic origin. See also *ploughman's lunch*.

public bar /ˌpʌblɪk 'bɑː(r)/ (daily life) The most popular *bar¹* in a *pub*, where drinks are sometimes cheaper and the atmosphere usually very lively. If *darts* is played in the pub, it will be in the public bar.

public bill /ˌpʌblɪk 'bɪl/ (government) A *bill* that affects the general public, as distinct from a *private bill*. See also *private member's bill*.

Public Lending Right /ˌpʌblɪk 'lendɪŋ raɪt/ **(PLR)** (law) A government scheme, first operating in 1984, by which payment is made from public funds to authors (including illustrators, translators and editors) whose books are lent out from public libraries. At present no author can earn more than £6,000 from the scheme in any one year.

public limited company /ˌpʌblɪk ˌlɪmɪtɪd 'kʌmpənɪ/ see *PLC* (finance)

Public Record Office /ˌpʌblɪk 'rekɔːd ˌɒfɪs/, **the** (government) An office in *London* that holds official (government) records, including those of *courts³* of law and of most government *departments*. Many of the documents it holds are of great national interest, such as the *Domesday Book* and the papers of the *Gunpowder Plot*. The office is open to members of the public.

public school /ˌpʌblɪk 'skuːl/ (education) **1** An *independent* (usually fee-paying) *school* for students aged 11 (or 13) to 18. Many of *Britain*'s public schools are long-established and have gained a reputation for their high academic standards, as well as their exclusiveness and snobbery. The boys' schools include such well-known schools as *Eton, Harrow, Westminster* and *Winchester*. (Many traditional boys' schools now take some girls, if only in the *sixth form*.) Among leading girls' public schools are *Roedean* and Cheltenham Ladies' College (see *Cheltenham*). Most of the members of the British *Establishment* were educated at a public school. See also *preparatory school*. ['public' since originally students could enter the school from anywhere in *England* and not just from the immediate neighbourhood] **2** The title occasionally used for a school in *Scotland* that is supported from public funds (ie, is non-fee-paying). It should not be confused with the better-known public school[1], which is an independent (fee-paying) school.

pudding /ˈpʊdɪŋ/ (food and drink) **1** A sweet dish cooked with flour, milk, eggs, fruit and other ingredients, and usually served hot. Examples are *Christmas pudding* and *plum pudding*. **2** A term for any sweet course or dessert at *lunch* or *dinner*. **3** A savoury dish usually made of pastry or batter and containing meat. Examples are *steak and kidney pudding* and *pease pudding*.

Pullman (train) /ˈpʊlmən (treɪn)/ (transport) A luxury *Inter-City train* with *first class[1]* seats only and with special comfort and facilities, such as meals and drinks served at a passenger's seat. [name ultimately derives from American railcar designer George M Pullman (1831–97)]

Punch and Judy

Punch and Judy /ˌpʌntʃ ən ˈdʒuːdɪ/ (tradition) A traditional play for puppets, popular with children, and mostly performed at seaside and other holiday resorts. The play, today usually performed by hand puppets, has historic origins in European popular comedies, notably the Italian 'commedia dell'arte' (with the character Punchinello). Its main characters are the hunch-backed, hook-nosed Punch, his wife Judy, with whom he quarrels, and their dog, Toby.

punt /pʌnt/ (sport and leisure) An open, flat-bottomed boat that is broad and square at both ends. It is used on shallow rivers and is propelled by someone standing at one end pushing against the river bed with a long pole. Punts are very popular at *Cambridge University* and *Oxford University*.

punt

punter /'pʌntə(r)/ (sport and leisure) **1** A person who bets on the results of horse races, *greyhound racing* and other sporting events in a *betting shop*, either on the course itself or by post from home (especially in the *pools*). **2** A customer of any kind, or simply a person in general.

Purcell Room /'pɜːsel ruːm/, **the** (arts) A recital hall on the *South Bank* site, *London*, used mainly for performances of chamber music. It is in the same complex as the *Queen Elizabeth Hall*, the *Royal Festival Hall* and the *Hayward Gallery*. [named after English classical composer Henry Purcell (?1659–95)]

putting /'pʌtɪŋ/ (sport and leisure) A simplified game of golf popular in public parks and at seaside resorts, where it is played on a course known as a 'putting green'. Compare *clock golf*.

PYO /ˌpiː waɪ 'əʊ/ (**pick your own**) (daily life) A roadside sign showing the location of a field, farm or *market garden* where people can pick their own fruit or vegetables, paying for the amount by weight. Such fruit is usually cheaper than in the shops or even in a market on *market day*.

Pytchley (Hunt) /ˈpaɪtʃlɪ (ˌpaɪtʃlɪ ˈhʌnt)/, **the** (sport and leisure) One of the best known *hunts*, founded about 1750 in the village of Pytchley, near Kettering, Northamptonshire.

QUEENSBERRY RULES

* QC /ˌkjuː ˈsiː/ **(Queen's Counsel)** (law) The title given to certain senior *barristers* by the *queen* (see *Queen Elizabeth*) on the recommendation of the *Lord Chancellor*. A QC is known as a 'silk' because of the silk gown he wears, and in *court³* he is entitled to sit 'within the *bar²*', in the special area reserved for the judge or *magistrate*. (Many QCs actually become judges.) Barristers who are not QCs are known as 'juniors', whatever their age. At present about one barrister in ten is a QC.

QE2 /ˌkjuː iː ˈtuː/**, the (Queen Elizabeth 2, the)** (transport) A large liner built by *Cunard* to operate as a cruise liner in the winter and as a passenger liner between Southampton and New York in the summer. The ship was launched in 1967 and entered service in 1969, replacing an earlier 'Queen Elizabeth' liner withdrawn from service in 1970.

QPR /ˌkjuː piː ˈɑː(r)/ (sport and leisure) The nickname of *Queen's Park Rangers football club.*

quadrangle /ˈkwɒdræŋgl/ (style) An inner courtyard of a *college¹*, especially one at *Oxford University*. Compare *court²*.

Quakers /ˈkweɪkəz/ (religion) The popular name of members of the *Society of Friends*, a religious body founded in *England* in 1668. Quakers are unlike other Protestants since they have no officiating *ministers¹* or order of service in their worship, which takes place in the form of 'meetings'. At these, anyone can offer spoken prayer, ministry or reading. All men and women Quakers are equal. Quakers are noted for their pacifism, their high but not rigid moral standards, their association with charity work and education, and their endeavours to abolish persecution and to aid the poor. [originally a derogatory

---

* In the reign of a king, 'Queen's' in these titles becomes 'King's' and 'QC' becomes 'KC'.

quadrangle

nickname: their founder, George Fox, had told a judge that he
and others should 'quake at the word of the Lord']
quality paper /ˌkwɒlətɪ ˈpeɪpə(r)/ (media) A daily or *Sunday*
newspaper aimed at the more intelligent reader. Quality
papers are usually broadsheet (with large pages, unlike
tabloids) and carry detailed news reports and a wide range of
topical articles and features, together with many job adverts.
They also usually have special pages or sections devoted to
arts and literary reviews, finance, and sport, as well as an
accompanying weekly magazine, with many colour
photographs and full-page advertisements. The daily quality
papers are the *Financial Times*, the *Daily Telegraph*, The
Guardian, The *Independent* and The *Times*. The Sunday quality
papers are the *Sunday Telegraph*, The *Independent on Sunday*,
The *Observer* and the *Sunday Times*. Compare *popular paper*.
quango /ˈkwæŋgəʊ/ (government) A semi-official term for
what is officially known as a 'non-departmental public body',

that is, a body that is funded by the government to oversee or develop activity in an area of public interest but is not ifself a government *department*. Examples of quangos are the *Arts Council (of Great Britain)*, the *British Council* and the *Commission for Racial Equality*. There are currently about 2000 quangos in *Britain*. [abbreviation of '*qu*asi-*a*utonomous *n*on-*g*overnmental *o*rganization']

quarter day /ˈkwɔːtə deɪ/ (law) One of four days in the year when certain payments such as rent and interest are due. In *England, Wales* and *Northern Ireland* they are 25 March (the church festival of the Annunciation of the Blessed Virgin Mary, more commonly known as Lady Day), 24 June (St John the Baptist's Day, often called *Midsummer Day*), 29 September (St Michael and All Angels' Day, more commonly known as *Michaelmas Day*) and 25 December (*Christmas Day*). In *Scotland* they are 2 February (Candlemas), 15 May (*Whit Sunday*), 1 August (Lammas) and 11 November (Martinmas).

queen /kwiːn/ (royal family) The title of a female sovereign and at present that of *Queen Elizabeth*. The queen is the official head of state, the head of the legal system of *Britain*, the commander-in-chief of all armed forces and the head ('supreme governor') of the *Church of England*. Many important government processes require the participation of the queen, including the summoning, *prorogation* and dissolution of *Parliament*. Several *bills*, too, require her official approval (so-called *royal assent*). She also gives many important honours and awards, mostly on the advice of the *Prime Minister*, although she herself personally selects the people who receive the *Order of the Garter*, the *Order of the Thistle*, the *Order of Merit* and the Royal Victorian Order. By convention she invites the leader of a party winning a *general election* to form a government. In international affairs, the queen has the power to declare war and make peace, as well as to recognize foreign states and governments, conclude treaties and annex or cede territory. The queen also appoints many important office holders, including government *ministers*[2], judges, diplomats and bishops in the Church of England. She also has the power to remit all or part of the sentence passed on a criminal (by granting a 'royal pardon').

Queen Anne (style) /ˌkwiːn ˈæn (staɪl)/ (style) **1** A style of furniture popular in the early 18th century and characterized by the use of walnut veneer, curved legs on chairs and an overall simplicity and elegance. **2** An architectural style similarly popular in this period, characterized by the use of red brick and simple, classical lines. [both typical of the reign of Queen Anne (1665–1714)]

Queen Elizabeth /ˌkwiːn ɪˈlɪzəbəθ/ (royal family) Queen Elizabeth II (born 1926) has been *queen* since 1953. Among her many royal duties are the regular visits she makes to foreign countries, and especially those of the *Commonwealth*[1], whose interests and welfare are very important to her. The Queen has done much to simplify the formalities of the monarchy, including allowing the *BBC* to make an unprecedented documentary film about the everyday life of the *royal family*. She also instituted the tradition of the 'walkabout', an informal feature of an otherwise formal royal visit, when she walks about among the public crowds and stops to talk to some people. The Queen has long been regarded with considerable respect and affection by many of her subjects. The annual *Christmas* broadcast made by the Queen on radio and television has become a traditional and popular feature of the season, and there were widespread celebrations and special programmes of events in 1977 to mark her Silver Jubilee. The Queen's husband is the *Duke of Edinburgh*, and her four children are the *Prince of Wales* (born 1948), Princess *Anne*, the *Princess Royal* (born 1950), Prince Andrew, the *Duke of York* (born 1960) and Prince Edward (born 1964). The Queen's mother is *Queen Elizabeth, the Queen Mother*.

Queen Elizabeth Hall /ˌkwiːn ɪˌlɪzəbəθ ˈhɔːl/, **the** (arts) A concert hall in *London* on the *South Bank* site, used chiefly for performances of classical music. It is in the same complex (built 1967) as the smaller *Purcell Room* and the nearby *Hayward Gallery* and *Royal Festival Hall*.

Queen Elizabeth, the Queen Mother /ˌkwiːn ɪˌlɪzəbəθ ðə ˌkwiːn ˈmʌðə(r)/ (royal family) The mother of *Queen Elizabeth* and widow of King George VI (died 1952). The Queen Mother (born 1900) is a very popular member of the *royal family*, greatly respected for her sympathy for and interest in her people. She holds many honorary titles, both civilian and military, and is still remembered by many for the morale-raising visits she made to many parts of *Britain*, together with her husband, in the Second World War. See also *queen mother*.

Queen Elizabeth 2 /ˌkwiːn ɪˌlɪzəbəθ ðə ˈsekənd/ see *QE2* (transport)

298

queen mother /ˌkwiːn ˈmʌðə(r)/ (royal family) The title of the widow of a former *king* who is also the mother of the reigning sovereign. The present queen mother is *Queen Elizabeth, the Queen Mother*. See also *queen*.

Queen of the South /ˌkwiːn əv ðə ˈsaʊθ/ (sport and leisure) A Scottish *football club* founded in 1919, with a stadium in Dumfries, southern *Scotland*.

Queen Victoria /ˌkwiːn vɪkˈtɔːrɪə/ (royal family) The *queen* who had the longest reign in British history and who did much to make the monarchy respectable after the unpopular reigns of a number of monarchs. Queen Victoria (1819–1901) came to be a unique symbol of the British monarchy in modern times, with a high sense of duty and loyalty to her people and a genuine sympathy for her poorer subjects. She came to the throne in 1837, and three years later married her cousin, Albert. After her husband's death in 1861, she mourned him constantly, and although at first her tragic widowhood attracted increased public affection and sympathy, her continuing avoidance of public appearances made her less popular with her people. The adjective '*Victorian*', which had come to be used in her lifetime to mean 'flourishing', 'potentially great', came to acquire the sense of 'over-strict', 'censorious', much as it means today. Victoria herself, too, is now remembered as a humourless, unsmiling queen (she is said to have replied 'We are not amused' when a groom playfully imitated her), instead of the happy, dutiful and popular sovereign and mother that she had originally been. See also *Prince Consort, Victoriana*.

Queen Victoria Memorial /ˌkwiːn vɪkˌtɔːrɪə məˈmɔːrɪəl/, **the** (London) A monument to *Queen Victoria* built in front of *Buckingham Palace, London*, in 1911.

* **Queen's Bench Division** /ˌkwiːnz ˈbentʃ dɪˌvɪʒn/, **the** (law) One of the three main divisions of the *High Court of Justice*, having the *Lord Chief Justice* as its president. It deals chiefly with actions for damages for breach of contract, actions for recovery of land or goods, election petitions and cases regarding the registration of electors.

* **Queen's Birthday** /ˌkwiːnz ˈbɜːθdeɪ/, **the** (royal family) At present, either the date of the true birthday of *Queen Elizabeth* II, 21 April, or of her *Official Birthday*, on the second Saturday in June. The *Union Jack* is flown on public

---

* In the reign of a king, 'Queen's' in these titles becomes 'King's'.

buildings, and the *national anthem* played on the Queen's true birthday, but it is not a *bank holiday*, and no particular annual ceremony is held.

Queen's Club /ˌkwiːnz ˈklʌb/, **the** (sport and leisure) A leading tennis club in west *London*, equally well known as a centre for *real tennis* and *rackets*. It was founded in 1886.

* **Queen's English** /ˌkwiːnz ˈɪŋglɪʃ/, **the** (language) Standard, correct English, as traditionally spoken by an educated southerner.

* **Queen's English Society** /ˌkwiːnz ˈɪŋglɪʃ səˌsaɪətɪ/, **the** (language) A small but active society set up in 1972 to campaign for the correct use of the English language at all levels, and to reintroduce the teaching of formal grammar in schools to all children up to the age of 16. In 1987 its members won the support of many famous people in a petition for their cause which they sent to the *Secretary of State* for Education and Science. Among those who signed were Iris *Murdoch*, William *Golding*, Ted *Hughes* and Sir John *Gielgud*. [named after the *Queen's English* which the Society regards as being the only correct English]

* **Queen's Gallery** /ˌkwiːnz ˈgælərɪ/, **the** (arts) An art gallery open to the public inside *Buckingham Palace, London*, where a (changing) selection of paintings and other works of art from the royal collections is on display. The Gallery was opened in 1962 and is housed in what used to be the private *chapel*[2] of Buckingham Palace.

Queen's Park Rangers /ˌkwiːnz pɑːk ˈreɪndʒəz/ **(QPR)** (sport and leisure) A popular *London football club*, founded in 1885 and having a stadium near White City in west London. [named after former stadium at Queen's Park, northwest London]

Queen's Prize /ˌkwiːnz ˈpraɪz/, **the** (sport and leisure) The main prize for rifle shooting at *Bisley*, founded by *Queen Victoria* in 1860.

* **Queen's Speech** /ˌkwiːnz ˈspiːtʃ/, **the** (government) The speech made by the sovereign (when a *queen*) at the opening of a session of *Parliament*, in which the government outlines its planned programme, and the policies it intends to follow. The speech is prepared for the sovereign to read by the *ministers*[2] of the government in power.

---

* In the reign of a king, 'Queen's' in these titles becomes 'King's'.

Queen's University /ˌkwiːnz juːnɪˈvɜːsətɪ/, **The** (education) The oldest university of *Northern Ireland*, founded in *Belfast* in 1845 as Queen's College, when it was part of the Queen's University of Ireland, and becoming a full university in 1908. It has about 9,200 students.

Queensberry Rules /ˌkwiːnzbərɪ ˈruːlz/, **the** (sport and leisure) The code of rules followed in modern boxing, relating to the length of rounds, composition of gloves, types of blows allowed and other similar matters. [rules originated by Marquess of Queensberry in 1869]

quid /kwɪd/ (daily life) A colloquial term for a *pound (sterling)*. The word does not take an 's' in the plural so that 'five pounds', for example, would be 'five quid'.

Quorn /kwɔːn/, **the** (sport and leisure) A well-known *hunt* in Leicestershire. [founded in the mid-18th century at Quornden Hall, a *country house* near Loughborough]

RAC /ˌɑːr eɪ ˈsiː/**, the (Royal Automobile Club, the)**
(transport) One of two leading motoring organizations in
Britain, the other being the *AA*. It was founded in 1897 and
offers a service similar to that of the AA, including the
publication of special guides for motorists. Unlike the AA,
however, it has an actual *club* in *London*. The RAC also
regulates motor racing in Britain.

race meeting /ˈreɪs ˌmiːtɪŋ/ (sport and leisure) A sporting event
at which horses or *greyhounds* race over a set course at set
times.

race relations /ˈreɪs rɪˌleɪʃnz/ (life and society) *Britain* has long
had ethnic and national minority groups, and a variety of
people have settled in the country, either to escape political
or religious persecution, or simply to seek a better life. The
largest single minority group in Britain are the Irish, while
many Jews have also settled in this country. After the Second
World War a large number of Eastern European and other
refugees came to Britain, and were followed during the 1950s
and early 1960s by large communities from the West Indies,
India and Pakistan. There are also sizeable communities of
Chinese, Greek and Turkish Cypriots, Italians and Spaniards
now in Britain, besides Americans and Australians. The
difficulties that many minorities face are partly dealt with by
a range of social programmes, and the legal rights of such
people were officially recognized by the passing of the Race
Relations *Act* of 1976, which established the *Commission for
Racial Equality*.

rackets /ˈrækɪts/ (sport and leisure) A game rather like *squash*
(*rackets*) played in an enclosed court with a hard ball by two
or four people. The game was officially adopted at *Harrow
School* in the early 19th century, and one of its main centres in

Britain today is at the *Queen's Club, London*. [named from the racket with which the ball is hit in the game]

RADA /'rɑːdə/ **(Royal Academy of Dramatic Art, the)** (education) A school that trains professional actors and actresses. It was founded in 1904, and has its headquarters in central *London*. The public are admitted to performances staged by its students in the Vanbrugh Theatre there (named after the 18th-century dramatist Sir John Vanbrugh).

Radcliffe Camera /ˌrædklɪf 'kæmrə/**, the** (education) The main reading room of the *Bodleian Library* at *Oxford University*, founded by the physician John Radcliffe (1650–1714). The domed building of the Camera is one of the landmarks of central *Oxford¹*. ['Camera' here in basic sense of 'vaulted room']

Radio Authority /ˌreɪdɪəʊ ɔːˈθɒrəti/**, the** (media) The body set up in 1991 to license and regulate all *ILR* and *INR* stations in *Britain*. Compare *ITC*.

Radio 5 Live /ˌreɪdɪəʊ ˌfaɪv 'laɪv/ (media) A national radio channel of the BBC introduced in 1994 and broadcasting mainly sports and news programmes.

Radio 4 /ˌreɪdɪəʊ ˌfɔː(r)/ (media) A national radio channel of the *BBC*, providing a varied service. It is the main channel for speech, as distinct from music, and thus many of its programmes are devoted to news and current affairs, plays, comedy shows, documentaries and panel games. It also broadcasts debates from *Parliament* and live reports from important public events. It is on the air from 6 am to after midnight.

Radio 1 /ˌreɪdɪəʊ 'wʌn/ (media) A national radio channel of the *BBC*, providing a service mainly of pop and rock music plus news bulletins. It broadcasts for 24 hours a day.

Radio 3 /ˌreɪdɪəʊ 'θriː/ (media) A national radio channel of the *BBC*, broadcasting mainly classical music, but also drama, poetry, short stories and talks, from 7 am to after midnight. In the early morning it often broadcasts *Open University* programmes, and in season it carries *test match* commentaries.

Radio Times /ˌreɪdɪəʊ 'taɪmz/**, the** (media) A weekly magazine published by the *BBC* to give detailed information of television and radio programmes on BBC, *ITV*, *Channel 4* and satellite channels, together with features relating to the particular week. Until 1991 it published BBC programmes only. It was first published in 1923 and has a current circulation of about 1.6 million. Compare *TV Times*.

Radio 2 /ˌreɪdɪəʊ 'tuː/ (media) A national radio channel of the *BBC*, broadcasting light entertainment and music programmes for 24 hours a day.

RAF /ˌɑːr eɪ 'ef/, **the (Royal Air Force, the)** (defence) The air force of *Britain*, formed in 1918 on the amalgamation of the Royal Flying Corps and Royal Naval Air Service. RAF fighter pilots won public admiration for their achievements in the Second World War. There are now about 86,000 RAF servicemen and women.

raffle /'ræfl/ (sport and leisure) A type of lottery held at *fêtes*, etc, in which the prizes are goods rather than money. Most raffles are held to raise money for a particular charity, or to help pay for the building of a new *club* or the buying of sports equipment for a school.

rag (week) /'ræg (wiːk)/ (education) A special week of entertainments arranged in some universities to raise money for charity. The highlight of the week is traditionally a procession through the streets of the town or *city*, in which open vehicles carry colourful scenes performed by students, while other students with collecting boxes collect money from the crowds lining the route.

Rail Rover /'reɪl ˌrəʊvə(r)/ (transport) A special ticket sold by *BR* for unlimited travel over a specified region for a specified period (usually a week or a fortnight).

railcard /'reɪlkɑːd/ (transport) A special card sold by *BR* to certain types of passengers, enabling them to travel at a reduced rate. They include *OAPs*, young people under 24, disabled people, and passengers travelling within the *Network SouthEast* region. The cards are valid for one year.

Rainbow (Guide) /'reɪnbəʊ (gaɪd)/ (sport and leisure) A girl aged 7 or under who is a member of the youngest branch of the *Guides Association*.

Rambert Dance Company /'rɑːmbeə(r) 'dɑːns ˌkʌmpənɪ/, **the** (arts) A leading ballet company, which specializes in performing modern ballets, and often tours abroad. It was founded in *London* in 1930 by the ballet dancer and teacher Marie Rambert (1888–1982) and until 1987 was called the 'Ballet Rambert'.

rambler /'ræmblə(r)/ (sport and leisure) A person who enjoys rambling, or going for long walks in the countryside, especially someone who is a member of the Ramblers Association, which encourages walking of this type and aims to keep open to the public those public footpaths that have been closed by farmers and other landowners.

Ranger (Guide) /'reɪndʒə(r) (gaɪd)/ (sport and leisure) A girl or young woman aged 14 to 25 who is a member of the senior branch of the *Guides Association*.

Rangers /'reɪndʒəz/ (sport and leisure) A popular Scottish *football club* with its stadium at *Ibrox Park* in *Glasgow*. It draws support especially from among the local Protestant community and its traditional rivals are *Celtic*.

Rattle, Simon /'rætl, 'saɪmən/ (people) Simon Rattle (born 1955) is one of *Britain*'s outstanding musical conductors who is respected and admired for his modesty and enthusiasm. His work has received international praise, and he is well known for his willingness to conduct complex modern compositions as well as traditional classical music. In 1980 he was appointed principal conductor of the City of Birmingham Symphony Orchestra, which has gained worldwide acclaim under his baton.

reader /'riːdə(r)/ (education) The title of certain senior lecturers at some universities. [originally, in 16th century, one who read learned works and explained them to pupils and students]

real ale /ˌrɪəl 'eɪl/ (food and drink) Another term for *draught beer*, especially beer which has been brewed and stored in the traditional way, and which has continued to ferment in its cask before being drawn. See also *CAMRA*.

real tennis /ˌrɪəl 'tenɪs/ (sport and leisure) An old form of (lawn) tennis played in a four-walled indoor court with a special hard ball and racket. The game is still played today by enthusiasts, and has one of its main centres at the *Queen's Club, London*. [originally 'royal' tennis; the name was not widely used until the 20th century, when lawn tennis, on open, outdoor courts, became the much more popular version of the game]

receiver /rɪ'siːvə(r)/ (law) An official appointed to manage the property or business of a person who has been declared bankrupt or insane.

reception room /rɪ'sepʃn ruːm/ (daily life) A formal term used by *estate agents* for a main *ground floor* room in a house, especially the *living room* (sitting room) or dining room. [so called as these are rooms in which visitors are received, as against the private rooms for family use only, such as the kitchen or bedroom]

recess /rɪ'ses/ (government) **1** The temporary closure of *Parliament* over a holiday or vacation period, such as the 'summer recess'. **2** The suspension of Parliament between a *prorogation* and the start of the next session.

Recorded /rɪ'kɔːdɪd/ (commerce) A special service of the *Post Office*, which for a small additional payment provides written proof that a letter has been posted and confirmation by telephone that it has been delivered, although not necessarily the following day. Compare *Special Delivery*.

recorder /rɪ'kɔːdə(r)/ (law) A *barrister* or *solicitor* who has been qualified for at least ten years, and who is appointed to act as a judge in a *crown court*.

rector /'rektə(r)/ (**1** religion **2** education) **1** A clergyman appointed to be in charge of a parish, originally one entitled to receive the whole of the tithes (income from the parish). **2** The title of the head of some schools, *colleges*[1,2] and universities.

rectory /'rektərɪ/ (religion) The residence of a *rector*[1].

red /red/, **the** (finance) A colloquial term for a money account such as a bank account that is overdrawn or in debit. Compare *black*. [such accounts were originally made in red ink, whereas credit accounts were written in black]

Red Arrow (bus) /ˌred 'ærəʊ (bʌs)/ (transport) A single-deck bus operated by *London Regional Transport* to run between the main *London* railway termini and the chief shopping and business areas. [from the colour of such buses]

Red Arrows /ˌred 'ærəʊz/, **the** (defence) A special aerobatics squadron of the *RAF* performing in red aircraft.

red biddy /ˌred 'bɪdɪ/ (food and drink) A colloquial term for an alcoholic drink made from cheap red wine and methylated spirits. It is an unpleasant and dangerous drink. [apparently from 'Biddy', a nickname for an old woman, since some female tramps enjoy the drink]

red book /'red bʊk/ (media) A colloquial term for one of a number of official directories of people, which are bound in red. Among such books are *Who's Who, Burke('s Peerage)*, the various *Kelly's (Directories)* and handbooks and similar annual or regular publications.

Red Devils /ˌred 'devlz/, **the** (defence) **1** The semi-official nickname of the Parachute Regiment of the British *Army*. [apparently first called this by the Germans in the Second World War] **2** A special team from the Army who give displays of sky-diving and parachuting.

Red Devils

Red Ensign /ˌred 'ensən/, **the** (transport) The ensign (flag) of the Merchant Navy, having a red background with the *Union Jack* in the top left quarter (nearest the flagpole).

Red Flag /ˌred 'flæg/, **the** (politics) The hymn or official song of the *Labour Party*, sung at the end of party conferences and other big meetings. [from, 'We'll keep the Red Flag flying here!', the last line of the song, composed in 1889 by the socialist James Connell]

Red Hand of Ulster /ˌred hænd əv 'ʌlstə(r)/, **the** (tradition) The badge of *Northern Ireland*, in origin that of the O'Neill *clan*. It is shown heraldically as an upright red hand severed at the wrist (hence its alternative name of 'Bloody Hand'). See also *shamrock*.

redbrick university /ˌredbrɪk juːnɪ'vɜːsətɪ/ (education) One of the universities founded in the late 19th century and the first half of the 20th century, as distinct from the older *Oxford University* and *Cambridge University*. Many such universities were built in red brick, contrasting with the mellow grey stone of the old foundations.

redcoat /'redkəʊt/ (sport and leisure) A steward and entertainer at a *Butlin's* holiday camp, who wears a red coat as part of his uniform.

Redgrave, Vanessa /'redgreɪv, və'nesə/ (people) Vanessa Redgrave (born 1937) is a powerful and versatile actress who first appeared on the *London* stage in 1958, together with her father, the renowned actor Sir Michael Redgrave (1908–85). She soon gained approval for her sensitive performances in all types of plays, from *Shakespeare* to the present day, and has won special praise for her ability to express strong emotions or excitement. From the 1960s, she has been involved with Marxist politics and anti-nuclear campaigning. This has been the cause of some controversy.

reg /redʒ/ (transport) A colloquial abbreviation for 'registration' in a car's *registration number*, after a letter of the alphabet that indicates the new car's year of sale. For example, an 'L-reg' car is one sold in the year from 1 August 1993 to 31 July 1994, while a 'K-reg' car is one sold the previous year.

Regency (style) /'riːdʒənsɪ (staɪl)/ (style) A style of furniture and architecture found in *England* at the end of the 18th century and beginning of the 19th. It was the equivalent of the French Empire style and was characterized by neo-classical designs and, in furniture, the use of rosewood and brass inlay work. [period overlapped 1811–20 when the future King George IV was *Prince Regent*]

Regent Street /'riːdʒənt striːt/ (London) A central shopping street in *London*, originally built as a processional way for the *Prince Regent* in the 19th century. Its fashionable stores include a range of jewellery, clothing, china and gift shops.

Regent's Park /ˌriːdʒənts 'pɑːk/ (London) A large park in northwest *London*, laid out in 1811 for the *Prince Regent*. It contains a boating lake, an open-air theatre, a large number of sports fields, tracks and courts, flower gardens and a central refreshment pavilion. On its north side is the *London Zoo*.

Regina /rɪ'dʒaɪnə/ (law) The term used for the prosecution in criminal proceedings during the reign of a queen, as in 'Regina v. Jones', since the *queen* is nominally the prosecutor in all criminal cases. The corresponding term in the reign of a king is 'Rex'. [Latin, 'queen']

regional electricity company /ˌriːdʒənl ɪlek'trɪsətɪ ˌkʌmpənɪ/ **(REC)** (commerce) One of the 12 private companies that supply electricity in *England* and *Wales*. They are named after the region in which they operate, such as Eastern Electricity, although some have abbreviated names. Manweb, for example, is short for *Merseyside and North Wales Electricity Board*, while Seeboard stands for *South-Eastern Electricity Board*, while punning on 'seaboard', as the company serves a coastal area of England. ('Board' has survived from the area electricity boards that were the RECs' nationalized equivalents before 1990.)

Regional Railways /'riːdʒənl ˌreɪlweɪz/ (transport) The business sector of *BR* that runs passenger services outside the *Network SouthEast* region.

Registered /'redʒɪstəd/ (commerce) A special service of the *Post Office* for sending money, jewellery, documents and other valuable items. The service guarantees delivery the following day, and if the item is lost, the Post Office pays compensation. Compare *Registered Plus*.

Registered Plus /ˌredʒɪstəd 'plʌs/ (commerce) A special service of the *Post Office* for sending items that are too valuable to be sent by the *Registered* service.

registrar /ˌredʒɪ'strɑː(r)/ (1 law 2 medicine) 1 The officer in charge of a local *registry office*. 2 A senior doctor in a hospital.

registration number /redʒɪ'streɪʃn ˌnʌmbə(r)/ (transport) The official number given to a motor vehicle when it is first registered. The number is shown on plates ('number plates') at the front and back of the vehicle (at the back only, on motorcycles and other two-wheeled vehicles). Some vehicles on the roads of *Britain* still have a registration number consisting of three letters (chosen to indicate the licensing authority of the area where the car is registered), three

registration number

numbers (less often one or two, indicating the serial number of the car with the licensing authority) and a final letter (which indicates the year of registration). From August 1983 the letter showing the year of registration was placed in front, beginning with A that year.

registry /'redʒɪstrɪ/ (religion) A place or room in a *church* where registers are kept, especially the register signed by a bride and groom immediately after their marriage ceremony in the church.

registry office /'redʒɪstrɪ ˌɒfɪs/ (government) An office where civil marriages are performed (as distinct from marriages performed in a *church*), and where births and deaths are recorded.

Regius professor /ˌriːdʒɪəs prə'fesə(r)/ (education) A university professor appointed to a professorship that was founded by a royal patron, especially one of the five founded by *Henry VIII* at *Oxford*² or *Cambridge*². [Latin 'regius', 'royal']

Reith lectures /ˌriːθ 'lektʃəz/, **the** (media) An annual series of lectures on a political, economic, scientific or other subject, broadcast on radio or television by the *BBC* and published in The *Listener*. The lectures were founded in 1947 by Lord Reith (1889–1971), first general manager of the BBC.

Relate /rɪ'leɪt/ (charities) A voluntary organization that works through a network of local centres to give practical advice to men and women whose marriage is in difficulties or has failed, or to young people planning to marry for the first time. [formerly Marriage Guidance Council]

remand centre /rɪ'mɑːnd ˌsentə(r)/ (law) A place of detention to which young offenders are sent while awaiting trial in court. At present there are nine such centres, one being a private remand prison. See also *young offender institution.*

Remembrance Sunday /rɪ'membrəns ˌsʌndɪ/ (tradition) The *Sunday* nearest to 11 November, *Armistice Day*. On this Sunday the dead of both world wars are remembered in special *church* services and civic ceremonies, the chief of which is the laying of wreaths at the *Cenotaph, London* by members of the *royal family* in the presence of leading statesmen and politicians (including the *Prime Minister* and *Leader of the Opposition*). See also *two-minute silence, Poppy Day.*

Remploy /'remplɔɪ/ (work) A non-commercial state company operating various workshops and centres where practical work is undertaken by people with physical handicaps.

Much of their work is making simple furniture and fittings for use in government and armed services establishments. [from 're-employ']

Restart /'riː‚stɑːt/ (work) A government scheme to help the unemployed. People who have been unemployed for six months or more are invited to a special interview to discuss ways in which they might find work, either with an employer or by starting their own business.

rest home /'rest həʊm/ (life and society) A common term for an old people's home.

Restoration /‚restə'reɪʃn/, **the** (history) The re-establishment of the monarchy in 1660, when Charles II became *king* after the collapse of the *Protectorate*. The name is also used for Charles's reign (1660–85), and for the flourishing of art and literature in that period.

restrictive practice /rɪ‚strɪktɪv 'præktɪs/ (**1** commerce **2** work) **1** A trading agreement against the public interest, for example, an agreement to sell to certain buyers only. **2** A practice of some trade unions, such as a *closed shop* or *work-to-rule*, that similarly limits trading.

retirement age /rɪ'taɪəmənt eɪdʒ/ (work) The age at which employed people normally retire from work, at present 65 for men, 60 for women. See also *OAP*, *old age pension*.

returning officer /rɪ'tɜːnɪŋ ‚ɒfɪsə(r)/ (government) The officer who presides at a *by-election* or, in a particular *constituency*, at a *general election*.

Reuters /'rɔɪtəz/ (media) The principal British world news agency, formerly owned jointly by a number of press organizations including the *Press Association* and the Newspaper Publishers Association. It was founded by the German telegraph promoter Baron Paul Julius de Reuter (1816–99), who opened his *London* office in 1851. In 1984 Reuters became a *PLC*.

Reverend, Rev. /'revərənd/, **the** (religion) The traditional title of a clergyman in the *Church of England*, and in most of the *Free Churches*. It is usually put before the first name, as 'the Reverend Peter Marshall' (or written, 'the Rev. Peter Marshall'), but also used (incorrectly, according to some) before the surname alone ('the Reverend Marshall') or even (also incorrectly) alone ('the Reverend'). See also *Right Reverend, Very Reverend.*

Revised Version /rɪ‚vaɪzd 'vɜːʃn/, **the (RV, the)** (religion) A revision of the *Authorized Version* of the Bible, prepared by two committees of British scholars, with American collaborators. The New Testament was produced in 1881, the Old Testament in 1885, and the Apocrypha in 1895. The older Authorized Version still remains popular in many *church*es and with many *Anglican*s.

RGN /ˌɑː dʒiː ˈen/ **(Registered General Nurse)** (medicine) A nurse who has successfully completed a three-year training course and who is qualified to look after a group of hospital patients, as well as give individual nursing care like an *EN*. Until 1983, the equivalent qualification was that of the *SRN* (State Registered Nurse).

rhyming slang /ˈraɪmɪŋ slæŋ/ (language) The slang way of speaking, originally popular among *cockneys*[2], in which a rhyming phrase, or part of it, is substituted for a standard word. An example is 'loaf of bread' (or simply 'loaf') for 'head', or 'apples and pears' (or simply 'apples') for 'stairs'. Some examples of rhyming slang have passed into spoken English generally, for example, 'use your loaf' means 'use your intelligence', 'think effectively'.

Rice, Anneka /raɪs ˈænəkə/ (people) Anneka Rice (born 1958) is a popular television personality who has been the central figure in a number of outdoor programmes. In 'Treasure Hunt', first broadcast by *Channel 4* in 1983, she flew by helicopter to search the countryside for a prize, guided by a list of cryptic clues and a map. In 'Challenge Anneka', first shown in 1989, she led a team of people to carry out various construction projects for charity in record time. In one programme, for example, her team took just two days to convert an old barn into a boathouse for the use of disabled children.

Richard, Cliff /ˈrɪtʃəd klɪf/ (people) Cliff Richard (born 1940), whose original name was Harold Webb, remains even today one of the most popular of pop singers. He is generally admired for his 'wholesome' image, his religious faith, and his youthful good looks. His songs make pleasant listening but are not particularly original.

Right Honourable, Rt Hon /raɪt ˈɒnərəbl/**, the** (life and society) The form of address used for people holding a number of titles or offices, among them an earl, a viscount, a baron, a *Lord Mayor* (also a *Lord Provost*) and a *Privy Councillor* (see p 470). The full title appears in the form 'The Rt Hon the Earl of Derby'. Compare *Honourable*.

right of way /ˌraɪt əv ˈweɪ/ (law) A public path or track across land that is otherwise private property, such as a farmer's field.

312

Right Reverend, Rt Rev /raɪt ˈrevərənd/**, the** (religion) The formal title of a bishop in the *Church of England*, appearing in the form 'The Rt Rev the (Lord) Bishop of Oxford'.

Ritz /rɪts/**, the** (London) A fashionable *London* hotel and restaurant in *Piccadilly*, founded in 1906 by the Swiss hotelier César Ritz.

RMT /ˌɑːr em ˈtiː/**, the (National Union of Rail, Maritime and Transport Workers, the)** (work) A trade union of railway, port and dock workers, formed in 1990 through the merger of two separate unions. The current membership of the RMT is about 110,000.

Robin Hood /ˌrɒbɪn ˈhʊd/ (tradition) A semi-legendary outlaw

Robin Hood

hero of English and Scottish ballads, said to have lived in the 12th or 13th century. He is still popular for his life-long policy of taking from the rich (by force, if necessary) and giving to the poor. According to tradition, he lived with his 'Merry Men' (companions) in Sherwood Forest, Nottinghamshire.

rock /rɒk/ (food and drink) A type of sweet in the form of a round, hard, brittle stick of peppermint sugar, with a white centre and a coloured edible coating. Such sticks are traditionally sold at seaside or other tourist resorts, where they often have the name of the resort inside in pink sugar, running from one end of the stick to the other. The sweet appears to have been first produced commercially in *Edinburgh*. See *Edinburgh rock*.

rock cake /'rɒk keɪk/ (food and drink) A small individual cake containing dried fruit, and thought to look like a rock.

Rockers /'rɒkəz/ (life and society) Groups of teenagers who rivalled the *Mods* in the 1960s. Rockers wore leather jackets, had long hair, and rode motorcycles. [from their addiction to *rock* music]

Roedean (School) /'rəʊdiːn (ˌrəʊdiːn 'skuːl)/ (education) A famous *public school*[1] for girls, near *Brighton*, East Sussex. It was founded in 1885, and has 475 students, all resident. [named after a place there, meaning 'rough valley']

Rogation Days /rəʊ'geɪʃn deɪz/ (religion) Special days set aside in the *Church of England* for solemn prayers asking for a good harvest. The days are the four days before *Ascension Day*, with the *Sunday* known as 'Rogation Sunday'. In some *churches* a special service is accompanied by a procession outside the church building, and the ceremony of *beating the bounds* may also be held (instead of on Ascension Day). [literally 'asking days', from the prayers offered]

Roget /'rɒʒeɪ/ **(Roget's Thesaurus)** (language) A well-known dictionary of synonyms of the English language, arranged in classified lists. The dictionary, which now exists in several different editions, was first published in 1853 by an English physician, Peter Mark Roget (1779–1869). [full title is 'Roget's Thesaurus of English Words and Phrases', with 'thesaurus' used in sense 'treasury', 'store-house' (ie, of synonyms)]

Roller /'rəʊlə(r)/ (transport) A colloquial name for a *Rolls(-Royce)* car. [pun on 'roll' as in 'move on wheels']

Rolling Stones /ˌrəʊlɪŋ 'stəʊnz/**, the** (people) Together with the *Beatles*, the Rolling Stones were one of the most important

British pop groups of the 1960s. The group formed in 1962, and the initial members were Mick Jagger (vocals) (born 1943), Keith Richard (guitar, vocals) (born 1943), Brian Jones (guitar, vocals) (1942–69), Bill Wyman (bass) (born 1936) and Charlie Watts (drums) (born 1941). The group arose from the members' interest in blues and rhythm-and-blues. The Rolling Stones were deliberately brash, anti-establishment and provocative. Their public behaviour was severely criticized by sections of the media for their alleged decadence. This 'shock effect' was precisely what they wished to achieve, and their powerful and uninhibited music was a major factor in the development of *Britain*'s 'alternative society'. The group's two most popular hits were 'Satisfaction' (1965)—'I Can't Get No Satisfaction', the full title, summarized their philosophy of frustration and ferocity—and 'Jumpin' Jack Flash' (1968). [name taken from a song by the American blues singer Muddy Waters]

Rolls(-Royce) /rəʊlz (ˌrəʊlz ˈrɔɪs)/ (transport) A well-known make of expensive motor-car famous for its luxury and its reliability. [firm founded in 1906 by Charles Stewart Rolls and Henry Royce]

roly-poly /ˌrəʊlɪ ˈpəʊlɪ/ (food and drink) A roll of baked or steamed suet pastry filled with jam or fruit, eaten as a dessert for *lunch* or *dinner*. The dish is a variety of *suet pudding* and is popular with children. [name, based on 'roll', suggests something round and fat]

Roman Catholic Church /ˌrəʊmən ˌkæθəlɪk ˈtʃɜːtʃ/, **the** (religion) The Roman Catholic Church became established in *Britain* in medieval times and its influence increased considerably after the *Norman Conquest*. However, after the Reformation and *Henry VIII*'s break with the church of Rome (he took the title of Supreme Head of the Church and Clergy of England), the position of the Roman Catholic Church in Britain altered dramatically, so that it was outlawed for a time and was no longer the sole Christian church. For many years, British Roman Catholics were served by missionary priests (Englishmen who had trained abroad), and had no bishops or archbishops. Today there are both bishops and archbishops, and many of the old religious orders, previously banned, have been restored. Even so, many of the highest posts in the country are still closed to Roman Catholics, and no member of the Church can become sovereign, regent or *Lord Chancellor*. The Republic of Ireland is a strongly Roman

Catholic country and there are still many Roman Catholics in *Northern Ireland*, although the majority of the population there are Protestants. In the *United Kingdom* as a whole Roman Catholics are the second largest religious community (after the *Church of England*).

Roman road /ˌrəʊmən ˈrəʊd/ (history) One of a number of roads or trackways in *England*, built by the Romans during their occupation of *Britain* in the 1st–4th centuries AD. Sections of the roads still survive, whether in their original form or as stretches of modern roads. They were particularly noted for their length and straightness. Among the best known Roman roads are the *Fosse Way*, *Ermine Street[1]* and *Watling Street*.

rose /rəʊz/ (tradition) The national emblem of *England* from the time of the *Wars of the Roses*. Compare *leek*, *thistle*, *daffodil*.

rosette /rəʊˈzet/ (clothing) A large artificial flower made of ribbons, either worn in the lapel to show that the wearer belongs to a particular organization, such as a political party, or given as a prize in a sports contest, such as a *gymkhana*. In a *general election*, *Conservative Party* candidates wear a blue rosette, while *Labour Party* candidates wear red and *Liberal Democrats* wear yellow.

Rotary Club /ˈrəʊtərɪ klʌb/, **the** (life and society) One of the *clubs* in *Britain* that belong to Rotary International, a world organization of business and professional men, founded in the United States in 1905. The organization has the self-stated aim to 'provide humanitarian service, encourage high ethical standards, and help build goodwill and peace in the world'. In Britain and *Ireland* there are over 63,000 members known as Rotarians, in over 1,600 clubs. [members originally met at one another's houses, in rotation]

Rotten Row /ˌrɒtn ˈrəʊ/ (London) A horse-riding track running along the south side of *Hyde Park, London*, from *Hyde Park Corner* to *Kensington Gardens*. [popularly supposed to be a corruption of French 'route du roi', 'road of the king', but probably meaning what it says, with 'rotten' in sense 'soft']

Round House /ˈraʊnd haʊs/, **the** (arts) A modern theatre in *Hampstead, London*, opened in 1968 in what was formerly a 'roundhouse', a circular building for servicing railway locomotives. In its early years it had a reputation as a centre for young people, who attended rock concerts, film shows and other modern entertainments there. The building today also contains a cinema, library and art gallery. There is now a scheme to develop the Round House as a centre for black performing arts.

Round Pond /ˌraʊnd 'pɒnd/, **the** (London) A pond in *Kensington Gardens, London* where both children and adults traditionally sail toy boats and yachts.

Round Table /ˌraʊnd 'teɪbl/, **the** (1 tradition 2 life and society) **1** In the stories about *King Arthur*, the table at which the *Knights of the Round Table* sat. A round table was deliberately chosen so that none of the knights sat in a more important place than any of the others. **2** One of a number of *club*s for young business and professional people, aged between 18 and 40, where discussions, debates and other meetings are held with the aim of undertaking community service and promoting international understanding. Such clubs were first organized in 1972.

Round the Island Race /ˌraʊnd ðiː 'aɪlənd ˌreɪs/, **the** (sport and leisure) An annual yacht race round the *Isle of Wight*.

rounders /'raʊndəz/ (sport and leisure) A ball game resembling American baseball, in which the players strike a hard leather ball the size of a tennis ball with a wooden bat, shorter than a baseball bat. They then try to run round four bases (making a 'rounder') before the ball is returned to the thrower ('bowler', as in *cricket*). If a player cannot complete the round, he or she must then stop at one of the bases, and can only move on when the next player hits the ball. The game is particularly popular with children.

Rover /'rəʊvə(r)/ (transport) One of the five main motor manufacturing companies in *Britain*, the others being Ford (including *Jaguar*), Vauxhall, Peugeot-Talbot and Nissan. It was founded in the 19th century as a firm making bicycles. It produced its first car in 1904, and in 1967 Austin Rover Morris merged with another company, the Leyland Motor Corporation, to become the British Leyland Motor Corporation (later, simply BL). In 1986 it reverted to its original name of Rover. [name originally denoted a bicycle intended for 'roving', or riding about]

Row /rəʊ/, **the** (London) A colloquial name for *Rotten Row*.

Royal Academy (of Arts) /ˌrɔɪəl ə'kædəmɪ (ˌrɔɪəl əˌkædəmɪ əv 'ɑːts)/, **the** (arts) The oldest society in *Britain* devoted entirely to the fine arts, founded in 1768 and well known for its annual summer exhibition of contemporary art held at its headquarters, *Burlington House*, in *Piccadilly, London*.

Royal Academy of Music /ˌrɔɪəl əˌkædəmɪ əv ˈmjuːzɪk/, **the (RAM, the)** (education) A school training professional musicians, founded in 1822, and having its headquarters in west *London*.

Royal Aircraft Establishment /ˌrɔɪəl ˈeəkrɑːft ɪˌstæblɪʃmənt/, **the (RAE, the)** (defence) An aircraft design and test establishment at Farnborough, Hampshire, under the control of the *RAF*. See also *Farnborough Air Show*.

Royal Albert Hall /ˌrɔɪəl ˌælbət ˈhɔːl/, **the** (London) The full name of the *Albert Hall, London*.

Royal and Ancient /ˌrɔɪəl ən ˈeɪnʃənt/, **the (R and A, the)** (sport and leisure) A leading golf *club* in St Andrews, *Scotland*, recognized (except in the United States) as the international headquarters of golf. It was founded in 1754, and adopted its present name in 1834 by permission of King William IV (in full, 'Royal and Ancient Golf Club of St Andrews').

Royal Ascot /ˌrɔɪəl ˈæskət/ (sport and leisure) A four-day horse-racing meeting held at *Ascot* each year in June. The event is one of the most important racing occasions in *Britain*, and members of the *royal family* always attend. The second day of the meeting is *Ladies' Day*.

royal assent /ˌrɔɪəl əˈsent/ (law) The official signing of an *Act (of Parliament)* by the sovereign, as a result of which it becomes law.

Royal Ballet /ˌrɔɪəl ˈbæleɪ/, **the** (arts) *Britain*'s national ballet company, with its centre at the *Royal Opera House, London*. It was founded in 1931, renamed the Sadler's Wells Ballet in 1941 (see *Sadler's Wells (Theatre)*), and became the Royal Ballet in 1956, when it merged with the Sadler's Wells Theatre Ballet, which had been formed in 1946. It performs both classical and English works.

Royal Ballet School /ˌrɔɪəl ˈbæleɪ skuːl/, **the** (education) The school for young professional ballet dancers entering the *Royal Ballet*. It is in west *London* in two separate centres, junior (residential) and senior.

Royal Bank of Scotland /ˌrɔɪəl ˌbæŋk əv ˈskɒtlənd/, **the** (finance) The largest Scottish bank, founded in 1727 and with branches in many Scottish towns and *cities* and with an increasing number in *England* (through its ownership of Williams and Glyn's, one of the smaller English banks).

Royal British Legion /ˌrɔɪəl ˌbrɪtɪʃ ˈliːdʒən/, **the** (charities) An organization of ex-service men and women, founded in 1921 and with membership open to all British men and women who have served in the armed forces. Its aim is to assist all ex-service personnel and their families both financially and materially. It gains most of its income from *Poppy Day*. Its current membership in *Britain* and overseas is 858,000.

Royal College of Art /ˌrɔɪəl ˌkɒlɪdʒ əv ˈɑːt/, **the (RCA, the)** (education) A *college²* in central *London* that offers art students a professional course at *postgraduate* level and awards *higher degrees* such as Doctor of Philosophy (PhD) and *MA*. It was founded in 1837.

Royal College of Music /ˌrɔɪəl ˌkɒlɪdʒ əv ˈmjuːzɪk/, **the (RCM, the)** (education) A *college²* in central *London* that offers professional training to students intending to take up music as a career, and makes academic awards in music. It was founded in 1883.

Royal Court (Theatre) /ˌrɔɪəl ˈkɔːt (ˌrɔɪəl ˌkɔːt ˈθɪətə(r))/, **the** (arts) A theatre in southwest *London* originally opened in 1870 and, after a series of closures, reopened in its present form in 1965. It gained a reputation for its experimental productions (by the *English Stage Company*), and today stages mainly contemporary plays.

royal duke /ˌrɔɪəl ˈdjuːk/ (royal family) A duke who is also a *prince*, since he is a member of the *royal family*. There are at present five royal dukes: the *Duke of Edinburgh*, the *Duke of Cornwall*, the *Duke of York*, the Duke of Gloucester and the Duke of Kent.

Royal Enclosure /ˌrɔɪəl ɪnˈkləʊʒə(r)/, **the** (sport and leisure) A special area of the stands at *Royal Ascot*. To gain a ticket for this enclosure one must apply well in advance to the Ascot office, who check every applicant, and their sponsors, for suitability. [in full, Royal Ascot Enclosure]

royal family /ˌrɔɪəl ˈfæməlɪ/ (royal family) The British sovereign and his or her immediate family, regarded as representing the highest aristocratic presence in the land, with each member attracting much popular interest and the constant attention of the media. At present the royal family is headed by *Queen Elizabeth*, and directly includes the *Duke of Edinburgh*, *Queen Elizabeth, the Queen Mother*, the *Prince* and *Princess of Wales*, the Queen's other three children (see *Queen Elizabeth*) and the Queen's sister, Princess *Margaret*. Outside this immediate circle, the royal family also includes the Queen's cousins, the Dukes of Gloucester and Kent (see *royal duke*), and the spouses and children of these and other relations apart from those already mentioned. When members of the royal family attend an official ceremony the *national anthem* is played and the *Union Jack* may be flown. See the Order of Succession to the throne on p 470.

Royal Festival Hall /ˌrɔɪəl ˌfestəvl ˈhɔːl/ (arts) A concert hall on the *South Bank* site, *London*, built in 1948–51 for the *Festival of Britain*. See also *Queen Elizabeth Hall*, *Purcell Room*.

Royal Greenwich Observatory /ˌrɔɪəl ˌgrenɪdʒ əbˈzɜːvətrɪ/, **the** (science and technology) An astronomical observatory established at *Greenwich*, *London*, in 1675, in order to provide navigational information for sailors. The growth of London, with its smoke and bright lights, adversely affected its work, however, so that in 1958 it moved to Herstmonceux Castle, in East Sussex. In 1990 it moved again to *Cambridge University*. The importance of the Observatory's work resulted in the adoption in 1885 of *GMT* and of the Greenwich Meridian as international standards of reference.

Royal Highland Regiment /ˌrɔɪəl ˈhaɪlənd ˌredʒɪmənt/ see *Black Watch* (defence)

Royal Highness /ˌrɔɪəl ˈhaɪnɪs/ (royal family) The form of address used for a member of the *royal family* (other than the sovereign), used as appropriate by 'Your', 'His', 'Her', etc. Compare *Her Majesty*.

Royal Horse Guards /ˌrɔɪəl ˈhɔːs gɑːdz/, **the** (defence) A regiment of the British *Army* raised in 1661, and known as 'The Blues' from the colour of their uniform. In 1969 they joined with the Royal Dragoons to form the *Blues and Royals*.

Royal International Agricultural Exhibition /ˌrɔɪəl ɪntəˌnæʃnəl ægrɪˈkʌltʃərəl eksɪˌbɪʃn/, **the** (daily life) An important agricultural exhibition held every July near Kenilworth, Warwickshire, enabling visitors to see the latest developments in British agriculture. Most manufacturers of agricultural machinery are represented, and the exhibition is also an important show of pedigree livestock.

Royal International Horse Show /ˌrɔɪəl ɪntəˌnæʃnəl ˈhɔːs ʃəʊ/, **the** (sport and leisure) An international show-jumping contest held annually at the *National Exhibition Centre*, Birmingham.

Royal Liverpool Philharmonic Orchestra /ˌrɔɪəl ˌlɪvəpuːl ˌfɪlɑːmɒnɪk ˈɔːkɪstrə/, **the (RLPO, the)** (arts) A well-known symphony orchestra founded in Liverpool in 1840.

Royal Mail /ˌrɔɪəl ˈmeɪl/, **the** (commerce) The department of the *Post Office* that handles the collection and delivery of letters. Compare *Parcelforce*.

Royal Marines /ˌrɔɪəl məˈriːnz/, **the (RM, the)** (defence)
Britain's 'sea soldiers', a corps first formed in 1664 and part of
the *Royal Navy*. The Royal Marines are best known for their
units of *Commandos*.

Royal Mews /ˌrɔɪəl ˈmjuːz/, **the** (London) A building near
Buckingham Palace, London, where the sovereign's coaches are
kept and horses stabled, ready for use on state occasions. The
three state coaches are of particular interest to the public,
who are admitted to the Mews for two hours twice a week.
['Mews' means 'stables', the word was originally used of
royal stables built on the site of hawks' mews (rooms) at
Charing Cross[1]]

Royal Mile /ˌrɔɪəl ˈmaɪl/, **the** (history) The central streets of
Edinburgh, Scotland, that run through the historic part of the
city (the 'Old Town') from *Edinburgh Castle* in the west to
Holyrood House in the east. [so named for the many *king*s,
*queen*s and *prince*s who have walked or ridden there in
historic times]

Royal Military Academy /ˌrɔɪəl ˌmɪlɪtrɪ əˈkædəmɪ/, **the (RMA,
the)** (education) A military establishment founded in 1799 to
train both officers and new entrants to the British *Army*.
Originally it was at High Wycombe, Buckinghamshire, but
eventually was re-established at *Sandhurst*, Berkshire.
Compare *Cranwell, Dartmouth*.

Royal Mint /ˌrɔɪəl ˈmɪnt/, **the** (finance) The state organization
that manufactures British coins (with the *Bank of England*
supplying the bank notes). In its present form, the Royal
Mint was founded on *Tower Hill, London*, in 1811, and moved
to a site near *Cardiff, Wales*, in 1968.

Royal Museum of Scotland /ˌrɔɪəl mjuːˌzɪəm əv ˈskɒtlənd/, **the**
(arts) A museum in *Edinburgh* formed in 1985 from the
combined premises of the Royal Scottish Museum (originally
opened in 1866, and housing a comprehensive collection of
art, natural history and other fields) and the National
Museum of Antiquities of Scotland (formerly part of the
National Portrait Gallery).

Royal National Institute for the Blind /ˌrɔɪəl ˌnæʃnəl ˌɪnstɪtjuːt
fə ðə ˈblaɪnd/, **the (RNIB, the)** (charities) A voluntary
organization that aims to provide specialized services for
blind people as the government provides only limited
services. The RNIB was founded in 1868.

Royal National Institute for the Deaf /ˌrɔɪəl ˌnæʃnəl ˌɪnstɪtjuːt fə
ðə ˈdef/, **the (RNID, the)** (charities) A voluntary body

Royal National Lifeboat Institution

founded in 1911 with the aim of making deaf people's lives easier by providing specialized services (including housing, employment, social communication and information), as the government provides only limited services.

Royal National Lifeboat Institution /ˌrɔɪəl ˌnæʃnəl ˈlaɪfbəʊt ɪnstɪˌtjuːʃn/, **the (RNLI, the)** (charities) A voluntary organization that operates a round-the-clock lifeboat rescue service round the coasts of *Britain* and *Ireland*. It was founded in 1824 and has 2,000 fund-raising branches and 100,000 members.

Royal National Theatre /ˌrɔɪəl ˌnæʃnəl ˈθɪətə(r)/, **the** (arts) **1** A *London* theatre opened on the *South Bank* site in 1976, and staging both classical and modern plays in its three auditoriums. **2** The theatre company based now at the Royal National Theatre[1] and formerly at the *Old Vic* (from 1963).

Royal Naval College /ˌrɔɪəl ˈneɪvl ˌkɒlɪdʒ/ see **Britannia Royal Naval College** (education)

Royal Naval Reserve /ˌrɔɪəl ˌneɪvl rɪˈzɜːv/, **the (RNR, the)** (defence) A volunteer force of service men and women who undergo regular training, and who can be called upon in time of war to serve with the *Royal Navy*.

Royal Navy /ˌrɔɪəl ˈneɪvi/, **the (RN, the)** (defence) The British navy, existing from historic times but formally established by

King *Henry VIII* in the 16th century. It is *Britain*'s smallest armed force, with a current strength of about 62,100, including the *Royal Marines*.

Royal Opera /ˌrɔɪəl ˈɒprə/, **the** (arts) A leading *London* opera company with its own orchestra. It was founded in 1946 and has its home, together with that of the *Royal Ballet*, at the *Royal Opera House*, London. See also *Covent Garden*[2].

Royal Opera House /ˌrɔɪəl ˈɒprə haʊs/, **the** (arts) The leading theatre of opera and ballet in *London*, also known, from its location, as *Covent Garden*[2]. The first theatre on this site was built in 1732. After this and a later building were burnt down, the present building was opened in 1858 and is now the home of the *Royal Opera* and *Royal Ballet* companies.

royal park /ˌrɔɪəl ˈpɑːk/ (London) Any of the 20 parks in *London* that are maintained by the *Crown*[2]. Among them are the five great parks that began as royal preserves, later opened to the public — *Green Park, Hyde Park, Kensington Gardens, Regent's Park* and *St James's Park*. Two further royal parks are *Kew Gardens* and the gardens at *Hampton Court*.

Royal Pavilion /ˌrɔɪəl pəˈvɪlɪən/, **the** (arts) A famous building in *Brighton*, East Sussex, noted for its many royal connections. It was originally built in the late 18th century for the *Prince Regent* but was rebuilt in the early 19th century in its present oriental style, with onion-shaped domes, spires and minarets. Today it is open to the public as a museum. Part of its interior is in the Chinese style, existing from the original building.

Royal Philharmonic Orchestra /ˌrɔɪəl ˌfɪlɑːmɒnɪk ˈɔːkɪstrə/, **the (RPO, the)** (arts) A leading *London* symphony orchestra, founded in 1946. It has regularly performed at *Glyndebourne*.

Royal Regiment /ˌrɔɪəl ˈredʒɪmənt/ see *Royal Scots* (defence)

royal salute /ˌrɔɪəl səˈluːt/, **the** (royal family) A ceremonial salute fired on the riverside at the *Tower of London* on a royal occasion. On the sovereign's birthday, and also on the anniversary of his or her accession (see *Accession Day*) and *Coronation*, 62 guns are fired, as they are at present on the birthdays of the *Duke of Edinburgh* and *Queen Elizabeth, the Queen Mother*. When the sovereign opens, prorogues (see *prorogation*) or dissolves *Parliament*, or passes through *London* in procession, 41 guns are fired. When a child is born to a member of the *royal family*, 41 guns are also fired, in *Hyde Park* as well as at the Tower of London.

Royal Scots /ˌrɔɪəl ˈskɒts/, **the** (defence) The senior regiment of the British *Army*, raised in *Scotland* in 1633 and formally known as the *Royal Regiment*.

Royal Shakespeare Company /ˌrɔɪəl ˈʃeɪkspɪə ˌkʌmpənɪ/, **the (RSC, the)** (arts) One of *Britain*'s leading theatre companies, presenting mainly plays by *Shakespeare*. It has two bases: at the *Royal Shakespeare Theatre* in *Stratford-(up)on-Avon* and at the *Barbican (Centre)* in *London*. See also *Swan (Theatre)*.

Royal Shakespeare Theatre /ˌrɔɪəl ˈʃeɪkspɪə ˌθɪətə(r)/, **the** (arts) The theatre in *Stratford-(up)on-Avon* that opened in 1879 as the Shakespeare Memorial Theatre for summer seasons of *Shakespeare*'s plays. It was destroyed by fire in 1926, and the present theatre was built in 1932 in its place. In 1961 the theatre was given its present name. See also *Royal Shakespeare Company, Swan (Theatre)*.

Royal Smithfield Show /ˌrɔɪəl ˌsmɪθfiːld ˈʃəʊ/, **the** (tradition) An annual exhibition of agricultural machinery and livestock held every December at *Earls Court, London*. [named for its historic connection with *Smithfield*]

Royal Society /ˌrɔɪəl səˈsaɪətɪ/, **the** (science and technology) The oldest and most important scientific society in *Britain*, originating in 1645 as the Royal Society for Improving Natural Knowledge, and functioning as the equivalent of a national academy of sciences. Election as a *Fellow*[3] of the Society is regarded as one of the greatest honours for an academic. The Society's headquarters are in central *London*.

Royal Society for the Protection of Birds /ˌrɔɪəl səˌsaɪətɪ fə ðə prəˌtekʃn əv ˈbɜːdz/, **the (RSPB, the)** (charities) A voluntary organization founded in 1889 with the aim of conserving and protecting wild birds. The Society has over 200,000 members.

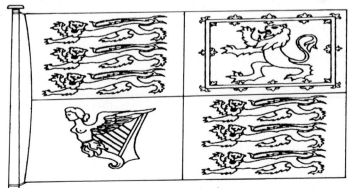

royal standard

royal standard /ˌrɔɪəl ˈstændəd/, **the** (royal family) A flag bearing the arms of the sovereign, and flown to show he or she is present in a particular place.

Royal Tournament /ˌrɔɪəl ˈtɔːnəmənt/, **the** (sport and leisure) An annual display given every summer by teams from the three armed services (the *Royal Navy*, the *Army* and the *RAF*) at *Earls Court, London*. One of the highlights is a contest in dismantling field guns, transporting them over obstacles and re-assembling them.

Royal Ulster Constabulary /ˌrɔɪəl ˌʌlstə kənˈstæbjʊlərɪ/ see *RUC* (law)

Royal Variety Show/Performance /ˌrɔɪəl vəˈraɪətɪ ʃəʊ/ pəˌfɔːməns/, **the** (arts) An annual variety and entertainment show held at a leading *London* theatre, with top artists and entertainers performing, in order to raise money for the Variety Artistes' Federation (part of *Equity*). The performance is traditionally attended by one or more members of the *royal family*, and is usually televised.

Royal Worcester /ˌrɔɪəl ˈwʊstə(r)/ (style) The term used for *Worcester* (*china*) made from 1862 by a factory in Worcester (Royal Worcester Ltd), originally founded in 1751 and known by a variety of names since then.

Royal Yacht /ˌrɔɪəl ˈjɒt/, **the** (royal family) A special ship of the *Royal Navy*, named *Britannia*[3], used for official visits overseas by members of the *royal family*. The ship can be converted into a hospital ship in wartime. It first entered service in 1954.

Royals /ˈrɔɪəlz/, **the** (1 defence 2 royal family) 1 The nickname of the Royal Dragoons, now joined with the *Royal Horse Guards*. See *Blues and Royals*. 2 A colloquial name for the *royal family*.

RP /ˌɑː ˈpiː/ **(Received Pronunciation)** (language) A non-regional accent of standard British English, often regarded as a prestige form. [traditionally called 'Received' in the sense 'accepted as standard']

RSA /ˌɑːr es ˈeɪ/, **the (Royal Society of Arts, the)** (education) A learned society founded in 1754 'for the encouragement of arts, manufacturers and commerce'. It arranges series of lectures on a wide range of subjects. The Society also arranges many examinations in *commercial subjects* and in various languages. These examinations are held both in *Britain* and in other countries.

RSPCA /ˌɑːr es ˌpiː siː ˈeɪ/, **the (Royal Society for the Prevention of Cruelty to Animals, the)** (charities) A voluntary organization founded in 1824 to promote kindness in the treatment of animals and to discourage, by *court[3]* prosecution if necessary, cruelty to them. The Society has 23,500 members.

RUC /ˌɑː juː ˈsiː/, **the (Royal Ulster Constabulary, the)** (law) The police force of *Northern Ireland*. It is supported by British troops in the fight against terrorism and has a current strength of about 8,200.

rugby football /ˌrʌɡbɪ ˈfʊtbɔːl/ (sport and leisure) A form of *football* different from *association football*. See *rugby league* and *rugby union*.

rugby league /ˌrʌɡbɪ ˈliːɡ/ (sport and leisure) A form of *rugby football* played by 13 players instead of 15, with professional players allowed. The game originated in 1893, when professionals were still banned, and is traditionally associated with the north of *England*. There are some differences in the rules and in scoring between rugby league and *rugby union*.

Rugby (School) /ˈrʌɡbɪ (ˌrʌɡbɪ ˈskuːl)/ (education) A leading *public school[1]* in the town of the same name in Warwickshire.

rugby union

It was founded in 1567, and currently has about 650 students. It was at Rugby that the game of *rugby football* was first played in 1823.

rugby union /ˌrʌgbɪ ˈjuːnɪən/ (sport and leisure) The standard game of *rugby football* (popularly known as 'rugger'), played by teams of 15, always amateurs. The game originated in 1871, when the *FA* banned handling the ball. (This had first happened at *Rugby* (*School*) when, one day in 1823, a player picked up the ball and ran with it.)

rugger /ˈrʌgə(r)/ see *rugby union* (sport and leisure)

Rule, Britannia /ˌruːl brɪˈtænjə/ (tradition) A patriotic British song, sung traditionally during the *Last Night of the Proms*, as well as on other occasions when strong (or even militaristic) patriotism is expressed. The song was written in 1740, and is well known for its last two lines: 'Rule, Britannia, Britannia rule the waves; Britons never, never, never shall be slaves'. See also *Britannia²*.

Russell, Ken /ˈrʌsl, ken/ (people) Ken Russell (born 1927) is a controversial film director who has become well known for his dramatic artistic effects and flamboyant, even shocking treatment of his subjects. At the same time, he has also produced a number of moving television documentaries on the lives of modern composers, including *Elgar*, Debussy and Delius.

Rutland /ˈrʌtlənd/ (geography) A former *county¹* in the *Midlands*, long famous as the smallest county in *England*. Its inhabitants protested vigorously when the county was merged in the much larger county of Leicestershire in 1974, on the reorganization of local government boundaries, and did all they could to preserve the name and the identity of the county, even erecting unofficial road signs saying 'Rutland'. In fact the name still exists for one of the administrative districts of Leicestershire.

Ryder Cup /ˌraɪdə ˈkʌp/, **the** (sport and leisure) A professional golf contest between Europe and the United States held every two years. Compare *Walker Cup*. [originally a contest between *Britain* and the United States, it was first held in 1927, the trophy presented by a Briton, Samuel Ryder]

Sadler's Wells (Theatre) /ˌsædləz ˌwelz ˈθɪətə(r)/ (arts) A
London theatre famous for its presentation of opera and ballet.
It was originally the home of the Sadler's Wells Ballet (which
became the *Royal Ballet* in 1956 on moving to the *Royal Opera
House, Covent Garden*) and the Sadler's Wells Opera Company
(which became the *English National Opera* in 1968 on moving
to the *Coliseum*). The Royal Ballet's sister company, the Royal
Ballet Touring Company, became the Sadler's Wells Royal
Ballet in 1976 when it took up a regular base at Sadler's Wells.
In 1990, however, it moved to the Hippodrome, Birmingham,
and became the Birmingham Royal Ballet. [original theatre
built by Thomas Sadler, who in 1683 discovered an old well
in the garden of his house and developed it as a 'spa']

Sadler's Wells

safe seat /ˌseɪf ˈsiːt/ (politics) A *seat* whose *MP* has been elected by a large majority, and which is therefore unlikely to change its political support in a future *general election* or *by-election*. Many *constituencies*, such as those in the south of *England* held by the *Conservative Party*, and some seats in northern industrial areas held by the *Labour Party*, have long been regarded as safe seats.

Sainsburys /ˈseɪnzbrɪz/ (commerce) A chain of privately owned, good quality supermarkets. The stores sell mainly food but some also sell other goods, such as cosmetics and clothing. [the first shop was opened in *London* in 1869 by dairyman John James Sainsbury (1844–1928)]

Saint . . . /snt . . . / see *St* . . .

sale of work /ˌseɪl əv ˈwɜːk/ (daily life) A sale of home-made goods such as knitwear, ornaments, furnishings, cakes and sweets, usually organized by a group of women or by a school in aid of a particular charity. Compare *bring-and-buy sale*.

Salisbury Plain /ˌsɔːlzbrɪ ˈpleɪn/ (geography) An extensive area of open land to the north of Salisbury, Wiltshire, owned by the *Ministry*[2] of Defence and used by the *Army* for military exercises. The main tourist attraction there is *Stonehenge*.

Sally Army /ˌsælɪ ˈɑːmɪ/, **the** (religion) A colloquial name for the *Salvation Army*. [based on girl's name, Sally]

Sally Lunn /ˌsælɪ ˈlʌn/ (food and drink) A flat, round cake made from flour, sugar, yeast, milk, butter and eggs. It is usually eaten hot. [said to be named after a girl who sold them in the streets of Bath, Avon in the 18th century]

saloon bar /səˈluːn bɑː(r)/ (daily life) A *bar*[1] in a *pub* which is more comfortable, and has slightly higher prices, than the *public bar*. Compare *lounge bar, private bar, snug*.

Salopian /səˈləʊpɪən/ (geography) **1** A native or inhabitant of the county of Shropshire. **2** A native or inhabitant of Shrewsbury, the *county town* of Shropshire. **3** A member, or former member, of *Shrewsbury* (*School*). [from Salop, the alternative name for Shropshire, in official use from 1974 to 1980 but also used in written addresses and other documents]

Salvation Army /sælˌveɪʃn ˈɑːmɪ/, **the** (religion) A uniformed religious movement organized on semi-military lines to carry out Christian evangelistic work and give practical aid and spiritual comfort to the poor and needy. It was founded in 1865 and is familiar for the plain, dark uniforms of its men and women members, its public prayer meetings and hymn singing and its lively brass bands. The movement, though of

Salvation Army

British origin, is now international.

Salvationist /sæl'veɪʃənɪst/ (religion) A member of the *Salvation Army*.

Samaritans /sə'mærɪtənz/, **the** (religion) An organization which befriends those in despair, especially anyone thinking of suicide. It is staffed almost entirely by volunteers and usually operates by telephone contact, after which a personal contact may be made. It was founded in 1953, and currently has 182 branches staffed by volunteers. [from the biblical story of the 'Good Samaritan', Luke 10 : 30–37]

Sandhurst /'sændhɜ:st/ (education) The short name of the *Royal Military Academy*, at Sandhurst, Berkshire.

Sandown Park /ˌsændaʊn 'pɑːk/ (sport and leisure) A race course near Esher, Surrey. [named after old house there]

Sandringham /'sændrɪŋəm/ (royal family) A village in Norfolk where the *royal family* has a country residence, Sandringham House.

sandwich course /'sænwɪdʒ kɔːs/ (education) A course at a university or other place of *further education* in which students alternate periods of full-time study with periods of supervised experience in a particular job. [study and work experience alternate like the layers of a sandwich]

sandwich man /'sænwɪdʒ mæn/ (commerce) A man who wears two advertising boards, one on his chest, the other on his

Santa Claus

back, joined by straps across the shoulders, and who walks along a pavement in a shopping street to publicize his advertisement. [boards suggest a 'sandwich', with the bearer as the 'filling']

Santa Claus /'sæntə klɔːz/ (tradition) The legendary patron saint of children, who brings them presents at *Christmas*. He is traditionally represented as a cheery old man, rosy cheeked and with a white beard, dressed in a scarlet robe and hood. In popular folklore he arrives from the North Pole (or some northern country such as Greenland) in a sledge drawn by reindeer and visits each child's house by coming down the chimney on *Christmas Eve* in order to leave his presents. He appears as a character in many *pantomimes,* and, commercially, is an attraction in many large department stores at Christmas, where he usually sits in a fairy-tale setting and runs a *lucky dip* for young children. He is also known as *Father Christmas.* He is not associated with the religious aspect of Christmas. [modification of Dutch dialect, 'Sante Klaas', 'St Nicholas']

Sarum /'seərəm/ (geography) The historical name of

Salisbury, Wiltshire. Today it is most commonly used in the names Old Sarum and New Sarum. Old Sarum is an Iron Age camp site to the north of Salisbury, where the *city* stood until the 13th century. New Sarum is an official name of the modern *cathedral city* of Salisbury.

SAS /ˌes eɪ 'es/**, the (Special Air Service, the)** (defence) A special force of one regular army regiment (see *Army*) and two *Territorial Army* regiments containing highly trained and experienced troops, whose main task is to cause problems behind enemy lines, usually by means of sabotage, etc. The Service originated in the Special Air Service Brigade formed in the Second World War.

Saturday girl /'sætədɪ ɡɜːl/ (daily life) A girl, often a schoolgirl or student, who works as a temporary shop assistant on Saturdays, when trade is busiest.

Saturday person /'sætədɪ ˌpɜːsn/ (daily life) A young person, male or female, who carries out the work of a *Saturday girl*.

sausage roll /ˌsɒsɪdʒ 'rəʊl/ (food and drink) A sausage, or filling of sausage meat, in a small roll of light flaky pastry, eaten either hot or cold.

Save the Children Fund /ˌseɪv ðə 'tʃɪldrən fʌnd/**, the** (charities) A voluntary organization founded in 1919 with the aim of rescuing children in disaster areas, and working for their welfare. The organization operates internationally, as well as in *Britain*, and its practical objectives change according to the country. In Britain it aims chiefly to provide homes, *club*s and *playgroups* for children where these are not fully provided by the *local authorities*.

Saver /'seɪvə(r)/ (transport) A special return ticket sold at a reduced rate by *BR* to people travelling over 50 miles. Compare *SuperSaver*.

Savile, Jimmy /'sævl, 'dʒɪmɪ/ (people) Jimmy Savile (born 1926) is a television personality who has become well known for his hosting of the children's programme 'Jim'll Fix It', in which children are granted the fulfilment of a wish, such as an interview with the *Prime Minister* or an appearance with a famous rock group. Jimmy Savile is also famous for his efforts to raise money for charity and for the *Stoke Mandeville* hospital. This work won him a knighthood in 1990.

Savings Certificates /'seɪvɪŋz səˌtɪfɪkəts/ see *National Savings Certificates* (finance)

Savoy (Hotel) /sə'vɔɪ (səˌvɔɪ həʊ'tel)/**, the** (London) A luxury hotel with a high-class restaurant, off the *Strand, London*.

[named, as are many streets there, after the Savoy Palace built for Peter of Savoy in 13th century]

Savoy (Theatre) /sə'vɔɪ (sə͵vɔɪ 'θɪətə(r))/, **the** (arts) A *London* theatre founded in 1881. For many years it was famous for its productions of *Gilbert and Sullivan operas* but now it puts on ordinary stage plays. [located in Savoy Court; see *Savoy Hotel*]

Savoy Operas /sə͵vɔɪ 'ɒprəz/, **the** (arts) A name for *Gilbert and Sullivan operas*, which were first staged almost exclusively at the *Savoy (Theatre), London*.

Saxon (architecture) /'sæksn (͵sæksn 'ɑːkɪtektʃə(r))/ (style) The earliest form of English architecture, also known as Anglo-Saxon, and covering the period 600–1086. It is a simple style, and is characterized by small, deep-set windows, rounded arches and alternate long and short angle stones.

scholarship /'skɒləʃɪp/ (education) A special financial grant given to a clever scholar at a fee-paying school.

school song /͵skuːl 'sɒŋ/ (education) A traditional song sung on special occasions, such as an end-of-term concert, at many schools, especially *public schools[1]*. The words of the song are usually intended to make students proud of their school and to describe the best enduring qualities of a public school education.

school tie /͵skuːl 'taɪ/ (education) The distinctive tie worn as part of the school uniform by members of a school and regarded as symbolic of the particular school and its educational values. School ties are typically designed with a repeated pattern such as a crest or stripe. Compare *old school tie*.

school welfare officer /͵skuːl 'welfeər ͵ɒfɪsə(r)/ (education) A *social worker* who aims to ensure that school children, especially those who are 'difficult' or needy, both attend school and receive their rights, such as school *dinners* and transport to and from school.

school year /͵skuːl 'jɪə(r)/ (education) The academic year, beginning in September and ending in late June or early July. It is divided into three *terms[1]*.

schooner /'skuːnə(r)/ (food and drink) A large, tall wine glass, especially one in which sherry is served in a *bar[1]*.

Science Museum /'saɪəns mjuː͵zɪəm/, **the** (science and technology) A famous museum in southwest *London*, housing collections that illustrate the history and development of science, medicine, engineering and industry,

with many working models. The museum, originally part of
the South Kensington Museum that developed after the *Great
Exhibition* of 1851, is particularly popular with children, for
whom it has a special Children's Gallery. A development of
the Science Museum is the *National Railway Museum*, York.

science park /ˈsaɪəns pɑːk/ (science and technology) A special
site, often at a university, where a science-based industry can
promote its technology to interested scientists. There are
currently 40 such parks. The largest, at *Cambridge[1]*, has about
85 companies on its site.

Scilly Isles /ˈsɪlɪ aɪlz/, **the** (geography) A group of islands off
the southwest coast of *England*, some 28 miles (45 km) from
Lands End. There are five sizeable inhabited islands (St
Mary's, Tresco, St Martin's, St Agnes and Bryher) and a large
number of small islands. The islands are popular with
tourists in the spring, when early flowers (especially
daffodils) are grown commercially. The unusually mild
climate makes the islands additionally attractive to visitors.

scone /skɒn/ (food and drink) A light, plain cake made of
flour, milk and very little fat and cooked either in an oven or
on a griddle (a flat iron plate). It is usually round in shape,
and eaten split and buttered. It is popular throughout *Britain*.

Scotch /skɒtʃ/ (food and drink) *Whisky* made in *Scotland*,
regarded by many as the only genuine kind. See also *whiskey*.

Scotch broth /ˌskɒtʃ ˈbrɒθ/ (food and drink) A thick soup
made from beef stock, chopped vegetables and pearl barley.

Scotch egg /ˌskɒtʃ ˈeg/ (food and drink) A hard-boiled egg
enclosed in sausage-meat and covered in fried bread crumbs,
eaten either hot or cold.

Scotch mist /ˌskɒtʃ ˈmɪst/ (daily life) A misty rain or drizzle,
regarded as typical of the weather over moorland in *Scotland*.

Scotch/Scottish terrier /ˌskɒtʃ/ˌskɒtɪʃ ˈterɪə(r)/ (animal world) A
small breed of terrier with long, black hair and erect ears and
tail, noted for its loyalty and companionship. It is familiarly
known as a 'Scotty'. [originally bred in the *Highlands* of
Scotland]

Scotch woodcock /ˌskɒtʃ ˈwʊdkɒk/ (food and drink) A savoury
dish of hot *toast* with anchovies and creamy scrambled eggs,
usually eaten at the end of a meal rather than as an
hors-d'oeuvre.

Scotland /ˈskɒtlənd/ (geography) The northernmost part of
mainland *Britain*, bordered on the south by *England*.
Although part of the *United Kingdom*, Scotland has its own

distinct legal and educational system and its banks issue their own banknotes. Its beautiful and varied countryside has made it popular with tourists, including visitors from England, who can enjoy sports facilities such as skiing that are not available locally. See also *Gaelic*.

Scotland Yard /ˌskɒtlənd ˈjɑːd/ (law) The former name of the headquarters of the *Metropolitan Police Force* in *London*, still in use for the present headquarters that are officially known as *New Scotland Yard*.

Scots Greys /ˌskɒts ˈɡreɪz/**, the** (defence) One of the best known Scottish *Army* regiments (in full, the Royal Scots Greys), raised in 1678 and named after the colour of their horses.

Scots Guards /ˌskɒts ˈɡɑːdz/**, the** (defence) One of the five *Army* regiments that form the *Guards Division*, originally raised in the early 17th century for service in *Ireland*, then reformed under its present name in 1660 as a regiment of the Scottish Army.

Scots, wha hae /ˌskɒts wʌ ˈheɪ/ (tradition) The opening words of the unofficial Scottish national anthem, taken from a poem by Robert Burns (see *Burns' Night*), published in 1798. [in full, 'Scots, wha hae' wi' Wallace bled' ('Scots, who have with Wallace bled'); the reference is to Sir William Wallace, the 13th-century Scottish patriot, who defeated the English in 1297 but was later himself defeated and executed]

Scotsman /ˈskɒtsmən/**, The** (media) A leading daily Scottish *quality paper*, first published in 1817. Its current circulation is about 90,000.

Scottish Certificate of Education /ˌskɒtɪʃ səˌtɪfɪkət əv edjʊˈkeɪʃn/ **(SCE, the)** (education) The *secondary school* examinations in *Scotland* that correspond approximately to the *GCSE* and *A level* in *England* and *Wales*. At the end of their fourth year, when they are about 16, students take the Standard grade examination at one of three levels: Credit (grade 1 or 2), General (grade 3 or 4) and Foundation (grade 5 or 6). Grade 7, the lowest, is awarded to students who merely complete the course. A year later, at about the age of 17, they take the Higher grade examination.

Scottish Hydro-Electric /ˌskɒtɪʃ ˈhaɪdrəʊ ɪˌlektrɪk/ (commerce) The independent company that generates and supplies electricity in northern *Scotland*. (Scotland's hydro-electric stations are mostly in the *Highlands*.) Compare *Scottish Power* and see also *Scottish Nuclear*.

Scottish Natural Heritage /ˌskɒtɪʃ ˌnætrəl ˈherɪtɪdʒ/
(geography) The rural conservation body in *Scotland* that
corresponds to the *Countryside Commission* in *England*.

Scottish Nuclear /ˌskɒtɪʃ ˈnjuːklɪə(r)/ (commerce) The
government-owned company that operates two nuclear
power stations in *Scotland*. It sells the electricity it produces
to *Scottish Power* and *Scottish Hydro-Electric* (who both
generate their own electricity).

Scottish Power /ˌskɒtɪʃ ˈpaʊə(r)/ (commerce) The independent
company that generates and supplies electricity in southern
Scotland. Compare *Scottish Hydro-Electric* and see also *Scottish
Nuclear*.

Scottish TV /ˌskɒtɪʃ tiː ˈviː/ (media) One of the 15 regional
television companies of the *ITC*, based in *Glasgow* and
broadcasting to central *Scotland*.

Scouse /skaʊs/ (**1** geography **2** language) **1** The nickname of a
native or inhabitant of Liverpool. **2** The characteristic dialect
of such a person. [from the dialect word 'scouse', used for a
type of Lancashire *hotpot*, itself a shortened form of
'lobscouse', a similar dish once popular with sailors]

Scout/scout /skaʊt/skaʊt/ (**1** sport and leisure **2** education) **1** A
boy aged 11 to 16 who is a member of the *Scout Association*. **2**
A *college*[1] servant at *Oxford University*.

Scout Association /ˈskaʊt əsəʊsɪˌeɪʃn/, **the** (sport and leisure) A
uniformed organization for boys founded in 1908 by Lord
Baden-Powell (as a world-wide movement) to encourage a
sense of adventure and of responsibility for others among
young people. The Association's British membership is
currently about 728,000. See *beaver, cub (scout), scout*.
Compare *Girl Guides Association*.

Scrabble /ˈskræbl/ (sport and leisure) The trade name of a
board game in which small tiles, marked with letters of the
alphabet, are arranged to form words, such words being
arranged as in a crossword puzzle. Each letter has a
numerical value with more 'difficult' letters, such as Q and X,
having higher values. The aim is to use all one's letters and
form high-scoring words.

scrip issue /ˈskrɪp ˌɪʃuː/ (finance) An issue of shares made by a
company to its shareholders without charge.

Scrooge /skruːdʒ/ (arts) The miser, Ebenezer Scrooge, is the
central character in Charles *Dickens*'s popular story 'A
Christmas Carol' (1843). The subject of the story is the
conversion of Scrooge from a mean and unpleasant man to a

cheerful and loving man. The name 'Scrooge' is now used to describe a very mean person.

Scrubs /skrʌbz/, **the** (law) A colloquial name for *Wormwood Scrubs* prison.

scrumpy /'skrʌmpɪ/ (food and drink) A kind of rough, dry cider brewed in the *West Country* of *England*.

SDLP /ˌes diː el 'piː/, **the (Social Democratic and Labour Party, the)** (politics) A party formed in *Northern Ireland* in 1970 as a reaction to the *Troubles*. Its supporters are largely Catholic and would like *Ireland* (ie, Northern Ireland and the Republic of Ireland) to be reunited as one country.

SDP /ˌes diː 'piː/, **the (Social Democratic Party, the)** (politics) The former political party that in 1987 merged with the *Liberal Party* to form the *Liberal Democrats*. See also David *Owen*.

Sealed Knot Society /ˌsiːld 'nɒt səˌsaɪətɪ/, **the** (history) An organization founded in 1971 that re-enacts battles of the *English Civil War* both for enjoyment and to raise money for charity. Members wear the military dress of the period and usually act out the battle on its original site. [named after a secret 17th-century organization that vowed to restore the royal house of Stuart to the throne after the *Commonwealth*[2]]

Sealyham (terrier) /'siːlɪəm (ˌsiːlɪəm 'terɪə(r))/ (animal world) A small breed of wire-haired terrier with white coat and short legs. [originally bred in the small village of Sealyham, near Fishguard in *Wales*]

season ticket /'siːzn ˌtɪkɪt/ (1 transport 2 arts) **1** A ticket for a form of public transport (usually train or bus) that allows regular travel over a particular route for a particular period (a week, a month, a quarter or a year) at a reduced rate. **2** A similar ticket giving regular admission to a series of concerts, performances or exhibitions.

seat /siːt/ (government) An alternative term for a parliamentary *constituency*, so called because it provides its *MP* with a seat in the *House of Commons*. See also *safe seat*.

second class /ˌsekənd 'klɑːs/ (1 transport 2 commerce 3 education) **1** Until 1987, the official name for the standard class of seat in a railway train, now named *standard class*. **2** The lower of two postal rates, providing delivery at a slower rate than *first class*[2] mail. **3** The second and most common class of *honours degree*, indicating high academic competence but not originality or excellence.

second reading /ˌsekənd 'riːdɪŋ / (government) The second presentation of a *bill* in the *House of Commons* or *House of Lords*, usually followed by a debate on it. Compare *first reading*, *third reading*.

secondary modern (school) /ˌsekəndrɪ 'mɒdn (skuːl)/ (education) A type of *secondary school* that offers a more general and technical and less academic education than a *grammar school*. Of all school children of secondary school age, only 4% attend such schools.

secondary picketing /ˌsekəndrɪ 'pɪkɪtɪŋ/ (work) Action taken by *pickets* at the premises of a firm where they are not themselves employed but which has trading links with their own workplace or which produces similar products or goods. Such action, which is legally an offence, is carried out to support pickets from a workplace's own employees.

secondary school /'sekəndrɪ skuːl/ (education) A *state school* or *private school* that provides education for school children aged between 11 and 18. Such schools are organized in a number of ways, with the most common type being the *comprehensive school*, attended by over 90% of school children of this age. Other types of secondary schools are *grammar schools*, *middle schools*, *secondary modern schools*, *technical schools* and *public schools*[1]. An extension of a state secondary school is the *tertiary college*. Most students leave their state secondary school at the age of 16, having taken one or more subjects in the *GCSE*.

Secretary of State /ˌsekrətrɪ əv 'steɪt/ (government) The title of the heads of many government *departments*, corresponding to *minister*[2]. In the *Cabinet* appointed by John *Major* in May 1993 there were Secretaries of State for Foreign and *Commonwealth* Affairs, the *Home Office*, Trade and Industry, Transport, Defence, National Heritage, the Environment, *Wales*, *Social Security*, *Scotland*, *Northern Ireland*, Education, Health, and Employment. The title is often shortened to 'Secretary' and follows the name of the department, so that the Secretary of State for Transport, for example, is called the 'Transport Secretary'. See also *Foreign Secretary*, *Home Secretary*.

select committee /sɪˌlekt kə'mɪtɪ/ (law) A committee set up on a temporary basis to consider a particular matter, especially from a legal point of view. The best known select committees are those of the *House of Commons*, where a committee will be attached to a particular *department*, such as agriculture, defence, transport, etc. At present the main select committee in the *House of Lords* is the one dealing with the European

Communities (such as the *EEC* and the European Atomic Energy Community).

self-governing school /ˌself ˈɡʌvənɪŋ ˌskuːl/ (education) A school in *Scotland* that is the equivalent of a *grant-maintained school* in *England* or *Wales*.

Selfridges /ˈselfrɪdʒɪz/ (commerce) *London*'s largest department store after *Harrods*, in *Oxford Street*. It is particularly famous for its food section, and also contains two restaurants and several cafés. [founded in 1909 by an American businessman, H Gordon Selfridge (died 1947)]

Sellafield /ˈseləfiːld/ (science and technology) The industrial installation of *British Nuclear Fuels* at Sellafield, in the north-west of *England*, where a reprocessing plant recovers unused uranium and plutonium from spent nuclear fuel. In 1983 there was public concern at a leakage of nuclear waste from the plant on to the nearby seashore. Until 1981 the site was known as *Windscale*, and this name is retained for the adjacent research establishment of the *United Kingdom Atomic Energy Authority*.

semi(-detached house) /ˈsemi (ˌsemi dɪˌtætʃt ˈhaʊs)/ (style) A house attached on one side only to another, usually very similar house. A house of this kind is less expensive than a *detached house*, but still offers a good standard of privacy and comfort. Compare *terraced house*.

semi(-detached house)

SEN /ˌes iː ˈen/ **(state enrolled nurse)** (medicine) A nurse having the qualification formerly equivalent to that of the *EN*.

senior citizen /ˌsiːnɪə ˈsɪtɪzn/ (life and society) A term, regarded by some as patronizing, for a person who has reached *retirement age*, otherwise called an *OAP*.

senior service /ˌsiːnɪə ˈsɜːvɪs/, **the** (defence) A name for the *Royal Navy*, which is the oldest of the three armed services.

sense of humour /ˌsens əv ˈhjuːmə(r)/ **(English/British sense of humour)** (daily life) The humour believed to be characteristic of the British, or specifically of the English (since there are also regional Scottish, Irish and Welsh senses of humour). It includes a love of 'double entendre' (a word or phrase meaning two things at the same time, one 'proper', one 'improper' or vulgar), self-mockery and an enjoyment of what is absurd and eccentric. Much English humour originated in the music-halls, and is seen today in the performances of comedians in *working men's clubs*, *pantomimes* and, most of all, on radio and television.

Sergeant/Serjeant at Arms /ˌsɑːdʒənt ˌsɑːdʒənt ət ˈɑːmz/ (government) Another title of *Black Rod*, in his capacity as an official in the *House of Lords*. He attends the *Lord Chancellor*, and is responsible for security and for accommodation and services in the house.

Serious Fraud Office /ˌsɪərɪəs ˈfrɔːd ˌɒfɪs/, **the** (law) A government body set up in 1987 to investigate and prosecute serious or complicated cases of criminal fraud. Its staff includes lawyers, accountants, *police* officers and other specialists. Compare *Fraud Squad*.

Serpentine /ˈsɜːpəntaɪn/, **the** (London) A lake in *Hyde Park, London*, artificially made in 1730 to be a centre for boating, fishing and swimming. [from the winding or 'serpentine' course of the former river Westbourne there]

SERPS /sɜːps/ **(State Earnings-Related Pension Scheme, the)** (finance) The state pension scheme in *Britain*, by which an employee is paid a basic weekly amount plus an additional amount related to his or her former earnings. At present the latter is fixed at 25% of the best 20 years of those earnings, but from 2000 it will be calculated at 20% of a lifetime's earnings.

servants /ˈsɜːvənts/ (life and society) Before the First World War and for a short time after it, servants were widely employed in even quite small households in *Britain*, especially as housemaids, cooks and gardeners. Such servants lived in their employer's house. Today some rich families with large houses still employ servants, only they are not usually called as such but are known by their type of employment, for example 'cook', '*nanny*', 'chauffeur', etc.

service area /'sɜːvɪs ˌeərɪə/ (transport) A place on a *motorway* where a number of facilities are available for drivers and travellers, usually including a *service station*, restaurant or café and toilets.

service charge /'sɜːvɪs tʃɑːdʒ/ (commerce) An amount, usually 10% of the total, that is often added to the bill in a restaurant or hotel as a charge for service. This is instead of the customer deciding how much, if anything, he will leave. Some restaurant menus indicate that no service charge is made, but add that the amount left (the 'tip') is for the customer to decide.

service flat /'sɜːvɪs flæt/ (daily life) A flat or apartment in a large residential block, especially in *London*. The rent paid for the flat includes such services as cleaning, laundry and delivery of meals.

service road /'sɜːvɪs rəʊd/ (commerce) A fairly narrow road running parallel to a main road and giving access to the rear entrances of shops, offices and factories built along it, so that deliveries and collections can be made without affecting traffic on the main road.

service station /'sɜːvɪs ˌsteɪʃn/ (transport) A commercial garage that not only supplies petrol, oil, air, etc, but also usually carries out repairs, services vehicles (eg, for the *MOT test*), and sells mechanical parts and other goods.

set-aside /'set əˌsaɪd/ (commerce) A piece of agricultural land taken out of production in order to reduce a surplus of crops or to control the prices paid for a particular crop. Farmers with a set-aside are paid a special subsidy as part of the revised *Common Agricultural Policy*.

set book /ˌset 'bʊk/ (education) A literary work, in English or a foreign language, (set) to be studied for a school-leaving examination such as the *GCSE*.

Severn /'sevən/**, the** (geography) *Britain*'s second longest river (180 miles, or 290 km), which rises in northeast *Wales* and flows east and south into the Bristol Channel. It is famous for its periodic 'bore' (tidal wave) which, for a short time, makes the water flow back up the part of the river nearest the sea. See also *Severn Bridge* and *Severn Tunnel*.

Severn Bridge /ˌsevən 'brɪdʒ/**, the** (transport) The bridge that carries the *M4* across the estuary of the river *Severn* between southwest *England* and south *Wales*. The bridge, opened in 1966, frequently has to be closed when strong winds are blowing as these are dangerous for tall vehicles. A second bridge over the Severn is planned to open in 1996. See also *Severn Tunnel*.

Severn Tunnel /ˌsevən 'tʌnl/, **the** (transport) The longest tunnel in *Britain*, taking the railway under the estuary of the river *Severn* on the main line from *England* to *Wales*. The tunnel is to the southwest of the *Severn Bridge*.

S4C /ˌes fɔː 'siː/ **(Sianel Pedwar Cymru)** (media) The television channel in *Wales* that corresponds to *Channel 4* in *Britain* as a whole. Many of its programmes are in Welsh. [Welsh for 'Channel Four Wales']

Shadow Cabinet /ˌʃædəʊ 'kæbɪnɪt/, **the** (government) The team of *ministers*[2] in the *Opposition* (the major political party not currently in power) who would probably form the *Cabinet* if their party won the next *general election*. Meanwhile, they individually deal with the same matters as the Cabinet ministers in the current government.

shadow minister /ˌʃædəʊ 'mɪnɪstə(r)/ (government) A *minister*[2] in the *Shadow Cabinet*. He will usually be called by his particular area of responsibility, eg, 'Shadow Chancellor', 'Shadow Home Secretary'. See *Chancellor of the Exchequer*, *Home Secretary*. However, the party leader is known as the *Leader of the Opposition*, not the 'Shadow *Prime Minister*'.

Shaftesbury Avenue /'ʃɑːftsbrɪ 'ævənjuː/ (London) A street in central *London*, running northeast from *Piccadilly Circus*, and famous for the many theatres and cinemas on it. The street was built only in the 1850s and is named in honour of the industrial reformer and churchman, Lord Shaftesbury (1801–85).

Shaftesbury Society /'ʃɑːftsbrɪ səˌsaɪətɪ/, **the** (charities) A voluntary organization founded in 1844 by Lord Shaftesbury (see *Shaftesbury Avenue*) to help physically handicapped, poor and needy children. The Society runs schools, homes, holiday camps and *club*s for the physically handicapped. A tradition has developed that physically able boys in the Home often join the *Royal Navy* or Merchant Navy.

Shakespeare country /'ʃeɪkspɪə ˌkʌntrɪ/ (geography) The towns, villages and other places connected with William *Shakespeare* (1564–1616), in particular *Stratford-(up)on-Avon*, Warwickshire and the surrounding countryside.

Shakespeare, William /ˈʃeɪkspɪə(r), ˌwɪljəm/ (people) William Shakespeare (1564–1616) is generally acknowledged to have been *Britain*'s finest playwright and one of her most accomplished poets. His plays show a great understanding of human activities of all kinds. In them, he very skilfully uses many different literary styles to express a wide range of emotions. The plays are usually described as comedies, tragedies and histories but this is an over-simplification as many of them do not fall neatly into any one category. His poems, especially his 'Sonnets', show his extraordinary powers of expression and his depth of emotional understanding. His work has had a great influence on English and many of his expressions have become part of the language, for example, 'a *winter of discontent*'[1,2]. Because the English language has changed so much since Shakespeare's day, many people (including school students obliged to read him for examination purposes) find his works difficult and 'dated'. There have been several recent attempts to present his plays in a more accessible way, either by modernizing the language or by printing the original text with cartoon illustrations. His birthplace at *Stratford-(up)on-Avon* remains a popular tourist attraction.

shamrock /ˈʃæmrɒk/ (tradition) The plant that is the national emblem of *Ireland*, and the equivalent of the English *rose*, the Welsh *leek* and *daffodil* and the Scottish *thistle*. According to legend, it was the plant chosen by St Patrick, patron saint of Ireland, to illustrate the Christian doctrine of the Trinity to the Irish.

shandy /ˈʃændɪ/ (food and drink) An alcoholic drink of beer mixed with lemonade, or sometimes ginger beer.

share shop /ˈʃeə ʃɒp/ (finance) A bank, *building society*, *stockbroker* or other financial specialist that sells shares to the public.

Shaw's Corner /ˌʃɔːz ˈkɔːnə(r)/ (arts) A 19th-century house in the village of Ayot St Lawrence, Hertfordshire, where the dramatist George Bernard Shaw lived for 44 years until his death in 1950. The house is now owned by the *National Trust*, and is open to the public.

She /ʃiː/ (media) A glossy monthly magazine for younger women, aimed at the needs and interests of the reader both as individual and as parent. It was first published in 1955 and has a current circulation of about 283,000.

Sheffield United /ˌʃefiːld juːˈnaɪtɪd/ (sport and leisure) A *football club* founded in 1889 with a stadium in south central Sheffield, South Yorkshire.

Sheffield Wednesday /ˌʃefiːld 'wenzdɪ/ (sport and leisure) A popular *football club* founded in 1867 with a stadium in northwest Sheffield, South Yorkshire. [so named as originally it played matches on a Wednesday]

Sheldonian (Theatre) /ʃel'dəʊnɪən (ʃelˌdəʊnɪən 'θɪətə(r))/, **the** (education) An historic building in *Oxford*[1] where degrees are conferred on *graduates* of *Oxford University*, special University ceremonies take place, and concerts are held. The building contains the chair of the *vice-chancellor* of the University, and was itself built in the second half of the 17th century by the clergyman Gilbert Sheldon (1598–1677).

Shell Centre /'ʃel ˌsentə(r)/, **the** (commerce) A 25-storey building in *London* near the *South Bank* site. It was built over the period 1957–62 as the headquarters of the Shell Transport and Trading Company.

Shelter /'ʃeltə(r)/ (charities) A voluntary organization founded in 1966 to provide homes for poor or needy people who have nowhere to live.

sheltered housing /ˌʃeltəd 'haʊzɪŋ/ (daily life) A form of housing for retired or elderly people in newly-built blocks of flats. They can feel safe in them, and can live without the worry of doing daily jobs such as cleaning and gardening, because such jobs are done for them. Each flat also has a special telephone on which the residents can call a warden, who lives in the block, for help at any time. Most housing of this type is built close to the centre of a town, near shops, bus stops and other places that the residents will wish to visit.

shepherd's pie /ˌʃepədz 'paɪ/ (food and drink) A hot savoury dish, also known as *cottage pie*, containing minced meat usually mixed with onions, carrots and gravy, topped with a layer of mashed potato, and then baked. [said to have been a common dish with shepherds]

Sheraton /'ʃerətən/ (style) A style of furniture popular from the 18th century, when it was invented by the cabinet-maker Thomas Sheraton (1751–1806). It is characterized by a neo-classical design and by its lightness and elegance, as well as the extensive use of inlay. Compare *Chippendale* and *Hepplewhite*.

sheriff /'ʃerɪf/ (**1** government **2** law) **1** In *England* and *Wales*, the chief state executive officer in a *county*, having mainly ceremonial duties. **2** In *Scotland*, a judge in a *court*[3] of law.

Shetland pony /ˌʃetlənd ˈpəʊnɪ/ (animal world) A small, sturdy breed of pony with a long mane and tail, popular for children because of its small size, although in fact the animal is often quite stubborn and can be difficult to control. [originally bred in the *Shetlands* in *Scotland* and used in the 19th century as work ponies]

Shetlands /ˈʃetləndz/, **the** (geography) The most northerly group of islands in *Britain*, which are part of *Scotland* and lie to the north of the *Orkneys*. The largest island is Mainland and the most northerly is Unst. For many centuries the islands were ruled by Scandinavia, and both the Shetlands and the Orkneys belonged to Scandinavia until the 15th century. This link is clear in the many Norse archaeological sites and place-names there. From the 1970s, the Shetlands have become an increasingly important centre of the *North Sea oil* industry.

shilling /ˈʃɪlɪŋ/ (daily life) A silver coin worth 12 pence (see penny) or one twentieth of a *pound (sterling)*, officially replaced in 1971 by the 5p piece (value 5 pence), which was the same size. The shilling is no longer found in circulation. The term is still occasionally used, especially among older people, for the 5p coin. See also *bob*.

shinty /ˈʃɪntɪ/ (sport and leisure) A game like hockey played chiefly in *Scotland*. The stick used is shorter and heavier than a hockey stick, and the game itself more vigorous and faster, since the ball is often hit when still in the air.

shire horse /ˈʃaɪə hɔːs/ (animal world) A large, strong, heavy breed of cart-horse formerly used all over *Britain* as a work horse on farms. [originally bred in the *Shires*]

Shires /ˈʃaɪəz/, **the** (geography) A traditional name for the *counties*[1] of the *Midlands*, long famous for their *hunts*. Those of Northamptonshire, Leicestershire and the south of Lincolnshire are especially famous. [from 'shire' in meaning of 'county'; the names of many counties still end in '-shire', with the first part of the name usually being that of the *county town*, so that 'Northamptonshire', for example, means 'county of Northampton']

shooting brake /ˈʃuːtɪŋ breɪk/ (transport) An alternative name for an *estate car*.

shooting stick /ˈʃuːtɪŋ stɪk/ (sport and leisure) A special kind of walking stick that has a point (for digging into the ground) at the lower end, and a folding seat at the top. It is chiefly used as a temporary seat by sportsmen when shooting game (see *gamekeeper*), watching horse-racing and attending shows.

shop steward /ˌʃɒp ˈstjʊəd/ (work) A trade union leader in a factory or other local work force.

shopping precinct /ˈʃɒpɪŋ ˌpriːsɪŋkt/ (commerce) An area in a town or *city* where there are a lot of shops and where traffic is banned to make shopping easier for people on foot.

shortbread /ˈʃɔːtbred/ (food and drink) A rich, crumbly biscuit made of flour and butter. It is also known as shortcake. ['short' in sense 'rich in fat' and therefore crumbly]

shorthorn (cattle) /ˈʃɔːthɔːn (ˌʃɔːthɔːn ˈkætl)/ (animal world) A stocky breed of beef and dairy cattle, in several regional varieties, with short horns.

shove-ha'penny /ˌʃʌv ˈheɪpnɪ/ (sport and leisure) A game popular in *pub*s and some *club*s, in which old (pre-1971) *halfpennies* or polished discs are pushed by hand on to marked sections of a smooth wooden board.

Shrewsbury (School) /ˈʃrəʊzbrɪ (ˌʃrəʊzbrɪ ˈskuːl)/ (education) A leading *public school*[1] in Shrewsbury, Shropshire, founded in 1552, and having 670 students. See also *Salopian*[3].

Shrove Tuesday /ˌʃrəʊv ˈtjuːzdeɪ/ (religion) The day before *Ash Wednesday*, once thought of as a last day of enjoyment before the fasting of *Lent* in the Christian year. Many people still traditionally eat *pancakes* on Shrove Tuesday, hence its popular name of *Pancake Day*. [named from a rare verb 'shrive', meaning 'to make one's confession': at this time Christians used to confess their sins to a priest before Lent; this is still done by many members of the *Roman Catholic Church* and some *Anglicans*]

sickness benefit /ˈsɪknɪs ˌbenɪfɪt/ (finance) A state payment made to self-employed or unemployed people when they are sick for at least four days. The benefit is payable for a period up to 28 weeks, after which it is replaced by *invalidity benefit*. Compare *statutory sick pay*.

sidesman /ˈsaɪdzmən/ (religion) A man appointed to assist the *churchwarden* in the *Church of England*. Among his duties are giving out prayer books and collecting money from the congregation during a *church* service. [so called as he 'stands beside' the churchwarden]

Silbury Hill /ˌsɪlbərɪ ˈhɪl/ see *Avebury* (tradition)

Silicon Glen /ˌsɪlɪkən ˈglen/ (commerce) A nickname for the low-lying region between *Glasgow* and *Edinburgh* in *Scotland*, where there are several computer firms. [from 'silicon chip' and 'glen' as a word for a Scottish valley; name was modelled on that of Silicon Valley, in California, USA]

silk /sɪlk/ (law) A term used to refer to the silk gown worn by a *QC*, and so to the QC himself, who is said to 'take silk' on reaching this rank as a *barrister*.

silly season /ˈsɪlɪ ˌsiːzn/, **the** (media) The summer season, traditionally regarded as a time when journalists, without important news in the holiday period and during the *recess[1]* of *Parliament*, fill their columns with amusing and unimportant reports.

Silverstone /ˈsɪlvəstən/ (sport and leisure) A racing track near Towcester, Northamptonshire, where the *British Grand Prix[1]* for motor racing is held every second year and where the *British Grand Prix[2]* for motorcycle racing is held every year. Many other important national and international races are also held there.

simnel cake /ˈsɪmnəl keɪk/ (food and drink) A small fruit cake covered in marzipan, traditionally eaten on *Mothering Sunday*, or in *Lent* or at *Easter*.

Single Market /ˌsɪŋgl ˈmɑːkɪt/, **the** (government) The unified economic federation introduced in the *EC* from 1993, thus creating a Europe without trade barriers in which countries can trade freely with one another. *Britain* remains unhappy about aspects of the Single Market and did not readily accept the *Maastricht Treaty* and the type of full economic and monetary union that it proposed.

Sinn Féin /ˌʃɪn ˈfeɪn/ (politics) The Irish republican movement that arose before the First World War and that campaigned for the economic and political separation of *Ireland* from *Great Britain*. Today it is the political wing of the Provisional *IRA*, and wants *Northern Ireland* to become part of the Republic of Ireland, by using force if necessary. In the *general elections* of 1983 and 1987 the president of Sinn Féin, Gerry Adams, was elected an *MP*. He never took his seat in Parliament, however, and in the 1992 elections he lost to an *SDLP* candidate. [Irish for 'we ourselves']

sir /sɜː(r)/ (life and society) A polite form of address to a man, used most commonly by schoolchildren to their teachers, junior military ranks to senior officers, and assistants, officials, etc, in shops, banks, *club*s, public transport vehicles, to their customers, clients and passengers. The form of address is becoming less common, however, and is more likely when the man so addressed is noticeably older than, or of apparent senior status to, the speaker.

Sir /sə(r) [unstressed]/ (life and society) The title of honour placed before the name of a knight or baronet, as 'Sir Edward Brown' (or 'Sir Edward', but never 'Sir Brown')

sit-down strike /ˌsɪt daʊn ˈstraɪk/ (work) A strike in which workers refuse to leave their place of work (where they may normally sit or stand while working) until settlement has been reached.

site of special scientific interest /ˌsaɪt əv ˌspeʃl ˌsaɪəntɪfɪk ˈɪntrəst/ **(SSSI)** (geography) A rural site that has been identified by *English Heritage* in *England* and equivalent bodies in *Wales* and *Scotland* as being of special interest because of its flora, fauna or geological features. There are currently almost 6,000 SSSIs in *Britain*.

sit-in /ˈsɪt ɪn/ (politics) A form of protest or 'civil disobedience' in which demonstrators occupy areas normally belonging to their management or superiors (as students in a staff common room, workers in a factory boardroom).

sixpence /ˈsɪkspəns/ (daily life) A small silver coin worth six old pence (see *penny*) and two and half (new) pence, not minted since 1970, although in circulation until 1980.

sixth form /ˈsɪksθ fɔːm/ (education) The most senior class in a *secondary school*, often divided into two years as a 'lower sixth' and an 'upper sixth'. The class is usually intended for students preparing for the *A-level* examination.

sixth form college /ˌsɪksθ fɔːm ˈkɒlɪdʒ/ (education) A *further education college*[2], sometimes an independent (fee-paying) one, for students who wish to prepare for the *A-level* examination or, in some cases, to retake the *GCSE*. Compare *tertiary college*.

Sizewell /ˈsaɪzwel/ (science and technology) A site on the east coast of *England*, in Suffolk, where a *nuclear power* station ('Sizewell A') was built in 1967 and where a second such station ('Sizewell B') is currently under construction. There has been much local opposition to Sizewell B on the grounds that the plant, a pressurized water reactor, could prove dangerous. It is due to open in 1994.

Sky /skaɪ/ (media) A popular short name for *BSkyB*.

Skye terrier /ˌskaɪ ˈterɪə(r)/ (animal world) A short-legged, long-coated breed of terrier, originally bred as a working dog on the island of Skye, *Scotland*.

Slade School of (Fine) Art /ˌsleɪd ˌskuːl əv (ˌfaɪn) ˈɑːt/**, the** (education) A *college*[2] of *London University* founded in 1871, and providing *higher education* courses in fine art. [named after art collector and benefactor Felix Slade (1790–1868)]

sleeping partner /ˌsliːpɪŋ ˈpɑːtnə(r)/ (finance) A partner in a business or company who does not play an active role but who merely provides the capital.

sleeping policeman

sleeping policeman /ˌsliːpɪŋ pəˈliːsmən/ (transport) A low bump built across a road to prevent drivers of vehicles from travelling too fast, usually in residential areas or, for example, in a university campus.

slip road /ˈslɪp rəʊd/ (transport) A short, narrow road linking a standard main road, such as an *A-road*, with a *motorway*.

Sloane /sləʊn/ (life and society) A colloquial term for a *Sloane Ranger*.

Sloane Ranger /ˌsləʊn ˈreɪndʒə(r)/ (life and society) A semi-humorous nickname for a fashionable *upper class* or *upper middle class* young person, especially a woman, who wears casual but expensive country-style clothes (often including *green wellies*), speaks in an affected tone of voice, and typically living in *London* in the week and in the country at the *weekend*. Ostentatious or loud-voiced Sloane Rangers are often known as *Hooray Henries* if male, and Hooray Henriettas if female. [name devised in mid-1970s by journalist Peter York as a blend of '*Sloane* Square', a fashionable square in southwest London, and '*Lone Ranger*', the name of a television cowboy character]

sloe gin /ˌsləʊ ˈdʒɪn/ (food and drink) A type of liqueur made from *gin* that has had the juice of sloes and sugar added to it.

smallholding /ˈsmɔːlˌhəʊldɪŋ/ (daily life) A small farm in *England* or *Wales*, especially one rented from a *local authority*. Compare *croft*.

Smash Hits /ˌsmæʃ 'hɪts/ (media) A fortnightly magazine for teenagers on pop and rock music. It was founded in 1979 and has a current circulation of about 391,000.

Smith, John /ˈsmɪθ, dʒɒn/ (people) John Smith (1938-94) was a Scottish politician who first became an *MP* for the *Labour Party* in 1970. He gradually rose to more senior posts, and in 1987 was appointed *Chancellor of the Exchequer* in the *Shadow Cabinet* and eventually leader of the Labour Party in 1992. John Smith was an intelligent and forceful speaker, but was regarded by some as not giving his party a firm enough lead. It is also said that, as a Scot, he did not always understand the English point of view. Politically John Smith stood on the right of the Labour Party.

Smith Square /ˌsmɪθ 'skweə(r)/ (London) A square in central *London* where the headquarters of the *Conservative Party* are. The *Labour Party* was also based here in *Transport House* until 1980, when it moved to Walworth Road. [square itself was laid out in 18th century on land belonging to Sir James Smith]

Smithfield (Market) /ˈsmɪθfiːld (ˌsmɪθfiːld 'mɑːkɪt)/ (London) The popular name of the Central Meat Market, *London*. [said to mean 'smooth field'; the site was originally used for fairs, tournaments and public executions]

Smith's /smɪθs/ (commerce) One of a number of chain stores selling newspapers, magazines, stationery, books, records, cassettes, home computers and confectionery. [in full *W H Smith* & Son (Holdings) Ltd; business was established in 19th century by newsagent father and son William Henry Smith]

snakes and ladders /ˌsneɪks ən 'lædəz/ (sport and leisure) A children's board game using dice and a board divided into 100 numbered squares. On the board are pictures of snakes and ladders, the snakes leading down from a higher number to a lower, the ladders leading up from a lower number to a higher. Each player moves a counter according to a throw of the dice: if a counter lands on the head of a snake, it moves down to the lower square where the snake's tail is; if it lands at the foot of a ladder it moves up to the square at the top of the ladder. The first player to reach the 100th square wins.

snap /snæp/ (sport and leisure) A children's card game using either ordinary playing cards or special picture cards. Players lay their cards face up on the table simultaneously: the first player to see two identical cards, or two of the same value, calls 'snap!' and wins his opponent's cards.

snatch squad /ˈsnætʃ skwɒd/ (law) A group of policemen sent

snakes and ladders

into a crowd of *pickets* or demonstrators in order to arrest
troublemakers when the gathering becomes unruly.

snooker /'snuːkə(r)/ (sport and leisure) A game like billiards,
played with 15 red balls, worth one point each, six coloured
balls (yellow, worth two points; green, three; brown, four;
blue, five; pink, six; black, seven) and one white cue ball.

snow pudding /ˌsnəʊ 'pʊdɪŋ/ (food and drink) A light sweet
dish containing whipped egg whites and a lemon gelatine
mixture.

Snowdonia /snəʊ'dəʊnɪə/ (geography) A *national park*
northwest *Wales*, famous for its picturesque mountain
scenery, and including the highest mountain in Wales,
Snowdon (1,085 m).

SNP /ˌes en 'piː/ , **the (Scottish National Party, the)**
(politics) *Scotland*'s chief nationalist party, campaigning for
the separation of Scotland from the *United Kingdom* in order
to safeguard the country's cultural and economic life. The
SNP was founded in 1934 and has had mixed fortunes in

recent years. It contests elections, and after the *general election* of 1992 had three *MPs* in the *House of Commons* (as against 11 in 1974).

snug /snʌg/ (daily life) A *private bar* in some *pubs*, offering an intimate ('snug') setting for a small number of people.

soapbox /'səʊpbɒks/ (**1** life and society **2** sport and leisure) **1** An improvised platform for a public speaker, once traditionally made from a wooden crate used for packing soap. Such speakers were known as 'soapbox orators'. See *Speakers' Corner.* **2** A child's home-made racing car made from a similar crate or box to which wheels and a steering device are fitted.

soccer /'sɒkə(r)/ (sport and leisure) A popular abbreviation for *association football.*

Social Democratic and Labour Party /ˌsəʊʃl deməˌkrætɪk ənd 'leɪbə ˌpɑːtɪ/ see *SDLP* (politics)

Social Fund /'səʊʃl ˌfʌnd/**, the** (finance) A government fund from which payments are made to people who, although receiving *income support,* find it difficult to meet their necessary expenses. The amounts paid are either 'regulated' (fixed), such as the 'cold weather' payment, made when the average outdoor temperature is 0°C or below, or 'discretionary' (variable, and depending on personal circumstances).

social security /ˌsəʊʃl sɪ'kjʊərətɪ/ (finance) Money given by the government in cases of sickness, old age and unemployment. The money is raised by means of taxation and insurance schemes (notably *national insurance*). See also *welfare state.*

social worker /'səʊʃl ˌwɜːkə(r)/ (life and society) A person employed by a *local authority* or a voluntary organization to give practical aid and advice to people in need, such as the sick, the handicapped, the elderly (especially any of these living alone), and to children at risk of neglect or ill treatment. Many social workers are employed by the *NHS.*

Society of Friends /sə ˌsaɪətɪ əv 'frendz/**, the** (religion) The formal name of the *Quakers.*

Soho /'səʊhəʊ/ (London) A district of west central *London* well known since the 19th century for its striptease *clubs* and sex shops. Recent local legislation has done much to close a number of these, although some still exist there. The area is also well known for its restaurants.

solicitor /sə'lɪsɪtə(r)/ (law) A person specially trained in legal matters, and who advises his clients on matters of law, draws up official documents, and acts in many court cases. Most people engage a solicitor for domestic matters, such as buying or selling a house, negotiating a will or bequest, or advising on some apparent legal injustice.

Solicitor General /səˌlɪsɪtə ˈdʒenrəl/, **the** (law) The state legal official who ranks next to the *Attorney General* and in effect acts as his assistant.

Somerset House /ˌsʌməset ˈhaʊs/ (London) A large 18th-century building in the *Strand, London*, which formerly housed the General Register Office (of all births, marriages and deaths in the country), the *Inland Revenue* and other important government offices. [built on the site of palace begun in 16th century for the Duke of Somerset]

Sotheby's /ˈsʌðəbɪz/ (commerce) An important firm of fine art auctioneers in *London*, specializing in rare books and manuscripts. It was founded in 1744 by a bookseller, Samuel Baker, with its present name coming from that of Baker's nephew, John Sotheby (1740–1807), who had become a partner of the firm. Compare *Christie's*.

South Bank /ˌsaʊθ ˈbæŋk/, **the** (London) A site on the south bank of the river *Thames* in central *London*, developed mainly for the 1951 *Festival of Britain*. The main complex there, called the South Bank Arts Centre, contains several famous concert halls, theatres and galleries, including the *Royal Festival Hall, Queen Elizabeth Hall, Royal National Theatre[1], National Film Theatre, Purcell Room, Hayward Gallery* and *Museum of the Moving Image*.

South Bank Show /ˌsaʊθ ˈbaeŋk ˌʃəʊ/, **The** (media) A weekly television programme on the arts, first broadcast by *ITV* in 1978. Its regular presenter is Melvyn *Bragg*. [named after the *South Bank, London*]

South Downs /ˌsaʊθ ˈdaʊnz/, **the** (geography) A range of chalk hills in southern *England*, extending from Hampshire (near Petersfield) in the west to East Sussex (near Eastbourne) in the east. See also *long distance footpath*. [named by contrast with the North Downs that run roughly parallel through Surrey and Kent]

Southdown (sheep) /ˈsaʊθdaʊn (ˌsaʊθdaʊn ˈʃiːp)/ (animal world) A breed of sheep with short wool and dark faces and legs. The breed is one of the oldest in *Britain*, and is still found mainly on the *South Downs*.

Spaghetti Junction /spəˈgetɪ ˌdʒʌŋkʃn/ (transport) The nickname of a complex *motorway* intersection on the M6 in

Spaghetti Junction

north Birmingham, properly known as the Gravelly Hill
Interchange. [from the air the complex of roads and flyovers
looks like spaghetti]

SPCK /ˌes piː siː ˈkeɪ/, **the (Society for Promoting Christian
Knowledge, the)** (charities) A society founded in 1698,
originally with the aim of providing children with a religious
education and generally promoting religion in the English
colonies. Later, the society started to publish religious works,
which it continues today, selling its publications, as well as
general books, through a number of bookshops in *Britain*. Its
missionary activity is today chiefly concentrated in
developing countries in Africa and Asia.

Speaker /ˈspiːkə(r)/, **the** (government) The chief officer of the
House of Commons, who is elected by *MP*s to preside over
proceedings and keep order. [in the *House of Lords*, the *Lord
Chancellor* acts as speaker]

Speakers' Corner /ˌspiːkəz ˈkɔːnə(r)/, **the** (London) The
northeast corner of *Hyde Park, London*, where at weekends
individuals or representatives of various organizations and
causes, which vary from the ordinary to the eccentric, make
public speeches from improvised stands (*soapboxes[1]*). The
area was set aside for such use in 1872 after Hyde Park itself
became a popular centre for orators.

Speaking Clock /ˌspiːkɪŋ ˈklɒk/, **the** (commerce) A service
(officially called *Timeline*) operated by *BT* enabling people to

call a special telephone number and hear a recorded voice announce the time every 10 seconds. The recording runs: 'At the third stroke, the time sponsored by Accurist will be [for example] twelve twenty-six and forty seconds'. Three 'beeps' follow.

Special Branch /'speʃl brɑːntʃ/, **the** (law) The department of the police force that deals with political security.

special constable /ˌspeʃl 'kʌnstəbl/ (law) A person who volunteers to carry out police duties in his spare time under the guidance of a particular police force. He receives no pay, but wears a standard police uniform with the letters 'SC' on the shoulder.

Special Delivery /ˌspeʃl dɪ'lɪvərɪ/ (commerce) A special service of the *Post Office* that guarantees delivery of a postal item the following day. The sender pays a fee additional to the cost of *first class* postage. Compare *Recorded*.

special school /'speʃl skuːl/ (education) A school catering for children with physical or mental handicap or emotional or behavioural disorders. Such schools can be either state (non-fee-paying) or private (fee-paying, or run by a voluntary organization).

Spectator /spek'teɪtə(r)/, **the** (media) A weekly right-wing political and literary magazine. It was founded in 1828 and has a current circulation of about 39,000.

Spectrum International Radio /'spektrəm ˌɪntə'naeʃnəl ˌreɪdɪəʊ/ (media) An *ILR* station based in *London*, first operating in 1990. By day it broadcasts a mixture of news and music in English, but in the evening it caters for London audiences who speak other languages, especially Arabic, Chinese, Greek, Italian, Spanish and Hebrew. [pun on 'spectrum' in special sense 'range of wavelengths' and general sense 'wide range']

speech day /'spiːtʃ deɪ/ (education) An annual day in many schools, usually at the end of the school year (in July), when prizes are presented, and a special speech is made by a distinguished visitor (who may be a former student of the school).

Speech from the Throne /ˌspiːtʃ frəm ðə 'θrəʊn/, **the** (government) A name for the *Queen's Speech* made at the opening of each session of *Parliament*.

speed limit /'spiːd ˌlɪmɪt/ (transport) Traffic on all public roads in *Britain* is restricted to a maximum speed, depending on the type of road. Cars must not travel at more than 30 miles an hour (48 kilometres an hour) in a *built-up area*, more than 60 miles an hour (97 kilometres an hour) on standard roads in country areas, or 70 miles an hour (113 kilometres an hour) on *motorways*. Other limits apply to other types of vehicles, such as buses and coaches.

Spitalfields /'spɪtlfiːldz/ (London) A permanent wholesale market for fruit, vegetables and flowers in *London*'s *East End*. [name can be understood as 'hospital fields': there was a 12th-century priory on this site]

Spithead Review /ˌspɪthed rɪ'vjuː/, **the** (defence) A ceremonial review of *Royal Navy* ships anchored in the Spithead channel between Portsmouth and the *Isle of Wight*. Before the Second World War this review was held each year; since then it has been held only on special occasions, such as the 1977 Silver Jubilee (25-year anniversary) of the reign of *Queen Elizabeth*.

Spitting Image /ˌspɪtɪŋ 'ɪmɪdʒ/ (media) A series of satirical programmes produced by *Central TV* for *ITV* since 1984, in which lifelike but grotesque puppets act out scenes relating to topical events and people in the news, including especially politicians and members of the *royal family*. The programmes have been criticized by some people for their poor taste, but praised by others for their inventiveness and originality. [Title is pun on phrase 'spitting image', meaning 'exact likeness', and sense of 'spit' meaning 'show contempt']

Spode (china) /spəʊd ('tʃaɪnə)/ (style) Fine porcelain manufactured by the pottery established in 1770 at Stoke-on-Trent, Staffordshire (see *Potteries*) by Joseph Spode (1733–97).

sponsored walk /ˌspɒnsəd 'wɔːk/ (charities) A walk undertaken to collect funds for a particular charity or cause. Beforehand, each walker draws up a list of people who agree to give a certain amount of money for each mile covered (or for completion of the walk). The walker collects the money after the walk. So similarly 'sponsored jog', 'sponsored run', 'sponsored climb', 'sponsored swim', etc. See also *fun run*.

sporran /'spɒrən/ (clothing) Part of the traditional costume of a *highlander[1]* or other Scot. It is a large leather or fur pouch worn in front of the *kilt*. It hangs from a narrow belt worn round the hips.

Sporting Life /ˌspɔːtɪŋ 'laɪf/, **the** (media) A daily newspaper devoted to the sport of horse racing. It publishes racing results and forecasts the performance of horses in future races. It was first published in 1859 and has a current circulation of about 95,000.

sports day /'spɔːts deɪ/ (education) An annual *open day* at a school, when one of the main events is a programme of sports in which children (and sometimes parents) compete. Sports days are particularly popular at junior schools such as *primary schools*.

sports jacket /'spɔːts ˌdʒækɪt/ (clothing) A man's informal jacket, often made of tweed, for both indoor and outdoor wear, usually worn with trousers of a contrasting colour and material. [as originally worn for some outdoor sports, walking, etc]

spotted dick /ˌspɒtɪd 'dɪk/ (food and drink) Another name for *spotted dog*.

spotted dog /ˌspɒtɪd 'dɒg/ (food and drink) A colloquial name for a steamed or boiled pudding in the shape of a roll. The pudding contains fruit such as raisins or sultanas, some of which can be seen on the outside of the roll, and give it a 'spotty' appearance. [the roll is thought to look like the body of a Dalmatian, also nicknamed 'spotted dog' from the black or brown spots on its white coat]

Spring Bank Holiday /ˌsprɪŋ bæŋk 'hɒlədeɪ/ (daily life) The *bank holiday* that falls on the last Monday in May.

spring double /ˌsprɪŋ 'dʌbl/ (sport and leisure) A bet placed simultaneously on the results of two annual horse races: the Lincoln Handicap, run at Doncaster, South Yorkshire (formerly run at Lincoln) and the *Grand National*. Compare *autumn double*.

Sprinter /'sprɪntə(r)/ (transport) A new type of fast diesel train introduced by *BR* in the mid-1980s for travel on provincial routes. Compare *Pacer*.

Spurs /spɜːz/ (sport and leisure) The nickname of the *football club Tottenham Hotspur*.

Square Mile /ˌskweə 'maɪl/ (London) A term for the *City (of London)*, whose area is approximately one square mile.

squash (rackets) /'skwɒʃ (ˌrækɪts)/ (sport and leisure) A game for two or, more rarely, four players in an enclosed court. It is played with a small rubber ball and rackets, like tennis rackets but with a smaller head and a longer, lighter handle. The ball is hit off any wall, but must strike the front wall above a line painted above the floor in order to count. Compare *rackets*, from which it evolved (probably at *Harrow School*) in the 19th century. [so named as the ball is soft and 'squashy' (easily pressed)]

SRN /ˌes ɑː 'en/ **(state registered nurse)** (medicine) A nurse

squash (rackets)

having the qualification formerly equivalent to that of an
RGN.

St Andrews /snt ˈændruːz/ (geography) An ancient town and
seaside resort in Fife, *Scotland*, where Scotland's oldest
university (founded in 1411) is situated. Also at St Andrews
is the famous *Royal and Ancient* golf *club*. [named after a holy
shrine there to St Andrew; see *St Andrew's cross*]

St Andrew's cross /snt ˌændruːz ˈkrɒs/ (tradition) The national
flag of *Scotland*, consisting of two diagonal white stripes
crossing on a blue background. The flag forms part of the
Union Jack, together with *St George's cross* and *St Patrick's
cross*. St Andrew is the patron saint of Scotland. See also *St
Andrew's Day*.

St Andrew's Day /snt ˈændruːz deɪ/ (tradition) 30 November,
the *church* festival of St Andrew, regarded as *Scotland*'s
national day (although not an official *bank holiday*). On this
day some Scotsmen wear a *thistle* in their buttonhole. See also
St Andrew's cross.

St Bartholomew's Hospital /snt bɑːˌθɒləmjuːz ˈhɒspɪtl/
(medicine) An important *teaching hospital* in *London*, and the
oldest hospital in *England*. [named after a church there
dedicated to St Bartholomew]

St Clement Danes /snt ˌklemənt ˈdeɪnz/ (London) A famous
London church designed by Sir Christopher Wren and built in

the 17th century on the site of a much older church believed to date back to a 9th-century Danish settlement. Although seriously damaged in the Second World War, the church, which is the central church of the *RAF*, was fully restored in the 1950s. The bells of the church play the melody of the song sung in the children's game *oranges and lemons*. (The song begins with the words 'Oranges and lemons, Say the bells of St Clement's'.)

St David's Day /snt ˈdeɪvɪdz deɪ/ (tradition) 1 March, the *church* festival of St David, a 6th-century monk and bishop, the patron saint of *Wales*. The day is regarded as the national holiday of Wales, although it is not an official *bank holiday*. On this day, however, many Welshmen wear either a *daffodil* or a *leek* pinned to their jackets, as both plants are traditionally regarded as national emblems of Wales.

St George's Chapel, (Windsor) /snt ˌdʒɔːdʒɪz ˈtʃæpl (snt ˌdʒɔːdʒɪz ˌtʃæpl ˈwɪnsə(r))/ (history) The main *chapel*[2] of *Windsor Castle*, built in the 15th and 16th centuries in the *Perpendicular* (*style*). The *Garter ceremony* is held in the Chapel, which also contains the tombs of many sovereigns and famous men and women. Together with the Castle, it is one of *Britain*'s most popular tourist attractions, and with its royal connections and dedication to St George (see *St George's cross*) is regarded as uniquely symbolic of *England*. Officially it is a *chapel royal*.

St George's cross /snt ˌdʒɔːdʒɪz ˈkrɒs/ (tradition) The national flag of *England*, consisting of a red cross on a white background. The flag is part of the *Union Jack*, together with *St Andrew's cross* and *St Patrick's cross*. St George is the patron saint of England. See also *St George's Day*.

St George's Day /snt ˈdʒɔːdʒɪz deɪ/ (tradition) 23 April, the *church* festival of St George, regarded as *England*'s national day (although not an official *bank holiday*). On this day some patriotic Englishmen wear a *rose* pinned to their jackets. See also *St George's cross*.

St James's Palace /snt ˌdʒeɪmzɪz ˈpælɪs/ (London) A famous palace in *Pall Mall, London*, built in 1532 by King *Henry VIII* on the site of a former leper hospital dedicted to St James, and the residence of British sovereigns from 1697 to 1837. Foreign ambassadors are still 'accredited to the Court of St James'.

St James's Park /snt ˌdʒeɪmzɪz ˈpɑːk/ (London) The oldest of London's *royal parks*, originally laid out as pleasure grounds for King Charles II on the site of a deer park adjoining *St*

James's Palace. Many regard it as *London*'s most attractive park, with its lake (containing an island with a bird sanctuary), walks, lawns and flowerbeds.

St John Ambulance (Brigade) /snt ˌdʒɒn ˈæmbjʊləns (brɪˌɡeɪd)/ (medicine) A voluntary organization providing first aid and nursing services in hospitals and residential homes, and also, when required, at public and sporting events and in theatres and concert halls. [name of religious nursing order, the Knights Hospitallers of St John of Jerusalem]

St John's, Smith Square /snt ˌdʒɒnz ˌsmɪθ ˈskweə(r)/ (London) A *church* in *Smith Square, London,* whose interior was destroyed in the Second World War, and which was restored in the 1960s to be an arts centre for concerts, exhibitions and lectures.

St Martin-in-the-Fields /snt ˌmɑːtɪn ɪn ðə ˈfiːldz/ (London) A famous *church* in *Trafalgar Square, London,* built in a neo-classical style in the early 18th century. The catacombs under the church were used as a bomb shelter in the Second World War, and are now used as a shelter for the homeless. The main church itself is frequently used for musical performances. See *Academy of St Martin-in-the-Fields.* [original church on this site stood on open land]

St Mary-le-Bow /snt ˌmeərɪ lə ˈbəʊ/ (London) A well-known *church* in the *City (of London),* famous for its *Bow Bells.* See also *cockney*[2]. [church was built over 11th-century crypt, thus was constructed on arches (bows) of stone]

St Mirren /snt ˈmɪrən/ (sport and leisure) A Scottish *football club* founded in 1876 with a stadium in Paisley, southwest *Scotland.* [named after nearby St Mirren Park]

St Pancras /snt ˈpæŋkrəs/ (transport) 1 A main line railway station and terminus in north central *London,* not far from *King's Cross*[1], from which trains run to the *Midlands* and north of *England.* The station is famous for its *Victorian Gothic* architecture. 2 An *Underground* station here (called King's Cross St Pancras).

St Patrick's cross /snt ˌpætrɪks ˈkrɒs/ (tradition) The national flag of *Northern Ireland* (and earlier, the national flag of *Ireland* before the establishment of the Irish Republic). It consists of two diagonal red stripes crossing on a white background, and is part of the *Union Jack,* together with *St Andrew's cross* and *St George's cross.* St Patrick is the patron saint of Ireland. See *Paddy, St Patrick's Day.*

St Patrick's Day /snt ˈpætrɪks deɪ/ (tradition) 17 March, the *church* festival of St Patrick, regarded as a national day in *Northern Ireland* and an official *bank holiday* there.

St Paul's (Cathedral) /snt 'pɔːlz (snt ˌpɔːlz kə'θiːdrəl)/ (London) One of *London*'s most famous landmarks, regarded as the 'parish *church* of the British *Commonwealth[1]*'. The present cathedral, built in the latter part of the 17th century and early part of the 18th, is the third on the site, the previous one having been destroyed by the *Great Fire of London*. The cathedral contains a number of famous tombs and memorials, including that of its architect, Sir Christopher Wren (1632–1723). One of its most popular features is the *Whispering Gallery*.

St Paul's Girls' School /snt ˌpɔːlz 'gɜːlz skuːl/ (education) A well-known *London public school[1]* for girls, opened in 1904, but tracing its origin back to 1509 and the founding of *St Paul's (School)* for boys. It currently has 620 students, all *day girls*. The headmistress has the special title of 'High Mistress'.

St Paul's (School) /snt 'pɔːlz (snt ˌpɔːlz 'skuːl)/ (education) A well-known *public school[1]* for boys in *London*, founded in 1509 by the *dean[3]* of *St Paul's (Cathedral)*, and having about 750 students. Its headmaster has the special title of 'High Master'.

St Swithin's Day /snt 'swɪðɪnz ˌdeɪ/ (daily life) 15 July, a day on which tradition says that, if it rains, it will rain for the next 40 days. [named after St Swithin, 9th-century bishop of Winchester, who was said to perform miracles, including the sending of prolonged rain in the summer when it was most needed]

St Thomas's Hospital /snt ˌtɒməsɪz 'hɒspɪtl/ (medicine) A *London teaching hospital*, founded in 1552.

St Trinian's /snt 'trɪnɪənz/ (arts) The name of a fictitious girls' school invented in 1941 by the cartoonist Ronald Searle (born 1920). In his cartoons, and in the subsequent books and films that evolved, the girls of St Trinian's school became comically famous for their scruffy uniforms, riotous behaviour and generally rebellious attitude to life and authority. [random name chosen to suggest a typical *private school* for girls; Searle's daughters had actually attended St Trinnean's school in *Edinburgh*]

stag night /'stæg naɪt/ (life and society) A dinner or drinks party for men only held by a bridegroom the night before his wedding. Compare *hen night*. [from 'stag' as a male animal]

stamp duty /'stæmp ˌdjuːtɪ/ (finance) A tax on the sale of property, especially a private house. If the value of the property is at least £30,000, duty is currently charged at a rate of 1%, that is, £1 for every further £100 (or fraction of £100).

Standard /'stændəd/ see *Evening Standard* (media)

standard class /ˌstændəd 'klɑːs/ (transport) The official term used from 1987 for the majority of seats on a railway train, as distinct from *first class[1]*.

standing order /ˌstændɪŋ 'ɔːdə(r)/ (finance) An order from a customer to his bank requesting that regular payments should be made from his account, usually monthly or annually, to the account of a named individual or organization. The amount of the payment is decided by the customer. It is a convenient way to pay regular subscriptions. Compare *direct debit*.

Stanley Gibbons /ˌstænlɪ 'ɡɪbənz/ (commerce) A well-known *London* firm of stamp dealers, who hold important philatelic auctions and publish annually a range of authoritative stamp catalogues. [firm founded by Stanley Gibbons in 1856]

Stansted (Airport) /'stænstɪd (ˌstænstɪd 'eəpɔːt)/ (transport) An international airport near Stansted, Essex. It is *Britain*'s third largest airport (after *Heathrow* and *Gatwick*), and the government intends to make it *London*'s third airport.

starting price /'stɑːtɪŋ praɪs/ (sport and leisure) The odds on a horse in a race as quoted by *bookmakers* as the horse is about to start the race.

State Opening of Parliament /ˌsteɪt ˌəʊpənɪŋ əv 'pɑːləmənt/, **the** (government) The official opening of a new session of *Parliament*, usually at the end of October or beginning of November, or after a *general election*. The sovereign travels in procession to the *Houses of Parliament* for the occasion, and there makes the *Speech from the Throne*.

state school /'steɪt skuːl/ (education) A school, usually a *primary school* or a *secondary school*, that is run by the state through a *LEA*, and so is non-fee-paying, as distinct from an *independent school*. About 93% of British schools are state schools.

stately home /ˌsteɪtlɪ 'həʊm/ (life and society) A term for a *country house*, especially one open to the public. [term comes from opening lines of a poem by Felicia Hemans (1793–1835): 'The stately homes of *England*, How beautiful they stand!']

statutory sick pay /ˌstætʃʊtrɪ 'sɪk peɪ/ **(SSP)** (finance) The payment that an employer is legally obliged to make to an employee when the latter is off work sick. There are two weekly rates of payment, depending on the employee's earnings. The payment is made for up to 28 weeks, after which it is replaced by *invalidity benefit*. Employees unable to get SSP for any reason can claim *sickness benefit* instead.

steak and kidney pie /ˌsteɪk ən ˌkɪdnɪ 'paɪ/ (food and drink) A savoury pie, usually eaten hot, made of meat and kidney in gravy baked in pastry.

steak and kidney pudding /ˌsteɪk ən ˌkɪdnɪ 'pʊdɪŋ/ (food and drink) A savoury dish eaten hot, made of meat and kidney in gravy cooked in a suet case.

Stena Sealink /ˌstenə(r) 'siː lɪŋk/ (transport) The shipping company that operates a passenger service between ports in *England* and continental Europe. The main routes are between Dover and Calais, Newhaven and Dieppe, and Harwich and the Hook of Holland. [in full, Sealink Stena Line]

Stewards' Cup /ˌstjuːədz 'kʌp/, **the** (sport and leisure) **1** An annual horse race run at *Goodwood*, and also the prize awarded to its winner. **2** An annual race for rowing fours at *Henley Regatta*, and also the prize awarded to the winners.

stiff upper lip /ˌstɪf ʌpə 'lɪp/ (tradition) The characteristic ability of the English to stay calm and unemotional in a crisis, especially when in pain or distress. [alluding to the concealing of emotion by compressing the lips]

stile /staɪl/ (geography) A step or steps over a wall or fence, usually leading from one field into another on a public *right of way*. The stile enables people to pass from one field to another but not animals such as cows or sheep.

Stilton (cheese) /'stɪltən (ˌstɪltən 'tʃiːz)/ (food and drink) A type of rich blue-veined cheese with a strong flavour. [originally sold, but not made, in the village of Stilton, Cambridgeshire]

Stock Exchange /'stɒk ɪksˌtʃeɪndʒ/, **the** (finance) The *London* financial centre, founded in 1802, where stocks and shares are bought and sold.

stockbroker /'stɒkˌbrəʊkə(r)/ (finance) A member of the *Stock Exchange* who buys and sells shares. The title was officially abolished in 1986, when the Stock Exchange was reorganized, so that members are now more usually known as *market-makers*.

stockbroker belt /'stɒkbrəʊkə belt/, **the** (geography) A colloquial name for the region south and southwest of *London*, especially the county of Surrey, where many rich *stockbrokers* and other professional people live.

stocking filler /'stɒkɪŋ ˌfɪlə(r)/ (tradition) A small, attractive present designed to be given as an 'extra' at *Christmas*, whether actually put in a 'stocking' (see *Christmas Eve*) or not.

Stoke Mandeville /ˌstəʊk 'mændəvɪl/ (medicine) A village near Aylesbury, Buckinghamshire, well known for its hospital in which there is a department that specializes in the treatment of spinal diseases and injuries (officially the National Spinal Injuries Unit).

Stone of Scone /ˌstəʊn əv 'sku:n/, **the** (tradition) The ancient stone coronation seat of the kings of *Scotland*, at present lying below the Coronation chair in *Westminster Abbey*, *London* to where it was taken from Scone, east Scotland, by King Edward I in 1296. The Stone has been removed more than once by Scottish Nationalists trying to return it to Scotland. See *SNP*.

Stonehenge /ˌstəʊn 'hendʒ/ (tradition) A prehistoric (megalithic) complex on *Salisbury Plain*, Wiltshire, regarded as one of the most important monuments of its kind in Europe, and very popular with visitors. The great circle of standing stones (many now fallen) is believed to have had some religious or astronomical purpose. The complex has become well known in recent years for the annual assembly there of *Druids*[2] at sunrise on *Midsummer Day* (since on this day the sun rises above a certain stone), and also for the summer camp nearby of *hippies*[2]. [the name is said to mean 'stone hanger', referring to the horizontal stone 'hanging' or lying across two vertical stones]

Stoppard, Tom /'stɒpɑ:d, 'tɒm/ (people) Tom Stoppard (born 1937) is a playwright who has gained a reputation for the original subjects of his plays and for his clever handling of the dialogues. Many of his plays are in effect a philosophical debate of some kind. For example, his first success, 'Rosencrantz and Guildenstern Are Dead' (1967), argued that the two main characters, who are actually minor parts in *Shakespeare*'s 'Hamlet', could not exist outside their original play.

Stormont /'stɔ:mɒnt/ (government) The large house on the outskirts of *Belfast*, Northern Ireland, where the *Northern Ireland* parliament was held from 1921 to 1972, when *direct rule* was introduced. The parliament buildings now form the administrative centre of Northern Ireland.

stout /staʊt/ (food and drink) A strong dark beer brewed with roasted malt.

Strand /strænd/, **the** (London) One of the main streets of central *London*, linking the *West End* with the *City (of London)* and containing several theatres and high-class shops and hotels. [from the 'strand' or bank of the river *Thames*, where it formerly ran as a riverside walk]

Strangers' Gallery /'streɪndʒəz ˌgælərɪ/, **the** (government) The galleries in the *House of Commons* and *House of Lords* to which members of the public are admitted, usually by invitation. ['stranger' in the sense of 'non-member']

strap-hanger /'stræp ˌhæŋə(r)/ (daily life) A colloquial term for a passenger in a public transport vehicle, especially an *Underground* train, who has to travel standing, holding on to an overhead strap.

Stratford-(up)on-Avon /ˌstrætfəd (əp)ɒn 'eɪvn/ (geography) A town in Warwickshire, famous as the birthplace of William *Shakespeare* (1564–1616) and for this reason alone a popular tourist centre. Buildings connected with Shakespeare in the town include the house where he was born, in Henley Street, Holy Trinity Church, where he was buried, *Anne Hathaway's Cottage*, and the *Royal Shakespeare Theatre*.

strathspey /ˌstræθ'speɪ/ (sport and leisure) A slow Scottish dance. [originating in Strathspey, the valley of the river Spey]

strawberries and cream /ˌstrɔːbrɪz ən 'kriːm/ (food and drink) A traditional English summer dish, often eaten during some special outdoor occasion or event, for example, at *Wimbledon*.

streaming /'striːmɪŋ/ (education) The division of schoolchildren into groups either according to ability or by subject.

Street /striːt/, **the** (media) A colloquial nickname for the television programme series *Coronation Street*.

strike pay /'straɪk peɪ/ (work) Money paid to strikers from the funds of their trade union.

striker /'straɪkə(r)/ (sport and leisure) An attacking player in *football*, especially one who stays near the opponents' goal in the hope of scoring.

Sturmer /'stɜːmə(r)/ (food and drink) A variety of eating apple with yellow-green skin and sweet, juicy flesh. [originating from the village of Sturmer, Essex]

suburbia /sə'bɜːbɪə/ (life and society) A suburban or outer residential district of a town or *city*, and thought of with regard to its residents and their social standing (sometimes said to be typically *middle class* and conservative).

suet pudding /ˌsuːɪt ˈpʊdɪŋ/ (food and drink) A name used for different kinds of boiled or steamed pudding made with suet, whether savoury (such as a *steak and kidney pudding*) or sweet (such as *spotted dog*).

Suffolk (sheep) /ˈsʌfək (ˌsʌfək ˈʃiːp)/ (animal world) A breed of black-faced sheep. [originally bred in Suffolk]

Suffolk punch /ˌsʌfək ˈpʌntʃ/ (animal world) A breed of draught horse with powerful body, relatively short legs and chestnut-coloured coat. [originally bred in Suffolk: 'punch' is the dialect word for a thick-set person or animal]

suffragan bishop /ˌsʌfrəgən ˈbɪʃəp/ (religion) A bishop who assists a senior bishop or an archbishop by being responsible for a certain district within his superior's area.

Sugar, Alan /ˈʃʊgə(r), ˈælən/ (people) Alan Sugar (born 1947) is one of *Britain*'s most successful businessmen. He started modestly, selling car aerials from a van, and shrewdly built up his electrical and electronics business. His company, Amstrad, started selling low-priced radio and television products, and then introduced a low-priced word processor and home computer, bringing these products into the homes of many people who previously could not afford them. In recent years he has also become well known for his involvement with *Tottenham Hotspur football club*, of which he became chairman in 1992.

Sullom Voe /ˌsʌləm ˈvəʊ/ (geography) *Britain*'s largest *North Sea oil* terminal and oil exporting port, in the *Shetlands*, *Scotland*. [named after inlet (*voe*) there]

Summer Bank Holiday /ˌsʌmər ˌbaeŋk ˈhɒlədeɪ/ (daily life) The *bank holiday* that falls on the last Monday in August. It is also sometimes known as the August Bank Holiday.

summer pudding /ˌsʌmə ˈpʊdɪŋ/ (food and drink) A sweet dish made from fruit, usually strawberries or raspberries, and red and black currants (sometimes with apples or blackberries) and bread. The fruit is boiled and then put in a bowl lined with bread. All the juice soaks into the bread, and the pudding is served chilled, usually with cream.

summer school /ˈsʌmə skuːl/ (education) A school or academic course such as a language course held in the summer months, often on the premises of a school or university whose regular students are on holiday. Many students of the *Open University* go on summer schools as part of their courses.

summer time /ˈsʌmə taɪm/ (daily life) A colloquial term for *BST*.

summons /ˈsʌmənz/ (law) An official order, often served by a *bailiff*, to a person to attend a *court*[3] of law, either to answer a charge or to give evidence.

Sun /sʌn/, **The** (media) A daily *popular paper* noted for its exposures of scandals and its popular features on celebrities such as pop stars and television personalities. It has many photographs, one of which is of its regular *page three* model. It was first published in 1964 and currently has the highest circulation of any daily newspaper in *Britain*, about 3.6 million (1972 – 2.6 million).

Sunday /ˈsʌndɪ/ (life and society) A distinctive day of the week in *Britain*, when most people are at home. Many people spend the whole day at home, although visits to friends and relatives are also popular, as are outings to a place of interest or leisure. Most people sleep later on Sunday than on any other day. Some people go to a religious service. Most shops and stores are closed for the day (except in *Scotland*, where legal regulations are different). However, many newsagents open in the morning to sell newspapers and magazines, and many *corner shops* are open all day. *Licensing hours* are shorter with many *pubs* opening at a later time, public transport services are less frequent, and entertainment facilities are restricted. Cinemas open, although later than on other days of the week, but it is still rare for theatres to be open on Sunday. Post offices (see *Post Office*) and banks are closed although letters are collected from main post offices and some post boxes. Sport is now more commonly played on Sunday than previously. The British Sunday still retains much of its 19th-century atmosphere of solemnity and respectability, and many young people find Sunday boring. There is, however, a general slow move towards a more lively and varied day, and strong support for the opening of some kinds of shop that at present remain closed. See also *Sunday roast*.

Sunday Express /ˌsʌndɪ ɪkˈspres/, **the** (media) A *Sunday popular paper* owned by the same company as the *Daily Express*. It is politically right of centre. It was first published in 1918 and has a current circulation of about 1.7 million (1972 – 4 million). It has a colour supplement, 'Sunday Express Magazine'.

Sunday Mirror /ˌsʌndɪ ˈmɪrə(r)/, **the** (media) A *Sunday popular paper* owned by the same company as the *Daily Mirror*. It is politically left of centre. It was first published in 1963 and has a current circulation of about 2.7 million (1972 – 4.4 million).

It has a colour supplement, 'Sunday Mirror Magazine'.

Sunday roast/joint /ˌsʌndɪ ˈrəʊst/ˈdʒɔɪnt/, **the** (life and society) The main ingredient of a traditional English family lunch on *Sunday*—hot roast beef (or other meat) with vegetables and gravy. The tradition of having meat on Sunday is a survival of a religious custom, when Sunday was a feastday and followed the austerity of Friday, when only fish was eaten (as it still is by devout Roman Catholics).

Sunday school /ˈsʌndɪ skuːl/ (religion) Religious instruction for children on *Sunday*s which is usually organized by the priest in a particular *church* or *chapel*[3]. Instruction is voluntary and is usually given in the church or chapel building itself, either by the priest or pastor or by a regular member of the congregation. Sunday schools are often held at the same time as the main Sunday morning service, so that parents can attend the service while their children attend the instruction.

Sunday Sport /ˌsʌndɪ ˈspɔːt/, **the** (media) A *Sunday popular paper* owned by the same company as the *Daily Sport*. It caters mainly for a young male readership and has many photographs of the *page three* type as well as popular articles on sport. It was first published in 1986 and has a current circulation of about 368,000.

Sunday Telegraph /ˌsʌndɪ ˈtelɪɡrɑːf/, **the** (media) A *Sunday quality paper* noted for its rather old-fashioned views and its detailed news reports and features. It is politically right of centre, and is owned by the same company as the *Daily Telegraph*. It is currently modernizing its image with the aim of attracting younger readers. It was first published in 1961 and has a circulation of about 561,000 (1972 – 753,000).

Sunday Times /ˈsʌndɪ ˈtaɪmz/, **the** (media) A *Sunday quality paper* owned by the same company as The *Times*. It is larger than any other Sunday paper, with several sections, some in magazine format, and a colour supplement, 'The Magazine'. It is politically right of centre, and has a reputation for its intelligent and authoritative features and its exposure of scandals. It first appeared in 1822 and now has a circulation of about 1.2 million (1972 – 1.4 million).

Sunrise Radio /ˈsʌnraɪz ˌreɪdɪəʊ/ (media) An *ILR* station broadcasting to Asian audiences across *London*. It officially opened in 1989 but operated illegally as a 'pirate' station before this. Its two main languages are Hindustani and English.

SuperSaver /ˈsuːpəˌseɪvə(r)/ (transport) A special return ticket sold at a reduced rate by *BR* to people travelling over 50 miles outside peak times (but not on Fridays or certain Saturdays in summer). Compare *Saver*.

supplementary benefit /ˌsʌplɪˌmentrɪ ˈbenɪfɪt/ (finance) The name used until 1988 for *income support*.

supply teacher /səˈplaɪ ˌtiːtʃə(r)/ (education) A teacher appointed temporarily by an *LEA* in place of another, regular teacher who is absent through illness or for some other reason.

Supreme Court (of Judicature) /suːˌpriːm ˈkɔːt (suːˌpriːm ˌkɔːt əv ˈdʒuːdɪkətʃə(r))/, **the** (law) The highest *court*[3] of law in *England* and *Wales*, formed in 1873 by the amalgamation of several courts[3] into two divisions, the Court of Appeal and the *High Court of Justice* (which consists of the *Chancery Division*, the *Queen's Bench Division* and the Family Division). The central office of the Supreme Court of Judicature (officially the Royal Courts of Justice, but popularly known as the Law Courts) is in the *Strand, London*.

surgery /ˈsɜːdʒərɪ/ (1 medicine, 2 politics) 1 The office in which a *GP* receives his patients, either in the morning or, for people at work during the day, in the early evening. 2 A date and time set aside by an *MP* in his *constituency* to receive local people who wish to consult him on any matter.

Sussex (hen) /ˈsʌsɪks (ˌsʌsɪks ˈhen)/ (animal world) A heavy breed of domestic fowl used mainly for its meat, but also for its eggs. There are several varieties, all originally bred in Sussex, among them Light Sussex, Red Sussex, Brown Sussex and Speckled Sussex (all named for the colour of its feathers).

Swan (Theatre) /ˌswɒn ˈθɪətə(r)/, **the** (arts) A theatre opened in *Stratford-(up)on-Avon* in 1986 as a new auditorium for the *Royal Shakespeare Company*. It was designed to resemble a playhouse of *Shakespeare*'s day, with a rehearsal room on an upper floor as large as the theatre itself. [named in honour of Shakespeare, the 'Swan of Avon']

swan-upping /ˌswɒn ˈʌpɪŋ/ (tradition) An annual ceremony held on the river *Thames*, near Windsor, Berkshire, when swans are driven upstream and marked (with small cuts on their beaks) to show who owns them. Those belonging to the *Crown*[1] (ie, the royal Swans) are marked with five cuts; those belonging to two *livery companies* (the Dyers' and the Vintners' Companies) are marked with two cuts.

sweepstake /ˈswiːpsteɪk/ (sport and leisure) 1 A term loosely

used for any horse race with a money prize for the winner.
2 A type of horse race in which the winner (and sometimes near-winner) receives a money prize from the combined entrance fees, forfeit payments (eg, for horses withdrawn from the race), etc. The first such race was held at Doncaster, South Yorkshire, in 1714. **3** A method of gambling on a horse race, in which the prize is the combined stakes (bets) of all who have taken part in the sweepstake, each person usually buying a ticket with the name of an individual horse. The winner is the person who has drawn the name of the winning horse.

Swiftair /'swifteə(r)/ (commerce) The express airmail service of the *Royal Mail* available on payment of a fee additional to the normal airmail postage.

Swiss roll /ˌswɪs 'rəʊl/ (food and drink) A thin sponge cake spread with jam, cream or some other filling, and then rolled up while still hot. [said to be of Swiss origin, but perhaps simply an alteration of 'sweet roll']

Switch /swɪtʃ/ (finance) A type of *debit card* issued by some banks. [from the 'switch' (transfer) of money from the cardholder's account, and also suggesting the 'swipe' (sweeping stroke) of the card through the electronic terminal]

sword dance /'sɔːd dɑːns/ (sport and leisure) A traditional

sword dance

Scottish dance in which a dancer performs fast dance steps over two crossed swords on the ground. It is usually performed by one dancer but occasionally two dancers dance together over the same pair of swords.

Synod /ˈsɪnəd/, **the** (religion) The *General Synod* of the *Church of England*.

T and G /ˌtiː ən ˈdʒiː/ see **TGWU** (work)

Tablet /ˈtæblɪt/, **The** (media) A weekly Roman Catholic magazine with articles of interest to both clergy and laity. It was first published in 1840 and has a current circulation of about 17,000. [probably named from 'tablet' in former sense of 'notebook']

tabloid /ˈtæblɔɪd/ (media) A term for a newspaper with small pages, as distinct from a broadsheet, with large pages. As most *popular papers* are of this size, the term 'tabloid' often applies to them, and in particular to the papers that are generally regarded as having the greatest *working class* appeal; the *Daily Mirror*, the *Daily Star*, and The *Sun*.

Taffy /ˈtæfɪ/ (tradition) A nickname for a Welshman, deriving from the supposed Welsh pronunciation of Dafydd, a common Welsh forename. (See *St David's Day*.) [Dafydd is the Welsh form of the English name, David]

Take a Break /ˌteɪk ə ˈbreɪk/ (media) A popular weekly magazine for women, with 'human interest' stories and features, competitions, pages of letters from readers, etc. It was founded in 1990 and has a current circulation of about 1.3 million.

takeaway /ˈteɪkəweɪ/ (food and drink) A restaurant or kitchen counter that provides ready-cooked meals for people to take away with them. Many takeaways specialize in Chinese dishes, and some of them have no dining-room but simply sell meals from a counter. The customer selects the dishes from a menu, and they are usually available in a few minutes while he either waits, or goes away and returns at a particular time.

take-home pay /ˈteɪk ˌhəʊm peɪ/ (finance) An employee's net pay after the deduction from his gross pay of *income tax* (see *PAYE*, *National Insurance*) and any other contributions. [reference to the pay that many workers take home weekly in a pay packet]

tam-o'-shanter /ˌtæm ə 'ʃæntə(r)/ (clothing) A Scottish flat wool cap without a brim but with a bobble on top, traditionally worn pulled down at one side. [named after Tam o'Shanter, the hero of Burns' (see *Burns' Night*) poem of that name, published in 1790]

Tannoy /'tænɔɪ/ (daily life) The trade name of a loudspeaker amplification and relay system. The name is often popularly used for any such system.

tartan /'tɑːtn/ (**1, 3** style **2** clothing) **1** The special checked design, of contrasting colours, used in Highland dress in *Scotland*. By long tradition, each Scottish *clan* has its own distinctive tartan. **2** Highland dress itself. **3** A similar design reproduced on Scottish souvenirs or other items such as postcards, badges and bookmarks.

Task Force /'tɑːsk fɔːs/ (government) One of a number of local organizations set up by the government from 1986 to improve conditions in *inner cities* by combining the efforts of *local authorities*, private businesses and local communities. A total of 16 Task Forces are currently in operation, and more are planned.

Tate (Gallery) /teɪt ('gælərɪ)/, **the** (arts) A well-known art gallery in *London*, opened in 1897 with the financial support of Sir Henry Tate, who gave many of his paintings. The Tate has a unique collection of British paintings from the 16th century, with many by Turner and Blake, as well as modern foreign paintings and sculptures. In 1988 the Tate opened a second gallery in Liverpool, and in 1993 another in St Ives, *Cornwall*. In 1992 the trustees of the Tate decided to split the main collection in two, keeping the present building for British art and establishing a gallery of modern art elsewhere in London.

Tattenham Corner /ˌtætnəm 'kɔːnə(r)/ (sport and leisure) A notorious sharp bend before the final straight on the race course at *Epsom*, regarded as a major obstacle in the *Derby*. [named after historic house there, Tottenham Lodge]

Tattersall's /'tætəslz/ (commerce) A famous firm of racehorse auctioneers, founded in 1766 by Richard Tattersall as a horse market in *London*, but today holding its annual auctions at Newmarket, Suffolk.

tax disc

tax disc /'tæks dɪsk/ (transport) A small, round, paper
document showing that a motor vehicle has been officially
licensed by the Department of Transport (see *department*)
totravel on the road. The disc is usually stuck to the bottom
left-hand corner of the windscreen inside the vehicle. Drivers
buy their tax discs (the fee varying with the type of vehicle) at
either a post office or a local office (known as a Local Vehicle
Licensing Office) of the *DVLC*.

Taxpayer's Charter /ˌtækspeiəz 'tʃɑːtə(r)/, **the**
(government) One of the first of the separate charters issued
after the publication of the *Citizen's Charter* in 1991. It sets out
the standards of service that people should expect from the
Inland Revenue and *Customs and Excise*.

tea /tiː/ (food and drink) 1 The traditional popular British
drink, usually taken with milk and sometimes sugar. It is
drunk at all hours of the day. It is especially popular on
awakening (when still in bed), at breakfast, during a working

morning (either for *elevenses* or as a 'tea break'), after *lunch* (or *dinner*), for tea[2] and during the evening. Coffee is now more popular for breakfast and in the middle of the morning. See also *cuppa*. **2** A light, usually uncooked meal, taken between four and five o'clock, and traditionally consisting of bread and butter and jam (or some other spread), cakes or biscuits, and tea[1] to drink. Instead of plain bread, various kinds of pastries or cakes are often preferred, such as *scones*, *crumpets*, *muffins* and *teacakes*, the last three eaten toasted (see also *toast*). In towns, tea is served in hotels and *tea-shops* as well as in restaurants and snack bars. **3** A light supper (sometimes called *high tea*), usually with a single cooked dish and with tea[1] to drink.

teacake /'ti:keɪk/ (food and drink) A light, flat, usually slightly sweet kind of bun, sliced horizontally into two halves and eaten toasted, with butter, for *tea*[2].

teaching hospital /'ti:tʃɪŋ ˌhɒspɪtl/ (medicine) A hospital in which medical students train to become doctors and nurses.

tea-shop /'ti:ʃɒp/ (daily life) A type of restaurant serving *tea*[2] and occasionally light evening meals. Such shops, which also usually serve coffee in the morning, are often old or 'quaint' in character with corresponding furnishings and furniture that are typical of the age of the building. See also *ye olde tea shoppe*.

tech /tek/ (education) A colloquial abbreviation for a *technical college*.

technical school /'teknɪkl sku:l/ (education) A state *secondary school* that provides an integrated academic and technical course. Such schools are attended by under 1% of all students of secondary school age.

Telecom Tower /ˌtelɪkɒm 'taʊə(r)/, **the** (London) The name of a tall tower 620 feet (176 metres) high in *London*. It was built by the *Post Office* in 1965 to transmit and receive radio, television and telephone communications in and out of London without interference from other tall London buildings. The Tower has two viewing galleries and a revolving restaurant at the top, usually open to the public.

Telegraph /'telɪɡrɑ:f/, **the** (media) The short name of the *Daily Telegraph* newspaper.

telemessage /'telɪˌmesɪdʒ/ (commerce) A form of telegram introduced by the *Post Office* in 1982 to replace conventional telegrams. It enables a message to be sent anywhere in *Britain* by telephone or telex so that it can be delivered the following day (although not on a *Sunday*). Telemessages can also be sent to the USA (and international telegrams to most countries abroad).

Teletext /'telɪtekst/ (media) The teletext service of *ITV* and *Channel 4*. Compare *Ceefax*.

Temple /'templ/, **the** (1 London 2 transport) 1 The historic buildings in the *City (of London)* that house two *Inns of Court*—the *Inner Temple* and the *Middle Temple*. [built on site of buildings owned by the Knights Templars in the 13th century] 2 An Underground railway station just west of there. See *London Underground*.

Temple Bar /ˌtempl 'bɑː(r)/ (London) The historic western entrance to the *City (of London)*, where a gate built after the *Great Fire of London* (1666) stood until 1878, and where now a memorial (the Temple Bar Memorial) stands to mark the site. When the sovereign visits the City he or she is met at this point by the *Lord Mayor*. [understood as '*Temple* Gate']

Temple Church /ˌtempl 'tʃɜːtʃ/, **the** (London) An ancient *church* in the *City (of London)* near the *Temple*, built in the 12th century for the Knights Templars.

10 pence (piece) /ˌten 'pens (ˌten pens 'piːs)/ (finance) A coin made from a mixture of copper and nickel that looks like silver. It is worth one-tenth of the value of a *pound (sterling)* and replaces the old *two-shilling piece* which was similar in appearance and had the same value. See p 472.

tenner /'tenə(r)/ (daily life) A colloquial term for a £10 note. Compare *fiver*.

term /tɜːm/ (1 education 2 law) 1 A division of the academic year in a school, *college*[1,2] or other educational establishment. Most schools and colleges have three terms in a year, with school terms extending from September to December (autumn term or *Christmas* term), January to March (winter term or *Easter* term) and April to July (summer term). College (university) terms are shorter and often have religious names (*Michaelmas*, Hilary, *Lent*, Trinity). 2 A similar division when law *courts*[3] are in session; January–March (Hilary Term), April–May (Easter Term), June–July (Trinity Term), October–December (Michaelmas Term).

terraced house /ˌterəst 'haʊs/ (style) A (usually small) house that is one of a continuous row in one block in a street. Many rows of terraced houses were originally built for workers in nearby factories or coalmines. A terraced house usually costs less than a *semi-detached* or *detached house* of similar size. ['terrace' in sense 'connected row of houses'; originally such a

terraced house

row overlooked a slope]

Territorial Army /ˌterətɔːriəl ˈɑːmɪ/, **the (TA, the)** (defence) A reserve force of about 91,000 volunteers who can be called up in time of national emergency to help the regular *Army*. The strength of the TA is gradually being reduced.

tertiary college /ˈtɜːʃəri ˌkɒlɪdʒ/ (education) A state educational *college²* that provides a range of specialized courses for students over 16 at *sixth form* or *further education* level. Compare *sixth-form college* and see also *secondary school*. ['tertiary' as the third level of education after primary and secondary]

TESSA /ˈtesə/ (finance) A *building society* investment account introduced in 1991, with all interest earned after five years free of *income tax* [short for *Tax Exempt Special Savings Account*]

test match /ˈtest mætʃ/ (sport and leisure) An international commercially sponsored series of five-day *cricket* matches played in summer between the *England* team and a visiting team from Australia, New Zealand, India, Pakistan, Sri Lanka or the West Indies. [matches are a 'test' of which is the better team]

TGWU /ˌtiː ˌdʒiː ˌdʌbljuː ˈjuː/, **the (Transport and General Workers' Union, the)** (work) A large trade union representing a wide range of industrial groups, including bus drivers. lorry drivers, engineers, dockers, clerical workers and technicians. It has a current membership of about 1.1 million.

Thames /temz/, **the** (geography) *Britain*'s best known and longest river, on which *London* stands. It rises in the Cotswolds, southwest *England*, and flows east for a distance of 210 miles (338 km) to London and out into the North Sea. Ocean-going vessels can sail up it as far as London, and smaller craft can sail up it for a further 86 miles (138 km). *Oxford* and Henley-on-Thames (see *Henley Regatta*) are also on the Thames.

Thames Barrier /ˌtemz ˈbærɪə(r)/, **the** (science and technology) A specially constructed flood barrier built across the river *Thames* in *London*. The barrier, which was officially opened in 1984, consists of ten gates which, when not in use, lie horizontally on the river bed, allowing ships to travel normally up and down the river. When the barrier is raised, the gates stand vertically so that the top of the barrier is more than 50 ft (15 m) above the river bed. The barrier was constructed to protect London from the serious flooding that has sometimes occurred in the past.

Thameslink /ˌtemzˈlɪŋk/ (transport) A railway link first operated by *BR* in 1988. The route uses a reopened tunnel in central *London* to enable passengers to travel from places north of the *Thames* to places south of the river without changing trains. This means, for example, that it is now possible to go by train direct from Luton (with its airport) to *Gatwick*.

Thatcher, Margaret /ˈθætʃə(r), ˈmɑːgrɪt/ (people) Margaret Thatcher (born 1925) first became a Conservative *MP* in 1959 and was elected leader of the *Conservative Party* in 1975. In 1979 she became Britain's first woman *Prime Minister*. She was re-elected in two further *general elections* and became Britain's longest-serving Prime Minister of the 20th century. Her government's economic policies, whose priorities were cutting public expenditure, controlling inflation, and privatizing nationalized industries became known as 'Thatcherism'. Her autocratic, sometimes abrasive, style became less popular in the late 1980s and her outspoken criticisms of the objectives of the *EC* lost her much support within the Conservative Party. She resigned as Conservative leader and Prime Minister in 1990 and was succeeded by John *Major*.

That's Life /ˌðæts 'laɪf/ (media) A popular weekly television programme that investigated scandals, campaigns for causes where ordinary members of the public have little influence, along with jokes and entertaining acts by people and animals. It was first broadcast in 1973 and ran until 1994.

Theatre Royal /ˌθɪətə 'rɔɪəl/, **the** (arts) The official name of the *Drury Lane* theatre in *London*.

Theatre Upstairs /ˌθɪətər ʌp'steəz/, **the** (arts) A *London* theatre on the *first floor* of the *Royal Court* (*Theatre*), staging mainly modern and experimental or 'avant-garde' plays.

theme park

theme park /'θiːm pɑːk/ (sport and leisure) A large park or leisure complex whose layout and exhibits are devoted to a particular theme, for example, maritime history. Such parks, which usually include restaurants, amusement facilities and special attractions for children, are mostly privately owned and became popular from the early 1980s.

third leader /ˌθɜːd 'liːdə(r)/, **the** (media) In The *Times*, the third editorial leading article which, traditionally, sometimes deals with a relatively unimportant topic, but is written in a witty style.

third reading /ˌθɜːd ˈriːdɪŋ/ (government) The final review of a *bill* in the *House of Commons* and *House of Lords*, after which, if agreement is reached between the two Houses, it is sent to the sovereign for the *royal assent*. On receiving this it becomes an *Act* (*of Parliament*) and part of the law of the land.

third-party insurance /ˌθɜːdˌpɑːtɪ ɪnˈʃɔːrəns/ (finance) A type of insurance that all drivers of motor vehicles must have. A person is insured against damage or injury caused to someone who is not party to the insurance policy. [the policy is agreed between two parties, the insured and the insurer, and anyone outside this agreement is thus a 'third party']

Thirty-Nine Articles /ˌθɜːtɪ naɪn ˈɑːtɪklz/, **the** (religion) A set of doctrines accepted by the *Church of England* in 1563. Since 1865 the clergy have been required to agree to them in general outline. [in full, the 'Articles agreed upon by the Archbishops and Bishops of both Provinces, and the whole Clergy, in the Convocation holden at London in the Year 1562, for the avoiding of Diversities of Opinions, and for the establishing of Consent touching true Religion']

This England /ˌðɪs ˈɪŋglənd/ (media) An illustrated quarterly magazine that aims to reflect current and (especially) traditional life in *England*, with many fine colour photographs. The subjects of the magazine include famous Englishmen and women, the English countryside, its historic towns and villages and its many customs and legends, especially rural ones. The magazine, which has a keen overseas readership, has a current circulation of about 180,000. [title is familiar quotation from Shakespeare's 'King Richard II': 'This blessed plot, this earth, this realm, this England']

This Is Your Life /ˌðɪs ɪz jɔː ˈlaɪf/ (media) A series of programmes shown on *ITV*. In each programme, the life story of a famous person is retold with the help of specially invited former colleagues, friends and members of his or her family. The guest himself, although the star in the programme, is told nothing in advance about it, and so it is a complete surprise. At the end of the programme he is presented with his 'biography' in a big red book. The programmes are among the most popular on British television.

thistle /ˈθɪsl/ (tradition) The national emblem of *Scotland*, apparently first used in the 15th century as a symbol of defence. Some Scotsmen wear a thistle pinned to their jackets on *St Andrew's Day*. See also *Order of the Thistle*.

Thomas, Dylan /'tɒməs, 'dɪlən/ (people) Dylan Thomas (1914–53), a Welsh-born poet, although knowing no Welsh himself, gained a popular following for his colourful personality and his fine, often passionate and highly evocative writings. One of his best-known works was the play written for radio, 'Under Milk Wood' (1954), later adapted for the stage. His legendary wild living and heavy drinking led to his early death, while on a lecture tour of the United States.

Threadneedle Street /θred'niːdl striːt/ (finance) A street in the *City (of London)* on which there are several large banks including the *Bank of England*. See *Old Lady of Threadneedle Street*.

Three As /ˌθriː ˈeɪz/, **the** (sport and leisure) A colloquial name for the *Amateur Athletic Association* and for the championship contest organized by it.

Three Choirs Festival /ˌθriː ˌkwaɪəz ˈfestəvl/, **the** (arts) A music festival, first held in 1724, held annually (in turn) in the cathedrals of Gloucester, Hereford and Worcester. The music consists of both choral and orchestral religious works (*church music*), and is performed by each cathedral choir, as well as special festival choirs and outside orchestras.

three-card trick /ˌθriː ˈkɑːd trɪk/ (sport and leisure) A gambling game occasionally played in the street. A man with a pack of cards invites members of the public to bet on which of three cards, laid face down, is the queen. The man with the cards always wins.

three-cornered fight /ˌθriː kɔːnəd ˈfaɪt/ (politics) A term for an election (either a *by-election* or a *general election*) in which the contest is between candidates from three political parties, usually *Conservative, Labour*, and *SLD* or *Green Party*. In certain areas of *Scotland, Wales* and *Northern Ireland*, the third party may be a local nationalist one, such as the *SNP, Plaid Cymru, Sinn Féin* or a *Unionist Party* in *Northern Ireland*.

three-day event /ˌθriː deɪ ɪˈvent/ (sport and leisure) A horse riding contest held over three days, usually comprising dressage (the control of horses in obedience) on the first day, cross-country riding on the second day and show jumping (in the ring) on the third. The event originated at *Badminton* in 1949. See also *eventing*.

three-legged race /ˌθriː ˈleɡɪd reɪs/ (sport and leisure) A race popular with children, in which two competitors run together, with the right leg of one tied to the left leg of the

three-legged race

other.

three-line whip /ˌθriː laɪn ˈwɪp/ (**1** government **2** daily life)
1 An urgent request by a *whip¹* to an *MP* to attend a
particular debate or to vote. **2** A similar request to a person to
attend a particular function or take part in a particular event.
['three-line' with reference to the triple underlining of the
written request, indicating its extreme urgency]

Throgmorton Street /ˌθrɒgˈmɔːtn striːt/ (finance) A street in the
City (of London) where the *Stock Exchange* is, and so also a
name for the Stock Exchange itself. [the street is named after a
16th-century diplomat]

tick-tack man /ˈtɪk tæk ˌmæn/ (sport and leisure) A *bookmaker*
at a race course who sends betting information to other
bookmakers by means of a special sign language, using his
hands and arms.

tied cottage /ˌtaɪd ˈkɒtɪdʒ/ (life and society) A cottage or house
whose occupant, such as a farmworker, can live in it only as
long as he works for the employer who owns it. In a few
cases, however, people who live in tied cottages can continue
to live there after they retire.

tied house /ˌtaɪd ˈhaʊs/ (daily life) A *pub* under contract ('tied')
to a particular brewery for its supplies of beer and other
alcoholic drinks. Compare *free house*.

Time Out /ˌtaɪm ˈaʊt/ (media) A weekly magazine of news,
reviews and entertainment in *London*, at one time noted for
its radical views. It was first published in 1968 and has a
current circulation of about 90,000.

Timeline /'taɪmlaɪn/ (commerce) The official name of *BT*'s Speaking Clock service.

Times /taɪmz/, **The** (media) A daily *quality paper* first published in 1785 (as the 'Daily Universal Register') and generally regarded as one of the most influential newspapers. It is noted for its regular features, and in particular for its editorial (including the *third leader*), readers' letters, *personal column* and crossword. It is officially independent politically, but many of its readers support the *Conservative Party*. Its current circulation is about 390,000 (1970 – 437,000). It has a weekly supplement, 'The Times Magazine'.

Times Ed, /ˌtaɪmz 'ed/ the(media) A colloquial name for the *Times Educational Supplement*.

Times Educational Supplement /ˌtaɪmz edʒʊˌkeɪʃnl 'sʌplɪmənt/, **the (TES, the)** (education) A weekly newspaper published by the owners of The *Times*. It is aimed mainly at teachers and those professionally concerned with education, and has an extensive advertising section for readers seeking a teaching post. It was founded in 1910 and has a current circulation of about 120,000. Compare *Times Higher Educational Supplment*.

Times Higher Educational Supplement /'taɪmz ˌhaɪer edʒʊˌkeɪʃnl 'sʌplɪmənt/, **the (THES, the)** (media) A weekly newspaper published by the owners of The *Times* for those involved in *higher education*. It first appeared in 1972 as a sister publication to the *Times Educational Supplement*, and has a current circulation of about 17,000.

Times Literary Supplement /ˌtaɪmz ˌlɪtərərɪ 'sʌplɪmənt/, **the (TLS, the)** (education) A weekly newspaper published by the owners of The *Times*. It is chiefly devoted to reviews of new books, and is noted for its readers' letters, many of which are from authors who feel their books have been unfairly reviewed. It was founded in 1902 and has a current circulation of about 30,000.

Tintagel /tɪn'tædʒəl/ (geography) A village near the north coast of *Cornwall*, where Tintagel Castle is the legendary birthplace of *King Arthur*.

tip and run /ˌtɪp ən 'rʌn/ (sport and leisure) A form of *cricket*, popular with children, in which the batsman must run to the opposite wicket every time his bat hits or touches ('tips') the ball. This rule speeds up the game considerably.

tipsy cake /'tɪpsɪ keɪk/ (food and drink) A kind of *trifle* made from sponge cake soaked with wine or sherry and usually decorated with nuts and crystallized fruit. [from colloquial 'tipsy', meaning 'slightly drunk'].

Titanic /taɪˈtænɪk/, **the** (history) A British passenger liner, at the time the largest vessel afloat, which collided with an iceberg on her maiden voyage to New York in 1912, and sank with the loss of all but 703 of her 2,206 passengers. Attempts to locate and raise the sunken liner have so far failed.

toby jug

Titbits /ˈtɪtbɪts/ (media) A monthly consumer magazine for men, mainly devoted to show business and items of general interest. It was first published in 1895 and has a current circulation of about 150,000.

toad-in-the-hole /ˌtəʊd ɪn ðə ˈhəʊl/ (food and drink) A savoury dish, usually eaten hot, consisting of sausages cooked in batter. [the sausage buried in batter is thought to look like a toad hidden in a hole]

toast /təʊst/ (food and drink) A traditional part of an *English breakfast*—slices of bread that have been lightly cooked and browned by exposure to heat, in an electric toaster, under a grill or by a fire. Toast is also eaten at *tea*² or supper (similar to *high tea*); in the latter meal often with a savoury covering, such as eggs or cheese.

toby jug /ˈtəʊbɪ dʒʌg/ (style) A mug or jug in the shape of a squat, seated man wearing a three-cornered hat and smoking a pipe. The spout is formed from one of the corners of the hat. Some people collect toby jugs and the old ones are valuable. [said to be derived from an 18th-century poem about a man called 'Toby Philpot']

Toc H /ˌtɒk 'eɪtʃ/ (charities) A Christian organization founded after the First World War to encourage comradeship and social service in the place of hatred and loneliness. The name comes from the former telegraphic sign for the letters 'T' and 'H', which stood for 'Talbot House'. The original Talbot House was opened in the small town of Poperinghe, west Belgium, in 1915, as a *chapel*² and *club* for soldiers and as a memorial to Gilbert Talbot, the brother of the organization's founder, Neville Talbot.

Today /təˈdeɪ/ (media) **1** A daily *popular paper* noted for its bright features and emphasis on the modern world. It is politically right of centre. It was first published in 1986 and has a current circulation of about 495,000 (1987 – 307,000). **2** A popular *BBC* radio programme broadcast every morning on *Radio 4* from 6.30 to 8.45. It is noted for its professional yet relaxed style, and consists mainly of comments on the news, topical interviews, travel information for people going to work, etc. It was first broadcast in 1975.

toffee apple /'tɒfɪ æpl/ (food and drink) An apple on a stick covered with a layer of brittle toffee. It is traditionally sold at *fêtes* or made for *Hallowe'en* parties.

tombola /tɒmˈbəʊlə/ (sport and leisure) A type of lottery in which tickets are drawn from a revolving drum. Tombola is often played at a *fête* or other entertainment with the aim of raising money for charity. [from Italian 'tombolare', 'to tumble']

Tommy /'tɒmɪ/ (tradition) A rather dated nickname for a British soldier. [said to derive from Thomas Atkins, a random name for a soldier used in instruction manuals giving directions for completing certain army forms]

top hat /ˌtɒp 'hæt/ (clothing) A man's or boy's tall, black or grey hat with a cylindrical crown and narrow brim, worn on some formal occasions (eg, at *Ascot*) or, in the case of boys, as part of the uniform at some schools such as *Eton* or *Harrow*.

Top of the Pops /ˌtɒp əv ðə 'pɒps/ (media) A weekly television programme on *BBC 1* in which a selection of recently released pop and rock hits is performed, including those in the *top ten*, either live or recorded, often with an accompanying video. The programme was first transmitted in 1964.

top shelf magazine /ˌtɒp ˈʃelf ˌmægəziːn/ **(media)** A pornographic or semi-pornographic magazine that is usually kept on the top shelf in a newsagent's or other shop so that young children cannot reach it or even see it properly.

top ten /ˌtɒp ˈten/**, the** (media) The top-selling pop and rock records released in a particular week, as established by market research and sales figures. The records are played frequently on *Radio 1* and several *local radio* stations. A selection, including the 'number one' best-seller, is performed weekly on *Top of the Pops*.

tor /tɔː(r)/ (geography) The word for a steep or rocky hill, especially in the names of such hills in the *West Country* and in the *Peak District*. Among the best known are Glastonbury Tor, Somerset, Rough Tor, *Cornwall*, and Mam Tor, Derbyshire. These and similar hills are popular with tourists.

torpids /ˈtɔːpɪdz/ (sport and leisure) The annual spring boat races between teams of eight oarsmen from each of the *colleges[1]* of *Oxford University*, held on the river *Thames* at *Oxford[1]*. [from 'torpid' in sense 'slow', 'sluggish'; the races were originally between the second eights of the colleges, which were slower than the main crews]

Tory /ˈtɔːrɪ/ (politics) An alternative term for Conservative, used either critically, as applied to an extreme Conservative, or simply as a convenient shorter word (eg, in newspaper headlines). See *Conservative Party*. [name was inherited from the former English right-wing political party in existence from the 17th century to the 1830s when the Conservative party was formed]

tossing the caber

tossing the caber /ˌtɒsɪŋ ðə ˈkeɪbə(r)/ (sport and leisure) A contest popular in Scottish *Highland games*, in which a heavy wooden pole ('caber') is thrown through the air as a test of strength.

tossing the pancake /ˌtɒsɪŋ ðə ˈpæŋkeɪk/ (tradition) A tradition marked on *Shrove Tuesday*, when either in a race (see *pancake race*) or among a group of standing participants, *pancakes* are tossed in the air out of a frying pan so that they turn over and are caught again in the pan. The custom developed from the days when Shrove Tuesday was a final day of feasting and enjoyment before the start of *Lent*.

Tote /təʊt/, **the** (sport and leisure) The usual short name of the Horserace Totalisator Board, a state-run body that operates a betting pool system at all British racecourses and that owns a chain of over 100 *betting shops*. Many of the bets placed through the Tote are made by a credit system or over the telephone. In 1988 plans were announced to privatize the Tote.

Tottenham Court Road /ˌtɒtnəm kɔːt ˈrəʊd/ (London) A street in central *London* well known for its shops selling radio, television and video equipment and home computers, as well as for its furniture dealers.

Tottenham Hotspur /ˌtɒtnəm ˈhɒtspɜː(r)/ (sport and leisure) A popular *London football club* with a stadium at *White Hart Lane*. The club was founded in 1882, originally as Hotspur Football Club. [named after district in north London where stadium is; 'Hotspur', meaning 'person of fiery temper', was the nickname of Sir Henry Percy (1364–1403), who led the English into battle against the Scots]

Tower Bridge /ˌtaʊə ˈbrɪdʒ/ (London) One of *London*'s best-known landmarks—the distinctive twin drawbridges with *Gothic* (*style*) towers over the river *Thames* near the *Tower of London*. The Bridge was built in the late 19th century, and is the farthest downstream of all London's bridges.

Tower Hill /ˌtaʊə ˈhɪl/ (London) The historic open space near the *Tower of London*, which was the main place where traitors imprisoned in the Tower were executed.

Tower of London /ˌtaʊər əv ˈlʌndən/, **the** (London) One of the oldest, best-known, and most imposing fortresses in *England*, on the north bank of the river *Thames* in *London*. The Tower was begun in the 11th century by William the *Conqueror*, and was added to and altered by later sovereigns. In the course of its history it has been a royal palace, a state prison, a citadel and an arsenal. Its many associations with English history make it a popular tourist attraction. Two important parts of it are the *Bloody Tower* and the *White Tower*. There also the *Crown Jewels* are on public display, and *Yeomen Warders* are on guard.

town and gown /ˌtaʊn ən ˈgaʊn/ (life and society) The term used for the native residents ('town') and students (and sometimes academic staff) ('gown') of some university *cities*, especially the older ones such as *Oxford*[2] and *Cambridge*[2]. The phrase also implies a culture clash between the two groups. See also *gown*[1,2].

Town Clearance /ˌtaʊn ˈklɪərəns/ (finance) A system for transferring high-value cheques between banks the same day. The system operates only in the *City of London*.

town clerk /ˌtaʊn ˈklɑːk/ (government) The title, officially abolished in 1974, of the secretary and chief administrative officer of a *town council*. He is now usually called the Chief Executive.

town council /ˌtaʊn ˈkaʊnsl/ (government) The *local authority* in a town (usually within a *district council*) that is headed by a *mayor* or *mayoress* and that has certain legislative powers, for example, to make *by-laws*. The secretary and chief administrative officer of a town council was formerly called the *town clerk*, but now usually the Chief Executive. Larger towns usually have a local authority that is a *borough council* or a district council.

town crier /ˌtaʊn ˈkraɪə(r)/ (tradition) **1** A person formerly employed to make public announcements in a town. **2** In modern times, a person who plays this role on special occasions, usually for publicity or when sponsored by a particular commercial promoter. See also *oyez*.

town hall /ˌtaʊn ˈhɔːl/ (government) The chief building in a town or *city* (where it may be called a city hall and be a more important building) in which local government business is carried out, and which usually has a public hall, which may be available for concerts or meetings. See also *council house*.[2]

town house /ˈtaʊn haʊs/ (style) A house in a town or *city*, either a fashionable one or (in *estate agents'* language) simply a *terraced house*.

Trade Descriptions Act /ˌtreɪd dɪˈskrɪpʃnz ækt/, **the** (law) An *Act* (*of Parliament*), passed in 1968 and later, according to which goods and services must be honestly and correctly described and not exaggerated through advertising or promotion.

trading estate /ˈtreɪdɪŋ ɪˌsteɪt/ (commerce) A district of a town, often on the outskirts, where several commercial or trading firms have their premises. Compare *industrial estate*.

Trafalgar /trəˈfælgə(r)/ **(Battle of Trafalgar, the)** (history) A decisive naval battle that took place off Cape Trafalgar, southwest Spain, on 21 October 1805. The French and Spanish fleets were defeated by the English under Admiral Nelson, who was mortally wounded. See also *Trafalgar Square*.

Trafalgar Square /trəˌfælgə ˈskweə(r)/ (London) The main square of central *London*, where there are a number of famous buildings and monuments, including the *National Gallery*, *St Martin-in-the-Fields* and *Nelson's Column*. The Square is popular with visitors, who come to relax by the fountains there or to feed the pigeons. Trafalgar Square is also a popular meeting place for political and other demonstrations. [named in commemoration of Nelson's victory at the Battle of *Trafalgar*]

traffic warden /ˈtræfɪk ˌwɔːdn/ (transport) A person whose job is to make sure drivers obey parking regulations. Wardens have the authority to issue *parking tickets*, and may also help to direct traffic. They wear a special black uniform with yellow cap bands.

transport café /ˈtrænspɔːt kæfeɪ/ (daily life) A café on a main road, such as a *motorway*, that provides good, inexpensive food, mainly for long-distance lorry (truck) drivers.

Transport House /ˌtrænspɔːt ˈhaʊs/ (politics) The building in *Smith Square*, *London* that houses the headquarters of the *TGWU*. Until 1980, it also housed that of the *Labour Party*. See *Walworth Road*.

Travelcard /ˈtrævlkɑːd/ (transport) A special ticket issued at a reduced rate by *BR* for travel within the *Greater London* area, including the *Underground*, for either one day (a 'One Day Travelcard') or seven days (a 'Seven Day Travelcard').

treasure trove /ˈtreʒə trəʊv/ (law) Precious objects such as jewels, coins, gold or silver discovered buried in the ground and of unknown ownership. Such treasure belongs to the state, and is traditionally offered to the *British Museum*. It is usual for the discoverer of the treasure to be recompensed for the full market value of the objects. *Britain*'s biggest treasure trove of Roman coins was that found in a Suffolk village in 1992, valued at over £1 million. [from Old French 'tresor trové', 'found treasure']

Treasury /ˈtreʒərɪ/, **the** (government) The state *department* responsible for the management of *Britain*'s finances and economy, officially headed by the *Prime Minister* (as First Lord of the Treasury) but actually the responsibility of the *Chancellor of the Exchequer*.

treble chance /ˌtrebl ˈtʃɑːns/ (sport and leisure) A method of betting in *football pools* in which the main aim is to pick the draws, which count more than wins. [from original three different possible results: a win away, a win at home, or a draw]

Trent Bridge /ˌtrent ˈbrɪdʒ/ (sport and leisure) A *cricket* ground in Nottingham where *test matches* take place. [ground is near bridge over river Trent]

Tribune /ˈtrɪbjuːn/ (media) A weekly political and literary magazine that gives the viewpoint of the left wing of the *Labour Party*. Its current circulation is about 10,000. It was first published in 1937.

Trident /ˈtraɪdnt/ (defence) A long-range missile, fired from a submarine, that can carry a nuclear warhead. Four *Royal Navy* submarines designed to carry Trident missiles are being built to replace the four that at present carry Polaris missiles. The first was completed in 1993.

trifle /ˈtraɪfl/ (food and drink) A sweet dish consisting of a sponge cake (sometimes soaked in wine) spread with jam or fruit, then covered with a layer of *custard*, and topped with cream. It is often decorated with nuts and more fruit.

trilby (hat) /ˈtrɪlbɪ (ˌtrɪlbɪ ˈhæt)/ (clothing) A type of man's soft felt hat with an indented crown. [named after the heroine of a dramatized novel (1893) by George du Maurier]

Trinity House /ˌtrɪnətɪ ˈhaʊs/ (transport) The authority (in full, Corporation of Trinity House) that controls light-houses and buoys, and some lightships, around the coasts of *England* and *Wales*. It is the largest English pilot authority, and is a charitable organization providing homes and financial support for retired mariners and their families. The Corporation was founded in 1514.

Trinity Sunday /ˌtrɪnətɪ ˈsʌndɪ/ (religion) The *Sunday* after *Whit Sunday*, and one of the major festivals of the Christian year.

Triple Crown /ˌtrɪpl ˈkraʊn/, **the** (sport and leisure) **1** The title awarded to the *rugby football* team of *England*, *Scotland*, *Wales* or *Ireland* that in one season defeats all three of its opponents. **2** The title awarded to a horse that has won the three races, Two Thousand Guineas, *Derby* and *St Leger*.

Triple Event /ˌtrɪpl ɪ'vent/**, the** (sport and leisure) The three horse races whose winner is awarded the *Triple Crown²*.

tripos /'traɪpɒs/ (education) At *Cambridge University*, the final *honours degree* examination in certain subjects. [said to derive from the nickname of 'Mr Tripos' given to an examination candidate who sat on a three-legged stool]

Trooping the Colour /ˌtruːpɪŋ ðə 'kʌlə(r)/ (tradition) An annual ceremony held on the *Official Birthday* of the sovereign on *Horse Guards Parade, London*, when regiments of the *Guards Division* and the *Household Cavalry*, parade ('troop') the regimental flag ('colour') before the sovereign. The ceremony dates from the 18th century, and was originally a guard-mounting ceremony.

Troubles /'trʌblz/**, the** (politics) The name used for the sectarian divisions between Roman Catholics and Protestants in *Northern Ireland* from the late 1960s, and for the terrorism that has resulted from such divisions. By mid-1992 the Troubles had claimed 3,000 lives, mainly those of civilians, but also including members of the British *Army* and of the *RUC* and *UDR*.

trunk road /'trʌŋk rəʊd/ (transport) A main road, especially one used by lorries (trucks) and other heavy vehicles. Trunk roads are usually *A-roads*.

Trustcard /'trʌstkɑːd/ (finance) The credit card issued by the *Trustee Savings Bank*.

Trustee Savings Bank /ˌtrʌstiː 'seɪvɪŋz bæŋk/**, the (TSB, the)** (finance) A leading commercial bank that originated as a number of locally managed savings banks but that now provides a full range of banking services. In 1986 all the TSBs were transformed into a single bank, the TSB Group, with shares sold to the public. See also *Trustcard*.

TT /ˌtiː 'tiː/**, the (Tourist Trophy, the)** (sport and leisure) An important annual series of motorcycle races held on the *Isle of Man*. The races were first held in 1907, originally for tourists visiting the Isle of Man, and currently comprise the Senior TT Race, for riders of 500cc machines, and the Classic Race for less powerful motorcycles.

tube /tjuːb/**, the** (transport) A colloquial term for the *London Underground* railway. [from its tube-shaped tunnels]

TUC /ˌtiː juː 'siː/**, the (Trades Union Congress, the)** (work) A voluntary association of trade unions, founded in 1868. The main aim of the TUC is to promote the interests of its members and improve the working and social conditions of working people. Union representatives meet annually, usually in early September, to discuss matters of common concern. The TUC currently represents about 78% of all trade union members in *Britain*, ie, some 7.8 million people.

Tudor (style) /'tju:də(r) (staɪl)/ (style) An architectural style of the late *Perpendicular* period, characterized in particular by half-timbered houses. [named after the 16th-century royal house of Tudor]

turf /tɜ:f/, **the** (sport and leisure) Horse-racing as a sport or industry. [from the turf of the race-course]

turf accountant /'tɜ:f əkaʊntənt/ (sport and leisure) A formal name for a *bookmaker*.

tutor /'tju:tə(r)/ (education) **1** A member of staff at a university responsible for the teaching and supervision of a fixed number of students in a particular subject or subjects. **2** A teacher who works with individual students or pupils and who is usually employed privately.

TV licence /ˌti: vi: 'laɪsns/ (commerce) The licence that must legally be held by anyone owning or renting a television. The present annual cost of the licence is £83 for a colour television (the majority) and £27.50 for one with only a black and white picture. The TV licence provides most of the income of the *BBC*. It is possible that the TV licence may be reduced in the near future, or even abolished altogether (as the former radio licence was in 1971).

TV Times /ˌti: vi: 'taɪmz/ (media) A weekly magazine with detailed schedules of television and radio programmes on *ITV, BBC, Channel 4* and satellite channels, together with features relating to the particular week. Until 1991 it published ITV and Channel 4 programmes only. It was first published in 1968 and has a current circulation of about 1.2 million. Compare *Radio Times*.

Twelfth Night /ˌtwelfθ 'naɪt/ (tradition) 6 January, the twelfth day after *Christmas Day* and the traditional end of the celebrations of *Christmas* and the New Year (see *New Year's Day*). On this day Christmas decorations are usually taken down, as are Christmas cards that have been on display since Christmas Day or earlier. Twelfth Night coincides with the *church* festival of the Epiphany.

12 /twelv/ (arts) A category introduced in 1989 by the *British Board of Film Classification* to show that no child under the age of 12 can be allowed to see the film. See also *15* (listed under *letter F)*, *18* (listed under letter E), *PG* and *U Certificate*.

20 pence (piece) /ˌtwentɪ 'pens (ˌtwentɪ pens 'piːs)/ (finance) A seven-sided coin made from a mixture of copper and nickel that looks like silver. It is worth one-fifth of the value of a *pound (sterling)*. See p 472.

Twickenham /'twɪkənəm/ (sport and leisure) A district of Richmond-upon-Thames (southwest *Greater London*) where international matches are played on the famous *rugby football* ground there. See also *University Match*.

2 pence (piece) /ˌtuː 'pens (ˌtuː pens 'piːs)/ (finance) A bronze coin that is worth one-fiftieth of the value of a *pound (sterling)*. See p 472.

twin set /'twɪn set/ (clothing) A woman's matching jumper and cardigan, often worn with a pearl necklace.

two pound coin /ˌtuː paʊnd 'kɔɪn/ (finance) A special coin with a value of £2 issued in 1986 to mark the Commonwealth Games, held in *Edinburgh* that year. The coin is sometimes given as a gift, but can be used in shops like any other coin. See p 472.

two-minute silence /ˌtuː mɪnɪt 'saɪləns/**, the** (tradition) A silence observed at the *Cenotaph, London*, and elsewhere in *Britain*, at 11.00 am on *Remembrance Sunday*, in order to remember the dead of both world wars.

two-shilling piece /ˌtuː ʃɪlɪŋ 'piːs/ see *10 pence (piece)* (finance).

Tyne Tees TV /ˌtaɪn ˌtiːz ˌtiː 'viː/ (media) One of the 15 regional television companies of the *ITC*, based in Newcastle upon Tyne and broadcasting to northeast *England*. [named after two rivers in this region]

Tynwald /'tɪnwɔːld/**, the** (government) The parliament of the *Isle of Man*. It has two houses: the Legislative Council and the House of Keys. After *bills* are passed through both houses they are sent for the *royal assent*.

U /juː/ (arts) A category in which a cinema film is placed by the *British Board of Film Classification*, to indicate that it is suitable for anyone to see, including children. Compare *12* (under letter T), *15* (under F), *18* (under E) and *PG*. [initial of 'universal']

UCCA /ˈʌkə/ **(Universities Central Council on Admissions, the)** (education) The organization through which students in their final year at school apply for admission to a degree course at a university. All universities in *Britain* belong to the scheme except the *Open University* and the independent University of Buckingham. The organization was formed in 1961.

UDM /ˌjuː diː ˈem/ **, the (Union of Democratic Mineworkers, the)** A trade union of miners formed as a 'breakaway' union from the NUM in 1985 after a lengthy miners' strike in Nottinghamshire. The UDM curently has about 20,000 members. It is not affiliated to the *TUC*.

UDR /ˌjuː diː ˈɑː(r)/, **the (Ulster Defence Regiment, the)** (law) A locally recruited and mainly part-time reserve force which supports the *RUC* on behalf of the *Army* in *Northern Ireland*.

UK /ˌjuː ˈkeɪ/ see *United Kingdom* (geography)

Ullswater /ˈʌlzˌwɔːtə(r)/ (geography) The second largest lake (after *Windermere*) in the *Lake District*. It is $7\frac{1}{2}$ miles long and half a mile wide, and is generally regarded as the most spectacular of the lakes.

Ulster /ˈʌlstə(r)/ (geography) A name for *Northern Ireland*, originally the name of a former kingdom there.

Ulster Defence Association /ˌʌlstə dɪˈfens əsəʊsiˌeɪʃn/, **the (UDA, the)** (politics) The largest Protestant paramilitary organization in *Northern Ireland*. It was founded in 1971 to counter the violence of the *IRA* by coordinating *working class* vigilante groups in *Belfast* and other urban areas. It was officially banned in 1992.

Ulster Democratic Unionist Party /ˌʌlstə deməˌkrætɪk ˈjuːnɪənɪst ˌpɑːtɪ/ (politics) A political party formed in *Northern Ireland* in 1971. The founders (who include Ian *Paisley*) disagree with many of the policies of the official Unionist Party (see *Ulster Unionist Party*). The Democratic Unionist Party is strongly Protestant and insists that *Ulster* should remain part of the *United Kingdom*. Ian Paisley is the current leader of the party and an *MP* in the *House of Commons*.

Ulster TV /ˌʌlstə tiː ˈviː/ (media) One of the 15 regional television companies of the *ITC*, based in *Belfast* and broadcasting to *Northern Ireland*. See also *Ulster*.

Ulster Unionist Party /ˌʌlstə ˈjuːnɪənɪst ˌpɑːtɪ/ (politics) A political party which has been active in *Northern Ireland* for very many years. Most of its supporters are Protestants who wish *Ulster* to remain part of the *United Kingdom*. After 1920, when Ulster and the Republic of Ireland became separate countries, the Unionists were the ruling party in the Northern Ireland Parliament until *direct rule* began in 1972. The party has regularly been well represented among the Northern Ireland *MP*s in the *House of Commons*.

Ulster Volunteer Force /ˌʌlstə ˌvɒləntˈɪə ˌfɔːs/**, the (UVF, the)** (politics) A Protestant terrorist organization in *Northern Ireland*. It was founded in 1913, initially in order to oppose those aiming to unite *Ireland* under Irish rule, but later specifically combatting the *IRA*. In the early 1990s it increased its attacks on the IRA and on Catholics in general. The UVF was officially banned in 1975.

unadopted road /ˌʌnədɒptɪd ˈrəʊd/ (geography) A public road not maintained by a *local authority*.

undergraduate /ˌʌndəˈɡrædʒuət/ (education) A university student studying for a first degree at any university. The word 'student' is probably more widely used in everyday speech. Compare *postgraduate*.

Underground /ˈʌndəɡraʊnd/**, the** (transport) An electric railway system operating largely underground in a city, especially the one in *London*. (See *London Underground*.) There is also a *Glasgow* Underground and one in Liverpool. See also *Metro, Metrolink*.

underwriter /ˈʌndəraɪtə(r)/ (finance) **1** An insurance agent

who decides how much a person should pay to insure
something, taking into account the degree of risk involved,
and charging more for the insurance when risks are high.
2 An official who undertakes (by 'underwriting' or
subscribing his name) to accept responsibility for any losses
that result from another person's insurance policy. 3 A
person who accepts financial responsibility for any shares in
a company that are offered to the public but not bought by
them.

unemployment benefit /ˌʌnɪmˈplɔɪmənt ˌbenɪfɪt/ (finance) A
state payment made to people without work, payable for up
to a year. The amount paid depends on whether the person is
married or single. People receiving unemployment benefit
must actively look for work. In some cases they may also do
voluntary work in the community without losing their
entitlement to the benefit.

unicorn /ˈjuːnɪkɔːn/ (tradition) A mythical animal that looks
like a horse with a long straight horn growing from its
forehead. It has appeared on the Scottish and British royal
coats of arms for many centuries, and is a symbol of purity.

Union Flag /ˌjuːnɪən ˈflæg/, **the** (tradition) The formal name of
the British national flag, more commonly known as the *Union
Jack*.

Union Jack /ˌjuːnɪən ˈdʒæk/, **the** (tradition) The national flag
of the *United Kingdom*, combining the *St George's cross* of
England, *St Andrew's cross* of *Scotland* and *St Patrick's cross* of
Ireland (now representing *Northern Ireland*). [properly the
Union Flag; 'Union' for the union of England and Scotland in
1606, 'jack' as flown on the jack staff (a small flagstaff) of ships
to show their nationality]

Unionist Party /ˈjuːnɪənɪst ˌpɑːtɪ/ see *Ulster Democratic Unionist
Party* (politics) and *Ulster Unionist Party* (politics)

Unison /ˈjuːnɪsn/ (work) One of the largest trade unions, to
which *NHS* staff and non-manual government employees
belong. It was formed in 1993 as the merger of three former
unions, and has a current membership of about 1.5 million.
[pun on 'union' and 'unison', with 's' for 'staff' or 'service']

unit trust /ˈjuːnɪt trʌst/ (finance) An organization that invests
money on people's behalf by selling them units and
distributing the income and profits amongst them.

United /juːˈnaɪtɪd/ (sport and leisure) The colloquial name of
any *football club* having 'United' in its name, especially
Manchester United.

United Kingdom /juːˌnaɪtɪd ˈkɪŋdəm/, **the (UK, the)**
(geography) The short name of the United Kingdom of *Great
Britain* and *Northern Ireland*, that is, *England, Scotland, Wales*
and Northern Ireland. Compare the *British Isles*. See map on
p 466.

United Kingdom Atomic Energy Authority /juːˌnaɪtɪd ˌkɪŋdəm
əˌtɒmɪk ˈenədʒɪ ɔːˌθɒrəti/, **the (UKAEA, the)** (science and
technology) The United Kingdom Atomic Energy Authority
was set up in 1954, with the aim of developing nuclear power
from a basic science to an essential part of the *United
Kingdom*'s energy supply. It conducts research to ensure that
nuclear power is both economic and safe, and that it will not
threaten the environment. Its research establishments
include *Harwell*, Risley (Cheshire), Winfrith (Dorset),
Windscale (adjacent to *Sellafield*) and Culham (Oxfordshire) in
England and Dounreay in *Scotland*.

United Reformed Church /juːˌnaɪtɪd rɪˌfɔːmd ˈtʃɜːtʃ/, **the**
(religion) A leading Protestant, non-*Anglican church* in
Britain, formed in 1972 by the union of the Presbyterian
Church and the Congregational Church. It is particularly
strong in *Wales* and has about 121,000 members.

Universal Aunts /ˌjuːnɪvɜːsl ˈɑːnts/ (commerce) A
long-established *London* firm providing private and domestic
services especially for non-Londoners, such as finding
accommodation, doing shopping, and escorting children
across London.

Universe /ˈjuːnɪvɜːs/, **The** (media) A leading weekly
newspaper for Roman Catholics, with features and articles of
interest to clergy and laity alike. It was founded in 1860 and
has a current circulation of over 100,000. [English 'Catholic'
comes from a Greek word meaning 'universal']

University College Hospital /juːnɪˌvɜːsəti ˌkɒlɪdʒ ˈhɒspɪtl/, **the
(UCH, the)** (medicine) A London *teaching hospital* founded
by University College, *London* in 1833.

Unknown Warrior /ˌʌnnəʊn ˈwɒrɪə(r)/, **the** (history) The grave
in *Westminster Abbey, London*, where the remains of an
unknown British serviceman killed in France in the First World
War are buried. [full title: Tomb of the Unknown Warrior]

unlisted securities market /ˌʌnlɪstɪd sɪˈkjʊərətɪz ˌmɑːkɪt/
(USM) (finance) The official term for the buying of stocks
and shares that are not listed on the *Stock Exchange*. Such
shares belong mainly to small or recently formed companies
that have not yet obtained a Stock Exchange listing or that are

unwilling to do so. UDM companies must prove that they have been trading for at least two years and that a minimum of 10% of all shares are in public hands. The UDM has been operating since 1980. Compare *unquoted company*.

unofficial strike /ˌʌnəfɪʃl 'straɪk/ (work) A strike not officially supported or called by a trade union.

unquoted company /ˌʌnkwəʊtɪd ˌkʌmpənɪ/ (finance) A small or new company whose shares are dealt with in the usual way on the *Stock Exchange* but which are not subject to any requirements, and which have no official status. Investments in such companies can have high rewards but also carry higher risks. Compare *unlisted securities market*.

upper class /ˌʌpə 'klɑːs/ (life and society) The class that occupies the highest position in the social scale, usually members of the aristocracy (such as the *royal family* or the *peerage*) with their wealth, breeding and air of exclusivity. See also *U*.

upper middle class /ˌʌpə 'mɪdl klɑːs/ (life and society) The social class that is higher than the *middle class* but not as high as *upper class*, usually regarded as including professional people such as politicians, surgeons, professors, company directors and senior *civil servants*.

upper school /'ʌpə skuːl/ (education) The senior classes in a *secondary school* or *public school*[1,2], usually including the *sixth form*.

urban development corporation /ˌɜːbən dɪ'veləpmənt kɔːpəˌreɪʃn/ **(UDC)** (government) A local body set up by the government in an *inner city* or similar region to reclaim derelict land for housing, businesses and recreation, much in the same way that a *new town* is planned. There are currently 12 UDCs, the first being set up in *London Docklands* and Merseyside (round Liverpool) in 1981.

Urban Programme /'ɜːbən ˌprəʊɡræm/**, the** (government) A major government spending programme organized in the 1980s to give help to *inner cities*. It arranges grants through *local authorities*, helps local businesses, and improves sites and buildings.

USDAW /'ʌsdɔː/**, the (Union of Shop, Distributive and Allied Workers, the)** (work) A trade union with members mainly in retail and wholesale distribution, but also in food manufacturing, chemical processing, catering and other service trades. It has a current membership of about 360,000.

V and A /ˌviː ən ˈeɪ/ see *Victoria and Albert Museum* (arts)

Valentine's Brook /ˌvæləntaɪnz ˈbrʊk/ (sport and leisure) One of the major jumps in the *Grand National* horse race, consisting of a thorn fence with a brook on the far side. [named after horse that fell there]

Variety Club /vəˈraɪətɪ klʌb/, **the** (charities) A theatrical organization founded to raise money for children's charities. Its president is the Chief Barker. [in full, Variety Club of *Great Britain*]

Varsity Match /ˈvɑːsətɪ mætʃ/ (sport and leisure) The traditional annual *rugby football* match at *Twickenham* between teams from *Oxford University* and *Cambridge University*.

VAT /ˌviː eɪ ˈtiː, also pronounced væt/ **(value added tax)** (finance) A tax charged on most goods and services that are paid for by the customer or consumer. VAT is not currently charged on most kinds of food and drink (though it is on 'leisure consumables' such as ice creams, sweets, potato crisps and alcoholic drinks), on public transport fares and postal services, or on children's clothing. VAT was not formerly charged on books and newspapers but it was imposed on these in 1993 and on domestic heating (electricity, gas and coal) from 1994. The present rate of VAT is 17.5%, added to the basic cost at the time of payment.

Vaughan Williams, Ralph /ˌvɔːn ˈwɪljəmz, reɪf/ (people) Probably more than any other British composer, Ralph Vaughan Williams (1872–1958) was the true founder of a nationalist movement in English music. His great interest was English folksong, and this, combined with his interest in early English music, enabled him to develop a style that was both typically 'English' and very original (eg, his 'Sinfonia

Antartica' of 1953). Many of his short pieces are very popular, such as the early song 'Linden Lea' (1902) and the stirring hymn-tune 'For All the Saints'. He was awarded the *Order of Merit* for his services to English music.

VC /ˌviː ˈsiː/, **the (Victoria Cross, the)** (defence) The highest British decoration, awarded for 'conspicuous bravery or devotion to the country in the presence of the enemy'. It was founded by *Queen Victoria* in 1856, and has been awarded fewer than 1,400 times since then (over 600 of these in the First World War). It shows the royal crown with a lion above it. Under the crown are the words, 'For Valour'.

vehicle licence /ˈvɪəkl ˌlaɪsns/ (transport) A licence issued by the *DVLC* stating that a vehicle is in a fit condition to be driven on a public road, and that it is insured. It is commonly called a *tax disc* or a 'road fund licence'.

verger /ˈvɜːdʒə(r)/ (religion) **1** An official in the *Church of England* who acts as a general caretaker in a *church*, and often also looks after the vestments (priests' robes) and church furnishings. **2** A similar official who carries a verge (rod) of office in front of a bishop or other important person in church services and ceremonies, usually in a cathedral.

Very Reverend /ˌverɪ ˈrevərənd/, **the (Very Rev, the)** (religion) The title given to a *dean*[3] in the *Church of England* (eg, 'The Very Reverend the Dean of Ely').

veteran car /ˌvetərən ˈkɑː(r)/ (transport) An old, usually carefully preserved, motor-car, technically one built before 1905. Compare *vintage car*, and see also *Veteran Car Run*.

Veteran Car Run /ˌvetərən ˈkɑː rʌn/, **the** (transport) An annual race of *veteran cars* from *London* to *Brighton*, organized by the *RAC*, and usually held on the first *Sunday* in November.

vicar /ˈvɪkə(r)/ (religion) A clergyman appointed to be the priest of a parish in the *Church of England*. Compare *rector*[1].

vicarage /ˈvɪkərɪdʒ/ (religion) The house provided by the *Church Commissioners* for a vicar in the *Church of England*. Compare *rectory*.

Vice Squad /ˈvaɪs skwɒd/, **the** (law) A police *department* dealing with prostitution, gambling, pornography and similar offences.

vice-chancellor /ˌvaɪs ˈtʃɑːnsələ(r)/ (education) The executive and administrative head of a university, usually elected or appointed for a fixed number of years from among the senior members of the university, in particular the heads of *colleges*[1]. Compare *chancellor*.

Victoria /vɪk'tɔːrɪə/ (transport) **1** A main line railway station and terminus in central *London*, from which trains run to southern *England*. **2** An *Underground* railway station there. [main line station, opened in 1860, was named in honour of *Queen Victoria*]

Victoria and Albert Museum /vɪk͵tɔːrɪə ən ͵ælbət mjuːˈzɪəm/, **the (V and A, the)** (arts) A famous museum in south central *London*, housing a national collection of fine and applied art of all countries and periods, especially collections of sculpture, water-colours, miniatures and a large art library. It grew out of the Museum of Manufactures established at *Marlborough House* in 1852, and was given its present name (in honour of *Queen Victoria* and her husband, Prince Albert) when founded in its present form, in 1899.

Victoria Cross /vɪk͵tɔːrɪə 'krɒs/ see *VC* (defence)

Victoria plum /vɪk͵tɔːrɪə 'plʌm/ (food and drink) A late-ripening dessert plum with round, dark red or yellow fruit and a delicious flavour. [named after *Queen Victoria*]

Victorian /vɪk'tɔːrɪən/ (history) A term used to refer to the times of *Queen Victoria* (reigned 1837–1901), who was considered to be, somewhat mistakenly, narrow-minded, hypocritical and humourless.

Victoriana /͵vɪktɔːrɪ'ɑːnə/ (style) Objects manufactured in the reign of *Queen Victoria* (reigned 1837–1901), in particular

Victoriana

ornaments, furnishings and household items. Such objects are sought after by many collectors and have, therefore, come to acquire a value and rarity much greater than their true worth.

Victory /'vɪktərɪ/, **the** (history) The flagship of Admiral Nelson at the Battle of *Trafalgar*, now preserved at Portsmouth, Hampshire, and open to the public.

village college /ˌvɪlɪdʒ 'kɒlɪdʒ/ (education) A centre, serving one or more villages, that provides educational and sports facilities, the former usually at post-school level. Such colleges grew up in the 1930s, and currently only five still exist, all in Cambridgeshire.

village green /ˌvɪlɪdʒ 'griːn/ (daily life) A grass area of common land found in or near the centre of many villages, and often serving as a recreational area or as a site for *fêtes* and other public gatherings.

village hall /ˌvɪlɪdʒ 'hɔːl/ (daily life) A kind of *community centre* in a village, often a smallish hall hired out for dances, *jumble sales*, public meetings, etc.

village idiot /ˌvɪlɪdʒ 'ɪdɪət/, **the** (tradition) A colloquial, somewhat dated, term for an eccentric or perhaps mentally disturbed person. The term was originally used for such a person who lived in a particular village and was well known to the other inhabitants.

vintage car /ˌvɪntɪdʒ 'kɑː(r)/ (transport) An old, usually carefully preserved, motor-car, technically one built between 1919 and 1930. Compare *veteran car*.

Viz /vɪz/ (media) A magazine of crude humour and satire published every two months. It consists chiefly of indecent cartoons and picture stories with obscene or irreverent captions. It first appeared in 1979 and has a current circulation of about 916,000.

Vogue /vəʊg/ (media) A monthly fashion magazine, with features and articles on a wide range of cultural and other subjects of interest to women. It was first published in 1916, and has a current circulation of about 181,000.

voluntary school /'vɒləntrɪ skuːl/ (education) A school maintained by an *LEA* but founded by a voluntary body, usually a religious denomination such as the *Church of England* or the *Roman Catholic Church*. Currently about one *state school* in three is a voluntary school. (The majority of other state schools are known as *county schools*.) See *church school*.

voting system /ˈvəʊtɪŋ ˌsɪstəm/ (government) In a *general election* or a local election, each voter casts one vote in a secret ballot for the candidate he or she wishes to support. The vote is normally made in person at a *polling station*. Voting is not compulsory, and in the general election of 1987 just over 75% of the electorate voted. The candidate who polls the most votes is elected (see *'first past the post'*), and in political elections there is no *proportional representation*, as in some countries.

V-sign /ˈviː saɪn/ (daily life) **1** A sign formed with the forefinger and middle finger of the hand (forming a 'V') with the palm turned outwards and the thumb holding down the third and fourth fingers, indicating victory (as in war, a match or an election). **2** A similar sign but with the palm turned inwards, and usually accompanied by an abrupt upward thrust of the arm, indicating contempt, defiance or general frustration. [in second sense, sign has sexual symbolism]

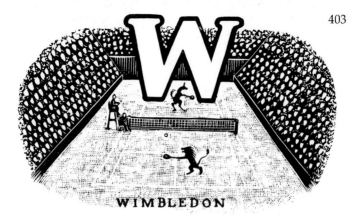

WIMBLEDON

W H Smith /ˌdʌblju: ˌeɪtʃ ˈsmɪθ/ (commerce) The full name of the chain-store stationery and record shops known more popularly as *Smith's*.

wakes week /ˈweɪks wiːk/ (tradition) An annual holiday in certain towns of the north of *England*, when factories and schools close for a week (occasionally two weeks).

Walker Cup /ˌwɔːkə ˈkʌp/, **the** (sport and leisure) A biennial golf tournament between amateur players of *Britain* and the United States, held since 1922 alternately in Britain and the United States. Compare *Ryder Cup*. [named after George H Walker, the American golfer who organized the event]

Wales /weɪlz/ (geography) The most westerly part of mainland *Britain*, bordered on the east by *England*. Wales (properly the 'Principality of Wales') is the smallest land of the *United Kingdom*, but has considerable variety, from the picturesque mountains of the north (including *Snowdonia*) to the mining and industrial areas of the south. Welsh is still spoken by about 19% of the population, mainly in the north and west. In recent years there has been increasing interest in encouraging the use of this Celtic language, especially in schools and by radio and television. See *S4C, eisteddfod*.

Wallace Collection /ˈwɒlɪs kəˌlekʃn/, **the** (arts) A collection of paintings, furniture and armour in central *London*, bequeathed to the nation by the widow of the art collector Sir Richard Wallace in 1897. A distinctive feature of the Collection is the French furniture and paintings of the 18th century.

Walworth Road /ˌwɔːlwəθ ˈrəʊd/ (politics) A road in south *London* where the headquarters of the *Labour Party* have been located since 1980, when they moved there from *Transport House*.

Wandsworth (Prison) /'wɒndzwəθ (ˌwɒndzwəθ 'prɪzn)/ (law)
The largest prison in *Britain*, founded in 1851 in the village
(now *London borough*[2]) of Wandsworth.

Wapping /'wɒpɪŋ/ (media) A district of east *London* where the
head offices of four of the five national newspapers owned by
Rupert *Murdoch* are located. These are The *Times*, The *Sunday
Times*, The *Sun* and the *News of the World*.

War on Want /ˌwɔːr ɒn 'wɒnt/ (charities) A charitable
organization collecting funds for the aid of poor and
underprivileged people in many countries of the world.

ward /wɔːd/ (government) A district of a *city*, town or other
area, used chiefly as an administrative unit in a political
election such as a *by-election* or *general election*, with each
ward having its own *polling station*.

warden /'wɔːdn/ (**1** education **2** daily life) **1** The head of
certain *colleges*[1,2] and higher or specialized educational
establishments (eg, All Souls College at *Oxford University* or
Lincoln Theological College). **2** The short title of a
churchwarden or *traffic warden*.

Wardour Street /'wɔːdə striːt/ (London) A central street in
London, famous for its many offices connected with the film
industry. [street named after family who built it in 17th
century]

Wars of the Roses /ˌwɔːz əv ðə 'rəʊzɪz/, **the** (history) The wars
in the second half of the 15th century between the house of
York (whose symbol was a white rose) and the house of
Lancaster (symbolized by a red rose). The aim of each side
was to win the throne of *England*, and each was sometimes
successful. The Wars ended in 1485 when Henry *Tudor* (house
of Lancaster) defeated Richard III (house of York) and became
Henry VII. Henry's marriage to Elizabeth of York united the
two sides and ended the fighting. See *rose*.

Wash /wɒʃ/, **the** (geography) A large but shallow inlet of the
North Sea (15 miles long, 12 miles wide) between
Lincolnshire and Norfolk. Much of the agricultural land
round the Wash has been reclaimed from the sea over a
period of many years.

watch night service /'wɒtʃ naɪt ˌsɜːvɪs/ (religion) A service held
in some *churche*s, or in a public place such as a square, on the
night of 31 December (*New Year's Eve*), to mark the passing of
the old year and to pray for what the New Year will bring.

Water Rat /'wɔːtə(r) ˌræt/ (charities) A show business
personality who belongs to the organization known as the

Grand Order of Water Rats. The organization, founded in 1889, has collected large sums of money for charity over the years and each November holds an eccentric variety show at the beginning of the *pantomime* season. Its officers have names such as 'King Rat', 'Scribe Rat', etc. [said to be named after the Water Rat, a winning racing pony at the time of the organization's foundation]

Waterloo /ˌwɔːtəˈluː/ (transport) **1** A main line railway station and terminus in *London*, south of the *Thames*, from which trains run to southern *England* and the *West Country*. **2** An Underground station there. [main line station is named after Waterloo Bridge, built over the Thames here in 1817 to mark the victory of the Battle of *Waterloo*]

Waterloo /ˌwɔːtəˈluː/ **(Battle of Waterloo, the)** (history) The final battle of the Napoleonic Wars, in which in 1815 near the village of Waterloo, Belgium, the English forces under the Duke of Wellington, with the support of Prussian forces under Field Marshal Blücher, gained a victory over the French army of Napoleon.

Waterloo and City Line /ˌwɔːtəluː ən ˈsɪti laɪn/, **the** (transport) One of the oldest *London Underground* railway lines (though with modern trains), linking *Waterloo[1,2]* with the *City (of London)*. It is used mainly by business people who live in the southern *Home Counties* (see *stockbroker belt*) and who travel daily to *Waterloo[1]*. The line, which is closed on *Sundays*, is operated by *BR*, not *London Transport*. See also *Drain*.

Watling Street /ˈwɒtlɪŋ striːt/ (history) One of the main *Roman roads* in *Britain*, running from Dover, Kent, through *Canterbury* to *London* and then north to St Albans, Hertfordshire and Wroxeter, Shropshire. [based on an old name of St Albans]

WEA /ˌdʌbljuː ˌiː ˈeɪ/, **the (Workers' Educational Association, the)** (education) An educational organization which runs courses for adults in a wide range of subjects. It does not support any particular political party or religious denomination. At present it has about 900 branches. When originally founded, in 1903, it aimed to provide education for *working class* people who might otherwise not have had it.

wedding breakfast /ˈwedɪŋ ˌbrekfəst/ (food and drink) A meal (not breakfast) served to guests at the reception that follows a wedding ceremony.

Wedgwood /ˈwedʒwʊd/ (style) A famous make of pottery and china. The most famous Wedgwood design has raised classical-style decorations in white on a pale blue background. [named after the potter Josiah Wedgwood (1730–95), who established a pottery near Stoke-on-Trent, Staffordshire in the late 18th century; see also *Potteries*]

weekend /ˌwiːkˈend/ (daily life) Traditionally, the period of relaxation and holiday between one working week and the next, extending from early Friday evening to *Sunday* night.

welfare officer /ˈwelfeər ˌɒfɪsə(r)/ (law) An alternative term for a *social worker* or *probation officer* who supervises the well-being and behaviour of a former juvenile criminal.

welfare state /ˌwelfeə ˈsteɪt/, **the** (government) A system by which the government provides the economic and social security of the population through its organization of health services, pensions and other facilities. In *Britain* the term applies mainly to the *NHS*, *national insurance* and *social security*.

welfare worker /ˈwelfeə ˌwɜːkə(r)/ (charities) A person who helps the underprivileged, poor or needy, especially the sick, elderly and handicapped, usually through a voluntary (charity) organization.

wellies /ˈweliːz/ (clothing) A colloquial name for *wellington boots*, whether worn by children or adults. See also *green wellies*.

wellington boots /ˌwelɪŋtən ˈbuːts/ **(wellingtons)** (clothing)

wellington boots

Knee-length (less often, calf-length) rubber boots, worn in wet weather or over wet ground. [they look like the leather boots worn by the Duke of Wellington (1769-1852)]

Wellington (College) /ˈwelɪŋtən (ˌwelɪŋtən ˈkɒlɪdʒ)/ (education) A large *public school[1]* at Crowthorne, Berkshire. It was founded in 1856 as a school for the sons of *Army* officers killed in battle, and was named in memory of the Duke of Wellington (see also *wellington boots*). It currently has about 800 students.

Welsh Guards /ˌwelʃ ˈgɑːdz/, **the** (defence) The most recently formed *Army* regiment of the *Guards Division*, established in 1915 from a group of Welshmen in the *Grenadier Guards*.

Welsh pony /ˌwelʃ ˈpəʊnɪ/ (animal world) A small, sturdy breed of pony, used mainly for *pony-trekking* but also for leisure riding. [originally bred in *Wales*]

Welsh rarebit /ˌwelʃ ˈreəbɪt/ **(Welsh rabbit)** (food and drink) A savoury dish consisting of melted cheese, sometimes with milk added, on hot *toast*. [originally 'Welsh rabbit', although never containing rabbit's meat]

Wembley /ˈwemblɪ/ (sport and leisure) A large sports stadium in northwest *Greater London*, where several important *football*, *rugby football* and hockey matches are held, including the *FA Cup* (see also *Cup Final*). In the large arena there matches and contests are held at international level in many other sports, such as badminton, basketball, boxing, cycling, ice hockey, show-jumping, tennis and table tennis.

Wendy house /ˈwendɪ haʊs/ (sport and leisure) A toy house that young children can play inside. [named after the house built for Wendy, the young heroine of the play *'Peter Pan[1]'* (1904) by J M Barrie]

Wensleydale (cheese) /ˈwenzlɪdeɪl (ˌwenzlɪdeɪl ˈtʃiːz)/ (food and drink) A white, crumbly cheese with a mild taste, originally produced in Wensleydale (a valley in North Yorkshire where the village of Wensley is located).

Wentworth /ˈwentwəθ/ (sport and leisure) A famous golf *club* and course in Virginia Water, Surrey. [on land formerly owned by a Mrs Wentworth (died 1816)]

West Brom /ˌwest ˈbrɒm/ (sport and leisure) The colloquial abbreviation for the West Midlands town of West Bromwich, especially when speaking of its *football club*, *West Bromwich Albion*.

West Bromwich Albion /ˌwest brɒmɪdʒ ˈælbɪən/ (sport and leisure) A popular *football club* founded in 1879, with a stadium (The Hawthorns) in West Bromwich, West Midlands. ['Albion' is a poetic name for *Britain* or *England*]

West Coast Line /ˌwest 'kəʊst ˌlaɪn/, **the** (transport) One of *BR*'s longest railway routes. linking *London* with *Britain*'s five most important cities: Birmingham, *Liverpool*, Manchester, *Glasgow* and *Edinburgh*. [north of Liverpool to the Scottish border the route is close to the west coast of *England*]

West Country /'west ˌkʌntrɪ/, **the** (geography) The southwest of *England*, especially the *counties* of *Cornwall*, Devon and Somerset.

West End /ˌwest 'end/, **the** (London) The area of west central *London* that contains the main fashionable shopping streets, *clubs*, high-class hotels, cinemas and theatres. Compare *East End*.

West Ham (United) /ˌwest 'hæm (ˌwest hæm juː'naɪtɪd)/ (sport and leisure) A well-known *football club* founded in 1900, with a stadium in Upton Park, near West Ham, east *London*.

Westcountry TV /ˌwest ˌkʌntrɪ tiː 'viː/ (media) One of the 15 regional television companies of the *ITC*, based in Plymouth and broadcasting to the *West Country*.

Western Approaches /ˌwestən ə'prəʊtʃɪz/, **the** (geography) The western shipping lanes of the English Channel, south of *Cornwall* and Devon.

Westminster /'westmɪnstə(r)/ (**1** London **2** government) **1** A *borough*[2] of central *London*, on the river *Thames*, containing several important buildings, including the *Houses of Parliament* and *Buckingham Palace*. **2** An alternative term for the Houses of Parliament, especially in the sense of the government of the day.

Westminster Abbey /ˌwestmɪnstər 'æbɪ/ (religion) One of the leading landmarks of *London*: a fine *Early English church* in *Westminster*[1] where almost all the English sovereigns have been crowned since the 11th century, and where many famous Englishmen and women are buried. (See also *Poets' Corner*, *Unknown Warrior*, *Stone of Scone*.)

Westminster Cathedral /ˌwestmɪnstə kə'θiːdrəl/ (religion) The principal *Roman Catholic Church* in *England*, in *Westminster*[1], *London*. The large church was built in neo-Byzantine style in the late 19th century and was opened in 1903.

Westminster Hall /ˌwestmɪnstə 'hɔːl/ (London) A large hall in *Westminster*[1], *London*, the only surviving part of the old *Palace of Westminster*[1], and one of the finest medieval halls in western Europe. The Hall was formerly a royal residence and in recent times the bodies of many sovereigns have lain in state there.

Westminster School /ˌwestmɪnstə ˈskuːl/ (education) A well-known *public school[1]* in *Westminster[1]*, *London*. It was founded in 1560 and has about 650 students.

wheel clamp

wheel clamp /ˈwiːl klæmp/ (law) A device used by the *police* or a private organization to prevent a car being driven when it has been illegally parked. The device, sometimes called a 'Denver boot' (from its original use in the city of Denver, Colorado, USA), is a strong clamp fixed to one wheel of the car. It is unlocked with a special key only when the driver has paid the fine.

wheelie bin /ˈwiːlɪ bɪn/ (daily life) A colloquial name for a large wheeled dustbin, especially one issued to householders by a *local authority* with the aim of simplifying the regular collection of refuse.

Which? /wɪtʃ/ (media) The monthly magazine of the *Consumers Association*, containing factual reports and details of the quality, content and performance of a range of consumer products and services. The magazine usually recommends a 'best buy' for each of the products it examines. 'Which?' is available only to members of the Consumers Association. It was first published in 1957, and now has several related supplements, eg, 'Holiday Which?', 'Gardening Which?', 'Car Buying Guide' and 'Tax-Saving Guide'. Its current circulation is about 650,000.

whip /wɪp/ (politics) **1** An *MP* in the *House of Commons*, or a *peer* in the *House of Lords*, appointed to organize the members of his party in parliamentary procedures, and in particular to ensure their participation in votes and debates. See also *Chief Whip*. **2** A schedule of parliamentary business sent out from time to time by a whip[1] to members of his party. See also *three-line whip*[1]. [term derives from 'whips' or 'whippers-in' employed by a *hunt* to control and discipline the hounds]

whippet /'wɪpɪt/ (animal world) A breed of thin, short-haired racing dog resembling (and probably originating from) a small *greyhound*. The dog is especially popular in the north of *England*.

Whipsnade (Zoo) /'wɪpsneɪd (ˌwɪpsneɪd 'zuː)/ (animal world) A large open-air zoo for over 2,000 animals near Dunstable, Bedfordshire, opened by the Zoological Society of London (see *London Zoo*) in 1931. The zoo occupies a park of 500 acres (200 hectares) in area. There are few cages at the zoo, and most animals are kept in open enclosures. [named after nearby village of Whipsnade]

whiskey /'wɪskɪ/ (food and drink) The usual spelling for *whisky* made in *Ireland* or the United States.

whisky /'wɪskɪ/ (food and drink) The traditional spirit drink of *Scotland*, made by distilling fermented cereals, especially malted barley. It is usually taken mixed with another drink, either alcoholic (eg, ginger wine, to make a *whisky mac*) or non-alcoholic (eg, soda water), although some whisky drinkers prefer the drink 'neat' (undiluted). Its country of origin gives it the popular alternative name of *Scotch*. Compare *whiskey*.

whisky mac /ˌwɪskɪ 'mæk/ (food and drink) A drink consisting of a mixture of *whisky* and ginger wine. ['mac' for the characteristic Scottish surname beginning 'Mac-' or 'Mc-' (as 'Macdonald' or 'McDonald')]

Whispering Gallery /'wɪspərɪŋ ˌgælərɪ/**, the** (London) A famous gallery in *St Paul's (Cathedral), London*. It runs right round the inside of the lower section of the dome. If someone who is standing near the wall on one side whispers some words, those words can be heard near the wall on the opposite side, 107 feet (32 m) away.

Whit Monday /ˌwɪt ˈmʌndɪ/ (tradition) The day following *Whit Sunday*, for many years (until the 1960s) one of the most popular *bank holidays* of the year. The name is still used unofficially for the *spring bank holiday* (which sometimes coincides with Whit Monday in the *church* calendar).

Whit Sunday /ˌwɪt ˈsʌndɪ/ (religion) A major festival in the Christian *church* that falls on the seventh *Sunday* after *Easter*. The day is named after the white robes formerly worn by converts to the church admitted at this time. The festival is still a popular occasion in some churches for the christening (baptism) of babies, also dressed in white.

Whitaker's Almanack /ˌwɪtəkəz ˈɔːlmənæk/ (media) A well-known annual reference book, containing a wide range of information, facts and figures about *Britain* and all the countries of the world. The Almanack also includes detailed astronomical data. It was first published by Joseph Whitaker in 1868 and is still issued by the publishing house he founded (today, J Whitaker & Sons).

White Ensign /ˌwaɪt ˈensən/, **the** (defence) The official ensign (flag) of the *Royal Navy*, consisting of a *St George's cross* on a white background with the *Union Jack* in the top left quarter (nearest the flagstaff). It is flown at the stern of all Royal Navy ships in daylight hours. It is also flown on the flagstaff of land naval establishments.

White Hart Lane /ˌwaɪt hɑːt ˈleɪn/ (sport and leisure) The stadium of *Tottenham Hotspur football club* in north *London*. [named after street where it is; street named after *inn* there]

white horse /ˌwaɪt ˈhɔːs/ (history) One of a number of large figures of horses carved out of the chalk hills at several points in the south of *England*, especially in the Vale of the White Horse, Berkshire and in Wiltshire. Many of the figures were made in prehistoric times.

white paper /ˌwaɪt ˈpeɪpə(r)/ (government) An official report setting out the government's policy on a matter being discussed, or about to be discussed, in *Parliament*.

white stick /ˌwaɪt ˈstɪk/ (daily life) A white stick carried by a blind or poorly sighted person and used for feeling the way ahead while walking. People who are both deaf and blind sometimes carry a white stick with two red reflective bands.

white tie /ˌwaɪt ˈtaɪ/ (clothing) A conventional indication on an invitation card that formal men's *evening dress* is to be worn.

White Tower /ˌwaɪt ˈtaʊə(r)/, **the** (history) The oldest part of the *Tower of London*, built in the 11th century and one of the largest *Norman* keeps in western Europe. The Tower, which is built in white stone imported from Normandy, is in the centre of the whole fortress and contains a fine collection of arms and armour. It is believed by some that the White Tower was the site of the murder of the *Princes in the Tower*, since the bones of two children were found there in the 17th century.

white-collar worker /ˌwaɪt ˈkɒlə ˌwɜːkə(r)/ (work) A person who does clerical or professional work, not manual work. Such people used to wear white shirts in contrast to the overalls (often blue) of a manual or *blue-collar worker*.

Whitehall /ˈwaɪthɔːl/ (**1** London **2** government) **1** A street in central *London* running from *Trafalgar Square* to the *Houses of Parliament* and containing many important buildings and government offices. **2** A term used for the government itself. [street named after former Whitehall Palace there, of which only the *Banqueting House* survives]

Whitehouse, Mary /ˈwaɪthaʊs, ˈmeəri/ (people) Mary Whitehouse (born 1910) became well-known in the 1960s and 1970s for campaigning against sex and violence on television. In 1964 she co-founded the Clean Up TV Campaign, and the following year the National Viewers' and Listeners' Association, with an initial membership of about 31,000. She later brought various legal charges against the media generally. She did not win all the cases, but she managed to overturn a proposal to abolish film censorship in *London* in 1975, convicted the magazine 'Gay News' of blasphemous libel in 1977, and stopped a National Theatre (now *Royal National Theatre*) production of the play 'The Romans in Britain' in 1982 on grounds of obscenity. In 1987 she launched a vigorous attack on the television series *Eastenders*, claiming its bad language and depiction of low moral values were a danger to viewers and their children. She retired from the National Viewers' and Listeners' Association in 1993.

Whitley Council /ˌwɪtli ˈkaʊnsl/ (work) An industrial council, at national or local level, that meets regularly to discuss and settle conditions of employment in the workplace. It is composed of representatives of employers and employees at all levels of a particular work force. [established as the result of a report made in 1917 by J H Whitley, an *MP*]

Who's Who /ˌhuːz 'huː/ (media) An annual biographical reference book of distinguished or titled (aristocratic) British people, giving (in the person's own words) details of his or her birth, family, career, posts held, special interests and current address and *club*. The work was first published in 1848, and today includes some entries for distinguished non-British people. However, few popular personalities are included. The interests ('recreations') given by some of the people are deliberately amusing, such as those of the writer Patricia Highsmith (snail-watching) or the actor John *Cleese* (gluttony).

WI /ˌdʌbljuː 'aɪ/**, the (Women's Institute, the)** (life and society) A local branch of the National Federation of Women's Institutes, an organization founded in 1915 with the aim of improving and developing the lives of women who live in rural areas. The Federation, through its many local branches, offers a wide range of social and cultural activities and courses. It also runs a number of country markets as part of the weekly markets held in *market towns* and *cities*. It has its own *further education* establishment. The WI currently has 355,000 members in over 9,000 local branches thoughout *England* and *Wales*.

Wightman Cup /ˌwaɪtmən 'kʌp/**, the** (sport and leisure) An annual contest between women tennis players of *Britain* and the United States, and also the prize awarded to the winning team. The contest was begun in 1923 by the American tennis champion Hazel Wightman. The matches are played alternately in Britain and the United States (in Britain, at *Wimbledon* regularly until the early 1970s).

Wigmore Hall /ˌwɪgmɔː 'hɔːl/**, the** (arts) A *London* concert hall opened in 1901 and used mainly for recitals of chamber music and songs. [in Wigmore Street]

William and Mary (style) /ˌwɪljəm ən 'meərɪ (staɪl)/ (style) A furniture style of the end of the 17th century, characterized by finely carved wooden chairs with upholstered seats, elegant tables and cabinets and a fashion for tallboys (high chests of drawers), with much use of walnut and exotic woods. [named after King William and Queen Mary who ruled together over the period 1688–94]

willow pattern /'wɪləʊ ˌpætn/ (style) A popular pattern on pottery and porcelain, usually in blue on a white background, and showing a stylized oriental scene of figures by a willow tree and a bridge over a river. [designed in the late 18th

willow pattern

century by the potter Thomas Turner]

Wilton (carpet) /ˈwɪltən (ˌwɪltən ˈkɑːpɪt)/ (style) A type of thick wool carpet. Most are plain and of just one colour, but some have an oriental pattern. They were first made at Wilton, Wiltshire.

Wimbledon /ˈwɪmbldən/ (sport and leisure) The short name of the *All England Club*, in the district of Wimbledon, southwest *Greater London*, where annual international tennis championships are held.

Winchester (College) /ˈwɪntʃestə(r) (ˌwɪntʃestə ˈkɒlɪdʒ)/ (education) A well-known *public school*[1] for boys in Winchester, Hampshire, founded in 1382 by the bishop of Winchester, William of Wykeham. It has 650 students. See also *Wykehamist*.

Windermere /ˈwɪndəmɪə(r)/ (geography) The largest natural lake in *England*, in the *Lake District*. It is $10\frac{1}{2}$ miles (16 km) long and 1 mile (1.6 km) wide. It is a popular tourist centre with many hotels and facilities for yachting, boating and fishing, and during the summer there is a regular boat service from one end to the other.

Windmill Theatre /ˌwɪndmɪl ˈθɪətə(r)/, **the** (London) A *London* theatre once famous for its non-stop variety shows with nearly nude girls, and for its slogan 'We never closed', referring to the fact that it was the only London theatre to remain open throughout the Second World War. Many well-known comedians began their career there. After a period as a cinema in the 1960s it reopened in the early 1970s, also as a variety theatre but with sex revues that today lack the former element of comedy. [named after a windmill there till the 18th century]

Windscale /'wɪndskeɪl/ see *Sellafield*

Windsor Castle /ˌwɪnzə 'kɑːsl/ (royal family) An official residence of the sovereign, in Windsor, Berkshire. William the *Conqueror* began to build the Castle in the 11th century, and it is now one of the most famous royal palaces in Europe. Some of the interior apartments are open to the public when the sovereign is not in residence, but the Albert Memorial Chapel is open throughout the year, being closed only on *Sundays*. *St George's Chapel*, however, is the better known of the two chapels, both because many members of the *royal family* go to a service there on *Christmas Day*, and because the *Order of the Garter* holds its special services there.

Windsor chair /ˌwɪnzə 'tʃeə(r)/ (style) A style of strong wooden chair popular from the late 18th century, with a shaped seat, a back containing slender, rod-shaped uprights and straight arm-rests. [originally made in Windsor, Berkshire, but later also in *Wales*]

Winnie the Pooh /ˌwɪnɪ ðə 'puː/ (arts) The toy bear ('of very little brain') who is the constant companion of the child hero, Christopher Robin, in the children's books by A A Milne (1882–1956), 'Winnie the Pooh' (1926) and 'The House at Pooh Corner' (1928). As with Lewis *Carroll*'s children's books, A A Milne's 'Pooh' books have come to be widely loved by adults. Christopher Robin was the author's young son, and Winnie the Pooh represents the boy's teddy bear that accompanied him everywhere.

Wisden /'wɪzdən/ (sport and leisure) A well-known *cricket* reference book. A new edition is published each year, giving full details of professional cricket matches and the performance of well-known cricketers. The book was first published in 1864 by the cricketer John Wisden. [full title, 'Wisden Cricketers' Almanack']

Woburn Abbey /ˌwəʊbən 'æbɪ/ (arts) An 18th-century *country house* near Luton, Bedfordshire, the home of the Duke of Bedford. The house and grounds are open to the public, who come to see the valuable collection of paintings and furniture in the house and the large deer park and bird sanctuary in the grounds. There is also an antiques market.

Wodehouse, P G /'wʊdhaʊs, 'piː ˌdʒiː/ (people) P G
Wodehouse (1881–1975) is best known for his comic novels of
upper class life about the young bachelor, Bertie Wooster, and
his manservant, Jeeves. The novels are set either in elegant
flats in *Mayfair, London*, or in grand baronial castles in the
country, and the same characters feature over and over again,
presenting a humorously exaggerated picture of English
aristocratic social life in the early part of the 20th century.
Wodehouse wrote more than 90 novels, and about a third of
these involve Bertie Wooster and Jeeves. Wodehouse also
wrote plays, musical comedy lyrics and film scripts. In 1955
he became an American citizen.

Wolverhampton Wanderers /ˌwʊlvəhæmptən 'wɒndərəz/ (sport
and leisure) A famous *football club*, founded in 1877, with a
stadium in Wolverhampton, West Midlands.

Wolves /wʊlvz/ (sport and leisure) The nickname of
Wolverhampton Wanderers football club.

Woman /'wʊmən/ (media) A popular illustrated weekly
magazine for women, containing a wide range of material
aimed at a broad readership. It was first published in 1937
and has a current circulation of about 860,000.

Woman and Home /ˌwʊmən ən 'həʊm/ (media) An illustrated
monthly magazine for women, containing articles and
features on fashion, beauty, home, cookery and travel, among
other topics. It was first published in 1926 and has a current
circulation of about 453,000.

Woman's Hour /'wʊmənz aʊə(r)/ (media) A daily hour-long
radio programme of topical and general interest to women,
broadcast each weekday on *Radio 4* since 1946.

Woman's Own /ˌwʊmənz 'əʊn/ (media) A popular illustrated
weekly magazine for women, containing short and serial
stories, often with a romantic theme, as well as practical
advice on the home, articles on fashion, and general features.
It was first published in 1932 and has a current circulation of
about 931,000.

Woman's Realm /ˌwʊmənz 'relm/ (media) An illustrated
weekly magazine for women, offering a wide range of
material, including 'human interest' articles, real-life love
stories, tales of adventure and the supernatural, and items of
general interest. It was first published in 1958 and has a
current circulation of about 483,000.

Woman's Weekly /ˌwʊmənz 'wiːklɪ/ (media) A popular weekly magazine for women, with a mixture of 'human interest' stories, features on film and television personalities, romantic fiction, and practical articles on the home. It was first published in 1911 and has a current circulation of about 905,000.

Wood, Victoria /'wʊd ˌvɪk'tɔːrɪə/ (people) Victoria Wood (born 1953) is a popular entertainer and writer who first became well-known in the early 1980s, when she appeared on television in sketches and plays that she had written herself. She was born in the *North (Country)*, and her sharp and often frank humour has made her a favourite with many.

woolsack /'wʊlsæk/, **the** (tradition) The seat on which the *Lord Chancellor* (as *Speaker*[2]) sits in the *House of Lords*. At present this is a large square cushion of wool, without back or arms, covered with red cloth. Originally there were four sacks of wool on which the sovereign's counsellor sat in medieval times.

Woolworth's /'wʊlwəθs/ (commerce) One of a large chain of stores, found in most towns in *Britain*, and developing in 1909 from the equivalent stores in the United States founded by Frank Winfield Woolworth in 1879. For many years the Woolworth stores sold goods at two cheap prices only (threepence and *sixpence*). Today, the stores stock a wide range of goods, from confectionery to home computers, and some of the bigger branches also have a restaurant. [in full, F W Woolworth & Co]

Worcester (china) /'wʊstə(r) (ˌwʊstə 'tʃaɪnə)/ (style) A type of superior porcelain made in Worcester since 1751, and particularly popular as table-ware.

Worcester sauce /ˌwʊstə 'sɔːs/ (food and drink) A strong-flavoured sauce made with vinegar and spices, originally produced in Worcester.

work-in /'wɜːkɪn/ (work) A form of strike in which workers occupy a factory that is due to close down, and attempt to continue working in it.

working class /'wɜːkɪŋ klɑːs/ (life and society) A social class of low status, made up almost entirely of manual workers but ranking above *lower class*. Some class-conscious manual workers are proud to be regarded as working class, seeing this as the productive base on which all the other social classes depend. Similarly, working class people who have risen to a higher class are often proud of their former status.

working men's club /ˌwɜːkɪŋ menz 'klʌb/ (sport and leisure) A

local *club* in a town or *city* for *working class* men, who meet
their work mates there to enjoy games such as *darts* and
cards, to drink, or to watch an entertainment of some kind
(often a comedy show, with or without a strip-tease act). The
working men's club is thus a blend of a modern *pub* and an
old-style music hall.

work-to-rule /ˌwɜːk tə ˈruːl/ (work) A form of strike or
industrial protest in which workers or employees keep
strictly to all the rules, thus slowing the rate of working or
production.

World Heritage Site /ˌwɜːld ˈherɪtɪdʒ ˌsaɪt/ (geography) A
unique or historic site that is listed by the World Heritage
Convention as a world site deserving protection. There are
currently 13 such sites in *Britain*, including *Avebury, Blenheim
Palace, Canterbury* Cathedral, the *Giant's Causeway, Hadrian's
Wall*, the *Palace of Westminster, Stonehenge*, the *Tower of
London* and *Westminster Abbey*.

World Service /ˌwɜːld ˈsɜːvɪs/ see *BBC World Service* (media)

Wormwood Scrubs /ˌwɜːmwʊd ˈskrʌbz/ (law) A large prison
for first-time male offenders, in northwest *London*. It was
opened in 1874. [name of original site there, with 'scrubs'
meaning 'woods']

Worship /ˈwɜːʃɪp/ (life and society) A title (preceded by
'Your', 'His' or 'Her') used to refer to a number of people of
high rank, in particular a *mayor* and a *magistrate*.

WRAC /ˌdʌbljuː ɑːr eɪ ˈsiː/, **the (Women's Royal Army Corps,
the)** (defence) The former women's branch of the British
Army, begun as the Auxiliary Territorial Service (ATS) in 1938
and renamed in 1949. The WRAC was finally disbanded in
1992. Women now belong to the Army and work in many of
the trade groups available to men.

WRAF /ˌdʌbljuː ɑːr eɪ ˈef/, **the (Women's Royal Air Force, the)**
(defence) The former women's branch of the *RAF*, originally
established in 1918, then disbanded in 1920 before being
re-formed as the Women's Auxiliary Air Force (WAAF) in
1939. The WRAF was formed out of the WAAF in 1949.
Women now work alongside the men in many trade groups,
but only rarely fly aircraft.

Wren /ren/ (defence) A name for a member of the *WRNS*.
[name based on initials WRNS, but influenced by the name
of the bird, noted for its small size, chattering and alertness]

writ /rɪt/ (law) A legal document requiring the person to
whom it is addressed to do some specific act, or not to do it. It

may be served by a *bailiff*.

WRNS /ˌdʌblju: ɑːr en 'es/, **the (Women's Royal Naval Service, the)** (defence) The women's section of the *Royal Navy*, first formed in 1917. It was disbanded in 1919 but was re-formed in 1939. Women work in many of the branches available to men, and now serve at sea in all ships except submarines and minelayers. The WRNS finally disbanded in 1994, so that women are now part of the Royal Navy. See also *Wren*.

WRVS /ˌdʌblju: ɑː vi: 'es/, **the (Women's Royal Voluntary Service, the)** (defence) An organization formed in 1938 to enable women not in the armed services to engage in war work, in particular in the Air Raid Precaution Services. After the Second World War, the WRVS changed its activities to cover welfare work for the armed services, the elderly (delivering *meals on wheels*), children (running holiday schemes and play centres) and the disabled. It also carries out welfare work in prisons. Another of its functions is to collect clothing and furniture, and to distribute them to people in need, and to help out in any local emergency such as a flood.

Wykehamist /'wɪkəmɪst/ (education) The name for a member, or former member, of *Winchester* (*College*), after the school's founder, William of Wykeham. ['Wykeham' is the historic spelling of Wickham, the village near Fareham in Hampshire where William was born]

X certificate /ˈeks səˌtɪfɪkət/ (arts) A certificate awarded until 1982 by the former British Board of Film Censors (now the *British Board of Film Classification*) to a cinema film that was regarded as unsuitable, because of its subject or because of particular scenes, for showing to people aged under 18. The title of the category was changed to *18* (listed under letter E).

Xmas /ˈkrɪsməs, also pronounced ˈeksməs/ (tradition) A conventional and commercial abbreviation of *Christmas*. [from the Greek letter 'X' that was used as a symbol for 'Christ' by early Christians]

Yard /jɑːd/, **the** (law) A colloquial term for *Scotland Yard* or *New Scotland Yard*.

ye olde tea shoppe /ˌjiː ˌəʊld ˈtiː ʃɒp/ (daily life) A mock Old English spelling of 'the old tea shop', used to refer to a *tea shop* in a historic building. The name is actually used by some tea shops in real or imitation historic buildings. ['ye', meaning 'the', originates from a mistranscription (as 'y') of an old letter representing 'th'; the spellings of 'olde' and 'shoppe' are regarded as typical of medieval English words]

Yearly Plan /ˌjɪəlɪ ˈplæn/ (finance) A government savings scheme operated by the *Post Office*, in which monthly contributions (from £20 to £400), paid over a fixed period, earn interest free of *income tax*. Payments must be made on fixed dates monthly by *standing order*.

yellow lines /ˌjeləʊ ˈlaɪnz/ (law) Yellow lines painted along the side of a road or street to indicate waiting restrictions for vehicles. A single yellow line means that no vehicle may wait (park) during the working day (usually from 8.0 am to 6.30 pm) except to load and unload. Two yellow lines close together normally mean that no vehicles may park there at any time.

Yellow Pages /ˌjeləʊ ˈpeɪdʒɪz/, **the** (commerce) A commercial telephone directory that lists subscribers according to their trade or business. It is printed on yellow paper and published by *BT*.

Yeoman Warder /ˌjəʊmən ˈwɔːdə(r)/ (tradition) One of the guardians at the *Tower of London*, who wears a similar uniform to that worn by the *Yeomen of the Guard*. Yeomen Warders have apparently existed since the 11th century, when the *White Tower* was built. A Yeoman Warder is popularly nicknamed a *Beefeater* (and this name is also sometimes used for a member of the Yeomen of the Guard).

Yeoman Warder

Yeomen of the Guard /ˌjəʊmən əv ðə ˈɡɑːd/, **the** (tradition) The men who form the bodyguard of the sovereign on state occasions. The bodyguard was first formed in the late 15th century, and the men still wear the red uniform of that period. Compare *Yeoman Warder*.

YHA /ˌwaɪ eɪtʃ ˈeɪ/ see *Youth Hostels Association* (sport and leisure)

YMCA /ˌwaɪ em si: ˈeɪ/, **the (Young Men's Christian Association, the)** (charities) A Christian organization offering a wide range of religious, educational, sports and social activities to young men of all races, religions and social backgrounds. It was founded in *Britain* in 1844, but now operates internationally. It is well known for its regional centres and hostels.

Yorkshire Post /ˌjɔːkʃə ˈpəʊst/, **the** (media) A daily *quality paper* published in Leeds, West Yorkshire, and covering much of the surrounding region. It is noted for its 'sober' style and content and right-wing views, but is one of the most influential regional papers in *Britain*. It was founded in 1754 (as the 'Leeds Intelligencer') and has a current circulation of about 93,000.

Yorkshire pudding /ˌjɔːkʃə ˈpʊdɪŋ/ (food and drink) A light savoury dish baked from a batter of flour, eggs and milk, and traditionally served with roast beef (usually for the main course of the midday meal on *Sunday*). See also *Sunday roast*.

Yorkshire Ripper /ˌjɔːkʃə ˈrɪpə(r)/, **the** (law) The nickname, widely used by the media, of the criminal Peter Sutcliffe (born 1946), from Bradford, West Yorkshire. He was convicted in 1981 of the murder of thirteen women. [so named from similarity of the crimes to those committed by *Jack the Ripper*]

Yorkshire Terrier /ˌjɔːkʃə ˈterɪə(r)/ (animal world) A small breed of terrier with a long, silky, steel-blue coat. [originally bred in the 19th century in West Yorkshire]

Yorkshire TV /ˌjɔːkʃə tiːˈviː/ **(YTV)** (media) One of the 15 regional television companies of the *ITC*, based in Leeds and broadcasting to the whole of Yorkshire, ie, the *counties²* of North, South and West Yorkshire. It is noted for the high standard of its programmes, especially plays, documentaries and comedies.

young offender institution /ˌjʌŋ əˈfendər ɪnstɪˌtjuːʃn/ A special place of detention for young offenders aged between 15 and 20. There are currently 30 young offender institutions in *England* and *Wales*.

Young Pretender /ˌjʌŋ prɪˈtendə(r)/, **the** (history) The nickname of Charles Edward Stuart, the Scottish prince (also known as *Bonnie Prince Charlie*) who was the pretender to (claimant for) the British throne in 1745. See the *Forty-Five*. [named by contrast with his father, James Francis Edward Stuart, nicknamed the Old Pretender]

Young Vic /ˌjʌŋ ˈvɪk/, **the** (arts) A theatre for young playgoers in *London*, founded in 1970 as part of the *National Theatre*. It was built in 1971 opposite the *Old Vic*.

youth club /ˈjuːθ klʌb/ (sport and leisure) A *club* for young people, usually one belonging to the National Association of Youth Clubs. Such a club offers a wide range of sporting and social activities for young people aged mainly between 14 and 21. They are run mainly by voluntary leaders and helpers, and they are frequently associated with a particular *church* or *community centre*.

youth court /ˈjuːθ kɔːt/ (law) A court of law for young offenders aged under 16. It is presided over by a *magistrate* and sits separately from any court for adult offenders.

youth hostel /ˈjuːθ ˌhɒstl/ (sport and leisure) A hostel run by the *Youth Hostels Association*.

Youth Hostels Association /ˈjuːθ ˌhɒstlz əsəʊsɪˌeɪʃn/, **the (YHA)** (sport and leisure) An organization first formed in *Britain* in 1930 (as a development of the movement founded in Germany in 1910) to provide cheap residential hostels for young travellers, in particular walkers and cyclists. The Association is now operated internationally, and in Britain, as in many other countries, membership is not restricted to young people.

Youth Training Scheme /ˌjuːθ ˈtreɪnɪŋ ˌskiːm/, **the (YTS, the)** (work) A government scheme that guarantees unemployed school leavers a training course for a trade or practical career.

Yule/yule log /ˈjuːl/ˈjuːl lɒg/ (tradition) A large log of wood traditionally used as the basis of a fire in a hearth at *Christmas*. Such fires are found in some *country houses*, hotels, and *pubs*, as well as larger private homes. [from 'yule', an old pagan festival held in mid-winter, and later replaced by the Christian festival of Christmas]

YWCA /ˌwaɪ dʌbljuː siː ˈeɪ/, **the (Young Women's Christian Association, the)** (charities) The sister organization of the *YMCA*, founded in 1855, and now operating internationally. It is well known for its hostels and flatlets, offering accommodation to young single women living or working away from home.

zebra crossing /ˌzebrə ˈkrɒsɪŋ/ (transport) A pedestrian crossing over a road, marked with alternating black and white stripes. Such crossings are indicated by *Belisha beacons*, and are often operated as a *pelican crossing*. [from black and white stripes like those of a zebra]

Index

British Film Institute
British Library
British Museum
Burrell Collection
Cheltenham Festival
Chichester Festival
choir
coffee-table book
Coliseum (Theatre)
copyright library
Courtauld Institute
  (Galleries)
Covent Garden
Dr Watson
Drury Lane
Ealing comedy
Edinburgh Festival
18
eisteddfod
Elgin Marbles
English Chamber Orchestra
English National Ballet
English National Opera
English Stage Company
15
Fitzwilliam Museum
Fringe
G and S
Geffrye Museum
Georgian poets
Gilbert and Sullivan operas
Globe (Theatre)
Glyndebourne
Gothic novel
Gray's Elegy
Greensleeves
Hallé (Orchestra)
Haymarket (Theatre)
Hayward Gallery
Her Majesty's Theatre
Holmes, Sherlock
Lake Poets

Lake School
Last Night of the Proms
Lilliburlero/Lillibullero
London Library
London Mozart Players
London Philharmonic
  Orchestra
London Symphony
  Orchestra
Londonderry Air
Magic Circle
Malvern Festival
Mermaid Theatre
Mersey sound
mod
Museum of Mankind
Museum of the Moving
  Image
National Film Theatre
National Gallery
National Portrait Gallery
National Youth Orchestra
National Youth Theatre
New Sadler's Wells Opera
Norwich School
Old Vic
Palladium
Penguin
Peter Pan
PG
Philharmonia Orchestra
Pinewood Studios
Poet Laureate
Poets' Corner
Pre-Raphaelites
Promenade Concerts
promenader
Proms
Purcell Room
Queen Elizabeth Hall
Queen's Gallery
Rambert Dance Company

Round House
Royal Academy (of Arts)
Royal Ballet
Royal Court (Theatre)
Royal Festival Hall
Royal Liverpool
  Philharmonic Orchestra
Royal Museum of Scotland
Royal National Theatre
Royal Opera
Royal Opera House
Royal Pavilion
Royal Philharmonic
  Orchestra
Royal Shakespeare
  Company
Royal Shakespeare Theatre
Royal Variety
  Show/Performance
Sadler's Wells (Theatre)
Savoy (Theatre)
Savoy Operas
Scrooge
season ticket
Shaw's Corner
St Trinian's
Swan (Theatre)
Tate (Gallery)
Theatre Royal
Theatre Upstairs
Three Choirs Festival
Times Literary Supplement
12
V and A
Victoria and Albert
  Museum
Wallace Collection
Wigmore Hall
Winnie the Pooh
Woburn Abbey
X certificate
Young Vic

charities
AA
Abbeyfield home
Age Concern
Alcohol Concern
Alcoholics Anonymous
almshouse
Amnesty International
ASH
Barnardos
British Legion
Charity Commission
Cheshire Homes
ChildLine
Christian Aid
Church Army
Church Urban Fund
Civic Trust
Crisis
Darby and Joan club
flag day
Gingerbread
Help the Aged
Lions Club
MENCAP
MIND
National Lottery
NSPCA
NSPCC
Oxfam/OXFAM
PDSA
Relate
Royal British Legion
Royal National Institute for
  the Blind
Royal National Institute for
  the Deaf
Royal National Lifeboat
  Institution
Royal Society for the
  Protection of Birds
RSPCA
Samaritans

Save the Children Fund
Shaftesbury Society
Shelter
SPCK
sponsored walk
Toc H
Variety Club
War on Want
Water Rat
welfare worker
WRVS
YMCA
YWCA

clothing
Barbour jacket
black tie
blazer
boater
boiler suit
bowler
brogues
Burberry
busby
cap
cavalry twill
cloth cap
deerstalker (hat)
dinner jacket
dog-collar
donkey jacket
duffle-coat
Eton suit
evening dress
Fair Isle
fancy dress
glengarry
gown
green wellies
guernsey
gum boots
Harris tweed

heather mixture
jersey
kilt
morning coat
morning dress
Moss Bros
paisley shawl
Peter Pan collar
pinstripe suit
plaid
plus-fours
pork-pie hat
rosette
sporran
sports jacket
tam-o'-shanter
tartan
top hat
trilby (hat)
twin set
wellies
wellington boots
white tie

commerce
bargain basement
Blackwell's
book token
British Philatelic Bureau
British Telecom
broker
BT
BTA
Bull Ring
cardphone
chamber of commerce
Christie's
Consumers Association
convenience store
Co-op
Co-operative Movement
Co-operative Wholesale
  Society

corner shop
Datapost
estate agent
F W Woolworth
first class
Fortnum and Mason
Foyle's
Freefone
Freepost
garden centre
gazumping
gift token
goodwill
GPO
Harrods
HMV
Ideal Home Exhibition
Liberty's
Luncheon Voucher
market garden
Marks & Spencer
Mercury
Milk Marque
Mount Pleasant
MRP
Muzak
national call
National Exhibition Centre
National Grid Company
National Power
nationalized industries
NCP
Nuclear Power
off-licence
Offer
Ofgas
Oftel
Ofwat
Olympia
Parcelforce
payphone
phonecard
Post Office

PowerGen
Recorded
regional electricity
  company
Registered
Registered Plus
restrictive practice
Royal Mail
Sainsburys
sandwich man
Scottish Hydro-Electric
Scottish Nuclear
Scottish Power
second class
Selfridges
service charge
service road
set-aside
Shell Centre
shopping precinct
Silicon Glen
Smith's
Sotheby's
Speaking Clock
Special Delivery
Stanley Gibbons
Swiftair
telemessage
Timeline
trading estate
TV licence
Universal Aunts
W H Smith
Woolworth's
Yellow Pages

daily life
A to Z
Advertising Standards
  Authority
allotment
A1
August Bank Holiday

avoirdupois
bank holiday
Bank Holiday Monday
bed and breakfast
bedsit(ter)
beer garden
bob
bottle bank
bring-and-buy (sale)
BST
CAB
Caff
Cambridge blue
CAMRA
car boot sale
chapel of rest
Chubb (lock)
community centre
conference centre
copper
council estate
council house
court
dialling code
DIY
dress circle
Easter Monday
Entryphone
ex-directory
fayre
fête
first floor
fiver
foolscap
foot
free house
front room
gallon
gill
granny flat
Green Cross Code
ground floor
guest house

happy hour
hatches, matches and
  dispatches
Heath Robinson
High Street
home help
housing estate
inch
inn
inn sign
Jiffybag
jumble sale
Kitemark
knees-up
landlady
licensing hours
lighting-up time
living room
local
local call
lodge
lollipop lady/man
lounge bar
market day
meals on wheels
Meccano
milkman
National Garden Festival
naughty postcard
Neighbourhood Watch
999
north of Watford
office party
open day
Oxford blue
paperboy/papergirl
pavement artist
paying guest
piggy bank
pint
playground
Portakabin
postcode

postman
private bar
private hotel
pub
public bar
PYO
quid
reception room
sale of work
saloon bar
Saturday girl
Saturday person
Scotch mist
sense of humour
service flat
sheltered housing
shilling
sixpence
smallholding
snug
Spring Bank Holiday
St Swithin's Day
strap-hanger
Summer Bank Holiday
summer time
Tannoy
teashop
tenner
three-line whip
tied house
tombola
transport café
village green
village hall
V-sign
warden
weekend
wheelie bin
white stick
ye olde tea shoppe

defence
Admiralty

Aldermaston
Army
Black Watch
Blue Ensign
Blues and Royals
Coldstream Guards
Commandos
D-notice
Edinburgh Military Tattoo
Fleet Air Arm
GCHQ
Gordon Highlanders
Green Jackets
Grenadier Guards
Guards
Guards Division
guardsman
highlander
HMS
Holy Loch
Horse Guards
Household Cavalry
Household Troops
Imperial War Museum
Irish Guards
Life Guards
MI5
MI6
NAAFI
Naffy
NATO
RAF
Red Arrows
Red Devils
Royal Aircraft
  Establishment
Royal Highland Regiment
Royal Horse Guards
Royal Marines
Royal Naval Reserve
Royal Navy
Royal Regiment
Royal Scots

Royals
SAS
Scots Greys
Scots Guards
senior service
Spithead Review
Territorial Army
Trident
VC
Victoria Cross
Welsh Guards
White Ensign
WRAC
WRAF
Wren
WRNS

education
academic year
academy
adult education
A-level
ARELS
AS-level
Aston (University)
ATL
BA
Backs
BEd
Billy Bunter
Birkbeck (College)
Britannia Royal Naval
  College
British Council
BSc
Cambridge
Cambridge Certificate
Cambridge University
cap
cathedral school
CFE
chancellor

Charterhouse (School)
choir school
Christ's Hospital
church school
city technology college
Clifton (College)
college
college of education
Common Entrance
commoner
comprehensive school
correspondence college
correspondence course
county school
CPVE
crammer
Cranwell
Dartmouth
day release
day boy
day girl
dean
dinner lady
don
Duke of Edinburgh's
  Award Scheme
Dulwich (College)
Edinburgh Academy
eleven-plus
Encyclopaedia Britannica
Eton (College)
fellow
fifth form/year
finishing school
first class
first degree
first school
fresher
further education
GCSE
general degree
Gordonstoun (School)
governor

gown
graduate
graduate student
grammar school
grant-maintained school
Greats
Greyfriars
Guildhall School of Music
  (and Drama)
half-term
hall
hall of residence
Harrow (School)
Heriot-Watt University
high school
higher degree
higher education
honours degree
house
housefather/housemother
housemaster
housemistress
independent school
infant school
kindergarten
King's School
LEA
lodge
London University
long vacation
lower school
LSE
MA
Marlborough (College)
master
mature student
Mays
middle school
Mods
mortarboard
National Curriculum
Natural History Museum
nursery school

NUS
NUT
old boy
old girl
old school tie
Open College
Open University
Outward Bound Trust
Oxbridge
Oxford
Oxford University
pass (degree)
PGCE
playgroup
playschool
polytechnic
postgraduate
prefect
prep school
preparatory school
pre-preparatory school
pre-school playgroup
primary school
private school
proctor
provost
PTA
public school
Queen's English Society
Queen's University
RADA
Radcliffe Camera
rag (week)
reader
rector
redbrick university
Regius professor
Roedean (School)
Royal Academy of Music
Royal Ballet School
Royal College of Art
Royal College of Music
Royal Military Academy

Royal Naval College
RSA
Rugby (School)
Sandhurst
sandwich course
scholarship
school song
school tie
school welfare officer
school year
Scottish Certificate of
  Education
Scout/scout
second class
secondary modern (school)
secondary school
self-governing school
set book
Sheldonian (Theatre)
Shrewsbury (School)
sixth form
sixth form college
Slade School of (Fine) Art
special school
speech day
sports day
St Paul's Girls' School
St Paul's (School)
state school
streaming
summer school
supply teacher
tech
technical school
term
tertiary college
Times Educational
  Supplement
tripos
tutor
UCCA
undergraduate
upper school

vice-chancellor
village college
voluntary school
warden
WEA
Wellington (College)
Westminster (School)
Winchester (College)
Wykehamist

finance
APR
BACS
Baltic (Exchange)
Bank of England
Bank of Scotland
Barclays (Bank)
base rate
bear
big four
black
blue chip
broker
building society
bull
bursar
capital gains tax
CHAPS
chartered accountant
child benefit
Christmas bonus
clearing bank
closing price
Clydesdale Bank
corporation tax
council tax
Coutts
death duty
debit card
direct debit
disability living allowance
discount house

dividend
divvy
dole
Ernie
Exchange Rate Mechanism
family allowance
family credit
50 pence (piece)
finance house
financial year
5 pence (piece)
Footsie
friendly society
FT Index
gilt-edged securities
giro
giro cheque
Girobank
ground rent
guinea
halfpenny
holding company
House
housing association
housing benefit
Income Bonds
income support
income tax
inheritance tax
Inland Revenue
insurance broker
invalidity benefit
investment trust
IOU
limited company
Lloyd's
Lloyds (Bank)
Lombard Street
Ltd
market-maker
maternity allowance
maternity pay
merchant bank

Midland (Bank)
MIRAS
mortgage
National Debt
national insurance
National Savings Bank
National Savings
  Certificates
National Westminster
  (Bank)
NatWest
old age pension
Old Lady of Threadneedle
  Street
ordinary shares
pay packet
PAYE
penny
PEP/Pep
PLC/Plc/plc
Post Office Counters
postal order
pound (sterling)
preference shares
Premium (Savings) Bonds
private company
private income
private limited company
private means
provident society
PSBR
public limited company
red
Royal Bank of Scotland
Royal Mint
Savings Certificates
scrip issue
SERPS
share shop
sickness benefit
sleeping partner
Social Fund
social security

stamp duty
standing order
statutory sick pay
Stock Exchange
stockbroker
supplementary benefit
Switch
take-home pay
10 pence (piece)
TESSA
third-party insurance
Threadneedle Street
Throgmorton Street
Town Clearance
Trustcard
Trustee Savings Bank
20 pence (piece)
2 pence (piece)
two pound coin
two-shilling piece
underwriter
unemployment benefit
unit trust
unlisted securities market
unquoted company
VAT
Yearly Plan

food and drink
bacon and eggs
bacon sarnie
Bakewell tart
Banbury cake
bangers and mash
bannock
bap
bar
bar snacks
Bath bun
Bath Oliver
Beaujolais Nouveau
bitter

black pudding
Blenheim Orange
Bloody Mary
Bramley's (Seedling)
bread and butter pudding
Bristol Cream
Bristol Milk
bubble and squeak
buck's fizz
bullseye
butterscotch
butty
Caerphilly
Cheddar (cheese)
Chelsea bun
Cheshire (cheese)
chippy
Christmas dinner
Christmas pudding
clotted cream
cock-a-leekie
Conference (pear)
continental breakfast
Cornish pasty
cottage loaf
cottage pie
Cox's (Orange Pippin)
cream cracker
crumpet
cuppa
custard
Devonshire cream
dinner
dog's nose
doorstep
double
double Gloucester (cheese)
draught beer
drop scone
Dundee cake
Dunlop
Eccles cake
Edinburgh rock

elevenses
English breakfast
fish and chips
fish fingers
fudge
Gaelic coffee
gin
gin and tonic
ginger biscuit
gobstopper
Granny Smith
gravy
griddle cake
Guinness
haggis
high tea
hot cross bun
hotpot
hundreds and thousands
Irish coffee
Irish stew
jelly
jugged hare
kipper
Lancashire (cheese)
lardy cake
Laxton's Superb
light ale
liquorice allsorts
lollipop
lunch
luncheon
Madeira cake
marmalade
Melba toast
Melton Mowbray pie
mild
mince pie
mincemeat
mock turtle soup
Mrs Beeton
muffin
mushy peas

oatcake
pancakes
pease pudding
Pimms
pinta
ploughman's lunch
plum pudding
porridge
pudding
real ale
red biddy
rock
rock cake
roly-poly
Sally Lunn
sausage roll
schooner
scone
Scotch
Scotch broth
Scotch eggs
Scotch woodcock
scrumpy
shandy
shepherd's pie
shortbread
simnel cake
sloe gin
snow pudding
spotted dick
spotted dog
steak and kidney pie
steak and kidney pudding
Stilton (cheese)
stout
strawberries and cream
Sturmer
suet pudding
summer pudding
Swiss roll
takeaway
tea
teacake

tipsy cake
toad-in-the-hole
toast
toffee apple
trifle
Victoria plum
wedding breakfast
Welsh rarebit
Wensleydale (cheese)
whiskey
whisky
whisky mac
Worcester sauce
Yorkshire pudding

geography
Aberdonian
Anglesey
area of outstanding natural
  beauty
Belfast
Ben Nevis
benchmark
B'ham
Black Country
Blackpool
Borders
Boston Stump
Bournemouth
Brecon Beacons
bridleway
Brighton
Brit
Britain
British Isles
Briton
Broads
Brum
Brummie
built-up area
Caernarfon
Cairngorms

Caledonia
Caledonian Canal
Cambria
Cambridge
Canterbury
Cardiff
cathedral city
Celtic fringe
Cerne Giant
Channel Islands
Cheltenham
Chilterns
Cinque Ports
city
Clyde
conference centre
conservation area
Constable country
Cornwall
Countryside Commission
county
county town
croft
dalesman
Dartmoor
Derwentwater
dewpond
Downs
East Anglia
Edinburgh
England
Fens
Fingal's Cave
forest park
Forth
garden city
Garden of England
garden suburb
garden village
Geordie
Giant's Causeway
Glasgow
Glaswegian

Gloucester
GMT
Gog Magog Hills
Goodwin Sands
Gorbals
Grampians
Granite City
Granta
Grasmere
Great Britain
Great Glen
green belt
Greenwich
Greenwich Park
Harrogate
Hastings
Hebrides
heritage coast
highlander
Highlands
Highlands and Islands
Holy Island
Home Counties
inner city
Inverness
Iona
Ireland
Isis
Isle of Man
Isle of Wight
John o'Groats
Kentishman
Lake District
Land's End
Liverpudlian
Loch Lomond
Loch Ness
Lough Neagh
Lowlands
Man of Kent
Mancunian
market town
metropolitan county

Middle England
Midlands
national grid
national park
national scenic area
nature reserve
New Commonwealth
new town
Newmarket
Norfolk Broads
North (Country)
North/South Divide
Northern Ireland
Ordnance Survey
Orkneys
Oxford
Peak District
Pennine Way
Pennines
Pilgrims' Way
postal district
Potteries
Princes Street
right of way
Rutland
Salisbury Plain
Salopian
Sarum
Scilly Isles
Scotland
Scottish Natural Heritage
Scouse
Severn
Shakespeare country
Shetlands
Shires
site of special scientific
  interest
Snowdonia
South Downs
St Andrews
stile

stockbroker belt
Stratford-(up)on-Avon
Sullom Voe
Thames
Tintagel
tor
UK
Ullswater
Ulster
unadopted road
United Kingdom
Wales
Wash
West Country
Western Approaches
Windermere
World Heritage Site

government
Admiralty
alderman
another place
backbencher
ballot paper
bill
Black Rod
borough
borough council
Boundary Commission
Budget
burgh
Cabinet
Chancellor of the Duchy of
  Lancaster
Chancellor of the Exchequer
Chancery
Chequers
Chiltern Hundreds
Citizen's Charter
City Action Team
civic centre
civil servant

Civil Service
Clerk of the House (of
  Commons)
COI
Common Agricultural
  Policy
Common Market
Commons
community council
constituency
constitutional monarchy
council house
councillor
Countryside Council for
  Wales
county council
County Hall
crossbencher
Crown
Crown Agent
Customs and Excise
department
Deputy Lieutenant
devolution
Diplomatic Service
direct rule
district council
division
Downing Street
duty-free
EC
English Heritage
English Nature
Euro-MP
Father of the House
first reading
Foreign and
  Commonwealth Office
Foreign Secretary
Forestry Commission
front bench
frontbencher
gangway

Great Seal
green paper
guillotine
Hansard
High Commissioner
HMG
HMSO
Home Office
Home Secretary
House
House of Commons
House of Lords
Houses of Parliament
Lancaster House
Leader of the House
Leader of the Opposition
local authority
Local Government
  Commission
London Gazette
lord
Lord Chancellor
Lord High Chancellor
Lord Lieutenant
Lord Mayor
Lord President of the
  Council
Lord Privy Seal
Lord Provost
Lords Spiritual
Lords Temporal
Maastricht Treaty
maiden speech
mayor
minister
ministry
Monopolies and Mergers
  Commission
MP
National Rivers Authority
Northern Ireland Assembly
Number Ten/No 10
ombudsman

Opposition
order in council
order paper
Palace of Westminster
parish council
Parliament
Parliamentary
  Commissioner
parliamentary private
  secretary
parliamentary secretary
parliamentary under-
  secretary of state
Patent Office
Paymaster General
President of the Board of
  Trade
Prime Minister
private bill
private member
private member's bill
Privy Council
Privy
  Councillor/Counsellor
Privy Seal
prorogation
public bill
Public Record Office
quango
Queen's Speech
recess
registry office
returning officer
seat
second reading
Secretary of State
Sergeant/Serjeant at Arms
Shadow Cabinet
Shadow minister
sheriff
Single Market
speaker
Speech from the Throne

State Opening of
  Parliament
Stormont
Strangers' Gallery
Task Force
Taxpayer's Charter
third reading
three-line whip
town clerk
town council
town hall
Treasury
Tynwald
Urban Programme
voting system
ward
welfare state
Westminster
white paper
Whitehall

history
Abdication
Act of Supremacy
Act of Union
ancient monument
Anne Hathaway's Cottage
Antonine Wall
Armada
Armistice Day
Battle of Britain
Battle of Britain Day
Black Prince
Blenheim
Blenheim Palace
Blitz
Bloody Mary
Bloody Tower
Boer War
Bonnie Prince Charlie
Boyne
Britannia

British Empire
Briton
Chartwell
Commonwealth
Conqueror
Conquest
Coronation
Coronation Chair
Culloden
Cutty Sark
D-day
Depression
Discovery
Domesday Book
Druids
Duchy of Cornwall
Duchy of Lancaster
Dunkirk
Edgehill
Edinburgh Castle
Eleanor Cross
English Civil War
Ermine Street
Festival of Britain
Fifth of November
Forty-Five
Fosse Way
Gaiety Girls
General Strike
Georgian
Glencoe Massacre
Globe (Theatre)
Glorious Twelfth
Golden Age
Golden Hind
Great Exhibition
Great Fire (of London)
Great Plague (of London)
Great Train Robbery
guinea
Gunpowder Plot
Hadrian's Wall
Hampton Court

Hastings
Home Guard
hundred
Industrial Revolution
Jack the Ripper
Jorvik Viking Centre
listed building
Long Man of Wilmington
Magna Carta
Martello tower
Merry Monarch
national service
Norman Conquest
Oak Apple Day
Offa's Dyke
Old Contemptibles
Penny Black
Prince Consort
Prince Regent
Princes in the Tower
Protectorate
Restoration
Roman road
Royal Mile
Sealed Knot Society
St George's Chapel
  (Windsor)
Titanic
Trafalgar
Unknown Warrior
Victorian
Victory
Wars of the Roses
Waterloo
Watling Street
white horse
White Tower
Young Pretender

language
A N Other
Anglo-Saxon

Basic English
BBC English
Brewer
clerihew
Estuary English
four-letter word
Fowler
Gaelic
ITA
limerick
Manx
Oxford accent
Oxford English Dictionary
Piccadilly Circus
pidgin English
Queen's English
rhyming slang
Roget
RP
Scouse

law
Act (of Parliament)
act of God
age of consent
age of discretion
Anglo-Irish Agreement
attendance centre
attorney
Attorney General
bailiff
bar
barrister
Black Maria
bobby
borstal
bound over
Bow Street
Broadmoor
by-law
capital punishment
caution

Central Criminal Court
chambers
Chancery
Chief Constable
CID
citizen's arrest
coming of age
common law
common law husband/wife
constable
copper
coroner
court
crown court
Crown Prosecution Service
Dartmoor
death penalty
decree absolute
decree nisi
detention centre
DPP
Flying Squad
Fraud Squad
governor
Gray's Inn
habeas corpus
H-blocks
High Court (of Justice)
Holloway (Prison)
immigration
Inner Temple
Inns of Court
internment
JP
jury
Law Lords
Law Society
legal aid
Lincoln's Inn
lord
Lord Chief Justice
magistrate
Master of the Rolls

Maze (Prison)
McNaughten Rules
Metropolitan Police
Middle Temple
minor
M'Lud
Moor
Murder Squad
naturalization
New Scotland Yard
not proven
Old Bailey
panda car
parish warden
Parkhurst (prison)
patrial
penal system
penalty points
Pentonville (prison)
planning permission
police
Prevention of Terrorism Act
prison visitor
private treaty
probate
probation
probation officer
probationer
procurator fiscal
Public Lending Right
QC
quarter day
Queen's Bench Division
receiver
recorder
Regina
registrar
remand centre
royal assent
Royal Ulster Constabulary
RUC
Scotland Yard
Scrubs

select committee
Serious Fraud Office
sheriff
silk
snatch squad
solicitor
Solicitor General
Special Branch
special constable
summons
Supreme Court (of
  Judicature)
term
Trade Descriptions Act
treasure trove
Vice Squad
Wandsworth (Prison)
welfare officer
wheel clamp
Wormwood Scrubs
writ
Yard
yellow lines
Yorkshire Ripper
young offender institution
youth court

life and society
BEM
Birthday Honours
blimp
bluestocking
Book Trust
bottle party
brother
Burke('s Peerage)
BYOB
cardboard city
chieftain
childminder
clan
club
College of Arms

Colonel Blimp
Commission for Racial
  Equality
commoner
Companion of Honour
constable
corporal punishment
Country Code
crofter
Dame
Debrett
Disgusted, Tunbridge Wells
Druids
duchy
Earl Marshal
English-Speaking Union
Enterprise Neptune
Equal Opportunities
  Commission
Establishment
fellow
freedom (of the city)
garden party
Garter
Garter ceremony
gaudy
GC
gentleman
gentleman farmer
gentleman-at-arms
gentleman's gentleman
Gentlemen-at-Arms
gentry
George Cross
George Medal
ginger group
glue-sniffing
God Save the Queen
Gold Stick
governor
Grace and Favour residence
Grand Old Man
greetings card

hall
hen night
hereditary peer
hippie
Honourable
Hooray Henry
in-laws
Joneses
lady
lager lout
laird
latchkey child
life peer
Lord Chamberlain
Lord's Day Observance
  Society
lower class
lower middle class
ma'am
madam
Master
mayoress
Men of the Trees
Mensa
Messrs
middle class
Miss
Mods
MORI
Mr
Mrs
Ms
My Lady
My Lord
nanny
national anthem
National Council for Civil
  Liberties
National Trust
National Trust for Scotland
New Year Honours
non-U

Norland nurse
Notting Hill Carnival
OAP
OBE
old boy network
one-upmanship
Order of Merit
Order of the Bath
Order of the Garter
Order of the Thistle
Oxford Group
peer
peerage
peeress
Peter Pan
race relations
rest home
Right Honourable
Rockers
Rotary Club
Round Table
senior citizen
servants
sir
Sir
Sloane
Sloane Ranger
soapbox
social worker
stag night
stately home
suburbia
Sunday
Sunday roast/joint
tied cottage
town and gown
upper class
upper middle class
WI
winter of discontent
working class
Worship

London

Palace of Westminster
Pall Mall
Park Lane
pearly king/queen
Peter Pan
Petticoat Lane
Piccadilly
Portobello Road
Queen Victoria Memorial
Regent Street
Regent's Park
Ritz
Rotten Row
Round Pond
Row
Royal Albert Hall
Royal Mews
royal park
Savoy (Hotel)
Serpentine
Shaftesbury Avenue
Smith Square
Smithfield (Market)
Soho
Somerset House
South Bank
Speakers' Corner
Spitalfields
Square Mile
St Clement Danes
St James's Palace
St James's Park
St John's, Smith Square
St Martin-in-the-Fields
St Mary-le-Bow
Strand
Tattersall's
Telecom Tower
Temple
Temple Bar
Temple Church
Tottenham Court Road
Tower Bridge
Tower Hill

Tower of London
Trafalgar Square
Wardour Street
West End
Westminster
Westminster Hall
Whispering Gallery
Whitehall
Windmill Theatre

media
agony aunt
Andy Capp
Anglia TV
annual
Any Questions?
Archers
Auntie
Autocar & Motor
BBC
BBC 1
BBC Television Centre
BBC 2
BBC World Service
Beano
Beeb
Bill, The
Blue Peter
Border TV
Brain of Britain
breakfast TV
British Broadcasting
  Corporation
BRMB
Broadcasting House
Brookside
BSkyB
Bunty
Bush House
Capital Radio
Carlton TV
Catholic Herald

Catholic Times
Ceefax
Central TV
Channel 4
Channel TV
Chat
Church Times
Classic FM
Company
Cook Report
Coronation Street
Cosmopolitan
Countdown
Country Life
Daily Express
Daily Mail
Daily Mirror
Daily Sport
Daily Star
Daily Telegraph
Dandy
Desert Island Discs
Doctor Who
EastEnders
Economist
Elle
Emmerdale
Evening Standard
Exchange and Mart
Exchange Telegraph
  Company
Express
Extel
Field
Financial Times
Fleet Street
fourth estate
free paper
FT
Gardener's World
Garnett, Alf
GLR
GMTV

Good Housekeeping
Goons
gossip column
GQ
Gramophone
Grampian TV
Granada TV
Grandstand
Guardian
Guinness Book of Records
gutter press
heavies
Hello!
HTV
Illustrated London News
ILR
In Britain
INR
Independent
IRN
ITN
ITV
Jazz FM
Just Seventeen
Kelly's (Directories)
local radio
LWT
Mail
Mail on Sunday
Man Alive
Mandy/Judy
Marplan
Mastermind
Melody Maker
Meridian
Mirror
Morning Star
Neighbours
New Scientist
New Statesman and Society
News at Ten
News of the World
Nine O'Clock News

NME
Observer
Old Moore's Almanack
page three
Panorama
People
personal column
pips
popular paper
Press Association
Press Council
Prestel
Prima
Printing House Square
Private Eye
quality paper
Radio Authority
Radio 5 Live
Radio 4
Radio 1
Radio 3
Radio Times
Radio 2
red book
Reith lectures
Reuters
Scotsman
Scottish TV
S4C
She
silly season
Sky
Smash Hits
South Bank Show
Spectator
Spectrum International
  Radio
Spitting Image
Sporting Life
Street
Sun
Sunday Express
Sunday Mirror

Sunday People
Sunday Sport
Sunday Telegraph
Sunday Times
Sunrise Radio
Tablet
tabloid
Take a Break
Telegraph
Teletext
That's Life
third leader
This England
This Is Your Life
Time Out
Times
Times Ed
Times Higher Educational
  Supplement
Titbits
Today
Top of the Pops
top shelf magazine
top ten
Tribune
TV Times
Tyne Tees TV
Ulster TV
Universe
Viz
Vogue
Wapping
Westcountry TV
Which?
Whitaker's Almanack
Who's Who
Woman
Woman and Home
Woman's Hour
Woman's Own
Woman's Realm
Woman's Weekly
World Service
Yorkshire Post
Yorkshire TV

medicine
Bart's
blood donor
BMA
BUPA
Charing Cross Hospital
cottage hospital
district nurse
donor card
EN
general hospital
general practitioner
government health warning
GP
Great Ormond Street
group practice
Guy's Hospital
Harefield Hospital
Harley Street
health centre
health visitor
hospice
King's College Hospital
Lancet
locum
matron
Medical Research Council
Middlesex Hospital
NHS
nursing home
Papworth Hospital
PPP
prescription
private patient
private practice
registrar
RGN
SEN
SRN
St Bartholomew's Hospital
St John Ambulance
  (Brigade)

St Thomas's Hospital
Stoke Mandeville
surgery
teaching hospital
University College Hospital

people
Adie, Kate
Amis, Kingsley
Ashdown, Paddy
Attenborough, David
Austen, Jane
Ayckbourn, Alan
Bacon, Francis
Beatles
Bellamy, David
Benn, Tony
Bennett, Alan
Betjeman, John
Birtwistle, Harrison
Black, Cilla
Blyton, Enid
Bowie, David
Bragg, Melvyn
Branagh, Kenneth
Britten, Benjamin
Burgess, Anthony
Carey, George
Carroll, Lewis
Cartland, Barbara
Christie, Agatha
Christie, Linford
Churchill, Winston
Cleese, John
Collins, Phil
Dickens, Charles
Drabble, Margaret
Elgar, Edward
Gielgud, John
Glover, Jane
Golding, William

Greene, Graham
Guinness, Alec
Gunnell, Sally
Heath, Edward
Henry VIII
Heseltine, Michael
Hockney, David
Hughes, Ted
Hume, Basil
John, Elton
King Arthur
Larkin, Philip
Lively, Penelope
Lloyd Webber, Andrew
Major, John
Milton, John
Morris, Desmond
Murdoch, Iris
Murdoch, Rupert
Olivier, Laurence
Owen, David
Paisley, Ian
Patten, Chris
Pinter, Harold
Potter, Dennis
Rattle, Simon
Redgrave, Vanessa
Rice, Anneka
Richard, Cliff
Rolling Stones
Russell, Ken
Savile, Jimmy
Shakespeare, William
Smith, John
Stoppard, Tom
Sugar, Alan
Thatcher, Margaret
Thomas, Dylan
Vaughan Williams, Ralph
Whitehouse, Mary
Wodehouse, P G
Wood, Victoria

politics
Alliance Party (of Northern Ireland)
blue
Bow Group
British National Party
by-election
Chief Whip
coalition
cod war
Commonwealth
Conservative Party
dry
electoral register
Fabian Society
first past the post
Friends of the Earth
fringe party
general election
Green Party
Home Rule
IRA
Irish Republican Army
Labour Party
landslide (victory)
Lib Dems
Liberal Democrats
Liberal Party
Loyalists
marginal constituency
marginal seat
National Front
Orangemen
Paisleyites
party political broadcast
Plaid Cymru
polling booth
polling day
polling station
polls
postal vote
presiding officer
Primrose League

proportional representation
Provisionals
proxy vote
Red Flag
safe seat
SDLP
SDP
Sinn Féin
sit-in
SNP
Social Democratic and
  Labour Party
surgery
three-cornered fight
Tory
Transport House
Troubles
UDR
Ulster Defence Association
Ulster Democratic Unionist
  Party
Ulster Unionist Party
Ulster Volunteer Force
Unionist Party
Walworth Road
whip

religion
Advent
Anglican
Anglo-Catholic
Archbishop of Canterbury
Archbishop of York
Ascension Day
Ash Wednesday
Authorized Version
Baptists
Book of Common Prayer
carol service
chapel
chapel royal
Christmas
church

Church Commissioners
Church House
Church of England
Church of Scotland
churchwarden
close
Crockford
curate
deacon
deaconess
dean
district visitor
Easter
Free Churches
General Assembly of the
  Church of Scotland
General Synod
Good Friday
grace
harvest festival
High Church
Hymns Ancient and
  Modern
Jerusalem Bible
King James Bible
kirk
Lady Chapel
Lady Day
Lambeth Conference
Lambeth Palace
lay reader
Lent
lord
Low Church
Low Sunday
Methodist
Methodist Church
minister
minster
Nonconformists
Oxford Movement
Palm Sunday

parish church
parish magazine
parish register
parson
Passion Sunday
PCC
Plymouth Brethren
presbytery
primate
Primate of All England
Primate of England
provost
Quakers
rector
rectory
registry
Reverend
Revised Version
Right Reverend
Rogation Days
Roman Catholic Church
Sally Army
Salvation Army
Salvationist
Shrove Tuesday
sidesman
Society of Friends
St Paul's (Cathedral)
suffragan bishop
Sunday school
Synod
Thirty-Nine Articles
Trinity Sunday
United Reformed Church
verger
Very Reverend
vicar
vicarage
watch night service
Westminster Abbey
Westminster Cathedral
Whit Sunday

royal family
Anne, Princess
Balmoral (Castle)
Britannia
Buck House
Buckingham Palace
Charles, Prince
Civil List
Clarence House
court circular
Diana, Princess
Duchess of York
Duke of Cornwall
Duke of Edinburgh
Duke of Windsor
Duke of York
Ferguson, Sarah
Glamis Castle
Her Majesty
Holyrood House
king
lady-in-waiting
Margaret, Princess
Master of the Horse
Master of the Queen's
  Music
Official Birthday
Palace
Philip, Prince
prince
Prince of Wales
princess
Princess of Wales
Princess Royal
Privy Purse
queen
Queen Elizabeth
Queen Elizabeth, the
  Queen Mother
queen mother
Queen Victoria
Queen's Birthday
royal duke

royal family
Royal Highness
royal salute
royal standard
Royal Yacht
Royals
Sandringham
Windsor Castle

science and technology
Astronomer Royal
BP
British Aerospace
British Association
British Gas
British Nuclear Fuels (Plc)
British Steel
British Technology Group
BSI
Geological Museum
Harwell
ICI
Jodrell Bank
National Physical
  Laboratory
North Sea gas
North Sea oil
nuclear-free zone
nuclear power
Porton Down
Royal Greenwich
  Observatory
Royal Society
Science Museum
science park
Sellafield
Sizewell
Thames Barrier
United Kingdom Atomic
  Energy Authority
Windscale

sport and leisure
accumulator

Admiral's Cup
Aintree
Alexandra Park
All England Club
all-in wrestling
Alton Towers
Amateur Athletics
  Association
Anfield Road
Arsenal
Ascot
association football
Aston Villa
autumn double
Badger
Badminton (Horse Trials)
ballboy/ballgirl
bar billiards
Barbarians
Beaver (Scout)
Becher's Brook
beer tent
betting shop
bingo
Bisley
blood sports
blue
Bluebird
Boat Race
Boat Show
bookie
bookmaker
bouncy castle
bowl
bowling
bowls
boy scout
Braemar Gathering
Brands Hatch
British Grand Prix
British Lions
British Open
  (Championship)

Brownie (Guide)
Butlin's
Cambridge blue
cap
Celtic
Chelsea
Cheltenham Gold Cup
Chief Scout
clock golf
colours
conkers
county cricket
coursing
Cowdray Park
Cowes (Week)
cricket
Crystal Palace
cub (scout)
Cup
Cup Final
cup tie
curling
darts
Derby
Devizes-Westminster race
Diamond Sculls
dinner dance
division
Dodgem
dogs
donkey derby
double
drive
each way bet
Edgbaston
egg-and-spoon race
Eights
eleven
Epsom
eventing
Everton
FA
FA Cup

Fastnet (Race)
field sports
fives
Flat
fly-fishing
Fontwell Park
football
Football League
French cricket
front
Fulham
fun run
gala
gamekeeper
gamesmanship
Gang Show
Gay Gordons
gillie
Girl Guide
Glorious Goodwood
Glorious Twelfth
Gold Cup Day
Goodison Park
Goodwood
Grand National
Greyhound Derby
greyhound racing
groundsman
grouse shooting
Guide
Guider
Guides Association
gun-dog
gymkhana
Hampden Park
Hampden roar
hare and hounds
hat trick
Head of the River Race
Heart of Midlothian
Hearts
Henley Regatta
Hibernian

Highland fling
Highland games
Highland gathering
hopscotch
hornpipe
Horse of the Year Show
hunt
hunt-the-thimble
Hurlingham
Ibrox Park
Isis
I-spy
jamboree
Jockey Club
jodhpurs
Kempton Park
Ladies' Day
League Against Cruel
  Sports
leisure centre
Liverpool Football Club
London Marathon
Lonsdale Belt
Lord's
Lord's Taverners
lucky dip
ludo
Mallory Park
Manchester City
Manchester United
master of foxhounds
master of hounds
Mays
MCC
Milk Race
Moor Park
morris dance
Murrayfield
musical chairs
National
national trail
nineteenth hole
Ninian Park

Norwich City
nursery stakes
Old Trafford
Oulton Park
Oval
Oxford blue
Paul Jones
pig in the middle
point-to-point
Pony Club
pony-trekking
pools
postman's knock
Premier League
Premiership
punt
punter
putting
Pytchley (Hunt)
QPR
Queen of the South
Queen's Club
Queen's Park Rangers
Queen's Prize
Queensberry Rules
Quorn
race meeting
rackets
raffle
Rainbow (Guide)
rambler
Ranger (Guide)
Rangers
real tennis
redcoat
Round the Island Race
rounders
Royal and Ancient
Royal Ascot
Royal Enclosure
Royal International Horse
  Show
Royal Tournament

rugby football
rugby league
rugby union
rugger
Ryder Cup
Sandown Park
Scout/scout
Scout Association
Scrabble
Sheffield United
Sheffield Wednesday
shinty
shooting stick
shove-ha'penny
Silverstone
snakes and ladders
snap
snooker
soapbox
soccer
spring double
Spurs
squash (rackets)
St Mirren
starting price
Steward's Cup
strathspey
striker
sweepstake
sword dance
Tattenham Corner
test match
theme park
Three As
three-card trick
three-day event
three-legged race
tick-tack man
tip and run
tombola
torpids
tossing the caber
Tote

Tottenham Hotspur
treble chance
Trent Bridge
Triple Crown
Triple Event
TT
turf
turf accountant
Twickenham
United
University Match
Valentine's Brook
Walker Cup
Wembley
Wendy house
Wentworth
West Brom
West Bromwich Albion
West Ham (United)
White Hart Lane
Wightman Cup
Wimbledon
Wisden
Wolverhampton Wanderers
Wolves
working men's club
YHA
youth club
youth hotel
Youth Hostels Association

style
Adam (style)
Bridge of Sighs
but and ben
Chippendale
close
Coalport
cottage
country house
court
Crown Derby
Decorated (style)

detached house
Doulton (pottery)
drive
Dutch barn
Early English
Elizabethan
folly
gate-leg(ged) table
Georgian (style)
gnome
Gothic Revival
Gothic (style)
Hepplewhite
Jacobean
Kidderminster (carpet)
Minton
Norman
paisley pattern
pebble dash
Perpendicular (style)
quadrangle
Queen Anne (style)
Regency (style)
Royal Worcester
Saxon (architecture)
semi(-detached house)
Sheraton
Spode (china)
tartan
terraced house
toby jug
town house
Tudor (style)
Victoriana
Wedgwood
William and Mary (style)
willow pattern
Wilton (carpet)
Windsor chair
Worcester (china)

tradition
Apprentice Boys' Parade

April Fools' Day
Auld Lang Syne
Aunt Sally
Avebury
Bampton fair
Bath and West
beating the bounds
Beefeater
bell ringing
best man
bonfire night
Boxing Day
Britannia
Burns' Night
busker
Canterbury bell
ceilidh
Ceremony of the Keys
change ringing
Chelsea Pensioners
Christmas Day
Christmas Eve
Christmas tree
corn exchange
cracker
Crown Jewels
daffodil
dame
Easter egg
farthing
Father Christmas
Father's Day
folk museum
Furry Dance
Goldsmiths' Company
Good King Wenceslas
Goose Fair
Great Tom
Gretna Green
guildhall
guy
Guy Fawkes' Day
Guy Fawkes' Night

gyp
Hallowe'en
Heart of Oak
Hogmanay
holly
Home, Sweet Home
Humpty Dumpty
It's a Long Way to
  Tipperary
Jack the Giant-Killer
Jack-in-the-box
Jerusalem
Jock
John Bull
Knights of the Round Table
Lambeth Walk
Land of Hope and Glory
Land of My Fathers
leap year
leek
lion
Liver bird
livery company
Loch Ness Monster
loyal toast
Lutine bell
Lyonesse
Maundy money
Maundy Thursday
May Day
May Queen
maypole
Men of Harlech
Merlin
Merry England
Michaelmas
Midsummer Day
Moonraker
Mothering Sunday
Mother's Day
nativity play
Nessie
New Year's Day

New Year's Eve
nursery rhyme
O Come, All Ye Faithful
oranges and lemons
other place
oyez
Paddy
Pancake Day
pancake race
pantomime
Poppy Day
principal boy
Punch and Judy
Red Hand of Ulster
Remembrance Sunday
Robin Hood
rose
Round Table
Royal Smithfield Show
Rule, Britannia
Santa Claus
Scots, wha hae
shamrock
Silbury Hill
St Andrew's cross
St Andrew's Day
St David's Day
St George's cross
St George's Day
St Patrick's cross
St Patrick's Day
stiff upper lip
stocking filler
Stone of Scone
Stonehenge
swan-upping
Taffy
thistle
Tommy
tossing the pancake
town crier
Trooping the Colour
Twelfth Night

two-minute silence
unicorn
Union Flag
Union Jack
village idiot
wakes week
Whit Monday
woolsack
Xmas
Yeoman Warder
Yeoman of the Guard
Yule/yule log

transport
AA
Air Miles
A-1
APEX/Apex
A-road
BAA
Beaulieu
Belisha beacon
Bentley
Bluebell Railway
box junction
BR
British Airways
British Leyland
British Shipbuilders
B-road
brown sign
bucket shop
bus pass
CAA
cat's-eyes
Channel Tunnel
Charing Cross
Chunnel
Clansman
Clapham Junction
clearway
Clifton Suspension Bridge
Concorde

Cornish Riviera
Cunard
Daimler
derv
disc parking
double decker
Drain
driving licence
DVLC
estate car
E-type
Euston
Farnborough Air Show
first class
Forth Bridge
freightliner
Gatwick
Golden Hind
Grand Union Canal
Great North Road
green card
Green Line Bus
GT
hackney carriage
Heathrow
HGV
Highway Code
hovercraft
hoverport
Hoverspeed
InterCity
ITC
Jaguar
juggernaut
King's Cross
Kiss 100 FM
L-driver
Liverpool Street
Lloyd's Register
LNR
London Airport
London Bridge
London Transport

London Underground
L-plates
Mansion House
Marylebone
Metro
Metrolink
M4
MG
midibus
Mini
M1
Montagu Motor Museum
MOT (Test)
Motability
Motor Show
Motorail
motorway
M25
mystery tour
National Railway Museum
Network SouthEast
Nightrider
orange badge
P & O
Pacer
Paddington
parking ticket
Parkway
pelican crossing
Penalty Fare
penny-farthing
Piccadilly Circus
Port of London Authority
Postbus
Prestwick
private road
provisional licence
Pullman (train)
QE2
Queen Elizabeth 2
RAC
Rail Rover
railcard

Red Arrow (bus)
Red Ensign
reg
Regional Railways
registration number
Roller
Rolls(-Royce)
Rover
Saver
season ticket
second class
service area
service station
Severn Bridge
Severn Tunnel
shooting brake
sleeping policeman
slip road
Spaghetti Junction
speed limit
Sprinter
St Pancras
standard class
Stansted (Airport)
Stena Sealink
Supersaver
tax disc
Temple
Thameslink
traffic warden
Travelcard
Trident
Trinity House
trunk road
tube
Underground
vehicle licence
veteran car
Veteran Car Run
Victoria
vintage car
Waterloo
Waterloo and City Line

West Coast Line
zebra crossing

work
ACAS
AEEU
Aslef
assisted area
ASTMS
blacking
blackleg
block release
block vote
blue-collar worker
British Coal
British Steel
CBI
chapel
clerk of works
closed shop
collective bargaining
Congress House
development area
Durham Miners' Gala
Employment Training
enterprise zone
Equity
father of the chapel
flying pickets
fringe benefits
ganger
General Council
girl Friday
GMB
golden handshake
go-slow
industrial action
industrial council
industrial estate

Institute of Directors
intermediate area
Jobcentre
Jobclub
jobs for the boys
lump
MSF
National Coal Board
National Farmers Union
NFU
nine-to-five job
NUJ
NUM
open shop
PA
Parkinson's law
pickets
probationer
Remploy
Restart
restrictive practice
retirement age
RMT
secondary picketing
shop steward
sit-down strike
strike pay
T and G
TGWU
TUC
UDM
Unison
unofficial strike
USDAW
white-collar worker
Whitley Council
work-in
work-to-rule
Youth Training Scheme

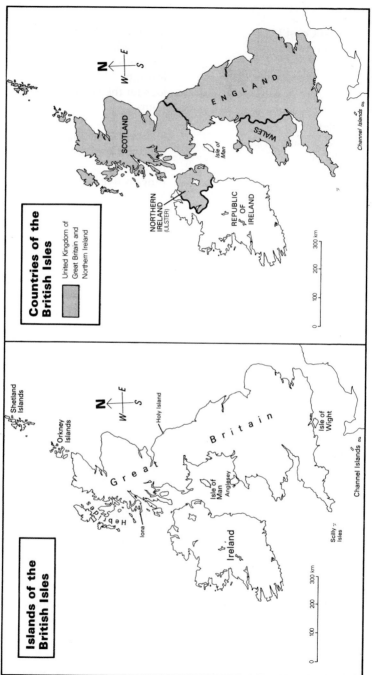

Countries of the British Isles

United Kingdom of Great Britain and Northern Ireland

SCOTLAND

ENGLAND

WALES

Isle of Man

NORTHERN IRELAND (ULSTER)

REPUBLIC OF IRELAND

Channel Islands

0 100 200 300 km

Islands of the British Isles

Shetland Islands

Orkney Islands

Hebrides

Iona

Great Britain

Holy Island

Isle of Man

Anglesey

Ireland

Isle of Wight

Scilly Isles

Channel Islands

0 100 200 300 km

467

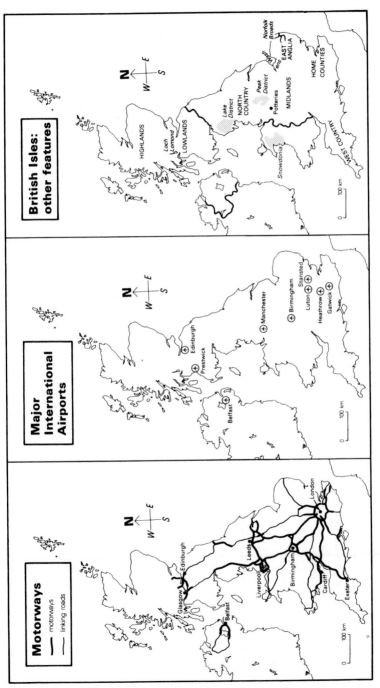

Motorways

— motorways
— linking roads

0 100 km

Glasgow · Edinburgh · Belfast · Leeds · Liverpool · Birmingham · Cardiff · London · Exeter

Major International Airports

0 100 km

Belfast · Prestwick · Edinburgh · Manchester · Birmingham · Stansted · Luton · Heathrow · Gatwick

British Isles: other features

0 100 km

HIGHLANDS · Loch Lomond · LOWLANDS · Lake District · NORTH COUNTRY · Peak District · Potteries · MIDLANDS · Snowdonia · Fens · Norfolk Broads · EAST ANGLIA · HOME COUNTIES · WEST COUNTRY

468

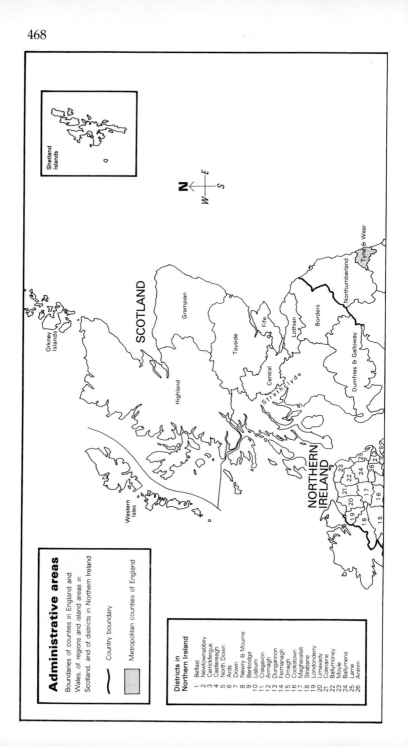

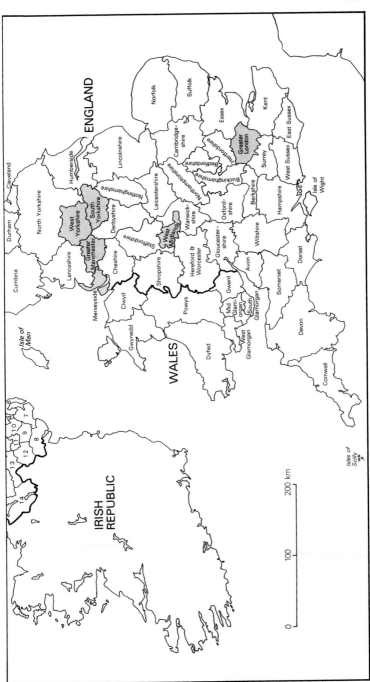

Peers in order of rank

(and current number of each)

Peers
royal duke (5)
duke (24)
marquess (35)
earl (195)
viscount (125)
baron (460)

Peeresses
countess (5)
baroness (16)

The figures are for hereditary titles only, not for life peers.

Order of succession to the throne

(first ten only)

1 Prince Charles, Prince of Wales (eldest son of the Queen), born 1948
2 Prince William (first son of Prince Charles), born 1982
3 Prince Henry (second son of Prince Charles), born 1984
4 Prince Andrew, Duke of York (second son of the Queen), born 1960
5 Princess Beatrice (first child of Prince Andrew), born 1988
6 Princess Eugenie (second child of Prince Andrew), born 1990
7 Prince Edward (third son of the Queen), born 1964
8 Princess Anne, Princess Royal (only daughter of the Queen), born 1950
9 Peter Phillips (only son of Princess Anne), born 1977
10 Zara Phillips (only daughter of Princess Anne), born 1981

Relative ranks of the armed forces (officers)

Royal Navy
Admiral of the Fleet
Admiral
Vice-Admiral
Rear-Admiral
Commodore
Captain
Commander
Lieutenant-Commander
Lieutenant
Sub-Lieutenant
Acting Sub-Lieutenant

Army
Field Marshal
General
Lieutenant-General
Major-General
Brigadier
Colonel
Lieutenant-Colonel
Major
Captain
Lieutenant
Second Lieutenant

Royal Air Force
Marshal of the Royal Air Force
Air Chief Marshal
Air Marshal
Air Vice-Marshal
Air Commodore
Group Captain
Wing Commander
Squadron Leader
Flight-Lieutenant
Flying Officer
Pilot Officer

Coins

penny

2 pence (piece)

5 pence (piece)

10 pence (piece)

20 pence (piece)

50 pence (piece)

pound (sterling)

Calendar of special days

New Year's Day	1 January
Twelfth Night	6 January
Burns' Night (Scotland)	25 January
St David's Day	1 March
St Patrick's Day	17 March
April Fools' Day	1 April
St George's Day	23 April
May Day	1 May
Mother's Day	second Sunday in May
Father's Day	third Sunday in June
August Bank Holiday	first Monday in August (Scotland)
	last Monday in August (England, Wales, N Ireland)
Guy Fawkes' Night	5 November
St Andrew's Day	30 November
Christmas Eve	24 December
Christmas Day	25 December
Boxing Day	26 December
New Year's Eve, Hogmanay (Scotland)	31 December

The dates of the following days depend on the date of Easter Sunday, which is variable—from mid-March to mid-April:

Shrove Tuesday (Pancake Day)	day before Ash Wednesday
Ash Wednesday	40 days before Easter
Palm Sunday	Sunday before Easter
Good Friday	Friday before Easter Sunday
Easter Sunday	variable—from mid-March to mid-April
Ascension Day	40th day after Easter
Whit Sunday	seventh Sunday after Easter

Common forenames

female names

Alison /ˈælɪsn/
Angela /ˈændʒələ/
Ann, Anne /æn/
Annabel, Annabelle /ˈænəbel/
Barbara, Barbra /ˈbɑːbrə/
Brenda /ˈbrendə/
Carol, Carole /ˈkærəl/
Caroline /ˈkærəlaɪn/
Christina /krɪˈstiːnə/
Christine /ˈkrɪstiːn/
Clare, Claire /kleə(r)/
Daphne /ˈdæfnɪ/
Deborah /ˈdebərə/
Diana /daɪˈænə/
Doreen, Dorene /ˈdɔːriːn/
Doris /ˈdɒrɪs/
Dorothy /ˈdɒrəθɪ/
Eileen /ˈaɪliːn/; Aileen/ˈeɪliːn/
Elaine /ɪˈleɪn/
Elizabeth, Elisabeth
  /ɪˈlɪzəbəθ/
Emma /ˈemə/
Evelyn /ˈiːvlɪn/
Fiona /fɪˈəʊnə/
Frances /ˈfrɑːnsɪs/
Gillian /ˈdʒɪlɪən/
Glenda /ˈglendə/
Hazel /ˈheɪzl/
Heather /ˈheðə(r)/
Helen /ˈhelən/
Jane /dʒeɪn/
Janet /ˈdʒænɪt/
Janice, Janis /ˈdʒænɪs/
Jacqueline /ˈdʒækəlɪn/
Jean /dʒiːn/
Jennifer /ˈdʒenɪfə(r)/
Joanna /dʒəʊˈænə/
Joyce /dʒɔɪs/
Judith /ˈdʒuːdɪθ/
Julia/ˈdʒuːlɪə/
June/dʒuːn/
Karen, Karin /ˈkærən/

Katherine, Catherine
  /ˈkæθrɪn/
Laura /ˈlɔːrə/
Lesley /ˈlezlɪ/
Linda /ˈlɪndə/
Louise /luːˈiːz/; Louisa/
  luːˈiːzə/
Margaret /ˈmɑːgrɪt/
Marian, Marion /ˈmærɪən/
Marilyn /ˈmærəlɪn/
Mary /ˈmeərɪ/
Maureen /ˈmɔːriːn/
Moira /ˈmɔɪrə/
Muriel /ˈmjʊərɪəl/
Nicola /ˈnɪkələ/
Pamela /ˈpæmələ/
Patricia /pəˈtrɪʃə/
Pauline /ˈpɔːliːn/
Rachel /ˈreɪtʃl/
Rita /ˈriːtə/
Rosemary /ˈrəʊzmərɪ/
Ruth /ruːθ/
Sally /ˈsælɪ/;Sal/sæl/
Samantha /səˈmænθə/
Sandra /ˈsɑːndrə/
Sarah, Sara /ˈseərə/
Sharon /ˈʃærən/
Sheila, Shelagh /ˈʃiːlə/
Silvia, Sylvia /ˈsɪlvɪə/
Stephanie /ˈstefənɪ/
Susan /ˈsuːzn/
Susanna, Susannah
  /suːˈzænə/
Sybil, Sibyl /ˈsɪbəl/
Teresa, Theresa /təˈriːzə/
Tracy, Tracey /ˈtreɪsɪ/
Valerie /ˈvælərɪ/
Vera /ˈvɪərə/
Veronica /vəˈrɒnɪkə/
Virginia /vəˈdʒɪnɪə/
Vivien, Vivienne /ˈvɪvɪən/
Wendy /ˈwendɪ/
Yvonne /ɪˈvɒn/

male names

Adam /'ædəm/
Adrian /'eɪdrɪən/
Alan, Allan, Allen /'ælən/
Alexander /ˌælɪg'zɑːndə(r)/
Alfred /'ælfrɪd/
Andrew /'ændruː/; Andy
  /'ændɪ/
Alistair, Alisdair, Alas–
  /'ælɪstə(r)/
Anthony, Antony /'æntənɪ/
Arnold /'ɑːnəld/
Arthur /'ɑːθə(r)/
Benjamin /'bendʒəmɪn/
Brian, Bryan /'braɪən/
Bruce /bruːs/
Charles /tʃɑːlz/
Christopher /'krɪstəfə(r)/
Clifford /'klɪfəd/
Clive /klaɪv/
Colin /'kɒlɪn/
Craig /kreɪg/
Daniel /'dænɪəl/
David /'deɪvɪd/
Dennis, Denis /'denɪs/
Derek /'derɪk/
Donald /'dɒnəld/
Douglas /'dʌgləs/
Edward /'edwəd/
Eric /'erɪk/
Francis /'frɑːnsɪs/
Frank /fræŋk/
Gary /'gærɪ/
Gavin /'gævɪn/
Geoffrey, Jeffrey /'dʒefrɪ/
George /dʒɔːdʒ/
Gerald /'dʒerəld/
Giles /dʒaɪlz/
Gordon /'gɔːdn/
Graham, Grahame, Graeme
  /'greɪəm/
Gregory /'gregərɪ/

Harold /'hærəld/
Henry /'henrɪ/
Howard /'haʊəd/
Hugh /hjuː/
Ian /'iːən/
James /dʒeɪmz/
Jason /'dʒeɪsn/
Jeremy /'dʒerəmɪ/
John /dʒɒn/
Jonathan /'dʒɒnəθən/
Keith /kiːθ/
Kenneth /'kenɪθ/
Kevin /'kevɪn/; Kev/kev/
Laurence, Lawrence /'lɒrəns/
Leslie /'lezlɪ/
Malcolm /'mælkəm/
Mark /mɑːk/
Martin /'mɑːtɪn/
Matthew /'mæθjuː/
Michael /'maɪkl/
Neil, Neal /niːl/
Nicholas, Nicolas /'nɪkələs/
Nigel /'naɪdʒl/
Norman /'nɔːmən/
Oliver /'ɒlɪvə(r)/
Patrick /'pætrɪk/
Paul /pɔːl/
Peter /'piːtə(r)/
Philip /'fɪlɪp/
Richard /'rɪtʃəd/
Robert /'rɒbət/
Roger /'rɒdʒə(r)/
Scott /skɒt/
Simon /'saɪmən/
Stanley /'stænlɪ/
Stephen, Steven /'stiːvn/
Stewart, Stuart /'stjuːət/
Terence /'terəns/
Thomas /'tɒməs/
Timothy /'tɪməθɪ/
Trevor /'trevə(r)/
William /'wɪlɪəm/

476

Acknowledgements

Alphabet illustrations by Robert Kettell
Cover illustrations by Iain McCaig

Location photography by
Emily Anderson, Nicky Dixon, Rob Judges, Julian Prentis

The publishers would like to thank the followir.g for their
permission to use photographs:
    Architectural Association
    H.M. Bateman/Cartoon Study Centre, University of Kent
    Birmingham City Council
    Britain on View photographic library (BTA/ETB)
    Camera Press
    Patrick Eager
    Mary Evans Picture Library
    Flambards Triple Theme Park
    Heath Robinson/Duckworth/Cartoon Study Centre,
        University of Kent
    The Hulton/Deutsch collection
    Liberty
    The Mansell Collection
    Metropolitan Police
    Nottingham City Council
    Oxford Times
    Pixieland Funpark
    The Red Devils
    Royal Doulton
    Royal Mint
    Royal National Lifeboat Association
    Salvation Army
    Scottish Tourist Board
    Sothebys
© Maps copyright Oxford University Press